of the Animal Kingdom

5.	6.	7.	8.
Worms	Coelenterates	Sponges	Protozoa

3. Molluscs

1.	2.	3.
Snails	Mussels	Cephalopods

5. Worms

1.	2.	3.
Segmented worms	Threadworms	Tapeworms

ANIMAL LIFE OF EUROPE

ANIMAL LIFE OF EUROPE

The Naturalist's Reference Book

DR. JAKOB GRAF

English version prepared by
PAMELA AND MAURICE MICHAEL

WITH ALMOST 400 SPECIMENS
ILLUSTRATED IN COLOUR
AND OVER 1600 DRAWINGS
IN BLACK AND WHITE

FREDERICK WARNE & CO. LTD: *London*
FREDERICK WARNE & CO. INC: *New York*

7232   0958   8

Printed in West Germany
by Buchdruckerei Universal, München

FOREWORD

This book introduces a new system of identification, based on prominent features and characteristics, which will help the amateur to recognise any wild animals, birds and insects which he may encounter, while being of equal use to the advanced student. The aim has been to illustrate everything completely, the drawings being placed in the margin next to the relevant descriptive text where possible, to avoid the inconvenience of cross references.

The order of arrangement is such that the beginner will easily be able to understand it. Classification is in accordance with habitat in the case of certain fish, some butterflies and many of the pests. Birds which are similar, and so likely to cause confusion, are dealt with in groups, both in the colour plates and text, and the silhouettes are an additional aid to quick identification. It is hoped that the division of beetles, moths and butterflies according to colour will make it possible for the amateur to recognise those he discovers by merely observing their striking features. Other insects have been classified by size, number of wings or method of progression. Insect larvae are placed separately, as many as 63 of the most common and conspicuous caterpillars being illustrated on one colour plate. One of the black and white plates shows only those caterpillars which have an anal horn or similar appendage, while others are arranged on the same principle as that used throughout the book. No special knowledge is required to determine the striking features of butterflies or insects, etc. and one need only be familiar with the grouping in the classification to turn at once to the part where the creature concerned is likely to be found. The birds' songs are divided into definite sections depending, for example, on place and time of singing.

The author wishes to acknowledge help received in compiling the book from M. Wehner and A. Graf, and in producing the illustrations from Fritz Bäuerle, Miss L. Hausdorff und Dr. Neubauer.

PUBLISHER'S NOTE

This book will commend itself instantly to all who have an interest in natural history, whether as amateurs or professionally. It has a wealth of accurate illustrations, both coloured and black and white, and makes use of clearly observable features and characteristics to simplify the identification of all common groups of animals.

Although originally intended for readers in central Europe, the scope of this edition has been widened by including descriptions and illustrations of most species which a visitor to almost any part of the Continent might encounter. It is hoped, therefore, that in its present form *Animal Life of Europe* will appeal not only to naturalists at home, but to the increasing number of English-speaking visitors to Europe as a useful travelling companion.

By including pests of farms and gardens, parasites of man and his domestic animals, insects and spiders found around the home, and an interesting and unusual section of birds' songs, this valuable and compact reference book should prove helpful to the farmer, gardener, teacher and householder.

No book previously published in this country has covered such a wide range of species so concisely, accurately yet so comprehensively. We are proud to have had the opportunity of presenting this remarkable volume to a wider public.

CONTENTS

INSTRUCTIONS FOR USING THIS BOOK

CONTRACTIONS AND SYMBOLS USED

♂	= Male	♀	= Female
♂ ♂	= Males (in plural)	♀♀	= Females (in plural)
♀	= Worker	♀♀	= Workers (in plural)
C	= Cry	*	= Not found in Britain

Before attempting to identify an animal study the table of contents so that you will be able to turn straight to the group in which you will find it. Groups can be quickly found by using the section headings which are printed at the top of each page. In the case of arthropods, by size or length of body is meant the distance from the front of the head (excluding antennae) to the end of the body (excluding tail).

ORDER, FAMILY, GENUS, SPECIES

See "Guide to the Classes of Animals" at the back of the book.

Each *CLASS* of animals is subdivided into various orders. The orders in the class of the mammals are carnivores, ungulates, rodents, insect-eaters, bats, etc.

Each ORDER is subdivided into Families, each FAMILY into Genera and each *Genus* into *Species*. Thus, for example, all feline carnivores are put in the cat family (FELIDAE), all canine ones in the dog family (CANIDAE) and all marten-like ones in the marten family (MUSTELIDAE). See the table on page 12.

In the cat family (FELIDAE), for example, a distinction is made between the cat genus *(Felis)* and the genus *Lynx*. In the marten family (MUSTE-LIDAE) a distinction is made between the marten genus *(Martes)* and the weasel genus *(Mustela)*.

Within each genus there are different species, e.g. the wild cat and the domestic cat are two different species because of the different characteristics they always have.

In order to make them understandable internationally, each has been given a Latin name. In this the name of the genus (e.g. *Felis*) comes first, the first letter always being a capital; then comes the name of the species, e.g. *silvestris*, the first letter of which is always written small.

The following shows how the carnivores included in this book are divided up into Family, Genus and Species:

ORDER CARNIVORA

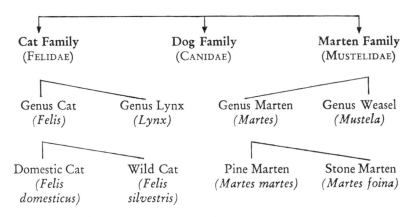

| Cat Family (FELIDAE) | Dog Family (CANIDAE) | Marten Family (MUSTELIDAE) |

Genus Cat *(Felis)*   Genus Lynx *(Lynx)*   Genus Marten *(Martes)*   Genus Weasel *(Mustela)*

Domestic Cat *(Felis domesticus)*   Wild Cat *(Felis silvestris)*   Pine Marten *(Martes martes)*   Stone Marten *(Martes foina)*

DIVISION VERTEBRATES

Body supported by an inner skeleton, the chief part of which is the gristly or bony spinal column, which is composed of numerous vertebrae one behind the other. From these, processes of gristle or bone protrude, and together form the spinal canal which encloses and protects the spinal cord. In front, this spinal cord enters the skull in which the brain lies. Brain and spinal cord are the main parts of the nervous system. Large numbers of nerves run out from both. Below the vertebrae lie the organs of circulation of the blood, breathing and digestion. The blood is coloured red by the red corpuscles in it. It flows through a closed network of vessels and is kept in motion by a hollow muscle, the heart. Breathing is performed by lungs or gills. As a rule there are two pairs of limbs; only exceptionally is one or perhaps both pairs missing.

Class   *MAMMALIA*   Mammals

Have bodies consisting of head, torso and limbs, the head and body being connected by the neck. Head covered with hair, seldom bare or scaly. Have lungs for breathing. Four-chambered hearts. Dual circulation. Blood warm or at constant temperature, as a rule about 37° C; considerable increases or decreases in temperature result in death; exception: the few species that hibernate. Highly developed brains. Viviparous (with the exception of the egg-laying duckbills) and suckle the young.

Dental formula: above the line is given the number of teeth in one half of the upper jaw, below the line those in one half of the lower jaw. From front to back: incisors, canines, pre-molars, molars.

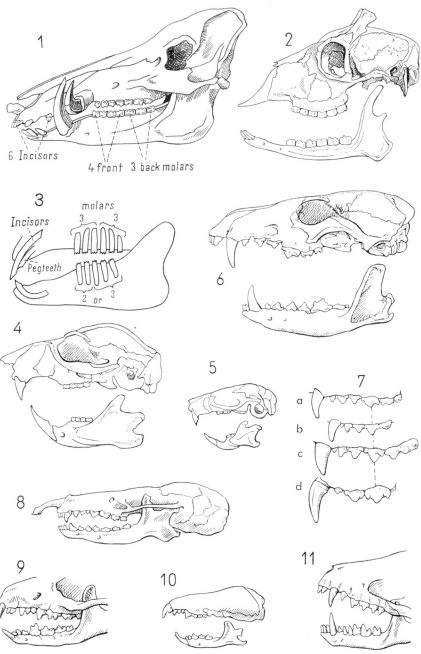

Fig. 1: Jaws of European Mammals: 1 Wild boar 2 Roe deer 3 Hare 4 Squirrel 5 House mouse 6 Fox 7 Teeth of left upper jaw of: a fox, b marten, c badger, d cat 8 Mole 9 Hedgehog 10 Field shrew 11 Bat

(In 7 the teeth for tearing are all in the same arrangement — see text for dental formulae)

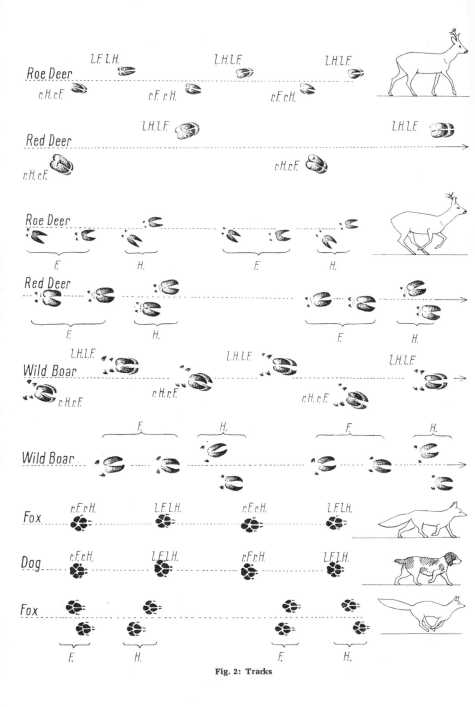

Fig. 2: Tracks

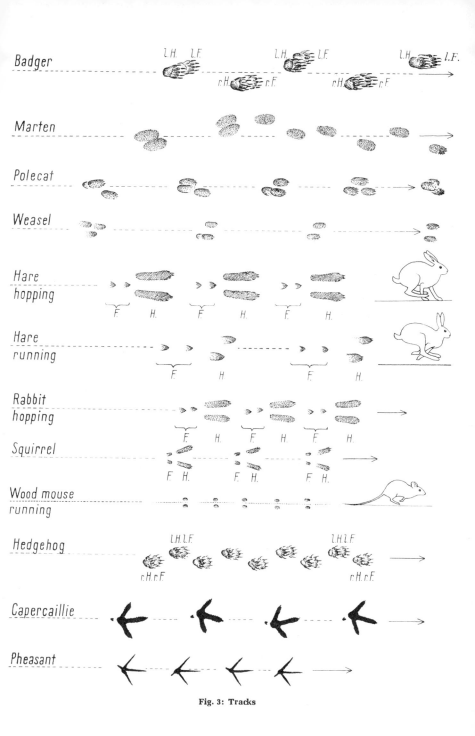

Fig. 3: Tracks

INDICATIONS AND "GIVE-AWAYS"

Sounds and voices of the woods

A hard, clear brittle snapping of dry twigs in the dark or in dense under-wood betrays the fact that wild animals are on the move nearby. A dull, barking sound is the warning cry of startled deer (roe, red and fallow) when surprised. A continuous, dull, explosive *bo bo bo* frequently repeated is the bellowing of roe deer, mainly heard at dusk and during the night during rutting (the mating season, from the end of July to the middle of August). A protracted *oo-oo-oo-aah,* loud and booming, heard at night during the rutting season (beginning of September to middle of October) is the *belling* or *roar* of the stag challenging his rivals to battle. A staccato, hoarse bark, similar to that of a dog, ending in a loud screech heard especially at night during February and March (mating time) is the voice of the courting fox.

Hunter's Jargon: Deer (red, fallow, roe), wild boar and moufflon are *hoofed* game. Other game have *paws,* except the hare, otter and fox which have pads. The deer's and boar's dew-claws are the false hoofs at the back of the ankle bone, which are really toes. A *print* is the impression of an individual foot. An impression so sharp and clear as to show every detail is called a *slot.* The prints of all four feet are called a *trace.* The prints of hoofed game that are aligned one behind the other are called the *spoor.* The same prints of beasts of prey, hares, rabbits, squirrels, mice and hedgehogs are called their *trail.* The prints of birds are called *tracks.* When the prints are almost in a line it is called *beading,* like a string of beads. When those of the right and left feet are exactly in front of each other, so that you get two lines of prints, giving a parallel or double track, looking like a zigzag line, it is called *cross-trace.* The cross is the distance between the two parallels. The hare's bound is the gait of almost all mammals when in flight: that is to say the prints of the hind feet are in front of those of the fore feet. Animals with elongated hind legs (hares, squirrels) can move only in this way, even when just hopping along.

The size of an animal's print will vary considerably as will the length of stride depending on the size of the specimen. The prints of any one animal will themselves vary with the state of the ground or snow, as also will its mode of progression. If a hoofed animal is in flight, its prints look very different from those when it is walking, quickly or slowly. In flight the hoof is forced wide open and deeper into the ground. Also in soft ground there will be the impression of the dew-claw, which is seldom the case with an animal moving while at ease, except in the case of the wild boar.

Roe deer tracks There is considerable similarity between the tracks of roe and red deer, except that in the former the measurements are all smaller. In addition with roe deer the sole continues further into the hoof than with the stag, so that the roe track is recognisable by the larger soles. The track of the doe is slighter than that of the buck. With the latter the two toes touch at their points, leaving a ridge in the middle of the slot: the thread. The points of the toes of roe deer turn away from each other. The roe deer moving when at ease, that is walking normally, will usually place the hind foot exactly in the print of the fore foot on its side. The stag when walking at ease does exactly the same, and its track then consists only of the impression of the hind hoofs. When trotting its tracks become irregular misprints and when fleeing roe and stag leave the print of all four feet. The width of bound of a fleeing roe deer can be anything up to 4 m, that of the fleeing stag up to 7 m. The track of a roe deer is scarcely 3 cm wide and some 4 cm long, that of the red deer from 3.5 cm to 6.5 cm broad and from 6 cm to 10 cm long.

Red deer tracks (Compare the tracks of the roe deer.) Prints of the stag and hind (Fig. 4) can easily be distinguished. The full grown stag is on the average heavier and broader than the hind. The length of step and width of trace (cross-trace) are greater with the stag than with the hind. As the stag's toes are broader and blunter than those of the hind, the prints of the two are quite distinct. Also an older stag will leave a stronger print than a younger animal and its cross-trace will be broader.

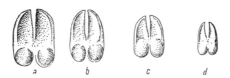

Fig. 4: Slots of (a) **Stag** (b) **Hind** (c) **Fallow deer** (d) **Roe deer**

Fallow deer tracks are similar to those of red deer, but its "slots" are slighter, longer and more pointed in front than those of the red deer.

Wild boar tracks Though resembling those of the red deer, the wild boar's track is recognisable by the shorter length of stride and above all by the impression of the dew-claws, which are visible whatever the animal's pace, though with stags only when in flight. The hind hoofs or toes of the wild boar are long and curved. Their impression is in the shape of a half moon and the interval between them is greater than in other hoofed game. In the wild boar the inner toes are usually shorter than the outer.

Hare tracks are unmistakeable because the impression of the fore feet, which are seen one behind the other, always come behind the much larger impression of the hind feet. This order is retained whether the hare is hopping, bounding or fleeing. The hare touches down with the fore feet only briefly, swinging the hind feet up outside the fore feet and then putting them down.

Rabbit tracks Very similar to those of the hare, only smaller prints. The impression of the hare's front feet are always one behind the other, those of the rabbit however often obliquely aligned. A rabbit's tracks usually end fairly soon at a hole in the ground, while a hare's goes on and on.

Squirrel tracks are much more delicate than those of the hare which they otherwise resemble. Here again the longer print of the hind feet comes in front of the smaller print of the fore feet, because the squirrel *hops*. The prints are in pairs, one beside the other, whether the animal is just hopping about or in flight.

Fox tracks Impression of four toe pads plus claws. Very similar to those of the smaller dogs, though the print of the fox's foot is distinctly longer than the rounder and broader print of the dog. When trotting or creeping the fox places its hind feet in the place where a moment before the corresponding fore-foot had been. Its track is thus recognisable, showing only the impression of the hind feet which are almost in a line. This is called registering. When stalking a prey the distance between the individual impression normally shrinks. Here a fox often makes a cross-trace, placing its prints one beside the other, turning the line of print into a zigzag. When fleeing at a gallop the print appears at considerable, regular distances. Unlike the cats, a fox leaves the impression of its claws, called studding. As a result the print of a fox is somewhat elongated, while that of a cat is circular. As the bare foot of the fox makes the impression of the pad much more sharp than that of the claws, you will find, especially in summer, tracks where there is no claw impression. Such tracks are very similar to those of the wild cat both in size and position of the pads.

Badger pad marks Only the badger has digging claws which leave such strikingly long marks.

Marten tracks Marten, polecat and weasel move along the ground by using the caterpillar principle, alternately contracting and stretching their slender bodies. In this the hind feet are placed in the tracks of the fore feet. The prints appear in pairs one beside the other. The track consists of nothing but twin prints. The track of the pine marten resembles that of the domestic cat. As the pads of the tree marten's paws are hairy, the print it leaves is not sharp, though that of the stone marten is. Even when fresh, the track of the pine marten is somewhat faded. When hopping the pine marten puts its feet down obliquely, but when in flight straighter. The tracks of marten often begin and end at a tree or wall, unlike those of the polecat.

Track of the polecat Prints in pairs obliquely adjacent and with a shorter interval between them than in the case of the marten, for the polecat takes relatively short bounds. In the track of the polecat you will quite often find so-called triple or quadruple prints between the normal double print. Polecat prints are often along ditches and the banks of streams.

Track of the weasel Nothing but dual prints, only seldom blurred as those of the polecat are.

Hedgehog tracks Only in the summer six months. An unmistakeable cross-trace track that shows quite distinctly the impression of the spread, clawed toes.

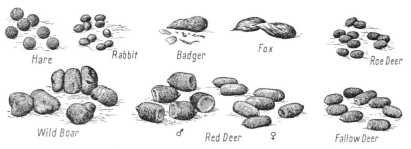

Fig. 5: Droppings on the forest floor

DROPPINGS

The droppings (crotels) of the hare are firm, spherical or egg-shaped; those of the rabbit are somewhat smaller. The roe deer's droppings are oval, green-black lumps; those of the stag (fewmets) are larger and acorn-shaped (glandiform) with a cup at one end and a plug that fits at the other. The wild boar's droppings (lesses) are fat and pulpy, like those of the domestic pig; cylindrical droppings like a dog's come from the fox (billetings). The cylindrical or pulpy droppings with the remains of beetles, and the husks and pips of berries come from the badger and are called fiants or fuants.

HAUNTS, PATHS AND LYING-UP PLACES OF GAME

You often see narrow trodden paths in the mossy floor of the forest leading through a thicket and, in winter time, numerous tracks in the snow all using the same narrow path. The prints and droppings on them will tell you whether they are those of hoofed game or those of hares called "muses", rabbits or the predators. Grass and moss pressed flat in some hidden-away place in a thicket will be the lair or ligging of a stag or roe deer. A shallow trough the length of the body of a hare with a deeper hollow at one end is the hare's "form". These are often found under a sheltering bush or in a furrow in a ploughed field. In the marshy ground with bushes, where you might expect to find wild boar, a well-ploughed lengthy depression, lined with moss, grass or rushes, in some raised, thus drier ground, will be the wild boar's "couch". A freshly kneaded mud hole with stirred-up, muddy water, numerous foot prints and hair along the rim and surroundings shows where a red or fallow deer or a wild boar has been wallowing. Look nearby for the rubbing-tree with its smooth place. The footprints, hair, droppings and height of the bare patch will tell you what animal used it. Roe deer do not wallow.

ROOTING AND GRUBBING PLACES

Places in the forest where the ground is furrowed as though by a domestic pig, and where there are footprints and droppings of the wild boar are called rooting places. Places, particularly on the skirts of a wood, with small, round hollows and rabbit droppings nearby are the "scratching places" of rabbits. The badger makes similar troughs in the ground. It prods with the long claws on the fore feet making small funnel-shaped holes as it digs for insects, worms and snails. When hunting mice the fox scrapes quite a deep hole.

HOLES IN THE GROUND

If there is no freshly scraped-out earth at the mouth or if there is a spider's web or undamaged plants growing in the entrance the earth will have been abandoned. If there are rabbit droppings lying round it, it will be a rabbit's burrow. If there are other holes in the immediate vicinity and bones and feathers lying about, it will be a fox's earth in use. If there is freshly dug out earth with a deep groove in it and roundabout small funnel-shaped holes and droppings containing the blue, black and brown chitinous parts of beetles, you have found a badger's set.

NIBBLING, BARKING, GNAWING AND FRAYING PLACES

If you find a lot of bitten off young shoots lying on the ground under a tree, it will be the work of a squirrel. When the tips of young spruces are eaten, this is usually the work of rabbits, roe deer or red deer. The barking places of the red and fallow deer are found mostly in summer. There are wounds in the bark, from the length of a hand to that of an arm, which, when fresh, are light and often have tatters of bark hanging from them. Tooth marks are clearly visible. When older these wounds become smeared with resin or grow black. These places are found on conifers, oak, beech and ash. The cause of this is the animal's need of tannic acid, or they may do it to relieve boredom. Gnawed places are found above all during and after a hard winter. If the bark of young trees and branches has been gnawed off all round, it will be the work of hares and rabbits. You will see the twin marks of teeth. Often there will be droppings on the ground there. Where the marks of the teeth are smaller and more slender, it will be the work of the bank vole *Clethrionomys glareolus* or dormouse. These wounds will not go right round and in the case of the dormouse will reach up into the twigs, while those made by the bank vole will not. In summer rubbing places can be seen on the young trees. There are scorings and scratches in the bark 50–100 cm above the ground, sometimes even higher, which are white when fresh. The roe buck chooses weaker trees against which to "fray" its horns. The rubbing-places of stags are generally higher than those of roe deer. The brushed-off coating of the new antlers, the velvet, is seldom to be found, because most stags are avid to eat it. At fresh rubbing-places you may, however, find cast body hair.

Order   CARNIVORA   Carnivores

Complete set of teeth, i.e. have all kinds of teeth, mostly adapted to a diet of meat. *Teeth:* dagger-like eyeteeth and mostly sharp cutting molars of which the carnassials (i.e. last upper pre-molar and first lower molar) are especially strong. Limbs have free, clawed fingers or toes. Fore 5, hind 4 toes. (Fig. 1, nos. 6 and 7.)

Sub-order   FISSIPEDIA

Family   CANIDAE   Dogs

Digitigrades with unretractable claws. Complete carnivore's teeth, and long smooth tongue. Fore 5, hind 4 toes. (Fig. 1, no. 6.)

FOX *(Vulpes vulpes)* Length up to 80 cm, tail 40 cm; height at shoulder 30 cm. *Shape:* slender body, legs thin and short, muzzle long and thin, ears erect and pointed, thick bushy tail (brush) held straight out when running. Teeth and tongue like a dog's, but eye-teeth thinner. Dental formula $\dfrac{3\ 1\ 4\ 2}{3\ 1\ 4\ 3} = 42$. *Colour:* back yellow grey-red, belly and tip of tail white, ears and paws black. *Movements:* quick, nimble run, extremely active, great endurance; takes long bounds; skilful in creeping, lurks almost lying on its belly; swims easily and quickly. *Cry:* dog-like barking or yelp, but not often heard, except in mating season or stormy weather; when frightened or angry a suppressed chatter (keckern); in pain a long drawn-out wail. Cubs cry and yelp when hungry or bored. *Earth:* deep hole with one or more branches, ending in a roomy den; often uses an abandoned badger set or even one that is still in use. Also has well hidden emergency hiding places. *Food:* all sorts of animals from beetles to fawns, but especially mice. On occasion will take songbirds, domestic poultry, pheasant, partridges or leverets. Acts as "hygiene officer of the woods"

in that it finishes off ill or weak animals. Also eats fruit and grapes. Hunts mostly during twilight and at night; excellent sense of smell, acute hearing and sharp sight. *Mating season:* January to March. Vixen has 3–12 cubs in the spring. *Life-span:* 10–12 years. Cannot be crossed with a dog (silver- and other foxes that are farmed are colour mutations). The most widespread beast of prey. Common throughout Europe.

WOLF *(Canis lupus)* Length of body 1.15 m. Height at shoulder 85 cm, tail 45 cm. Considerable resemblance to Alsatian dog, but of stronger build, wider head, slanting eyes and stouter eye-teeth. *Dental formula:* as fox's. Coat yellowy-browny-grey mixed with black on top. Underside yellowy grey-white: colour varying with age, territory and season of the year. Ears erect, black at edges. Tail long, bushy and drooping. Is one of the ancestors of our dogs. Wolf and domestic dog can be crossed successfully. Hides during the day, roams widely at night. *Cry:* a doleful howl. Hunts in packs, hares, birds, smaller animals; runs down stags and roe deer, breaks into flocks of sheep and, when starving, will even attack people; in an extremity will eat potatoes and fruit. Scandinavia, Russia, Poland, Serbia, Carpathians, Balkan mountains, Pyrenees. Last native wolf killed in Britain in the 18th Century, in Germany in the 19th (1841). Stray wolves from the East occasionally appear in East Prussia and the Rhine country. No wolves now in the Ardennes or Vosges.

Family   FELIDAE   Cats

Digitigrades with retractable claws, incomplete set of teeth, with few cheek-teeth but long and sharp canines; jaws adapted to slice meat with an up and down movement only and not sideways; rough tongue furnished with backward-pointing "hooks".

WILD CAT *(Felis silvestris)* Body length 70–90 cm. Tail 30–35 cm. Height at shoulder 35–42 cm. Carnivore living alone largely nocturnal in habits. Shape like that of domestic cat, but much larger and stronger. Lithe

body; wide, round-rectangular head; tail of the same thickness throughout, no narrowing at the tip, but looks as if shorn off, relatively short, thick haired; sharp retractable claws. Teeth of a carnivore; long whiskers; thick long coat. *Colouring:* male fawn-grey to black-grey; female yellowy-grey; yellowy-white patch on throat, faded dark transverse stripes on the sides. Yellowish body. Tail rust-grey with 7–8 dark or black rings. Round black patch on sole of hind feet. *Movements:* noiseless in prowl, patient lurking, assured pounce; sure climber. *Food:* principally mice and small birds, will also attack hares, rabbits and fawns; in winter will go into village henhouses and dovecots. *Mating season:* February to March. Kittens April to May, 2–4 kittens, born blind. *Life-span:* up to 12 years. Individuals in wooded mountain regions of the Middle Rhine, Harz and Taunus mountains, Alps, Scottish Highlands etc. More frequent in the Balkans and Spain. Prefers extensive, dark woods, crags, holes in trees; will hide in an abandoned earth or set. Not to be confused with domestic cat gone wild. Domestic cats are probably descended from the Egyptian fallow cat.

*EUROPEAN LYNX *(Lynx lynx)* Length of body up to 105 cm, tail 15–20 cm. Height at shoulder up to 75 cm. *Build:* powerful, lithe, compact body; sturdy legs with large paws. Pointed ears topped with black tufts of hair; stub tail, looking as if docked, with black tip. Mane-like cheek fringes short in summer, long in winter; long, stiff whiskers; thick, soft fur. *Colouring:* reddish grey mixed with white on top; scattered round red and grey-brown spots everywhere, inside of legs, front of neck, lips and surrounds of ears white; reddish face; winter fur lightly tinged with white. *Action:* great endurance in walking, runs in long bounds, very good climber. Hunts only in the twilight and at night. *Food:* from the smallest mammals or birds up to roe deer and capercaillie. *Mating season:* February to March. 2–3 young, blind at birth. *Life-span:* 12–14 years. *Distribution:* Scandinavia, Russia, Siberia, Balkan mountains, very occasionally in East Prussia

Family   Ursidae   Bears

Plantigrades, each broad, flat foot bearing 5 toes with non-retractile claws. Flat crowned and broad molar teeth but no special carnassial teeth. On the whole omnivorous animals.

*BROWN BEAR *(Ursus arctos) Length:* up to 210 cm. *Shape:* heavy build, weighing up to 200 kg; small ears, very short tail. *Colour:* variable, ranging from pale fawn to dark brown. *Activities:* brown bears are active mainly at night and live solitary lives. They hibernate in a den excavated in rocks or under a tree–the time varying from September in the far north of its range to December in the south (Pyrenees). *Food:* mainly vegetable–roots, fruits, nuts, fungi etc. but its diet also includes sheep, eggs and fish. They are particularly voracious in autumn when they build up a thick layer of subcutaneous fat to tide them over hibernation. *Mating season:* July, the young being born in the winter den in January or February. Two cubs usual. *Life-span:* 30 years. *Distribution:* now only in small numbers in wilder parts of Carpathians, Swiss Alps, Balkans, Scandinavia, Finland and the Pyrenees. More abundant in U.S.S.R. The brown bear became extinct in Britain in 10th Century and in the French Alps about 1937.

Family   Mustelidae   Martens etc.

Tread on half the sole (except the badger which treads on the whole sole); claws slightly retractable. Small canine (tearing) teeth with only one uneven molar behind.

PINE MARTEN *(Martes martes)* Length of body 45 cm, tail 25 cm. True tree animal, mainly nocturnal. *Build:* very slender, lithe, elastic body. Short legs; long bushy tail for balancing; round head with low, wide ears and long hair whiskers. *Colouring:* skin yellow-brown; thick woolly hair between whiskers, reddish-grey at base, slightly rusty-yellow at the tip; yellow throat patch reaching to the chest, not forked. *Action:* expert climber, jumper, stalker. *Food:* from very young roe deer and hares down to mice, especially squirrels, dormice; also birds and fledglings as well as the berries of the mountain ash and fruit. *Mating season:* end of July to beginning of August. 3–5 young born blind at the end of March or beginning of April. *Life-span:* 8–10 years. *Habitat:* particularly dense, gloomy woods well away from people. Rare. Lives in hollow trees, fissures in rocks, abandoned nests of squirrels and birds of prey. Widely distributed in Europe and Asia. In Britain now restricted to north-west Scottish Highlands, Lake District, Wales and Ireland.

* STONE BEECH MARTEN *(Martes foina)* Body 44 cm. Tail 29 cm. Mainly nocturnal beast of prey that can cause great slaughter among poultry. Similar to the foregoing

in shape and colouring but legs shorter, head longer, ears smaller, coat shorter and lighter in colour. Fur grey-brown: light grey woolly hair between whiskers. Throat patch mostly white, always forked at bottom and reaching the middle of the inside of the forelegs. Ears rimmed with short whitish hairs. *Action:* quick and nimble; can take wide leaps, climb high up smooth tree trunks and walls, swim well, crawl and squeeze through narrow slits. *Food:* mice, rats, rabbits, birds and their eggs, squirrels, reptiles, dormice, fruit. *Mating season:* July to August. 3–5 young born blind at the end of April or early May. *Life-span:* 15 years. On the continent not so rare as the pine marten, but does not occur in Scandinavia or the British Isles. Lives in barns, sheds, old walls, heaps of stone or wood, hollow trees. In Germany may be hunted during January.

BADGER *(Meles meles)* Body 75 cm. Tail 18 cm. Height at shoulder about 30 cm. Mainly nocturnal. Very greedy. *Build:* thickset body, long head with snout-shaped pointed muzzle; thick neck, broad back; short tail, stiff hair; short, strong legs, bare soles, strong claws (track on page 15); small eyes; small but visible ears; thick, coarse coat. *Colouring:* back grey,

belly and feet black-brown, head white with two broad, black longitudinal stripes, running down over the ears and eyes. Gait deceptively shuffling and awkward. Expert at digging. Grunting cry. Lives underground in a *set,* in lonely places, the southern slopes of a wooded hill; one entrance passage and perhaps six exits, several vertical ventilation shafts and a spacious den lined with leaves and moss as well as a special privy pit in which dung and rubbish is buried. The den is from 1.5 m to 2 m or even up to 5 m underground. In an emergency the exits serve as escape passages. Tremendously clean. *Food:* turnips, beech nuts, acorns, berries, fruit, mushrooms, insects, snails, worms, grubs, at times birds eggs, fledglings, mice, frogs, lizards, snakes, baby rabbits. Useful in destroying forest pests.

Dental formula: $\dfrac{3\ 1\ 4\ 1}{3\ 1\ 4\ 2}$ $= 38$. Omnivorous with carnivore's teeth; molars

wide, uneven; 4 eyeteeth less pointed than those of its relative, the marten. Retires in winter, but not real hibernation; retains its body temperature and ability to move, emerging now and again to eat. *Mating season:* July to August: 3–5 young born blind in set early in March, living with the mother until autumn or sometimes over the winter. *Life-span:* 15 years. *Distribution:* everywhere.

STOAT *(Mustella erminea)* Body length up to 29 cm, tail up to 10 cm. *Build:* long slender, very lithe body; small head; very short legs with sharp claws. Summer coat: browny red on back, underparts white, clearly distinguished; winter coat in north of range white all over except for black tip to tail; further south the change to full white is rare, and a coat like the summer one but denser is more usual. *Action:* very assured and swift; runs and leaps most agilely, excellent climber, squeezes through narrow holes and fissures, slips between stones and through bushes, will swim wide stretches, starts hunting as dusk falls. *Food:* mice, moles, hamsters, rabbits, birds and fledglings, snakes, squirrels, lizards. *Mating season:* February to March; June to July. 4–7 young born blind in nest May to June. *Distribution:* throughout the northern hemisphere.

WEASEL *(Mustela nivalis)* Length of body: of male 26–35 cm; of female 23–26 cm; tail of male up to 8 cm, female up to 5 cm. Bloodthirsty and fearless. Also hunts by day. *Build:* long, thin, very lithe body; very short legs, sharp claws, wide, rounded ears. Small eyes. *Colouring:* back reddish brown, white underparts. In winter either whitish brown speckled with white or, in north, entirely white. Point of tail not bushy or black. *Action:* like stoat. *Food:* mice, hamsters, rabbits, leverets, frogs, lizards, snakes, birds up to pigeon size; robs birds' nests. *Mating season:* mostly in May. Often two litters a year of 5–10 young, born blind. *Life-span:* 8–10 years. *Habitat:* fields and woods everywhere. Hides in holes in trees, mole runs, under heaps of stones, and, in winter, in barns and sheds.

AMERICAN MINK *(Mustela vision)* Length of body: 30–43 cm; tail 12.7–22.9 cm. *Colouring:* normally rich dark brown all over but light-coloured specimens sometimes found wild; many colour varieties raised in captivity. *Food:* fish, birds, small mammals, frogs, toads, snails and insects. *Mating season:* single litter of 4 to 6 young born in April or May in hole in bank, hollow tree etc. *Life-span:* about 10 years. *Habitat:* mainly an

aquatic animal and frequents rivers and streams where most of the food is caught. Normally silent animals, they may shriek when alarmed or purr during the mating season. Can emit an offensive odour as defence.

This N. American species has been kept on fur ranches in many parts of the world and escaped animals have become established in some countries

including Britain where it was first recorded as breeding
in the wild state in 1956, on the River Teign in Devon.
Has now spread to many countries.

*EUROPEAN MINK *(Mustela lutreola)* Closely related
to the previous species with similar life-history and
behaviour. A decreasing animal in Europe it occurs now
only in eastern Europe, Finland and possibly in western
France.

POLECAT *(Mustela putorius)* Body about 40 cm, tail
30 cm. Nocturnal. Sprays attackers with a stinking fluid
from anal glands. *Build:* similar to the marten and between
it and the stoat in size. A little plumper. *Colouring:* black-
brown with light under-hair shining through. Legs and tail
dark brown. Whitish about the lips, chin and on either side
of the nose; ears dark with light rims. *Action:* swift and
agile. Expert climber, crawler and swimmer. Cunning, but
cautious; brave and fierce when attacked. *Food:* mice, rats,
moles, frogs, snakes, fish, birds and their eggs, insects,
worms, poultry. *Mating season:* March to June. Has 3–7
young born blind, usally in May. *Life-span:* 8–10 years.
Distribution: in Great Britain mainly confined to central
Wales, fairly common on continent. In summer lives in
holes in the earth, hedges, hollow trees, fox's earths, rabbit
burrows; in winter in old walls and buildings.

FERRET *(Mustela putorius furo)* Size of a polecat.
Whitish or yellowish fur. Bright red eyes: an albino.
Otherwise as the preceding. The ferret is a domesticated
variety of the Asiatic polecat and is not found wild.
Mostly kept for hunting rabbits. Frequently crossed with
polecat, the cross, called a polecat-ferret, or fitchet, is
coloured rather like a wild polecat and is frequently mistaken for one.

OTTER *(Lutra lutra)* Length of body up to 100 cm, of
tail up to 50 cm. Height at shoulder about 30 cm. Weight
up to 12 kg. Very shy and cautious. Hunts at night, spends
day mostly asleep in its den, called a *holt,* or occasionally
sunning itself on the ground. *Build:* like a marten's; head
broader and flatter with a rounded muzzle. Flat, slender
body. Rounded tapering tail with a thick root; uses this

as a rudder. Short, powerful legs, broad webs between its clawed toes. Ears almost completely hidden in the fur. Nostrils and eyes high up on head. Long whiskers on upper lip and at the corners of its mouth. Thick close fur consisting of coarse shiny bristles, upper hair und very fine, thick wool. *Colouring:* back dark brown, glossy, underparts somewhat lighter; front of neck and sides of head whitish grey-brown; lips and edges of ears light. *Dental formula:* $\dfrac{3\ 1\ 4\ 1}{3\ 1\ 3\ 2} = 36$. *Action:* on land a fast waddle; when submerged nostrils and ears are closed; surfaces every few minutes to breathe. Expert swimmer and diver. The holt is a natural hole or one the otter has dug itself in the banks of river, stream or lake, with several passages: roomy living chamber above level of the water, lined with dry grass etc. and provided with ventilation shaft to ground level. Entrance always under water. Other exits and entrances recognisable by tracks and remains of food: bones and scales of fish in them. *Food:* fish, crabs, frogs, water rats, birds. *Mating season:* end of February or early March. A clear whistle heard at night is its alarm signal. Has 9–10 young (whelps) in May. These are blind for 35 days and after about 8 weeks go fishing with their mother. Valuable fur. Numbers on the decline but occurs throughout Europe.

Sub-order   PINNIPEDIA   Seals, sea-lions, walrus

Marine mammals with spindle-shaped bodies, no visible transition between neck and torso, the shortened hind legs being turned right back near the small tail. The clawed toes, namely 1 and 5, are elongated and connected with web-skin and haired. On land they move on their bellies with clumsy jerks of the body, using their front-flippers as supports. Masterly swimmers. Circulation adapted to life in water: when submerged heart beat is reduced and certain sections of the system can be "disconnected" leaving more oxygen for blood and brain. Fore- and hind-feet used for steering. No external ear. Ears and nostrils can be sealed with flaps of skin. All three kinds of teeth, though now only for gripping; points often directed backwards. Gestation period a little over 11 months. Fat content of milk 53%. Mate on land or in water a few weeks after birth of young. Short, stiff coat. Skin has a thick layer of blubber. Fish-eaters.

Family   PHOCIDAE   Seals

GREY SEAL *(Halichoerus grypus)* Length up to 3 m. Weighs up to 150 kg. Females much smaller. Long head with long broad muzzle; lips sometimes thick; molars in upper jaw have only one point, curved backwards in a hook: *Colouring:* basic colour grey, in old males almost black, with irregular brown to black spots. Pups, 60–100 cm long, in Baltic February to March. In Atlantic pups in autumn, Sept. to Oct. 1 sometimes 2 pups with white woolly coat shed after 4–5 weeks, when weaned.

Distribution: North Atlantic; in Britain Scottish Islands, Farne Islands, Scorby Sands, Scilly Isles, Pembrokeshire and Ireland.

COMMON SEAL *(Phoca vitulina) Length:* up to 180 cm. Weight up to 68 kg. Roundish head; short, broad muzzle; molars in upper jaw have several points. All molars set obliquely. *Colouring:* silvery or yellow grey with small black spots; under parts lighter and have fewer spots; light ring round the eyes. Pups in North Sea in June and July. Pup about 80–95 cm in length has adult coat at or soon after birth.

Distribution: North Atlantic coasts, North Sea, western Baltic. *Breeding centres in Britain:* Wash and East Anglia, Scottish Islands and N. Ireland.

Order   ARTIODACTYLA   Even-toed ungulates

Vegetable eaters (at times omnivorous). Even number of horn-covered toes, of which toe 3 and 4 touch the ground; many also employ toe 2 and 5 in treading, but these are not so well formed as 3 and 4.

Sub-order   RUMINANTIA   Ruminants   (Fig. 1, no. 2)

Teeth and intestines adapted to purely vegetarian diet. Stomach consists of four parts; in most ruminants the upper jaw lacks both incisors and eyeteeth. Food goes almost unchewed straight to paunch or rumen, then into honeycomb, where cellulose dissociation by bacteria takes place; food is then returned to the mouth to be properly chewed; on being swallowed a second time it passes through the gullet into the manyplies for further mechanical treatment and so to the belly for actual digestion.

Family   Bovidae   Horned Ruminants

Hollow horns on long frontal knobs, which are not shed. *Dental formula:*

$$\frac{0\ 0\ 3\ 3}{3\ 1\ 3\ 3} = 32$$

* CHAMOIS *(Rupicapra rupicapra)* Total length from 130 to 145 cm, of which 8–10 cm is tail. Height at shoulder 70–80 cm. *Build:* powerful, thickset body; two main toes, hoof capable of opening wide, concave on the underside and edges almost as hard as steel; a further two subsidiary toes or dew-claws on each foot, which do not touch the ground where the surface is level, but on steep grassy slopes give added security to the stance. Track identifiable by the separate impression of the toes (Fig. 6) Horns of both sexes about 25 cm long rising straight up from skull with points curved backwards in shape of a hook; growth-rings; horns of billy somewhat larger, thicker and more curved. Eyes large, brown, somewhat protuberant, sparkling. Upright, mobile ears the shape of a paper-screw. No beard. Sparse, dry hair, short, fine curly undercoat and largish, straight guard-hairs up to 16 cm long in winter. Strikingly thick, long hair on back. *Colouring:* summer coat yellow-brown, underparts and legs brown-black; winter coat darker, uniform black-brown,

Fig. 6: Seals of Chamois (left), **Ibex, Roe Deer, Stag** (right)

with light underparts, also thicker and longer. Narrow blackish back stripe and blackish bar above the eye.

Action: swift run, good jumper and climber. *Cry:* peculiar hoarse whistle through the nose given by both sexes as a warning signal to the others. Billies also give a strange grunting bleat during the rut, when the billies try do drive each other from the flock and collect the females. *Food:* in summer principally grasses, herbs, mountain hay; in winter buds, twigs, bark, lichens, moss, pine-needles.

Mating season: November to December. Produces 1–2 kids end of April to June; kids have thick, pale dun-red hair. *Life-span:* 20–25 years. *Habitat:* upper limits of tree zone, knee-timber belt, and mountain areas up to 10,000 ft. In summer also above the tree line, even up to snow line; prefers northerly or easterly grassy slopes; in winter mostly retreats to upper tree zone and grazes on southerly and easterly slopes. Frequents same area, preferably in flocks of nannies, kids, one-year olds and young billies, usually 10–20, but also up to 30–40 in number. No leader. Every member on the alert. Warning signal: stamps with fore-hoof or whistles. Diurnal. Sportsmen distinguish them by the type of territory: rock and

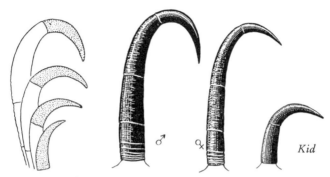

Fig. 7: Development of a chamois' horns

wood, scree, glacier, etc. The first are somewhat lighter in colour and better game. Formerly common in Alps, but now restricted to certain areas. Also in Appenines, Carpathians and Asia Minor. Good to eat; provide buckskin and horn.

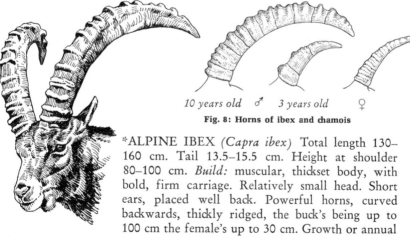

10 years old ♂ 3 years old ♀

Fig. 8: Horns of ibex and chamois

*ALPINE IBEX (*Capra ibex*) Total length 130–160 cm. Tail 13.5–15.5 cm. Height at shoulder 80–100 cm. *Build:* muscular, thickset body, with bold, firm carriage. Relatively small head. Short ears, placed well back. Powerful horns, curved backwards, thickly ridged, the buck's being up to 100 cm the female's up to 30 cm. Growth or annual rings that permit accurate estimate of age. Powerful necks and sturdy, medium length legs. Short, steel-hard hoofs, underside rough, wide expansion. Short tail, held upright. Thick coarse hair; in winter longer and with fine wool under-coat. Summer coat is shorter, softer, glossy and close-lying. Mane-like growth only in buck; and then on nape and the upper side of neck, in old bucks also on back of head and lower jaws, which in winter grow a beard of 5 cm in length at the most; this the younger bucks and females do not have. *Colouring:* in summer reddish-grey, in winter

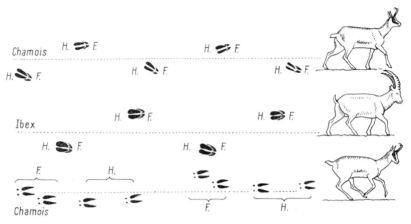

Fig. 9: Tracks of walking and running Chamois and Ibex

yellowy-grey. Neck, chest, flanks, legs are blackish brown, belly and buttocks white. Eyes amber-yellow with horizontal black pupil stripe; sight the most important sense. Forms flocks. *Action:* quick, enduring run; wonderfully powerful leap in crossing deep ravines, incredibly agile and sure-footed. *Cry:* whistling sound when threatened similar to that of mountain goat, but sharper and not so drawn-out; when frightened a strange note like a short, sharp sneeze. Kids have a high-pitched slender bleat. *Food:* herbs, grasses, young shoots, willow, birch, strawberries, rhododendron; in winter yellow grass, dry herbs, lichen. Needs lots of salt and licks rocks containing salt. *Mating season:* in January and has 1, rarely 2 kids at end of June or early July. These are able to clamber about after a few hours. *Life-span:* up to 30 years. *Habitat:* in alpine regions from upper fringes of the forests to the snow line preferring dwarf pine woods, high pastures and grassy strips among rocks. Usually lives above the "goat-line" only seeking shelter of the higher woods in exceptionally severe weather. Prefers rocky areas free of snow or thick dwarf pine. Females and kids and young bucks form herds of varying size. Older bucks will also group in herds outside the rut; only very old bucks are solitary. Will cross with domestic goat. Now only in the Gran Paradico massif of south Aosta valley (Northern Italy), and in Germany round Berchtesgaden.

* MOUFFLON *(Ovis musimon)* Length of body 120 cm. Height at shoulder 65–70 cm. Larger and stronger than a roe deer. Short tailed. Ram has a short mane like a stag's. Summer coat is foxy reddish-brown with a dark-brown tinge on its back. Ashen grey of the head fading into white on the muzzle. Underparts and legs white. Grey or white saddle on the back. Winter coat is darker: reddish-brown to chestnut. Colouring of the female less vivid, more dun-coloured. Horns curved backwards and outwards with numerous rings up to 80 cm in length; female either has none or they are short, like those of the young rams. *Cry:* soft bleat when grazing; a shrill whistle when frightened. *Food:* coarse grasses, heather, broom, leaves and spruce-tips, in autumn also acorns and beech nuts. Does not go on to open

land, does not bark trees. Feeds in the evening and morning, mostly in flocks of 20–30 led by a ram. *Mating season:* October to December. Lambs end of March to middle of April usually 1 lamb (rarely 2) that is able to run straightaway. *Life-span:* up to 15 years. A wild sheep native to the mountains of Corsica and Sardinia, but successfully introduced into Germany and other parts of Central Europe. Must have woods; prefers to lie hidden in thickets. Difficult to stalk, as the moufflon is very cunning and sharpsighted and can see a man 1,500–2,000 metres away. Meat very tasty.

*EUROPEAN BISON (WISENT) *(Bison bonasus)* Length of body up to 3.50 m. Tail 80 cm. Height at shoulder 1.90 m. Extinct in wild state, only surviving in national parks. Dangerous. Large, heavy body, strongly curved from the nape to the middle of the back; narrowing and slighter towards the hindquarters. Moderately large head with high, broad brow; blunt muzzle, bare nose; short, rounded ears; small eyes; very powerful, short, high neck with dewlap extending to the chest; long tail. Thick coat; shaggy mane on back of head, chest and nape; distinct ridge along the back. Chin has tufted pendent beard. Winter coat shed in spring in shaggy shreds. Round pointed horns, curving outwards, upwards and then forwards, points turned towards each other. Coat chestnut-brown. *Action:* swift walk; lumbering gallop that covers ground quickly. *Food:* grass, leaves, buds, bark of trees, branches, lichens. *Mating season:* August to September. Has one calf in May or early June. *Life-span:* up to 30 years.

200 years ago common in great forests of the continent. A herd of 700 survived in Polish forest of Bialowieza into this century. Almost exterminated in First World War. In 1923 "International Society for the Preservation of the Wisent" founded to promote planned breeding in parks etc. (Springe, Darsz, Shorfheide, Waren, Neandertal). Now about 160 pure-bred animals in Europe.

Family   CERVIDAE   Antlered Ruminants or Deer

Have on the head, mostly of males only, solid branching horns which are renewed every year and carried on frontal studs, called pedicles. The shaft of the antler is the equivalent of the bony horn-studs of horned cattle and the cuticle corresponds to the horn-case. The lowest, disc-shaped part of the shed antler with its bead-like ring of pustules (pearls) is known as the burr. (*Teeth:* See Fig. 1, no. 2.)

ROE DEER *(Capreolus capreolus)* Length of body 1.3 m. Tail 2 cm.
Height at hindquarters 75 cm. Our smallest and most graceful ungulate.
Lives mostly in families. Very timid. *Build:* slender hindquarters; tall very
slender, sinewy legs with small narrow hoofs and well-opened dew-claws.
Slender, but strong neck carrying a narrow pointed head with large erect
ears and large bright eyes. *Colouring:* in summer rust-red, short hair with
faint yellowish patch on hindquarters; in winter browny-grey thick coat

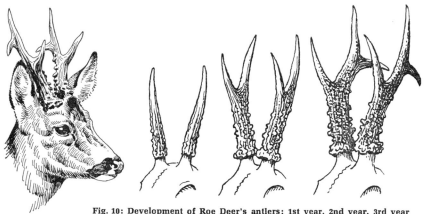

Fig. 10: Development of Roe Deer's antlers: 1st year, 2nd year, 3rd year

with distinct white patch on hindquarters. Kid has reddish background
colour with numerous round white or yellowish spots in rows for camouflage. *Antlers:* in first autumn small budlike "horns" shed after 2–3 months.
In first winter, from February on, proper antlers each of 1 prong or tine.
(Figs. 10 and 13.) The buck sheds its antlers in late autumn. In second
winter forked antlers each with 2 tines, in third winter each with 3 tines;
four and five tines are rare. The skinny covering (velvet) shrivels and
peels off in strips and is rubbed off. *Action:* quick, agile, graceful. *Cry:*
warning a deep barking bleat: "bö, bö", staccato, from both bucks and does;
during the rut bucks also have challenging roar. Also a snore/cough of
mating bucks. The roe in the rutting season and the kid that has lost its
mother both give a ringing bleat: "mfieh – mfieh". When afraid, a plaintive "pee-eh, pee-eh". *Food:* grass, leaves, young shoots of trees, acorns,
beech-nuts, wild forage plants. Rut late July to mid August; sometimes a
second rut at end of November or early December. Produced 1–2, rarely
3, kids May to June. *Life-span:* up to 16 years. *Habitat:* woods with plenty
of undergrowth; frequently in country with standing corn. In mountainous
country seeks the valleys at the onset of winter. Lies in thickets by day
emerging to feed at dusk, returning in the morning. In the summer lives

mostly in family groups of 4–10 consisting of does, kids, and younger bucks. The older bucks are unsociable, surly and solitary. In winter congregate in herds of up to 30, which like the family groups are led by a doe. Permanent only when it feels quite safe. *Range:* Northern Europe and Northern Asia.

RED DEER *(Cervus elaphus)* Length of body 1.85–2.15 m. Tail 15 cm. Height at shoulder 1.2–1.5 m. *Build:* long body, broad straight flat back. Slender neck, long narrow head; medium-long legs, slender yet very strong, with narrow hoofs and pendent dew-claws which do not touch the ground. The hind is much smaller than the stag which, as well as antlers, has a dark mane, its "collar". Antlers can be up to 1.3 m long. Short tail, its "single", half the length of its ears. *Colouring:* in summer hair is short, thin and reddish-brown; winter coat is thicker, longer and much darker with a grey tone and dark longitudinal stripes down the back. Colouring of calves same as that of roe kids. Occasional white stags are not neces-

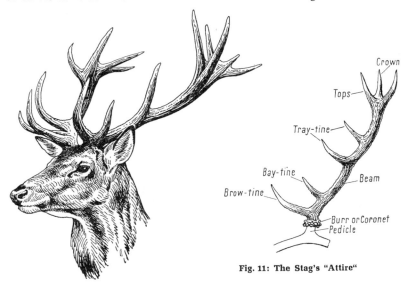

Fig. 11: The Stag's "Attire"

sarily albinos with red eyes. Rump patch bright rust colour all the year round. *Antlers:* at the end of first winter mere knobs of cartilage covered with "velvet" some 20–25 cm long. After about 4 months 2 simple shafts without burrs (broach). (Fig. 13.) After another 5 months, when stag is 2 years old, the broach antlers are shed and in May of the stag's third spring, when it is 2 years old, it grows antlers that often have six tines or "points". Unlike the roe buck, the stag almost always skips the 2-prong stage. The next year after being a "six-pointer" the stag becomes an eight-

Fig. 12: Stag: The older terms for stags' antlers as above were
Top: **pricket, brocket, staggard, stag.** Middle: **hart.** Now known by their "points" ten-
pointer, twelve-pointer etc. Below: **a twenty-pointer is very rare; in a very old stag the
procedure is reversed and the antlers shrink**

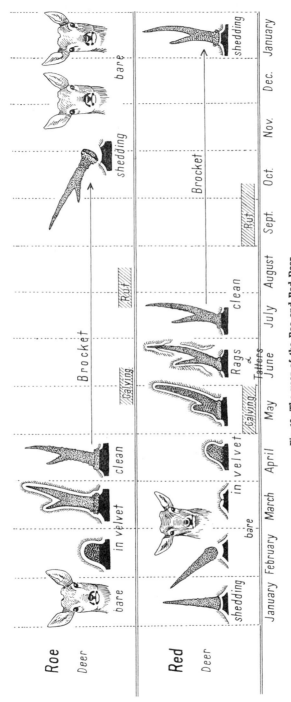

Fig. 13: The year of the Roe and Red Deer

pointer, then a ten-pointer, twelve pointer and so on. Antlers with 30 or 40 points are very rare. Old stags shed their antlers in February or March at the latest, and the new ones are complete by the end of July. Young stags, one-year olds in particular, often retain their antlers until May and have the new ones by August. Summer coat comes with the new antlers; when the hind is changing her coat she also drops her calf. At about 15 a stag is getting senile and it then has miserable antlers. A stag which fails to develop antlers is called a "hummel", or in Somerset and Devon a "nott". *Cry:* deep, powerful roar in rut, a sort of *ra* sound. *Food* differs with the seasons: buds, young shoots, grass and plants in spring; later roots, plants, standing corn, potatoes, beech-nuts; acorns; in winter sown corn, buds, bark, blackberry leaves, heather. Can cause considerable damage to crops and young trees. *Rutting season:* early September to middle of October, when stags roar and duel with rivals; the outcome of the duel decides the ownership of the harem. Rooting-places: leaves, needles, grass and moss often brushed away leaving the bare earth. The roe buck also roots. At the end of May or early June hind drops 1, rarely 2, calves. *Life span:* up to 20 years. Large woods, especially deciduous. Generally sticks to same haunts. Voluntary change of territory usually only with growth of new antlers or due to lack of food or during rut. Young stags and hinds without calves usually live in herds led by a hind which has calved. Even adult stags go about in groups. Old stags are solitary.

SIKA DEER (*Cervus nippon*) Length of body 1.5 m. Height at shoulder 82–90 cm. Tail 10 cm. Closely related to red deer with antlers similar but simpler. *Colouring:* warm brown in summer, darker in winter; rump white with black border. Calves like fallow deer but with smaller spots. *Cry:* sharp scream by both stag and hind when alarmed, repeated several times; stag has characteristic whistle during rut. *Food:* mainly grass and low plants but sometimes bark and tree shoots. *Rutting season:* early October; single calf (usually) born late May or June. Comes out mainly in the late evening; not so gregarious as red deer and single animals often seen.

This eastern Asiatic deer was introduced into parks in several European countries about the mid-19th Century. Feral populations are now found in many parts of Britain, Ireland, Denmark, France, Germany and Austria.

FALLOW DEER *(Dama dama)* Length of body 130–140 cm; tail 16–19 cm. Height at shoulder 85–90 cm. Smaller and not so stately as red deer. Despite strong hindquarters legs are shorter and not so strong; also the neck and ears are shorter than those of the red deer. Buck has no mane. Summer coat of adults is brown-red with round white spots. Black stripe along the spine. Winter coat has no spots, the back is then a darker, the underparts a lighter grey-brown. All black and all white specimens more frequent than with other deer. Rump patch rimmed with black. *Antlers:* broad, six-point etc. (Fig. 14). From the age of 5 on, the shaft of the antler broadens into a blade. There are no bay-antlers: the brow-antler is above the burr. Sheds its antlers in April or May. *Cry:* in rut a short, staccato, jarring sound, a sort of "belch". *Food:* same as red deer. Not so destructive as red deer. Very fond of salt, which is put out for them in salt-licks. *Rut:*

mid-October to mid-November. Drops 1–2, seldom 3, fawns from June to late July. *Life-span:* 20–25 years. *Range:* truly wild only in Mediterranean countries but commonest park deer in Britain and many parts of Europe. Lives mostly in herds, larger than those of roe deer. Easy to keep in parks; very trusting and easy to tame.

Fig. 14: Horns of Fallow Deer: (a) 2nd year–Pricket, (b) 3rd year – Sorel, (c) 4th year–Sore, (d) 5th year–Buck

Chinese Muntjac
or Barking Deer

CHINESE MUNTJAC or BARKING DEER *(Muntiacus reevesi)* Length of body: 110 cm. Height at shoulder: 37.5–42.5 cm. Rounded back and run with head held low down. A small deer which can readily hide from view in summer among bracken and low bushes. *Colouring:* in summer bright, foxy-red is usual; in winter olive-brown but tail and legs remain as in summer. Fawns dark brown with white spots on flanks. *Antlers:* short and simple with single brow tine; pedicles hairy and long; from them dark lines of hair continue on to the face. No definite period for shedding antlers. In bucks, the upper canine teeth are tusk-like and curved. *Cry:* dog-like bark when disturbed; more prolonged during the rut. Occasionally a prolonged cry of alarm. When moving a series of soft growl-like barks. *Food:* grass, shrubs but not usually bark. *Rut:* between October and March; one, or sometimes two fawns born in late summer.

These deer live singly or in pairs throughout the year. They are most often seen at dusk or in early morning. The species was introduced to Britain from China about 1900 as a park deer and either alone or crossed with the closely related Indian Muntjac *(M. muntjak)* is now feral in many counties.

*EUROPEAN ELK *(Alces alces)* Length of body 2.8 m; tail 10 cm. Height at withers 1.9 m. *Build:* large and heavy; body relatively short, thick, very high at the withers, broad chest. Legs strong, very long, with

narrow, deeply cloven hoof joined by a web of stretchy skin. Short powerful neck; large long head; long thick distended muzzle with a thick, considerably enlarged, very flexible upper lip that protrudes far beyond the lower jaw; small eyes; big, long, brow, pointed ears; long, thick, stiff hair. Mane on nape, neck and fore-legs. *Colouring:* coat dark brown; mane black-brown; legs whitish ashen-grey. Only bull has antlers, span up to 145 cm. Each of the 2 thick stems carries large single flat triangular "scoops" with numerous outward-facing points that form a wide basket of prongs. Indication of age as with red and roe deer. *Cry:* hoarse, plaintive, not very loud cry in rut. *Food:* leaves and bark of juicy deciduous trees such as birch, willow, poplar, elder, ash, also pine, juniper, larch; also grasses, herbs. *Rutting season:* September. Produces 2 calves (seldom 1) in May. *Life-span:* up to 20 years. *Habitat:* forest areas with lakes and bogs. Found in Northern Europe.

REINDEER *(Rangifer tarandus)* Length of body 107–122 cm. Height 91–107 cm. *Build:* straight bodies, short tail, rather long legs with very broad hoofs which splay out to enable them to travel easily over snow.

Long noses and small ears covered with soft hair as a protection against the cold. *Colouring:* greyish long hair with thick woolly undercoat. Underparts paler whitish-grey. Some all white specimens, but not albinos. *Antlers:* unique among deer in that male and female carry antlers. Shed annually, the hind retaining them longer than the stag for the calf's protection. *Rutting season:* early autumn one calf born per birth. *Life-span:* 15 years. *Habitat:* Lapland and southern Norway, Siberia. Introduced into Cairngorms in Scotland in 1952 and a small herd has become established there. *Food:* reindeer moss, leaves, grass, water-plants and lichens. They scrape for food beneath the snow with their hoofs and noses. Largely domesticated in Lapland where they are used for food, transport and clothing. Wild in southern Norway, Siberia.

Sub-order   SUIFORMES   Non-ruminant ungulates

Full set of teeth including all three kinds. Incisors and canines in upper and lower jaw. Canines large, rootless, always growing. Molars fairly uniform, the hinder ones have rugged surface. (Fig. 1, no. 1.) Metatarsal bones 3 and 4 not merged. No horns or antlers.

Family   SUIDAE   Swine

Have disc snouts. Omnivorous. Single stomach. Foot rests on toes 3 and 4. Toe 1 has disappeared. Dew-claws 2 and 5 rather long.

*WILD BOAR *(Sus scrofa)* Body length (of adult boar) 1.50 m. Height at shoulder: up to 1 m. Tail 25 cm. Sow is smaller. *Build:* powerful, compact wedge-shaped body, sloping down at rear. Short powerful legs, but longer legged than domestic pig. Small eyes, upright ears; short, flexible

snout with cartilage disc and nostrils in front. Long thin tail. Very thick skin; ridge of longer bristles on back, which stands up when boar is excited. *Colouring:* changes: bristles in summer fallow to rust brown, in winter black-grey. Canine teeth of adult boar outside the mouth tusks; the two lower ones are long and directed upwards, slightly curved, pointed and sharp; these are the boar's weapons and dangerous ones they are; two upper canines are short. Canines of sow not nearly so stout and seldom protrude. *Dental formula:* $\dfrac{3\ 1\ 4\ 3}{3\ 1\ 4\ 3}$ = 44. (Fig. 1 no. 1.) Swift, enduring run. Sows, young boars and barren live in herds; only old boars live on their own. Boars rest during the day in "couches" made with the snout in some thicket, or in a wallow; with dusk they sally out together to feed, using their snouts to search for roots, bulbs, acorns, beech-nuts, mushrooms, worms, snails, insects. *Mating season:* November to January. Sow has a litter of up to 12 in April or May; young have light striped coat of bristles. *Life-span:* 20–25 years. To be found in most of the great forests of the continent, especially in regions with thick underwood and boggy places, but now in much reduced numbers.

Order   LAGOMORPHA   Hares and rabbits

These animals were formerly classified as rodents but in a separate suborder, the DUPLICIDENTATA, because of the presence of two pairs of incisor teeth in the upper jaw, compared with one pair in the true rodents. They are now regarded as a separate order, characterised by the small second pair of (functionless) upper incisors, lying behind the functional pair (Fig. 1, no. 3); they have continously growing first incisors and a long space, the diastema, between the incisors and the rootless cheek-teeth, of which there are six on each side of the jaw. The lagomorphs are vegetarian.

Family   LEPORIDAE   Hares

Dental formula $\dfrac{2\ 0\ 3\ 3}{1\ 0\ 2\ 3}$ = 28. Fore-feet not used to hold food. *Food:* vegetables, grasses, herbs, twigs, bark.

BROWN HARE *(Lepus europaeus)* Total length 75 cm of which tail 8 cm. Height 30 cm. Jack-hare is slightly smaller in body then the doe. Very timid, which makes it appear more stupid than it is. *Build:* long body with strikingly long hind legs, large ears which, when laid forward, extend beyond its nose. Large, protuberant eyes. Thick, very mobile lip with deep cleft; strong whiskers. Forefeet 5-toed, hind feet 4-toed. Thick sole of feet slightly haired. Rough coat; short, thick, very curly wool undercoat and long, strong whiskers. *Colouring:* either true fallow earth-colour, or reddish-brown; back browny-yellow sprinkled with black-brown; underparts white. Yellow-brown eyes, surrounded by external lighter ring; ear has black tips; tail (scut) black on top, white underneath. *Action:* swift run in wide bounds, as the hind feet are much longer than the fore; swerves when pursued. *Cry:* a scream like the cry of a child when, e.g. caught by a dog. Scrapes its "form", a shallow hollow in the ground, in a dry sheltered place. "Freezes" to avoid attention. Long mobile ears which catch noises from a long way off. Is guided more by its delicate hearing than by its sight, which is not especially good. Nonetheless can see when a person is carrying a gun. Spends much of the day in its form.

When asleep eyes are not open, but are veiled by eyelids. *Food:* grass, plants, turnips, clover, young corn; in winter also bark. *Mating season:* mainly in spring when males indulge in antics such as boxing each other. Produces young March–August; has 3–4 broods: 1st. brood 1–2, 2nd.

brood 3–4, 3rd. brood 3, 4th. brood 1–2, with hair, eyes open; suckled for 2–3 weeks. *Life-span:* 8–12 years. Prefers open, grassy country. Is seldom found in large woods, but in smaller woods between fields and pastures.

MOUNTAIN or VARYING HARE *(Lepus timidus)* Total length 63–67.5 cm of which 5.3–6.5 cm is tail. Hind foot 13.8–14.8 cm. Ear 9.8–10.6 cm. More gay, lively and bold, lighter in its movements and less stupidly timid than the brown hare. *Build:* smaller, slighter, narrower body than brown hare's; head shorter and rounder, nose thicker; skull domed; ears shorter, hind legs longer, hind foot wider and more powerful, deeply cloven with long spreading toes with long, pointed curved claws (for moving on frozen snow) and stiff hairs. Bearing surface is thus greater. *Colouring:* uniformly white. Tail of woolly hair, top has at most a few grey hairs in summer. Summer coat is grey-brown, lighter on the sides; head brown, belly, lower jaw and throat white-grey; never has the yellow-mustard shade of the brown hare. In the far north the fur is often white throughout the year. By contrast the Irish race is brown always. Elsewhere the change begins in November. White hairs then grow over the brown; hair does not fall out. Brown colouring the result of white hair falling. *Action:* similar to brown hare. Makes the same "form" in shallow earth in a sheltered place. *Track:* like brown hare's, though the actual print is larger. *Food:* clover, grass, yarrow, bark and leaves of dwarf trees. Feeds in early morning and at dusk. *Mating season:* February onwards in the south, but not until April in the north. Produces young April to August. 1st litter end of April or early May; 2nd litter July to August; in each 2–5 leverets, with hair and eyes open. *Life-span:* 8–10 years. *Habitat:* throughout the Alps from about 1,300 to 3,600 m. In summer in the treeless, stony areas of the dwarf-tree zone up to the snow line; in winter in the

Fig. 15. Track: left **Brown hare**; right **Mountain hare**

upper tree zone. By day in its "form" under bushes. Will sometimes let itself be covered with snow, when it will scrape a free space under the snow, gnaw roots and leaves and only emerge when the frost has made the snow so hard that it will bear it. Also found on high ground in Scotland, Scandinavia and Ireland. Introduced into N. England and Wales.

RABBIT *(Oryctolagus cuniculus)* Total length *circa* 40 cm of which tail (scut) 7 cm. Gregarious, lives in colonies. More clever at swerving than the hare and also more cunning. *Build:* much smaller than the hare, more compact body, shorter head, shorter ears, shorter hind legs which are only slightly longer than fore legs. Ears not so long as head and when pressed down do not reach to nose. *Colouring:* grey fur, more yellow-brown on back, more reddish-yellow in front, light rust colour on flanks, underparts white. Ears do not have the hare's black tip. Tail black on top, white underneath. *Action:* rapid run, but not able to cover long distances. Lives in burrows, mostly dug in sunny parts among bushes; burrow has a fairly deep chamber and twisting passages with multiple exits. Single nest passage dug by doe and lined with wool plucked from her belly. *Food:* grass, clover, young corn, shoots and bark of young trees. *Mating season:* February to June. Produces 3–5 litters a year between March and October each of 4–12 naked, blind young, that are able to see after 10 days. *Life-span:* 5–8 years. *Habitat:* originally Mediterranean countries, especially Spain. Introduced from France into Germany in 1149; since when has spread all over Central Europe and to Great Britain. Regarded as a pest. Since the virus of myxomatosis was introduced in France in 1953 the population of rabbits in western Europe has decreased considerably, and although resistant strains have restored numbers somewhat, the density is much lower than before the epidemic.

Order	RODENTIA	Rodents, or gnawing animals

The largest order of mammals: the most characteristic feature is the dentition; single pair of incisors in each jaw growing continuously and kept in check by wear in use. They have enamel only on the front surface so that they sharpen to a chisel-like edge. There are no canines and there is a long space (diastema) between the incisors and cheek-teeth which are never more than four below and five above. Rodents are mainly vegetarian in diet, but some take animal food.

Family	MURIDAE	Mice, rats and voles

Tail scaly or with sparse hair. Largest group of mammals represented in every part of the world. Prolific, rapid reproduction. Short life-span.

FIELD VOLE *(Microtus agrestis)* Length of body: 9–11.5 cm; tail 3–4.6 mm; blunt muzzle, short furred ears and tail. Back yellowish to deep brown; underside grey to buffish. This grassland species is one of the most abundant voles and is found throughout Europe, except Russia, in fairly dense ground cover, unlike the following species which frequents open grassland. It makes prominent runs through the grass and also sometimes underground tunnels, but the nest is usually above ground under a log or stone. The field vole is active both by day and night. *Food:* stems and leaves of grasses, rushes and sedges; in winter roots and bark. *Mating season:* produces a succession of litters of between 3 and 6 blind, naked young from spring to autumn. The young may begin to breed when six weeks old. *Life-span:* about 2 years. *Habitat:* rough grassland, marshy ground and young forestry plantations, in which the voles may do much damage.

M. agrestis is the only species of *Microtus* on the mainland of
Britain. It occurs also on most of the Hebridean islands but
not in Orkney or Shetland.

COMMON VOLE *(Microtus arvalis)* Length of body: 11 cm,
tail 3 cm. Rather plump; very short tail; small ears. Back
yellow-, brown- to black-grey; underparts dull yellowy white.
Digs innumerable runs with 4–6 different entrance holes, connected above ground by paths trampled or eaten through grass;
in winter paths run below surface of snow; has both subterranean
and above-ground nest, ball-shaped structure of chewed straws,
grass and moss; also a store-room with grain, acorns and berries.
Food: grain, potatoes, roots, berries, fruit, nuts, acorns. Produces between spring and autumn 5 to 7 broods of 4–8 blind,
naked young in nest. A pair of field voles has progeny of up to
200 a year. *Life-span:* 2–3 years. *Habitat:* treeless areas, fields,
pastures, more seldom on skirts of woods or in glades. In mountains up to 6000 ft. May migrate when become too numerous.
Can be a plague. This is a more southerly species than *M. agrestis*
and is not found in Scandinavia, Finland or the mainland of
Britain. The large forms that occur in the Orkney Islands and
on Guernsey are believed to have been introduced by human
agency probably in prehistoric times.

HOUSE MOUSE *(Mus musculus)* Body 7 cm; tail 9 cm. Long
ears and tail. *Colouring:* uniform grey, somewhat darker on
back. Speedy, splendid climber, makes wide jump, often moves
by short hops; able to jump straight in the air; makes good use
of tail in climbing; can also swim. *Food:* anything we eat. Makes
nest of straw, hay, paper, feathers and other soft materials which
it takes to some recess. Between spring and late autumn has
4–5 litters each of 4–10 blind, naked, pink young in nest; which
are themselves able to produce young after 6 weeks. *Life-span:*
2–4 years. *Habitat:* everywhere in buildings, also in gardens and
fields. (White and other colours bred as pets and for scientific
research.) Originally from Central Asia but the species has followed everywhere as man has spread. There are many subspecies
and races differing somewhat in colouring and size. The western
European race is *Mus musculus domesticus,* whereas east of a
line from Venice to Hamburg the race is *M. m. musculus.*

HARVEST MOUSE *(Micromys minutus)* Body 6.5 cm; tail 6 cm. Dainty. Tail appears bare; is prehensile and used in climbing. Upper parts yellowy-brown-red; underparts and feet white, distinct line of demarcation. Colouring varies. Very swift run; agile climber among thin branches of bushes and stalks of grass or corn. *Food:* grain, seeds, plants, small insects. Nest size of a goose egg; clever structure of grass woven round tall grasses, reed and sedge stalks; or made of 20–30 sedge leaves woven together. Inside lined with wool from catkins, reedmace and flower panicles. In summer produces 2–3 litters each of 5–9 blind young in nest. *Life-span:* 2–3 years. Found in cornfields, among bushes, reed-banks, rushes; in winter in barns and granaries. Sleeps in cold weather, but not proper hibernation.

BANK VOLE *(Clethrionomys glareolus)* Body 10 cm, tail 4.5 cm. Upper parts brown-red, underparts white. Blunt head. Ears half the length of the head, protrude from fur. Agile climber; digs burrow; makes ball-shaped nest of grass stalks and similar materials mostly above ground in thick bushes or in the earth. *Food:* insects, worms, seeds, roots, bulbs, young bark. Lives in light woods, deciduous or mixed; particularly in bushes or fringes of trees.

WOOD or LONG-TAILED FIELD MOUSE *(Apodemus sylvaticus)* Body up to 9.2 cm; tail up to 8.7 cm. *Colouring:* brown above, white below but variable usually yellow spot on chest. Large ears and eyes. *Action:* runs quickly or takes big leaps; climbs well. *Habitat:* deciduous woodland, in runways below and above the litter, but also in gardens and hedgerows. Will come into houses and buildings. Nests below ground but makes platform above, often an old bird's nest, for feeding places. Food stores below ground. *Breeding season:* March to October; 5–6 young born 25 days after mating and leave nest at 15 days old. *Food:* grain, seedlings, fruit, nuts, snails etc. *Distribution:* deciduous zones of Europe; common in all parts of British Isles.

YELLOW-NECKED MOUSE *(Apodemus flavicollis)* Larger than preceding species. Body up to 11.5 cm; tail up to 11.1 cm. *Colouring:* upper part rust to chestnut-brown; abrupt transition to white of underparts. Yellow collar. Distinguishing marks:

darker patch on heel conspicuous against the white. Long ears. Tail mostly longer than body. *Action:* moves in great arching bounds; good climber. *Habitat:* deciduous woods. Will come into houses in winter. Nest is a hole in the earth. *Distribution:* deciduous woodland zones of Europe but rare in France and the low countries. In Britain restricted mainly to parts of southern England and Wales.

*STRIPED MOUSE (*Apodemus agrarius*) Body length up to 11.5 cm. Tail up to 8 cm. Short ears (1.2 cm). Tail looks bare. *Colouring:* summer coat rusty-brown, grey-toned in winter. Underparts whitish-grey with sharp demarcation. Narrow clear-cut black stripe down back. *Action:* clumsier than that of its relatives. *Food:* grain, seeds, plants, bulbs, insects, worms. Lives in holes in the ground. Between spring and late summer produces 3–4 litters, each of 4–8 naked, blind young born in a nest. *Life-span:* 2–4 years. *Distribution:* mainly eastern European species; in Germany found everywhere east of the Rhine, in fields, on the fringes of woods, among bushes; in winter in farm buildings, barns, etc.

*ALPINE VOLE (*Microtus nivalis*) Total length 18 to 21 cm. Tail 6–7.5 cm. *Colouring:* upper parts brownish-grey with somewhat darker back; underparts grey-white. Tail greyish or pure white, about half as long as its body. Ears relatively large, rounded. Feet white. *Food:* roots, alpine plants, grass, hay; enters Alpine huts for food, even meat. Stores food for winter in underground passages. Does not hibernate; digs passages under the snow from plant to plant; with the snow to hide it does not require to be white in winter. Short alpine summer allows only 1 to 2 litters each of 4–7 naked, blind young born in warm nest. *Habitat:* highest living mammal of the Alps. Seldom seen below 1,500 m, most common near the snow line, and can be seen on the highest peaks. Prefers clumps of rhododendron, stone pine, dwarf pine, larch. Digs its nest mostly under stones. Will also live in mountain huts. The Alpine vole is found in most of the high mountain ranges of Europe.

BLACK RAT (*Rattus rattus*) Body 20 cm; tail up to 25 cm, thin, with 260–270 scaly rings, longer than body. *Colouring:* upper parts dark brown-black, underparts a somewhat lighter grey-black. White ones not uncommon. Ears large (2.5 cm) bare, thin-skinned, about half the length of the head. Skull not so blunt as that of brown rat. Mates and produces young from spring till autumn, having 2 or more litters every year each of 8–20, blind, naked, born in a nest. *Life-span:* 7 years. *Distribution:* all over Europe, but in northern countries driven out by the stronger, more pugnacious brown rat, and exists only in small pockets especially near seaports.

BROWN RAT (*Rattus norvegicus*) Body 25 cm. Ears 2 cm long. Tail bare and appears thick, has about 210 scale rings. *Colouring:* upper parts reddish grey-brown, lower parts sharply contrasting grey-white. Good swimmer: *Food:* will eat anything, even refuse; will attack poultry. Produces yearly 2–7 litters each of 5–20 blind, naked young. *Life-span:* 3–5 years. Lives in cellars, stables, river banks, sluices, mills, canals, ditches. Does great damage. Spreads the parasitic round worm *Trichina spiralis*. *Distribution:* world-wide, occurring abundantly near human habitations.

WATER VOLE (*Arvicola terrestris*) Body up to 17 cm, tail 10 cm. Ears scarcely rise above its fur. *Colouring:* size and colouring vary considerably: upper parts grey-brown or brown-black, darkest down the line of the middle; gradually fading into the lighter, whitish or grey underparts. Short, thick round head. *Food:* mainly roots and vegetable food, but also water-insects, frogs, fish, crab, mice, baby birds, eggs. In autumn makes a store of peas, beans, potatoes, onions. Produces 3–4 litters a year each of 2–7, in underground, spherical nest lined with warm dry grass. *Habitat:* found on river banks and most watery places, but also in drier ground, gardens, etc. *Distribution:* a wide spread species but with considerable variations in different regions. The large form (*A. t. amphibius*), found in Britain and northern Europe, favours aquatic habitats whereas the smaller forms that occur in central Europe (*A. t. scherman* and *A. t. enitus*) are often found away from water and dig tunnels like those of moles. The water vole does not occur in Ireland.

*MUSK-RAT *(Ondatra zibethica)* Body 30 cm, tail 20 cm. *Build:* compact body, rather short and broad; thick, blunt nose, long whiskers; ears almost hidden by fur, covered with short hairs, can be sealed against water; tail is flat-sided, with distinct upper and lower edge; a sideways motion of the tail provides main motive power when swimming. Broad hind feet. Thick, close-lying fur, soft and glossy. *Colouring:* upper parts brown, sometimes yellowish; underparts grey, sometimes with a hint of red; tail black; toes edged with white swimming bristles. Glands which are near the sexual organs secrete an oily fluid smelling of civet. Similar in many respects to the beaver.

Nests by the bank: either a subterranean den with several entrances, the mouths of which are under water, or a conical nest built on mud above the surface of the water, with one passage opening below the water. *Food:* water plants and at times also small aquatic creatures (shell fish), rarely fish or birds. Its tunnelling does considerable damage to dykes and dams. Produces 3–4 broods every year each of 2-8 naked, blind young. Generally confined to water; can travel considerable distances overland. *Distribution:* originally a North American species bred in captivity in many countries for its valuable fur. Some escaped or were released in many parts of Europe and multiplied rapidly. It was feral in Britain between 1927 and 1937 but was then exterminated because of the damage it caused to river banks by tunnelling.

*COMMON HAMSTER *(Cricetus cricetus)* Body 20–22 cm. Tail 5 cm, shorter than the head. *Build:* stocky body, thick neck, fairly pointed head; medium length ears, large eyes, short legs and claws. Thick, close-lying fur, slightly glossy, short wool-hair and longer, stiff sparser guard hairs. *Colouring:* upper parts light browny-yellow; edges of ears, lips, tips of muzzle, throat and feet white; underparts and stripe across the brow black. Variations of colouring, even all black and all white. *Action:* active and nimble; when angry long bounds and high leaps; expert digger; uses fore feet cleverly like hands, raises food to its mouth in them. Puts food in cheek-pouches to take it to nest. Nest consists of living-chamber 1–2 m underground, 1 sloping exit tunnel and 1 horizontal entrance (bolt-hole), 1 store room. Nest of the female has 2–8 bolt-holes. Hibernation sometimes interrupted.

Body temperature drops to 4° C. *Food:* pretty well omnivorous: cultivated plants, invertebrates and small vertebrates. Winter store of up to 15 kg of grain, roots, potatoes, cabbage. *Breeding season:* May to July; has 2–3 broods annually each of 4–18 blind, naked young in nest. *Life-span:* 6–10 years. *Distribution:* western Europe from Belgium east to Siberia; common in central Germany, but never in northern or southern Germany. Distribution varies considerably as it will migrate. Has to have permanent home, so avoids both sandy and hard, stony ground, preferring good, firm dry soil. Can become a plague.

GOLDEN HAMSTER *(Mesocricetus auratus)* This popular pet and laboratory animal is smaller than the common hamster and originated in Syria. All those now in captivity are the progeny of 1 female and 12 young sent to England in 1931.

*LEMMING *(Lemmus lemmus)* Length 12.5 cm. *Build:* short legs, lithe body, covered with rather short, soft fur. *Colouring:* yellow-brown coat marked with darker brown spots. *Action:* most spectacular feature is their periodic migration or irruption, following exceptional increase

in population which causes serious food shortage. They make their way in countless swarms across country in all directions, climbing mountains, swimming rivers and lakes, eating their way through fields of corn and grass until eventually some may reach the sea, plunge in and continue their journey swimming, until they drown. Normally they choose dry places to make their burrows in which they spend the day sitting near the entrance. If an intruder appears they sit up on their hind quarters and chatter excitedly. Will attack the legs of those who come too close to their holes. *Food:* grass, reindeer moss, birch catkins, and roots. *Breeding:* normally two litters of five or six young are born in summer in nests of dry grass lined with hair. *Distribution:* mountains of Scandinavia.

Family   SCIURIDAE   Squirrels

Mainly small animals, the family including the flying squirrels and the marmots. Four genera are represented in Europe.

*COMMON GROUND SQUIRREL *(Citellus citellus)* Body height at shoulder up to 9 cm. Almost the size of a hamster. *Colouring:* upper parts yellowy grey; underparts rust yellow, chin and front of neck white; light ring round the eyes which are rather large. Small, short ears. Final half of tail bushy. Diurnal. *Food:* delicate plants, roots, grain, podded seeds, berries. Builds a winter store during the autumn. Has cheek pouches. Holds its food between its fore paws in semi-upright position. *Action:* like marmot's. *Cry:* shrill whistle. Lives in groups. Each individual digs itself a burrow. Den 1–1.5 m beneath the surface, with a diameter of some 30 cm. Hibernates. *Breeding season:* April to May. Produces 1–2 broods every year each of 3–8 young. *Life-span:* 4–5 years. Animal of the steppes. Range: south-eastern Europe but with a patchy distribution. Avoids woods and damp ground, loves the open field. Rather rare, but more common in Russia.

RED SQUIRREL *(Sciurus vulgaris)* Body about 25 cm. Tail 20 cm. "Sciurus" means "shading tail" or "he who shades himself with this tail". *Build:* slender, very elastic, light body (weighs only about 250 g). Long hind legs; fore paws with 4 movable fingers, 1 stumpy thumb, bare palms with several pads for gripping branches. The 5-toed feet also have pads. Broad head, pointed muzzle, ear tufts. Large, protuberant eyes. Tail bushy. Rodent's teeth. *Colouring:* in low country summer coat mostly rust-red on upper parts, belly sharply distinguished white; winter coat grey-brown. In mountains brown-black to black. Variants to brown, grey and black are common. *Action:* never runs or trots, but always bounds in swift leaps, both when climbing and on the ground. Agile climber, even descending swiftly head downwards. Tail used as rudder and when making a long leap with all four legs widespread also as parachute. *Cry:* when scared a loud *duck, duck, duck;* when pleased and excited a shrill whistle, when put-out or angry a peculiar grumbling. Builds a nest or "drey" (page 81) mostly on a forked branch close to the trunk, with twigs and branches cleverly woven into a closed sphere with the main entrance from underneath. Often has an escape hole, close to the trunk; inside is lined with moss and wool. In winter the bolt-hole is blocked up. Also uses old nests of crows and birds-of-prey. *Food:* hazel nuts, acorns, beechnuts, buds, young shoots, conifer seeds, berries, mushrooms, bird's eggs, baby birds. Makes store in autumn (hazel nuts etc.) in cracks in trees, holes it has dug itself, under stones, etc. but does not hibernate. Does damage by nibbling trees and plundering nests. *Breeding season:* spring to summer. Has 2–5 litters every year each of 3–7 young which remain blind for 30 days. *Life-span:* 10 years. *Distribution:* All over Europe in dry shady specially coniferous, woods, but now rare or absent in much of Midlands and south-east England. Occurs, however in Isle of Wight, and East Anglia. Disease was the main cause of the decline.

GREY SQUIRREL *(Sciurus carolinensis)* Body about 26 cm. Tail 21 cm. *Build:* sturdier than red squirrel and with slightly longer skull. *Colouring:* grey colour is made up of hairs black at base, then with bands of

brown and black and finally a white tip. In winter there is a yellow-brown streak down the middle of the back and short brown hairs on the face. In summer there are bright russet streaks on flanks and limbs which often lead the uninitiated observer into thinking the animals are red squirrels, or hybrids, but the red and grey squirrels do not interbreed. *Action:* similar to red squirrel but spends more time on the ground. Builds in summer a leafy platform out on a branch. In winter the true nest (drey), a domed structure of twigs with a side entrance and lined with grass, leaves etc. is built in a large fork of the tree nearer the main trunk and as much as 12 m up. *Food:* similar to red squirrel; surplus food similarly buried. Does not hibernate. *Breeding season:* mating takes place late December or January and again late May to June. Two litters every year of about three young.

Life-span: 6–10 years. *Distribution:* a N. American species which was introduced into Britain on several occasions between 1876 and 1930 and has now become established throughout most of the lowlands of Britain and in much of Ireland. It is more typical of broad-leaved woodlands as well as parks and gardens. It has replaced the red squirrels in most of England but by superior adaptability rather than by actual destruction.

*ALPINE MARMOT *(Marmota marmota)* Body 48–52 cm, tail 18–20 cm. Height 15 cm. Weight up to 5 kg. Pliny called it *mures alpini*, "mountain mouse", hence the Roman *murment* from which name our word marmot comes. *Build:* plump, thickset body; thick rounded head with no brow. Cheeks have long hair and appear puffed up. Short, thick neck. Upper lip furnished with long whiskers. Small, rounded ears. Very short strong legs with powerful curved claws, 4 toes on each fore foot, 5 on each hind. Thick coarse coat of short wool hair and longer guard hairs. Tail bushy. *Colouring:* pale-grey fur; back more browny black, underparts more browny-grey; in winter grey blended. Occasionally black, white or white-spotted. Gnawing teeth brown-red. Eyes shiny black. *Action:* waddling gait; often sits back on hind legs and peers round. In digging scuffles loose earth out behind it with hind feet, shoving this out of the hole with its backside. *Cry:* a ringing shrill whistle to give warning of danger,

produced in larynx with mouth open. Its main or winter quarters a passage 8–10 m long leading inwards to a round den lined with grass, some 1.5–3 m below the surface. When hibernating up to 15 can be found together in one nest. Before hibernation 1–2 m of the entrance passage is blocked up with stones and earth (protection against cold and flooding). Has short lateral passages used as privies. *Summer quarters:* a branching passage 1–4 m long without a living burrow and usually with several openings; inhabited by marmot babies. *Food:* juicy alpine plants, grass, roots. *Mating season:* end of April to early May. Produces 2–5 young, at first naked and blind. Suckles for 4 weeks. *Life-span:* 15–20 years. Lives in colonies in the Alps and Carpathians, not so common in Eastern Alps. Lives above the tree line, usually above the dwarf tree zone up to near the snow line. In autumn retreats lower down. Prefers sunny boulder-strewn slopes in lonely places for its summer quarters. Hunted for its "grease" used locally as embrocation for rheumatism, gout, chilblains. *Distribution:* in Europe in the Alps and Carpathians and in Asia corresponding alpine regions of central and north-east Asia. Also in the Rockies, N. America.

Family   MUSCARDINIDAE   Dormice

Round tail covered with hair throughout its length. Climb in trees and bushes. Nocturnal. Hibernate.

DORMOUSE *(Muscardinus avellanarius)* Total length 14 cm, of which almost 7 cm is tail. Slightly smaller than a house mouse. *Colouring:* yellowy-red fur; chest, throat and feet white. Bushy tail. Black protruberant eyes. *Action:* climbs agilely on the thinnest twigs. Sleeps by day, searches by night for nuts, acorns, hard seeds, juicy fruit and leaf buds. Favourite food hazel nuts. Produces 3–4 young in August. Retires before middle of October into its winter nest with its accumulated stores. Hibernates. Lives in woods. Not restricted to hazel bushes. Round underground nest of grass, moss, wool, under bushes. Protected. *Distribution:* throughout Europe except Denmark and Iberian peninsula. In Britain mainly in the south.

EDIBLE or FAT DORMOUSE *(Glis glis)* Body 16 cm. Smaller than a squirrel. *Colouring:* upper parts blue-grey. Underparts white. *Build:* head pointed in front. Large eyes surrounded by a dark ring; broad, erect, almost hairless ears; long whiskers (nocturnal); bushy tail. *Action:* quick, graceful movements. Sleeps by day; at night searches for acorns, beechnuts, hazel nuts, chestnuts, berries, fruit, insects. Bites off young shoots, plunders birds' nests. Causes damage in orchards by barking young trees. Produces 3–5 naked, blind young in June to August. Hibernates in groups by middle of October at latest. Rolls up tightly. Remains cold and rigid for 7 months in warm nest. *Distribution:* central and southern Europe (not in the north). Prefers mountainous or hilly country; deciduous woods, parks, orchards. Introduced into the Chiltern Hills in England in 1902 and has become established there.

*GARDEN DORMOUSE *(Eliomys quercinus)* Body 14 cm. Tail 12 cm. Build: smaller than the edible dormouse. *Colouring:* upper parts reddish grey-brown; underparts white; dark ring round eyes and black stripes reaching to neck. *Distribution:* from France to Russia, south to Mediterranean in deciduous and conifer woods. In autumn enters houses, outdoor storehouses, etc.

Family CASTORIDAE Beaver

BEAVER (Castor fiber) Body up to 82 cm. Tail up to 38 cm in length and 10–12 cm wide. Up to 30 kg in weight. *Build:* plump, strong, much broader behind than in front. Curved back; short, thick neck; short, blunt head; small, short ears almost hidden by its fur; eyes small, with inner eyelid for use under water; upper lip grooved in the middle and with an upward running cleft; short, powerful legs; feet have five toes and the hind feet broad webs between the claws making them splendid paddles; two hind toes have twin claws for grooming its fur. No clear demarcation between tail and body; tail round at root, otherwise flat, as though squashed flat from on top, egg-shaped, with sharp edges, sometimes called its trowel; this acts as a rudder, especially when swimming up or down, also as a support for the body when sitting up. *Colouring:* upper parts dark brown, lower parts somewhat lighter. Thick, delicate undercoat and thin, erect, stiff, glossy guard hairs in many places over 5 cm long. Tail naked, with black-grey skin-scales. Gnawing teeth have orange-coloured edges.  *Activity:* lives in water and banks; expert swimmer and diver; nose and ears can be sealed. Wipes out its tracks by dragging its tail behind it. Prefers special places for landing, called "beaver-exits", makes "beaver paths" to its felling places, when at a distance; on mud and boggy ground these become trodden into canals. *Food:* bark, leaves, soft saplings of willow, poplar, ash, birch; less frequently of alder, elm, oak. Fells trees of up to 60 cm diameter making a cut shaped like an hour glass. Builds an underground house (lodge) in the bank consisting of two entrance tunnels up to 6 m long with their mouths under water. One living-room above the level of the water lined with fine gnawed saw-dust. In lonely woods lodges of barked branches and earth haphazardly thrown up; oven-shaped mound 2–3 m high with living room and larder. Stores consist of branches, the thickness of an arm with the bark on. Excavated passages ending in deep water. In the autumn plasters its house with mud brought from the bank by shoving it forward with its chest and fore-feet. Builds a dam if the level of the water varies considerably: irregular layers of sticks padded out with turf and clay; worked with mouth and paws; does not use its tail as a trowel. Draining channel regulates the height of the water, so that the entrances and exits are always under water. Gregarious. Nocturnal. Does not hibernate. *Mating season:* February to March. Produces by May one brood of 2–4 young. *Life-span:* about 50 years. *Distribution:* on the Rhône, some still in nature parks on the Elbe between Magdeburg and Wartenburg. Also in Scandinavia. Exterminated in Britain probably by 13th Century. Valuable fur. Secretes a reddish-brown greasy substance (castoreum) to attract the opposite sex. This used to be used in medicine as a sedative and in perfumery.

COYPU *(Myocastor coypus)* Body up to 58 cm; tail up to 34 cm; weight up to 6.4 kg. *Build:* with humped back and large head; ears hairy with central black tuft; tail thick, round and scaly. Short front legs with strong claws; longer hind legs with webbed feet, black underneath. *Colouring:*

dark brown or nearly black; belly fur, from which the "nutria" of commerce is obtained, is greyish and soft. Large orange-coloured incisor teeth. *Activities:* lives in water making runways through the marsh plants and short burrows for shelters in the banks; active mainly between dusk and dawn; solitary. *Food:* marsh and water plants, root crops. *Breeding season:* throughout the year; the young, 5 or 6 to a litter, are well developed at birth and suckle in the water from teats along the mother's sides. Sexually mature after about 3 months. *Life-span:* 3–6 years.

This rodent is a native of South America and has been kept in captivity in many countries for its fur. Feral populations are established in much of Europe including Great Britain where the main concentration is in East Anglia.

Order   INSECTIVORA   Insect-eaters

Small plantigrades (walking on the sole of the feet) most with 5 toes with claws. Complete set of teeth with all three kinds of tooth, small eye-teeth and pointed molars: adapted for eating insects. (Fig. 1, nos. 8, 9 & 10.)

Family   TALPIDAE   Moles

Have rooting snouts and front digging feet. Dental formula: $\dfrac{3\ 1\ 4\ 3}{3\ 1\ 4\ 3} = 44$
(Fig. 1, no. 8).

COMMON MOLE *(Talpa europaea)* Body 15 cm, tail 2.5 cm; cylindrical snout, conical in front with trunk-like bare muzzle. Fur velvet soft, thick, smooth, grey-black to grey; point of nose and soles of feet bare, flesh-coloured. Very small eyes hidden in fur; ears scarcely visible. Delicate

sense of smell. *Teeth:* strong, sharp eye-teeth; pointed, ridged molars; meat diet. Short legs 5 toes on feet; fore feet broad with strong digging claws, bare soles turned outward; narrow hind feet. Extensive branching structure of tunnels with galleries and nest-chamber, the whole called its fortress, tunnels just below the surface in search of food, surplus earth being thrust out upwards in mole hills. *Food:* worms, snails, cockchafer grubs and other insects. Stores food. Does not hibernate. Digs deeper into frost free ground. Keep strictly to their own territory. Mating takes place mostly in March and April. Has from 2 to 6 young born in nest in April and May. These are blind and naked at birth. Common nearly everywhere. Found in Alps up to 2,400 m. The Mediterranean mole *(Talpa caeca)* replaces the commoner species along the northern shores of the Mediterranean. It is smaller.

Family   ERINACEIDAE   Hedgehogs

Have prickles on their backs. Dental formula $\dfrac{3\ 1\ 3\ 3}{2\ 1\ 2\ 3} = 36$. (Fig. 1, no. 9.)

COMMON HEDGEHOG *(Erinaceus europaeus)* Body 25–30 cm; tail 2.5 cm. Height 12–15 cm. *Build:* plump body, very short legs. Walks on the soles of its feet. Back and sides covered with spines that can be erected.

Colouring: grey-brown. Sleeps most of the day in bushes, under heaps of twigs, among roots and abandoned burrows. Hunts by night mice, insects, worms, snails; on occasion also young birds, birds' eggs; will not despise a mole or a snake, but it is not immune to snake poison, though very resistant. Insect-eater jaws with nothing but pointed little teeth. Very delicate sense of smell and hearing. Deep, uninterrupted hibernation in nest lined with moss and leaves. Rolls up and erects it prickles when danger

threatens. Has 1 or 2 broods each of 3–8 young with white, soft prickles. *Life-span:* 6 years. *Distribution:* throughout Europe and western Asia. *Cry:* a cough-like grunt or snore. The young have a shrill squeak.

*ALGERIAN HEDGEHOG *(Erinaceus algirus)* A north-west African species has been recorded from the Mediterranean coasts of France and Spain, but has probably been introduced. It has a slightly wider spine-free area in the centre of the crown.

Family   SORICIDAE   Shrews

Among the smallest mammals. In size, build and appearance like mice. Have rooting snouts but not digging paws. Insect-eater jaws with numerous pointed teeth. *Food:* insects, worms, snails, mice and other small mammals, on occasions also small birds. Voracious, cannot go long without food. Do not hibernate. When threatened stink glands produce musk-like smell that does not always turn an enemy away, but is enough to make dogs, cats, etc. leave a dead shrew alone, though owls will take them.

Genus   *Sorex*   Terrestrial red-toothed shrews

Dental formula: $\dfrac{3\ 1\ 3\ 3}{2\ 0\ 1\ 3} = 32.$

COMMON SHREW *(Sorex araneus)* Body 6.5–8 cm. Tail 4.5 cm. *Colouring:* upper parts black-brown, underparts greyish-white, not sharply distinguished. Reddish-brown points to teeth. *Habitat:* lives in woods, rough grasslands and moorland, though

in winter will come in to farm buildings. Inhabits abandoned mouseholes, mole-runs, and tunnels it digs for itself. Active both by day and night. Eats insects, spiders, woodlice, worms and snails. Breeding continues through summer; gestation about 20 days; litter size usually 6 or 7. *Distribution:* throughout Europe except for Mediterranean region. Not found in Ireland or the Outer Hebrides.

PYGMY SHREW *(Sorex minutus)* Body 3.5 cm. Tail 3.4 cm. Smallest mammal north of the Alps. *Colouring:* upper parts glossy grey-brown, a little yellower on the flanks, underparts ashen-grey, otherwise as previous species. *Distribution:* as for *Sorex araneus* but occurs in Ireland and Hebridean islands.

*ALPINE SHREW *(Sorex alpinus)* Body up to 7.5 cm. Tail up to 8 cm. *Colouring:* upper parts black-grey, with a brown shade toning into the somewhat lighter colouring of the underparts. Ears hidden by the fur. Tail evenly haired throughout its length. *Habitat:* lives in woods throughout the Alps, Balkans, Carpathians and in the Riesengebirge, Hartz Mts., Jura; often in bushes beside a stream, mainly in upper tree and dwarf tree zones, from 1,000 to 2,000 m. The Alpine shrew is the largest European species of *Sorex* and is easily recognised by the tail, which is as long as the head and body. Little is known about its life-history.

Genus   *Crocidura*   White-toothed shrews   (Fig. 1, no. 10)

Dental formula: $\dfrac{3\ 1\ 1\ 3}{1\ 1\ 1\ 3}$ = 28. Points of teeth white. When threatened the young follow the mother, each fastening its teeth onto the tail of the one in front.

* HOUSE SHREW *(Crocidura russula)* Body 8.1 cm. Tail 4–5 cm. *Colouring:* upper parts grey-brown, in the young ones blackish-grey, fading into light grey on the underparts; browny-white lips and feet. *Food:* eats insects, snails, worms, mice. Breeding continues from March to September; several litters, normally of 4 young, born naked and blind in a nest. Lives in gardens, fields, and in winter in buildings. Also eats meat, bacon, etc. *Distribution:* the commonest shrew in most parts of Europe but absent from British Isles, Denmark and the Baltic coast.

*FIELD SHREW (*Crocidura leucodon*) Body 7–8 cm. Tail 3.5–4 cm. *Colouring:* upper parts slate grey to black-brown; underparts sharply distinguished yellow-white. Teeth quite white. Produces several broods of about 6 young, born blind and naked in nest.

Distribution: deciduous woodland zones of Europe, but not in Schleswig-Holstein; on mountains up to 1,200 m; fields, gardens, buildings. Makes nest of grass with a side entrance; often found in compost heaps under or above ground. Two other species of white-toothed shrews occur in Europe: *Crocidura suaveolens* resembling *C. russula* but slightly smaller; and *Suncus etruscus* the smallest of all shrews, mainly a Mediterranean species.

Genus   *Neomys*   Water shrews

Dental formula: $\dfrac{3\ 1\ 2\ 3}{2\ 0\ 1\ 3} = 30$

NORTHERN WATER SHREW (*Neomys fodiens*) Body up to 8 cm. Tail up to 6.5 cm. Teeth have reddish-brown points. Fringe of long stiff hairs on side of foot to help in swimming. Tail has short hair on top, and down the middle of the under side a line of stiff long bristles that serves as a rudder when swimming. *Colouring:* very thick fur, mostly dark-brown to black on upper parts; underparts sharply distinguished grey-white or whitish; small white spot below the eye. Digs tunnels. Good swimmer and diver. Thick velvety fur keeps water out. 2 flaps of skin inside the ear-shell enable it to close the ear opening on the outside. Breeding season from April to September; in Britain; up to 3 litters of 6 or 7 blind, naked young in an underground burrow. *Food:* water insects, worms, molluscs, crabs, small fish, birds; produces a poison capable of paralysing prey. Not confined to aquatic habitats and will go ashore in fields, gardens, mills, barns etc. *Distribution:* throughout Europe except for Mediterranean lowlands and in the north beyond Arctic Circle.

*SOUTHERN WATER SHREW (*Neomys anomalus*) Occurs mainly in the Pyrenees, Alps and Balkan mountains. In eastern Europe, however, it occurs on plains and steppes. It is found mainly in marshes and along streams. Both the northern and southern water shrews occur together in some areas.

Order   CHIROPTERA   Bats

Flying mammals of nocturnal habit. Limbs adapted to flight.
Forearm, upper arm and 4 fingers (but not thumb), as well as
lower segment of leg and tail vertebra, are elongated into thin
rods which support the stretched wing-membrane. Short thumbs
with strong claws for holding on while crawling and hanging up.
Wide mouth with an insect-eater's teeth (Fig. 1, no. 11) which
are pointed for holding on to prey and crushing chitinous armour.

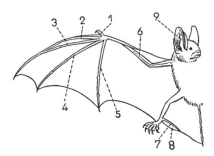

Fig. 16: Bat: 1–5 fingers; 6 forearm; 7 spur;
8 membrane flap on spur; 9 tragus

Ears erect when flying, folded back and hidden under wings
when asleep. *Food:* moths, beetles, flies, gnats, caterpillars, seized
in flight and consumed at once. Prey and obstacles located by
hearing and touch. *Cry:* continual emission of high, shrill cries
inaudible to most people *(ultrasonic).* Sound-waves thrown back
by prey and obstacles are heard as echo. Orientation by echo-
location. Thus the flitting flight, like groping using the sense
of hearing; helped by the sense of touch of the big wing-membrane and ears. Hibernates in colonies. Young suckled for several
weeks; at first taken on mother's flight, clinging to her fur; then
hung up in place of safety.

Family   VESPERTILIONIDAE   Typical bats

Nose has no border of skin. Tragus or prolongation of inner-
rim of ear-shell important in distinguishing the different species.
Milk teeth at birth.

LONG-EARED BAT *(Plecotus auritus)* Total length up to
10 cm, of which tail up to 5 cm. Wing-span up to 25 cm. Plump
body; broad, short wings light grey brown in colour; fur on
upper parts grey-brown, underparts dirty white. Very long

ears up to 3.6 cm, rounded at the tip, light grey-brown in colour, numerous transverse ridges on outer rim with rounded indentations on main body of ear. Narrow, slightly pointed tragus half the length of the ear. *Dental formula:* $\dfrac{2\ 1\ 2\ 3}{3\ 1\ 3\ 3} = 36$. In warm weather in noiseless, swift, zigzag flight from late evening until morning, especially on edges of woods, in glades, orchards, avenues and where houses are surrounded by lots of bushes and trees. Spends the day in hollow trees, lofts, behind beams, shutters, mostly solitary. Hibernates hanging in cellars, in galleries of mines, on roofs or walls. *Breeding season:* mainly in April and May; single young born June or July. *Distribution:* whole of temperate Europe. Common in Britain.

WATER or DAUBENTON'S BAT *(Myotis daubentoni)* Flies from early March to end of October. Total length up to 9 cm, of which tail up to 4 cm; ear about 1.3 cm. Wing-span up to 24 cm. Wing-membrane to middle of sole of foot. Ear short, but longer than it is broad, with longish narrow tragus. Fur on upper parts reddish-grey-brown, on underparts dull white. Wing-membrane and ears grey-brown. Hair two-coloured: black at roots, light reddish-grey-brown (from the top) at the ends or white (from underneath). Nostrils shaped like half moons, opening in front in the point of the muzzle. Gregarious; flies soon after sunset close above the surface of stagnant or sluggish waters hunting for mayflies and gnats; at times the bats hang up to rest in large numbers on branches of a tree. Spends day in hollow tree, caves, ruins, and hibernates in similar places either singly or in groups, hanging free from the roof. Lives in areas with plenty of water. Sometimes numerous. Young born June or July. *Distribution:* most of Europe; occurs in most counties of Britain and Ireland.

NOCTULE *(Nyctalus noctula)* Total length 11 cm, tail 4 cm. Wing-span 35–40 cm. Big powerful shape with round head, roundish ears, and long, narrow wings. Fur on upper parts reddish brown, underparts lighter. The earliest bat to start flying, mostly before sunset. Flies swiftly and very high and thus is often thought not be a bat. Lives in summer in hollow trees and buildings. Hibernates in similar places. In Britain single young born June or July. Twins not uncommon on continent. *Distribution:* most of Europe; common in England and Wales, but rarer in Scotland.

PIPISTRELLE *(Pipistrellus pipistrellus)* Body 3.6 cm. Tail 3.1 cm. Wing-span 17–18 cm. Smallest European bat. Weighs only 3–4 g. Fur brown on upper parts with lighter underparts. Very small ears. Narrow wings. Seen on edges of woods, in glades, orchards and villages. Lives in hollow trees, holes in walls, arches. Sometimes thousands can be found hibernating in the attics of a church. Preyed on by birds-of-prey, especially kestrels. Single young born late June to mid-July. *Distribution:* whole of temperate Europe; commonest species over the whole of British Isles.

MOUSE-EARED BAT *(Myotis myotis = Vespertilio murinus)* Total length up to 12 cm of which 5–6 cm tail; wing-span up to 38 cm. Largest European bat. Fur light smoky-brown with hint of rust on upper parts, underparts dirty white. Ear relatively short, up to 2.8 cm with 9–10 horizontal folds, light grey-brown, translucent. Tragus long, slim almost straight, narrowing from the bottom third up, pointed end reaches half way up the ear. Wing-membrane reaching to middle of the sole of the foot. Tip of tail protrudes from wing membrane. Appears in late spring, flying in late evening in slow, low, rather laboured flight. Lives in cellars and attics of buildings, where it also hibernates. Found in Alps up to 1,400 m. *Distribution:* common in many parts of the continent; in Britain rare winter vagrant but may be resident.

WHISKERED BAT *(Myotis mystacinus)* Body 4.6 cm. Weight 4–6 g. Fur brown on upper parts with longer silky hairs; underside greyish-white. Flies low and comes out early in the evening. Lives in buildings and trees and hibernates in cellars, caves etc. Prey often picked from leaves. Single young born in June or July. *Distribution:* most of Europe; common in England and Wales, rarer in Scotland.

NATTERER'S BAT *(Myotis natteri)* Body 4.3 cm. Weight 8–9.5 g. Fur greyish-brown above, underside white with clear-cut division from ear to shoulder. Flies low in woodland and other timbered areas. Single young born late June or early July. Like previous species sometime picks spiders, insects etc. from foliage. *Distribution:* most of Europe; common in most of England and Wales, rarer in southern Scotland and Ireland.

SEROTINE *(Eptesicus serotinus)* Total length 12.5 cm, of which 5.5 cm tail. Wing-span 32–35 cm. Upper parts smoky-brown, underparts yellowish-brown. Broad wings, dark black-brown in colour. Tip of tail protrudes about 7 mm under wing-membrane. Light-coloured tips to hairs on back, otherwise colour uniform. Ear dark blackish-brown pointed. Tragus rather narrow, smaller at the base, has a pointed "tooth" on its outer rim. Common in plains and hilly country, but rare in Alps. Appears late in the evening, low flight. In gardens, avenues, etc. Long hibernation in hollow trees, buildings, etc. *Breeding:* single young observed in June and July. *Distribution:* widely over Europe. In Britain confined to southern counties of England.

BARBASTELLE *(Barbastella barbastellus)* Total length 9-10 cm, of which 5 cm tail. Wing-span 33 cm. Large broad ears that grow together at the base. Narrow, pointed tragus; outer rim has tooth. Broad, short, snout; exaggerated black cheeks covered with hair. Nostrils on top of point of snout. Fur dark, black-brown on upper parts, lighter grey-brown on lower parts. Individual hairs are black at root, fawn at tip. Wing-membrane and ears black-brown. Narrow wings; quick, agile flight. Appears early in evening from early in year to autumn. During summer lives in cracks in walls, behind shutters, etc. Hibernates singly in caves, cellars, etc. *Distribution:* most of Europe but not common. In British Isles rather local in woodland areas in England and Wales as far north as Cumberland.

Family   RHINOLOPHIDAE   Horseshoe bats

Nose has an additional growth of skin in the shape of a horseshoe. No tragus.

LESSER HORSESHOE BAT *(Rhinolophus hipposideros)* Total length 7 cm of which tail 3 cm. Wing-span 22 cm. Fur grey-white with upper parts darker than underparts. Broad wings. Tail almost entirely enclosed in wing-membrane. Ears drawn-out into a point; no tragus. Skinny addition to nose in the shape of a horseshoe. Waits for dark to fly. Low, awkward flight. Lives in caves, ruins, cellars, attics. Hibernates. Gregarious. Found up to tree line but not north of Hartz mountains and Thuringia; common in Taunus and along the Rhine and Lahn. *Breeding:* single young born late June or July. *Distribution:* throughout Europe; in Britain as far north as Midlands and Yorkshire, Wales and Western Ireland.

GREATER HORSESHOE BAT *(Rhinolophus ferrumequinum)*
Total length 10 cm of which tail 4 cm. Wing-span about 35 cm.
Upper part grey-brown in male, reddish-brown in female; underparts pale-grey in male, reddish-grey in female. Very large
"horseshoe"; ears fairly large, no tragus. Broad wings. Habits
as lesser horseshoe. Found up to 2,000 m. Appears early in year.
Low, clumsy flight as darkness falls. Same summer and winter
quarters as lesser horseshoe. *Distribution:* central and southern
Europe; in Britain southern counties of England and Wales.

Class   *AVES* Birds

Feathered. Fore limbs transformed into flying organs. Plumage made
up of flight feathers of the wing (remiges) and of the tail (retrices)
and covering feathers mostly of symmetrical structure; these are
collectively called contour feathers. Pinion and tail feathers unsymmetrical;
narrow half turned ouwards. Many species shed their feathers (moult)
twice a year: courting or mating plumage worn from early spring
until towards the end of the breeding season; then winter or plain
dress. *Legs:* upper thigh, shin, ankle bone and toes. The upper part
of the thigh (femur), is short and does not protrude beyond the plumage.
Lower part of the leg has shin bone (tibia) and fibula, the latter
very stunted and merged with the tibia. Three of the bones of the instep
(metatarsus) have grown together along their length to form the ankle
bone, which is mostly unfeathered. As birds walk on their toes (digitigrade)
the ankle bone is set so erect that one is tempted, as with hoofed animals,
to take the heel (instep) for the knee. Ankle bone and toes are covered
with horny scales. Number of toes never exceeds 4, often only 3. Breathe
through lungs; constant temperature; lungs have air sacs. Eggs have shells
of calcium. Nest young have to be tended. Some birds stay all year where
they have bred; others fly in autumn to warmer areas in the south and
return in the spring. Others leave the place where they were bred and
move about in search of food.

ARRANGEMENT OF EUROPEAN BIRDS INTO ORDERS

Order   PASSERIFORMES   Perching birds

Sub-order   OSCINES   Song birds

Small, sometimes also medium sized birds externally differing considerably. The order contains the most accomplished songsters. They are mostly arboreal, hence they have feet with well-developed toes and claws for grasping twigs and branches; this is also true of other species that often run. Back toes are often longer than the middle fore toe. Legs feathered as far as the heel.

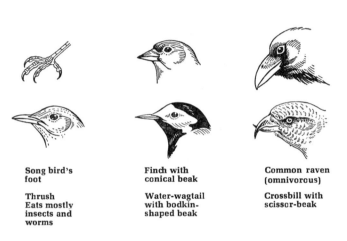

Song bird's foot

Thrush
Eats mostly insects and worms

Finch with conical beak

Water-wagtail with bodkin-shaped beak

Common raven (omnivorous)

Crossbill with scissor-beak

Beak adapted to type of food taken, being differently shaped according to family.

Order   PICIFORMES   Woodpeckers

Range in size from that of a sparrow to that of a jay. Specially adapted for clambering in trees. Strong feet with 2 toes pointing in front and 2 pointing behind. Sharp claws. Short ankle bones. Short, stiff, wedge-shaped tails that act as a support. Powerful chisel-beaks used to split bark and rotten wood in the search for food and to hollow out the nesting hole. Very long sticky tongues with barbs. Nest in holes. Young hatch out naked. The wryneck is the one exception. (See page 149). Picture shows: Great spotted woodpecker.

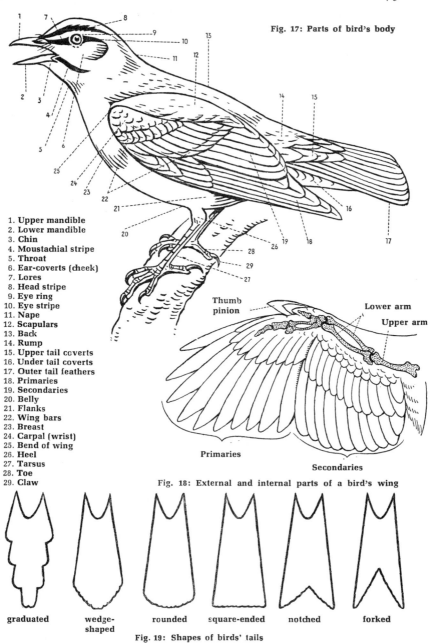

Fig. 17: Parts of bird's body

1. Upper mandible
2. Lower mandible
3. Chin
4. Moustachial stripe
5. Throat
6. Ear-coverts (cheek)
7. Lores
8. Head stripe
9. Eye ring
10. Eye stripe
11. Nape
12. Scapulars
13. Back
14. Rump
15. Upper tail coverts
16. Under tail coverts
17. Outer tail feathers
18. Primaries
19. Secondaries
20. Belly
21. Flanks
22. Wing bars
23. Breast
24. Carpal (wrist)
25. Bend of wing
26. Heel
27. Tarsus
28. Toe
29. Claw

Thumb pinion

Lower arm

Upper arm

Primaries

Secondaries

Fig. 18: External and internal parts of a bird's wing

graduated

wedge-shaped

rounded

square-ended

notched

forked

Fig. 19: Shapes of birds' tails

Order   APODIFORMES   Swifts

From starling size to that of blackbird; dark colouring. Very
long, narrow, sickle-shaped wings. Small beak; wide gape. Short
feet with 4 sharp-clawed toes that can turn in all directions, all
pointing forward. Live in tall stone buildings, cliffs and woods
with tall trees. Picture shows: Swift.

Order   CORACIIFORMES

Kingfishers, bee-eaters, rollers and hoopoe

Mainly birds with brilliant plumage, nesting in holes and laying
white or light-coloured eggs. Young hatch out naked and blind,
except hoopoes which have down covering. There is a tendency
for the three forward-pointing toes to be united.
Picture shows: **Kingfisher.**

Order   CAPRIMULGIFORMES   Nightjars

Larger than blackbird; bark-coloured; twilight and nocturnal,
thus large eyes. Plumage like an owl's, not close-lying. Long,
narrow wings. Small beak, but wide gape, surrounded by edging
of long, strong, bristles. Weak short feet with 3 toes facing forward and 1 behind, though it can be turned forward. Young
hatch out with down, soon move about.
Picture shows: Nightjar.

Order   STRIGIFORMES   Owls

Mainly nocturnal birds whose plumage makes them look large,
but which in reality have slender bodies. Large, broad heads with
short hooked beaks; large eyes directed forwards; large ear-
opening protected by flap that can be opened and shut. Most
have a disc of stiff bristly feathers round the eyes, their "veil".
Soft plumage and saw-toothed forward edge to flight feathers 1,
2 and 3 give noiseless flight. Long leg feathers down to claws
which are long, very curved and sharp; outside toe can be turned
either forwards or backwards. Some owls have striking feather
tuft "horns". Usually very clumsy on the ground, but agile in
trees. *Flight:* slow with numerous wing beats or gliding. Adopt
a great variety of positions: ducking down, stretching up, turning
and bending their heads, when their face can be pointed backwards. *Cry:* usually loud, infrequent and at night only. Swallow

their prey straight down. Eat only what they have caught alive. No crop and so cannot store food. Feathers, hair and bones are compressed into pellets which they disgorge after a short time. Make nests. Picture shows: Barn owl with ear-flap open.

Order   CUCULIFORMES Cuckoos

A little larger than blackbird; slender; long tail; long, pointed wings; movable toes, predator-like flight. Brood parasitic. Picture shows: Cuckoo.

Order   FALCONIFORMES Birds of prey

Large, strongly built birds with powerful beaks, the upper mandible of which hooks down over the lower. Powerful, strong curved claws. Most are exclusively carnivorous. Gullet enlarged in middle of its length like a crop. Bones completely digested. Tear off feathers and hair before eating. Pellets contain no bones, though claws of birds and mice. Most build their own nests (eyrie). Young hatch out with eyes open and have thick down for first few weeks; first plumage usually very different from adult plumage. Most are vagrant. In those which prey on birds (peregrine, goshawk, sparrow hawk) the female is larger than male and tends the young; the male hunting, the female guarding and dismembering prey and feeding it to young. Picture shows: Falcon, griffon vulture, buzzard's foot.

Order   COLUMBIFORMES Pigeons

Rounded bodies, small heads; weak bill has sharply defined "join" with brow, soft at base, horny tip, base enlarged round the slit-shaped nostrils. Drink by sucking, closing the nostrils with "flaps". Lively on ground, nodding its head at every step. Short feet; 4 toes with short, only slightly curved claws. Compact, firm, close-lying plumage. Fast flight. Deep, coo-ing cry. Always lays 2 eggs. Mate for life. Young have down, fed first with "milk" from mother's crop, then with softened seeds, etc. Vagrant.

Picture shows: Pigeon.

Order GALLIFORMES Gallinaceous birds

Most are big, heavy birds of thick-set build. Small heads with powerful beaks turned down at tip; short or medium-length necks; wings mostly short, rounded and arched; strong walking legs: blunt, powerful claws for scratching in ground. Male larger, more colourful, sometimes distinguished by comb, wattles and spur on leg. Swift, enduring run. Heavy flight. Spend most of the time on the ground scratching in search of grain and bits of plants, insects, worms, etc. Young are not confined to the nest. Picture shows: Partridge (head) and pheasant's foot.

Order GRUIFORMES Bustards, rails, cranes etc.

Family OTIDIDAE Bustards

Long-legged, terrestrial birds the size of the domestic hen or larger; live in open country (grassy steppe or fields). Hen-like appearance. No hind toe. Old males have a striking feathery "beard". Dignified gait. Very shy. Run swiftly but not agile fliers. Silhouette in flight characterised by broad wings and large body. Picture shows: Great bustard.

Family RALLIDAE Rails

Small to medium sized. Darting, secretive marsh birds. Bodies "squeezed in" at sides; short rounded wings; short tails. Short flight with legs dangling. Water rails have long, crakes short, beaks. Coots have thicker bodies, smaller heads and wide lobes on toes; moorhen has long toes for running on aquatic plants. Pictures show: Water rail and Moorhen.

Family GRUIDAE Cranes

Large, long-legged terrestrial birds, superficially resembling storks and herons. Beak somewhat longer than head. Long neck and long legs outstretched in flight. Very small hind toes, articulated higher up than the 3 fore toes; cannot grip a branch and so does not perch. The inner, elongated secondaries hang down over the tail. Nests on ground; lays only 2 well-speckled eggs. Young soon leave nest. Gregarious outside breeding season. Vagrant. Fly in V-formation.

Picture shows: Grey crane.

Order CICONIIFORMES (=GRESSORES) Herons etc.

Larger to medium-sized, mostly long-necked birds with long, straight beaks with sharp edges and no cere, only slightly set off from head. Long, wader-like legs, bare well above the heel bone, with fore toes connected by skin. Hind toes shorter, but just as powerful and have strong claws. Vagrant. Nest-bound. Represented in Europe by storks, herons, bitterns, and flamingo.
Picture shows: White stork.

Order   CHARADRIIFORMES   Waders, gulls

Sub-order   CHARADRII   Waders

There are 3 main groups of waders: plovers, sandpipers and snipe.

PLOVERS have short necks, large heads, big eyes; short beaks, soft at base, hard and somewhat thickened at tip. Heel joint somewhat thickened. Most have only 3 fore toes, but many also have a 4th very small hind toe. Pointed wings; short tail; colourful plumage. Distinctive flight and cry.
Picture shows: Lapwing.

SANDPIPERS have beaks as long, or slightly longer than head; mostly straight, soft, narrow, weak, 4-toed feet, naked to far above heel; medium length, pointed wings.
Picture shows: Common sandpiper.

SNIPE have long, pliant, soft beaks covered with skin in which are many nerves making it a tactile tool. Wings usually pointed and angled. Slim feet, naked to beyond the heel. Hind toes articulated somewhat higher; absent in some kinds. Short tails. In snipe themselves the eyes are set extraordinarily far back.
Picture shows: Common snipe.

Order   ANSERIFORMES   Ducks, etc.

There are 4 groups of this order: ducks, geese, swans, mergansers. Broad, spoon-like beaks that sieve, feel and cut. Numerous horny teeth and a fringe on the edges of their large, fleshy tongues that, together with the transverse horny laminae of the beak edge, act as a filter. Grooves for water to run off. Soft skin covering the upper mandible and large number of tactile structures in the tip of the beak allow the bird to find its food in dark mud. Aquatic. Webbed feet. Expert at swimming and, sometimes, diving. All fly well, live in flocks. Leave water to shake, stretch,

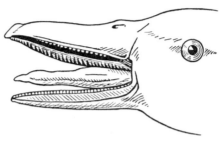

Fig. 20: Duck's beak

oil themselves and preen; rest sitting, but, like frog, always facing the water. Thick down protects them from cold. Oil from oil-glands situated above caudal vertebra keeps out wet. Covert oiled by beak. Wings when closed lie in a guard of feathers curving out from side of the breast. If water gets in under wings, the bird draws itself erect and flaps its wings violently to shake off the drops. Lays a number of relatively large, always monochrome white or lightly coloured eggs. Nests mostly on the ground. Before nesting season the female grows special "nest down" on her underparts used for lining nest, which is felted together with dry nest material to make a quilt that is used to cover eggs, when leaving nest. Only female sits. Young not bound to nest. Ducklings are the best able to look after themselves of all baby birds.

Picture shows: Mallard.

Order   PELECANIFORMES   Cormorants and gannet

Large up to goose size. All 4 toes point forward and are joined by web. Young remain for long time in nest.

Picture shows: Cormorant.

Order   PODICIPITIFORMES   Grebes

Body strikingly broad and flat. Short wings and legs. Short, straight pointed beak with sharp edges and small, slit-like nostrils that can be closed. Live only on water. Good at diving, but not at flying. Legs not suited for running. On land hold their bodies erect, because their legs are set far to the back. Feet not webbed, but have lobes with flaps of skin along each side of their toes. Tail reduced to small bunch of tattered feathers. Make large floating nests; white eggs. Down of young mostly striped. Young often carried on parent's back.

Picture shows: Great crested grebe.

Family   LARIDAE   Gulls and Terns

GULLS: rather pigeon-shaped, long-winged swimming birds. Point of beak curves down. Tail squared or rounded. Web straight. Pointed wings. Most kinds are white with grey or black backs and similarly coloured wings, most with dark tips. White headed kinds often have dark stripes on head in winter; the black-headed kinds lose their dark mark in winter.

Picture shows: Herring gull.

TERNS: more slender-bodied, narrower-winged and shorter legged than gull; swallow-shaped; beak slimmer and sharply pointed, pointing downwards in flight. Forked tail. Web excised, Graceful, often hovering flight; plunge for fish. Gulls and terns are gregarious.

Picture shows: Common tern.

Family   ALCIDAE   Auks

Duck-sized sea birds, short-winged, swimming and diving birds. Beak compressed at sides. Short tail. Short feet with 3 toes joined by web. 4th hind toe lacking or rudimentary. Plump. Fish-eater. Feathered wings still enable some kinds to fly (guillemot), others only use them for "rowing" (auk).

Picture shows: Guillemot.

Order   GAVIIFORMES   Divers (Loons)

Large aquatic birds with long bodies and thick necks. Bills sharply pointed and straight; front toes fully webbed. Frequent lakes and slow rivers in summer, but in winter seen off the coast singly. Submerge rapidly and when alarmed only the head or even the bill may be seen. Eggs usually two and laid in shallow depression in marshy ground. Clumsy on land and take flight with difficulty, although when aloft they have powerful flight.

Picture shows: Red-throated diver.

BIRDS' NESTS, NEST-HOLES AND EGG-LAYING

(Squirrel's nest included here owing to its resemblance to a bird's nest)

I. NESTS IN TREE-TOPS

1. *Large stick nests or eyries.*

BUZZARD Up to 60 cm across; usually deep in a wood and more often in conifer than deciduous tree; 8–20 m above ground; on side branches close to trunk, or in fork of branch or curve; built of thick sticks, bowl of thinner twigs, straw, moss, bark, always carpeted with a few fresh green sprigs from the tree in which it is built. April to May, 2 to 4 white eggs with brown speckles. (5.5 × 4.1 cm.)

HONEY BUZZARD 70–100 cm across; near edge of wood, mostly in deciduous trees; often uses old nest of buzzard or goshawk as foundation. 15–22 m above ground. Made of dry sticks; bowl carpeted with leaves; always lined with fresh leafy twigs. May or June to June or July 2 yellowy-white eggs with lots of faded brown spots. (5.1 × 4.1 cm.)

GOSHAWK 1–1.2 m across; deep in wood, mostly in a conifer, 15–20 m up; close to stem, well-hidden; often by a glade or stream where steep approach is possible: made of strong sticks, bowl out of twigs; rim heightened with green twigs. An old nest can be up to 1 m deep. April and May 3–5 greeny-white eggs, mostly without speckles or with only a few muddy-yellow, faded spots. (5.8 × 4.5 cm.)

SPARROW HAWK 25–40 cm across in medium sized mixed wood. Only 4–8 m up, in the lower crest area, close to trunk, well hidden, flat nest of stout and thin fir twigs. Bowl unlined, at most some bits of bark and moss. No green "decoration". An old crow's, pigeon's or squirrel's nest is often used as a foundation. May to June 4–6 round, white eggs, well speckled with chocolate-brown. (4 × 3.2 cm.)

KITE 70–100 cm across. In conifer or deciduous tree in small wood. Very high. Often in a fringe tree and near water. Old crow's nest or buzzard's nest often used as foundation. Bowl upholstered with rags, bits of paper and any old rubbish. No green decoration. April to May mostly 2, rarely 3 or 4, white eggs sparsely speckled with reddish-brown. (5.6 × 4.5 cm.)

*BLACK KITE 70–100 cm across, near water. Mostly in a conifer, 8–25 m up (seldom in deciduous tree). Built of stout sticks and branch twigs; bowl as kite's. April to May 2–3 white eggs with a few brown speckles, towards bottom end. (5.3 × 4.3 cm.)

OSPREY About 1 m across and 2 m deep in a tall tree near large lake; made of thick sticks and branches mostly fished out of water. 2–3 rough-shelled eggs (6.2 × 4.6 cm) pale-bluish in colour with large brown-red spots; others bright red with rufous red speckles; very variable.

*WHITE-TAILED EAGLE Large structure of sticks about 1 m deep and 2 m across, built in top of highest pine-tree or on cliff, or ground. 2–3 eggs (7.3 × 5.8 cm) white with slight gloss and deep pores.

2. Stick nests in colonies.

HERON About 1 m across. In very high tree in which it looks as if it had been whitewashed. 5–6 sea-green eggs (about 6 × 4.2 cm). End February to April.

ROOK In small wood, often more than one in a tree (rookery). About 20 cm across and 14 cm deep. Base made of dry sticks, straw often bound together with clay; bowl lined with wool, hair, straw and rags. 3–5 light green, dark-speckled eggs. (4 × 3 cm) March to May.

CORMORANT Generally on cliff ledges or rocks. Occasionally in trees. Tree nests of sticks, grass and other plants; coastal nests of sticks and seaweed. 4–6 bluish-white eggs April to May (7 × 4 cm).

3. Smaller stick nests.

Squirrel nest or drey, (pictured). A covered round of sticks built on a forked branch close to the trunk. Entrance from underneath; also a bolt-hole close to tree trunk. Inside lined with moss, wool etc. Squirrels will also use old rooks' nests or those of a bird of prey.

JAY Not very large stick nest built in thicket of small conifers or deciduous trees high above ground and mostly close to stem, though sometimes out on a branch. Bowl made of fine roots and hair, but no earth is used. April to May 5–7 eggs, grey-green with lots of grey-brown speckles, black stripes and scribbles. (3.4 × 2.4 cm.)

CARRION CROW Stick nest, some 20 cm × 14 cm deep in tall tree, mostly conifers. Base of thin twigs, grassy roots cemented with earth; bowl lined with wool, hair, grass, and even rags. 3–5 eggs (4 × 3 cm), blue-green base with olive-green and brown mottling. April to May.

MAGPIE In poplars, fruit and other tall trees and bushes, roofed round nest of sticks and mud lined with roots. From middle of April 6–8 greenish-grey eggs (3.3 × 2.3 cm) mottled with brown. Often build bits of glass and other things that sparkle, into nest.

WOOD PIGEON Flat, loosely built nest of thin sticks, mostly lowish in young tree or tall bush, or by stem of stout tree. 2 glossy white eggs (4 × 3.3 cm) April to August. 2 or more clutches.

TURTLE-DOVE Very loosely built, flat structure of dry sticks, roots, heather, in tall bush or small tree in wood or field; seldom in a conifer. May to July 2 white eggs (3 × 2.3 cm) detectable from below.

LONG-EARED OWL Often nest in abandoned nests of crows or birds of prey; also in brambles and sometimes on ground. March to April 4–6 round, faintly shiny white eggs. (4 × 3.2 cm.)

KESTREL Frequently nests in old crows' nests. 5–6 almost spherical yellowish-buff eggs (3.9 × 3.1 cm) thickly covered with reddish-brown spots and mottling.

HOBBY In tall trees, mostly firs, near edge of wood, 12–15 m up. Uses old nests of other birds (carrion crow, jay, buzzard). June to July 2–4 light yellow eggs (4.2 × 3.3 cm) thickly mottled with reddish-brown.

GREEN SANDPIPER Uses old nests (of rooks, squirrels, jays, pigeon, thrush) as base; sometimes nests on ground in bowl lined with straw and heather. Mostly near walls. April to May 4 yellowy-grey eggs with small red-brown speckles.

4. *Nests of small birds* (smaller than pigeon).
    (a) Nests of larger small birds, mostly in deciduous trees.

*GREAT GREY SHRIKE In deciduous trees on edge of wood or in fruit trees; high up; seldom in bushes; fairly firm structure of sticks, straw, roots, moss lined with animal hair and feathers;

25 cm across and 12 cm deep. Bowl 9–12 cm across, flat. April to May 4–7 eggs (2.8 × 2 cm), dirty-white ground with brown splodges.

*WOODCHAT SHRIKE In fruit trees or in blackthorn. Externally rather loose structure of a few sticks; rest dry grass interwoven with light-coloured, strongly scented herbs; bowl more firmly woven and lined with fine straws, wool and feathers. 14 cm across (bowl 8 cm and 5.2 cm deep). May to end of June 1 brood: 5–6 eggs (2.3 × 1.7 cm) with yellowy base flecked with grey and brown spots.

*LESSER GREY SHRIKE 12–14 cm across and 7–9 cm deep; bowl 7.9 cm × 3–5.5 cm. Always in an old deciduous tree, mostly near edge of wood, seldom less than 4 m up; often in holes more than 8 m up. Thick walled structure of straws and roots mingled with light-coloured, fragrant herbs; bowl lined with hair and feathers. May to June mostly 6 yellow-greeny-white eggs (2.5 × 1.8 cm) flecked with grey and brown, often arranged in a sort of ring round the blunt end.

HAWFINCH In trees, sticks mixed with moss and grasses, lined with vegetable wool and fine grass. May to June 5–6 eggs (2.5 × 1.7 cm) blue with grey and black flecks and scribbles, especially towards the blunt end.

BLACKBIRD and SONG TRUSH (often in bushes, see p. 85 and 86).

MISTLE THRUSH In woods in conifers, sycamores, beeches, oaks; mostly very high up often in fork of tree; bowl of dry grass and moss stiffened with lots of earth; lined inside with straws. Rim of nest firmly woven and built. 3–5 eggs (3 × 2.2 cm) with light green, often bluish ground flecked with rust-red or violet-grey. 2 broods between April and mid-June.

*FIELDFARE In all kinds of trees, mostly 4–8 m up in wood or fields, often in conifers or upland moors; also in fruit trees; often in colonies. Nest made of moss, twigs, roots, straw, firmly built, stiffened with clay and lined with grass. May to June 5–6 greeny-blue eggs (2.8 × 2.1 cm) finely flecked with rust-red and difficult to distinguish from eggs of blackbird.

(b) Nests of smaller birds mostly in deciduous trees.

CHAFFINCH Builds in lower branches of deciduous trees, often out on a branch; moss, grass, hair cleverly woven into a deep semi-spherical bowl decorated on the outside with lichens or fragments of birch bark. Outer walls always disguised with a plaiting of the tree itself. Bowl 4–4.7 cm deep and 5 cm across, lined with animal hair, sometimes also feathers. 4–7 eggs (1.9 × 1.5 cm); ground light blue, grey-blue or red-brown flecked with black-brown often ringed with red. April to June.

GOLDFINCH Smaller, semi-spherical nest of fibre, lichens and moss in smaller deciduous trees on fork under the crest. 4–6 eggs (1.7 × 1.3 cm) blue-white ground with a few pale reddish-brown flecks and dark scribbles.

GREENFINCH Well built bowl-shaped nest, mostly 1–4 m up in young conifers, small fruit trees, or climbers, seldom in bushes. Outside made of twigs, moss, roots, straw; inside lined with hair and feathers. April–July or August 5–6 yellowy-white eggs (2 × 1.5 cm) with a few red-brown and black specks and dots on blunt end. 2 broods.

*SERIN In conifers, vines, hornbeam, about a man's height up; made of straw, roots, lichens, closely woven; deep bowl upholstered with plant-wool and feathers. May and June to July 3–5 blue-white eggs (1.7 × 1.2 cm) with rust red flecks.

LONG-TAILED TIT (mostly in bushes, see p. 88).

(c) Hanging nests built into fork of branch or a twig.

GOLDEN ORIOLE Always nests in deciduous trees, mostly high up, in the fork of a horizontal branch, from which it hangs like a basket. Woven of bark fibre and straw and lined with wool, feathers, straw. 4–5 smooth-shelled, glossy, pure white eggs (3 × 2.1 cm) often with a hint of pink and a few black-brown to deep black dots and flecks. May to June.

GOLDCREST In fir woods and mixed woods, well hidden away among thick fir or pine twigs, a small, pendant almost round nest at the end of a long branch, made of lichens, moss, hair and caterpillar silk, lined with small feathers that also cover part of the small opening at the top. Externally 8–11 cm across, internally 6 cm; about 4 cm deep. 7–10 or more tiny eggs, brownish-white ground with reddish-brown speckles. Eggs as firecrest but darker brownish-white ground.

*FIRECREST Similar nest to above. 8–11 fragile tiny eggs (1.4 × 1 cm) yellowy, slightly flesh-coloured or white ground with darker nebulae thickening into a ring towards the blunt end. May to June. 2 broods.

*PENDULINE TIT Hanging, closed, egg-shaped nest with funnel-shaped entrance pipe; hangs free like a pouch from an outer twig, mostly above water, often more than 10 m up; filled with poplar and willow-wool. April or May. 5–8 matt white long eggs (1.5 × 1 cm) 2 broods.

(d) Nests built only in conifers.

CROSSBILL Small nest with deep cup in a wood of tall conifers. Wall about 3 cm thick woven of moss and lichens with outside of interwoven twigs, heather, grasses, inside lined with a few feathers, grasses, conifer needles. 3–4 eggs (2.2 × 1.6 cm) with white ground with tinge of blue or green and pale rust-coloured powdering and sharp red-brown or black spots and squiggles.

SISKIN Built in the thick branches of a tall conifer, always far out from stem, well made of lichens, straw, little roots, cobweb; deep cup lined with hair, feathers or plant-wool. Towards early May 4–6 blue-white eggs (1.5 × 1.2 cm) with brown dots and squiggles, like a goldfinch's.

II. Nests in Bushes

SONG THRUSH Larger cup of straw and moss, inside always plastered with mud, dust of rotten wood and cow dung, not lined with grass etc. In very young trees or bushes. 4–7 greeny-blue eggs (2.7 × 2 cm) with occasional black specks. April to July. 2 clutches.

BLACKBIRD Largish cup of grasses and moss often lined with a mixture of earth and powdered rotten wood, carpeted with grass; found in a great variety of places, even on the ground or a balcony etc. 3–5 yellowy-green eggs (2.9 × 2.2 cm) with delicate red-brown mottling. April to June. Several clutches.

NIGHTINGALE Loosely built nest of grass, leaves, moss with thick walls and open top, often lined with hair; built in thick undergrowth of shrubby copses close to the ground. 4–6 eggs (2.1 × 1.6 cm) semi-matt, greeny-brown-grey, blue-green or blue. May to June.

BULLFINCH In conifers, preferably young spruce, on edge of wood or in park, often quite low, 1.5–2 m up; foundation of twigs on which sits nest proper of roots, straws, lichens, often lined with hair. May to June or July 4–5 bluey-white eggs (2 × 1.5 cm) with red-brown and black dots and specks. 2 clutches.

LINNET Seldom higher than a man, mostly on young spruces or thick bushes (gorse, hawthorn, wild-rose, ivy) or in piles of twigs or stacks of wood. Often nest in company. Trim, delicate structure of straws, roots, fibre, moss, lined with hair and feathers. Starting end of March, 5–6 bluey-green eggs (1.8 × 1.3 cm) with brownish blotches. At least 2 clutches.

SERIN (mostly in trees, see p. 84.)

YELLOWHAMMER Thick walled, coarse nest of grass, open topped with hair; in bushes, gorse and hedges close to or on ground under jutting stone or earth. 4–7 white-yellow eggs (2.2 × 1.8 cm) with brown to black squiggles and fine lines. May or June and August. 2 clutches.

CIRL BUNTING Typical bunting nest of grass, little roots, etc. Seldom actually on the ground, rather in low bushes several feet up. From end of April 4–5 pale-green to grey-blue eggs (2.1 × 1.6 cm) with lots of dark red blotches.

GARDEN WARBLER Thin walled, very loose structure of grasses, stalks and stems, open at top, often plastered with moss outside and inside left mostly unplastered, though sometimes hair is used. In low bushes, brambles, herbage. June or July 5–6 whitey-yellow eggs (2 × 1.5 cm) sparsely flecked with grey to olive-brown.

BLACKCAP Like preceding nest, only of finer materials and lined inside with hair and fine grass. In hedges, undergrowth, thick bushes, often far out on branch, but well hidden, close to ground. May to June 4–6 browny-white eggs (1.9 × 1.5 cm) with blurred brown-red and olive-brown mottling that is very variable.

LESSER WHITETHROAT Most loosely constructed nest of all warblers; very thin walls, often transparent, made of stalks and fibres, interwoven on inside with fine roots. In thick bushes in gardens, parks and in open woods; placed higher than other warblers, often up to 2 m and more. May to June 5–6 whitish eggs (1.6 × 1.2 cm) with brown and green speckles.

WHITETHROAT Loose structure, yet firmer than other warblers, made of stalks with fairly deep cup, here and there lined with plant-wool and hair. In thorn bushes, undergrowth in deciduous woods, thickets; sometimes in tangled weeds (nettles, brambles); not high up. May to July 2 clutches. 4–6 grey-green eggs (1.8 × 1.4 cm) with brown and grey flecks often in a ring round blunt end.

*BARRED WARBLER Nests in bushes, mostly in thorn hedges, fairly extensive, loose structure, 5 grey-white eggs (2.1 × 1.5 cm) with grey or brownish specks. Only 1 clutch. June.

CHIFFCHAFF Loose, round nest with side entrance, high-domed, made of grass, moss, lined with leaves, mostly close to ground, often in thick undergrowth. Eggs visible through hole. April to June 5–7 white eggs (1.5 × 1.2 cm) with dark red-brown dots.

*ICTERINE WARBLER Nests in tall bushes (elder, hornbeam, currants) outside often has white birch bark or pieces of paper in it. June or July 3–6 pink eggs (1.8 × 1.3 cm) with black dots.

WILLOW WARBLER Nests mostly on the ground. See p. 90.

HEDGE SPARROW Neat, deep cup of fresh moss, fine stalks and hair lined with moss. In bushes, hedges, evergreens, low down, mostly between .5 and 1.5 m off the ground. April to June 2 clutches of 4–6 deep greeny-blue eggs. (1.9 × 1.5 cm.)

RED-BACKED SHRIKE Thick-walled nest made of roots and twigs and moss inside, cup of fine roots and stalks often lined with wool and animal hair. Deep in thorn hedge, brambles or gorse. May or June to August 2 clutches of 5–7 eggs (2.2 × 1.7 cm), varying ground colour: can be grey, green, greeny-yellow, yellowy-white; reddish, ring of brownish speckles low down towards pointed end.

WREN Spherical nest of moss and leaves with entrance at side; when used for hatching lined with small feathers; under overhanging tree roots, by ditches, streams and in hedges; usually low down. April to July 2 clutches of 6–8 white eggs (1.6 × 1.2 cm) with brick-red specks.

LONG-TAILED TIT In bushes or trees; some 10 cm across and 24 cm deep, oval nest, closed at top, made of moss and plastered outside with lichens; opening at side. 7–12 brittle, small eggs (1.4 × 1.1 cm) with pale rust-red specks on a white ground. March and June. 2 clutches.

III. Hanging Nests in Reeds, Bushes, Shrubs, Corn

*GREAT REED WARBLER Nest built on waterside of reed bank, never far in, sufficiently high up for water never to reach it; mostly built between 5 reeds, very firmly woven of bark fibre and dry sedge grass, deep bowl-like hanging nest with thick walls and inward curving rim to prevent eggs and young falling out; cup made of reed fibre often lined with cotton-grass, wool and feathers; 4–6 blue-green eggs (2.2 × 1.6 cm) with olive-brown and black-brown or grey speckles. May to July. 1 clutch.

REED WARBLER Often built in sparse or small reed beds, even away from water, in willows, elder and lilac; built between 2–3, seldom more stalks; mostly made of reed pedicles, only the foundation being made of dry sedge leaves and bark fibre. 3–5 greeny-white eggs (1.8 × 1.4 cm) with lots of olive and brownish spots, often in a ring. May or June to July. 1 clutch.

MARSH WARBLER Nest always over dry ground, on edge of ditch, in shrubs, spiraea, nettles, willowherb, sometimes also in corn; very seldom on reeds; much looser than preceding; made of dry grass; bottom of nest unusually thick made of fibre, stalks and hair, never of feathers; 4–6 bluish or light green eggs (1.9 × 1.4 cm) with dark grey to black spots.

IV. Nests on Ground

1. *In woods or glades.*

ROBIN Nest made of moss and grass, feathers and hair; either on or just off the ground; any hole or cavity, in tree stump, hole in bank; where there is no overhead cover will build a roof and make entrance at side. 4–7 yellowy-white eggs (1.9 × 1.5 cm) with reddish-brown mottling and dots. April to July. 2 or 3 clutches.

WOOD WARBLER Round nest, often domed, with entrance at side, made of moss, stalks and leaves, lined with hair; always in woods of big trees, on ground under grass, bracken or other undergrowth (bilberry). 4–7 whitish eggs (1.6 × 1.3 cm) with lots of dark brown dots. May to June. 1 clutch.

WILLOW WARBLER Domed nest on or just off the ground among grass (tuft); lined with hair and feathers. 5–8 yellowy-white eggs (1.5 × 1.2 cm) with light mustard speckles. May to June.

CHIFFCHAFF (also off the ground, see p. 87.)

TREE PIPIT Nest often open, made of grass, moss and leaves, lined with hair; always on ground; in glades, on edge of woods, mostly under long grass, bracken, etc. 4–6 eggs (2 × 1.5 cm) varying in colour: dark brown, reddish, greenish or bluey-white with darker dots, lines, squiggles. May to July. 2 clutches.

WOOD LARK On ground beneath or among scrub, often near trees, made of straws, moss, roots delicately woven and lined with plant-wool and feathers. April to June. 2 clutches of 3–5 glossy eggs (2 × 1.6 cm) with brown mottling on white ground.

* ORTOLAN BUNTING On ground or just off. Mostly in corn-fields or edge of ditches; carefully made of grass, roots, etc. Usually lined with hair. May to June, mostly 5 eggs (1.9 × 1.5 cm) with black-brown speckles and squiggles on ash-grey or reddish-grey ground.

YELLOWHAMMER (mostly on ground, see p. 86.)

COAL TIT; CRESTED TIT Mostly in holes in trees and walls. Sometimes even in rabbit holes, or in tree stumps. See 10 and 11 p. 101.

NIGHTJAR On dry ground in heather, commons, wooded and waste land; no actual nest is built. 2 dirty-white glossy eggs (3.1 × 2.2 cm) with yellow-brown blotches. May to June 2 clutches.

WOODCOCK Cavity in ground under a bush, branches or beside a trunk, sparsely lined with leaves and moss. April to June Mostly 4 eggs (4.4 × 3.3 cm) reddish-brown mottling on cream coloured ground. 2 clutches.

CAPERCAILLIE Shallow bowl scratched out of ground, 30 cm across, 6 cm deep, beside the trunk of a tree, or beneath undergrowth, sparsely lined with dry leaves and moss. May to June. 6–10 yellowy-grey eggs (4.9 × 3.6 cm) with lots of small red-brown spots and speckles.

BLACK GROUSE In heath and moor, especially on outer fringe of a wood; in the Alps up to or above tree line. Shallow bowl in ground lined with twigs, leaves or moss. May to June 6–10 ochre yellow eggs (4.9 × 3.6 cm) with lots of red-brown spots and blotches. One clutch.

*HAZEL HEN In mixed woods, heaths and moors; especially in the forests of the Mittelgebirge. Simple nest under thick growth; fairly flat bowl (17 cm across by 6 cm deep). May to June. 8–12 yellowy to browny eggs. (4.2 × 3 cm) with sparse brown mottling.

2. On ground in fields.

SKYLARK Well-hidden under grass, loosely made of straws, roots, moss and hair lining. April to August. 2–3 clutches of 3–5 cream-coloured eggs (2.3 × 1.7 cm) with grey-black mottling.

*CRESTED LARK Loose nest of straw lined with fine grass, usually in depression in dry open country away from houses, also in rubbish dumps, etc. April to June. 2 clutches of 3–5 yellow-white eggs (2.2 × 1.7 cm) with brown mottling, easily confused with those of the skylark.

CORN BUNTING On dry ground, made of grasses lined with hair; larger and looser than yellow hammer's; in hedges, banks, ditches, often under bushes or tufts of grass. March to July. 2 clutches of 4–5 grey-white eggs (2.4 × 1.7 cm) with rust-red mottling and black squiggles.

PARTRIDGE Mostly in cultivated fields, but also in meadows, low moors, sand-dunes; shallow depression, natural or scratched out; sparsely lined with grass and leaves. 10–20 eggs (3.5 × 2.6 cm) top-shaped, slightly shiny, olive-yellow. One clutch.

RED-LEGGED PARTRIDGE Has slightly larger eggs than the previous species with buff ground, fine reddish-brown specks and larger spots.

QUAIL In cornfields, clover, open waste land, in scratched out hollow, sparsely lined with grass and moss. 7–14 pear shaped eggs (3 × 2.3 cm), yellow-brown with large black spots.

PHEASANT In hedges or woods in shallow depression, either natural or scratched out, sparsely lined with dry leaves and grass. May to June. 1 brood of 6–18 plain brown/grey-green eggs (4.5 × 3.6 cm).

3. *Ground nests on pasture.*

MEADOW PIPIT In damp meadow or moor in depression in ground among loose tangle of plants; made of grass and moss lined with hair. May to June. 4–6 light green or browny eggs (2 × 1.5 cm) covered with brown-black vertical lines.

ROCK and WATER PIPIT Lays on ground in dry headland under overhanging stone or vegetation. 4–6 light grey eggs (2.14 × 1.6 cm) with fine dark vertical lines.

YELLOW WAGTAIL In wet grass or clover, in grassy glades; also hollow in bank or in fence; made of grass, moss and plant fibres, lined with hair. May to June. 4–6 yellowish eggs (1.9 × 1.4 cm) with reddish-olive mottling almost all over. 2 clutches.

QUAIL (see above) 2 clutches.

GRASSHOPPER WARBLER In bushes or tall grass, plants, marshes or wet wasteland; longish, deep bowl of sedge grass well smoothed down. May to June 5–6 faintly red eggs (1.7 × 1.3 cm) thickly dotted with rust red.

CORN BUNTING (see p. 91.)

4. *Ground nests on waste land, stony common, bare hillsides and vine-slopes.*

STONECHAT Firm structure of grass and hair well hidden under a clump of grass, furze, bramble or heath; 2 clutches of 5-6 bluey-green eggs (1.8 × 1.4 cm) with delicate, faintly red mottling.

WHEATEAR Mostly under a boulder, in a bank or wall, rabbit burrow, etc., loose structure of grass and roots lined with feathers and hair; 1 clutch of 5–6 light-blue, or nearly white eggs (2 × 1.5 cm). May to June.

* ROCK BUNTING Among stones, near tussocks, in vineyard walls, mostly in hilly country; grass and roots lined with finer grass and hair. May to June. 4–5 greeny-white eggs (2.6 × 1.6 cm) with black squiggles.

TAWNY PIPIT Largish nest, well-concealed in hollow near clods of earth, under tuft of grass, etc. From mid-May 4–5 glossy eggs (2.1 × 1.6 cm) with white, greenish or yellowish ground sparsely mottled.

SKYLARK (see p. 91.)

* ALPINE ACCENTOR Made of moss, grass, feathers, hair. Rather careless structure between stones or in hole in rock. 5 pale, greeny-blue eggs (2.3 × 1.7 cm). In mild years 2 clutches

5. *Ground nests in boggy ground or water meadows.*

SNIPE Deep hollow in moist ground lined with dry grass, well hidden by overhanging grass, heather, bracken. End of April July 2 clutches of 4 pear-shaped greeny-brown-yellow eggs (4 × 2.9 cm) with large dark brown splodges mostly towards the blunt end.

LAPWING In rough pasture, ploughed field, moor or marsh, in a scraped out hollow sparsely lined with vegetable matter. March to May, one clutch of 4 pear-shaped browny-olive green eggs (4.6 × 3.3 cm) with light grey and brown-black mottling. Eggs all lie with point inward. Picture shows nest seen from above.

CURLEW Scratched out bowl in moist grassland, moor, heath or fallow field and lined sparsely with grass, etc. April to May one clutch of 4 large pear-shaped olive-brown eggs (6.8 × 4.8 cm) mottled with dark brown and grey.

REDSHANK Bowl in grass near water lined with a few straws. End April to early May 4 yellowy-grey glossy eggs (4.4 × 3.1 cm) with dark red-brown mottling and dots. One clutch.

RUFF Nest like lapwing's on dry place in swampy ground or grass, usually near water. 4 pear-shaped, olive-brown or light yellowy-grey eggs (4.4 × 3 cm) mottled with brown.

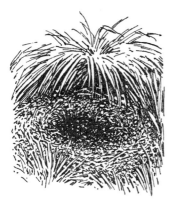

←

MALLARD Made of reeds, grass, leaves, breast feathers, mostly a little way from water among thick growth, reeds, hedge etc. in quiet dry spot, also in hole in tree, old crow's or other nest (off the ground), 8–14 greeny to browny-white eggs (5.7 × 4 cm). One clutch, April to June.

TEAL, GARGANEY, SHOVELLER Have nests like mallards', but eggs are smaller.

POCHARD Nests in reed bed in such a way that nest is surrounded by water.

TUFTED DUCK Nests in companies by lakes and ponds. One clutch.

←

BLACK-HEADED GULL Prefers islands or marshy banks, inland marsh, often in colonies. Largish nest with base of reeds, sticks, grass, etc. and bowl of dry sedge. April to May 2–3 pale olive-green eggs (5 × 3.6 cm) with brown mottling of different shades. One clutch.

SHORT-EARED OWL Simply lays eggs in a hollow in grass, heather, bracken, sedge or in loose heap of dead leaves and grass. May to June 4–7 pure white eggs (4 × 3.1 cm). One clutch.

*CRANE In swamps, moors, wet grassland, alder-swamp; flat, untidy nest of dry grass, moss, reeds, sedge. April to May one clutch of 2 reddish-brown or light browny-green eggs (9.6 × 6.2 cm) with reddish-brown or reddish-grey mottling. Often has dark squiggles on blunt end.

* WOOD SANDPIPER Beside lakes, ponds, on river banks, in swamps and moors. Hollow in moss, heather, grass, scantily lined with grass, etc. April to May, 4 light greenish eggs (3.8 × 2.6 cm) with brown dots and mottling.

GREEN SANDPIPER Sometimes nests on ground. See p. 82.

6. *Nests close to or on water, in reed or sedge-beds, willow or alder thickets.*

MARSH HARRIER Nests near water or on water among reeds, or close to or on ground; usually in reed-bed, but also in a willow or in cornfield near water; rather tall structure of twigs, rushes, sedge, grass etc. with shallow bowl. 4–5 eggs (5 × 3.9 cm) grey- to greeny-white. Unmarked. One clutch.

MALLARD, TEAL, TUFTED DUCK See p. 94.

MUTE SWAN Rather large, stout nest of reeds, rushes and other aquatic plants close to water or floating in water. Often several nests close together. Bowl upholstered with white down. April to May. One clutch of 6–8 very large, stout-shelled dirty-white or dirty pale green eggs (11.5 × 7.4 cm) with rough, coarse-grained surface.

GREY LAG GOOSE In marsh or large lake, in reeds or heather, mostly in colonies. Extensive heap of reeds, rushes, heather, twigs, etc. April to May. One clutch of 5–10 matt white-yellow eggs (8.5 × 5.8 cm) tinged with yellow or creamy buff.

*LITTLE BITTERN Nests in reed beds or osiers, often several in a group; rarely in open water; fairly deep bowl of rush and aquatic plants. May to June. 5–6 white eggs (3.5 × 2.6 cm) tinged with bluey-green.
←

BITTERN In reed-beds in inaccessible places, on bent reeds or rushes above the water; sometimes on mounds of earth or islands of reeds; rarely floating. Tall untidy lump of dry sedge, reeds, etc. lined with panicles and dry grass. April to June. 3–5 olive-green, matt eggs (5.3 × 3.9 cm).

←
WATER RAIL Large nest in reeds or under willows in inaccessible places, made of reed, rush, sedge, grass with deep bowl. Roof of dry stalks. May to June. 5–11 glossy, whitey-yellow eggs (3.5 × 2.6 cm) mottled with grey and a few red dots.

SPOTTED CRAKE Well made of rush, sedge, grass in thick vegetation, often covered by overhanging plants. About 15 cm across with bowl 3–7 cm deep. June to July 8–14 shiny, light brown eggs (3.5 × 2.5 cm) mottled with grey and thickly covered with sharp brown dots.

*LITTLE CRAKE Very small nest, preferably under willows or sedge, reached by swimming; or close to water; made of dry sedge leaves and grass; sedge leaves and rush drawn together over it like a hood. May to June. 6–8 grey-white or light brown eggs (3 × 2.2 cm) with rust-yellow or brownish mottling. Mostly 2 clutches.

*BAILLON'S CRAKE Like preceding nest, often covered approach; made of cotton grass leaves, roots, and dry sedge leaves. June to July, 6–8 very shiny yellowish or browny eggs (2.8 × 2.1 cm) mottled brown; darker than other crakes.

COOT By ponds, lakes, rivers. In reeds or rushes on bank; large, fairly deep bowl of rush, reed and other aquatic plants; on clumps of sedge grass or bent-over reeds, usually a foot above water; either on bank or floating. April to July. 7–12 grey-yellow eggs (5 × 3.5 cm) with lots of black and grey dots. 2 or 3 clutches.

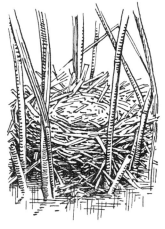

←
MOORHEN Similar kind of nest to coot's; either on water or among bushes; mostly on clumps of sedge, seldom floating; always made of reed and sedge. 6–9 rather long yellowy-brown eggs (4.1 × 2.9 cm) with dark dots and mottling. 2 or 3 clutches.

GREAT CRESTED GREBE Nests on the water, either free or attached to a few stalks; or built among reeds and rushes. About 30 cm across, 15 cm high made of dry rushes and other aquatic plants, damp and decaying; only a hand's breadth above water. 3–5 eggs (5.3 ×

3.6 cm) lying half in water. Pure white at first, then stained with damp. Late April to July. Often 2 clutches.

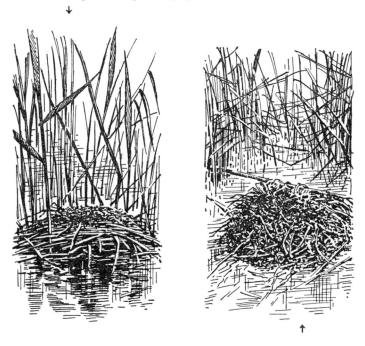

LITTLE GREBE Untidy heap of dry and green plants, floating among rushes and other plants, often quite free, always as far as possible from bank of pond. 4–6 eggs (3.8 × 2.6 cm) blue-white or cream, becoming stained by material of nest. 2 clutches.

BEARDED TIT Nest has deep cup. On ground in a clump of grass or dead vegetation with some blades of sedge and reed woven in. Top edge always slightly overhanging. Lining of plant wool and feathers. From middle of April 2 or 3 clutches of 5–7 shining white eggs (1.7 × 1.4 cm) lined and speckled with brown.

REED BUNTING Nests among vegetation on bank, in clump of sedge or on the ground beside a bush or reeds, usually hidden by overhanging plants; built of grass and other plants, often lined with hair. 2 clutches, May to July, of 4–6 brownish eggs (2.1 × 1.5 cm) with dark squiggles.

SEDGE WARBLER On or just above ground in thick bank vegetation, or in thick grass under overhanging sedge. Supported from beneath. Outside plant stems, moss, etc. lined with hair and feathers. May to July. 1 clutch of 4–6 light grey or yellowy eggs (1.7 × 1.3 cm) with hair streaks and speckles.

7. Ground nests on flat shore with banks of gravel, sand, or mud.

→

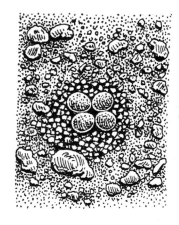

LITTLE RINGED PLOVER On bare, sandy-gravelly ground near fresh water; especially on boulder-islands or in flooded gravel pits; bowl dug out and lined with little stones. April to May, 4 rust or browny-yellow eggs (3 × 2.2 cm) like gravel, mottled grey and with lots of blackish specks.

COMMON SANDPIPER Nests on sandy or gravelly, overgrown bank of river or pool under vegetation, usually well hidden; made of stalks, leaves, grass and moss. April to May, 4 clay-coloured eggs (3.6 × 2.5 cm) with brown mottling, mostly round blunt end.

COMMON TERN On sandbanks in rivers, on islands in lakes, sand dunes or banks of shingle, etc. In small colonies. Makes a hollow in shingle; often unlined, May to June, 1–3 gravel-like, yellowy-brown eggs (4.2 × 3 cm) with brown mottling and dots.

8. Ground nests on or above tree-line.

PTARMIGAN June to July scrapes a shallow hollow under a rock or boulder, rarely under a bush; scantily lined. Lays 6–12 whitey-yellow eggs (4.4 × 3.1 cm) with large black and black-brown mottling.

*ROCK PARTRIDGE Nests in similar places to preceding, but lines the bowl well with grass and feathers. June to July, 9–15 yellowy-green eggs (4.4 × 3.2 cm) with scattered reddish dots.

V. Nests in Natural or Artificial, Holes, Beam-heads etc.

Nos. 3–19 have the description of their nest and eggs given with that of the bird itself.

1. *Nests in specially made holes in trees.*

(a) Without nesting material.

*BLACK WOODPECKER Makes hole mostly in beech trees, fairly high up; almost arm's length in depth: oval entrance 8–10 cm wide by 13 cm high; often like an arched window because bottom edge of entrance is flat and level. April to June, one clutch of 4–5 glossy white, almost pear-shaped eggs (3.7 × 2.6 cm).

GREEN WOODPECKER Only in deciduous trees, in thick woods, orchards, parks. Usually elaborates a natural hole. Circular entrance (6.5 × 6.4 cm) sometimes used year after year. End of April one clutch of 5–7 shiny white, pear-shaped eggs (3.1 × 2.3 cm) bedded, if at all, on wood chips and dust.

* GREY-HEADED WOODPECKER In old deciduous trees in woods; circular entrance up to 6 cm in diameter. From mid-May 6–7 white, very shiny eggs (2.8 × 2 cm).

GREAT SPOTTED WOODPECKER In rotten deciduous tree or conifer, seldom in fruit trees; entrance about 4.6 cm in diameter. April to May, 1 clutch of 4–8 glossy white eggs (2.6 × 1.9 cm). Will use abandoned holes of other woodpeckers.

* MIDDLE SPOTTED WOODPECKER Holes as those of preceding, but more often in fruit trees; makes holes in old deciduous trees, willows and poplars. Entrance about 4 cm. April to May, one clutch of 5–6 glossy white eggs (2.3 × 1.8 cm).

LESSER SPOTTED WOODPECKER As well as mixed woods often in orchards, parks; Entrance 3.2 cm in diameter. In May, one clutch of 5–6 glossy eggs (1.9 × 1.4 cm).

(b) With nesting material.

WILLOW TIT Self-made hole in rotten alder and willow. Nest itself of willow bark fibre. April to June, 1 clutch of 7–8 eggs (1.5 × 1.6 cm) very similar to marsh tit.

2. *Entrance hole reduced to body width with mud.*

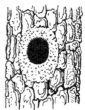

NUTHATCH Nests in holes in trees, abandoned woodpecker holes, sometimes hole in wall. Entrance hole always plastered with mud to reduce it to body size. Layer of mud can be up to 6 cm. If hole too deep it is filled up with leaves and bits of bark (especially of conifers) and bark fibre. April to May 6–8 shiny white eggs (1.9 × 1.5 cm) mottled rust-red. One clutch.

3. *Nests in self-made holes on bare bluff or wall of loam pit:* kingfisher and sand martin.

4. *Nests always in or on buildings or rock faces.*
   a) in buildings: swallow, barn owl.
   b) on buildings or rock faces: house martin, swift, *Alpine swift.

5. *In holes in trees, often in nesting boxes or woodpeckers' holes:* stock dove, wryneck.

6. *Always in holes in trees, especially old woodpeckers' nests:* *Tengmalm's owl, *pygmy owl, *roller.

7. *Mostly in holes in trees, seldom in buildings or in old crows' nests:* tawny owl, little owl, *scops owl.

8. *In holes in trees or in nesting boxes, seldom in buildings:* *fieldfare, *hoopoe.

9. *In holes in trees, nesting boxes or under tiles:* redstart, starling, pied flycatcher.

10. *In woodpecker's hole in tree, nesting box, also in hole in wall:* nuthatch, coal tit, blue tit, marsh tit, great tit, crested tit.

11. *In rabbit holes:* crested and coal tit.

12. *In holes it has excavated, also in rabbit holes or badger sets:* sheldrake.

13. *In holes by water:* goldeneye, smew, goosander.

14. *In crevices in bark or trunks, sometimes under tiles or in crevices in rock:* *wall creeper, tree creeper, *short-toed tree creeper.

15. *In buildings or holes in rock, seldom in holes in trees:* house sparrow, jackdaw, kestrel.

16. *Nests on beam-heads, in holes in walls:* sparrow, redstart, spotted flycatcher, white wagtail.

17. *In crevices or on trellis:* spotted fly-catcher.

18. *Under bridges, in caves:* redstart, dipper, grey wagtail.

19. *Eyrie or eggs laid on ledge of rock:* peregrine falcon, golden eagle, raven, kestrel, Alpine jackdaw, eagle owl.

EASILY RECOGNISABLE EGGS.

1. *Bluey-green:* hedge sparrow, redstart, pied flycatcher, starling, *Alpine accentor, wheatear, whinchat (very few red specks).

2. *Eggs with squiggles:* all buntings and finches.

3. *Usually 4 top-shaped, strongly mottled eggs, arranged in a cross:*
    a) in sedge bogs: snipe, curlew, lapwing;
    b) in damp wooded areas: woodcock;
    c) on gravel banks: little ringed plover, common sandpiper.

FEEDING PLACES AND PELLETS

TEARING AND PLUCKING

Bits of flesh with feathers that have had part cut clean off lying on the ground will be the work of *fox, marten, polecat* or *weasel.*

Feathers plucked out complete or tufts of animal hair spread over several places (3–6) several hundreds of metres apart, will be the work of a *bird of prey,* which if disturbed moves on with its prey a short distance before tearing at it again.

Bits of pigeon, partridge, pheasant, magpie, crow, domestic hen, duck is the work of the *goshawk.* Long trails of excrement are characteristic.

Feathers on tree stump or elevation in the ground, also feet, beaks, bits of breast-bone or humerus of birds from thrush-size up; bits of smaller birds. Long trails of excrement. The work of *sparrow hawk.*

Rings of feather caused by the plucker continually moving round its prey, so as to keep an eye on its surroundings, with such typical remains as shoulder with primaries still attached, a round patch of excrement (thrown down and not behind as with goshawks and sparrow hawk) is the work of the *peregrine falcon.*

Pellets

Grey, woolly, sausage-shaped lumps an inch or so in length lying on the ground. In these are bits of hair, shell and jawbones of mice (recognisable by pointed rodent teeth), claws of mice and birds, feathers and beaks:

in a wood under a tall or old tree, are the pellets of an owl: *long-eared owl, tawny owl.*

in a clearing, on edge of wood or stones in field: from a *bird of prey.*

with husks of corn: from *crows.*

under the tree carrying a goshawk's eyrie, but containing no bones (these have been digested) but claws of mice and birds: from *goshawk.*

a

Woodpecker's Smithy

Pine or fir cones with split scales heaped at foot of a tree, in whose bark another cone is fixed into a crack or a hole made by a woodpecker. The woodpecker plucks one cone after the other from the crest, places it in the holes, removes the seeds and then throws it to the ground (a).

Cones Lying on the Ground

Fir and pine cones, more or less damaged, lying scattered about the ground can be that of various creatures.

When the cone has been "chiselled" from the tip down and split without the scales being removed:

b   **c**

(a) *Great spotted woodpecker*

Ground covered with scales and shank of fir and pine cones which have been bared up to the upper rings of scales. The gnawed-off scales lying separately on the ground:

(c) *Squirrel*

Pine cones from which many scales have been split clean in half up the middle, the two halves being still in the shank (d) is the work of a *crossbill.*

Pine cones from which the seed scales have been gnawed-off on one or all sides (b) is the work of *mice.*

d

DISTINGUISHING THE DIFFERENT KINDS OF BIRDS

SPARROW Short body, thick conical beak, stumpy wings; tail scarcely notched at end. Short, sturdy feet; hops heavily on ground. *Flight:* short distances straight; greater distances in flat arc. Male house sparrow: grey crown and black throat; tree sparrow: chocolate crown, black spot on cheek. Flight noise: house sparrow – *cheep, cheep;* tree sparrow – short *teck teck.*

Fig. 21: Sparrows, Finches, Buntings
From left to right: **House Sparrow, Chaffinch, Corn Bunting**

FINCH (chaffinch pictured) Size of sparrow; body somewhat elongated, slimmer than house sparrow's; medium length pointed conical beak; short neck; short legged; wings and tail medium length; tail has shallow notch at end, shorter than a bunting's. Hops, occasionally steps. Undulating flight. Flight call: chaffinch a soft *chwink-chwink;* greenfinch a soft *ten ten;* goldfinch a repeated *swilt-wilt-swilt-wilt;* linnet a soft, somewhat chattering twitter.

BUNTING Size of a sparrow, looks plump; rather short, pointed conical beak. Fairly long tail curved at end. Short-legged. Hopping, sometimes

Fig. 22: Starling, Thrush, Thrush-like (= Chats, Wheatears)
From left to right: **Starling, Blackbird, Robin**

stepping gait. Flies in medium-length arcs; fanned tail. Flight call: yellow-hammer a clear *chip chip;* cornbunting a climbing *zeep zeep zeep.*

STARLING Somewhat smaller than blackbird; sturdy, short neck, thickset. Long, straight, pointed beak; medium length strong legs; medium length pointed wings; short tail. Steps, waddling gait; does not hop. Flies in straight line, swift, whirring; glides on occasion.

THRUSH Strongly built, holds itself erect; beak shorter than head, straight and pointed, only upper mandible slightly curved; long pointed wings, when closed cover only half the tail, which is almost straight, gently rounded, longer than a starling's. Slender legs; feet for walking, but mostly hops. Straight-line flight (blackbird) or in flat undulations (song, mistle, fieldfare).

Of thrush shape, but only size of sparrow or smaller, with long, thin legs, erect, thin beaks, which flick their tails and bob, have hopping gait and fly mostly in flat undulations, are: redstart, nightingale, robin, wheatear.

Fig. 23: Warblers
Left to right: **Grass, Leaf, Reed Warbler**

GRASS-WARBLERS About sparrow-size, inconspicuous grey and brown of slender body, bowed, horizontal stance; slim bodkin-shaped beak, slightly hooked in front, much shorter than head; rather short feet; medium length wings, rounded; tail varies; action on ground or flying in open, mostly skulking in bushes; undulating flight. In mating season barred warbler and whitethroat have song-flight.

LEAF-WARBLERS Smaller than sparrow; upper parts greeny-yellowy-grey, underparts yellowish. Slim body, almost horizontal stance; bodkin-shaped beak; medium length feet, weak; rather long wings, medium-long tail, cut off straight or slightly down-curved; live in bushes or trees.

REED WARBLERS About the size of a sparrow; slim body, elongated, flat-browed head; fairly long pointed beak. Clamber in reeds, seldom sit in open. Fly with spread tail. In mating season sedge warbler and marsh warbler have short song-flight.

LARKS Size of sparrow, strongly built, earth-coloured, terrestrial; slim, conical beak with slightly curved ridge, rather thin as with insect eaters; that of skylark is stouter; long, broad wings; medium-length tail; low legged; walking feet; gait tripping step and run, does not hop. Slightly undulating flight or fluttering song-flight. Skylark has a loud *chir-r up*.

Fig. 24: **Larks, Pipits, Wagtails**
Left to right: **Skylark, Tree Pipit, White Wagtail**
Below: **Skylark, White Wagtail, Tree Pipit**

PIPITS Sparrow size, terrestrial, similar to lark in colouring, but body, beak and legs slimmer, like wagtail's. Flies in great arcs, slightly undulating. In song-flight sings on upward glide.

WAGTAILS Size of sparrow, strong excellent runner, terrestrial; very slim body; long-legged; upright stance; long, straight, thin, bodkin-shaped beak; long, pointed wings; long tail which it frequently flicks; *gait:* quick run; *flight:* deep waves; flight sounds: white wagtail *tchizzik;* yellow wagtail *tsip-tsip-tsipsi . . .*

TITS Small, stocky, plump; powerful, short pointed bodkin-shaped beak; upper mandible slightly hooked; wings mostly fairly short, rounded; tail mostly straight edged or slightly curved; sometimes long gymnastics on twigs. Whirring flight, short arcs, seldom for much of a distance. Flight call *sit sit.*

Fig. 25: Tits, Goldcrest, Wren
From left to right: **Tit, Goldcrest, Wren**

GOLDCRESTS Tiny, plump, olive-green tree-dweller; yellow erectile crest; climbs like tit along thin twigs, flutters round, hovers. *Call:* light *zee-zee-zee.*

WREN Tiny, round body; inconspicuous brown; short, round wings; short, mostly cocked tail; skulks in bushes; darts about the ground; swift flight, whirring; over a distance in short, flat arcs. *Song:* very loud clear shrill warble.

Fig. 26: Shrikes, Flycatchers
From left to right: **Red-backed Shrike, Flycatcher**

SHRIKES Vividly coloured, somewhat larger than sparrow, stocky build; fairly broad head; strong beak; upper mandible hooked at tip. Stiff, upright stance; strong fairly long legs. Medium-long, rounded wings; long tail either straight or graduated, well-rounded at end or wedge-shaped; waves or fans tail. Hops. Indifferent, irregular flight, that of red-backed shrike and woodchat shrike undulating.

FLYCATCHERS Size of sparrow; near upright stance; short, bodkin-shaped beak, looking broad from above. Frequent flicking of tail. Short, fluttering hunting flights from vantage point with audible snap of beak.

SWALLOWS Slim, slight, stream-lined body with broad chest, short neck, flat head, very short shallow beak, wide gape. Long, narrow, pointed wings, that, when folded, cross over the forked tail. Awkward stumbling run. Fly in daring sweeps with swift turns. Flight call: swallow, a high *twsit;* house martin, a soft sibilant *tchichirrip;* sand martin, a soft dry *tchrrip.*

Fig. 27: Swallow, Swift, Nightjar
From left to right: **Swallow, Swift, Nightjar**

SWIFT Swallow-like shape, only more slender, sickle-shaped wings, and short forked tail; small beak; short feet. Fiercely swift flight in great swoops with lightning turns, uttering shrill *sree-sree.*

NIGHTJARS Size of a blackbird, nocturnal, with owl's plumage; procumbent body, short neck, broad, low head, small beak with wide gape; tiny feet, long, narrow wings; big straight tail; undulating flight; strange churring sound and wing-clapping in flight at night.

Fig. 28: Treetrunk climbers
Tree Creeper, Nuthatch, Woodpecker

TREE CREEPERS Small, bark-coloured; long, thin, curved beak; jerky spiral climb, stiff tail action as support on bark.

NUTHATCH Small, stocky, ashen-blue upper parts; strong, pointed woodpecker-like beak; big, strong feet; climbs in spurts, up and down; short tail not used as support.

WOODPECKERS Ranging from sparrow to jackdaw size; strong, chisel-beak; strong feet; short, stiff tail acts as support. Flight undulating with deep troughs (green woodpecker) or straight or faintly undulating (black woodpecker).

Fig. 29: Crows, Pigeons, Partridges, Cuckoo
From left to right: top, **Crow, Pigeon, Partridge, Cuckoo**
bottom, **Crow, Pigeon, Cuckoo, Partridge**

CROWS Black or black head with grey body; procumbent but powerful bodies; beaks as long as the head, strong, thick, curved down at end; long, strong legs; rounded wings; rounded tail. Rather waddly walk. Straight flight, regular, slow wing beats. Seldom glide. Flight calls: rook, a rough, deep *kaaa,* less croaking than carrion crow's.

PIGEONS Plump bodies, small heads, short, weak beaks, distinct demarcation line of beak and head; slight down-curve at tip. Long, pointed wings; fairly long tail, gently rounded. Short legs; walks continually moving neck. Quick flight with agile turns. Deep coo.

PARTRIDGES Plump, terrestrial; stocky, round shape; small head; short, strong, curved beak; short, broad tail, rounded; strong legs; walks crouching or running swiftly with head held high, before taking wing. Low, quick, straight flight alternating between whirring wing-beats and gliding. Tires quickly. *Flight call:* as it takes wing nine loud *krrr-ic,* repeated as *kar-wic.*

CUCKOO Rather smaller than pigeon; procumbent stance; beak as long as head; slender, slightly curved; long, pointed wings; long, rounded tail; short legs, feathered at top; climbing feet. Light delicate flight like a falcon's. In flight-silhouette and colouring like a sparrow hawk. Compare Figs. 29 and 30. See Plate 4.

Fig. 30: Buzzards, Accipiters, Falcons
From left to right: **Buzzard, Sparrow Hawk, Kestrel**

BUZZARDS Powerful bodies, plump of appearance; large heads with relatively small beaks; short, broad, rounded tail; broad wings; in-drawn head gives rather heavy silhouette. *Flight:* slow wing-beats, interrupted by gliding; flight calls: buzzard a high *pee-oo;* honey buzzard a rapid *kikiki* or squeaky *kee-er.*

ACCIPITERS Like falcons, but smaller heads and short, round wings; tails longer; long legs; quick wing-beats alternating with brief glides. Low, very swift, twisting flight. Flight calls: goshawk a buzzard-like mew and a chattering *gig-gig-gig;* sparrow hawk usually *kek-kek-kek.*

FALCONS More dashing; fairly large heads, broad shoulders; when closed wings reach the end of tail; extremely swift flight; quick pigeon-like, but shallow wing-beats, interrupted by occasional long glides. *Flight silhouette:* long narrow, pointed, sickle-shaped wings and long, narrow tail, slightly narrower at end. Flight call: kestrel, shrill *kee kee kee.*

KITES Buzzard-size, sombre colours; look fat when sitting with head drawn in; tail does not hang down straight, but has a slight forward curve; weak beak with a fairly long hook; angled wings; forked tail; short legs; long sailing flight.

Fig. 31: Kites, Harriers, Ospreys
a) **Black Kite**   b) **Marsh Harrier**   c) **Osprey**

HARRIERS Slender; small heads with short beaks; long, slightly angled wings; long tails; long, thin legs; rocking flight with long, undulating glides, when wings held above the body in a shallow V.

OSPREY Large and powerful; rather short beak with very long hooked-tip; long, narrow, angled wings, protruding far beyond the tail when folded; bent (L-shaped) posture, same when hovering; slight crest on head; dark upper parts, but snow-white underneath. Stout legs.

Fig. 32: Storks, Herons, Cranes
a) White Stork b) Heron c) Crane

STORKS Large, long-legged; long necks and long, straight beaks; often stand on one leg; measured walk; fly with slow wing-beats or sail, neck and legs outstretched.

HERONS Stork-like waders, with long legs, long necks, medium length pointed beaks. Elongated plumage on nape and neck. Slow heavy flight with head pulled in and legs outstretched. Flight call: a hoarse *frarnk*.

CRANES Large birds with long necks and legs; straight pointed beaks slightly longer than the head; body almost cylindrical. Elongated inner secondaries droop bushily over the short tail. Necks and legs outstretched in flight. Fly in wedge-formation or in line, uttering trumpeting flight-call.

BITTERN   Size of a domestic hen, brown-yellow reed-dweller; stocky body; long neck, in-drawn head and loose plumage make it appear fat: relatively short legs; straight, pointed beak the length of the head; broad wings; short tail. Walks in crouching posture; clambers among reeds, slow, fluttering flight. *Call:* deep booming, audible for long distances.

LAPWING   Size of pigeon; contrasting colouring; wader's legs with thickening at heel joints; erectile feather-crest; steep brow; straight beak; somewhat shorter than the head; long, narrow wings, blunt fore-edge; agile walk; flight exceptionally nimble and twisting; flight-call loud clear *keewi* and variants on it.

RAILS   Size of a thrush; browny-grey; hen-shaped; long beaks, short, blunt wings; very short, narrow tails; skulking; poor, low flight with legs dangling.

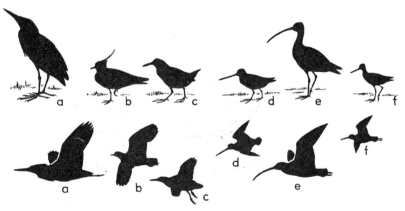

Fig. 33: Marsh birds up to size of Domestic Hen
a) **Bittern**   b) **Lapwing**   c) **Water Rail**   d) **Snipe**   e) **Curlew**   f) **Redshank**

SNIPE   Roughly thrush size; nocturnal marsh bird; long, straight beak; domed head; slender feet; medium-length, pointed wings; short, rounded tail; stormy zig-zag flight; diving courtship display with "drumming", tail making *huhuhuhu* sound.

CURLEW   Big wader the size of a crow with the colouring of a lark; slim, very long, thin, downward curved beak; slim, long legs, bare to well above heel; strong; quick, agile flight with measured wingbeats and soaring when draws neck in and stretches its legs out; flocks fly high or V. Flight call: full flute-like *cour-li* or *crwee*.

REDSHANK Size of thrush; grey-brown upper parts, white below; slim; long, red legs; long, straight, red beak; narrow, pointed, angled wings. Takes large steps, nodding head and flicking tail. Light agile flight. Flight call: musical *tuuu* or *tu-hu-hu*.

WOODCOCK Size of pigeon; rust coloured; camouflage plumage; squat, short body; domed head with high brow; very long, straight beak with rounded somewhat wider tip; short neck; short, broad wings; short, rounded tail; short stocky legs; quick, wobbling flight with beak held pointing down. In display flight (roding) makes low, croaking sound and a thin *tsiwick*.

OWLS Bark coloured nocturnal birds with large heads, hooked beaks and large, curved claws; mostly stooping posture; noiseless flight; that of barn owl wavering; of little owl low, quick in deep undulations. Loud barking call; tawny owl, prolonged *hoo-hoo-hoo* and a sharp *kewick*.

Fig. 34: Birds of Dusk and the Night: Snipe, Long-eared Owl

SNIPE (See Fig. 33 d)   NIGHTJAR (See Fig. 27)

SWANS Big, plump-looking bird with a very, long, slender S-shaped neck and a straight beak the length of its head; black bumps where it joins the head; short tail; short stocky legs set far back. Heavy waddling gait; quick, straight flight with slow, regular wing-beat, neck outstretched and head pointing slightly down, making a thrumming-swish; no gliding; flocks mostly fly in V-formation; when swimming neck is gracefully bent.

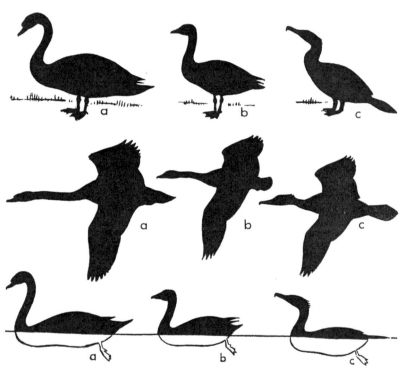

Fig. 35: a) **Mute Swan** b) **Goose** c) **Cormorant**

GEESE Squatter in the body, with shorter necks and beaks than the swan; longer in the legs which are set more in middle of the body. Lighter gait than that of swan or duck. Long, broad, pointed wings; flies with neck outstretched in oblique line or V-formation. Flight call of grey lag goose raw, nasal *gangangang;* bean goose a trumpeting *kagakak,* not so deep as grey lag.

CORMORANT Size of a goose; very long in the body; strong, long beak with hooked tip; neck shorter than swan's or goose's. Upright stance, often spreads its wings. Waddling gait. Swims deep in the water with beak tilted slightly up, tail level with the surface. Very quick straight flight.

SURFACE-FEEDING DUCKS Slim bodies; short to medium length necks; thick heads; beaks as long as heads; low legs set well back; heavy waddling gait; swim high in the water, tail very visible: take off immediately; swift flight, shallow wing beats. Do not normally dive, but "up-end".

DIVING DUCKS Short, plump bodies; short thick necks; large heads; beaks somewhat shorter than head; rather upright posture on land, since legs are set far back. In water hind end is submerged, tail trailing on the surface. Can dive for minutes at a time; run along the surface in taking off.

MERGANSERS Very long in the body, slender; thin, medium-length necks; large heads with feather-crest; long straight beaks; low legs set far back thus rather upright posture; waddling gait. Deep in water when swimming. Dive. Duck-like flight.

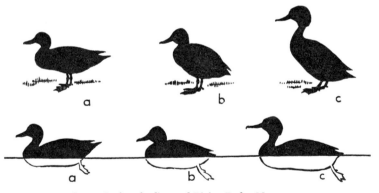

Fig. 36: Surface-feeding and Diving Ducks, Mergansers
a) **Surface-feeding** b) **Diving Duck** c) **Mergansers**

GULLS Thick-set bodies, long wings, but longer in leg and broader in wing than terns. Beaks slightly hooked. Tails cut straight or rounded.

TERNS Bodies more slender and wings narrower than gulls; beaks thinner and more pointed, pointing down in flight. Forked tails.

Fig. 37: Gulls and Terns

GREAT-CRESTED GREBE Broad, flat body; straight pointed beak rather shorter than the head; short legs set well back and thus almost vertical stance on land; has black twin-pointed ear tufts extended in male to frills; long, thin neck mostly held as an S; short, narrow wings; no tail. Lobed feet. Good diver and swimmer; poor flyer; straight, whirring flight.

COOT Plump, black, water bird, smaller than a duck, larger than a pigeon; small head; white cone-shaped beak, much shorter than its head; long strong legs; long toes with lobes; nods its head as it swims, quite slowly, sitting high in the water but without cocking up its tail. Dives and re-emerges at the same spot; flops pattering across the surface; reluctant to fly: in flight outstretched legs protrude behind tail.

Fig. 38: a) **Great Crested Grebe** b) **Coot** c) **Moorhen** d) **Blackheaded Gull**

MOORHEN Size of a partridge; more slender than coot; small head; cone-shaped beak; short high-set tail; long legs with long toes; walks on leaves of water plants; easy swimming action nodding its head and flicking its tail; surfaces at a distance from where it dived; fluttering, not quick, straight flight with dangling wings. Runs pattering across surface to take off.

Order   PASSERIFORMES   Perching Birds

Sub-order   OSCINES   Song Birds

SPARROWS, FINCHES AND BUNTINGS (Plate 1)

Family   PASSERIDAE   Sparrows

Distinguished from finches and buntings by their eggs, structure of nest and indifferent song.

HOUSE SPARROW *(Passer domesticus)* Plate 1 Grey crown; male has black throat, whitish cheeks and brown nape; female no black throat. Upper parts rusty dull brown. Heavy wide-legged hop with drooping wings and tail slightly raised. Flies straight with whirring wings and effort, over short stretches, but in flat arcs over longer distances. Quick flight, seldom high. Call: *cheep;* in agitation: *chissis.* During courtship song is a dreadful grating twitter with other chirping sounds. *Food:* omnivorous; insects especially in breeding season, various seeds, shoots of plants, buds of flowers and berries, ripening wheat grain, cherries, grapes, etc. *Nests:* in holes in buildings, in roofs etc. holes in trees, old nests of other birds or builds its own in ivy and bushes; shapeless clump of straws, rags etc. often hanging down untidily; lined with a great deal of feathers and hair. From April 3–4 clutches of 5–6 white eggs with dark mottling. Permanent resident. Gregarious in winter. Also near human habitations. *Distribution:* Europe generally and has spread to many other parts of the world which Europeans have colonised.

TREE SPARROW *(Passer montanus)* Smaller and more delicate than house sparrow. Colouring of sexes the same: rich chocolate brown crowns with black spot on whitish ear-coverts; white collar. Gait more agile, flight lighter, voice higher and softer than house sparrow's. *Call:* short, metallic *chik;* in flight *tek, tek. Song:* a quick, pleasant twitter. *Food:* the same as house sparrow, though more of an insect eater; eats more seeds of weeds. *Nests:* in holes in trees, walls, and in trees. *Eggs:* from April to May 2 (rarely 3) clutches of smaller, glossier eggs and with browner base colour than house sparrow. Nests similar to the latter's. Lives in copses in fields, deciduous woods, orchards, parks, less often in villages. Permanent resident. Unlike the house sparrow remain paired during winter. *Distribution:* Europe generally; in Britain widespread but local.

Family   FRINGILLIDAE   Finches and Buntings   Fig. 21

Powerfully built song birds roughly the size of sparrows with upright posture. Sexes usually distinguishable. Largely grain-eaters. Cone-shaped

Chaffinch

Tree
Sparrow

House Sparrow

Hawfinch

Goldfinch

Bullfinch

Crossbill

Linnet

Siskin

Serin

Greenfinch

Yellowhammer

Reed
Bunting

Corn
Bunting

Bäuerle

beaks, usually thick at base, straight tip and sharp edges for husking and crushing seeds. Wings and tail medium-long. Good fliers. Undulating flight. Medium length legs, fairly short torso. *Gait:* half hopping, half running; very agile at hopping. Mostly pleasant song. Nests mostly open with thick walls, neatly lined, made of plant material and hair.

CHAFFINCH *(Fringilla coelebs)* Plate 1 Best known of all finches; brightly coloured sociable bird with gay, though vehement, quarrelsome behaviour. The size of a sparrow but slimmer. Males have slate-blue crown and nape, pinkish-brown chest, striking double white wing-bars and green rump. Females and juveniles much less striking with olive-brown upper parts and pale-grey-brown underparts. Call: *chwink* and *chwit;* flight-call *tsip tsip. Song:* clear vigorous run of a dozen notes. On the ground either hops or runs; likes perching sideways on branches; quick flight in neat, flat undulations; longer distances at a height, shorter ones low down. *Food:* seeds, in summer lots of insects. *Nest:* see p. 84. *Habitat:* woods, gardens, hedges. Permanent resident and vagrant. Flocks in March and October. *Distribution:* everywhere.

BRAMBLING *(Fringilla montifringilla)* Size of sparrow, deeply notched tail, very colourful. Differs from chaffinch in striking white rump and less white on wings. *Male:* throat, chest and shoulders rust-yellow, head and mantle dark; wings dark with 2 white bands and yellowish feather-edgings. Female's head is not so dark and colouring duller. *Food:* seeds. *Habitat:* beech woods and farm-lands. Nests on skirts of wood, usually birch, mostly in Scandinavia. Winter visitor to rest of Europe.

GOLDFINCH *(Carduelis carduelis)* Plate 1 Smaller than sparrow, neat, slim. Head black, white and red; wings conspicuous black and yellow; black and white tail. Female almost identical to male, but smaller. Reluctant to go on to the ground, where it is rather clumsy. Climbs like a tit, hangs agilely upside down on twig or thistle head, often for minutes at a time, while it picks out seeds. Light, quick, undulating flight. *Call:* repeated high *swilt-wilt-wilt; song:* short gay twitter. *Food:* insects, especially greenfly; thistle and seeds. *Nest:* see p. 84. *Habitat:* orchards, hedges, fringes of woods, fields. Ever on the move. *Distribution:* Europe generally except in Norway and all but south of Sweden; resident and generally distributed in Britain except in parts of Scotland.

HAWFINCH *(Coccothraustes coccothraustes)* Plate 1 Larger than sparrow; stout; much thicker beak; short tail. Upper parts brown, under parts grey-white. White bars on wings. Female paler than male. Hops and runs in upright posture in little spurts. Slightly undulating flight. Recognisable in flight by large head and short tail. *Call:* a sharp *ptik* or *tzeerp. Song:* a slight metallic chatter, seldom heard. *Food:* fruit stones, seeds, insects. Cracks cherry stones and eats the inside. *Nest:* see p. 83. *Habitat:* mainly trees in mixed woods, orchards, etc. *Distribution:* most of Europe; in England a resident generally except in extreme west; breeds locally in parts of Scotland.

BULLFINCH *(Pyrrhula pyrrhula)* Plate 1 Larger than sparrow; stout; thick rounded beaks. Male has black cap, red underparts; female not so conspicuous: back and chest brown. (The northern European bullfinch is distinctly larger and brighter.) Hops and runs erect, discreet and cautious on ground; climbs nimbly in trees. Flight light, in slow loops. *Call:* a soft, plaintive *wheek* or *boot boot.* Song of both sexes subdued twitter with creaking noises. Also has a soft musical song. *Food:* young green things: buds, weed-seeds, berries, insects for the young. *Nest:* see p. 86. *Habitat:* woods, parks, gardens. Most frequent in coniferous woods on mountains. Sociable, secretive seldom coming out of cover. *Distribution:* most of Europe; generally distributed in England and Wales, rarer in Scotland.

LINNET *(Carduelis cannabina)* Plate 1 Somewhat smaller than a sparrow. Brown upper parts; back of head and neck ash-grey; reddish breast. Wing and tail-feathers edged with white. Crown and upper chest of male blood red, especially during mating season. Female has no red. Gait on ground a tripping run and also a hop. Swift flight in wide arcs. *Call:* a soft plaintive *tsooeet.* Song of both sexes a muted twitter interspersed with harsher notes. *Food:* greenstuff, seeds, berries; insects for its babies. *Nest:* see p. 86. *Habitat:* woods, gardens, hedges of farmlands. Sociable. Congregates in large flocks in winter, especially on waste ground. Partial migrant. *Distribution:* Europe generally. Common and widely distributed in Britain.

CROSSBILL *(Loxia curvirostra)* Plate 1 Gregarious, arboreal, seldom on ground. Slightly larger than sparrow, stocky, rather heavy large head; very strong, thick pointed, very curved beak with crossed mandibles; strong, short climber's feet with long, powerful toes, hooked, sharp claws and rather long, narrow wings. *Colouring:* male is brick red above and below, wings and tail black-brown. Female greenish-grey, no red, yellowish rump. Climbs agilely in tree tops using feet and beak like a parrot, breaking pine and fir cones open. Rapid flight in strong undulating line. *Call:* loud *chip-chip. Song:* a pretty twittering and flute notes. *Food:* conifer seeds. *Nest:* see p. 85. *Habitat:* coniferous woods mostly on mountains. Vagrant, often in large flocks. *Distribution:* Europe generally; in Britain has nested in most counties, usually following periodic irruptions of continental birds during summer.

PARROT CROSSBILL *(Loxia pityopsittacus)* Somewhat larger than the preceding and similar in appearance and habits, except that it prefers pines. *Distribution:* breeds in S. Finland, Scandinavia and N. Scotland.

GREENFINCH *(Chloris chloris)* Plate 1 Gay, trusting, friendly bird about the size of a sparrow; usually holds its body horizontal; short, slightly down-curved tail. *Colouring:* olive-green, striking yellow stripe on wings, yellow on sides of tail and yellow-green rump. Female less yellow and green, more sparrow-like grey and shorter tailed. Agile hop, occasionally running. Rather light undulating flight, wavering before alighting. Reluctant to fly far. *Call:* a prolonged *fswe-e-e,* also *chup* or *teu.* *Song:* a loud quick trill mixed with callnotes. *Food:* seeds, berries, buds, greenstuff. *Nest:* see p. 84. *Habitat:* gardens, farm-lands, deciduous woods. Resident and vagrant. *Distribution:* Europe generally; common throughout the year in Britain.

SISKIN *(Carduelis spinus)* Plate 1 Dainty, gay not shy. Smaller than a sparrow; beak drawn out to a point; deeply notched tail. Male has greenish upper parts, yellowish underparts; two yellow bars on dark wings, black crown, yellow stripe behind the eye. Female and juveniles have no black on crown, less yellow, whitish underparts and yellow-green upper parts with stronger dark stripes. Runs on ground or quick hops. Agile climber among branches, like tit. Finch-like flight but very light and quick. Courtship flight in early spring, when spirals high up with spread tail fluttering singing. *Call:* a quick *fsy-zi.* *Song:* a continuous musical twitter ending in a long wheezy note. *Food:* seeds, insects. *Nest:* see p. 85. *Habitat:* conifer woods, beech and alder. Resident and vagrant. Gregarious with redpolls in winter. *Distribution:* Europe generally; in Britain mainly a winter visitor but breeds in Scotland, N. England, N. Wales and Ireland.

SERIN *(Serinus canarius)* Plate 1 The dwarf of the finches and easily overlooked in the tree-tops. Male more noticeable as it likes to sing from twig or wire, or in courtship flight. Dainty, smaller than sparrow. Short, thick beak. Rump, brow, eyestripe, throat and breast bright yellow in male; in female less bright, more striped, browner on upper parts, greyer underneath. Running gait, only on ground to feed. Swift undulating flight. Batlike courtship flight, zigzagging while it sings. *Call:* a rapid *si-twi-twi-twi* or hard *chit-chit-chit. Song:* a twittering chirp with occasional trills. *Food:* mainly wild seeds, also greenfly. *Nest:* see p. 84. *Habitat:* garden, field-hedges, orchards, vineyards. Partial migrant. *Distribution:* N. W. Africa and parts of Europe; in Britain an annual vagrant during winter months.

YELLOWHAMMER *(Emberiza citrinella)* Plate 1 Head and underparts yellow, rump chestnut, back and sides streaked with brown. In flight the white on outer tail feather is conspicuous. Female darker in colour, more streaked. Very nimble gait, hops and sometimes runs. Likes sitting high up, flicking its long tail. Swift flight, irregular over short distances, otherwise in regular shallow dips *Call:* a ringing *zick-zick*, also in flight. Mournful but pleasant song: *chi-chi-chi-chi-chi--chi-chwee*. *Food:* in summer mostly insects, and wild seeds. *Nest:* see p. 86. *Habitat:* hedges of fields and roadside, open country. Resident and vagrant. *Distribution:* Europe generally; in Britain widely distributed throughout the year.

CORN BUNTING *(Emberiza calandra)* Plate 1 Almost the size of a starling, heavy; female smaller. Upper parts grey-brown, underparts light grey with short black streaks. No white on wings or tail. Sedate tripping movements on ground, flicking its tail. Flies over short distances with trailing legs, appearing awkward; over longer distances whirring, arching flight. Sits motionless on telephone wires or posts. *Call:* a short *chip* or *zeep*. Flight call a loud twitter. Industrious winter singer. *Food:* mainly weed-seeds; in summer also insects. *Nest:* see p. 91. *Habitat:* open farmlands, hedges, wastelands. Resident. *Distribution:* breeds in Europe from southern Norway to Mediterranean; in Britain locally abundant.

ORTOLAN BUNTING *(Emberiza hortulana)* Size of sparrow. Underparts pinkish-buff, yellow throat; olive-green head and chest; back reddish-brown; yellow moustachial stripe; pink beak; yellow ring round eyes. Female less colourful. *Food:* mainly weed-seeds, insects in summer. *Nest:* see p. 90. *Habitat:* farmland and open hilly country, scrub. *Distribution:* breeds northern Scandinavia to Mediterranean; occurs each year as a vagrant on east coasts of Britain.

CIRL BUNTING *(Emberiza cirlus)* Resembles yellowhammer, but rump olive-green. Male has black throat. Flight call: *sissi-sissi-sip*. *Song:* hurried jingle on one note. Nests low down in hedges and banks. Bird of the vineyards. *Distribution:* breeds mainly in the south of Europe; in Britain breeds in southern and western counties of England and Wales; elsewhere rare vagrant.

ROCK BUNTING *(Emberiza cia)* Upper parts brown with black stripes; grey throat and head, black streaks on head; underparts cinnamon-brown. Habits like yellowhammer. *Call:* a sharp *seep. Nest:* see p. 93. *Habitat:* rocky hillsides. Resident and migrant. *Distribution:* southern Europe; vagrant to Britain.

REED BUNTING *(Emberiza schoeniclus)* Plate 1 Sparrow size, but longer in tail. Rather short, conical beak, medium length wings. Black head and throat; white collar. Upper parts dark brown with black streaks; underparts grey-white with brown streaks on belly; grey rump: outer tail feathers edged with white. Female and juveniles inconspicuous grey, brown, black. Quick hop. Agile climber in reeds, often flicking tail and wings. Quick easy flight in graceful swoops. *Call:* a loud *tseek,* alarm note *chit. Song:* stuttering, begins slowly and ends hurriedly. *Food:* insects and seeds. *Nest:* see p. 98. *Habitat:* reed-beds, alders, willows. Resident and migrant. *Distribution:* across central Europe; generally distributed in Britain in aquatic habitats.

TWITE *(Carduelis flavirostris)* Rather like linnet, but throat is warm buff and male has pink rump. Beak greyish-yellow in summer, light yellow in winter. *Habitat:* moors and high wastelands. *Distribution:* Scandinavia; breeds locally on moorlands in northern England and is seen further south in winter.

REDPOLL *(Carduelis flammea)* Smaller than sparrow. Streaked grey-brown with red forehead and black chin. Male has pink flush on chest. Gregarious. Larger race on Continent (mealy redpoll) has paler plumage. Arctic redpoll *(Carduelis hornemani)* has white rump and underparts and paler-greyer back; also crimson crown. *Habitat:* copses of alder, willow; northern forests; rocky outcrops above tree line. *Distribution:* most parts of Europe; breeds in most counties of England and Wales but rarer in the west.

SNOW BUNTING *(Plectrophenax nivalis)* Larger than sparrow. Broad white patches on wings and tail make it look almost pure white in flight. Summer plumage of male: black back, primaries and middle tail feathers, rest snow white; in winter head and breast are light brown, back brown flecked with black: female and juveniles browner. High "dancing" flight. Gregarious. *Song:* almost lark-like. Sings on gliding descent from spiral courtship flight. *Nests:* in crevices. *Habitat:* open coastal regions, occasionally inland. *Distribution:* breeds in Scandinavia; mainly winter visitor to Britain, especially in coastal areas, but a few breed on mountains in northern Scotland.

THRUSHES AND THRUSH-LIKE BIRDS   Plate 2

Family   STURNIDAE Starlings   Fig. 22

STARLING *(Sturnus vulgaris)* Plate 2 Stocky, short neck, long pointed beak; short tail; pointed wings; plumage closely speckled in winter,

124 *Birds*

especially female's. In spring male has glossy black plumage shimmering with green and purple and lemon-yellow beak (dark in winter). Waddling gait. Straight, quick, whirring flight. Flocks in autumn and winter. *Call:* harsh *tcheeer,* also mixture of whistles, clicks and rattlings. Imitates other birds and noises; flaps wings in upright posture with beak wide open. *Food:* caterpillars, grubs and other insects; berries, grapes and other fruits. *Nest:* in tree-holes, crevices, in roofs, etc. Untidy structure of straws, leaves, roots, etc. April to June 2 clutches of 5–6 light-blue eggs. *Distribution:* Europe generally; in Britain generally distributed except in parts of western Wales and western Ireland.

ROSE-COLOURED STARLING *(Sturnus roseus)* Similar to starling in shape, flight and habits, but plumage unmistakeably rose-pink with glossy black head, wings and tail, and a distinctive crest. Juveniles light brown; no crest. *Habitat:* farm-lands, steppe. *Nest:* in holes among stones or in woods. *Distribution:* S. E. Europe; vagrant to Britain.

Family   Oriolidae   Orioles

GOLDEN ORIOLE *(Oriolus oriolus)* Plate 2   Size of blackbird; long wings, short legs. Male yellow with black wings and tail. Female and juveniles inconspicuous grey-yellowy-green. Seldom on ground. Quick light flight over distances in long, woodpecker swoops; shorter distances, fluttering; also flutters from branch to branch instead of hopping. *Call:* loud, fluting *weela-weeo;* alarm: harsh *chr-r-r. Nest:* see p. 84. *Food:* insects (only off trees), fruit. *Habitat:* woods, copses, orchards. Very shy. Mostly hidden in treetops. *Distribution:* breeds from southern Sweden to the Mediterranean; in Britain mainly a passage-migrant in late April and May, but has bred in a number of counties.

Family   Cinclidae   Dippers

DIPPER *(Cinclus cinclus)* Plate 2   Shape like a wren's, but almost the size of a starling. Long legs, short wings and tail. Slate grey upper parts, white throat and chest, reddy-brown belly. Both sexes alike. Agile run, wades into water and runs along submerged with head lowered, often remains under for 50 seconds or longer running and swimming, covering 18 metres. Upstream uses wings as paddles. Low, whirring flight with rapid wing beats; low over water. Sings almost the year round. Perches on stones and bobs spasmodically. *Food:* water and bank insects; tiny fish. *Nest:* domed with low side entrance, in crevices, water banks, always near running water. 4–6 white eggs, April to June. Adapted to aquatic life: able to seal nostrils; lots of down feather in plumage; preen glands. *Habitat:* swift streams, especially in hills. Occasionally on coast in winter. *Distribution:*

breeds from N. Scandinavia to Spain and Portugal; generally distributed in localities with streams in N. and W. England, Scotland, Wales and Ireland.

Family   TURDIDAE Thrushes   Fig. 22

Rather long legged, upright stance. Slender, pointed beak; large eyes; long, pointed wings. Feed mainly on ground. Hop. Noisy call and alarm notes. Melodious song, ringing flute notes. Open nests. Resident and vagrant.

BLACKBIRD *(Turdus merula)* Plate 2 Strong beak. Male black with yellow beak; female blackish-brown, dark speckles on lighter ground on throat; brown beak. Both hop and run on ground. Quick, straight flight, repeatedly closing wings; cocks and fans tail on alighting with drooped wings. *Call:* a thin *tsee;* alarm note: *tchina tchink tchwink. Song:* loud, melodious, fluting notes, mostly from tree or roof top. *Food:* insects, worms, snails, fruit. *Nest:* see p. 86. *Habitat:* woodlands, gardens, hedges. *Distribution:* breeds Scandinavia to Mediterranean; common all over British Isles throughout the year.

SONG THRUSH *(Turdus philomelos)* Plate 2 Smaller, slimmer, shorter in tail than blackbird. Upper parts olive-grey; underparts light with dark speckles. Runs in spurts or hops taking quick, long jumps. When notices something stands very erect, flicking its wings. Low undulating flight. *Flight call:* short, soft *sip.* Song loud, musical with repeated flute-like phrase. *Food:* insects, grubs, worms, snails, also berries. *Nest:* see p. 85. *Habitat:* woods, hedges. *Distribution:* N. Scandinavia to N. Spain; generally distributed in Britain throughout the year.

FIELDFARE *(Turdus pilaris)* Size of blackbird. Recognisable by flight-call: *tchak-tchak-tchak.* Pale grey head and rump, brown saddle, almost black tail; throat and breast rusty-yellow with black streaks. Sides strongly speckled with brown. Female smaller. Flat undulating flight. *Song:* harsh squeaky twitter, often in flight. *Food:* insects, worms, berries, especially juniper. *Nest:* see p. 83. Often in colonies in fields and woods. Flocks in February to April and in autumn. *Habitat:* fields and open country. *Distribution:* breeds N. Norway to Switzerland and Hungary; winter visitor to Britain between late September and mid-December, returning end of March to early May.

MISTLE THRUSH *(Turdus viscivorus)* Plate 2 Largest of the thrushes. Like song thrush but larger. Speckles on underparts rounder and thicker. Attitude more upright. Whitish tips to outer tail feathers. Back greyish, rump browny-grey, yellow-white breast. *Call:* a rasping *tue-tue-tue* and a thin *see-ip.* Loud song, like a blackbird's but without its variety. Sings in all weathers from highest tree-tops. *Food:* insects, worms, snails, berries. *Nest:* see p. 83. *Habitat:* woods, gardens. Small flocks in autumn. *Distribution:* breeds N. Sweden to Mediterranean; widely distributed in Britain, except in mountainous districts.

REDWING *(Turdus musicus)* Smallest common thrush. Distinguished from song thrush by creamy eye-stripe, chestnut sides, streaked breast and chestnut beneath wings. *Habitat:* winter visitor to open farmlands and woods. *Food:* worms, insects, berries. *Nest:* (northern Europe) in bushes, trees, on ground. *Distribution:* Iceland and N. Scandinavia to Germany as breeding species; winter visitor to Britain, arriving late September and leaving by mid-April. A few pairs have nested in N. Scotland.

RING OUZEL *(Turdus torquatus)* Distinct by reason of broad white crescent across breast; otherwise dull black plumage. Female browner. Juvenile no crescent. *Call:* piping *pee-u* or scolding blackbird's *tac-tac-tac.* *Food:* as other thrushes. *Habitat:* hilly moorlands and mountain above 305 metres. *Nests:* among heather, juniper, rocks, often by streams. On Continent within tree limit. 4–5 blue-green eggs with rufous blotches. *Distribution:* breeds in Scandinavia and Finland; in Britain nests in hilly districts of S.W. England, Pennines, N.E. Yorkshire, Wales, Scotland and Ireland.

REDSTART *(Phoenicurus phoenicurus)* Plate 2 Breast, sides and tail rust red; black throat; white forehead; bluey-grey upper parts. Female grey-brown upper parts, blue-reddish-brown underneath, no black throat. Continual flickering of tail and rump. Light, quick flight. Call: *whee-tic-tic.* *Nests:* in holes in trees, walls, buildings; loosely made structure of straw, hair; bowl open lined with feathers. 2 clutches of 5–7 greeny-blue eggs (April to July). *Food:* insects, berries. *Habitat:* old orchards, woodlands, heather with bushes. *Distribution:* N. Norway to Spain; widely distributed summer migrant to Britain but not in extreme south-west.

BLACK REDSTART *(Phoenicurus ochrurus)* Plate 2 Constantly flickers rust-red tail and bobs. Much darker colouring than redstart. Male, dull black-grey, white wing patch, light belly. Female, sooty-grey; juvenile lighter. Upright posture. Prefers to perch on roofs and rocks. Light, quick flight. *Call: tiditic. Song:* short, quick 3 phased. *Food:* insects, worms, snails, berries. *Nests:* in holes in walls, rocks, outbuildings. Bowl lined with feathers. 2 clutches of 4–6 white eggs (April to June). *Habitat:* near houses, quarries, rocky slopes, vineyards. Summer visitor. *Distribution:* S. Scandinavia to Mediterranean; breeds in Britain in increasing numbers.

Starling in Spring

in Autumn

♀ Golden Oriole ♂

♂ Blackbird ♀

Song Thrush

Mistle Thrush

Dipper

♀ ♂ Black Redstart

♂ ♀ Redstart

Robin

hinchat ♂ ♂

Stonechat

♀ Bluethroat ♂

Wheatear ♂

Nightingale

Bäuerle

ROBIN *(Erithacus rubecula)* Plate 2 Rounded body on long legs. Upper parts and tail olive-brown. Throat and breast red. Large eyes. Takes long easy hops. Agile flight. *Call:* sharp *tic tic. Song:* melancholy with high whistling notes and trills. *Nest:* see p. 89. *Food:* insects, worms, small snails, berries (especially spindle). *Habitat:* woods, gardens, wherever there are bushes and trees. *Distribution:* N. Scandinavia to mid-Spain and parts of central Europe; generally distributed in Britain, except in Shetlands.

WHINCHAT *(Saxicola rubetra)* Plate 2 Smaller than sparrow, stocky, short tail. Upper parts grey-brown with dark streaks. Rust-yellow throat and breast. White stripe above eye and below black cheek. White patch on dark-brown wing and white sides to tail feathers (visible in flight). Female has white underparts. Quick run. Not shy. Perches upright on tall plants, bushes or telephone wires looking for food. Quick nimble flight. *Call:* repeated short *wee-tic.* Song rather like redstart's. Ardent singer. *Food:* insects, small snails. *Nest:* of grass, moss and hair; on or near the ground. *Habitat:* commons, marshes, open country, moors. *Distribution:* breeds from N. Scandinavia to N. Portugal; widely distributed but somewhat local visitor to Britain.

STONECHAT *(Saxicola torquata)* Plate 2 Smaller than sparrow. Black-brown upper parts; head and throat black; white patch on side of neck, white wing stripe, dark tail, rust-red breast. Female's colouring duller. Upright stance; likes sitting high up, flirting fanned tail; not shy; takes big hops. Quick buoyant flight in flat loops. *Call:* a persistent *wheet tsack tsack.* Song like whinchat's but not so melodious. *Food:* insects and their larvae. *Nest:* see p. 93. *Habitat:* commons and open gorseland country; dry hillsides, scrub, railway embankments with hedges. *Distribution:* central and southern Europe; resident in Britain, mainly in coastal areas but some arrive as summer visitors from the Continent.

WHEATEAR *(Oenanthe oenanthe)* Plate 2 Size of a sparrow. Striking white root to tail and visible in flight. Male has black streak across eye and ear; upper parts ash-grey, but in autumn brownish, like female. Rump, wings, and middle tail feathers black; underparts yellowy-white. On stony ground colouring is protective. Sits on stones and clods in upright attitude, often bobbing and giving a slow flick with fanned tail, as it does when darting about open ground. Very agile flight; catches insects on wing. *Food:* insects and larvae. *Call:* a hard *chack,* often followed by softer *weet-chack. Nest:* see p. 93. *Habitat:* lonely stony slopes, moors, cliffs, dunes. *Distribution:* Europe generally; summer visitor to most parts of British Isles.

NIGHTINGALE *(Luscinia megarhynchos)* Plate 2 Just over sparrow size; long-legged, reddish-brown upper parts; light grey beneath, browny-red tail. Hops. Stops to stand erect with tail cocked up and drooping wings. Quick easy flight: flatly undulating over longer distances, but mostly just from bush to bush; never across open by day. *Call:* a protracted *wheet* and a loud *tac.* Song is soft, flute-like and musical. Also sings at night; mostly in early morning. *Food:* insect larvae, worms, beetles, spiders, flies, also berries. *Nest:* see p. 86. *Habitat:* deciduous woods and thickets; hedges. Rather unsociable. Skulking. *Distribution:* Denmark to Mediterranean; in Britain summer visitor, breeding south of a line from Severn to Humber, except in Cornwall.

BLUETHROAT *(Cyanosylvia svecica)* Plate 2 Rather larger than a sparrow, long-legged; posture mostly upright. Frequently flicks and fans its red tail with dark end. Male earth-brown upper parts and dirty-white underparts; in spring throat and crop have azure blue patch separated from breast by a black and rust-red band; the Scandinavian variety has a chestnut star in the middle of the blue throat *(Cyanosylvia svevica svevica)* and that of central Europe has a white one. In autumn the blue fades almost to white. Female is less conspicuous, has only the white star on throat. *Call:* a soft *wheet wheet* and a sharp *tac tac.* Perches free to sing very musical varied song. Imitates other birds, quacking of frogs and queer cries. *Food:* insects, acorns, autumn berries. *Nest:* on ground in tangled growth near water; banks of ditches, streams, among willows, birch, juniper. *Habitat:* swampy scrub and heath, usually in mountains (though in lowlands of north and eastern Germany). Migrant. *Distribution:* Scandinavia, central Europe; autumn passage-migrant to Britain.

WARBLERS

Family   SYLVIIDAE Warblers   Fig. 23

Less than sparrow-size (except great reed warbler); slim, inconspicuously coloured. Active little birds mostly hidden in bushes, seldom on the ground. Slender beaks; rather short legs. Insect-eaters. Nesting in low bushes and other vegetation. Sexes mostly alike.

BLACKCAP *(Sylvia atricapilla)* Plate 3 Size of sparrow but slimmer. Male has black, female chestnut cap to eye level; otherwise grey-brown upper parts, grey side of head and underparts. Seldom on ground. Undulating flight. *Call:* distinct *tac tac. Song:* a rich warble in two parts. *Food:* insects, berries (especially elder). *Nest:* see p. 87. *Habitat:* woods with plenty

Plate 3

Garden Warbler

Lesser Whitethroat

Blackcap

♀

♂

Barred Warbler

Whitethroat

Chiffchaff

Hedge Sparrow

Willow Warbler

Wood Warbler

Icterine Warbler

Reed Warbler

Great Reed Warbler

Sedge Warbler

Marsh Warbler

Grasshopper Warbler

Bäuerle

of undergrowth, gardens, parks, hedges. *Distribution:* Europe generally; summer visitor to most parts of England and Wales, except in the north-west; less frequent in Scotland.

GARDEN WARBLER *(Sylvia borin)* Plate 3 Just under sparrow size. Olive-brown upper parts; underparts lighter. *Call:* clicking *check check.* *Song:* pleasant sustained, organ-like; mostly from thick bushes. *Nest:* see p. 87. *Habitat:* woods with undergrowth, hedges, thickets, bramble patches. *Distribution:* Europe generally; summer visitor to most parts of Britain, except the far north.

WHITETHROAT *(Sylvia communis)* Plate 3 Smaller than sparrow. Chestnut upper parts, white chin and throat, longish tail with white outer feathers; grey cap. Will fly over open areas. Darts about with spread tail. When excited feathers on crown rise up. *Call:* repeated *check* or quiet *wheet, wheet.* Song begins quietly, ends loudly; is more a quick chattering twitter. In courtship sometimes rises vertically out of bushes to dive back steeply ending song in bush. *Nest:* see p. 87. *Habitat:* copses and hedges. *Distribution:* Europe generally; summer visitor to Britain but scarce in N. Scotland.

LESSER WHITETHROAT *(Sylvia curruca)* Plate 3 Ash-grey head, white throat, wings and back brown-grey; outer tail feathers partly white. *Call:* like whitethroat's. Song starts with twitter, then loud rattling on one note. *Nest:* see p. 87. *Habitat:* wherever there are bushes. *Distribution:* as for preceding species.

BARRED WARBLER *(Sylvia nisoria)* Plate 3 Larger than sparrow. Underparts barred with dark half-moon shaped markings on lighter ground; upper parts ash grey-brown. Female browner and less distinctively barred. *Call:* a loud sharp *tchack* and a grating *tcharr, tcharr.* Sings partly perched, partly in flight, similar to garden warbler's but mingled with rasping *rerr. Nest:* see p. 87. *Habitat:* bushy thickets, glades. *Distribution:* breeds from Denmark to N. Italy; passage migrant in north and east Britain; mainly in September.

LEAF WARBLERS (Fig. 23)

Neat and dainty. Live in trees. Dome-shaped nests.

CHIFFCHAFF *(Phylloscopus collybita)* Much smaller than sparrow. Plumage duller than willow warbler's. Upper parts olive-brown, underparts dirty-white; long, light eye stripe. Dark brown or blackish legs. *Call:* a soft *hweet.* Song monotonous, staccato *chiff chaff, chiff chaff. Food:* mostly insects. *Nest:* see p. 87. *Habitat:* gardens, parks, woods, trees more than bushes. *Distribution:* Europe generally; summer visitor to most of Britain.

WILLOW WARBLER *(Phylloscopus trochilus)* Much smaller than sparrow. Plumage slightly yellower than chiffchaff. Upper parts olive-browny-green; pale yellow underparts, belly almost white. Light eye stripe. Yellowy-brown or pink legs. Call-note like chiffchaff. *Song:* a liquid musical cadence, starting softly and descending to end with a flourish. *Nest:* see p. 90. *Habitat:* bushes, especially in woods and clumps of trees, but very general. *Distribution:* as for previous species.

WOOD WARBLER *(Phylloscopus sibilatrix)* Plate 3 Larger than chiffchaff with bodkin-shaped beak; medium-length legs, short toes, fairly long wings, medium length tail. Yellowish-green upper parts, yellow breast, white belly, yellow stripe above eye. Brown wings with yellow edges to feathers. Restless moving about bushes. *Call:* a soft *piu* or *whit, whit. Song:* several *pius* ending in a long trill *stipstipstip.* Sings from bush or in flight from tree to tree. *Food:* insects caught on the wing; greenfly, caterpillars, etc. taken off leaves; does not feed on ground. *Nest:* see p. 89. *Habitat:* trees, especially beeches and oaks; preferably in confusion of branches half way up tree. *Distribution:* breeds from S. Scandinavia to central France; summer visitor to Britain and well distributed in well-wooded areas but rare in East Anglia.

ICTERINE WARBLER *(Hippolais icterina)* Plate 3 Smaller than sparrow. Sulphur-yellow underparts, yellowish eye stripe; upper parts yellowy-white. Blue-grey legs. Seldom flies in open or goes on ground. *Call:* musical *deederoid.* Industrious singer of a loud sustained mixture of musical and discordant notes, including imitations of other birds, while sitting erect with beak wide open. *Food:* insects, worms and berries. *Nest:* see p. 88. *Habitat:* gardens, parks, deciduous woods. *Distribution:* Europe as far south as eastern France and Italy; passage migrant in small numbers to Britain mainly in September but sometimes in spring.

*MELODIOUS WARBLER *(Hippolais polyglotta)* Very similar, except for more hurried babbling song and shorter rounded wings, and its range being restricted to the Iberian Peninsula, France and Italy.

Reed Warblers (Fig. 23)

Have rather long pointed beaks without apparent division between them and skull, giving the latter a peculiarly pointed appearance. *Acrocephalus* means "pointed head". Mostly in reed-beds.

GREAT REED WARBLER *(Acrocephalus arundinaceus)* Plate 3 Somewhat larger than sparrow, but smaller than starling. Upper parts yellowish-brown, throat and belly light grey; prominent white eye stripe. Usually sings perching freely on reed or telephone wire, often with spread tail and drooping wings. Strident voice. *Call:* a hard *krik krik* or *karra-karra,* tone like a frog's or duck's. *Nest:* see p. 89. *Habitat:* reed-beds and marshes. *Distribution:* breeds from S. Sweden to Mediterranean; rare vagrant to Britain.

REED WARBLER *(Acrocephalus scirpaceus)* Plate 3 Similar to preceding only much smaller. Plumage more rust-yellow-brown; eye stripe indistinct; dark legs. Stooping attitude with in-drawn head is characteristic. Round tail spread and depressed when in short flight across water. *Song:* similar to preceding. Sings day and night; loudest in June. *Call: churr;* alarm strident *skurr. Nest:* see p. 89. *Habitat:* reed-beds everywhere. *Distribution:* Europe generally, from the Baltic south; summer visitor to England and Wales where there are suitable reed-beds.

SEDGE WARBLER *(Acrocephalus schoenobaenus)* Plate 3 Striking cream-coloured eye stripe and streaked back distinguish it from the preceding. Song-flight during courtship, flying up obliquely and returning to its starting point singing all the time. *Nest:* see p. 99. *Habitat:* avoids extensive reed-beds in preference for thickets in swampy places, wet areas of sedge grass, field crops. *Distribution:* breeds N. Norway south to central France; summer visitor and generally distributed in England, Wales and Ireland; local in Scotland.

GRASSHOPPER WARBLER *(Locustella naevia)* Plate 3 Smaller than sparrow. Dark lengthwise streaks on back, broad wedge-shaped tail; upper parts olive-brown, whitish throat. Underparts dirty-grey. Creeps like a mouse on the ground in thick undergrowth. Seldom flies in the open. *Call:* a soft, sharp *twhit. Song:* a churring *sirrirrir,* like a grasshopper, going on for minutes at a time. Sings day and night. *Food:* insects and small worms. *Nest:* see p. 92. *Habitat:* water meadows and woods with bushes and tall grass, bushy banks, fields and heath. *Distribution:* Baltic to N. Spain; late summer visitor to England and Ireland; rarer in Scotland and Wales.

MARSH WARBLER *(Acrocephalus palustris)* Plate 3   Inconspicuous. Smaller than sparrow. Similar to reed warbler only plumper and upper parts more ochre-yellow, underparts and legs lighter, as legs almost flesh-colour. Also song is unusually musical, including imitations of other birds. *Food:* insects and, in autumn, berries. *Habitat:* reeds and marshes, corn fields and thickets of willow, other low vegetation on margin of lakes and rivers. *Distribution:* Baltic to S. France and N. Italy; late summer visitor to few southern counties of England.

*CETTI'S WARBLER *(Cettia cetti)*   Skulking and seldom seen, but has a very loud burst of song like *settee settee*. Sings from dense vegetation. In Iberian Peninsula, Italy, Balkans.

DARTFORD WARBLER *(Sylvia undata)*   Very dark plumage and long constantly cocked or fanned tail. Male has slate-grey head with raised crown feathers (characteristic); underparts are dark purplish brown; chin and throat spotted with white in autumn. Eye orange-red. Skulking. Poor flight with whirring wings. *Habitat:* open common and heath with heather and gorse; dwarf oak, etc. *Nest:* of any grass, gorse and roots, lined with hair and wool. 4–6 eggs, nearly white with light-grey and brown mottling. (April to July.) *Distribution:* Iberian Peninsula, western parts of France; Sicily, Italy (except north). Very local resident in parts of Hampshire, Dorset, Sussex, Surrey, Berks. and Wilts.

Family   PRUNELLIDAE   Accentors

Drab, grey-brown plumage, looking like sparrows, but have slender, pointed beaks. Prefer to be on ground, take short hops; low flight. Short, high, jingling song. Markings and behaviour like those of the finches.

DUNNOCK or HEDGE SPARROW *(Prunella modularis)* Plate 3 Inconspicuous, skulking and solitary, smaller than sparrow. Upper parts dark brown with black streaks; head, neck and lower parts grey; crown and ear-coverts browny. Seeks food on ground; crouching short hops with raised tail; frequently twitches wings. *Call:* a sharp *tseep*. Sings from bushes or treetop a sort of low whisper like a wren's song. Sings almost all year. *Nest:* see p. 88. *Food:* insects, especially in summer, also seeds. *Habitat:* hedges, gardens, bushes. *Distribution:* Europe generally; resident and widely distributed in Britain.

Family   CORVIDAE   Crows

CROWS (Fig. 29)

Big, stocky birds with strong thick beaks somewhat hooked at the tip. Nostrils covered with bristle-feathers. In flight wings and tail are rounded. Slow, regular flight, seldom gliding. Long legs, strong blunt claws. Omnivorous. Loud-voiced. Sociable. Nest in trees.

CROW-LIKE BIRDS

ROOK *(Corvus frugilegus)* Slimmer than other crows with beak slighter and more pointed. Base of beak is white and bald, except in the juvenile. Plumage black with a magnificent purple sheen. Somewhat waddling gait. Flight appears heavy, but is actually buoyant and enduring and straight. Regular wing-beats quicker than those of carrion crow. *Call:* deep, harsh *caw,* but less "whining" than the carrion crow's. *Food:* insects, snails, worms, mice, corn and sprouting grain. Fruit (little damage). *Nest:* (see p. 81) in colonies. *Habitat:* woods, parks, fields. *Distribution:* southern Scandinavia to central France and N. Italy; resident and widely distributed in Britain.

CARRION CROW *(Corvus corone corone)* Size of the rook, but no white base to its beak. All black plumage. *Food:* largely insects. *Habitat:* woods, fields, pastures. *Nest:* alone mostly in a tree in a wood. See p. 81. *Distribution:* western Europe; resident and common in England and Wales and parts of Scotland.

HOODED CROW *(Corvus corone cornix)* Size as preceding, and now regarded as a race of the same species. Black with a grey mantle and underparts. *Habitat:* woods, parks and fields. One clutch of 4–6 eggs with bluish-green ground with streaks and blotches of black and brown. *Habitat:* moorlands and empty country. *Distribution:* N. and E. Europe south to Italy, Sicily and the Caucasus; west to the river Elbe in Germany; in Britain breeds in N. and N. W. Scotland and south to Clyde, Solway, Tay, Dee and Moray areas; also throughout Ireland.

MAGPIE *(Pica pica)* Size of pigeon. Black and white with a long tail with wedge-shaped end. The black feathers have a reddish-green shimmer. Walks sedately, but occasionally hops flicking up its tail. Irregular, fluttering flight that appears heavy. Call is harsh, piercing *chak-chak-chak-chak. Food:* insects, snails,

berries, fruit, grain and also eggs and young song birds. *Nest:* see p. 82. *Habitat:* near human habitation; woods, thickets, farmlands. *Distribution:* Europe generally; resident and widely distributed in Britain.

JACKDAW *(Corvus monedula)* Smaller than crows, about pigeon size; slim body; black plumage with grey neck. Movements brisker and more lively than the crows. Quick, agile flight. Sociable. Often with rooks and starlings. *Call:* loud, clear *chak,* when excited run together *chakachakachaka. Food:* insects, worms, fruit, refuse. *Nest:* in colonies in holes in trees, buildings; shapeless nest made of grass, straw, lined with hair, feathers, rags; foundation often of twigs. April to May 1 clutch of 3–5 light blue-green eggs (3.5 × 2.5 cm) well flecked with brown or grey. Rounder than crows' eggs. *Distribution:* Europe generally; resident and common in Britain.

JAY *(Garrulus glandarius)* Size of a pigeon; elongated erectile crown feathers; short, strong beak, slightly hooked at tip. Upper parts rust-coloured; underparts grey. Wing-coverts striking black-white-blue bands; black tail, white rump visible in flight. Takes long hops on ground; equally agile among branches. Heavy flight; reluctant to fly far. *Call:* a raucous *shraaak,* drawing attention of other birds to approach of people. Imitates voices of buzzard, roe-deer, and humans. *Nest:* see p. 81. *Food:* insects, worms, snails, young birds, acorns, cherries. Stores food and often forgets where. Great propagator of oaks. *Habitat:* mainly woods and copses. Vagrant. *Distribution:* Europe generally; resident and common in England and Wales but local in Scotland. In Ireland breeds in most counties.

CHOUGH *(Pyrrhocorax pyrrhocorax)* Larger than jay; long, curved red bill and red legs; glossy black plumage. Strong flight. *Habitat:* cliffs and rocks near sea, or in mountains. April to May 3–6 yellowish-white eggs spotted with grey and brown. *Nest:* in crevice or cave. *Distribution:* France, the Alps, Pyrenees, Iberian Peninsula; in Britain now restricted as a resident breeding species to a few cliffs in Wales, in the Isle of Man and the Inner Hebrides. Common in Ireland.

RAVEN *(Corvus corax)* Black all over. Largest of the crow family. 66 cm long; tail 25 cm; wing 45 cm. Powerful beak. Elongated, pointed feathers on throat. Very stout legs. Calm flight with head outstretched like bird of prey. Well rounded tail. *Call: prruk. Food:* fruits, grain, insects, small animals from mouse to hare, birds from fledgling to capercaillie; any carrion. Single clutch of 4–6 bluish-green eggs freely blotched with black and brown. *Nest:* made of sticks, heather, earth, moss, seaweed depending on locality. *Habitat:* cliffs and mountains, in summer mostly above tree-line. *Distribution:* Europe generally; in Britain resident and breeding in S. W. England, Hereford, Shropshire, Staffordshire, Lake District, Wales, Scotland and Ireland.

Larks, Pipits and Wagtails

Family   Alaudidae   Larks

Brown, streaked terrestrial birds with widely splayed front toes and a long, straight, or almost straight hind toe with a very long claw, for swift walking on loose earth. They have an agile stepping gait, and do not hop. Appearance of sexes similar.
Large, broad wings suitable for long-flight. Delight in dust baths. Beaks between those of the insect and grain eater; feed on both insects and seeds. Different voices, but musical. Nest on ground. Nestlings very downy.

SKYLARK *(Alauda arvensis)* Larger than a sparrow, but slimmer and longer in the body than other larks. Upper parts earthy-grey-brown with dark longitudinal streaks; underparts creamy white with dark streaks on breast. Tail has white outer edges. Female somewhat smaller than the male. Trips about nodding its head. Runs in a stooping attitude. Very nimble quick flight in shallow undulations, alternately flapping wings and shooting forward with closed wings. Courtship flight. *Call:* a loud *chir-r-up*, often as early as February. Song a musical sustained trill, mostly in courtship flight, only occasionally from the ground or some low vantage point. *Food:* seeds, insects, in spring delicate shoots. *Nest:* see p.91. *Habitat:* open grassland, farmland, marshes and moorland. *Distribution:* Europe generally; in Britain common and widely distributed as a breeding species but these birds leave in autumn and are replaced by winter visitors from N. and central Europe.

CRESTED LARK *(Galerida cristata)* Larger than sparrow and lighter in colouring than skylark. Has a pointed jutting crest. Upper parts only slightly streaked. Agile on ground. Usually runs before taking wing, when it flies in flat arcs, with irregular wing beats. *Call: twee-tee-too,* emphasis on *too;* from ground or in flight (early in year). *Food:* as skylark. *Nest:* see p. 91. *Habitat:* prefers steppe-like deserted country, roadsides; often near human habitations. Often vagrant. *Distribution:* central and southern Europe; vagrant to England.

WOOD LARK *(Lullula arborea)* Size of a sparrow. Shorter in body and beak than other larks. Very short tail. Often drops crown-feathers over eye-stripe. Upper parts light brown with dark streaks. Creamy-yellow streak round head, like a chaplet. Underparts yellowish-white with dark brown streaks. Unlike other larks often perches in trees. Soars like other larks, but never very high; oblique, not steep ascent. Once up, describes fluttering circles. *Song:* a melodious *lu-lu-lu-lu. Call: toolooeet.* Loveliest at night. *Food:* mostly insects, preferably grasshoppers; also seeds. *Nest:* see p. 90. *Habitat:* fringes of woods, sandy clearings in conifer woods; heath, hillsides. *Distribution:* Europe from S. Scandinavia south to Mediterranean; resident but local in England, mainly in the south.

SHORT-TOED LARK *(Calandrella cinerea)* Size of a sparrow. Underparts buffish-white without streaks, short yellowish bill. Low undulating flight. *Call:* short *tchi-tchirrp. Habitat:* open wastes, steppes and fields. Nests on ground. *Distribution:* Iberian peninsula, Italy, S.W. France, Balkans; annual vagrant to Britain, usually in autumn.

Family   MOTACILLIDAE   Pipits and wagtails

Long-legged terrestrial birds that do not hop, but walk and run. Pipits are earth-coloured with dark brown streaks and have long claws on their hind toes; relatively short tails. Appearance of sexes similar. Nest on ground. Sociable in winter. Wagtails have slender bodies, legs and beaks, long tails which they frequently flick, quick tripping gait. Nests are well concealed, mostly near ground.

TAWNY PIPIT *(Anthus campestris)* Rather larger than sparrow. Yellow-grey or sandy-brown largely uniform. Cream eye stripe. Mostly on the ground. Swift flight in big arcs. *Call:* a musical *tzi-uc. Song:* a pleasant repetitive *chivee, chivee,* usually on downwards glide of courtship flight. *Food:* insects, small snails. *Nest:* see p. 93. *Habitat:* arid wasteland and heath. Migrant. *Distribution:* S. Scandinavia to Mediterranean; annual vagrant to south coast of England, usually in September or October.

TREE PIPIT *(Anthus trivialis)* Size of a sparrow. Olive-brown upper parts with dark streaks. Pale rust-yellow breast with black streaks. Hind claw shorter. Song flight. Also sings from top of tree. Ascends steeply to glide down with rigid wings and hanging legs, singing a lovely, varied, rather canary-like song. *Food:* insects, spiders, worms, small seeds. *Nest:* see p. 90. *Habitat:* clearings in woods, sunny hillslopes. *Distribution:* N. Scandinavia to N. Spain and Greece; summer visitor to Britain and locally common in England, Wales and southern Scotland.

MEADOW PIPIT *(Anthus pratensis)* Breast less yellow than tree pipit's, and has a long hind claw. *Song:* a thin piping trill, almost only in downward glide of flight. *Food:* land and water insects, tiny snails. *Habitat:* upland pastures and moors, in winter marshes and coast. *Distribution:* breeds from Iceland and N. Europe to the south of France and Sicily; resident and common in open country in Britain.

ROCK PIPIT and WATER PIPIT *(Anthus spinoletta)* Larger than sparrow. Inconspicuous lark-like bird; grey-white underparts, reddish in summer. A number of races of this species occurs; birds from the mountains of central and southern Europe are called water pipits. Our native rock pipit is found in coastal areas. Sings only in flight. *Nest:* see p. 92. *Habitat:* mountains above tree-zone and marshes and rocky coasts. *Distribution:* Europe generally; resident and generally distributed on rocky shores in Britain.

PIED WAGTAIL and WHITE WAGTAIL *(Motacilla alba)* Size of sparrow, but slimmer. Striking black-white plumage, slender legs and long black tail. Two races, pied wagtail breeding

mainly in Britain, white wagtail on Continent. Pied wagtail has black back in the male or very dark in the female. The white wagtail has a light grey back; crown, throat and breast black (in summer) or white with black throat stripe (winter); outer tail feathers white. Forehead, sides of head and belly white. Juvenile dirty-grey. Quick tripping gait, body held horizontal, accompanied by nodding of head and flicking of tail. Flight easy and quick, in low loops. *Call:* a sharp *tchizzik. Song:* a pleasant twitter. *Food:* insects, snails and larvae in mud of bank or in plough. *Nest:* under a stone, in holes in wall, tree, bank, etc. 2 clutches of 4–6 whitish eggs covered with grey speckles (2 × 1.7 cm). *Habitat:* open country, often near water, farms, gardens. *Distribution:* pied wagtail resident and widely distributed in Britain; white wagtail a passage migrant along the coast from March to June; it breeds on the Continent from Iceland to the Mediterranean.

GREY WAGTAIL *(Motacilla cinerea)* More delicate and graceful than the pied wagtail with a longer tail. Upper parts ash-grey, underparts sulphur yellow. Throat of male black in summer, whitish in winter. White eye stripe. Male has white chin stripe. Green-yellow rump. Rocking gait; runs with quick tripping step. Lovely curved flight. *Call: see-eet* mostly in flight. *Nest:* on bank of water or nearby, under bushes, bridges, overhanging roots, also in holes in banks, walls, etc. 2 clutches of 4–6 greeny-yellow eggs (1.9 × 1.4 cm) with reddish-brown flecks. April to July. *Habitat:* by swiftly running water or vicinity, in both hills and lowland. *Distribution:* S. Scandinavia to the Mediterranean; resident and widely distributed in Britain.

YELLOW WAGTAIL and BLUE-HEADED WAGTAIL *(Motacilla flava)* Size of a sparrow, slim, long-legged. Tail not so long as the preceding. Yellow underparts, grey head, white eye stripe; olive-green upper parts and browny-black wings. Female much duller in colour. Males of central European race *(Motacilla flava flava)* have bluish crown, white eye stripe and white chin. *Food:* insects and larvae and worms. Relieve sheep and cattle of parasites. *Nest:* see p. 92. *Habitat:* pastures, damp meadows, farmlands. *Distribution:* blue-headed wagtail breeds S. Scandinavia to central France; occasional passage migrant in Britain. Yellow wagtail, summer visitor to Britain breeding in England and Wales but rarely in west and few places in southern Scotland and northern Ireland.

Family   BOMBYCILLIDAE   Waxwing

WAXWING *(Bombycilla garrulus)* The size of a starling. Plumage light pinkish brown, short tail with yellow tip, black throat, distinct yellow and white markings on wings and scarlet "sealing-wax" tips to secondaries from which the bird is named. Prominent crest on head. *Call:* weak trill *zirrr. Food:* berries (in winter when seen). *Habitat:* gardens and similar places where there are berried trees or shrubs. *Distribution:* N. Norway to Siberia; regular winter visitor to all parts of Britain but more often in east.

SHRIKES AND FLYCATCHERS   (Fig. 26)

Family   LANIIDAE   Shrikes

Big, strikingly coloured song-birds with stiff, erect carriage. Upper mandible hooked and with a tooth-like prominence in front which fits into notch in lower mandible for crushing the armour of larger insects. Medium-length rounded wings; long tail rounded or wedge-shaped. Slow, irregular flight, fairly low over ground. Strong, fairly long legs. Sharp claws. Hop. Usually sit upright on some vantage point, flicking and fanning their tail. Monotonous musical song; harsh call; often spear their prey on thorns to await their pleasure. Good mimics.

RED-BACKED SHRIKE *(Lanius cristatus)* Slightly larger than sparrow; plump; thick head; male has red-brown back, ash-grey head with black stripe over eye; black tail edged with white; white underparts. Female browny with brown eye streak and dark bars on lighter underparts. Slow flight. Usually hunt along a hedge gliding and hovering. "Larders" its food. *Call:* a hoarse *chee-uk.* Soft twittering song. *Nest:* see p. 88. *Food:* insects, especially beetles, baby mice, birds, frogs, etc. *Habitat:* thorn hedges in woods, clearings, round ponds, in fields, etc. Migrant. *Distribution:* breeds central Scandinavia to N. Spain, Sicily and Greece; summer visitor and passage migrant to Britain, breeding in parts of central and southern England.

WOODCHAT SHRIKE *(Lanius senator)* Top of head and nape browny-red; back, long tail, side of head black; shoulders, wing patch and underparts white. White rump conspicuous in

flight. Flight and hunting technique as red-backed's. *Call:* a harsh *shek-shek*. Song often mingled with other bird's notes. *Nest:* see p. 83. *Habitat:* orchards, bushy areas, open country, olive groves. *Distribution:* central Europe to Mediterranean; annual passage vagrant in S. and E. England.

GREAT GREY SHRIKE *(Lanius excubitor)* the largest of the shrikes, about the size of a blackbird. Striking black-white colouring; back and forehead grey. Broad black stripe from beak across head to beyond eye. Double white wing patch. Low flight, frequent hovering. In the old days falconers used them to help catch their birds as the shrike is afraid of birds-of-prey and utters warning cries when they see one. Soft musical song, often with mimicry of others. *Food:* small birds, lizards, beetles, mice. *Nest:* see p. 82. *Habitat:* woods and trees in fields, orchards, heather, hedges. *Distribution:* central and northern Europe; autumn and winter visitor to eastern Britain.

LESSER GREY SHRIKE *(Lanius minor)* Similar to the above but smaller; black forehead, underparts tinged with pink, relatively large wings (migrant) with only one white wing-bar and white edges to tail. Hovers frequently. *Call:* a harsh *rräh rräh*; also *kviell*. *Food:* almost only insects, especially beetles; seldom young mice or birds. *Nest:* see p. 83. *Habitat:* open country with scattered bushes, roadsides and commons in Italy, Balkans and S. central Europe; rare vagrant to S.E. England, usually in spring.

Family   MUSCICAPIDAE   Flycatchers

Small birds with broad beaks (seen from above) that often flick their tails. Usually sit upright on some vantage point waiting for a fly which they catch on the wing with an audible snap of the beak. Rather bad songsters. Nest mostly in holes.

SPOTTED FLYCATCHER *(Muscicapa striata)* Size of a sparrow. Dark speckles on forehead and whitish breast. Grey-brown upper parts, dull white underparts. Seldom on ground and rather awkward on it. Catches its prey on the wing. Sits upright and motionless on low vantage point, occasionally twitching wings and tail, and taking off in fluttering pursuit of an insect. In bad weather takes its prey from house walls. *Call:* a sharp *tzee* often with *tuc-tuc* added. *Song:* a soft twittering. *Food:* insects, rarely berries. *Nest:* in espalier wires, jutting balconies, open sheds, behind creepers, etc. Also in holes. 4–5 nearly white eggs with light red spots. May to July. *Habitat:* woods, lanes, gardens. *Distribution:* N. Norway to Mediterranean; summer visitor and passage migrant to Britain, nesting in most areas.

PIED FLYCATCHER *(Muscicapa hypoleuca)* Smaller than a sparrow. Upper parts black, underparts white; white patch on wing. Gay, active bird, ever on the move. Takes insects off leaves (and the ground) but only in flight. In hot weather goes up high to hunt flies, gnats, etc. *Nest:* in holes in trees or under tiles. Lines its nest carefully with straw, moss, and hair. 2 clutches of 5–7 delicate, light-blue eggs. (1.8 × 1.3 cm) unflecked. *Habitat:* woods, parks, gardens. *Distribution:* Europe from far north to S. France; summer visitor and passage migrant to Britain breeding in Gloucestershire and Wales and other localities in the Pennines, the North and Midlands.

TITS AND OTHER SMALL SONG-BIRDS

Family   PARIDAE   Tits   Fig. 25

Small dumpy bodies, short beaks for chiselling out seeds and smashing insects. Strong feet for clambering in search of food. Plumage of sexes similar. Inept on ground, but nimble in foliage, hopping and skulking often chirruping. Whirring flight often in a short arc, seldom going very far. Nest mainly in holes (exceptions long-tailed, bearded and penduline tits). Numerous progeny, 8–15 eggs.

GREAT TIT *(Parus major)* Restless, colourful, far from shy, is the size of a sparrow with head and neck a glossy blue-black, white cheeks; lower parts yellow with black stripe lengthwise down the middle. Upper parts greenish blue-grey. Seldom on ground; acrobatic in bushes. *Call:* a clear *tsink tsink* or *tchair tchair. Food:* insects and their eggs, fruits, seeds. *Nest:* in holes in trees, walls, etc. April to July 2 clutches of 6–13 white eggs (1.8 × 1.3 cm) with pink dots. *Habitat:* woods, gardens, parks. Resident. *Distribution:* Europe generally; a resident common and widely distributed in Britain.

BLUE TIT *(Parus caeruleus)* Smaller than sparrow. Blue crown, white cheeks, yellow underparts (no black stripe down middle). Black line through eye and around cheek and nape to chin. *Call: tsee-tsee-tsee-tsit. Song:* a clear *tsee tsee* ending in a trill. *Food* and *Nest* as great tit. 2 clutches of 7–9 white eggs (1.5 × 1.2 cm) with bright red dots, April to July. Pairs remain together during winter. *Habitat:* as great tit. *Distribution:* Europe generally; a resident common and widely distributed in Britain.

CRESTED TIT *(Parus cristatus)* Smaller than sparrow. Pointed crest speckled black and white. Curving black line from eye beyond cheek and down; black collar and bib. *Nest:* in holes in trees, etc. even rabbit holes. Nest made of grass, moss, lichen lined with hair and wool. End of April 7–10 white eggs (1.6 × 1.2 cm) with brown-red flecks (larger than on other tits' eggs). *Habitat:* mostly in conifer (pine) woods; thickets. *Distribution:* Europe generally; in Britain confined mainly to the Spey valley in Scotland.

COAL TIT *(Parus ater)* Similar in appearance to great tit, but has white patch on nape and underparts are light-grey instead of yellow. *Nest:* like crested tit. End of April 2 clutches of 6–11 white eggs (1.5 × 1.2 cm) with a lot of fine red specks. *Habitat:* wooded country and gardens. *Distribution:* Europe generally; a resident, common and widely distributed in Britain.

MARSH TIT *(Parus palustris)* Smaller than great tit, graceful. Glossy black pate and throat. Pure white cheeks, back of neck and underparts dull grey-white; upper parts grey-brown. Clever acrobat. Flies with slight whirr of wings. *Call:* a loud *pitchew* or *pitichewee. Food:* insects and small seeds. *Nest:* in holes and trees, even in earth. Builds with moss, straw, fibre, lined with hair. May to June 2 clutches of 7–9 white eggs (1.7 × 1.3 cm) with red speckles. *Habitat:* woods, hedges, gardens. (The name "marsh" is misleading.) *Distribution:* Europe generally except in the south-east; in Britain a somewhat local resident in England and Wales.

LONG-TAILED TIT *(Aegithalos caudatus)* Smaller than sparrow; very long graduated tail. Upper parts dark, underparts white, head white with dark stripe over eye (western variety) or all white (eastern variety). *Call:* a very high *tsee-tsee* or a deep *tsirrup. Nest:* see p. 88. *Habitat:* bushy woods and gardens. *Distribution:* Europe generally; in Britain a resident generally distributed.

BEARDED TIT *(Panurus biarmicus)* A little larger than the long-tailed tit. Upper parts tawny, very long tawny tail, underparts grey but white in middle. Male's head is ash-grey with a broad, black stripe, under tail feathers black. Female's head is browny or black and without "beard". Agile climbers among reeds. *Call:* a silvery *tching. Food:* in summer insects; in winter seeds of sedge and marsh plants. *Nest:* see p. 98. *Habitat:* confined to reed beds. *Distribution:* Europe, south and west of the Baltic; in Britain confined as a resident to Norfolk and Suffolk; elsewhere it is a rare vagrant.

WILLOW TIT *(Parus montanus)* Like marsh tit but has a dark sooty-brown crown and pale patch on wings. *Call:* a nasal *eez-eez-eez. Nest:* in holes in old trees. *Habitat:* marshy thickets. *Distribution:* Scandinavia and central Europe; in Britain a resident widespread in England and Wales but local, rarer in Scotland.

*PENDULINE TIT *(Remiz pendulinus)* Greyish-white head and throat with black eye mask. Reddy-brown back; cream-coloured belly. Agile in bushes and reeds. *Call:* a protracted *seeou. Food:* insects or their eggs; in winter seeds of reeds, etc. *Nest:* see p. 85. *Habitat:* marshy, swampy places. *Distribution:* eastern Europe, Italy and S.E. Spain.

Family   REGULIDAE   Goldcrests

GOLDCREST *(Regulus regulus)* Tiny. Saffron-yellow top of head with black border. Upper parts lime-green; underparts dull whitish-brown; greenish flanks. Two white bars and a broad black band on wing. Flies nimbly from tree to tree searching for insects. *Nest:* see p. 85. *Habitat:* woods and copses, mainly of conifers. *Distribution:* Europe generally except Spain; generally distributed resident in Britain.

FIRECREST *(Regulus ignicapillus)* Tiny. Red crown, black streak through eye, bold white stripe over eye. Upper parts green, underparts whitish. *Nest:* see p. 85. Otherwise like goldcrest. Migrant. *Habitat:* less confined to conifers; bracken, low bushes, etc. *Distribution:* Denmark and Poland south to Mediterranean; in Britain regular but scarce passage migrant in October and March to April, mainly on south coast.

Family   SITTIDAE   Nuthatches   Fig. 28

NUTHATCH *(Sitta europaea)* Plate 4 Perfect tree trunk climber. Stocky bird the size of a sparrow; strong, pointed beak like a woodpecker's but not used for chiselling holes, only for paring off bark. Short tail not used as a support when climbing. Short legs, big, sharp, curved claws. Grey-blue upper parts, cream underparts with chestnut flanks; white cheeks and throat; black stripe through eye. Climbs by means of a series of little jumps with its head up or down. *Call:* metallic *chwit, chwit, chwit,* a repeated *tsit* or a trill. *Food:* insects and their larvae which it taps out of the bark with its beak; seeds the larger ones of which (hazel nuts, beechnuts, acorns, sunflower seeds) it wedges in bark and then splits with its beak. Stores food (and forgets it). *Nest:* see p. 101. *Habitat:* old deciduous trees. *Distribution:* S. Scandinavia to Mediterranean; resident but local in southern and central England.

Family   TROGLODYTIDAE   Wrens   Fig. 25

WREN *(Troglodytes troglodytes)* A bustling little bird with a small round body, short tail and wings. Brown plumage, darker on upper parts, closely barred. Darts about like a mouse under bushes, seldom still. Sits with tail cocked up and breast low. Often bobs. Very quick, whirring flight, usually low, from bush to bush. Shallow dips over longer distances. *Call:* a hard *tit-tit-tit.* Loud song, fiery and trilling. Sings almost all year. *Food:* insects, spiders, etc. *Nest:* see p. 88. *Habitat:* low undergrowth and hedges in gardens, woods, rocks. *Distribution:* Europe generally; resident and generally distributed in Britain.

Family   CERTHIIDAE   Creepers   Fig. 28

Small lively birds with long, curved, slender beaks for searching out insects in crevices and cracks. Climb tree trunks or rocks but never head down. Sexes similar in appearance. *Nest:* in holes in trees or rocks.

TREE-CREEPER *(Certhia familiaris)* Not quite as large as a sparrow. Upper parts grey-brown, underparts white, curved beak. Climb spirally in spurts. *Call:* thin *tsee* or *tsit.* Always nests in a wood, in a crack in a tree; nest made of twigs, moss, straw, lichen, fibres; 2 clutches of 5–7 white eggs (1.6 × 1.2 cm) with browny-red spots mostly at blunt end. *Habitat:* woods and trees in fields and gardens. On Continent often above 900 m. Often in company of tits, goldcrests, nuthatches and woodpeckers after nesting. *Distribution:* Scandinavia and E. Europe; resident and widely distributed in Britain.

*SHORT-TOED TREE-CREEPER *(Certhia brachydactyla)* Has brown sides and less rust on rump than the tree-creeper, otherwise appearance is similar. Call is louder and fuller (see p. 545 and 552). Its hind claws are shorter and beak longer. No flecks on forehead. *Nest:* in trees, as above, but also in orchards, under tiles, in walls, barns, etc. Foundation of twigs, sides of moss, roots, hair etc. lined with feathers. May and June to July 2 clutches of 5–7 white eggs (1.6 × 1.2 cm) with more and larger browny-red spots. *Habitat:* orchards, woods, etc. Usually not beyond 1,525 m. *Distribution:* central and southern Europe.

*WALL CREEPER *(Tichodroma muraria)* See p. 206.

SWALLOWS AND MARTINS

Family HIRUNDINIDAE Swallows Fig. 27

Slim, streamlined bodies with broad chests, short necks, flat heads, very short, flat, triangular beaks. Gape extending to level of front of eye. Long, narrow, pointed wings, crossing over the tail when folded. Long, deeply forked tail. Swift, graceful, twisting flight. Hunt, drink and bath on the wing. Short feathered legs. Tiny feet just for clinging to nest and for perching. Clumsy tripping gait when on ground. Song a pleasant twitter. Sociable.

SWALLOW *(Hirundo rustica)* Long, forked tail with spike-shaped outer feathers which are not drooped when perching. Upper parts blue-black; forehead and throat rust-red, underparts reddish-white; steel-blue collar. Seldom on ground and then only to obtain nesting material from puddles. Flies at furious speed in elegant swoops with lightning turns, often even touching the surface of the water. *Call:* a high *tswit.* Sings from roof, telephone wire, a pleasant babbling twitter. *Nest:* always in buildings, especially where animals are; open nest of mud and straw placed on rafter or ledge, often used year after year by same couple. May to August 2 clutches of 4–5 small white eggs (2 × 1.3 cm) with dark brown speckles. *Habitat:* farms and farmland. Migrant. *Distribution:* Europe generally; summer visitor to most parts of Britain.

HOUSE MARTIN *(Delichon urbica)* Slightly smaller than swallow; shorter, slightly forked tail with the swallow's "spikes", mostly drooped when perching. Upper parts glossy black-blue; throat and underparts and rump white; feathered legs. Sexes similar in colouring. Flight not so fierce as a swallow's, but more fluttering and often higher. *Call:* a soft clear *tchirrip. Song:* a soft pleasant twittering both when perched and in flight, but seldom heard. *Nest:* in groups usually hemispherical (closed) structure of mud, saliva and straw under an eave or other over-hang; has entrance hole at top. April to August, 2 clutches of 3–5 white eggs (1.2 × 1.3 cm) faintly freckled with violet-grey and red. *Habitat:* villages and farmsteads, country houses. *Distribution:* Europe generally; summer visitor to many parts of Britain but more local than swallow.

SAND MARTIN *(Riparia riparia)* Smallest European swallow, very like the others in build and behaviour. Slightly forked tail; matt plumage. Upper parts earthen-brown, underparts white, grey collar. Flight more gliding and flitting, sometimes appearing fluttering. Often 30–40 nests close together, entrance a hole 4–6 cm across in steep wall of sand or gravel pit, river bank, etc., leading in 60–100 cm and excavated with beak and feet. *Nest:* of straw and feathers. May to June one clutch of 5–6 glossy white eggs (1.8 × 1.3 cm) speckled with violet-grey and red.

Habitat: open country with ponds, rivers, etc. Migrant. *Distribution:* Europe generally; summer visitor to many parts of Britain.

Order   APODIFORMES

Family   APODIDAE   Swifts   Fig. 27

Similar to swallow but not related; have all 4 toes directed forward for clinging to vertical faces. No song.

SWIFT *(Apus apus)* In appearance and behaviour similar to swallow. Long in body, head flat, beak short, legs short; wings more narrow and sickle-shaped than swallow's; short, forked tail; smoky-black plumage; only white at throat. Does not go on ground. Cannot walk or creep; only at home in the air. Flies at a furious speed with lightning turns; tireless, can fly from early morning to late evening. During breeding season will chase round roof tops screaming a shrill *srich. Food:* only flying insects, preferably beetles. *Nest:* usually in buildings, under eaves, in cracks in walls, holes in trees also in old house martins' nests. Structure of straw and feathers cemented with saliva. May to June one clutch of 2 oval all-white eggs (2.5 x 1.5 cm). *Habitat:* where suitable nesting sites are. Migrant. Returns each year to same nesting place. *Distribution:* Europe generally; summer visitor to Britain everywhere except N.W. Scotland.

*ALPINE SWIFT *(Apus melba)* See p. 206.

Order   PICIFORMES   Fig. 28

Family   PICIDAE   Woodpeckers

GREAT SPOTTED WOODPECKER *(Dendrocopus major)* Plate 4 Size of a blackbird. Male has crimson back of head and under tail-coverts. Upper parts black with big white shoulder patches. Area of eyes and cheeks white. Underparts whitish without markings. Female has no red on the back of her head. Juvenile red crown with black edging. Seldom goes on ground; hops, climbs up and down trees in a series of long, quick leaps, but always with its head pointing up. *Call:* a loud hard *tchick,* repeatedly when excited. Both male and female "drum" with swift pecks on a dry springy branch which is thereby set vibrating. *Nest:* see p. 100. *Food:* larvae of wood-boring insects, conifer nuts, hazel nuts, fruit stones. Smithy, see p. 103. *Habitat:* woods, deciduous and pine, farmlands, wherever there are scattered trees. Will not tolerate rivals in its territory. *Distribution:* Europe generally; resident, well distributed in England, Wales and most of Scotland.

* MIDDLE SPOTTED WOODPECKER *(Dendrocopus medius)* Plate 4 Size of a blackbird. Plumage black-white-red. Crown and back of head crimson; belly pink; back black; underparts speckled, white shoulder patches. *Call: ptik-tenk. Food:* small insects, spiders; otherwise as the others. *Nest:* some 10–12 m above the ground with circular opening; see p. 100. *Habitat:* as above. *Distribution:* central and southern Europe (not Spain).

LESSER SPOTTED WOODPECKER *(Dendrocopus minor)* Plate 4 Smallest European woodpecker. Size of a sparrow. Crown of male's head crimson, of female's white. Upper parts closely barred black and white; no crimson on under tail-coverts. Retiring behaviour; mostly high up in tree. *Food:* ants and other insects. *Nest:* see p. 100. *Habitat:* as great spotted. *Distribution:* Europe generally; resident but local in southern England, Midlands and parts of Wales; rare elsewhere.

GREEN WOODPECKER *(Picus viridis)* Plate 4 Just under pigeon size. Olive-green with crimson from crown to nape. Deep, looping flight, with wings shut between each ascent. *Call:* 7–12 clear, staccato notes like *kjack* sounding like a piercing laugh. Frequently feeds on ground, pecking holes in ant-heaps to eat them and their grubs. Also eats beetles and larvae in rotten tree trunks. *Nest:* see p. 100. *Habitat:* woods and farmlands. *Distribution:* Europe generally; generally distributed resident in England and Wales and becoming established in Scottish border counties.

* GREY-HEADED WOODPECKER *(Picus canus)* Plate 4 Similar to green woodpecker but smaller and has much smaller cheek stripes and grey neck and head with red only on front half of crown. Female has no red. *Call:* mellower and descending, 8 syllables at least. Drums more often than green woodpecker. *Nest:* like green woodpecker; will often feed on the ground; will sit on walls. *Habitat:* as green woodpecker. *Distribution:* central Scandinavia and central and eastern Europe.

♂

Great
Spotted
Wood-
pecker

♀

♂

Green Woodpecker
♀

♂

Lesser
Spotted

Middle
Spotted

Wryneck

Black
Wood-
pecker

♀

♂

♀

Grey headed
♂   Wood-
pecker

Kingfisher

Nuthatch

Hoopoe

Roller

♀

Cuckoo   ♂

Nightjar

BÄUERLE

* BLACK WOODPECKER *(Dryocopus martius)* Plate 4 Size of a pigeon. All black but for crimson crown. Ringing call: *krri-krri-krri. Song:* a strident *choc-choc-choc.* Shy and seldom seen. *Food:* ants and insects on or in trees. *Nest:* see p. 100. *Habitat:* the quiet woods and forests of northern Europe and the Alps and other mountainous areas.

WRYNECK *(Jynx torquilla)* Plate 4 More often heard than seen. When in danger stretches neck out and slowly turns it like a snake, fanning its tail and wings and raising the feathers on the crown of its head. Size of a big sparrow; largish rounded tail; woodpecker's feet: 2 toes forward, 2 behind. Upper parts bark-coloured; underparts lighter. Feeds on ground, hopping with long leaps and cocked tail; perches lengthwise or horizontally on branch. Clings to tree trunk like woodpecker, but moves amongst branches like a songbird, hopping and fluttering. Flies in shallow undulations. *Call:* a repeated loud *kyink kyink. Food:* insects, especially ants and their grubs, which it culls out with long sliding tongue. *Nest:* in natural holes in trees or walls. No foundation to nest; see p. 72. May to June 7–12 glossy white eggs. *Habitat:* woods, orchards, parklands. *Distribution:* central and southern Europe but not Spain; scarce summer visitor to Britain now mainly to Surrey and Kent as a breeding bird.

Order   CUCULIFORMES

Family   CUCULIDAE Cuckoos   Fig. 29

CUCKOO *(Cuculus canorus)* Plate 4 Shy, unsociable tree bird, the size of a pigeon. Slim body, small gently curved beak; long, pointed wings; very long rounded tail; short legs; can turn toes so that 2 point forward and 2 back. Upper parts ash-grey; underparts lighter with dark bars; yellow legs. Nimble, buoyant, straight flight; much flatter wing beat than a sparrow-hawk's. *Call: cuc-coo,* also a loud sniggering *wow-wow-wow. Food:* insects of all kinds, caterpillars a favourite. Caterpillars' hair ejected as pellets. Brood-parasitic laying one egg in the nests of any 10–20 songbirds all of the same species, which hatch and feed the young bird. (Hosts can be reed warblers, red-backed shrikes, pied wagtails, various warblers, pipits, flycatchers, redstarts, wrens, robins, hedge-sparrows, tits, finches or yellowhammers.) Egg mostly deceptively like that of host in size, colour and markings. *Habitat:* woodlands, bushy places. *Distribution:* Europe generally; summer visitor to all parts of British isles.

Order   CORACIIFORMES

Family   UPUPIDAE Hoopoes

HOOPOE *(Upupa epops)* Plate 4 Almost the size of a pigeon with erectile crest and black tips to its cinnamon-coloured feathers; long, thin,

curved beak. Earth-coloured (pinkish) plumage; wings and tail barred
with black and white. Nimble tripping gait on ground. Heavy, undulating,
fluttering flight, in which the white bars on the broad wings glint. *Call:*
a deep 3-syllable *poo-poo-poo*. *Food:* beetles, larvae, worms, cockchafer
grubs picked out of ground and droppings of animals, and insects from
crevices in rock and dead leaves. *Nest:* in open deciduous woods, or the
fringes, in hollow trees, buildings, under roofs, etc. May to June 6–7 eggs
(2.6 × 1.7 cm) of varying colour, but mostly olive-grey with light speckles.
Female and nestlings squirt a dirty-yellow fluid with a revolting smell
from anal glands when threatened. *Habitat:* pasture with old trees, open
glades, orchards. Migrant. *Distribution:* central and southern Europe;
regular passage migrant in southern counties of England where it has
occasionally nested.

Family   CORACIIDAE   Rollers

ROLLER *(Coracias garrulus)* Plate 4 Size of a pigeon, strong, jay-like,
with powerful beak and short legs. Head, neck, underparts and wing
coverts a gorgeous delicate sky-blue with a shimmer of green; back a
shiny chestnut; black edge to wings visible in flight; black-brown beak;
yellow legs. Flies restlessly from tree to tree; catches prey on the wing.
Tumbling courtship flight. *Call:* loud, crow-like *kr-r-r-r-ak*. *Food:* insects,
especially beetles, grasshoppers, occasionally frogs, lizards, mice. *Nest:* in
holes in old trees in open woods, often in woodpeckers' holes. About end
of May one clutch of 4–5 white eggs. *Habitat:* old woods and fairly
open country with trees. *Distribution:* S. Europe north to south of France;
vagrant to Britain mainly in the south-east in May to July and September to October.

Family   MEROPIDAE   Bee-eaters

BEE-EATER *(Merops apiaster)* Length 28 cm. Swallow-like in flight,
with pointed wings and middle tail-feathers projecting beyond the others.
Brilliantly coloured; throat yellow, upper parts chestnut, underparts
greenish-blue, wings blue-green and brown; long tail greenish. Hawks for
insects on wing which form the main food. *Nest:* in tunnel in cliffs, banks,
sandpits etc. Eggs 4–7 white, May to June. *Distribution:* S. W. Europe
north to N. Italy; in Britain a vagrant most years; bred in Sussex in 1955.

Family   ALCEDINIDAE   Kingfishers

KINGFISHER *(Alcedo atthis)* Plate 4 Size of a large sparrow, stocky,
colourful. Relatively large head; long, straight pointed beak, red at base.
Very slim, short bright red legs; short wings and tail. Smooth, close-lying
plumage; compact, upper parts; brilliant metallic blue-green upper parts,
rust-red underparts; yellowy-white throat. Swift, whirring flight; flies

close to water always at same height; sometimes hovers, plunging into water after fish or insects. Paddles with wings under water for a short distance, emerging and rising again in whirring flight. Perches for hours motionless on branch, stick or stone watching for its prey; regurgitates chitinous bits of insects as well as bones and scales of fish as pellets. Kingfisher pellets are white and silvery and crumble when touched; found below its perches. *Nest:* often in walls of sand or clay pits near water with plenty of fish, excavating with beak a tunnel 5 cm across and 0.5 to 1 m long opening into a round nest, the floor of which is covered with regurgitated bits of fish. Occupied hole recognisable by trickle of white excrement and nasty fishy smell rising from it. May to August 6–8 glossy white, almost spherical eggs (2.3 × 1.9 cm). *Habitat:* prefers small streams with steep banks and clear water; in mountains up to 1,800 m. In winter vagrant to coast and open water. *Distribution:* Europe generally including N. Scandinavia; resident, generally distributed in England, Wales and S. W. Scotland. Rare in Ireland.

Order   CAPRIMULGIFORMES

Family   CAPRIMULGIDAE   Fig. 27

Nocturnal, insect-eating birds with big eyes, huge gapes and very small feet; long wings and tails. They spend the day perching motionless lengthways along a branch or on ground.

NIGHTJAR *(Caprimulgus europaeus)* Plate 4 Size of a blackbird; head the shape of a swallow's; long, narrow wings; big eyes; tiny beak, but with a huge gape, surrounded by long bristle-hairs. Plumage the colour of bark and dead leaves. Nocturnal. Flight rocking to the accompaniment of strange noises. Strikingly long in evening or at night: a sustained whirring purr. *Call:* soft *goo-ek.* In courtship flight strikes its wings loudly together like a pigeon. *Food:* flying insects caught on wing. *Nest:* see p. 90. *Habitat:* heath, moors, open woodlands (pines), glades with bracken. Migrant. *Distribution:* Scandinavia to S. Europe; summer visitor to Britain and breeds in most suitable localities except the islands in the north of Scotland.

Order   FALCONIFORMES Birds of Prey, Owls   See p. 75

Family   FALCONIDAE   Eagles, Buzzards, Hawks, Kites, Falcons

Heads and necks feathered. Powerful toes and long, strong, curved sharp claws (talons) used in seizing and killing prey; beaks used to dismember prey; feed largely on prey they have caught, seldom on carrion. The smaller ones with short beaks curved from the base are the falcons; the larger ones with longer beaks that are straight at the base, are the eagles. (See p. 158–160.)

BUZZARDS   Fig. 30

BUZZARD *(Buteo buteo)* Powerful body: 50–60 cm; wing span 120–125 cm. Tail 26 cm. Beak for tearing and cutting; upper mandible pointed and hooked, very sharp; edges of beak notched. Talons for seizing and killing small animals. Colouring varies considerably: upper parts, brown, black-brown or lighter; underparts mostly lighter and occasionally mottled; underside of wings and tail have, dark, narrow bands. Feet and cere are yellow. Eyes have nut-brown iris. *Cry:* like a cat's mew. *Flight:* slow wing beat interrupted by long soaring glides. *Courtship flight:* circles high up with wing tips upturned and makes daring dives. Its broad wings, broad short tail and tucked-in head give it a rather stumpy silhouette. Hovers. Rather heavy flight, because of its scoop-shaped wings. Hunts by pouncing from flight or vantage point on prey on ground (mice, moles, weasels, rats, hamsters, leverets, rabbits, hedgehogs, young magpies, partridges, frogs, grasshoppers). Will also eat carrion. Indigestible parts (hair, feathers, claws) regurgitated as pellets. Talons protected by stout horny shields. *Eyrie:* see p. 80. *Habitat:* rocky coasts, moors, plains, mountain slopes; farmland with scattered woodland. *Distribution:* Europe generally; breeds in most counties of England, Wales and Scotland lying west of a line from Edinburgh to London.

HONEY BUZZARD *(Pernis apivorus)* Size of a buzzard, but has smaller head, longer tail; black bars at root and end of tail further apart. Upper parts dark brown; underparts lighter with dark-brown mottling on bars. Old males have grey heads. *Call:* a squeaky *kee-er* or rapid *kikiki;* quite unlike buzzard's. Flight like buzzard's, but sails and hovers less. Often on ground, where has a crow-like gait. *Courtship flight:* high circling with both birds circling above and below each other. Flight silhouette has narrower wings, longer tail, smaller head, longer neck and more distinct under markings; head stretched well out. *Food:* larvae

of wasps, hornets, bumble bees and the adults themselves, when
it bites off the sting before swallowing them; also caterpillars,
beetles, worms, frogs, snakes, small birds and their eggs, also
berries, fruit and buds. *Eyrie:* see p. 80. *Habitat:* skirts of open
woods, heaths, farmlands. Migrant. *Distribution:* Europe, from
N. Scandinavia to Mediterranean; irregular passage migrant to
Britain in September or October and May or June, but has bred
in England.

GOSHAWK *(Accipiter gentilis)* Body 55 cm; wing span 110 cm;
tail 22 cm. Female much larger (70 cm). Small head, short rounded wings, long tail. Edges of beak notched and very sharp.
Claws of inner fore-toe and hind toe particularly developed
and act like blacksmiths' tongs; these two especially kill prey
almost instantly. Back ash-grey; white stripe above and behind
the eye; underparts whitish with dark brown bars. Iris light
yellow or orange. Beak black, cere yellow; bright yellow eyes,
yellow legs. Juvenile has lighter upper parts, yellowish underparts with streaks instead of bars. *Call:* a buzzard-like mew and
a long *gig-gig-gig.* Low flight, very swift over short distances.
Agile doubling, even among bushes and branches, possible because
of long tail. *Flight silhouette:* short, round wings, long, barred
tail; conspicuous white under tail coverts. *Hunting flight:* mostly
low between trees; swift wing beats with gliding. *Courtship
flight:* circling high in the air with swift wing beats and almost
vertical upward swoops with wings and spread under tail coverts
showing white. Hunts by stalking flight and sudden pouncing.
Will take birds from nest while on wing. In open country flies
low over ground in order to knock down mice, partridges, weasels.
Also swoops on pigeons. *Eyrie:* see p. 80. *Habitat:* woods, especially conifers, heaths, moors, open farmland. *Distribution:*
N. Scandinavia to Pyrenees and east to Russia; rare vagrant to
Britain, but a few are resident in widely separated localities.

SPARROW HAWK *(Accipiter nisus)* Length 32 cm; wing-span
64 cm; tail 15 cm. Female 8–9 cm longer in body and 12–15 cm
wider wing-span. A goshawk in miniature, but does not "mew".
Middle toe conspicuously long, specially adapted for seizing
birds. Underparts of male rust-brown, of female dark-brown or
grey with bars. Long, yellow legs. Flight silhouette like goshawk's.

Also has stalking flight and pounce. Stormy flight, gliding over long distances interspersed with a few rapid wing beats. Doubles and twists through branches, seizing birds off perch or in flight. *Eyrie:* see p. 80. Like goshawk male only brings prey to edge of eyrie. Female feeds the young birds, offering small pieces; if it dies, the babies starve. Young about 4 weeks in nest. *Food:* mainly small birds, mice; the male catches those of wren and thrush size; the much stronger female, pigeon, partridge. *Habitat:* woodlands and farmlands. *Distribution:* Europe generally; in Britain it is a widely distributed resident but numbers have now decreased seriously.

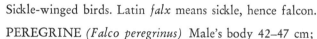

FALCONS   Fig. 30

Sickle-winged birds. Latin *falx* means sickle, hence falcon.

PEREGRINE *(Falco peregrinus)* Male's body 42–47 cm; wing-span 84–104 cm; tail 20 cm; female 47–52 cm; wing-span 110–120 cm; tail 20 cm. Recognisable when perching by big, black, lobe-shaped moustachial stripe. Neat body. Fairly large, round head and broad shoulders. Long, narrow pointed wings that, when folded, reach the ends of the tail. Powerful beak, broad, short and curved like a buzzard's. Behind the hook on each side a stud, the so-called falcon's tooth, which fits into a notch in the lower mandible. Prey-holding talons with long, wiry fore-toe; stocky hind toe with strong claw for stabbing its prey. Upper parts slate-grey; breast and belly whitish or reddish-yellow with dark horizontal mottling. Juvenile brown with dark streaks down breast and belly. Eye rings and feet light yellow. Never builds a nest, but uses those left by crows and other predators, or some suitable place in church towers, crevices in rock, quarry, etc. Lays 2–3 eggs closely mottled with reddish-brown. Flight is swift and pigeon-like with rapid, powerful wing beats, interrupted by occasional lengthy glides. *Silhouette:* falcon shape; long, narrow pointed sickle wings; long, narrow tapering tail. Hunts birds when on the wing only: stoops almost vertically at great speed, wings almost closed. If bird not killed by hind claw, bites through its spine or the back of its head. The male in summer hunts mostly starlings, the female crows or pigeons, but anything from swallow to goose can be their victim. *Habitat:* open country, especially when wild. *Distribution:* Europe generally; in Britain breeds mainly on the coast in S. and S.W. England, Wales, N. England, Scotland and Ireland but numbers have decreased seriously.

KESTREL *(Falco tinnunculus)* Length 33 cm, wing-span 70 cm; tail 16 cm. Female about 3 cm longer and wider in span. Slender shape; big head; broad shoulders; falcon beak. Sits on trees, rocks, telephone poles, etc. Upper parts reddish-brown with black-grey speckles. Underparts yellow-brown with spattering of black-grey spots. Underside of wings lighter with dark bars. Tail has dark, white-edged bands. *Flight:* frequent hovering; strong, rapid, shallow wing beats interspersed with short glides. Hovers facing upwind. *Silhouette:* long, pointed, narrow wings and fairly long tail; often mistaken for sparrow hawk. Hunts by hovering while watching ground below, or flies slowly along; stoops steeply on prey on ground. *Call:* high-pitched *kee-kee-kee* or deeper *kee-ke*. *Food:* mainly mice, also beetles, grasshoppers, sparrows. Very useful bird. *Nest:* see p. 82. *Habitat:* farmlands, open woods, moors and coastal areas; even in cities. *Distribution:* Europe generally; a widely distributed resident in Britain.

HOBBY *(Falco subbuteo)* The swiftest of the falcons, formerly used in falconry. Somewhat smaller than a pigeon, shaped rather like a small peregrine, but the wings look longer at the tail. The female some 4 cm larger. When folded the wing-tips reach to the end of its longish tail. Upper parts blue-black; greenish head; nape speckled white; underparts heavily "streaked" or "trousered"; rump and under tail feathers rust-red; wonderfully nimble, swift flight; rather like a swallow's; rapid wing beats. *Call:* a high, clear *kew* or *ket*. Stoops on birds in flight; also eats insects. *Nest:* see p. 82. *Habitat:* open country with scattered trees and light woodlands. *Distribution:* Europe generally; in Britain a summer visitor, breeding in small numbers in a few southern counties of England.

MERLIN *(Falco columbarius)* Male slightly larger than a thrush, but female about size of hen kestrel. Plumage: male, slatey-blue upper parts; underparts and nape buff; tail has broad dark band at the end; female: dark brown upper parts, underparts whitish and streaked with brown. Dashing flight, quick wing-beats and occasional glides. *Cry:* harsh *quek-ek-ek*. *Food:* small birds and mammals, insects. *Nest:* on ground among heather or sometimes in old nests of crows in trees, four eggs, May. *Habitat:* moors and hill country during breeding season, but marshes, sand dunes etc. at other times. *Distribution:* Europe generally; in Britain resident, breeding in N. England, Wales, Scotland and Ireland.

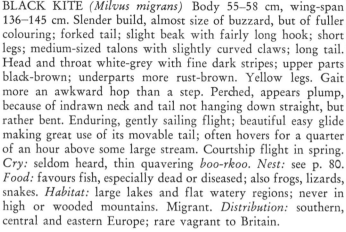

KITES   Fig. 31

BLACK KITE *(Milvus migrans)* Body 55–58 cm, wing-span 136–145 cm. Slender build, almost size of buzzard, but of fuller colouring; forked tail; slight beak with fairly long hook; short legs; medium-sized talons with slightly curved claws; long tail. Head and throat white-grey with fine dark stripes; upper parts black-brown; underparts more rust-brown. Yellow legs. Gait more an awkward hop than a step. Perched, appears plump, because of indrawn neck and tail not hanging down straight, but rather bent. Enduring, gently sailing flight; beautiful easy glide making great use of its movable tail; often hovers for a quarter of an hour above some large stream. Courtship flight in spring. *Cry:* seldom heard, thin quavering *boo-rkoo. Nest:* see p. 80. *Food:* favours fish, especially dead or diseased; also frogs, lizards, snakes. *Habitat:* large lakes and flat watery regions; never in high or wooded mountains. Migrant. *Distribution:* southern, central and eastern Europe; rare vagrant to Britain.

KITE *(Milvus milvus)* Length 61 cm. Similar in appearance and habits to the black kite, but slighter build, more deeply forked tail; lighter, reddish-brown plumage, streaked whitish head; in silhouette wings are steeply angled. *Call:* a buzzard-like whimpering mew with variations. *Food:* mice, larger insects, amphibians, fish, young birds, leverets. *Nest:* see p. 80. *Habitat:* not so dependent on water as black kite. Migrant. *Distribution:* similar to black kite; resident central Wales where, by careful protection, a few pairs nest.

HARRIERS   Fig. 31

MARSH HARRIER *(Circus aeruginosus)* Body 48–56 cm. Wing-span 136 cm. Female 3–4 cm larger and span 7–9 cm broader. Slim figure with small head; long, thin legs; rather long wings; long tail, short beak. Face feathers form a "veil", a wreath of stiff feathers such as owls have. Sharp edges to beak. Clasp of falcon kills. Each toe has short, curved, powerful claw. *Plumage:*

male's upper parts dark chestnut; head, nape and breast streaky yellow, tail light grey, secondaries contrasting with black primaries; female usually without grey; rather uniform dark brown with yellowy-white head and shoulders. Flight is more gliding than with other birds of prey, usually low over the ground; rocking action with long, undulating glides and occasional wing beats; pounces from low down into reeds. *Courtship flight:* an undulating glide with wings held high. In flight, normally holds its wings up in a shallow V. Hunts its prey from the air, when its "veil" helps it catch sound. Wonderful hearing. Can hear an unhatched coot chick peeping in shell and will break shell open. *Call:* a high-pitched *quee-a*, with variations. *Food:* mice, rats, etc. up to leveret and rabbits; birds from reed-bunting to coot; in emergency frogs, fish and insects. *Nest:* see p. 95. *Habitat:* marshes with large reed beds. Migrant. *Distribution:* Baltic south to Portugal and the Balkans; in Britain a few pairs breed in Norfolk and Suffolk and winter there, but mainly a summer visitor.

HEN HARRIER *(Circus cyaneus)* Body 46 cm, wing-span 113 cm, tail 21 cm. Female 6 cm longer and 9 cm wider span. Male's upper parts, throat and breast olive-grey, underparts white; tips of wings black; female's upper parts brown, underparts rusty yellow with brown streaks. Barred tail. *Call:* a shrill quavering *pee-a*. *Nest:* on ground. One clutch of 4–5 white (sometimes speckled) eggs. Otherwise like marsh harrier. *Habitat:* open country, moors and coast, marshes, fields. Partial migrant. *Distribution:* similar to preceding species; it breeds in the Orkneys, Outer Hebrides and on the Scottish mainland. A few pairs breed in Ireland. Present throughout the year.

MONTAGU'S HARRIER *(Circus pygargus)* Slighter and somewhat smaller than the hen harrier, but wing-span 125 cm and wings 48 cm. Male like male hen harrier but has black wing bar and brown streaks on breast. Female like female hen harrier only its rump is not so white. Wings narrower; tail longer. Call and habits similar to hen harrier. *Nest:* on ground. *Habitat:* marshes and fens or farm land. Migrant. *Distribution:* S. Sweden south to Mediterranean; summer visitor breeding mainly in S. W. England and Scotland but in small numbers.

EAGLES   Fig. 31

OSPREY *(Pandion haliaetus)* Body 53–56 cm, wing-span 156–164 cm. Between a white-tailed eagle and a kite. Fairly short beak starting to curve at cere. Very long downward hook. Strong legs, scarcely feathered beyond heel. Thick, close-lying plumage, wings reaching well beyond tail. Head has a small crest of sharp-pointed feathers. Easily distinguishable by dark upper parts and snow white underparts. Upper parts: black-brown feathers with lighter edge; underparts white with dark breast line bars. White crown with dark streaks; wide dark eye stripe running to middle of neck. *Cry:* high, often descending *keg-keg-keg. Flight-silhouette:* long, narrow, clearly angled wings; ends like spread fingers; white underparts, head, barred tail. Hunts usually perching near water, hunting some 20 m above the water, hovering then plunging obliquely into water with feet out to catch fish, sometimes going right under. Takes off with flapping wings, shaking water from feathers and holding fish with its head in front. *Nest:* see p. 81. *Habitat:* wooded country with big lakes or rivers. Seldom on coast. Migrant. *Distribution:* N. Scandinavia to Mediterranean; one or two pairs nest every year in Inverness-shire but the bird is also a regular passage migrant.

WHITE-TAILED EAGLE *(Haliaetus albicilla)* Body up to 95 cm, wing-span up to 2.4 m. Brown plumage: head light brown; short, wedge-shaped tail, white in age; yellow beak and legs;

big, broad plank-shaped wings; end-feathers spread. *Food:* fish and water birds; also mammals and carrion. *Nest:* see p. 81. *Habitat:* rocky coasts and remote inland waters. *Distribution:* Ireland, N. Scandinavia south to N. Germany and the Balkans; a vagrant appearing on the east and south coasts of England most years.

*SHORT-TOED EAGLE *(Circaetus gallicus)* Larger than buzzard with longer wings and much larger, owl-like head. Grey-brown upper parts and white underparts. Majestic soaring flight. Hovers. *Cry:* a plaintive *jee. Habitat:* mountains, marshy plains and secluded woods. *Distribution:* south and central Europe.

GOLDEN EAGLE *(Aquila chrysaëtos)* Length 80–95 cm. Wing-span 190–220 cm, tail 35 cm. Female larger than male. Powerful, squat body. Strong limbs. Powerful curved, hooked beak; great feet with very curved, sharp talons; feather-trousers to toes. *Plumage:* at nape a golden sheen; brown "trousers", white root to tail, broad black band at end of tail. Reaches adult colouring when 5–6 years old; majestic, soaring flight, seldom interrupted by wing beats; broad, up-curved primaries. Often hunt in couples, or more. Quarters ground in hunting and pounces on prey. *Food:* hares, marmots, ptarmigan, capercaillie, even a kid or lamb. Will take sick or even dead in preference. Builds eyrie of sticks and twigs, in inaccessible parts under jutting rock, making it up to 1 m high and 1.3–2 m across. March to April, 1–2 dirty white eggs (7.7 × 6 cm) with yellowy and brown spots. Originally inhabitant of the Northern forests and a tree-nester. 120 years ago lived in most great forests of the Continent, now has retreated to inaccessible mountains away from man's persecution. Does *not* attack climbers near nest. Very shy. *Voice:* seldom heard, a sort of yelping *kya. Distribution:* N. Norway to Mediterranean; resident and breeds in Highlands of Scotland, Inner and Outer Hebrides, Ireland and N. England. Elsewhere a rare vagrant.

*IMPERIAL EAGLE *(Aquila heliaca)* Has a pale yellowy crown and nape and a few white feathers on wings. Tail barred with grey. In Iberian peninsula has white shoulders. Big and heavy in appearance. Builds big conspicuous nest in tree top. *Habitat:* plains and marshes. *Distribution:* Spain, Portugal, most of Balkans, Hungary and Roumania.

*BONELLI'S EAGLE *(Hieraëtus fasciatus)* A little smaller than white-tailed. Dark brown upper parts, white patch on back; long tail; creamy underparts. Rapid flight. *Food:* rabbits, birds, etc. *Call:* like goshawk's. *Habitat:* rocky mountain country. *Distribution:* Spain, S. Italy, Greece.

*BOOTED EAGLE *(Hieraëtus pennatus)* Much smaller; square-cut tail. Upper parts dark brown, reddish head, centre parts whitish. Long yellow legs. Rapid, graceful, often weaving flight. *Nest:* in tall trees. *Food:* small birds and animals. *Habitat:* forests, deciduous and pine. *Distribution:* S. Iberian peninsula, N. Balkans, Roumania, Hungary.

Order   STRIGIFORMES Owls   Fig. 34

Family   Strigidae Owls

Largely nocturnal birds of prey with big heads, flat faces and forward-facing eyes. Noiseless flight; mostly large eyes and feathered feet.

BARN OWL *(Tyto alba)* Smaller than crow, but larger than pigeon. Familiar from ghost-like twilight flight; easily overlooked when sitting motionless asleep during day. Lengthy body, long legs; white face with heart-shaped "veil". Upper parts yellowish, finely speckled; white underparts. *Food:* almost only mice, which they will even store; seldom birds (sparrows). *Cry:* loud harsh screech, also a loud snore with hissing and clapping sounds. *Nest:* in buildings, does not construct an actual nest. Several clutches of 4–9 white eggs (3.9 × 3.1 cm), March to June. *Habitat:* farm buildings and human habitations; church towers, etc. *Distribution:* S. Sweden to Mediterranean; resident and widely distributed in Britain but not in great numbers.

LITTLE OWL *(Athene noctua)* Often seen by day sitting on high vantage point watching for prey. The ancient Greeks considered it the bird of the goddess of wisdom (Athene). About the size of a blackbird, plump, has a low forehead that makes it look

flat-headed. Upper parts dull grey-brown; underparts whitish with yellow-brown vertical streaks. Large yellow eyes. Indistinct veil. Low, noiseless flight. *Food:* mice, bats, moths, also birds. No actual nest, but lays in any suitable hollow in rock, old building, hollow tree, etc. April to May, 4–5 pure white eggs (3.5 × 2.9 cm). *Habitat:* orchards, open woods, villages, farms. Resident. *Distribution:* western Europe from Holland to Portugal; introduced into Britain late 19th Century and now a widespread resident in England and Wales.

TAWNY OWL *(Strix aluco)* Definitely nocturnal. In summer sleeps on branch close to trunk; in winter in a hollow tree. Larger than a pigeon; thick, fat head; dull plumage; "veil" round face. Large dark brown eyes. Underparts yellowish brown with dark streaks. Swooping flight. Short, rounded wings. *Cry:* shrill *ke-wick.* *Song:* a deep *hoo-hoo-hoo;* during mating staccato and hollow. *Food:* mice, moles, leverets, birds and the larger insects. *Nest:* in old trees, often a squirrel's without any bed for eggs. February to May, one clutch of 4–5 white eggs (4.3 × 3.9 cm) *Habitat:* woods and parks with old trees. *Distribution:* central Scandinavia to Mediterranean; widely distributed resident in Britain.

TENGMALM'S OWL *(Aegolius funereus)* Similar in size and flight to little owl, but has a larger head, longer, lighter-coloured face. Short legs with long, white feathers. Upper parts grey with large, whitish flecks; crown flecked with white. Underparts light with transverse brown streaks. Very erect posture. Flies at dusk. *Call:* high *poo, poo, poo. Food:* mice, larger insects, also an occasional small bird. *Nest:* in hollow trees; also uses old woodpeckers' nests. April to May, 4–6 white eggs (3.3 × 2.6 cm). *Habitat:* woods, especially mountains. *Distribution:* N. Scandinavia south to mountains regions of France to Bulgaria; rare vagrant to N.E. and E. coasts of England.

LONG-EARED OWL *(Asio otus)* Often in groups outside of breeding season. Size of a pigeon, slim with long feather ear-tufts (at least 3 cm) and a very distinct "veil". Upper parts yellowish-brown speckled with grey-brown. Underparts rusty yellow with dark streaks and delicate bars. Yellow eyes. Often sits on branch close to trunk during day. Agile, swooping flight. *Cry:* a loud, high howl *koo-oo.* Male claps its wings during courtship flight.

Food: mice, frogs, insects, birds. *Nest:* see p. 82. *Habitat:* conifer woods. *Distribution:* Europe generally; widely distributed resident in Britain but becoming scarcer; more common in Ireland.

SHORT-EARED OWL *(Asio flammeus)* Size of a pigeon. Whitish-grey "veil"; short, scarcely visible ear-tufts. Yellower than long-eared and has no bars on underparts. Upper parts rusty yellow with dark brown flecks; underparts yellowish white with dark streaks. Light yellow iris. Grey-black beak. Sits mainly on ground, about which it moves clumsily and only a little. Rolling flight with deep wing beats and much gliding. Also flies by day; swiftly and easily, like a falcon, from which it is distinguished by round head and short tail. Hunts at much greater height than other owls, hovering and stooping. When in danger cowers close to the ground. *Cry:* a bark-like *kee-aw*. *Song:* in courtship flight a deep *boo-boo-boo*, clapping its wings together over its back. *Nest:* on ground, no proper nest. One clutch of 4–8 dull white eggs. Hides by day in reeds and grass; hunts at dusk, mostly mice and larger insects, occasionally birds. Sits on posts, stones, etc. waiting like a cat. *Nest:* see p. 94. *Habitat:* avoids woods. Open marsh lands. Partial migrant. *Distribution:* Iceland and N. Scandinavia south to France and Sicily; resident and also winter visitor to Britain, nesting in Wales, England (south of Lancashire), Scotland and Ireland.

EAGLE OWL *(Bubo bubo)* Body 66–71 cm. The largest and rarest of the owls. Two erectile tufts on head looking like ears. Upper parts rust-brown with black-brown flame-shaped streaks; breast yellowy-brown with black streaks. Large eyes with golden irises. Flies close to the ground in evening and night. *Call:* a loud deep *ooo-hu*. *Food:* mice, but also takes any game it puts up, birds, hares, partridges, even fawns. *Nest:* in niches in rock, also on ground, a flat nest in thick woods. April 2–3 white eggs (6 × 5 cm). *Habitat:* crags and mountains in great forests. *Distribution:* Arctic Circle south to Pyrenees, Sicily and Greece; very rare vagrant to Britain.

SCOPS OWL *(Otus scops)* A little larger than pygmy owl; inconspicuous ear-tufts. Grey-brown streaky plumage. Largely nocturnal. *Call:* monotonous *kyew*. *Food:* mainly insects. *Nest:* in holes. *Habitat:* near human dwellings. *Distribution:* most of central and southern Europe; rare vagrant to Britain.

PIGEONS AND DOVES

Order   COLUMBIFORMES Pigeons

Family   COLUMBIDAE Pigeons

WOOD PIGEON *(Columba palumbus)* The largest pigeon. Has broad white band across wing and small white patch on each side of green-purple neck, which in old birds becomes a ring. Head and upper parts grey-blue. Claps its wings as it takes off. Recognisable in flight by white band in middle of big, long tail and white on neck and wings. *Call: coo-coo-roo-coo-coo. Food:* seeds of pines, firs, acorns, beechnuts, fruit, berries, grain and greenstuff. *Nest:* see p. 82. *Habitat:* all woods, farmland, etc. *Distribution:* Europe generally; widely distributed and resident in Britain.

TURTLE DOVE *(Streptopelia turtur)* Small, shy, colourful pigeon. Slim and neat; rounded black tail with white tip. Upper parts red-brown with black in middle of feathers. Sides of neck black and white stripes. Front of neck, crop, upper breast wine-red, rest of underparts bluey-red grey becoming grey-white. *Call:* crooning *roor-r-r* from tree top. *Food:* seeds of pines, birches, insects, weed seeds. *Nest:* see p. 82. *Habitat:* woods, porkland, thickets. *Distribution:* Europe generally; summer visitor breeding chiefly in the south, east and Midlands; small numbers in Scotland and Ireland.

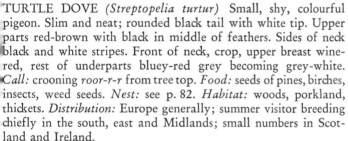

STOCK DOVE *(Columba oenas)* Very shy. Couples stick together. Smaller and darker than wood pigeon; no white on feathers. Wing bars blue-green and black. Crop area wine-red; sides of neck metallic green. Whistle of wings audible in more rapid flight. *Call:* monotonous *oo-roo-oo. Nest:* in holes in trees. April to June 3 clutches of 2 white eggs (3.7 × 2.8 cm). *Food:* all kinds of grain. *Habitat:* woods in old trees. Partial migrant. *Distribution:* Europe generally except far north; local but widely distributed resident in England, Wales and Ireland; spreading its range in Scotland.

ROCK DOVE *(Columba livia)* Has whitish rump, white beneath wings and two broad black bands over secondaries. Blue-grey plumage with green and lilac on neck. Flight low and faster than wood pigeon's. *Nest:* in crevices or caves in rock. *Habitat:* sea cliffs and rocky places. *Distribution:* southern Europe, Brittany, etc.; resident but decreasing in Scotland and Ireland.

COLLARED DOVE *(Streptopelia decaoto)* Larger than a turtle dove. Pale grey-brown upper parts with paler head; soft grey below. Narrow black line at the back of neck. Call of male *coo-cooo-cook. Nest:* in trees, especially conifers. Eggs white and glossy, two in number; two broods. *Food:* grain, seeds, fruit. *Habitat:* near human habitations, gardens, parks, chicken-runs. *Distribution:* originally an Asiatic bird but since 1900 it has spread from the Balkans right across Europe and is found in most countries adjoining North Sea; reached Britain in 1955 and has now become resident in many counties.

Order   GALLIFORMES   Gallinaceous Birds

Family   TETRAONIDAE   Grouse

Nostrils hidden by feathers. Legs almost wholly feathered (protection against cold). Mostly polygamous. Males have magnificent plumage.

CAPERCAILLIE *(Tetrao urogallus)* Male up to 112 cm, female up to 78 cm. Very shy. Rounded, fan-shaped tail. Male has bright red "rose" of skin round its eye. Yellow beak. Crown and throat black; neck dark grey; back brown; steely grey breast. Females inconspicuous black-brown and rust-yellow. Noisy flight, usually only for a short distance. *Call:* female, a pheasant-like *kok-kok.* From March or April to May cock begins to display at first light: strange, soft 4-phased song *telac-telac,* getting quicker and quicker and ending with explosive *titock* like a "pop"; then a soft "whetting" like sharpening a scythe. All accompanied by posturing: stretching up head, puffing out feathers, drooping wings, fanning the tail, excited tripping up and down or turning in circles. *Food:* berries, insects, worms; in winter pine needles, buds and shrubs. *Nest:* see p. 91. *Habitat:* wooded hills and mountains, where there is plenty of undergrowth and berry-bearing bushes. *Distribution:* coniferous forests of N. and E. Europe; resident which became extinct in Britain *c.* 1750 and was reintroduced in early part of 19th Century. Breeds in several Scottish counties.

BLACK GROUSE *(Lyrurus tetrix)* Body 60–65 cm, wing 30 cm, tail 20 cm. Female (greyhen) 15 cm shorter. Male (blackcock) has glossy blue-black plumage, lyreshaped tail; white wing bar and under-tail coverts. Greyhen rust brown band and flecked with black; white wing bar. Both have red wattle over the eye. Often on ground; roosts in trees. Blundering flight. Both sexes assemble in spring at special display grounds called "leks". Call of sociable greyhen a short whistle or soft *back back*. Courtship song of blackcock, in evening and early morning: a strange "whetting" audible for a considerable distance, then rapid gobbling from some vantage point. *Food:* berries, buds; insects, worms and snails for the chicks in summer. *Nest:* p. 91. *Habitat:* trees on or near moorland, rocky heather-clad hills. *Distribution:* Europe generally; resident but greatly reduced in numbers in N. Devon, Somerset, Wales, English border counties, north Midlands and Scotland.

*HAZEL HEN *(Tetrastes bonasia)* Size of a partridge. Rust-red flecked with white and brown, short tail. White bands down side of throat and on scapulars. Male has black throat bordered with white; female whitish throat. Black band on grey tail conspicuous in flight. Perches in trees. *Call:* high clear whistle: *tsissi-tseri-tsi, tsi, tsi.* *Nest:* see p. 91. *Habitat:* mixed woods of oak, birch, alder, beech. Heath and moor. *Distribution:* Scandinavia and eastern Europe.

RED GROUSE *(Lagopus scoticus)* A little larger than hazel hen. Short wings, dark nut-brown plumage. Legs white feathers. Red wattle above eye. Rapid flight; whirring wing beats and long glides on downcurved wings. *Call:* kowk-ock-ock-ock. Mating call of male, *go-bak-bak-bak-bak.* *Nest:* on ground among heather, bracken, grass. One clutch of 6–10 creamy or pinkish-buff eggs speckled and mottled with reddish-brown. *Habitat:* Great Britain and Ireland, usually above 300 m on moorland. Probably a race of the following species.

*WILLOW GROUSE *(Lagopus lagopus)* Very similar to ptarmigan, but found at lower altitudes, though above those of hazel hen. Confined to Norway, N. Sweden, Finland and Eastern Baltic.

PTARMIGAN *(Lagopus mutus)* See p. 99.

Family   PHASIANIDAE   Partridges, Quails, Pheasants   Fig. 29

Nostrils uncovered; unfeathered legs.

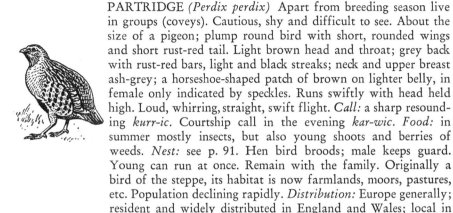

PARTRIDGE *(Perdix perdix)* Apart from breeding season live
in groups (coveys). Cautious, shy and difficult to see. About the
size of a pigeon; plump round bird with short, rounded wings
and short rust-red tail. Light brown head and throat; grey back
with rust-red bars, light and black streaks; neck and upper breast
ash-grey; a horseshoe-shaped patch of brown on lighter belly, in
female only indicated by speckles. Runs swiftly with head held
high. Loud, whirring, straight, swift flight. *Call:* a sharp resounding *kurr-ic.* Courtship call in the evening *kar-wic. Food:* in
summer mostly insects, but also young shoots and berries of
weeds. *Nest:* see p. 91. Hen bird broods; male keeps guard.
Young can run at once. Remain with the family. Originally a
bird of the steppe, its habitat is now farmlands, moors, pastures,
etc. Population declining rapidly. *Distribution:* Europe generally;
resident and widely distributed in England and Wales; local in
Scotland and Ireland.

RED-LEGGED PARTRIDGE *(Alectoris rufa)* Very similar to
partridge, but slightly larger and has red beak and legs, also
long white stripe above the eye. Wings barred with reddish-
brown, black and white. *Call: chuck, chuck-er* or *tschrek. Distribution:* western and south-western France, Iberian peninsula.
Switzerland and Italy; resident in S. and E. England, north to
Yorkshire, the Midlands and N. Wales. Almost indistinguishable
from it, except by its distinctive call of *whit-whit-whit,* is the
ROCK PARTRIDGE *(Alectoris graecca),* which is confined to
stony hillsides and wooded high slopes. *Nest:* among rocks.
Distribution: Italy, Switzerland, Austria, Balkans.

QUAIL *(Coturnix coturnix)* More often heard than seen. Shy,
ground-dweller. Stays still during day and begins to move about
towards sunset. The size of a thrush, it has a short, rounded tail;
back is partridge-coloured; underparts yellowish with light and
dark streaks on flanks; long cream-coloured streak above the
eye. Male has a black patch on his throat. Runs with quick
tripping gait and head pulled in. Quick, whirring flight. Reluctant to fly longer distances. Courtship call is 3-syllable *quic,
quic-ic. Food:* insects, tips of leaves, seeds especially of weeds.
Nest: see p. 92. Young do not stay in nest. *Habitat:* fields and
rough pasture. *Distribution:* Europe generally except N. Scandinavia; rare summer visitor mainly to southern Britain.

PHEASANT *(Phasianus colchicus)* Length 80 cm, wings 25 cm, tail 40 cm. Head and neck green shot with blue. Breast, belly and flanks reddish-brown with purple sheen. Female uniform yellow-brown with dark mottling. *Call:* unmusical crow, like *karrk-kok*. Feeds on ground: insects, buds, shoots, etc. Polygamous. Roosts at night. Originating in the coastal areas of Caspian Sea, the name comes from the river Phavis in the land of Colchis. Introduced into Europe by the Greeks and Romans because of its decorative and culinary excellence. *Nest:* see p. 92. *Habitat:* woods and farm lands, shrubberies, etc. *Distribution:* introduced to most European countries for sport; its introduction to Britain probably dates from Roman times and it is now generally distributed.

A variant *(Phasianus c. torquatus),* introduced later from China, has a white ring round its neck, but is otherwise identical. The two often cross.

Order   GRUIFORMES   Cranes, Rails, Bustards

Family   OTIDIDAE   Bustards

GREAT BUSTARD *(Otis tarda)* Length 1 m; weight 14–16 kg. Strikingly large, very shy terrestrial bird of turkey-like appearance and ways; larger than a goose. Thick, long neck, large head, wedge-shaped beak of medium length; very strong legs, 3 toes; large, slightly hollow wings. Head and neck light grey upper parts reddish-brown barred with black; underparts white; breast brownish; white wing patch. Male has a "moustache" of whitish bristles. Female lacks brown on breast and is altogether smaller and less colourful. Slow, sedate walk with head up; runs swiftly when alarmed. *Flight:* goose-like with slow wing beats; takes two or three bounds before taking off. In flight neck and legs are outstretched. Wings have black tips. *Food:* greenstuff and grain; as a chick insects. *Nest:* in tall corn, scratching a shallow depression. Lays 2–3 eggs. *Habitat:* flat, open, treeless farmlands; steppe. *Distribution:* breeds in Portugal, S. Spain and E. Europe; died out in Britain over 100 years ago and now very rare vagrant.

LITTLE BUSTARD *(Otis tetrax)* Less than half the size of the great bustard. The male has a conspicuous black and white collar; blue-grey face. Flight is swift with quick, whistling wing beats. In flight looks almost white. Flies higher than great bustard. Usually in small flocks. *Habitat:* the same as for great bustard. *Distribution:* France, Spain, Portugal and eastern Europe; occasional vagrant to Britain.

RAILS   Figs. 33 and 38

Family   RALLIDAE   Crakes, Rails and Coots

SPOTTED CRAKE *(Porzana porzana)* Size of a thrush; dull brown, dainty marsh bird; close-lying plumage; very short tail; beak shorter than head, pointed, yellowish, with orange root; yellowy-green legs. Upper parts dark olive brown, strikingly streaked and spotted with white; grey breast with white speckles. Female is smaller and less colourful. Swims and dives; poor, reluctant flight with dangling legs. *Call:* a high *quilt, quilt. Nest:* see p. 96. *Habitat:* swampy places generally, ponds, rivers, etc. *Distribution:* Europe generally; rare summer visitor and passage migrant to Britain and has bred in several counties.

LITTLE CRAKE *(Porzana parva)* Smaller than spotted crake but very similar; has a few white streaks on under wing coverts, uniform slaty underparts; green beak with red root and yellow tip. Under tail coverts dark ashen-grey barred with white. Red iris. Behaviour and flight same as spotted crake. *Call:* a clear *quek, quek,* repeated several times. *Food:* insects, worms, molluscs, etc. *Nest:* see p. 97. *Habitat:* boggy meadows, reedy dykes, ponds. *Distribution:* central and eastern Europe; vagrant to Britain mainly on south and east coasts.

BAILLON'S CRAKE *(Porzana pusilla)* Smallest of European marsh birds, roughly the size of a lark. Very similar to the little crake, but its beak has no red on it, and its upper parts are streaked with white; its flanks strongly barred with black and white. *Call:* quicker and more jarring than that of little crake. *Nest:* see p. 97. Behaviour, etc. as little crake. *Distribution:* Germany and south to Mediterranean; vagrant to Britain.

WATER RAIL *(Rallus aquaticus)* Size of a thrush, dull grey-brown bird with long legs, long, slender beak somewhat squeezed in at the sides; arched wings, but short and blunt; very short tail. Upper parts dark brown with dark mottling; face, throat and breast bluey-grey; flanks strikingly barred white and black; red beak with black tip; reddish-brown legs. Slips agilely through reeds, often through shallow water; swims with ease, dives well;

nods its head as it swims and flicks its short tail upwards; avoids large open expanses; takes cover half flying, half pattering across water, if hotly pursued will dive. Poor, low flight and never flies far; stretches wings far out and moves them in slow beats. Very secretive and skulking. More nocturnal than diurnal. *Food:* insects, worms, snails, also reeds and bits of green plants. *Nest:* see p. 96. *Habitat:* reed and osier beds, overgrown water generally. Migrant. *Distribution:* Europe as far north as S. Scandinavia; resident and breeds in most marshy areas of Britain.

CORNCRAKE *(Crex crex)* Solitary, skulking bird of the dusk and twilight, distinctive by its peculiar *rerrp-rerrp* cry. A little smaller than a partridge. Short, strong beak, medium length legs, rough-shaped wings, short soft tail, smooth plumage. Upper parts black mottling on brown ground; throat ash-grey, sides of neck and flanks browny-grey with rufous brown bars on flanks, rust brown wings. Quick, straight low flight with dangling legs, only over short distances. Not easy to get it to take wing. *Food:* insects, worms, small seeds. *Nest:* see p. 92. *Habitat:* flat country, standing crops, meadows etc. *Distribution:* Europe generally; summer visitor to Britain but becoming scarce except in parts of Ireland and Scotland.

COOT *(Fulica atra)* 41 cm. Smaller than a duck. Plump, black water bird with bare, white frontal shield; beak white, pointed, of medium length. Red eyes; grey-green, long, strong legs; toes have double-edged lobes. Rides high on water; nods its head as it swims rather slowly; stays in one place, often with others. Leaps a little way into air in order to dive in head first; reappears at same spot. Does not remain submerged for long. Patters across surface when taking cover or in order to take off. Reluctant to fly. *Call:* a loud *tewk.* Sociable. *Food:* worms, snails, insects, aquatic plants, frog and fish spawn. Couples stay together and build nest together, take turns to brood. *Nest:* see p. 97. *Habitat:* ponds and slow-flowing fresh water. *Distribution:* Europe generally; resident and widely distributed in Britain.

MOORHEN *(Gallinula chloropus)* Dainty, blackish bird the size of a partridge with a bare, red frontal shield; red base to wedge-shaped beak which has yellow tip. Yellow-green legs with red band. White streak on flanks. Short tail. Runs agilely over leaves of water-lily, etc. While swimming holds its tail high with end well above water. Swims easily and gracefully, nodding its head and jerking its tail. Will dive and swim under water and re-emerge elsewhere. Heavy, fluttering slow flight, usually low with trailing legs and neck outstretched. Takes off after a long pattering and flopping run. Hides by day, emerging in early morning and evening. *Nest:* see p. 97. *Habitat:* ponds, slow rivers, marshes. *Distribution:* Europe generally; resident and common in Britain.

| Family | Gruidae Cranes | Fig. 32 |

Large terrestrial birds like herons. Inner secondaries so elongated as to droop over tail. Long neck and legs, extended in flight. Trumpet-like voices. Migrate in V or line formation.

CRANE *(Grus grus)* 1.2 m. Conspicuous by long pinions that hang below the tail proper as a black feather duster tail. Beak shorter than that of heron or stork. Long neck, powerful legs; bare well above heel. Wader's feet, only the middle and external fore-toes webbed. Slate grey plumage, curving white streak on side of black head and neck. Male has red crown. Neck and feet outstretched in flight. Continual trumpeting cry while in flight, serving to keep individuals grouped. Feeds in early morning and evening in meadows, fields. *Food:* berries, grain, peas, insects, worms, mice. *Nest:* see p. 95. *Habitat:* river banks, lagoons, steppe. *Distribution:* Scandinavia and Germany east to the Volga; isolated colonies in S. E. Europe; vagrant to Britain and has wintered occasionally.

| Order | PHOENICOPTERIFORMES |

| Family | Phoenicopteridae Flamingo |

FLAMINGO *(Phoenicopterus ruber)* Very large, very slender wader with extra long legs and neck and beak curved almost at a right angle. Neck and legs outstretched in flight. Plumage white and pink, black outer flight feathers. Sedate gait. Gregarious. *Habitat:* shallow coastal lagoons, flooded areas, lakes and mudflats. *Distribution:* breeds now in S. France, and possibly S. Spain; very rare vagrant to Britain.

Order   CICONIIFORMES

Family   CICONIIDAE   Storks   Fig. 32

WHITE STORK *(Ciconia ciconia)* White plumage with black flight feathers; long, red beak and legs. Very long, strong legs for wading. Outer and middle toe webbed half way up. Feathers on upper breast longer, larger and jutting. Slow, deliberate walk. Perches in trees or on houses, often on one leg. When perched head is drawn in slightly. Glides and flies easily and often at great heights; slow wing beats. Needs one or two leaps to take off from ground. Neck and legs outstretched in flight; does not fly in any special order. *Call:* a hoarse hiss; claps its beak to express its feelings. *Food:* grasshoppers, snails, beetles, larvae of dragon-flies swallowed straight down, larger creatures first killed with a quick blow from its beak: squirrels, lizards, snakes, mice, moles, salamanders, eggs of ground-nesting birds; then swallowed or taken in pouch to young. *Nest:* mostly on buildings, seldom in trees, 2 m wide and 1 m or more deep, made of stout branches, twigs, reeds, straw lined with earth. Used many years running, new material being added. Mid-April 4–5 white eggs (7.3 × 5.2 cm). *Habitat:* marshes, water-meadows. *Distribution:* Baltic to Mediterranean but numbers on the decline; rare vagrant to England, usually in East Anglia and S. England.

BLACK STORK *(Ciconia nigra)* Head, neck and upper parts browny-black shot with a golden green and purple; underparts white; beak and legs red; otherwise like the white stork. Eats almost only fish. Builds nest of branches and twigs in a tall tree, sometimes using an old nest as foundation. End of April lays 3–5 white eggs (6.6 × 5 cm). *Habitat:* lonely forest areas with bog or marsh. Keeps away from humans. *Distribution:* Spain, Portugal, the Baltic and E. Europe; very rare vagrant to Britain, mainly on east and south coasts.

Family   PLATALEIDAE

SPOONBILL *(Platalea leucorodia)* Length about 87 cm; white colouring and characteristic spatulate bill. In flight both neck and legs are stretched out. Legs black. Silent bird. *Food:* small fish, molluscs, crustacea etc. *Habitat:* marshes, mud flats; breeds in reedy lagoons. *Distribution:* Holland, Denmark, S. Spain and south and east from Austria. Regular visitor to East Anglia, often in small numbers, and to other coastal areas.

GLOSSY IBIS *(Plegadis falcinellus)* Length about 55 cm. Curved bill like that of curlew. Dark purplish-brown plumage shot with green and purple. Flies with neck and legs extended. *Voice:* a grating *gra-a-k*. *Food:* molluscs, worms, insects. *Habitat:* reedy lagoons but feeds on mud-flats. *Distribution:* western Mediterranean and S. E. Europe; vagrant to Britain occurring mainly on S., E. and S. W. coasts of England.

Family   ARDEIDAE   Herons   Fig. 32

HERON *(Ardea cinerea)* Length 90 cm; long neck, medium length yellow, pointed beak; long legs bare far above heel; ash-grey plumage; black spots on front of neck; long, black crest feathers. Large flight feathers black. Legs are stretched out behind in flight, neck drawn in in shape of S. Slow, deep wing beats. *Call:* a hoarse *frarnk*. *Food:* fish up to 20 cm in length; frogs, snakes, shellfish, beetles, mice, moles, snails, worms, which it conveys to babies in a roomy pouch. *Nest:* see p. 81. Nests in colonies (heronries), where ground and trees are white with excrement and there is a smell of fish in the air. February to March 3–5 greenish-blue eggs. Colonies sited in woods near water. Hunts in ponds, ditches, streams, shallow rivers, mud flats. Partial migrant. *Distribution:* Europe generally; resident and widely distributed in Britain.

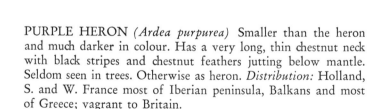

PURPLE HERON *(Ardea purpurea)* Smaller than the heron and much darker in colour. Has a very long, thin chestnut neck with black stripes and chestnut feathers jutting below mantle. Seldom seen in trees. Otherwise as heron. *Distribution:* Holland, S. and W. France most of Iberian peninsula, Balkans and most of Greece; vagrant to Britain.

LITTLE EGRET *(Egretta garzetta)* Smaller again than purple heron. Snow-white with black beak and legs, yellow feet. *Habitat:* marshes, lagoons, swamps. *Distribution:* Balkans, parts of S. France, Portugal; vagrant to Britain.

SQUACCO HERON *(Ardeola ralloides)* Smaller than little egret. Stocky and thick in the neck. Plumage pale brown, white wings, long crest. Dark tip to beak. Greeny legs. *Nest:* singly or in scattered groups. *Habitat* etc.: as little egret. *Distribution:* S. and S. E. Europe; rare vagrant to Britain.

BITTERN *(Botaurus stellaris)* Brown, heron-like inhabitant of reed-beds. Stocky body the size of a hen's; long neck made to look short by thick soft plumage on it; narrow, pointed beak, the length of the bird's head; legs feathered almost to heel, large toes, broad wings; short tail. Colouring that of the reed beds: ochre-yellow ground streaked and marked with a rich black-brown. Slow, deliberate gait; runs stooping with head drawn in; moves through reeds without touching ground, clutching the reeds with its long toes. Slow, noiseless flight, always moving wings. Courtship call of the male a dull repeated *woomp,* like the bellowing of a bull, audible up to a mile away. *Food:* frogs, water-beetles, leeches, worms, caterpillars, small fish, even mice and young birds. Mostly rests by day. When frightened assumes camouflaging "stick" posture with feathers drawn close to rigid body, head thrown back, neck outstretched with beak pointing vertically upwards. The whole is an excellent imitation of old reeds with shadows on them. Bird of the twilight. Only hunts at night. *Nest:* see p. 96. *Habitat:* reed beds. Migrant. *Distribution:* Europe generally; resident and breeds in East Anglia, N. Lancashire and elsewhere.

LITTLE BITTERN *(Ixobrychus minutus)* Size of a pigeon with very slim body, powerful wedge-shaped beak, long legs feathered to the foot-joint; relatively long wings and short tail. Colouring that of reed beds. Male has top of head, back, mantle and secondaries black shot with green; wing coverts rust yellow, underparts yellowish-white with a few long reddish-brown streaks; yellowish beak; green legs. In female the entire breast is streaked with brown, looking like reeds. In danger adopts "stick" posture like the bittern. Climbs agilely in reeds, clutching 3 at a time with its long toes. *Call:* a not very loud or deep *ump pump.* Bird of twilight, except in breeding season. *Food:* frogs, small fish, worms, insects; will rob nests. *Nest:* see p. 96. Very low flight with quick wing beats. *Habitat:* reed beds or water overgrown with tall bushes; small ponds and marshes. *Distribution:* Europe generally; vagrant to Britain in early summer and autumn.

Order CHARADRIIFORMES Marsh Birds – Waders Fig. 33

Family   HAEMATOPODIDAE Oystercatchers

OYSTERCATCHER *(Haematopus ostralegus)* Length about 43 cm. Striking black and white plumage, pink legs and long, orange-red bill. Characteristically a bird of sea-shores. *Call:* a loud and shrill *kleeep* and sometimes a short *pic-pic-pic. Food:* crustacea, molluscs, worms. *Nest:* in shingle or on rock with or without nesting material; 3 or 4 eggs. *Distribution:* Europe generally; in Britain present all through the year; breeds mainly on north and west coasts of England, throughout Scotland, Ireland and Wales.

Family   CHARADRIIDAE Plovers

LAPWING *(Vanellus vanellus)* Size of a pigeon with greeny-black and white plumage and long erectile, upward curved crest with twin points. Steep forehead, black beak, long narrow wings with blunt ends. Dirty dark red wader's legs somewhat thickened at heel joint and half-feathered. Top of head, crest, front of neck, top of breast and end of tail a brilliant black; back dark green shot with blue and purple; sides of neck and underparts contrasting white; under tail coverts dark rust-yellow. Female has shorter crest and neck flecked in front with white and black. Delicate, graceful gait. Twisting and turning agile flight; slow wing beats in acrobatic courtship flight; makes a dull thrumming sound like *woowoowoo* with its wings. *Call:* a clear *kee-wi* or *kee-r-wee. Nest:* see p. 93. *Habitat:* farm lands, moors, marshes and estuaries. *Distribution:* Europe generally; resident and generally distributed in Britain.

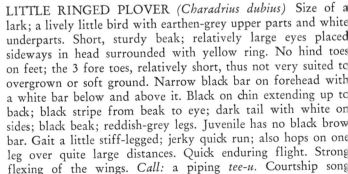

LITTLE RINGED PLOVER *(Charadrius dubius)* Size of a lark; a lively little bird with earthen-grey upper parts and white underparts. Short, sturdy beak; relatively large eyes placed sideways in head surrounded with yellow ring. No hind toes on feet; the 3 fore toes, relatively short, thus not very suited to overgrown or soft ground. Narrow black bar on forehead with a white bar below and above it. Black on chin extending up to back; black stripe from beak to eye; dark tail with white on sides; black beak; reddish-grey legs. Juvenile has no black brow bar. Gait a little stiff-legged; jerky quick run; also hops on one leg over quite large distances. Quick enduring flight. Strong flexing of the wings. *Call:* a piping *tee-u.* Courtship song specially in late summer. *Food:* snails, insects, worms, larvae. *Nest:* see p. 99. *Habitat:* gravelly banks especially of rivers and lower reaches of streams. Not marshes. Flocks in winter. Migrant. *Distribution:* Europe generally; in Britain now a regular summer visitor which has spread in small numbers to most English counties north to Yorkshire, frequently nesting in gravel pits.

RINGED PLOVER *(Charadrius hiaticula)* Slightly larger than the above and very similar to it, distinguished by broader band across breast, white wing bars (conspicuous in flight); orange-yellow beak with black tip; orange-yellow legs. *Call:* a flute-like *too-li,* quickly repeated in rocking courtship flight. *Food:* small insects, molluscs. *Nest:* a mere hollow scraped out by female in some gravelly site; 3–4 yellowish eggs spotted with dark brown. One clutch, April to June. *Distribution:* Europe generally; resident and breeds in most sandy coastal areas.

GREY PLOVER *(Charadrius squatarola)* Length 28 cm. Similar to golden plover but slightly larger and distinguished by darker wings, whitish rump and white bar on wing. *Call:* tee-oo-ee. *Food:* molluscs, worms etc. *Habitat:* estuaries and mud flats. *Distribution:* breeds Arctic Russia; winter visitor and passage migrant to Britain on east and south coasts, less on west coasts; Ireland all coasts.

GOLDEN PLOVER *(Charadrius apricarius)* Slightly smaller than a lapwing; has dark upper parts richly spotted with gold. A northern variety has jet-black face and underparts clearly separated by wide white stripe running from forehead, down neck and sides to flanks. In the southern variety the dividing lines are blurred. *Call:* a liquid *tlui.* *Nest:* on ground on a moor. 4 buff eggs heavily blotched with dark brown, very pointed. May. *Habitat:* moors, fields, mud flats, estuaries. *Distribution:* Europe generally; resident breeding in N. Pennines and northward throughout Scotland, Wales and (more rarely) in Ireland.

KENTISH PLOVER *(Charadrius alexandrinus)* Same size as little ringed plover but has a blackish beak and legs and a small dark patch on each side high up on the breast. Has a narrow white wing bar, and male bird has a narrow stripe of white above its eyes and a rufous crown. *Call:* poo-eet or *wit-wit-wit.*

Nest: on shingle. *Habitat:* mainly coastal. *Distribution:* S. Scan
dinavia to Mediterranean; rare passage migrant on south an
east coasts of England.

TURNSTONE *(Arenaria interpres)* Smaller than lapwing
Plumage tortoise-shell; legs orange, beak black, sturdy an
pointed. Underparts white with broad dark band across breast
Turns over stones etc. when searching for food, sandhoppers
shellfish, etc. *Call:* a staccato *tuk-a-tuk. Nest:* a mere hollow i
the ground. 4 glossy, pale green eggs (3.8 × 3.0 m) flecked wit
brown. *Habitat:* coasts, mainly pebbly. *Distribution:* breeds i
coastal areas in Scandinavia and Baltic; resident on all coast
in Britain but does not breed.

DOTTEREL *(Charadrius morinellus)* Slightly smaller than th
turnstone. Not shy. It has a white band between brown breas
and orange-brown underparts; broad white eye stripes joined o
nape in a V. *Call: titi-ri-titi-ri. Nest:* in a hollow in the ground
3 olive-yellow, pear-shaped eggs (4.0 × 3.0 cm) flecked wit
black and brown. *Distribution:* Arctic Europe, Scandinavia an
high ground in central Europe; summer visitor to Britain in smal
numbers and breeds in Cairngorm and Grampian Mountains an
possibly in Cumberland and Westmorland.

Family   SCOLOPACIDAE   Sandpipers, Curlews etc.

COMMON SANDPIPER *(Tringa hypoleucos)* Size of a lark
upper parts olive-brown with a shimmer of green and dar
arrow-shaped streaks and white edging to the feathers; whit
underparts; neck and breast faintly streaked; brown iris, grey
black beak. Holds body horizontal; likes to perch on eminences
quick run; trots rather than walks, all the time flicking its tail
Easy, swift flight, usually low over water; wings curve back
In flight the white patches on pinions are conspicuous. Shallow
wing beats. Zigzag courtship flight. If necessary will plunge int
water; swims rapidly, or dives, paddling quickly with wing
and emerging at a distance. *Call:* shrill *wee-wee* as it rises. *Food*
insects, small worms; takes prey on the wing, off leaves or from
ground. *Nest:* see p. 99. *Habitat:* rivers, streams and lakes wit
sandy shores and plenty of bushes. River estuaries. *Distribution*
Europe generally; summer visitor to Britain breeding mainly i
N. England, Midlands, Scotland, parts of Wales and Ireland.

REDSHANK *(Tringa totanus)* Slim wader the size of a pigeon.
It has red legs, a long, straight red beak with a black tip. Female
is larger than the male. Hind toes prevent its feet sinking into
mud. A distinct web between outer and middle toe. Upper parts
greyish-brown flecked and streaked with darker colour; underparts white with roundish brown spots on sides, head and breast.
Winter plumage: deep grey upper parts; underparts more strongly
flecked. Takes very large steps, nodding its head and tail. Light,
agile flight. In the air its back, rump and back edge of wings show
white. Wades in shallow water. Swims well. *Call:* a pure, flute-
like *tleu-hu-hu. Nest:* see p. 94. *Food:* aquatic insects, larvae,
worms, molluscs. *Habitat:* lakes and marshes, moors, estuaries.
Distribution: N. Scandinavia south to S. Spain; resident and
breeding in most counties of England, Scotland and Ireland,
except in the south.

RUFF *(Philomachus pugnax)* Larger than a blackbird with long
legs, straight soft beak; leg slim and bare to well above heel;
middle and outer toes webbed. Winter plumage dull brown-grey
with brown-black flecks on upper parts; belly white. In spring
male has a "ruff" of big erectile feathers; eartufts of black, white,
brown or chestnut; well developed "warts" on face conspicuous
by their colourfulness. Ruff and warts disappear with the moult.
Female (reeve) is much smaller: has no ruff; upper parts a
reddish-grey with dark mottling; underparts more or less white.
Gait: a graceful walk. Very swift, often soaring flight with easy,
swift, wheeling turns. Sociable; becomes very lively as night falls.
Feeds in evening and morning on insects, larvae, worms; in
autumn and winter also seeds. *Nest:* see p. 94. *Habitat:* inland
marshes, lake shores, estuaries, tundra. *Distribution:* N. Scandinavia south to W. France and Hungary; passage migrant to
Britain from March to October but some now winter here.

GREEN SANDPIPER *(Tringa ochropus)* Shy, solitary bird with
conspicuous black and white looking plumage. Size of a thrush,
slim, long, beak and legs, its upper parts are deep black-brown
with light spots; white rump and tail, which latter has 3 or 4
bands of black across the end of it. Underparts white with dark
spots on head and sides of belly; underneath of wings blackish.
Legs green. Jerky movement of head and tail. *Call:* a high *titti-
looi, titti-looi;* warning cry: *tluitt, weet weet. Food:* worms,
insects, small snails. *Nest:* on the bushy banks of small lakes or
ponds. See p. 82. *Habitat:* marshes, lakes, streams, seldom on
coast. *Distribution:* breeds from Arctic Circle south to Denmark
and S. Russia; passage migrant to Britain.

WOOD SANDPIPER *(Tringa glareola)* Similar in appearance and habits to green sandpiper, but is much smaller, being only the size of a lark. Upper parts black-brown, in spring speckled with white. Underwings white with brown flecks; tail white with 8–10 bars of black. When flushed cry is a shrill *chiff-iff-iff Nest:* see p. 95. *Habitat:* marshes, lakes, tundra. *Distribution:* N. Norway south to Holland and central Russia; passage migrant to Britain.

GREENSHANK *(Tringa nebularia)* Slightly larger than the redshank, but its plumage is altogether paler and it has green legs which stick out well beyond the tail when flying. It has no white wing bar. Its beak turns up very slightly. Its call is not so shrill as the redshank's *tew-tew-tew*. Otherwise its habits, etc. are the same as the redshank's. *Distribution:* north and central Scandinavia, Baltic states, N. Russia; summer visitor and passage migrant to Britain, nesting in small numbers in N. Scotland.

Family   RECURVIROSTRIDAE   Avocets and Stilts

AVOCET *(Recurvirostra avosetta)* Length 42 cm. Distinguished by long, slender upward curving bill, lead-blue legs and black and white plumage. Legs protrude well beyond tail when flying. Graceful, quick walk. Feeds in shallow water moving head from side to side, but will also wade deep or swim. Breeds in colonies among scrub near water, on sand banks, low islands or in water meadows. *Habitat:* estuaries, mudflats, etc. *Distribution:* breeds locally on coasts of North Sea and Baltic, inland in central Europe and on the Mediterranean and Black Seas; in Britain breeds on Havergate Island and other parts of Suffolk; some birds winter in Devon and Cornwall.

BLACK-WINGED STILT *(Himantopus himantopus)* Has enormously long pink legs protruding some 16 cm beyond tail when in flight. Upper parts black, underparts white. In summer back of male's head is black. Deliberate gait taking long steps. Very nervous. *Nest:* in colonies, building on tussocks or mud in shallow water. *Habitat:* wet marshes, lagoons, flood-waters. *Distribution:* S. E. and S. W. Europe north to central France and Hungary; rare vagrant to Britain on south and east coasts of England.

Family   BURHINIDAE   Stone Curlews

STONE CURLEW *(Burhinus oedicnemus)* Large and rather ungainly bird with distinctive round head; has large yellow eyes, short yellow and black beak, stout yellowy legs, plumage streaks of pale brown and white. Two white bars on wings. Flattens on ground to hide; low flight with slow wing beats and occasional long glides. *Habitat:* bare heather and open, stony, barren ground, sometimes marshes and cultivated land. *Distribution:* Baltic to Mediterranean; summer visitor to Britain, breeding sparingly in S. and E. England.

Family   SCOLOPACIDAE   Snipe   Fig. 33

SNIPE *(Gallinago gallinago)* Roughly the size of a thrush; brown, nocturnal bird of the marshes with a long, straight beak, somewhat thickened at the tip. Domed head, eyes placed well back. Upper parts brown-black with broad, rust-yellow lengthwise streaks from head down; underparts white, throat and breast grey flecked with brown. (Colouring of the ground.) *Flight:* stormy take off in initially zigzag flight. Beak points downwards when flying. *Call:* when flushed a hoarse *schape. Song:* a *chic-ka, chic-ka* rather like a clock, that seems to fill the moors, for all birds of both sexes start and stop together as though at a word of command; both while perching or in the air. The soft tip of the beak is full of nerves and is an organ of touch as well as a pincer for taking hold of worms, snails, insects underground and pulling them out. Feeds at dusk and during the night. Crouches flat to the ground when anxious. During courtship flies by day in a wonderful display of oblique dives when the spread outer tail feathers produce a drumming sound like *huhuhuhuhu. Nest:* se p. 93. Juveniles migrate early in year, followed by parents considerably later. *Habitat:* marshes, water-meadows, flooded fields. *Distribution:* Europe south to N. Portugal; resident in Britain, breeding in all suitable habitats but rarer in south.

GREAT SNIPE *(Gallinago media)* Appears heavier and darker than the snipe; in flight the adult bird has more white on outer tail feathers. Flight is slower and not zigzag; usually rises silently. Otherwise similar.

JACK SNIPE *(Lymnocryptes minimus)* The smallest snipe, only a little larger than a skylark. Has a much smaller bill and slower, straighter flight than other snipe. Silent rise from ground. No white on tail. Usually solitary. *Nest:* on a tuft, a hollow lined with grass. 4 olive-green eggs (3.5 × 2.5 cm) flecked with grey and brown. Otherwise as snipe. *Distribution:* N. Europe south to N. Germany and Poland; winter visitor and passage migrant to Britain.

CURLEW *(Numenius arquata)* Slender build, with very long, thin downwards curved beak; the largest European wader. Long slender legs, bare to well above heel; distinct web between toes. Female usually the larger. Upper parts brown with lengthwise darker streaks; underparts yellow-grey with delicate black streaks; white rump. Takes large steps; will wade in water up to its body. Strong, swift, agile flight with measured wing beats; rather gull-like; glides, especially before landing. In flight draws its neck in and stretches its legs out; large, pointed wings. In flocks it usually flies high, in line or V. Unmistakeable ringing *cour-li,* or *crwee;* also heard outside breeding season in early morning and at night. Song in courtship slow, musical trilling repetition of call. Very shy and cautious. *Food:* insects, worms, snails, also fish, berries. *Nest:* a little grass etc. on ground among rushes or heather; April to May, 3–4 buff or greenish-yellow eggs (6.5 × 4.6 cm) flecked with brown. *Habitat:* mud flats and estuaries, moors and sand dunes. *Distribution:* N. Scandinavia south to France and east to Russia; resident breeding in northern counties of England, Scotland and Wales.

WHIMBREL *(Numenius phaeopus)* Like a curlew but smaller and with shorter bill; two broad dark streaks on top of head divided by a narrow lighter line. *Call:* quite different, a rapid tittering sound. Wing-beats rapid. Otherwise as for curlew. *Distribution:* breeds in Iceland, Faeroes and N. Europe; passage migrant to all coasts of Britain and sometimes inland. Has bred in N. Scotland and isles.

WOODCOCK *(Scolopax rusticola)* Very shy, solitary bird of the woods, the size of a pigeon. The colour of fallen leaves, thus extremely difficult to see. Has a long, straight beak with a soft sensitive tip. Large eyes placed well back; high forehead. Small, weak legs. Relatively short, but broad, rounded wings. Stooping, slinking gait. Swift, rocking flight with agile turns, dips and ascents, weaving through branches. Rises with a swish and soon dives back into cover. In courtship flight (roding) male puffs out its feathers and uses soft wing beats so that it looks like an owl, though its beak will give it away. *Food:* insects larvae, worms, for which it pokes in soft ground. *Nest:* see p. 90. *Call:* courtship, soft *orrrtporrrt* or a high *fsiwick. Habitat:* woods with wet overgrown places. *Distribution:* N. Scandinavia, south to Pyrenees and Bulgaria; resident and breeds in many English counties (except west), Scotland, S. Wales and Ireland.

BLACK-TAILED GODWIT *(Limosa limosa)* Size of a pigeon; very long, straight beak; long legs that trail behind when flying, white tail with bold black band; broad white wing bar; head and breast rufous-brown; yellowy-white stripe through eye; flank and belly white with dark bars. *Call: reeta-reeta-reeta. Nest:* a hollow in a tussock; 4 olive-brown eggs (5.5 × 3.5 cm) flecked with black-grey and grey-brown. *Habitat:* moors, water-meadows, sand dunes, lakes and estuaries. *Distribution:* S. Sweden, Denmark, N. and E. Germany to Roumania and Russia; passage migrant and resident breeding in small numbers in East Anglia.

BAR-TAILED GODWIT *(Limosa lapponica)* Similar to previous species but lacks white bands on wings and tail; has shorter legs, so that they do not project so far behind tail when flying and bill slightly upturned. *Call:* a low *kirruk, kirruk. Habitat:* more exclusively marine than previous species. *Distribution:* N. Scandinavia to N. Siberia; passage migrant and winter visitor to almost all coasts of Britain.

DUNLIN *(Calidris alpina)* A bird of the shore, has a large black patch on lower breast, rufous-brown crown and upper parts, white breast with fine streaks. Fairly long, down-curved beak. Has a white wing bar and sides of rump and tail are white and visible in flight. *Nest:* on a moor in a tuft, lined with grasses, etc. 4 blue or pale-green eggs (3.5 × 2.5 cm) blotched with brown. May to June. *Call:* a high *treer. Habitat:* sea-shore and estuaries; inland waters. *Distribution:* Arctic Europe; mainly winter visitor and passage migrant to Britain but some are present all through the year and breed on northern moors in England, Scotland, Wales and Ireland.

SANDERLING *(Crocethia alba)* Slightly larger than dunlin, it appears to chase the waves as they recede. Conspicuous in flight by long, white stripe on its dark wing. Tail dark with white sides. Head, breast and upper parts pale chestnut in summer, belly white. In winter, upper parts are grey. *Call:* a short *twick. Distribution:* Arctic Europe; passage migrant and winter visitor to Britain.

KNOT *(Calidris canutus)* Much larger than dunlin; short straight black bill, short legs. Winter plumage grey and white and tail uniformly coloured. In breeding plumage, black and chestnut mottling on back and chestnut head and under-parts. *Calls:* a deep *knut* from which the name is derived and a whistle *twit-wit. Habitat:* sandy shores and estuaries, usually in large flocks. *Distribution:* breeds mainly in Siberia; in Britain passage migrant and winter visitor mainly to N., E. and W. coasts of England, E. coast of Scotland and E. and N. coasts of Ireland.

SWIMMING AND DIVING BIRDS

Order   ANSERIFORMES   Swans, Geese and Ducks

SWANS   Fig. 35

Large, white swimming birds with very long necks, straight beaks as long as their heads with a round "nail" at the tip. Short, stumpy legs placed well back and thus waddling gait. Small, weak hind toe that does not touch the ground. Very large webs. Very close, soft small feathers, velvety on head and neck; thick, almost fan-like on underparts. Do not dive. Feeding almost solely while swimming in shallow water. Live in large lakes, fens and marshes with open water.

Family   ANATIDAE

MUTE SWAN *(Cygnus olor)* Beak orange-red on black ground black knob and base. Lower mandible, nail and rim of upper mandible black; legs dark grey, short and stumpy; while swimming neck is gracefully bent with beak pointing up; feet paddle alternately. Does not dive. *Flight:* slow, regular wing beats, no sudden turns, swift and enduring; no gliding; neck outstretched, extended legs are hidden under tail; musical deep thrum of wings. Flies in line or V formation. *Call:* only during breeding season a trumpeting call like *karr;* otherwise lives up to its name and at the most hisses. *Food:* water plants, worms, insects, larvae, etc. *Nest:* see p. 95. 4 cygnets introduced to water on first day will swim behind mother; sometimes climb onto her back where, as at night, they shelter under a raised wing. Ready to fly at 4¹/₂ months; till then they live as a family. Their plumage is not completely white until they are 3 years old. *Habitat:* if truly wild frequent remote marshes and lakes, or sheltered coasts in winter. *Distribution:* breeds in wild state in the Baltic region, Poland and E. Europe; resident and widely distributed in Britain.

WHOOPER SWAN *(Cygnus cygnus)* Stocky shape; holds neck stiff and erect, not in an S; yellow beak with black tip and no knob. Loud, ringing whooping or trumpeting. No noise from wings in flight. No aggressive posture. *Nest:* a large structure of reeds, etc. on shore or islet: 4–6 creamy white eggs (11.6×7.3 cm). *Habitat:* sea-coasts, lakes, large rivers, tundra. *Distribution:* Iceland, N. Scandinavia, N. Finland and Russia; winter visitor to Britain but a few nest in N. and W. Scotland.

BEWICK'S SWAN *(Cygnus columbianus)* Much smaller and shorter in neck than other swans; has less yellow on beak. Behaviour, etc. like the whooper. Nests in Arctic Russia; winter visitor to Britain.

GEESE   Fig. 35

Large, noisy water birds with stocky bodies, shorter necks than swans; fairly short beaks, thick at base but higher than they are wide, falling in a straight line from forehead, tip extended in a broad arched sharp-edged "nail". Edges of beak have sharp horny "teeth" for cutting plants, grazing. Legs sited more in middle of body. Well developed down feathers. Sexes coloured alike. Leg medium length, feathered almost to heel; foot completely webbed and has strong, short claws. Better at walking than all other birds of duck family, though they are not such good swimmers. Easy flight: migrate over large distances mostly in lines or V formation, make a swishing sound and utter cries. Mostly in flocks. While grazing they post sentries. Male (gander) leads the family.

GREY LAG GOOSE *(Anser anser)* Largest of the wild geese. Silver grey plumage. Beak flesh-pink at base, waxy-yellow at tip (nail). Legs pale pink. Only dives to avoid danger or in play. On water quite distinct from duck; hind parts higher out of water than breast. On land in single file. Long, broad, pointed wings. Good, strong enduring flyers, with necks and legs outstretched, the latter hidden under tail. *Call:* various, like the domestic goose. 3–7 part *ackng-ung-ung* used to maintain contact between

individuals during flight, grazing or swimming. Feeds almost solely on land. *Food:* greenstuff, roots, seeds; often spend the entire night feeding on grassland or field. *Nest:* see p. 96. Mate for life. Almost unique in bird world in that if one of a pair dies, the other remains solitary all its life. Life-span up to 80 years. *Habitat*: grasslands, arable near coast, marshes, estuaries. *Distribution:* Iceland, N. Scandinavia south to Denmark and Macedonia; winter visitor and passage migrant to Britain but some resident in N. Scotland where they breed. Now being bred artificially and released.

BEAN GOOSE *(Anser arvensis)* Plumage browner and darker than grey lag goose's; beak black with orange markings and black "nail". Reddish-yellow legs. In flight looks darker than grey lag. *Call:* a resounding *ung-unk*. Migrant. *Habitat:* same as grey lag, but seldom on arable land. *Distribution:* Scandinavia, N. Finland, N. Russia; winter visitor to Britain.

BRENT GOOSE *(Branta bernicla)* Nearly the size of a mallard. Sooty black head, neck and breast; white rump and white patch on side of neck. One form has dark grey-brown belly, the other paler, nearly white. More birds of the sea than other geese. Very gregarious. Rests on water. Often up-ends to feed. Swift flight in very loose or no formation. *Distribution:* far north, Spitzbergen, Greenland etc.; winter visitor to Britain but in decreasing numbers.

BARNACLE GOOSE *(Branta leucopsis)* A little larger than the brent. Plumage black and white; striking white face and forehead; black on neck and throat and on to breast; lavender upper parts with black bars edged with white; white rump; tail black. Legs and back black. Small beak. Mainly nocturnal. More terrestrial than brent. *Habitat:* seldom seen far inland: estuaries, salt marshes, islands. *Distribution:* N. E. Greenland and Spitzbergen; winter visitor to Britain mainly to the Hebrides, Solway and N. and W. coasts of Ireland.

CANADA GOOSE *(Branta canadensis)* Largest European goose. Grey-brown with black head, long black neck, white breast, broad white patch from throat on to cheek. Chiefly a freshwater bird. Introduced into Europe and now breeds in Britain and Sweden, etc. *Distribution:* a native of N. America.

PINK-FOOTED GOOSE *(Anser brachyrhynchus)* Like a small bean goose but has pale blue-grey upper parts, very dark head and neck; small beak, black and pink; pink legs. *Habitat* etc.: as grey lag. *Distribution:* Greenland, Iceland and Spitzbergen; winter visitor to N.W. England, Solway, Clyde, Inner Hebrides and the east coast of Britain.

WHITE-FRONTED GOOSE *(Anser albifrons)* Smaller than grey lag and darker. Has a bold white patch at base of pink beak, orange legs and wide, straggly black bars on belly. Flight, behaviour, etc. as grey lag. *Distribution:* N. E. Russia, Siberia; winter visitor to several areas including Severn Estuary, W. Scotland and Ireland.

SHELDUCK *(Tadorna tadorna)* Goose-like shape. Male has knob on beak. Brilliant dark green head and neck; white body with broad foxy belt round front of breast and shoulders; large, black patch on each shoulder; dark central stripe down white underparts; pinions grey-black; red beak; flesh-pink legs. Female less showy and without knob. Rather heavy gait. Goose-like flight with slower wingbeats than a duck's. Good at swimming and diving. *Call:* a hoarse *quack. Food:* all sorts of small animals and plants. *Nest.* in holes it excavates itself or rabbit holes, fox earths, etc. 7–12 white eggs (6.5 × 4.7 cm). *Habitat:* sandy, muddy coasts. *Distribution:* N. Scandinavia south to N. France and the Balkans; resident and common in many coastal areas of Britain.

On the Danish island, Schleswig etc. the shelduck is domesticated.

On Sylt and on the coast artificial nesting holes are put out in order to collect eggs and feathers.

1. *Surface-feeding Ducks* (See Fig. 36, p. 116)

Mainly vegetarian; broad, shallow bodies as though flattened. Short to medium length necks; thick heads, beaks the length of their heads, of same width throughout their length or somewhat broader at tip. Legs set far back and short; feathered to heel. Narrow wings of medium length, pointed. Colouring varies with sex and season. Most have a colourful rectangular patch (speculum) on the hind edge of wing. Male keeps breeding plumage most of the year, but juvenile and summer (eclipse) plumage (June–September) resembles duller garb of female. 2 moults a year. Small feather moult in autumn gives winter plumage, in female darker down suitable for making nest. In summer moult sheds wing feathers and while thus unable to fly the drake remains hidden among reeds etc. Female moults only when young birds have grown up. Heavy walking gait. Good swimmer, riding high on water, so that neck and tail are well in view. Rises at once and easily from surface to fly. Quacking call, that of drake always different from that of duck. *Habitat:* lakes, fens, inland water and, in winter, coasts.

MALLARD *(Anas platyrhynchos)* Length 63 cm. Broad spoon-shaped beak. Drake has curly decorative feathers before its tail. Breeding plumage: head and neck shimmering metallic green; narrow white ring round neck; deep brown breast; violet patch on wing fringed with white; underparts light grey; tail edged with white; beak greeny-yellow with black nail; legs pale red. Juvenile and eclipse (June to September) plumage light brown with dark arrow markings; blue wing patch edged in front and behind with white; orange legs; grey-green beak with black nail, orange on either side. Reluctant to dive, but if necessary can swim under water paddling with its wings. Dabbles with stern up in air. Swift, enduring flight with quick shallow wing beats making piping *wee-wee-wee-wee* sound, by which it can be recognised in the dark. *Flight silhouette:* long, pointed wings, legs stretched out behind covered by short, pointed tail. Fly in chains, the ducks in front. *Call:* a fairly quiet *yeeb* (male) female quacks. Very greedy and will eat almost anything: delicate leaves, buds, shoots, seeds, etc. of water and marsh plants; worms, snails, frog and fish spawn, etc. *Nest:* see p. 94. *Distribution:* Europe generally; resident and widely distributed in Britain. Passage migrants and winter visitors arrive from N. and N. W. Europe mid-August to late November and leave March to May.

TEAL *(Anas crecca)* Length 32 cm. Smallest and loveliest European duck. Only the size of a dove. Shiny green speculum; drake has horizontal white stripe on its shoulder; head and top of neck deep chestnut, with magnificent metallic green stripe through eye, edged with white reaching to back of neck. The under tail coverts on either side have a yellowy-red spot. Plumage in eclipse like that of duck; yellowy-brown with dark arrow-head markings; speculum as in mating plumage: green framed with velvety black on one side and white and rust-yellow on the other. Very swift, noiseless flight; mostly low down in compact groups. *Call:* a short, low *krrit*. *Nest:* made of herbage and dark brown feathers on the ground in a wood or among rushes; 8–12 buff or greenish eggs (4.5×3.3 cm). *Distribution:* Europe generally; winter visitor and breeds in most British counties.

GARGANEY *(Anas querquedula)* Length 38 cm. Over pigeon size. Drake easily distinguished by broad white stripe curving from eye to nape and by the elongated, drooping black-white shoulder feathers. Under neck and breast brown, standing out sharply from belly. In eclipse has blue shoulders, but otherwise like the female, which has greyer wings than teal and no black in speculum. Very swift, darting, noiseless flight; acrobatic. Call of the drake is a dry rattling noise; of the female a soft, high quack. Prefers shallow water with plenty of vegetation. Not shy. *Nest:* on ground near water; 7–10 cream-coloured eggs (4.7 × 3.2 cm). *Distribution:* Finland and Scandinavia south to S. France and eastwards; summer visitor to Britain breeding mainly in eastern and south-eastern coastal counties.

PINTAIL *(Anas acuta)* Length 64 cm. Slim build; long, thin neck; protracted (especially in drake) pointed tail. Chocolate coloured head and back of neck; breast and neck white tapering to vertical stripe reaching almost to eye level; upper parts and flanks grey; feet and beak blue-grey. The middle (black) tail feather up to 9 cm longer than the others which are grey. In eclipse head, neck, breast rust-coloured with dark spots; upper parts dark brown; female much lighter in colouring, no shimmery speculum, grey back. *Flight:* very swift and agile; short, quick slightly sibilant wing beats. Over longer distances in wedge formation. Silhouette in flight shows long thin neck and spike-like tail. *Nest:* made of herbage and brown down on ground among vegetation: 7–10 greenish-yellow eggs (5.4×3.7 cm). *Distribution:* Iceland, Faeroes south to S. Spain and Hungary; resident and breeding in Scotland, East Anglia and Ireland. Passage migrant and winter visitor regularly in certain localities.

SHOVELER *(Spatula clypeata)* Length 50 cm; differs from all other ducks in its large, broad shovel-shaped beak. *Drake:* head and upper neck glossy green; lower neck and breast white; flanks and belly chestnut; upper part of wing light blue, behind it a green speculum. In eclipse yellow-brown with dark mottling, the colouring of the female. Beak conspicuous in flight which is rather ponderous; noise of wings deeper and quieter than mallard's. *Call:* drake a quiet *wonk. Nest:* made of vegetation and blackish down on ground in herbage; 8–12 greenish-white eggs (5.2 × 3.7 cm). *Distribution:* Baltic to Mediterranean and eastwards; resident breeding in England, Wales, Scotland and Ireland. Passage migrants and winter visitors arrive from Continent.

WIGEON *(Anas penelope)* Length 54 cm. Steep brow, short neck. Drake has rufous-brown head with cream-coloured crown; grey back and flanks; white shoulders; metallic dark green speculum; grey legs; blue-grey beak with black nail. In eclipse upper parts mainly dark grey-brown; female more yellowy-grey with grey speculum. Light easy, quick walk, scarcely waddling. Swift flight, perhaps the swiftest of the ducks; piping noise from wings. *Call:* high *whee-oo. Nest:* made of herbage and down near water, hidden in vegetation. 5–10 creamy-white eggs (5.5 × 3.7 cm). *Distribution:* Iceland, N. Europe south to Germany; resident and widely distributed in Britain and has bred. Passage migrant and winter visitor common on all coasts.

2. *Diving Ducks* (See p. 116)

Shorter, plumper bodies; short, thick necks; large heads, broad medium length beaks, slightly shorter than head; short legs set well back and feathered to heel, large webs; hind toe has wide pendant lobe. Because of set of legs must adopt fairly erect posture on land. When swimming rump is deep in the water and only a narrow strip of the back is unsubmerged; tail lies on surface. In diving the body is propelled head first downwards by a single upward stroke of both wings and continues more or less vertically to the bottom; emerges after minutes in almost the same spot. In taking off runs paddling across the water. Flight more of an effort than with swimming ducks: on reaching a height fly swiftly with quick wing beats. *Call:* is hoarser and creakier than that of swimming ducks.

POCHARD *(Aythya ferina)* Length 55 cm. Head and tail chestnut; breast black; body light grey; no striking speculum; black beak with grey-blue bar. Female has reddish-brown head and neck; black breast, flanks yellowy-grey with dark moon-shaped mottling; belly and wings grey. Blue bar on beak. Eclipse plumage of drake and duck similar, though the former's colouring is more vivid. Seldom on land; rests by day on the water. Dives frequently, remaining under for some 25 seconds. Call seldom heard, a hoarse wheeze. *Nest:* made of rushes and down on the ground near water; 6–12 greenish (or yellowy-white) eggs (6.0 × 4.3 cm). On the Continent is considered so tasty it is in places called the table duck. *Distribution:* Baltic south to Mediterranean; resident but breeds mainly in east of Britain; winter visitors arrive from the Continent between September and April.

TUFTED DUCK *(Aythya fuligula)* Length 40 cm. Has drooping crest of feathers at back of head. *Drake:* black and white with very long black heron's crest; in eclipse duller and crest undeveloped. In female the darker colouring is more brown. In loud swishing flight shows white bar almost the entire length of wing. *Nest:* made of reeds, etc. and dark down on the ground among vegetation near water; 8–10 olive-green eggs (5.6 × 4.1 cm). *Distribution:* Iceland south to Holland and Germany; resident and breeds in most parts of Britain; native stock augmented by winter visitors from Continent.

GOLDENEYE *(Bucephala clangula)* Length about 50 cm. Short neck, short beak, thick head; that of the drake has puffed out feathers during courtship that make it appear larger still *(Bucephala* means ox-head). Drake has black-green head with striking, white round spot at base of beak; black back and tail; white neck, underparts, speculum and wing coverts. In eclipse black-brown head, no white spot; marbled black-grey upper parts; white underparts; female has similar colouring, only often her black-grey beak has a yellow spot before the nail. Legs of both sexes orange. On land the ducklings are able to run and climb straight away which is necessary as the goldeneye nests in holes. Sits deep in water, often holding head and beak just above it; dives suddenly attacking prey from underneath. Swift, whirring flight (that of old drakes makes a tinkling sound) much faster than that of other diving ducks. Usually silent, but has a deep quack. *Nest:* in hollow trees, old woodpeckers' nests, rabbit and other holes in banks or near woods. 7–10 greenish eggs (6.0 × 4.2 cm). *Distribution:* Arctic south to E. Scandinavia, Germany, Yugoslavia and N. Bulgaria; passage migrant and winter visitor to Britain.

EIDER *(Somateria mollissima)* Mostly maritime. Larger than mallard, distinctive by its long, heavy body and long head. Drake has white back, black belly, breast flushed with pink; white head with black crown and green nape; greenish-yellow beak; olive-green legs. Female brown thickly barred with black. *Flight:* alternating wing beats and gliding; usually low, in single file. Swims and dives superbly. *Call:* drake a melancholy *coo-roo-uh;* female a peculiar *kor-r-r. Food:* shellfish and other sea creatures. *Nest:* in colonies in vicinity of sea on islands, etc. June to July 4–9 greeny-grey eggs (7.2×5.0 cm). Occasionally breeds on inland lakes, but mostly on coast or rocky islands. In places artificial nesting hollows are made to facilitate the collection of valuable down with which it lines its nest (eiderdown). *Distribution:* Iceland, Faeroes, Holland, N. W. Europe; resident, breeding in northern isles of Britain, east and west coasts of Scotland, Farne Islands, Counties Donegal, Down and Antrim.

GADWALL *(Anas strepera)* Length 50 cm, thus smaller and slighter than mallard. Both drake and female have white speculum, conspicuous when flying. Drake is grey with rufous-brown wing coverts, white belly and black tail coverts; bill grey, legs orange-yellow; in eclipse drake resembles the female. Flight like mallard's. *Nest:* in vegetation (on ground) near water; 7–12 cream-coloured eggs (5.4 × 4.0 cm). *Distribution:* Iceland and S. Scandinavia south to Mediterranean; resident and breeds in East Anglia, Surrey and parts of Scotland and Ireland. Winter visitors augment native population.

MANDARIN *(Aix galericulata)* Size of a wigeon; length 44 cm; has distinctive erect orange "sails" on wings, rufous-brown side-whiskers and colourful drooping crest. Female is a quiet brownish-grey with large white spots on breast and white marking behind eyes and around beak. *Nest:* in trees. *Distribution:* native of E. Asia but introduced to Europe and now breeds in a feral state in many parts including Britain.

Male

SCAUP *(Aythya marila)* Length 48 cm. Head, front and rear are black; back pale grey; flanks and underparts white. Blue-grey beak. In flight both sexes show white bar on wing. Expert at diving, will even do so in rough sea. Flies in close flocks, or in line. *Habitat:* maritime except when breeding. *Nest:* often in small colonies on islands in lakes surrounded with grass; on ground, often under a bush. 10–14 greenish yellowy-grey eggs (7.0 × 4.6 cm). *Distribution:* Iceland, Faeroes, N. Europe; passage migrant and winter visitor to all coasts of Britain.

Female

LONG-TAILED DUCK *(Clangula hyemalis)* Much smaller than a mallard, length including tail (20 cm) 56 cm. Female smaller. In winter drake has white head, neck, belly and scapulars; breast, back and wings blackish-brown; large dark patch on side of neck; beak has bands of pink and black. In summer drake is mostly dark brown with white belly and white round eye. Female has normal length tail and, in winter, is dark above and white underneath with black crown, dark spot on cheek. *Nest:* in colonies on inland islands; on ground near water: 5–8 light grey-green eggs (5.1 × 3.8 cm). Mainly maritime. *Distribution:* Iceland, Norway; winter visitor to Britain.

VELVET SCOTER *(Melanitta fusca)* Length 52 cm. Male black, female brown. Both sexes have white wing patch easily seen when wings are opened. Red feet (seen when diving). Drake has small patch of white below eye. *Nest:* among tall vegetation or bushes on the ground. 8–12 creamy eggs (7.5 × 5.1 cm) with a hint of red. Maritime except when nesting. *Distribution:* N. Europe and the Baltic; passage migrant and winter visitor to Britain although some birds are on the coast throughout summer.

COMMON SCOTER *(Melanitta nigra)* Length 48 cm. Unique among ducks in being entirely black; black bill has orange patch and large knob at base. Females and juveniles are dark brown with whitish cheeks and throat. Buoyant in water; often with

Male

Female

tail raised. Strong flight, usually in wavy lines or groups. *Nest:* under a bush near water. 6–9 creamy eggs (6.4 × 4.2 cm). Maritime except when nesting. *Distribution:* Iceland, N. Europe south to central Norway; winter visitor to east and south coasts of Britain but some birds are resident and breed on the north Scottish coasts.

MERGANSERS   Fig. 36

Very long, slender bodies; medium length, thin necks; large crested heads; long, straight beaks almost cylindrical with sharp horny toothed edges (saw-bills) for holding on to fish, which are their food. Legs sited well back, hence waddling gait with roughly horizontal body. Very pointed wings of medium length; soft, thick, beautifully coloured plumage. Swim deep in the water and strongly; dive with utmost ease, remaining submerged for a long time; noisy take-off from water with the help of their legs. Light, easy, quick flight; duck-like, diving obliquely into water and going under at once. Silhouette in flight shows body, neck, head and beak in one horizontal line. Voice is a strange rasping croak. *Habitat:* lakes, rivers, reservoirs.

GOOSANDER *(Mergus merganser)* Length 80 cm. Dark head, long red beak. Red legs. Erectile crest of feathers on head and nape. Drake has head and upper neck of glossy black-green; black back; grey flanks and tail; white breast and underparts white with a tinge of salmon-pink; white speculum. In eclipse head and neck a deep brown. Female has rufous-brown head and crest, white throat and neck; blue-grey upper parts; grey flanks; underparts white with a hint of salmon-pink. Fish eater. Often feeds in groups, hunts under water, twisting and turning. Will also eat frogs, toads, newts, etc., aquatic insects. *Nest:* in holes in trees, banks, etc., abandoned crow's nest; or on ground between reeds or under trees. 7–12 cream-coloured eggs (6.8 × 4.7 cm). *Distribution:* Iceland, N. Europe south to Denmark, Switzerland and Yugoslavia; winter visitor and resident, some breeding in N. Scotland and N. England.

RED-BREASTED MERGANSER *(Mergus serrator)* Length 60 cm. Long red beak. Drake has velvety-black head (and crest) and upper neck with metallic green shimmer; white collar; black back; white upper wing coverts; reddish-brown breast. In eclipse drake resembles the more sombre female which has brown head and upper neck; grey beak and breast. *Nest:* on ground under bushes, among rocks etc. but near water. 7–12 browny-yellow eggs (6.5 × 4.5 cm). *Distribution:* Iceland, Faeroes, N. Europe south to N. Germany, Poland; winter visitor to Britain and also resident, breeding in Scotland, N. England, N. Wales and Ireland.

SMEW *(Mergus albellus)* Length 41 cm. Smallest of the mergansers. Drake mainly white; striking dark eye patch; back and the band across back of head black with shimmer of green; small hanging black and white crest feathers. In eclipse drake has brown head and nape; grey upper parts. Short tuft on back of head. Female similar. *Food:* small fish, crabs, insects. *Nest:* in hollow trees beside water. June, 7–9 creamy-yellow eggs (5.2 × 3.8 cm). *Distribution:* Arctic N. W. Europe and E. Europe south to Roumania; winter visitor to Britain.

Order PELECANIFORMES

Gannets, Cormorants and Pelicans

Family SULIDAE Gannets

GANNET *(Sula bassana)* Size of a goose. Broad black tips to its long narrow wings; longer neck and more pointed, larger beak than a gull's, pointed tail. Low flight, exept when wheeling and diving vertically for fish while feeding. *Habitat:* the sea. Breeds in great colonies on ledges on steep cliffs. *Distribution:* islands of the N. Atlantic; large colonies in Scotland on Bass Rock (Berwickshire), Shetlands, Orkney, Outer Hebrides, St. Kilda, Ailsa Craig; in Wales in Grassholm (Pembrokeshire); and in Ireland at Bull Rock (Cork) and Little Skellig (Kerry).

Family PELECANIDAE Pelicans

*WHITE PELICAN *(Pelecanus onocrotalus)* White with black primaries and a huge wing-span. Long yellowish beak with throat pouch; pink legs. Both sexes have shaggy crest on back of head and rosy tint to plumage. Red eyes; tuft of yellow feathers at base of neck; black tips to wings. Leisurely flight with long glides; flies in lines; often at great height; dives vertically with wings not quite closed, hunting for fish. *Habitat:* inland waters, marshes, coastal lagoons; nests in colonies. Bulgaria, Roumania, Greece (in winter).

Family   PHALACROCORACIDAE   Cormorants   Fig. 35

Have longer tails than divers and beaks with hooked tips. Fly in line or wedge, like geese; neck held somewhat above the horizontal; swim with beak tilted up. Fish-eaters. Mainly maritime.

CORMORANT *(Phalacrocorax carbo)* Almost the size of a goose. Long beak and black, webbed feet. Bronze-black plumage. Body very long and rounded, but strong. Small head with white chin and cheeks; long, slender neck, strong beak with hooked tip. Webs on feet extending to hind toe. White patch on thigh. Very short legs; pointed claws enable it to cling on firmly and to perch on thick branches. Waddling gait. Sits always erect, supported on tail, often with half spread wings. Swims with its body low in water, so that its long tail lies on the surface, and holds head and neck erect; beak slightly up-tilted. Dives for up to 71 seconds and will go down to 13 m. Swims well under water holding wings closed, never using them to paddle (unlike shag). Very quick, straight flight. Silhouette in the air like a cross; very long, strong tail; wings considerably longer than those of other divers; also long head and beak. Flies either in line or in V formation. *Voice:* a deep, rough *r-rah.* Dives for fish. (The Continental variety has, during breeding season, almost completely white head and neck.) *Nest:* in old crows' or herons' nests; in colonies, mostly in tall trees, but also on ledges of rock near lakes or rivers. Ground littered with fish remains and an obnoxious smell everywhere. 4–5 greenish-white eggs (6.8 × 4.1 cm). *Distribution:* rocky coasts of Europe as far south as N. Spain and Italy; resident and widely distributed on British coasts, breeding in many areas.

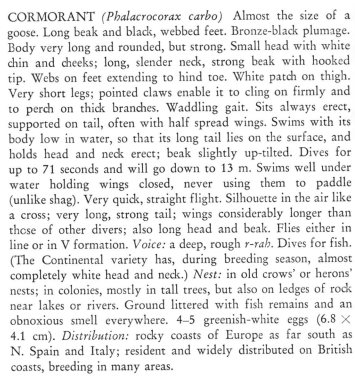

SHAG *(Phalacrocorax aristotelis)* Smaller than cormorant; has no white on its face. Plumage greeny-black instead of bronze-black. Pale blue-green eyes. Makes nest of seaweed on cliff or rocky ledge: 2–5 nearly white eggs. April to May. Only maritime. *Distribution:* west coast of Europe from N. Norway to Portugal, Mediterranean and Black Sea; resident and widely distributed on the Atlantic coasts of Britain and also breeds on the east of Scotland, the Farne Islands.

Order   PODICIPITIFORMES   Grebes   Fig. 38

Family   PODICIPITIDAE

GREAT CRESTED GREBE *(Podiceps cristatus)* Length 53 cm. Has black twin-pointed crest and in breeding season chestnut and black feathery frills on each side of its head. Pink beak with small, closeable slit nostrils. Upper parts grey-brown; underparts white. In winter almost all white. Shallow body; lies deep in water; can alter its swimming position at will by moving feathers away from or closer to body. Swims deeper when there is danger, leaving only line of back or even just its eyes and nostrils above the surface. When diving uses only its feet. Dives quickly and frequently; speedy under water, remaining submerged from 20–75 seconds; goes down to 8 m. Swishing, straight, low flight. Paddles before it takes off; has difficulty in taking off from the ground, at times cannot do so. *Food:* fish and shell-fish. When off nest (see p. 97) covers eggs with bits of plants. Chicks use the female's pinions as cradles, even when swimming, diving and flying. They learn to swim and dive from their mother's back. *Habitat:* lakes, reservoirs and slow rivers with reeds, etc. In winter on coast. *Distribution:* Europe generally; resident and breeding in most counties of England and Scotland but is scarcer in Wales and S. Ireland.

LITTLE GREBE or **DABCHICK** *(Podiceps ruficollis)* Smallest grebe (36 cm), the size of large blackbird. Rounded body, short neck with short beak. No crest. Sides of head and front of neck reddish-brown; yellow-green base of beak; upper parts browny-black; underparts black grey. Masterly in the water. Low flight. *Food:* insects and their larvae, small fish, frogs, spawn. *Nest:* see p. 98. *Habitat:* ponds, lakes, etc. *Distribution:* Europe generally; resident and generally distributed in Britain, although scarcer in N. Scotland.

RED-NECKED GREBE *(Podiceps griseigena)* Rather large. Has whitish cheeks, black crown, yellow base to beak and chestnut neck. Upper parts grey-brown, white underparts. Habits as great crested. *Nest:* as great crested, 4–5 greeny-white eggs (5 × 3.4 cm). *Distribution:* Europe east from Denmark, north nearly to Arctic Circle and south to Bulgaria; winter visitor to the east and south coasts of England.

SLAVONIAN GREBE *(Podiceps auritus)* Larger than little grebe; has black glossy head with a broad golden streak through eye, chestnut neck and flanks; white underparts and dark upper parts. White bar on wings. Beak held straight. *Nest:* as great crested. 4–7 greeny-white eggs (4.5 × 3.1 cm). *Distribution:* Iceland, N. Scandinavia, the Baltic and N. Russia; regular winter visitor to Britain and also breeds on lochs in Inverness-shire.

BLACK-NECKED GREBE *(Podiceps nigricollis)* Has a black neck and a tuft of golden feathers on either side of head. High black forehead and black crown. Does not have a floating nest. *Distribution:* S. Scandinavia to Mediterranean; resident and breeds in scattered localities in England, Wales, Scotland and Ireland.

Order   CHARADRIIFORMES   (see also p. 174)

Family   Laridae Gulls and Terns   Figs. 37 and 38

BLACK-HEADED GULL *(Larus ridibundus)* 41.5 cm. Long, tapering wings with white edge and black tip, jutting beyond tail when closed; short neck; crimson beak as long as head with sharp-edged rims. Webbed feet. Back and shoulders bluey-grey; head chocolate, in summer white with brown markings; neck, underparts and tail white. Red legs. Quick walk. Easy, circling flight, normally with legs outstretched. Rounded tail. Graceful, though not fast swimmer. Flies low above water catching insects and small fish; flies to arable fields and follows the plough like a crow eating grubs, worms, etc. *Nest:* see p. 94. *Habitat:* coasts and inland waters. *Distribution:* Iceland and N. Russia, south to France and Bulgaria; resident and breeds in nearly all coastal counties of England, Wales, Scotland and Ireland.

HERRING GULL *(Larus argentatus)* Length 60–67 cm. Blue-grey back and wings; head, neck, tail and underparts white; broad black stripe on primaries. Yellow beak with red spot on lower mandible. Flesh-coloured legs. Voice is a dry *gah-gah-gah*. *Nest:* in colonies on rocks, cliffs, islands. Nest of dry grass, seaweed, etc. 3–4 greeny-grey eggs (8.4 × 4.9 cm) flecked with dark brown and grey. *Distribution:* Europe generally; common resident, breeding on suitable rocky coasts around Britain. (In Mediterranean and E. Scandinavia the herring gull has yellow legs.)

KITTIWAKE *(Rissa tridactyla)* Size of a common gull; has triangular black covering wing tips, black legs and yellow beak. Tail slightly forked. Usually lives out at sea, but breeds in vast colonies on cliffs and caves round the coasts. *Distribution:* Arctic Europe south to Brittany; birds are present all through the year in Britain; the main breeding concentration is on rocky cliffs of the E. and W. coasts of Scotland, but there are colonies in many other parts of Britain.

COMMON GULL *(Larus canus)* Length 42–45 cm. Head, neck, underparts and tail white; wings blue-grey; black and white wing tips; dirty yellow beak (no red); grey-green legs. *Nest:* of grasses, twigs, seaweed; 3 grey or olive eggs (5.8 × 9.3 cm) with dark brown mottling. *Distribution:* Europe south to Holland and east to Russia; resident but only common as a breeding bird in Scotland.

LESSER BLACK-BACKED GULL *(Larus fuscus)* Size of a herring gull. Slate-grey mantle; head, neck, underparts white; yellow legs; black tips to wings. Untidy nest of seaweed etc. 3–4 grey-green eggs (7.7 × 5.5 cm) mottled with black and brown. *Nest:* in colonies on rocks, islands, etc. *Distribution:* northern Europe; mainly a summer visitor to Britain breeding on suitable sites around the coasts of England, Wales, Scotland and Ireland. In winter there are now substantial numbers among which may be seen the Scandinavian race which has a much darker back.

GREAT BLACK-BACKED GULL *(Larus marinus)* Much larger than herring gull (60–74 cm). Slaty blue-black mantle; tips of wing feathers, head, neck, tail, underparts white; grey-white legs; beak as herring gull's. 3–4 eggs (7.8 × 5.5 cm). *Distribution:* Europe east to Russia and south to Brittany; resident and breeding on south and west coasts of Britain, in Wales, Scotland and Ireland; winter visitors from Continent arrive in autumn.

LITTLE GULL *(Larus minutus)* Length 28–29 cm thus the smallest gull. Like miniature black-headed gull, but has black head, rather rounded wings with blackish under surfaces; underparts white with faint pink flush. Dark red beak, red feet; dark brown eyes. 2–3 olive-brown eggs (4.0 × 3.0 cm) flecked with dark brown. *Distribution:* Holland and Denmark eastwards and S. E. Europe; autumn and winter visitor.

Family   STERCORARIIDAE   Skuas

GREAT SKUA *(Catharacta skua)* Length 58 cm. Like a large, dark gull. Plumage dark brown with prominent white patch at the base of the primary feathers of the wing. Bill and legs blackish. *Call:* loud laughing, *ha-ha-ha,* and a deep clucking sound when attacking intruders to its territory. *Nest:* on ground among grass or heather. Eggs 2, May to June. *Habitat:* In breeding season moorland near sea; at other times off-shore. *Food:* like all skuas mainly by harrying other seabirds and forcing them to disgorge fish. *Distribution:* Iceland, Faeroes; summer visitor to N. Scotland and islands where it now breeds in large numbers.

ARCTIC SKUA *(Stercorarius parasiticus) Length:* 43 cm. More hawk-like than preceding species. Two plumage phases: one is dark brown all over except for lighter neck and face; the other has much lighter neck and underparts, the head remaining dark. In flight two long feathers project from the wedge-shaped tail. Habits similar to great skua. *Distribution:* northern coasts of Europe to the Arctic; in Britain summer visitor, passage migrant and breeds in many places in the northern islands of Scotland.

COMMON TERN *(Sterna hirundo)* Length 36–42 cm. Very deeply forked tail, the end of which does not protrude beyond tips of closed wings. Mantle and shoulders bluey ash-grey; sides of head, neck, rump and underparts white. Has black cap in

summer; orange beak with black tip. In winter white forehead, black on head only from eye to nape. Blackish beak with red base; red legs. Very graceful flight; "back-pedals" with its wings; skims the water or hovers and dives in vertically. *Food:* small fish, frogs, larvae, worms, insects; feeds on ground or in flight. *Nest:* see p. 99. *Habitat:* rivers, lakes, coasts. *Distribution:* Arctic Ocean to Mediterranean; summer visitor breeding in many places on coast of Britain except S. Wales.

ARCTIC TERN *(Sterna macrura)* Similar to common tern but with bill in breeding season blood-red and without black tip; in winter bill is mainly black; shorter legs than common tern. Otherwise similar to latter. Usually 2 eggs, May to June. *Distribution:* Arctic south to Mediterranean; summer visitor, breeding on all coasts of Scotland and Ireland and in N. England and N. Wales, Scillies and Norfolk.

SANDWICH TERN *(Sterna sanvicensis)* The largest of all species of terns mentioned; black bill with yellow tip, legs black, and black feathers longer at the base of crown, sticking out from head. *Habitat:* similar to other terns but although noisier bird, it is less aggressive to intruders. *Distribution:* Denmark and S. Baltic to Mediterranean; summer visitor, breeding in large colonies in N. Lancashire, Farne Islands, Suffolk and Norfolk; Anglesey in Wales; many places in Scotland and Ireland.

LITTLE TERN *(Sterna albifrons)* Length 21–22 cm. Distinctive by miniature size; yellow beak with black tip; yellow legs and white forehead. Black crown and black streak through eye. Tail short. Relatively narrower wings, quicker wing beat and more hovering than with other terns. *Nest:* in hollow in sand or shingle. 3 grey-yellow eggs (3.3 × 2.4 cm) with grey and brown-black mottling. *Distribution:* S. Baltic to Mediterranean; summer visitor breeding on all coasts of Britain except Cornwall.

BLACK TERN *(Chlidonias niger)* Length 24–26 cm. The only tern with blackish (breeding) plumage all over except for white under-tail coverts. Black beak; reddish-brown legs. Flits about skimming water picking off insects. On land has horizontal posture with head pulled in. Deeply forked tail. Seldom walks or swims. Light, graceful, varied flight. *Food:* insects, larvae, small fish, frogs. Gregarious. *Nest:* in colonies on marshy ground or on floating vegetation in shallow water. 2–3 greeny-brown eggs (3.5 × 2.5 cm) flecked with grey and black-brown. Migrates in groups of 20–1,000. *Habitat:* inland waters. *Distribution:* Denmark, S. Finland and Russia south to Spain and the Caspian Sea; a passage migrant to Britain.

Family   ALCIDAE   Auks

Salt-water diving birds with short, thick necks, thick heads. Very short, narrow wings; legs set far back; webbed feet; good swimmer and diver, using its wings only to propel itself under water. Whirring flight, seldom straight for any distance; straddles feet before landing. Erect posture on land. *Food:* small fish, crabs. *Nest:* on cliffs and rocks. Pointed beaks.

GUILLEMOT *(Uria aalge)* Comes to land only to nest; otherwise always at sea. Length 42–47 cm. Powerful body; slim, pointed beak. 3-toed feet with large webs; short tail. Head, front of neck and upper parts velvety brown; underparts white. Narrow, light-coloured bars on wings. In winter front of neck and cheeks are white. Black beak; leaden-grey legs. Normal gait a slither on soles of feet; occasionally runs on toes with help of wings. Quick flight with whirring wing beats. Expert diver remaining submerged for several minutes. *Nest:* in thousands on ledges on steep cliff faces, laying eggs on bare rock: only one top-shaped white or blue-green egg (8.0 × 4.8 cm) with brown and black flecks and streaks. *Habitat:* coastal waters up to 70° N. The ringed or bridled guillemot is a variety with a white ring around the eye and a white line from it over the sides of the head; the proportion of these birds increases northwards in its range. *Distribution:* N. Europe to Portugal; in Britain breeds in enormous numbers on suitable cliffs.

BLACK GUILLEMOT *(Cepphus grylle)* Much smaller, 34–37 cm. All-black plumage except for large white wing patch. Red feet. Remains closer to shore than guillemot and in smaller numbers. *Nest:* singly or scattered groups, fairly low down. 2 white eggs (6.0 × 4.0 cm) flecked with black, brown or grey. *Distribution:* N. Europe east to Russia and south to the Baltic; resident, breeding mainly in Scotland.

RAZORBILL *(Alca torda)* Duck size (39–46 cm), thick head, short, thick neck, beak pressed in at sides with upward curving, then down-hooked tip to upper mandible with angular, jutting lower mandible. White vertical line down beak. Narrow white stripe from beak to eye. White wing bars; upper parts and throat black; breast and belly white. Very clumsy on land. Good climber on cliff; masterly swimmer and diver, remaining submerged for minutes. *Nest:* on ledges or niches in rock, laying on bare rock one dirty-white egg (8.0 ×5.0 cm). *Habitat:* coastal waters. *Distribution:* Faeroes south to Brittany; birds seen all the year, they breed on similar cliffs to guillemot on all coasts except S. E.

PUFFIN *(Fratercula arctica)* Length 30–35 cm. Triangular red, blue and yellow beak, stumpy head, black and white plumage and orange feet. Perches upright, but rests in horizontal position. Breeds in colonies in rabbit or other burrows, or holes it excavates in turf on cliffs or grassy islands; one dirty-white egg (6.5 × 4.5 cm) with more or less distinct grey flecks. *Habitat:* coasts and off-shore waters. *Distribution:* Faeroes south to Brittany; breeds on rocky cliffs on all coasts of Britain except S. E. coast of England.

Order   PROCELLARIIFORMES   Shearwaters

Family   PROCELLARIIDAE

Oceanic birds visiting land only to breed; have tube-shaped external nostrils, slender bills, long narrow wings.

MANX SHEARWATER *(Procellaria puffinus)* Length 35 cm. Upper parts sooty-black, underparts white. Usually in groups gliding on rigid wings, following contour of waves. When breeding, nocturnal. Breeds in dense colonies in burrows on islands and cliff tops. *Distribution:* Faeroes and Iceland south to Madeira and Azores; summer visitor to Britain, breeding on islands off the west coast.

STORM PETREL *(Hydrobates pelagicus)* Length 15 cm. Could be mistaken for a house martin but has a square tail, slightly hooked bill and tube-nostrils. Plumage sooty-brown, white rump. Usually seen following in wake of ships during the daytime. *Food:* probably plankton and fish. *Nest:* in crevice in old walls or among stones and detectable by musty smell; single egg, dull white, June. *Distribution:* breeds on western isles, Faeroes south to Mediterranean; in Britain on islands to the west of Scotland, Wales, Devon and Scillies.

FULMAR *(Fulmarus glacialis)* Length 46 cm. Like a stocky gull, but has typical shearwater flight; thick neck and no black tips to wings. Plumage white with grey mantle and tail. Yellow beak, bluish legs. Tube-shaped external nostrils. *Distribution:* islands of the N. Atlantic; central Norway; summer visitor to Britain arriving at breeding places as early as November. St. Kilda was the only breeding site in Britain until 1878 but the bird has spread to suitable cliffs all around the coast.

Order   GAVIIFORMES   Divers or Loons

Family   GAVIIDAE

Large, heavy birds with sharp-pointed bills, thick necks, webbed feet and small, pointed wings. Clumsy on land but dive readily and swim under water. Frequent lakes for breeding and in winter are seen off the coast.

RED-THROATED DIVER (*Gavia stellata*) Smallest of the divers. Up-tilted bill most characteristic feature at all seasons. Breeding plumage: red throat, grey head and greyish-brown and uniform upper parts. In winter upper plumage grey-brown and speckled with white, underparts white. *Nest:* near water's edge with or without nesting material; 2 eggs greeny-brown, May to June. *Call:* guttural quack. *Food:* fish, molluscs etc. *Habitat:* breeding-time on both large and small lakes; in winter off-shore. *Distribution:* Europe from S. Sweden northwards; in Britain breeds N. Scotland and islands, and possibly N. W. Ireland. Otherwise regular winter visitor to all our coasts.

BLACK-THROATED DIVER (*Gavia arctica*) Very slightly larger than red-throated diver and with straight bill. Breeding plumage: grey head and back of the neck, black throat with narrow white stripes on sides of neck and breast, squarish white spots on upper parts divided into two patches. In winter darker uniform colouring of upper parts. *Nest:* usually on a small islet but may be on shore of lake. Two eggs, May. *Call:* similar to red-throated diver. *Food:* fish, molluscs etc. *Habitat:* usually on larger, deeper lakes than red-throated diver; mainly on the sea in winter. *Distribution:* Scandinavia and N. Germany north to Arctic; in Britain breeds in small numbers in N. Scotland; winter visitor (rare) elsewhere.

GREAT NORTHERN DIVER (*Gavia immer*) Largest of the divers, about 19 cm. Distinguished in breeding season also by black head and neck and by white spots spread all over upper-parts. In winter similar to black-throated diver but lighter back and greater size distinguish it. A silent bird in the winter. *Food:* as for other divers. *Habitat:* mainly off-shore but sometimes on reservoirs and lakes. *Distribution:* breeds Iceland and Greenland; mainly a winter visitor commoner off northern coasts in Britain but some non-breeding birds may be seen on the coasts in summer.

BIRDS OF THE ALPS

Order FALCONIFORMES Birds of Prey

Family FALCONIDAE Falcons

GOLDEN EAGLE *(Aquila chrysaëtos)* See p. 159.

Family AEGYPIIDAE Vultures

Have much longer wings and smaller tails than eagles, also small naked heads. They are carrion eaters and used to prevent the spread of scab, etc. in goats and sheep by eating the bodies.

*GRIFFON VULTURE *(Gyps fulvus)* Length 112 cm, wing-span 256 cm. Long goose-like neck going straight into longish head and only sparsely covered with white downy bristles. Pale brown plumage; white ruffle of long, narrow crumpled feathers.

← Griffon Vulture

Lammergeyer →

Black tail. In flight head is pulled in, primaries spread out widely at end of long, broad wings. Breeds in the mountains of Hungary, the Balkans, Italy and Spain. Being southern and heat-loving, in Europe they always choose a southern-facing cliff on which to sleep.

*BEARDED VULTURE or LAMMERGEYER *(Gypaetus bar-batus)* Length 115 cm, wing-span 267 cm. Largest bird-of-prey in Europe. Very big, long tail. Black upper parts, rust-yellow underparts; black beard-like feathers on lower mandible; black

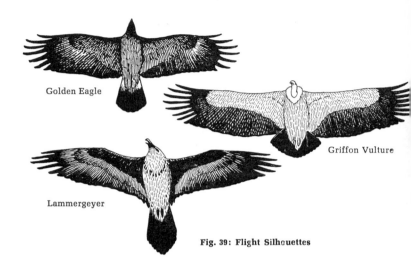

Golden Eagle

Griffon Vulture

Lammergeyer

Fig. 39: Flight Silhouettes

stripe through eye. *Flight silhouette:* long, fairly narrow angled wings and long, wedge-shaped dark tail. Eats only carrion with a preference for bones. *Call:* a thin, plaintive cry. Confined to high mountains. *Distribution:* Spain, Greece, Sicily, Sardinia and Corsica.

Order   PASSERIFORMES

Sub-order   OSCINES   Song Birds

*ALPINE RING OUZEL *(Turdus torquatus alpestris)* Like a blackbird. The male is black with a white ring round its breast; the female is less colourful; feathers of the underparts more or less lighter-edged. When disturbed, flies off with a loud warning *deck deck.* Song like the blackbird's. *Nest:* in scanty groups of trees or in dwarf scrub on hillsides. Nest, 1–2 m above the ground, made of stalks, straws and green moss cemented with moor-earth or cow dung; bowl lined with fine grasses. Migrant. Only bad weather drives it down into valleys.

ALPINE ACCENTOR *(Prunella collaris)* Length 18 cm. Tail 7 cm. Rather smaller than a starling. Looks rather like a lark. Brown plumage with white and black dots on throat and white-streaked flanks. Flicks its tail. Song rather like a lark's. Sings as it ascends and descends; also hovers and soars just above the ground. Really terrestrial. Hops about eagerly, eating seeds, insects, spiders. Untidy nest between stones or in a hole in rock: 5 pale, greeny-blue eggs; in mild weather at least 2 broods. *Habitat:* the higher mountains of southern and central Europe up to 3,000 m; often close to glacier.

*SNOW FINCH *(Montifringilla nivalis)* Larger than a sparrow. Inconspicuous plumage. Ash-grey head, brown back, black throat; dirty-white underparts; beak of adult male black; of female and juveniles orange. White wing patch conspicuous in flight. *Call:* repeated *treetree*. *Song: sitticher-sitticher,* soft and rather staccato. *Food:* looks for seeds, green things on places swept free of snow; good flyer. In summer also eats insects. *Nest:* in inaccessible crevices or holes. *Habitat:* boulder-strewn slopes of high mountains, moraine, snow-ridges, etc. *Distribution:* Pyrenees, Alps, Balkans.

*ALPINE CHOUGH *(Pyrrhocorax graculus)* Length 37 cm. Yellow beak shorter than its head and slightly curved. Red legs. Velvety black plumage. Gregarious. Sailing flight. Clear, shrill call, *skree*. Striking in its easy flight and lack of shyness. *Food:* insects, snails, berries, buds and other bits of plants. *Nest:* of roots, hay and hair built in colonies in inaccessible crevices in rocks. *Habitat:* high mountains, mostly above the tree line up to snow line. *Distribution:* Alps, Spain and S. E. Europe.

*ALPINE CROW *(Pyrrhocorax pyrrhocorax)* A race of the chough, see p. 134. Length 40 cm. Feet and long, thin, curved beak red. Plumage glossy greeny and blue-black. Shrill call. Only in western Alps close under snow line. *Nest:* in crevices.

RAVEN *(Corvus corax)* See p. 135.

NUTCRACKER *(Nucifraga caryocatactes)* About the size of a dove. Dark brown plumage sprinkled with white flecks. White bar at end of short tail. Slow flight on broad wings. Clear rasping *krair* repeated 5–6 times in quick succession. *Habitat:* coniferous forests of the Alps and the north; residence depends on presence of stone-pines, the seeds of which are its favourite food. Sometimes descends into valleys. Occurs sometimes in Britain as a vagrant chiefly to south and east England.

WALL CREEPER *(Tichodroma muraria)* Size of a sparrow with a very long, thin beak, very curved and pointed. Ash-grey with crimson wing coverts on blackish rounded wings. Throat black in summer, white in winter. Butterfly-like flight. Broad, short, black tail with white end band. Rock climber. Climbs half walking, half fluttering without the support of its tail, picking insects out of cracks and crannies. In winter comes to valleys and feeds on south faces of church towers and walls. *Voice:* a clear *da-du-dia-doi*. *Nest:* in inaccessible crevices. *Habitat:* steep, bare rock-faces; in the Alps up to 4,000 m. *Distribution:* all the high mountains of central and southern Europe.

Order   APODIFORMES   Swift

ALPINE SWIFT *(Apus melba)* The swiftest of all the European birds. Size of a blackbird and larger than swift. White under-parts broken by grey-brown throat band. Upper parts grey and sombre brown with metallic sheen. Very short feathered legs. 4 toes all facing forward for clinging. Short beak, huge gape. Flight silhouette shows wings strongly curved in sickle shape. Wonderfully easy, often furious flight; long periods of soaring interrupted with a few quick wing beats. Shrill, trilling cry, while in flight. *Call: ziep ziep.* Untiring flyer in search of insects. *Habitat:* cliffy areas up to snow line. *Nest:* in colonies of up to 100 pairs on inaccessible rock faces, also in ruins and towers. *Distribution:* S. Europe north to Germany.

Order   PICIFORMES   Woodpeckers

THREE-TOED WOODPECKER (Picoides tridactylus) Somewhat smaller than great spotted woodpecker. Only 3 toes on each foot, 2 directed forwards and one back. Colourful plumage, but without red. Black wings with narrow white bars. Black cheeks with narrow white stripes above and below. Broad white stripe down the back from nape to rump. Underparts white. Male has yellow in middle of crown; the female has black crown with white forehead. *Call:* seldom heard, like great spotted's, also a *kek-ek-ek.* Drums much more slowly than other woodpeckers. *Habitat:* coniferous woods of high mountains, especially spruce woods, from 1,000–2,000 m. *Distribution:* Alps, Scandinavia and E. Europe.

Order   GALLIFORMES   Game birds

ROCK PARTRIDGE (Alectoris graeca) Slightly larger than ordinary partridge with a white throat rimmed with a black band. Red beak, iris and legs. Upper parts blue-grey with red shimmer; underparts rust-brown with chestnut mottling. On taking wing a peculiar whistle like *pitchi-i-pitchi-i.* Noiseless flight. Gregarious in winter in large coveys. *Food:* as ptarmigan. Strictly monogamous. *Nest:* a simple bowl. A true mountain bird. *Habitat:* live in pairs on rocky, sunny, grassy slopes; from upper tree region to snow line. Prefers dwarf trees and rhododendrons. *Distribution:* Switzerland, Italy, Roumania and the Balkans.

PTARMIGAN *(Lagopus mutus)* A little smaller than red grouse. White wings and belly, white feathered feet, red wattle over eye. Male has mottled black-brown upper parts, breast and sides (grey in autumn), underparts white; female is yellowish-grey. In winter both sexes are pure white except for black tail and male has a black streak from beak through eye. *Nest:* beside rock or in a clump of vegetation. May to June, one clutch of 7–10 eggs similar to those of red grouse. *Habitat:* rocky slopes and tops of mountains over 1 m. *Distribution:* Northern Scandinavia, Iceland and Scotland.

Class   *REPTILIA*   Reptiles

Vertebrates that breathe with lungs and have skins covered with horny
scales or shields; 4 legs well-developed or degenerate even to being absent
altogether. Fore and hind legs, when they exist, have 5 toes and the toes
have claws. The heart is imperfect, divided longitudinally. Cold-blooded.
Torpid in winter in temperate regions. Reproduction mostly by eggs with
porous or hard shells which are either laid and hatched by heat of sun or
retained in female or hatched out in process of laying. No larval state.
Most species require a hot climate.

Order   SQUAMATA   Scaly Reptiles

Elongated bodies covered with horny scales. Use sight and smell to obtain
food. Darting tongue conveys smell to sense-organs in roof of mouth.

Sub-order   SAURIA   Lizards

Eyelids separate from eyes and able to move freely. Eyes can be shut.
Tongue ending in two short flaps. Belly covered with several longitudinal
rows of ventral shields. Both halves of lower jaw fused together and
immovable. *Food:* insects, worms, molluscs.

Family   LACERTIDAE   True Lizards

SAND LIZARD *(Lacerta agilis)* Body length up to 20 cm. Short
head with a blunt nose; thick, short tail. Upper parts brown or
grey with longitudinal dark stripes and several rows of light-
coloured spots. Underparts of female yellow with black speckles.
In spring male's back and belly (sometimes the whole body) a
vivid green dotted with black "eyes". Occasional darting out of
two-pronged tongue. Behind its gleaming eyes is a dark skin,
"drum-skin". No external ears. 2 lids and nictitating membrane
close the eye (as with birds). Numerous tiny teeth with points
slanted backwards serve to hold on to and kill the insects, spiders,
worms it eats. In summer the female buries 5–14 white oval eggs
the size of a hazel nut with parchment-like shells in loose earth,
which are then hatched out by the sun. The young emerge August
to September and are agile from the first. Several sloughings
during summer. Tail fragile and will break off easily if taken
hold of, to be soon replaced by the growth of another, but shorter
tail, the vertebrae of which will consist of cartilage (regeneration).

The bloodless loss of the tail is an example of autotomy (purpose being to save the creature's life when threatened by enemy seizing tail). *Habitat:* glades, fringes of woods, sunny mounds, hedges and fences. In rain or cold weather in holes in ground or other hiding places, where it will also hibernate. *Distribution:* France, Belgium, Switzerland, Germany, S. Sweden and W. Russia; in Britain parts of Hampshire, Dorset, Surrey and Lancashire.

*GREEN LIZARD *(Lacerta viridis)* Length 30 cm, but up to 50 cm in the south. Big, slender body; long tail. Upper parts a vivid green; underparts light yellow. Top of head brown or oily green, often speckled with yellow. Male's throat in spring is often blue. In female all these colours are "faded". Colouring can vary considerably. Some are black. *Habitat:* clearings in woods. Really Mediterranean. *Distribution:* central and S. Europe.

COMMON or VIVIPAROUS LIZARD *(Lacerta vivipara)* 16–18 cm long with a short, thick tail. The smallest European lizard. Back brown with dark, longitudinal stripes down the middle and on the sides. Underparts brown to black-brown; but yellow-red with black spots in male. Female's colouring is not so vivid. Occasional black ones. Young are born alive, measuring 1.5 cm. Has adapted itself to the short Alpine summer. The mother will go into the sun whenever possible, thus helping the eggs developing in her body. *Habitat:* moors and mountains up to 3,000 m (higher than any other reptile). *Distribution:* Europe generally; in Britain common and widely distributed everywhere except Ireland.

*EYED LIZARD *(Lacerta lepida)* Up to 70 cm or more in length; long tapering tail; grey-brown or grey-green upper parts with sky-blue "eyes" ringed with black; green head and yellow belly. Waits at the mouth of its hole for large insects, lizards, birds, and field mice. *Distribution:* S. coast of France, Spain and Portugal.

*WALL LIZARD *(Lacerta muralis)* Up to 19 cm; slender body, long tail, long, tapering head; grey-brown upper parts with the back covered with black patches; brown band with light edges along each side. Underparts whitish or yellowish. Females lay 2–8 eggs in holes which they dig in ground. *Habitat:* dry, rocky country, ruins etc. *Distribution:* central and E. Europe with many varieties confined to limited geographical regions.

Family   GECKONIDAE   Geckoes

Geckoes are sub-tropical, as well as tropical, and thus some are found in southern Europe. Their fingers and toes are flattened and equipped with adhesive plates (lamellae) so that they can go up vertical surfaces and even walk upside down. They have large eyes covered with transparent membrane, as do snakes. Tail fragile.

*WALL GECKO *(Tarentola mauritanica)* Up to 15 cm. Toes uniformly flat with a single row of broad, lateral lamellae underneath. Has claws only on toes 3 and 4. Light grey to brown or even dull black. *Habitat:* rocks and walls mostly near coast. Often seen in gardens. *Distribution:* shores of the western Mediterranean and eastwards to Crete and Egypt.

*DISC-FINGERED GECKO *(Hemidactylus turcicus)* Up to 10 cm. Only about half of its fingers and toes are enlarged and bear a double row of suckers. Back dirty flesh colour but variable. *Habitat:* in clefts of rock and under stones. Often comes into houses. *Distribution:* Mediterranean countries.

Family   ANGUIDAE   Slow-Worms

SLOW-WORM *(Anguis fragilis)* Length up to 50 cm. Long, legless body. Upper parts blue-grey to grey-brown; belly black. Being a lizard has 2 movable eyelids; back and belly have smooth, similar scales. *Food:* slugs, insects, worms. In summer produces 8–20 young, fully developed in egg membrane which they break through at once. Hibernate. *Habitat:* woods with plenty of undergrowth, tall grass, loose stones. Hides under fallen leaves, moss, in humus, under old tree-stumps, roots, etc. *Distribution:* central and W. Europe; in Britain widely distributed over England, Wales and Scotland.

Sub-order   SERPENTES   Snakes

Snakes have no limbs and cannot shut their eyes as the eyelids have grown back, the lower now covering the eye as a transparent, immovable skin. Belly has only 1 longitudinal row of broad plates. Both halves of lower jaw movable and joined by sinew, thus enabling the snake to swallow large prey.

Family   COLUBRIDAE   Colubers

Head runs into body gradually. Roundish pupils; long upper jaws with numerous teeth. Top of head has 9 large symetrically arranged shields. Eye placed by edge of shield of upper lip.

GRASS SNAKE *(Natrix natrix)* Female up to 150 cm. Male up to 100 cm but thicker. Back grey, but can be brown. On each side of back of head a half-moon shaped yellowy-white patch edged in front and behind with black.White underparts with faint black checkering. Occasional individuals are all black or black with light-coloured spots. Has ventral shields that make contact with the ground and help it to coil. Diurnal. Hunts frogs and other amphibians, rarely small fish, which it consumes whole and alive. Can swim far and dive. Not venomous and quite harmless; does not bite when grasped but hisses, emptying stink glands at root of tail. Lays 2–30 soft-skinned eggs, which are often joined together like a string of beads, in loose earth or moss. Three weeks later the young hatch out, 15 cm long and independent from the start. Sloughs several times in year. Hibernates. *Habitat:* damp woods, bushy marshes and moors, slow-flowing streams with overgrown banks. *Distribution:* central and S. Europe; in Britain widely distributed in England and Wales but rarer in the north; in Scotland only in S. W.

*DICE or TESSELATED SNAKE *(Natrix tessellata)* Length up to 100 cm but in south will reach 150 cm. Narrower, longer head than the grass snake's. Basic colour of upper parts olive-grey, green or light brown with dark brown checkered markings; underparts yellow or reddish with black checkers. Water is its element and it comes ashore only to sun or hibernate, fleeing into water if danger threatens. Harmless; does not bite; hisses when caught and empties the stink glands it has at the root of its tail. Diurnal. Often lies in the water motionless waiting for its prey (fish, or an occasional frog) which it seizes swiftly and swims to land devouring it. In July leaves the water and deposits 5–25 eggs in damp place e.g. under leaves; these are not in a string, but in a lump. *Distribution:* central and S. Europe.

SMOOTH SNAKE *(Coronella austriaca)* Up to 75 cm long; upper parts of male brown, of female grey; underparts of male reddish-yellow; of female steel-grey. Throat and adjacent parts underneath more white. Has a dark patch on the nape and two rows of dark-brown splodges running down its back. *Food:* lizards and slow-worms, occasionally mice or birds. Seizes its prey in a lightning grip by the head, coils round it and strangles it and then swallows it head first. Viviparous. Diurnal. Bites when caught, but is not venomous and otherwise harmless; often mistaken for adder. *Habitat:* sunny, stony slopes with bushes; quarries and hilly country. *Distribution:* Norway, Sweden, central Europe, N. Portugal, Switzerland, Balkans; in England in Hampshire, Dorset, Surrey, Sussex and Wiltshire, but rare.

*AESCULAPIAN SNAKE *(Elaphe longissima)* Up to 180 cm or, in southern Europe, 200 cm long. Upper parts shiny brown; has a yellow patch on either side of the back of its head; underparts yellowish-white. Climbs well. *Food:* mice, occasionally birds. Diurnal. Non-venomous and harmless, except that it bites when caught. *Habitat:* light, deciduous woods. *Distribution:* France, Spain, Switzerland, Germany, Austria, Czechoslovakia, Hungary, Poland, the Balkans.

Family   VIPERIDAE   Vipers

Vipers have a more or less distinct "join" between head and body; horizontal pupils, short upper jaws and on each side just one large, erectile, hollow poison fang and behind at least one small substitute poison fang. Top of head covered with numerous small, irregularly arranged shields. Eyes separated by shield from upper lip shields.

ADDER or VIPER *(Vipera berus)* Length up to 80 cm. Rather thick-set with fairly short, pointed tail. Basic colour various tones of grey and brown. Upper parts of male silvery to browny-grey; female yellowy to reddish-brown. Black or dark brown zigzag stripe down the back from nape to tail, and on the head a dark X-shaped mark reminiscent of a cross. Underparts dark grey to black. Individuals can be all black. Seeks out sunny places. Hunts mice in the evening and by night, killing its prey with a lightning bite with the hollow poison fangs in its upper jaw, before swallowing them. Fears man. Hibernates, often in considerable numbers, under tree-roots and stumps. Lays eggs from which live

young hatch at once. *Habitat:* sparse woods, heath and moor-
lands; in Alps mostly between 1,000 and 2,000 m. *Distribution:*
N. and central Europe; in Britain common in most parts except
Ireland.

*ASP *(Vipera aspis)* 50–60 cm in length, recognisable by its
slightly tip-tilted, sharp-edged snout (no horn) and the yellow
underside to the tip of its tail. Cylindrical body. Basic colour
varies between grey, yellow and brown. Dark marks on back
in the form of narrow bars, which, when contracted form a
zigzag stripe like that of the adder, which it also resembles in
behaviour. Slow, heavy movements. Will try to escape and bites
only if touched. Venomous. *Food:* mostly mice, lizards and
worms. *Habitat:* hilly country. *Distribution:* France, Pyrenees,
Alps, Black Forest (rare) and Italy.

Order   TESTUDINES (= CHELONIA)

Permanent armour on back and belly consisting of bone with
large horny plates. Fat body. Head has horny covering; limbs
and tail covered with stout scales. Round eggs with chalky shell
laid in hole it digs and covers over itself. Does not brood. Lives
to a great age.

Family   TESTUDINIDAE   Land and Pond Tortoises

*TERRAPIN *(Emys orbicularis)* Total length 32 cm, of which
8 cm is tail. Shell some 17 cm × 12 cm. It has 5 fingers and
5 toes with webs and claws, and can both walk and swim.
Carapace upper shell egg-shaped and only slightly curved;
brown or greeny-black; on some plates it has numerous yellow
dots or strokes radiating out from corner to edges. Plastron
(under shell) mostly uniform yellow. Male has whistling call
during the mating season. Suns on land, diving into water when
danger threatens; lively at night and then mostly in the water.
Good swimmer, catching and eating insects, snails, amphibians,
fish and worms. Toothless but can crunch up insects with sharp
horn-rims of its jaws. Drifting air-bubbles suggest its presence.
During June buries 15–30 hard-shelled eggs (some 3 × 1.8 cm)
by night on the shore, digging a hole with the tail and hind feet.
Habitat: stagnant or slow-flowing water. *Distribution:* southern
and central Europe as far north as N. Germany.

Class   *AMPHIBIA*   Frogs, Toads and Newts

Cold-blooded vertebrates with bare, moist skins, rich in glands, the secretions from which are not harmful to humans. All European amphibia have 4 legs, the fore legs with 4 toes, the hind with 5; no claws. In the juvenile stage as tadpoles they live mostly in the water and breathe through gills. (Certain salamanders retain their gills all their lives.) Those that hatch from eggs undergo metamorphosis, gradually achieving the shape of the perfect animal, most of which are terrestrial and breathe with lungs and skin. Lay eggs covered with transparent jelly or, like the salamander, produce live young. Larval state usually lasts 2–4 months, but in the newts may last longer.

Order   SALIENTIA (= ANURA)   Tail-less Amphibia

Squat bodies; grow up without tails. Land and fresh water. Mostly hop on land, paddle in water; many can climb; others dig. Apart from the midwife toad, they lay eggs in water. Tadpoles eat plants (algae) and have a long gut; adults are flesh eaters with short guts; they seize small creatures in their jaws or on an extendible sticky tongue. In breeding season call of male is amplified by external or internal vocal sacs; attain full maturity at the age of 3 or 4.

Family   RANIDAE   Frogs

Smooth skins few warts. Toes have no finger-pads.

EDIBLE FROG *(Rana esculenta)* Male about 7.5 cm, female up to 9 cm, even 12 cm. Smooth skin. Green upper parts with black or yellowish-brown spots and usually 3 yellow or greeny-white longitudinal stripes; occasionally uniform colour. Hind parts marbled black and yellow. Wholly webbed. Eardrum not in black stripe. Male can inflate large, blue-grey vocal sacs on both sides of its head; belly white or faintly yellow, unspotted; has finger-pads. Underparts of female spotted grey. *Voice:* hollow croak, like *quarr,* interspersed with clear *brekekek,* especially on warm summer evenings. Spawns end of May to early June; spawn in lumps that sink to bottom. Eggs brown on top, bright yellow below, 1.5 mm or, with jelly 6 mm. Tadpole spotted brown on top, white underneath, silvery speckles on the sides.

Food: snails, worms, insects, spiders, fry. Eats only live things it has caught itself. From October to April embedded in mud at the bottom of pond, etc., where lives on accumulated fat and breathes through skin. *Habitat:* ponds, bogs, ditches, parts of slow rivers, etc. *Distribution:* France, Belgium, Germany, Italy, S. Sweden, Hungary, Roumania and W. Russia; introduced into Britain in East Anglia and elsewhere but few survived.

COMMON FROG *(Rana temporaria)* Length up to 10 cm. Smooth skin. Blunt front to head. Eardrum in longitudinal black stripe. Web on hind feet extends only to 2/3rds of the way up the toes. Back brown or yellowy with brown patches; sometimes all one colour, rarely with light stripes framed in darker colour. Dark patch on temple. Hinder parts are not marbled. Hind legs have dark bars; underparts white or yellowish, flecked with reddish-brown or marbled. Male has vocal sac in mouth. *Voice:* faint grunt or growl. Tadpole at first black, then brown with metallic patches on belly. Spawn in clumps. Eggs brown-black, up to 1 cm with jelly; spawns in March. *Habitat:* streams, moors and marshes, gardens, woods. Will go farthest from water.

*MOOR FROG *(Rana arvalis)* Up to 6 cm long. Very closely related to common frog, but head has almost pointed "muzzle". Upper parts light brown and the back stripe is usually yellowy-white with a dark rim on either side; milky belly, unspotted; sides of rump marbled black; dark neck spot. Back of male often blue during mating season, early April. *Habitat:* edges of moors etc. inland. *Distribution:* Belgium, France, Denmark, Sweden and eastwards.

MARSH FROG *(Rana ridibunda)* 15 cm. Largest European frog. Colouring olive green or olive brown, underparts whitish with grey patches. Spawns in late April or May. Croaking of males very loud. *Food:* aquatic insects, crustaceans, newts, frogs, fish and even small mammals and birds. *Habitat:* on Continent lakes, marshes and rivers; fond of basking in the sun. *Distribution:* E. Europe, N. and central Germany, Holland; introduced into Britain from Hungary 1935 and has colonised the Romney Marsh area of Kent, where it lives in the drainage dykes.

Family   HYLIDAE   Tree Frogs

Smooth skin, granulated on belly. Toes have finger-pads.

*GREEN TREE FROG *(Hyla arborea)* Length 4.5 cm. Brilliant green in colour, which it can vary to shades of grey, blue or black, according to food eaten, state of health, surroundings, weather, nervous condition, sloughing, mating, e. g. after sloughing, which occurs every 14 days, skin is ash-grey. Juveniles do not change colour. Black streak from nostril to eye across eardrum to where hind leg joins the body. White belly. Male's throat is puckered, golden brown, and when croaking has a large vocal sac to amplify the sound. Female's throat is violet-grey. Can swim well, jump and climb. Croak is a loud, quick, clear *krack krack krack,* especially at night. Spawns end of May to early June. Spawn in several lumps the size of walnuts which remain on the bottom till the tadpoles hatch. Eggs are yellowy as are the tadpoles. *Food:* fish, spiders, beetles, butterflies, smooth caterpillars. From October to April hibernates in a hole in the ground, tree stump. *Habitat:* ponds with plenty of vegetation. *Distribution:* central and S. Europe.

Family   BUFONIDAE   Toads

Warty skins. Glandular swelling behind the eye (parotid).

COMMON TOAD *(Bufo bufo)* Length of female up to 15 cm, male much smaller and slimmer. Squat, plump body; short, thick legs; slow crawlers. Toes of hind feet half webbed. Upper parts yellow, reddish or grey-brown or dirty green, sometimes with dark flecks. Underparts yellow-brown or grey, those of female have dark flecks; the male's are uniform. The legs have black finger-pads. Red iris, horizontal pupil. Male's voice a soft rumbling *reck.* Spawns March to April, not in lumps but in strings 4–5 m in length twined round aquatic plants. Eggs are browny-black and about 1 mm across. Tadpoles are black and often have tiny golden speckles. Largely nocturnal, hiding by day in shelter or some hole it has dug. Hunts at night, only exceptionally by day; eats only live worms, caterpillars, slugs, spiders, beetles. Very greedy. *Habitat:* walls, tree trunks. *Distribution:* Europe generally except Mediterranean region; in Britain widespread and common.

NATTERJACK TOAD *(Bufo calamita)* Length up to 8 cm. Very small webs. Upper parts olive green or brown; narrow, yellow stripe down middle of back to its rump. Underparts grey-white with dark speckles. Greenish iris with black spots. Horizontal pupil. Male has dark grey throat extended with large, round vocal sac when croaking. On warm evenings from April to June, loud *errrr-errr.* Not so plump and stocky as the common toad. Instead of hopping, swims and climbs well. Spends day in holes in ground, wall or under stones. Spawns April to June, strings 5–6 feet long. Tadpoles like those of common toad. Tadpoles blackish, develop into toads in 5–6 weeks; fully mature at 4 or 5 years. *Habitat:* dry, sandy places. *Distribution:* France, Spain, Portugal, Switzerland, Denmark, S. Sweden, Poland and W. Russia; in Britain restricted to a few localities, mainly in sand dune areas.

*GREEN TOAD *(Bufo viridis)* Up to 9 cm long, slighter build than common toad; quick hops on long hind legs; hind feet are half-webbed. Upper parts grey with distinct, dark green flecks. Underparts whitish-grey or yellow with dark flecks. Iris greeny with narrow gold edge. Horizontal pupil. Male has vocal sac. Voice, a continuous trilling *oorrr-oorrr.* Spawns April to June; eggs in strings. Can be seen during the day, especially after warm rain or near water. *Distribution:* mainly E. Europe and as far north as S. Sweden.

Family   PELOBATIDAE   Toad Frogs

More like frogs than toads. Hind legs relatively long.

*SPADEFOOT TOAD *(Pelobates fuscus)* Length up to 8 cm. Female larger of the two. Stocky build. Vertical pupil. Toes of hind feet webbed to the end. Trim smooth skin on upper parts, which, in male, are light brown, in female light grey with irregular patches of brown or olive-green. Whitish belly often with grey or grey-brown flecks. Large, knife-sharp horny callous in front of smallest toe on underside of hind foot, serving as spade for digging. When disturbed exudes a secretion that smells of garlic. In Germany they are called garlic toads. No vocal sac. Voice of the male a deep rumbling *quack* thrice repeated. Nocturnal. By day digs itself a hole in the ground, also for hibernation. *Food:* worms, slugs, soft-skinned insects. Spawns April to May; a short, thick string. Tadpole blackish at first, then lighter; olive-brown on back growing to up to 17 cm. *Distribution:* central and E. Europe.

Family DISCOGLOSSIDAE

Rounded tongues joined throughout. Triangular or roundish pupils.

*MIDWIFE TOAD *(Alytes obstetricans)* Up to 5 cm. Thick-set body. Hind feet have very short webs. Upper parts blue-grey with small pimples; underparts light-grey or white. Vertical pupil. No vocal sac. Voice of male is loud like a glass bell, keeping to same note and interval; heard in spring and summer in the evening and at night from holes in walls or the ground. Hides during the day. *Food:* insects, worms, snails. Spawns in May. String of eggs in which the male tangles his hind legs and so carries them round with him for weeks, scraping them off into the water shortly before they are due to hatch. Hind legs then look as though fettered with dried egg-string. *Habitat:* hilly or mountainous country. Under stones, in walls, quarries, under roots or in holes in the ground. Not far from water. *Distribution:* S. W. Europe from Spain and Portugal to France, Belgium, W. Germany and Switzerland.

*FIRE-BELLIED TOAD *(Bombina bombina)* Up to 4.5 cm. Slim build. Hind feet fully webbed. Skin very warty. Round or triangular pupils. Eardrum invisible. Underparts blue-grey to blue-black with red or orange patches and white dots. Upper parts black-grey with black flecks. Male has internal vocal sac which extends to throat when croaking. *Voice:* a quite melodious *unk-unk* with frequent pauses; often goes on all night. *Food:* worms, snails, insects. Hibernates under stones, roots of trees, etc. Runs well on land, good swimmer; when threatened creeps into mud. When prevented from escaping bends the head back displaying vivid colouring of under parts, then flings itself on its back and its glands secrete a white, poisonous fluid with a strong smell. Spawns May to June. Eggs are laid either singly or in small lumps, attached to bottom or water plants. *Habitat:* ponds, ditches, etc. *Distribution:* Denmark, S. Sweden, Germany, Roumania, Yugoslavia, Bulgaria and east to Ural Mts.

*ORANGE-SPECKLED TOAD *(Bombina variegata)* Up to 4.5 cm. Squat. Shorter and more rounded muzzle than the other toads. Warty skin. Feet webbed to tips of toes. Underparts have large, yellow splodges on blue-grey or almost black ground. Upper parts light or dark grey, sometimes with dark mottling. Male has no vocal sac. *Voice:* like soft bells coming from a distance. Spawns mid-April to August, otherwise as other toads. *Habitat:* small ponds, etc. in hilly or mountainous areas. *Distribution:* France, Holland, Belgium, Germany, Alps, N. Italy.

Order   CAUDATA (= URODELA)

Salamanders and newts

Long bodies; well-developed tail. Land and freshwater; crawl slowly using legs; swim by wriggling tail.

Family   SALAMANDRIDAE   Newts and Salamanders

NEWTS

Newts have paddle-tails pressed in at the sides and in the breeding season the males have a crest down the back and tail. Adults only in water during mating season; otherwise hide in holes in the ground, under stones, etc. Female lays 100–400 eggs surrounded by transparent jelly, mostly at night, depositing them on leaves. Larvae live in water and, exceptionally, can retain gills up to sexual maturity and reproduce even as larvae. No voice. Live up to 30 years in captivity.

CRESTED or GREAT WARTY NEWT *(Triturus cristatus)* Male up to 13.5 cm in length, female up to 16 cm or even 18 cm. Lizard-like build. Tail as, or nearly as, long as the rest of the body, pressed in at sides with upper and lower seams. Large head, blunt muzzle; relatively large eyes; small nostrils opening in front of muzzle; no gills in adult state; 4 rather weak legs, the fore-feet have 4 toes, the hind 5. Moist, soft, warty skin. During mating season male has a high, serrated crest along its entire back with a deep gap at the base of the tail; and long silvery-blue-white streaks along each side of its tail. The crest disappears in summer. Female has no crest, just a seam of skin on her tail. Upper parts black-brown with or without dark spots; throat blackish with white dots, like the sides. Belly orange with large black blotches. Eggs adhered individually to waterplants. Larvae hatch out after 2–3 weeks, feeding at first on the tiniest aquatic creatures, later on worms, insect larvae, snails, etc. From June to July leave the water temporarily in search of hiding places on bank, but still feeding in the water. Young leave the water about September. Adults spawn from mid-March to May. Larvae have very fine tails with pointed ends; very long fingers and toes. On either side of the back of the head a cluster of external gills. *Habitat:* clear, but not running water, with plants in lowland and hills up to 600 m. *Distribution:* central and N. Europe; in Britain widely distributed but local.

SMOOTH NEWT *(Trituris vulgaris)* Length of male up to 11 cm, of female up to 9.5 cm. Rather slim build. Skin smooth or finely granulated. Male in mating season has a tall, serrated crest continuing along its tail without a gap at the root of the tail. The toes on the hind feet of the male have broad skin-seams. Male's upper parts brown or olive green with round, black spots; middle part of belly yellow to orange, flanks whitish with large, round blackish spots; lower skin-seam flecked alternately with blue and orange. Female's upper parts clay colour with dark spots sometimes running into each other to form two longitudinal stripes; belly straw-coloured to orange with dark patches. Appears in water sometimes as early as February, even in tiny puddles of dirty water; leaves water sometimes as late as September, then for the entire winter. The skin-seams disappear when it leaves the water. Spawns from mid-March to May. Usually in low country, but is found up to 1,000 m. *Distribution:* N. and central Europe; in Britain widely distributed in England, Wales, Scotland and W. Ireland.

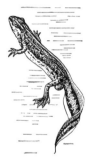

PALMATE NEWT *(Triturus helveticus)* Length of male up to 7.5 cm, of female up to 9.2 cm. Fairly slim; tail rather larger than rest of body with a skin-seam. Smooth skin. Blunt end of tail with a thread-like tip some 8 mm long. Very low crest. During mating season has web between toes of hind feet. Upper parts brown or olive green, mostly with small dark dots; on each side of head a dark lateral stripe through the eye. Belly yellow, usually unspotted, in the middle round dark patches on the sides, not merging to form a band. Spawns from March on. *Habitat:* slow-flowing streams, ditches, ponds and lakes. *Distribution:* France, N. Spain, Switzerland, W. Germany, Belgium, Holland; in Britain widely distributed but local in England, Wales and Scotland.

*ALPINE NEWT *(Triturus alpestris)* Length of male up to 11 cm. Thickset. Tail as long as, or shorter than body, with skin-seams top and bottom. Smooth skin. During breeding season male has a low crest, not serrated and with no gap at root of tail. Female has no crest. Upper parts of male light blue-grey, sometimes marbled; back seam banded with black and yellow. Sides of head, neck and rump white with round black spots: streak of blue along flank. Throat and belly uniform bright orange. Female has grey-blue upper parts with dark marbling; no blue streak on flanks. Sides of tail black spotted with bluey-white. Winter colouring very dark, almost black, upper parts and fairly warty skin. Spawns by end of May or up to July in mountains. Common on mountains. Takes to land shortly after reproduction. *Distribution:* central Spain and French Alps across central Europe to N. Italy and N. Greece.

SALAMANDERS

Round tapering tails. No crest. Nocturnal and only active by day in rainy weather. Mate only on land. Viviparous. Hibernate in sheltered holes.

*SPOTTED SALAMANDER *(Salamandra salamandra)* Length up to 20 cm. Plump body; broad head; tail shorter than rest of body. Slimy, shiny skin with 2 rows of glandular pores. Upper parts black with irregular bright yellow spots. Usually only in mountains. Emerges by night or in rainy weather to feed on worms, slugs and larvae of insects. Slow movements. Changes colour to intimidate. Secretion of skin glands fatal to small mammals or birds. Gives birth to 20–40 live young in water; these are 2–3 cm long, black-grey, with 4 limbs and laterally compressed paddle-tails, and breathe through branched gills not yet having lungs as the fully developed salamander has. Hibernates often in numbers in some place sheltered from frost. *Habitat:* damp, shady woods in gorges or narrow valleys; under roots; in quarries. *Distribution:* S. E. Europe, Appenines, Alps and central and southern Germany.

*ALPINE SALAMANDER *(Salamandra atra)* Length 11–16 cm. Shiny uniformly black, no spots; round tapering tail. Stiff gait. Mostly seen only in wet weather. Lives in groups. Hides in moss, under wet stones and bushes. Produces 2 live young each year, which spend the entire larval stage in the mother's body; on being born take to dry land at once, thus adapted to shortness of Alpine summer. *Food:* slugs, worms, spiders, caterpillars. *Habitat:* Wet woods, gorges on and above tree zone up to 3,000 m; none below; never under 600 m. *Distribution:* mainly in Alps.

Class   *PISCES*   Fish

Vertebrates that live in the water, whose blood is of variable temperature, are almost all covered with scales and a thick layer of slime. They breathe with gills: delicate membranes with many blood vessels able to conduct gases. Fertilisation in water. Female lays eggs (spawn) in water, where-

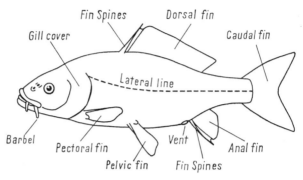

Fig. 40: Parts of a fish

upon the male squirts so-called milt (sperm cells) over them. The paired pectoral and pelvic fins steer the fish up or down or to either side. (Fig. 40.) Dorsal, caudal and anal fins maintain its balance. The tail (caudal fin) is the most important means of propulsion. Newly hatched fish or larvae have hard fin seams which gradually develop into dorsal, caudal and anal fins. The size, shape, position and colouring of the fins is important in distinguishing species. All fins are supported by soft rays or hard spines, the number of which also helps to differentiate species, as does the length of the lateral line, the number of scales in this line and the number of rows of scales above it.

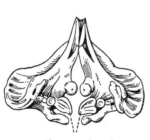

Pharyngeal teeth

**Fig. 41:
Throat-teeth of the Carp**

The mouth opening (Fig. 42) can be what is called superior (at the top), inferior (underneath) or in the middle of the snout. Some teeth are stronger, conical canine teeth or fangs, others are small, closely spaced bristle-like hackle teeth. Practically all the bones in the mouth of a fish can carry teeth. In carp the last pair of gill-bones has developed into throat-teeth (Fig. 41). The gill structure consists of 4 bony bars, roofed by movable bones of the gill cover. The inner side of the gill plates have sifters, which are very long and close together in the plankton-eaters. On either side there are at least 5 gill slits, through which the water taken in for breathing is discharged. Most fish have a "swim-bladder", which is a protrusion of the front gut and in most species remains linked to it by an air duct. In perch and stickleback it is completely closed. Ground fish such as bullhead, blenny, flounder, lamprey, have none.

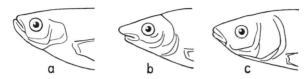

Fig. 42: **Mouth opening can be** a) **superior** b) **inferior** c) **in the middle of snout**

In tench the swim-bladder is elongated and one-chambered; in carp it consists of 2 linked chambers. When the swim-bladder is open gas can escape, also when fish snatches air on the surface; when the bladder is closed the quantity of gas is reduced by means of the "oval", a thin part of the bladder's wall with numerous blood-vessels which will conduct gas. The amount of gas in the bladder is only increased or diminished when the difference in depth is considerable. Minor alterations of specific gravity are adjusted by means of the bladder's muscles for rising or sinking. The

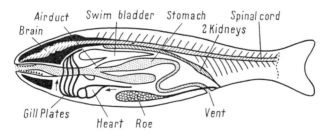

Fig. 43: **The inner structure of a fish**

"lateral line" is the seat of a kind of sixth sense, and is recognisable by the pores in the scales along it. From these pores short lateral channels lead into a slime-filled longitudinal channel which has tiny sensitive hairs or sense cells, from which nerves lead. Thus the fish feels any change in the pressure of the water, e. g. caused by the approach of a solid body, and also changes in the strength and direction of the current. The entire surface of the body is also covered with sense cells which transmit touch impressions.

SNAKE-LIKE ELONGATED FISH

Lampreys are no longer regarded as true fish, but as a special group of round-mouthed fish.

Sub-class   *CYCLOSTOMATA*   Round-mouthed

The group compromises fish of primitive type; skeleton of cartilage (gristle), no bones; snake-like body; no scales; very slimy skin; no pectoral or pelvic fins, no swim-bladder. Round sucker mouth without jaws, but have horny teeth. 7 gill holes on either side. Only one nostril.

Family   PETROMYZONTIDAE   Lampreys

LAMPREY *(Lampetra fluviatilis)* Length up to 50 cm, weight up to 100 g. Spawns April to May. Round worm-shaped body; full-grown the thickness of one's thumb. Tail pressed in at the sides. Single fin-seam divided into 2 dorsal fins and a small caudal fin; ventral fin only just indicated. Fully opened mouth is almost circular with a fleshy rim instead of lips. Cavity of mouth has numerous horny teeth and a rasp-like tongue; also teeth in front. Behind each of the two small eyes are 7 gill openings, and in the middle of the head a single nostril. Upper parts a shiny greeny-blue, sides yellowish white; belly silver; fins violet. *Food:* smaller creatures on the bottom and organic remains in slime. Will also prey on other fish, attaching itself by mouth disc and boring deep holes with its rasp-teeth; will

also attach itself to corpses. Buries itself in mud for the winter and emerges in March. Swarms can be seen in stony streams attached to stones in couples for spawning. Eggs hatch after 1 week into 4 mm long larvae, ammocoetes, difficult to distinguish from worms; have tiny heads, eyes hidden under the skin and mouths without teeth or tongue. Bury themselves in mud. Spend 4–5 years in larval stage. Fully developed they go to the sea, where they feed on fish spawn, fish and the lower aquatic creatures. Return to stream, even lakes and larger rivers to spawn. Larvae used as bait, adults as food.

LAMPERN (BROOK LAMPREY *(Lampetra planeri)* Length 8–36 cm. Spawning March to June. Body the thickness of a pencil. Second dorsal fin comes immediately after the first. Distinct anal fin. Back slate-grey or grey-brown to blue-green; sides lighter; belly silver with reddish or yellow tinge. Fins slightly lighter than back. Otherwise as the lamprey. Spawns in sandy or gravelly parts of small streams. Digs a hole for spawn. Larvae without teeth or eyes. Gill openings still covered with skin. Feeds on plants and animal particles in mud, in which it lives for 3–4 years. Upper reaches of even smallest streams.

SEA LAMPREY *(Petromyzon marinus)* Length up to 1 m; weight up to 3 kg. Spawns March to May. Elongated body round almost to the ends. A large gap between first and second dorsal fins. Upper parts whitish

marbled with black-brown or dark olive green. Belly white. Otherwise as lampern. December to May ascends rivers on Atlantic coasts. Excellent eating.

Order   APODES (Teleostei)

Bony skeleton. Paired and vertical fins. Almost always scaled. Swim-bladder (except in perch family).

Family   ANGUILLIDAE Eels

EEL *(Anguilla anguilla)* Male up to 50 cm; female up to 150 cm. Spawns in early summer. Fore part of body round, hind part slightly compressed at sides. Dorsal, caudal and anal fins form one fin. Small eyes. Small, oval scales, not connected, deeply embedded in thick skin or absent

altogether. Very small gill slits. Back is dark grey to olive; underparts yellowish or grey-white with a silvery sheen. Crawls and swims by sideways undulating movements of its long tail. Spawns in the Sargasso Sea. Male weighs up to 180 g; the female 1–2, even up to 6 kg. *Development:* journey to shores of Europe as transparent, leaf-shaped larvae 7 mm long at a depth of 27 fathoms in ocean currents; reach the coast at the age of 4, as transparent snake-shaped elvers, 6–8 cm long, the thickness of a knitting needle, with dark dots in front of the eyes. Ascend the rivers in swarms, mostly close to the surface, close to the bank. During this ascent they become coloured, grey or grey-green, and begin to eat, which they have not done before. (Where weirs, etc. have been built eel ladders are sometimes made.) Ascent finishes in ponds, ditches, tiny streams. Nocturnal, spending day in holes in the bank, under roots, in mud with only the head protruding; hunt at night, feeding mostly on small creatures and spawn. After 7–10 years in fresh water they are fully developed, they change colour: the belly becoming silver, the back darker and the whole body metallic; and they stop eating. This takes 3–4 months while they make their way by night, covering up to 50 km in 24 hours, back to the sea; where they make for the Sargasso Sea to spawn. This journey takes a year, during which time they do not eat, yet develop larger eyes and sexual organs; colouring darkens.

Family   COBITIDAE   Loach

*POND LOACH or MUDFISH *(Misgurnus fossilis)* Up to 30 cm in length. Spawns April to June. Long and eel-like, almost cylindrical in front, somewhat pressed in at sides towards the rear. Small head, narrow undercut mouth; six largish barbels on the upper, and 4 smaller ones on the

lower lip. Very small eyes. Small scales buried in the skin and covered with a thick layer of slime. Rounded fins. Dorsal fin set well back. Colouring varies. Upper parts and sides yellowy-green; underparts orange. Several dark brown longitudinal stripes and numerous black flecks and dots Burrows in bottom for snails, mussels, etc. using barbels. Is supposed to know of thunderstorms 24 hours in advance. Very sensitive to delicate shifting pressure. If lacking oxygen, being both a gill and an intestinal breather, it rises to the surface to swallow air. The middle section of the intestine has a close network of blood vessels and is an organ for breathing, obtaining oxygen from air forced into it, thus enabling the mudfish to live in stagnant water and pools. Exists through periods of drought by digging itself into the mud. *Distribution:* widely distributed in Europe, but does not occur in the British Isles.

SPINED LOACH *(Cobitis taenia)* Up to 12 cm long. Spawns April to June. Elongated body, compressed at sides. Under each eye is an erectile spike with a locking joint. Mouth undercut and narrow. 6 very short barbels on upper jaw, 4 in front and 2 above the corner of the mouth. Very small scales. Sandy camouflage colouring, rows of brown patches on yellow ground. A brown-black streak through the small eye to the tip of

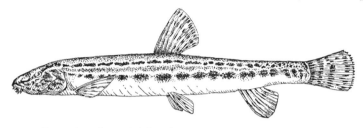

the snout. Dorsal and caudal fins have rows of dark spots; anal, pectoral and ventral fins yellowish-white. By day buries itself up to the head in sand. Swallows sand and blows it out through the gills, swallowing the tiny creatures sieved out in the process (worms, larvae and vegetable matter). *Habitat:* brooks, ditches, stagnant water with sandy or muddy bottom.

STONE LOACH See p. 244.

FISH WHOSE SHAPE AND APPEARANCE CANNOT BE CONFUSED

Family   ESOCIDAE   Pike

PIKE *(Esox lucius)* Up to 100 cm long. Spawns in mid-February to late April. Long, cylindrical body; dorsal and anal fins opposed, near to tail.

Very long snout, somewhat like a duck's beak. Protruding lower jaw. Broad mouth with a deep gape. Numerous larger and smaller hackle-teeth. Colouring varies with location: back olive, browny or grey-green; sides may have light or dark oblique streaks; in first year of life mostly light green. Very greedy predator that lies in wait and darts out suddenly on prey. Smaller fish, frogs, birds, mammals swallowed whole; even swallows 10-spined sticklebacks. It will kill, but not swallow a 3-spined stickleback. Can live for 20–30 years, grows to 2 m in length and weighs 70 lb. Found in lakes and most slow-flowing rivers. *Distribution:* found in most parts of Europe.

Family   Cottidae   Bullheads

MILLER'S THUMB or BULLHEAD *(Cottus gobio)* Up to 20 cm long. Spawns February to May. Its grotesque appearance is unmistakeable: broad, flat head, broad mouth, round body which has no scales except on lateral line. Strikingly large pectoral fins; two long dorsal fins, rounded caudal fin, short spines on gill cover. Camouflage colouring depends on

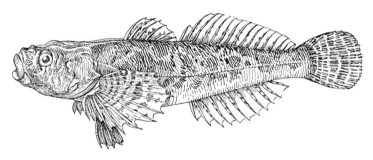

location: lives on bottom; shy. By day under or beside a stone and scarcely distinguishable. No swim-bladder. Crawls slowly about the bottom feeling for worms, larvae of dragon-flies and gnats, then suddenly darts away to another place. Male guards and defends eggs, adopting a threatening attitude if a trout comes along, increasing the size of its head by opening its gillspikes wide. Prefers clear, quick flowing water and stony, gravelly bottom. In trout areas under stones even in the tiniest brooks and also in lakes up to 2,000 m. Often found in turbulent water under weirs. Very greedy. *Distribution:* Europe, generally in lowland areas but not in mountainous regions.

*ALPINE BULLHEAD *(Cottus poecilopus)* Ventral fins strikingly long and narrow, reaching to the vent. Lateral line runs above the middle line of the body, while in the above it runs below it.

Family   Siluridae   Catfish

WELS *(Silurus glanis)* Up to 3 m long and weighing up to 250 kg. Spawns May to June. The second largest river fish in Europe. Body cylindrical and thick in front, in the rear compressed at the sides. Broad flat head; very large mouth, as wide as its body with a large number of hackle-teeth; has 2 long worm-shaped barbels that it can move at will on its upper lip, and 4 short barbels on the lower lip. Its skin is scaleless and slippery, its eyes small, sited above the corners of its mouth. Dorsal fin very short and placed well to the front; anal fin very long; caudal fin rounded. Small paired fins. Colouring varies considerably: upper parts dark with olive-

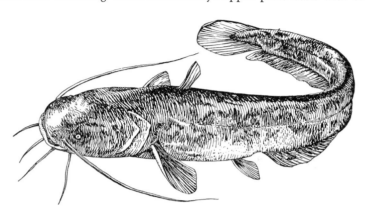

grey tinge; sides and belly lighter. Blackish marbling from the back on to the sides and on to the anal fin. Lurks by day in holes under jutting parts of the bank or on a dark muddy bottom, feeling and savouring the water with its barbels. Greedy predator. *Food:* fish, crabs, frogs, water birds, water mammals. Hunts by night. Spends winter in deep holes in mud, often several together, in a sort of hibernation. Prefers rivers or deep lakes with plenty of vegetation and boggy bottom; spends most of its time in still deep water. *Distribution:* Danube basin and eastern Europe. Young wels have tasty flesh, but that of old fish is tough and somewhat oily. The roe is prepared as caviar. Introduced into England.

Family   GADIDAE   Cod

BURBOT *(Lota lota)* Length up to 60 cm. Weight up to 8 kg. Spawns November to March. Cylindrical body, somewhat compressed at sides near the tail. Broad, flattened head; wide mouth with small hackle-teeth:

1 barbel thread on the chin and 1 short barbel on each nostril. Small scales. 2 dorsal fins, the second of which is very long; long anal fin and rounded caudal fin. Small pelvic fin placed under the throat in front of the pectoral fin and serving as a ground-support. Upper parts brown to oily-green; sides lighter; underparts dirty white to yellow. Blackish-brown marbling especially on upper parts. Very greedy predator, dangerous to all small fish. As a juvenile eats small aquatic animals, then fish that it can master, even sticklebacks and its own kind. Unsociable except at spawning time. Flesh is tender and tasty and relatively free of bones. The liver is accounted a delicacy, but it requires plenty of cooking as the undeveloped tapeworm *(Dibotriocephalus)* can occur in it. Strictly a bottom fish. Nocturnal. Found in flowing and stagnant water. Prefers deep water. Found up to 2,000 m.

Family   PLEURONECTIDAE   Flat-fish

FLOUNDER *(Platichthys flesus)* Length up to 50 cm with flattened asymmetrical body and both eyes on top side (mostly righthand side). Colouring of the upper part adjusted to that of the bottom it is on; brown

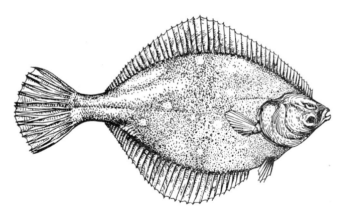

to dark olive green with yellow spots, under (blind) side being light yellow to yellowish-white with fine black spots. Spawn January to May return to the sea. *Food:* mussels, snails, worms, larvae of insects, crabs small fish. *Habitat:* coastal and brackish waters, but also ascending rivers Very tasty flesh. Large numbers are caught on their way back to the sea and in the sea.

FISH FOUND BOTH IN STAGNANT AND RUNNING WATER

Family   CYPRINIDAE   Carp

COMMON CARP *(Cyprinus carpio)* Length up to 1 m. Weight can be over 20 kg. Spawning season May to June. Stout build with highly arched back. Happily omnivorous, thick-lipped mouth capable of being "turned back", with 4 stout barbels that serve as organs of touch while burrowing in slime for food. Very large eyes; one long dorsal fin with 17–22 soft

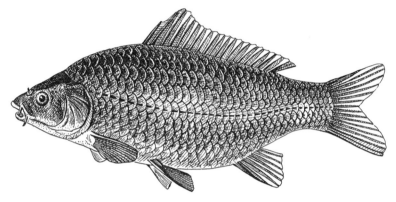

rays. No teeth in jaws, but pharyngeal or throat teeth. Colouring and shape vary according to race and geographical location. Back usually blue-green to dark, or brown-green; sides golden-yellow turning into blue. All except dorsal fins, grey to blue-grey with a hint of red. Several varieties of carp are farmed commercially for food; there are also leather carp which have almost no scales, and mirror carp with enlarged silvery scales. Carp feed on larvae of gnats, worms, molluscs etc.; also plant food. Small carp catch small crustaceans. Carp do not eat during the cold season remaining in deep water in a form of hibernation. In warm night during May and June the females move into shallow water to spawn, laying, it has been calculated, 700,000 eggs for every half kilogram they weigh. Originally came from Black Sea area, Central Asia, China and Japan. Prefers shallow, muddy sunny waters with plenty of plants, and avoids quick-flowing, clear, overshadowed or cold water.

IDE *(Idus idus)* Length up to 80 cm. Weight up to 8 kg. Spawns April to July. Resembles the chub which is the same size and lives in the same waters, but its head and mouth are smaller. The ide has a stocky body, rather compressed at the sides; mouth rather oblique and narrow in middle position. Colouring varies according to age, location and season of the year. Back usually dark grey-blue or black-blue; sides lighter, silvery belly. During spawning its sides shine like brass. A domesticated variety is the golden orfe, the back and sides of which are orange or the colour of red lead, the underparts silvery, and on the sides are broad violet longitudinal stripes. Its fins are red at the base, white at the top. Sociable, mostly seen near the surface especially in clear, not too shallow water. Feed on plankton and insect larvae, crustaceans, snails; also leap for

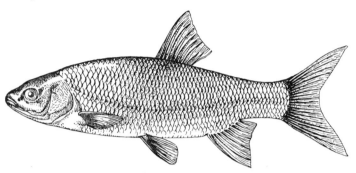

insects in the air. Spawns with much splashing among plants and stones near sand, banks. Common in all Continental lakes and rivers of any size north of the Alps and Pyrenees. Tasty flesh, but has lots of bones.

ROACH *(Rutilus rutilus)* Length up to 40 cm. Weight up to 1.5 kg. Spawns April to May. Dainty, fairly high-backed and yet slender white fish, compressed at sides. Short head. Mouth central, narrow and rather

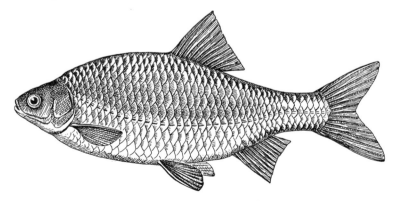

oblique. Red iris. Upper parts grey or blue-green; lighter on the sides towards the belly, silvery. Fins red. Sociable. As juvenile eats algae and plankton; then worms, insects, crustaceans, fish spawn, small fish and aquatic plants; also sucks out shellfish. Found in both stagnant and flowing water in shoals; seeks deeper water in winter. Very bony flesh and of little value as food.

BREAM *(Abramis brama)* Length up to 70 cm, weight up to 6 kg. Spawns May to July. Very compressed at sides; very high back with belly similarly curved; very small head; short dorsal fin and long anal fin. I row of throat teeth. Upper parts leaden grey to black; lighter sides,

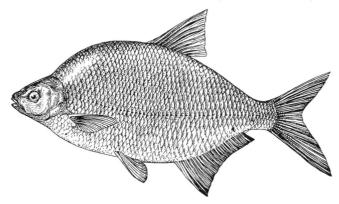

white belly. Fins grey or blue-black. Finds food in mud on bottom, reed-worms, larvae of various insects, snails and small mussels; in doing so its snout, which it can protrude, leaves small funnel-shaped holes. Lives in shoals in warm lakes or lower reaches of rivers; likes deep, quiet water with muddy bottom. Very good to eat.

TENCH *(Tinca tinca)* Length up to 70 cm. Weight up to 6 kg. Spawns May to July. Stocky and colourful; thick lips; one tiny barbel at each corner of its mouth; rounded fins; very small scales beneath a thick layer of slime. Male has elongated ventral fin, the second rays of which are thick and curved. Colouring varies according to surroundings: upper parts

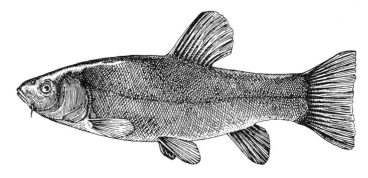

dark or light olive green shot with gold; underparts light or reddish grey with violet sheen; dark fins. A magnificent variant is the golden veil which is green shot with gold and has a red rim to its mouth. Lives on bottom and likes to stay in one place. Food and reproduction very much as the carp's. Stagnant and slow-flowing water with muddy bottom and plenty of vegetation. Both the golden veil and the tench are farmed commercially on the Continent. The tench keeps the carp clear of fish-leeches and "opens the ground" so that young carp are better able to get at their food. Good to eat.

GUDGEON *(Gobio gobio)* Length up to 15 cm. Spawns May to June. Spindle-shaped, almost round body with a thick head and a blunt arching snout, mouth in inferior position with 2 barbels. Upper parts grey-green with dark mottling (gravel colour) especially along the lateral line;

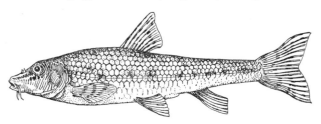

underparts silver with a reddish tinge. Dorsal and caudal fins. Yellowy with patches of black-brown, which the pectoral fins often have as well. Pelvic and anal fins yellowish-grey. Almost always in dense shoals that dart about the bottom keeping together in a remarkable way. It purses its sucker mouth forward, sucks up mud and ejects it again after obtaining from it tiny creatures, fish-spawn, particles of plants. Found in lakes, rivers, streams; prefers clear water with a sandy or gravelly bottom. Good to eat.

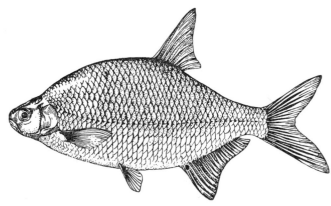

WHITE BREAM *(Blicca björkna)* Up to 40 cm long, weighing up to 1 kg. Spawns May to June. Easy to confuse with the bream, but differs from it in that its skin feels hard, that of the bream soft and slimy; the bream's fins are grey, while the white bream's pectoral and pelvic fins are reddish at the base. Habits are those of the bream. Very bony and not very good to eat.

Family   PERCIDAE   Perch

PERCH *(Perca fluviatilis)* Up to 35 cm long. Spawns March to June. Stocky, torpedo shape; has 2 adjoining dorsal fins, the front one of which has sharp spine, the second rays. Pelvic fin has one spine and 5 rays; the anal fin 1 spine and 8 rays. Gill-cover has 1 spine. Mouth in central position, has wide gape and numerous teeth. Large eyes. Scales have a spiky

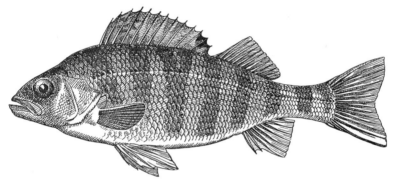

point on the hind edge so that the fish is rough to the touch. Upper parts dark and greenish, sides turning brown or yellow, and have broad dark vertical bars (camouflage among reeds). Whitish belly. Dorsal fins grey, the front one having a dark patch on its rear edge. Pectoral fins yellowish; pelvic and anal fins red; caudal fin partly red. Colouring varies with surroundings. Predator. Juveniles eat crustaceans, insect larvae; on attaining 15 cm, which often means not till the age of 8, they become fish-eaters eating fish up to finger-length as well as amphibians. Found in clear rivers and streams, lakes, ponds; usually in small shoals swimming close to the surface. Good to eat.

POPE or RUFFE *(Gymnocephalus cernua)* Up to 25 cm long. Spawns March to May. Stocky body not so high in the back as the perch; and the division between its 2 dorsal fins is not so distinct. Fat head with large eyes. Fore dorsal fin has stout spines. The rear of gill-cover ends in a spine; the front has short spines. Upper parts olive to browny-green with irregular dark patches often making vague longitudinal streaks. Underparts whitish; shimmer of red on pectoral region. Dorsal and caudal fins have dark spots. Large shoals at certain seasons in various areas. Prefers clear, deep lakes. Is attracted by noise and Baltic fishermen smack their boats to entice them. Very good to eat.

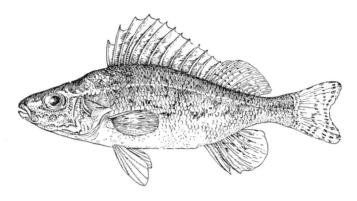

PIKE-PERCH *(Stigostedien lucioperca)* Up to 130 cm long and weighing up to 10 kg. Spawns April to early June. Pike-like build; elongated head, but pointed and smaller than that of a pike. Small crest scales. Spine fins. The front dorsal fin has stout spines. Mouth in central position, large. Elongated fangs between numerous small bristle-teeth. Back and sides

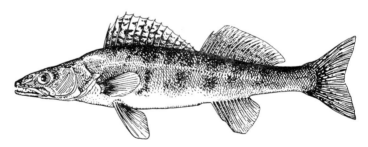

greenish-grey; juveniles have vertical streaks over back onto sides, which later becomes blurred and faded. Belly silvery white. Fins not red, but grey to yellowy-grey. Dorsal fins have longitudinal rows of blackish dots. Caudal fin has vertical line of black spots. Greedy predator. Lives in lakes and slow-flowing rivers. Really belongs to the Danube basin; introduced into Rhine etc. in the 1880's. Eggs are very hard and can be transported. Pike-perch first feed on small aquatic creatures, then small plankton-eating fish. Very good to eat; they are also "farmed".

Family   GASTEROSTEIDAE   Stickleback

THREE-SPINED STICKLEBACK *(Gasterosteus aculeatus)* Up to 9 cm long. Spawns late March to June, out of which period it is an inconspicuous, dainty and lively little fish with a slim pressed-in shape. Its dorsal fins consist of 3 separate stiff spines; the pelvic fins consist of 1 spine and 1 ray; the anal fin of 1 spine and a row of soft rays. The body is scaleless

but mostly armoured with bony plates instead. Upper parts olive green to blue-black, white underparts. But during the breeding season the male has a bright green back with a shimmer of blue; shiny red throat and at the sides of the belly; emerald eyes. *Food:* insect larvae, worms, small fish; also fish-spawn (not its own). Builds a nest of straws and roots which it collects in its mouth and cements with a sticky secretion from the kidneys produced from vent. Then, with its snout, it bores a hole in this potato-sized nest. The female, ready to spawn, is then led to the nest and introduced, when she lays 60–120 eggs the size of poppy seeds. The male fertilises the eggs and thereafter defends the nest and eggs; with its tail fans fresh water over them, takes any that die in its mouth and spits them out outside; makes holes in the roof of the nest to improve the circulation of water. The eggs hatch after 8–10 days. The male still looks after them, taking any that stray too far in its mouth and returning them to the nest. Lives sociably by banks of rivers and lakes, among plants and stones; in pools and ditches with sandy bottoms. (In certain places they are fished commercially for making fishmeal and oil.)

Family   SALMONIDAE   Salmon

SMELT *(Osmerus eperlanus)* Up to 30 cm long. Spawns end of February to end of May. Fleshy (adipose) fin above the tail. Spindle-shaped body. Wide mouth with pointed teeth in jaws; lower jaw protrudes. Caudal fin deeply notched. Scales small and transparent, as they lack the substance that provides the silvery gloss. Back grey-green; sides silvery, belly white. In live fish the ribs, intestines and brain can be seen through the skin. Eats plankton, small bottom-creatures and fish. The Continental river smelt found in lakes attains only 15 cm, while the sea smelt attains 30 cm. Flesh excellent, though has a distinctive smell. Also used as animal fodder.

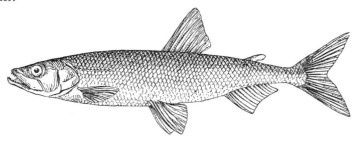

FISH FOUND ONLY IN STAGNANT OR SLOW-MOVING WATER

Family   CYPRINIDAE Carp

RUDD *(Scardinius erythrophthalmus)* Up to 30 cm long; spawns April to June. Differs from roach in that the arch of the back is higher; the scales between the pelvic and anal fins are bent down like a roof, forming a

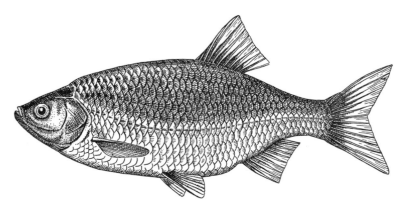

sharp keel-like edge to the belly. Very steep mouth-opening; sides shine like copper; rainbow-coloured gold-gleaming skin. Pelvic, anal, dorsal and caudal fins orange to red, but black-grey at base. 2 rows of throat-teeth. Otherwise as the roach.

CRUCIAN CARP *(Carassius carassius)* Length up to 50 cm, weighing up to 1 kg. Spawns May to June. Differs from ordinary carp in having a higher back, being more pressed in at the sides, having no barbels and a very tall, long dorsal fin. Mouth in central position, small. Caudal fin

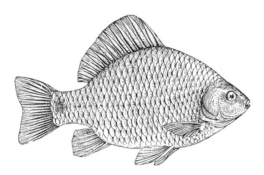

only slightly notched. Colouring often varies: upper parts mostly dark olive green, sometimes shot with steel-blue, getting lighter down the sides; underparts brassy-yellow. Pectoral, pelvic and anal fins have tinge of red. Dark patch at root of tail. Bottom fish. *Food:* worms, larvae, rotting vegetable matter. Common in most of Europe. Prefers still water, especially shallow lakes with marshy shores, marshes and bogs; will even be content with a tiny, dirty pool if the muddy bottom has enough vegetation growing in it. Good to eat.

GOLDFISH *(Carassius auratus gibelio)* Differs from the crucian, which it greatly resembles, in having larger scales and no black patch at the root of tail. Tends to have silver or gold colouring. It is the basic goldfish.

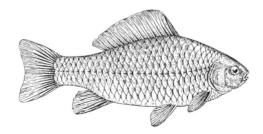

Originated in eastern Asia. It will be content with almost any water and can be fed on table scraps, so it can be domesticated. As well as deep red there are variants patterned with black and white, and others checkered and barred with various colours.

BLEAK *(Alburnus alburnus)* Up to 20 cm long. Spawns April to June. Dainty, slim, pressed-in fish, usually about the length of a finger; it has a small, oblique mouth in superior position. Back blue-green, sides and belly white with lots of silver. Often shoots out of water to snap at gnats or to avoid attack. *Food:* insect larvae, isopods, *Cladocera,* plankton, flies, gnats. Large shoals at spawning time congregating in shallow, gravelly

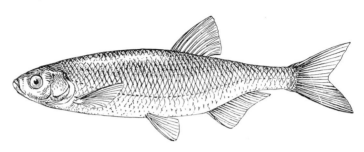

areas. Common in ponds, lakes etc. Sociable; lives near surface, playing just under the surface in hot, windless weather. No good to eat, but used as manure and fodder. Scales used to make artificial pearls.

*MODERLIESCHEN *(Leucaspius delineatus)* Up to 12 cm in length. Spawns April to May. Pretty, little fish with low, torpedo-shaped body thickening somewhat in front; narrow, steeply superior mouth and protruding lower jaw. Large eyes. Short, incomplete lateral line ending close to the head by the 8th or 12th scale. Scales detach easily. Deeply notched

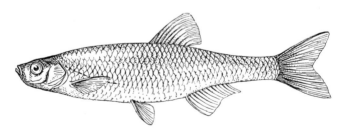

caudal fin. Belly sharp-edged behind the pelvic fins. Back and top of head greeny-brown, sides of head and body striking silver with steel-blue longitudinal streaks towards the rear. Fins yellowy or whitish. In shoals; often go over on their sides allowing a glint of silvery underparts. Eat small aquatic creatures and algae. Found in small, stagnant or sluggish waters in central, eastern and northern Europe; is even found in pools in peat-bogs and heaths.

Fish Found Only in Running Water

BITTERLING *(Rhodeus amarus)* Up to 9 cm long; spawns in the spring. So named because its flesh has a bitter taste. Dainty fish with high back, very pressed-in sides, that swim about in shoals. Short head, small mouth in central position. Incomplete lateral line extending only to scale 5 or 6. Usually grey-green back and silvery sides. Distinctive shining blue-green

horizontal streak from middle of side to tail. Fins pink, except for a caudal fin which has a grey base. In breeding season the male's back is steel-blue and violet, its belly a glowing orange-red, the side streaks a magnificent emerald, while a black edging emphasises the red of its dorsal and anal fins. The female retains her modest colouring but acquires a reddish-yellow ovipositor 3 cm long, which she pushes into the evacuatory opening of a mussel and lays her eggs in its gill-cavity; the male then squirts its milt over the mussel's breathing vent so that sperm cells enter with the water the mussel takes in thus fertilising the eggs. When hatched the bitterlings remain among the mussel's gills until they are able to swim. The mussel gets its own back by having its own progeny spend their final stage on the skin of bitterlings. Live in clean, sluggish water with muddy or sandy bottom and overgrown banks.

MINNOW *(Phoxinus phoxinus)* Up to 10 or 12 cm. Spawns April to June. Surface fish always in large shoals. Tiny, almost invisible scales. Torpedo shape; pressed-in at sides near tail. Colouring varies considerably with location. Back olive green to dirty grey with dark spots; sides silvery

or greeny-yellow often with dark vertical streaks; gold-glittering longitudinal streak running from behind the eye above the lateral line. Breast
and belly yellowish or white, sometimes scarlet; fins pale yellow, the
dorsal, anal and caudal fins often tinged with black; pectoral pelvic and

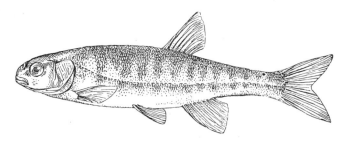

anal fins can be purple-red. Eats plant food, worms, insects. At spawning
moves in great shoals. Lives in streams and rivers with sandy, or gravelly
stretches.

BARBEL *(Barbus barbus)* Up to 70 cm and weighing up to 12 kg. Spawns
May to July. Elongated shape with trunk-like snout, mouth in inferior
position, thick, fleshy lips with 4 barbels on the rim of the upper one.
Notched caudal fin; short dorsal fin with 7–9 rays. Colouring varies: upper
parts grey-green; greeny-white on sides and belly with a golden gleam.

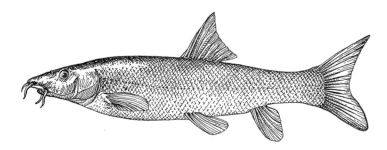

Dorsal and caudal fins grey-green; pectoral, pelvic, anal fin and lower
part of caudal fin tinged with red; sometimes the barbels are a strong
yellow. Spends the day on the bottom among aquatic plants, feeds by night
on worms, snails, mussels, insect larvae; also spawn and fry. Moves up
river in shoals to spawn. In autumn and winter take to holes or go
behind stones and stay there in shoals. Prefers river with swift-flowing
water and sandy, gravelly bed. Edible but very bony. Roe poisonous
especially at spawning, causing vomiting and diarrhoea if eaten.

CHUB *(Squalius cephalus)* Length up to 60 cm. Weight to 5 kg. Spawns April to June. Long, almost round body; in older fish stout and "chubby". Big, broad heads; mouth deeply cleft in central position, pouting lips. Large scales. Upper parts black-green, sides yellow-green; belly white to

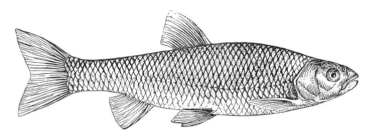

yellowish, cheeks and gill-cover on pink ground. Golden shimmer. Dorsal and caudal fins dark grey with tinge of red or yellow. Anal and pectoral fins bright red. Sociable near surface; but when old tends to be more solitary and seek deeper, open water. Likes to shelter under overhanging banks, stones, etc. As juvenile eats small animals, plants; also rises to feed; then becomes a predator eating small fish, frogs, crustaceans and trout spawn. Prefers strongly running water. Very bony flesh.

DACE *(Leuciscus leuciscus)* Length up to 30 cm. Weight to above 300 g. Spawns March to May. Very similar to chub, but has narrow mouth in inferior position; lighter basic colour with stronger silvery gleam, and paler

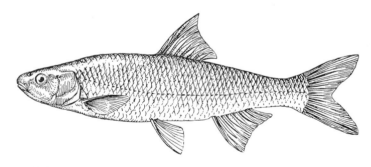

fins; and the outer edge of the anal fin is concave. Back black-blue; sides and belly yellowish or white. Paired fins pale yellow-orange; dorsal and caudal fins grey to dark grey. Sociable; hunts on surface for disabled flies; also eats plankton, insect larvae, aerial insects, snails, etc. Prefers quick-running water. Flesh very bony.

NASE or SHAD *(Chondrostoma nasus)* Length up to 50 cm. Weight up to 1.5 kg. Spawns March to May. Snout protrudes and looks like a nose (which is what it is called in Germany). Mouth in inferior position with sharp, horny rims. Elongated body. Back black-green to dark grey-blue;

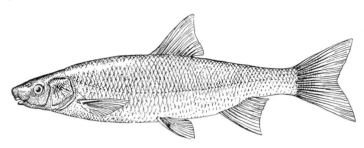

sides silver-white; underparts yellowish to white. Fins tinged with pink. Mostly in large shoals. Frequently heels over so that its silvery sides gleam. Eats plant matter, small creatures, sieved through gill-covers. When caught spits out lots of slime. Moves in shoals up river and into brooks and streams to spawn, which it does over gravel. Found north of the Alps. Bony flesh, but edible.

Family   COBITIDAE   Loach

STONE LOACH *(Nemacheilus barbatulus)* Up to 15 cm long. Spawns April to May. Elongated body, fore-part round. Somewhat pressed-in at the sides towards the tail. No free spine. Mouth in inferior position, narrow. 6 barbels on upper jaw, 4 in front and 2 at corners of mouth. Tiny scales. Most have dark brown-green backs with light grey or grey-yellow sides

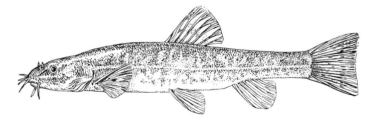

and underparts. Black patches scattered about its back and also on its dorsal, caudal and pectoral fins. (Camouflage.) Distinct lateral line. Spends the day mostly in a hollow under a stone, roams about at night in search of fish-spawn and small creatures to eat. Clear water, on firm and strong bottom, shallow brooks, ditches and flat lake shores. Good to eat.

Family   SALMONIDAE   Salmon

Distinguished by having a small, ray-less adipose fin behind the dorsal fin.

BROWN TROUT *(Salmo trutta [forma fario])* Length 25–40 cm. Spawns October to January. Predator: arrow-shaped, almost round body. Short blunt muzzle; mouth split extending to behind the eyes. Between dorsal and caudal fin is a small, stumpy adipose fin, often red at the tip. Caudal fin deeply forked as a juvenile, in maturity almost straight: in older males the lower jaw becomes slightly bent upwards; it has numerous sharp,

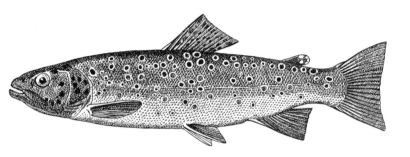

slightly curving teeth. Colouring varies with surroundings. Back is dark or blue-green; sides becoming lighter and lighter towards the belly. Head and sides have a shimmer of yellow or gold and spotted with black and red, the latter ringed with mostly blue or white. In shady streams the colouring is darker; in sunny streams lighter; thus, on the continent, they can be called "black", "white", "stone", "forest" and "mountain" trout according to their location and colouring. In small, quick-flowing brooks they are at the most 40 cm long and 1 kg in weight; in deeper water or in lakes and ponds where there is plenty of food they can be up to 90 cm and weigh 5–6 kg. Juveniles have 8 or 9 dark vertical streaks. Mostly in the shadow of an overhanging bank or just above the bottom; head pointing upstream. Eat only live, moving prey: tadpoles, minnows, water fleas, worms, insect larvae, snails, fry; also rise to mayfly etc. that have alighted or are flying just above it. Spawns first in its 2nd or 3rd year, going upstream until it finds a suitable place with clear water and a gravelly bed. At this season the male becomes more colourful and will bite to drive other males away. Female scoops out a trough with her tail anything from 20–50 cm across (depending on her size) and oval; here she lays her yellow eggs, the size of peas, which adhere to the gravel. The male then fertilises them, whereupon the female covers them up with gravel. Likes cold, mud-less water with plenty of oxygen; thus mountain (or northern) streams and lakes fed with spring water. Spends the day in one spot, moving away only in morning or evening dusk, but returning to its lie later. Very good to eat. Farmed commercially since 1763.

RAINBOW TROUT *(Salmo gairdneri)* Up to 50 cm in length, 5 kg in weight. Spawns December to May. Shape similar to trout; colouring varies back blue-green or green; sides lighter, browny-yellow with rainbow-glinting reddish longitudinal streaks that are especially vivid in the male a

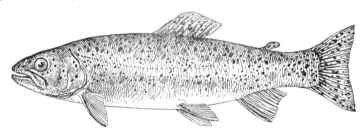

spawning time. Back, sides, dorsal, adipose and caudal fins all well speckled with black. Introduced from America in 1882. Will endure higher temperatures and more pollution than the brown trout. Feeds and lives as brown trout. Very good to eat, and thus also farmed.

BROOK TROUT *(Salvelinus fontinalis)* Length 20–45 cm. Weight up to 5 kg, but mostly about 1 kg. Spawns October to March. Shape like char. Mouth split extends to behind the eyes. Black brown or olive green with

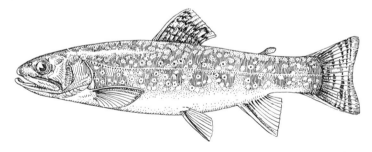

lighter marbling; sides lighter with lots of small yellow and a few red spots; belly white to dirty orange. Dorsal and adipose fins coloured and marked like the back; pectoral, pelvic and anal fins red with fore-edge fringed with white and black. During spawning the male's belly is a beautiful orange. Behaves like a trout, but is more sociable and not so shy; also more lively in its hunting. Introduced from North America in 1882. Likes even colder water than the brown trout.

SALMON *(Salmo salar)* Up to 150 cm long. Spawns from October to January. Long, spindle-shaped body, somewhat compressed at the sides. Head relatively small with a long jutting snout. During spawning the male's lower jaw is curved in an upward hook. Colouring very variable: back blue-green; sides silvery with a few black spots, as has the head; underparts white and shiny. Male at spawning time has a deep black back;

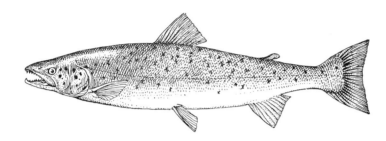

head and sides tinged with blue and flame-red spots; belly is a vivid red or orange; the fins are partly chrome-yellow. Young salmon have red spots, like trout, and also 10–12 browny or blue-grey vertical bands or oval patches running from the back down over the sides. Predator. At the age of 1–3 years the young salmon, called smolt, let themselves be carried downstream in the spring to the sea, which journey can take several months. In the sea with its wealth of food they grow rapidly and, reaching maturity, they leave the sea and enter the river from which they originally came, many even ascending to the very stream in which they were hatched. (This has been proved by tagged fish.) They ascend the rivers slowly during the winter and spring, not eating, and surmounting weir, sluices and such obstacles by leaps of 2–3 m. Some places artificial step-like ladders are built to help them. The journey from the mouth of the Rhine to Basel in Switzerland takes 45–60 days. They spawn in clear water some 50 cm deep on a gravel bottom. Males fight each other for the females, making good use of their hook-like lower jaws. The female fanning with her tail scoops out a hollow about the length of a man and in its she lays 10,000 to 40,000 reddish-brown eggs, while the male fertilises them with his milt. The eggs are then covered up by the female. The salmon then make their way back to the sea, but many are too exhausted to do so and die. Those that reach the sea soon recover and, when their time comes, go up their river once again. These fasting journeys in fresh water leave narrow dark frayed areas visible between the yearly growth rings of the salmon's scales, thus it has been possible to discover that 10 per cent at most make a 2nd or 3rd spawning journey, while to make 4 journeys is rare. The age of a salmon is 8 at the most. The distances between feeding grounds in the sea and spawning place in the river may be very great. The journey up river occurs at such different times that, for example in the Rhine, salmon can be caught throughout the year. (The flesh of the descending fish is worthless.) Salmon go up most rivers that mouth into the coast of the Atlantic and Arctic Oceans, North and Baltic Seas.

GRAYLING *(Thymallus thymallus)* Length up to 50 cm. Weight up to about 1.5 kg but usually between 0.5 and 1 kg. Elongated body with small pointed head and a strikingly tall and long dorsal fin. Narrow mouth with fine bristle-teeth inside. Deeply notched caudal fin. Colour varies: back

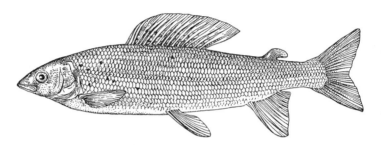

greeny-grey or blue-grey to ash-grey (hence its name), turning into silver or brassy-yellow on the sides; irregularly scattered black spots and dark yellow longitudinal streaks. During spawning has a golden-green shimmer over its whole body: dorsal, caudal and anal fins deep purple; pectoral and pelvic fins dirty-yellow. Otherwise rather like the trout, though it does not live in the same way, but lies in free water, just off the bottom and mostly alone. Only the juveniles form shoals. *Food:* larvae of gnats, worms, small water-snails, mussels, insects that alight on, or fly just above the surface of the water; on occasion even fish. Life span 14 years. Spawns in gravelly places with 30–60 cm of water. When hatched, the young fish are kept together in shoals by their distinctive smell (like thyme). A true river fish, it avoids lakes and large ponds. Prefers definite sections of small rivers. Good to eat.

ARTHROPODS

External skeleton of chitin, a horny substance, made up of rigid segments, linked together by thin chitinous skin; the armoured limbs (appendages) are also jointed. The individual segments of the chitin armour are moved by muscles attached to the inner walls: inner muscles (Fig. 44) in contrast

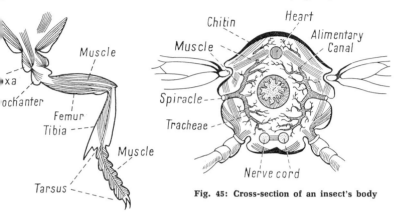

Fig. 44: Leg of an insect:
outer articulation and inner muscles

Fig. 45: Cross-section of an insect's body

to the outer muscles and inner skeleton of the vertebrates. The position of the principal organs inside the arthropod's body is exactly the opposite of that in the vertebrate's body. The heart is dorsal (lies along the back); the nervous system is ventral (on the belly side), a double nerve cord running the whole length of the body, the two cords being linked in each segment of the body by a transverse cord, the whole being rather like a rope-ladder (Fig. 45). In each segment of the body the nerve-cords have a knot-like thickening: a ganglion. The nerve-cords are joined in front with a ring of nerves encompassing the gullet. This gullet-ring has a large thickening on top, which may be called the insect's brain. The dorsal heart is round, or rather, tube-shaped. Most of the white blood plasma enters and leaves this tube by openings in the side and circulates freely in the body cavity. Most arthropods lay eggs, though a few are viviparous. The arthropods are divided into 4 related classes (see front end-papers).

CHARACTERISTICS OF THE 4 CLASSES OF ARTHROPODS

. INSECTS

Bodies distinctly articulated into regions: head, thorax, abdomen. Thorax has 3 segments each with 1 pair of legs; the 2nd and 3rd may also carry a pair of wings each. The abdominal segments are flexible. 3 pairs of jaws varying in shape according to what the insect eats, enabling it to bite and chew or to pierce and suck. Breathe through air tubes: tracheae. 2 compound eyes composed of a number of individual eyes and several simple eyes in

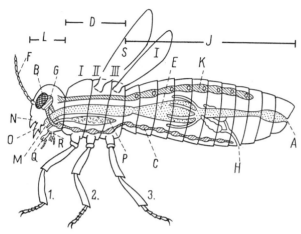

Fig. 46: Structure of an insect's body. A) vent B) eye C) nerve-cord D) thorax E) alimentary canal F) antenna G) brain H) reproductive vent I) rear wing J) abdomen K) heart L) head M) mouth N) maxillary palpus O) mandibles P) salivary glands Q) maxilla R) labial palpus S) front wing 1, 2, 3) the 3 pairs of legs

forehead etc., 1 pair of antennae or organs of smell. Feeling organs are the maxillae (second jaws) and the labium (third pair of jaws joined to form one lower lip). Reproduction by means of eggs from which larvae hatch undergo metamorphosis, either complete, that is to say including a pupa stage, or incomplete, when there is no pupal stage.

2. CENTIPEDES AND MILLIPEDES

Long arthropods with a large number of similar or nearly similar body segments and multiple pairs of legs. 1 pair of antennae. No wings. Breathe through tracheae.

3. SPIDERS

Head and thorax are fused together to form a cephalo-thorax (head-chest). No wings or antennae. 2 pairs of mouth organs and 4 pairs of legs. No compound eyes, only simple eyes situated on top, never the front, of the cephalo-thorax. True spiders usually have 4 pairs of eyes. Well equipped

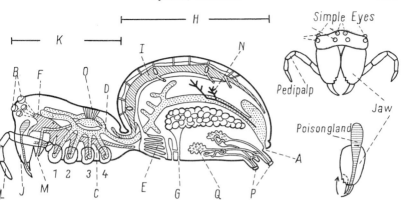

Fig. 47: Body structure of a spider. A) vent B) eye C) nerve-cord D) gut E) lung-book F) brain G) reproductive opening H) abdomen I)heart J) chelicera (jaw) K) cephalo-thorax L) pedipalp M) mouth N) kidney O) stomach muscle P) spinnerets Q) silk glands 1, 2, 3, 4) the 4 pairs of legs

with tactile organs (long stiff hairs [setae] on the body), legs and a pair of palpi (pedipalps), etc. Breathe through tracheae, either tubes or fan-tracheae (lung-books). The latter are sacs in the abdomen which contain fan-shaped thin leaves layered one on top of the other and filled with blood. The tube-tracheae are branching channels lined with a spirally thickened layer of chitin, each starting at a spiracle or breathing hole (stigmata). No pupal stage. The young spider grows in a series of moults.

4. CRUSTACEA

Arthropods with anything up to 20 body segments. External skeletons made of chitin strengthened with calcium salts. On each segment at most 1 pair of limbs, but together always more than 4 pairs. 2 pairs of antennae

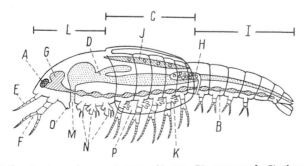

Fig. 48: Body structure of a crustacean. A) eye B) nerve-cord C) thorax D) gut E) antenna F) antennule G) brain H) reproductive opening I) abdomen J) heart K) gills L) head M) mouth N) mouth parts O) upper lip P) carapace

(the other arthropods have only 1 pair, if that) as organs of smell and taste, also main seat of touch. Breathe by gills or use the whole surface of the body. No tracheae. Mostly aquatic.

Class   *INSECTA*   Insects

Types of Larvae and Pupae of Insects

Metamorphosis The chitin armour does not grow with the young insect and thus has to be shed. Where the young are hatched as miniatures of the adult, maturity is achieved after several moults. This is the case with the primitive wingless insects (silverfish, spring-tail). Where there are juvenile

Fig. 49: Incomplete metamorphosis of the Great Green Grasshopper

stages, different in structure and way of life to the adult state, the process of change is called metamorphosis. The first of these stages is the larval. Some larvae are considerably different from the adult. Where metamorphosis is in steps (may-fly, dragonfly, grasshoppers, earwigs, lice, true bugs) it is called incomplete metamorphosis. In these juvenile stages the insect resembles the adult; but where there is a stage of rest, that of pupa, it is called complete metamorphosis (*Hymenoptera*, beetles, lacewings, butterflies and moths, two-winged flies, fleas). These have a larval stage quite different from the adult insect (the imago).

TYPES OF LARVAE

A. Larvae without abdominal legs.

1. Larvae with 3 pairs of well-developed thoracic legs.

a) Soft skinned, little chitin, mostly whitish, e.g. larvae of cockchafer.

b) More or less strong chitin; thoracic segment usually distinctly separated from the other segments and larger and stronger; head usually has simple eyes at the sides, e. g. ground beetles, water-beetles, carrion-beetles, etc.

2. Larvae with only slightly developed or vestigial thoracic feet; still the sole means of progression, e.g. many beetles and the larvae of wood wasps.

3. Thoracic legs wholly retrogressive.

a) With head-capsule and typical development of mouth-parts (chewing). Many are soft-skinned, whitish, live in seclusion: bark-beetles, bees, wasps, ants, etc.

b) Larvae without head-capsule, strongly retrogressive or transformed mouth parts, mostly soft skinned, whitish. Maggots, e.g. flies. Fly maggots have only crawling pads, no feet.

B. Larvae with abdominal feet as well as 3 pairs of thoracic feet. Long bodies of equal segments, definite head. Well-developed chewing mouth parts.

1. The caterpillars of butterflies and caddis flies.

2. The pseudo-caterpillar of the sawfly.

Difference: true caterpillars have only 2 or 5 pairs of abdominal feet. Pseudo-caterpillars have 8 pairs of soft abdominal feet on the 2nd to 9th abdominal segments, making a total of 11 pairs of feet as a rule.

TYPES OF PUPAE

1. Exarate or free. Limbs lie free along the body; e. g. beetles, *Hymenoptera, Neuroptera.*

Fig. 50: Types of pupae: a) **exarate or free (beetle)**; b) **obtect or mummified (butterfly)**; c) **coarctate barrel-shaped puparium of a fly**

2. Obtect or fused. Covered or mummified pupae have the limbs firmly stuck on to the body by a tough hardening secretion and are only visible in relief, e.g. butterflies.

3. The pupae of some flies are enclosed in the hardened last larval skin which is retained as a barrel-shaped puparium. See also "Beetle Family" (p. 256) and "Butterfly Family" (p. 256).

IMPORTANT DISTINGUISHING FEATURES OF INSECTS

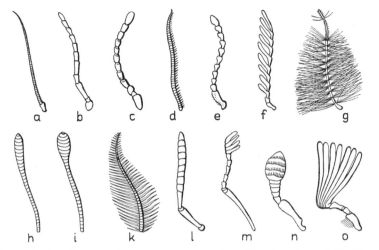

Fig. 51: **Various forms of insects' antennae:** a) **thread-like (grasshopper)** b) **filament (ground-beetle),** c) **string of bead-shaped** d) **serrated (hawk-moth)** e) **serrate (click beetle)** f) **comb-shaped (click beetle)** g) **spirally-haired (male gnat)** h) **club-shaped** i) **stud-shaped** k) **feathered** l) **elbowed (hornet)** m) **elbowed lash with multiple comb-club (stag beetle)** n) **elbowed lash with simple club (bark beetle)** o) **elbowed with fan-club (maybug)**

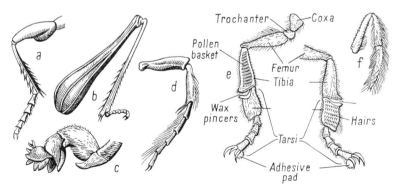

Fig. 52: **Shapes of insects' legs:** a) **for running (ground beetle)** b) **for leaping (grasshopper)** c) **for digging (mole cricket)** d) **for swimming (water beetle)** e) **honey bee (back leg of a worker — for collecting), left viewed from outside, right from inside** f) **for grooming (butterfly)**

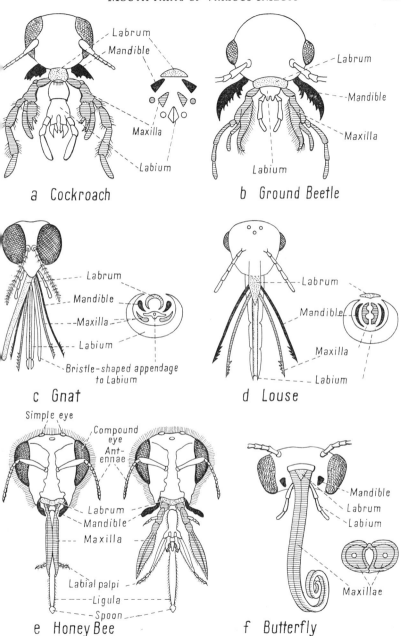

a Cockroach

b Ground Beetle

c Gnat

d Louse

e Honey Bee

f Butterfly

Fig. 53: **Parts of the mouth: a) chewing mouth of a plant-eater, beside it its cross-section b) chewing mouth of a flesh-eater c) and d) piercing/sucking mouths e) licking/sucking f) sucking (upper lip lined; upper jaw black; lower jaw hatched, lower lip white)**

The Orders of Insects in Brief

Order   COLEOPTERA   Beetles

Minute to very big. Head, thorax and abdomen easy to distinguish. Body mostly strongly chitinised; most have walking legs, but some have swimming, digging and leaping legs. 4 wings: the fore wings or elytra are horny cases – wing-cases, hard or leathery, often shortened; the hind or flight wings are membranous, usually hidden under the wing-cases, often degenerate. 2 compound eyes. 2 antennae, most with 11 sections and very different in shape. Chewing mouth parts. The 2nd thoracic segment carries the scutellum, a small, often triangular horn-shield that is inserted between the wing-cases. The abdomen is mostly covered by the wing-cases. Lay eggs. Larvae of varying structure, but long, with 1–6 simple eyes, short antennae, 3 pairs of legs (the wood-boring ones are legless). Complete metamorphosis: free pupa. *Beetles and larvae:* plant or carrion-eaters, robbers; also many are miners. Picture shows: maybug or cockchafer.

Order   LEPIDOPTERA   Butterflies and Moths

Small to very large; often highly coloured. Head, thorax and abdomen distinct. 3 pairs of legs; 2 pairs of membranous wings covered with scales; scales carry the colour; antennae of various shapes. 2 compound eyes; often 2 simple eyes. Sucking mouth part. Lay eggs. Complete metamorphosis. *Larvae:* long caterpillars; body has 13 ring-shaped segments, of which the 3 front ones each have a pair of jointed thoracic legs; also 2 or 5 pairs of unjointed pro-legs on the segments of the abdomen; 2 abdominal legs on the penultimate ring (pusher), though in some these are lacking. On either side of the head 6 or fewer simple eyes; jaws for biting. Often able to spin silk. 4–5 moults. Mummy-like pupa, often in cocoon. Adults mostly feed on nectar; caterpillars eat plants; many are leaf-miners or leaf-rollers. Terrestrial. See p. 316. Picture shows: scarce swallow tail.

Order   TRICHOPTERA   Caddisflies

Small to medium; mothlike. 4 large wings covered with fine hairs or almost bare, a few have hairy scales. Long, filament-shaped antennae. Mouth organ for sucking and licking. Complete metamorphosis. Eggs laid in or on water in gelatinous mass. *Larvae:* aquatic; caterpillar-like; able to spin; many build protective cases out of particles of plants, grains of sand, snail shells, etc.

Bushy tracheae-gills on abdomen. Many live free or in funnel-shaped tunnels of silk. Most are vegetarian, but a few are carnivorous. Pupate in cases which are fixed to some object in the water. Picture shows: *Limnephilus rhombicus.*

Order   NEUROPTERA   Lacewings

Medium sized, long bodies inconspicuously curved. Legs for walking. 4 similar, large, delicate wings, veined in a net pattern, held roof-wise when at rest. 2 compound eyes, sometimes also frontal eye. 2 filament-shaped feelers. Chewing mouth part. Complete metamorphosis. Larvae mostly have pointed mouth parts adapted for biting or sucking; carnivorous. Pupae curved. Terrestrial and aquatic. Picture shows: common lacewing.

Order   HYMENOPTERA   Sawflies, Ants, Wasps, Bees etc.

Tiny to very large; 4 membranous wings, in rest spread flat over the abdomen, often degenerate or lacking. Legs for walking. Often a deep "waist" between 2nd and 3rd abdominal ring; but not in the case of the wood wasps and sawflies. Compound and simple eyes. Antennae variously shaped. Mouth-parts adapted for chewing or licking-sucking. Egg-laying organ often jutting free or adapted for stinging. Carnivorous or vegetarian (pollen, nectar). Many of the bees, wasps and ants are sociable and organise division of labour; by giving superfluous larvae of the females special food turn them into "workers". Complete metamorphosis. *Larvae:* pseudo caterpillars (p. 252) or head and footless maggots; many are able to spin; free pupae, often in a cocoon. Vegetarian, carnivorous parasites or feed on pollen and nectar. Some form, or live in, galls. Terrestrial. Pictures shows: honey bee, bumble bee, wasp, ant, sawfly.

Order   DIPTERA   Two-winged Flies

Tiny to medium in size. 2 pairs of membranous wings, the hind pair reduced to knobs on stalks for balancing. 2 compound eyes; mostly have simple eyes as well. Antennae mostly brush-shaped. Mouth-parts for licking or piercing-sucking. Legs for walking often with a pad between the claws. Terrestrial; blood-suckers, predators, external parasites, eating pollen or sucking plant juices. Complete metamorphosis. Larvae have no feet; the lower forms have a head and mouth-part; the higher forms have no head-capsule but greatly modified mouth-parts (fly-maggot); mostly terrestrial, seldom aquatic. *Food:* carrion, excrement, plant material (miners, gall-producers, predators or internal parasites). Free pupa, or mummified or barrel-shaped.

1. Sub-orders BRACHYCERA and CYCLORRHAPHA Flies
Mostly thick-set bodies. Antennae are short and have 3 joints. Wings and legs relatively short. Mouth-parts adapted for piercing or licking-sucking. Larvae have degenerate or no head-capsule: maggots, barrel-shaped puparium. Picture shows: housefly.

2. Sub-order NEMATOCERA Gnats, Crane-flies etc.
Slim bodies; long wings and legs; antennae with multiple joints, long. Larvae have head-capsule. Mostly free or "mummified" pupa. Picture shows: midge.

Order APHANIPTERA Fleas

Small; with leathery chitin; flattened at the sides; hind legs for leaping; free, mobile thoracical segments, no wings; mouth-parts for piercing-sucking. Parasites on warm-blooded creatures. Complete metamorphosis. Larvae have no feet, but have a head-capsule and live on detritus. Exarate pupa, in silken cocoon.

Order HEMIPTERA True Bugs

Small to very large in size. Flattened or wedge-shaped bodies. 4 wings, often degenerate. Legs for walking, leaping or paddling. Mouth-parts adapted into "beak" for piercing-sucking, forming an articulated proboscis that folds back in the throat-channel when not in use; contains inside 4 piercing bristles that slide forwards or backwards. Antennae brush-shaped or very short. Incomplete metamorphosis. *Food:* plant or animal juices; some are terrestrial or aquatic predators.

Sub-order HETEROPTERA Plant Bugs and Water Bugs

Front wings mostly horny to beyond the middle, the tips being membranous. Bodies mostly flat. Stink glands and nauseous smell. Suck plant juices; predators. Some are external parasites. Groups a) terrestrial; b) aquatic. Picture shows: red-footed shield bug.

Sub-order   HOMOPTERA   Aphids, Leaf-hopper, etc.

Both pairs of wings the same; transparent, membranous. Bodies laterally compressed. Suckers of plant juices; many cause gall. Groups a) cicadas; b) plant-lice; c) white flies; d) aphis; e) scale insects. Picture shows: common (rose) greenfly.

Order   ANOPLURA   Biting Lice and Sucking Lice

Small, flat bodies; no wings; legs are bent clutching instruments each with 1 pair of powerful claws. Mouth-parts either for biting or for piercing-sucking; short antennae. Lateral simple eyes or blind. Incomplete metamorphosis. External parasites on mammals and birds.

Sub-order   SIPHUNCULATA   Sucking Lice

Tiny, louse-like and wingless; original mouth-parts atrophied and now consist of a pair of stylets for piercing and sucking. Thoracic segments fused and spiracles for breathing on the back. Blood-sucking parasites of mammals. Picture shows: head louse of man and eggs (nits) attached to hair.

Sub-order   MALLOPHAGA   Biting Lice

Tiny, louse-like, always without wings; flat egg-shaped or rod-like hairy bodies; short clutching legs; mouth-parts for chewing and biting. Degenerate compound eyes; short antennae. Incomplete metamorphosis. External parasites on birds or mammals, but do not suck blood, instead feed on feathers, hair, particles of skin. Picture shows: dog louse.

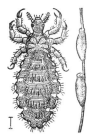

Order   THYSANOPTERA   Thrips

Minute, mostly only 1 mm. Slim, flat or wedge-shaped. 4 wings with hairy fringes all round, laid over the body when at rest; many lack wings. Short antennae; large compound eyes; often with 3 simple eyes. Mouth-parts for piercing-sucking, proboscis. Feet have 1 adhesive pad that it pushes out between its curved

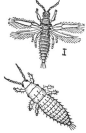

claws. Incomplete metamorphosis with several stages as nymph, when it has wing-cases. Suck mainly plant juices. Picture shows: greenhouse thrips.

Order   PSOCOPTERA   Bark Lice and Book Lice

Tiny; most have 4 delicate wings, closing roof-like over their bodies in repose; often degenerate; mouth-parts adapted for chewing; long, thread-like antennae; legs for running; able to spin. Incomplete metamorphosis. Terrestrial. *Food:* lichen, fungus spore, dust, etc. Picture shows: bark louse.

Order   ORTHOPTERA   Grasshoppers etc.

Medium to large in size; compound and simple eyes; 1 thoracic segment freely movable, covered by pronotum; 2nd and 3rd thoracic segments each carry one pair of wings, often atrophied and sometimes lacking. Wing-cases thin to leathery, not creased; hind wings membranous, generally with longitudinal folds. Mouth-parts for chewing. Incomplete metamorphosis.

1. Family GRYLLIDAE Crickets

Cylindrical bodies; long bristle-shaped antennae. 3-jointed tarsi long, jointed cerci. Ovipositors mostly straight, lance-shaped. Sound-producing apparatus: in males each front wing has two hardened parts that vibrate when rubbed together. Sound-receiving organs on fore-legs each of which has an opening on each side of the tibia. Hind-wings fold in. Spends most of its life in the dark, in passages it digs itself. Predator and plant-eater. Picture shows: field cricket.

2. Family TETTIGONIIDAE Bush Crickets or Long-horned Grasshoppers

Bodies slightly pressed-in at the sides; long, bristle-shaped antennae usually longer than the body. 4-jointed tarsi. Hind legs for leaping. Sound-producing apparatus on front wing; sound-receiving apparatus on front of fore-legs. Wings lie roof-like over the body or are lacking. Female ovipositor, usually long and pressed-in at the sides. Lays eggs mostly in the ground. Eats both plant and animal foods. Picture shows: oak bush-cricket.

3. Family ACRIDIDAE Short-horned Grasshoppers

Bodies slightly pressed-in at sides; short antennae, half the length of the body at the most, filament shaped. 3-jointed tarsi. 3 simple eyes as well as a compound eye. Short pincers, acephalous. Female has short ovipositor consisting of 4 short separate valves. Narrow wing-cases; wings lie roof-like over the body, sometimes atrophied or lacking; abdomen wedge-shaped; 1st segment carries one pair of sound-receiving organs. Sound-producing apparatus: hard veins on front wings against which points on hind legs rub. Eggs laid as bottle-shaped packages in ground. Migrates. Picture shows: rufous grasshopper *(Gomphocerippus)*.

4. Family BLATTIDAE Cockroaches

Flattened bodies; head hidden under front of thorax. Long, thin antennae. Kidney-shaped compound eye. Tough wing-cases spread flat over the abdomen; sometimes atrophied; wings, if present, thin and delicate, sometimes greatly reduced. Legs for running with stoutly horned front. Female has no ovipositor. Lays her eggs in egg-case (ootheca). Feeds on vegetable and animal matter. Picture shows: common cockroach.

Order   DERMAPTERA   Earwigs

Medium size, long somewhat flattened bodies. Head free. Filament-shaped feelers. Round compound eyes. Rectangular neckshield. Fore-wings reduced, leathery; hind-wings folded lengthwise and across, covered by forewings; top of rear of abdomen uncovered; equipped with heavily chitin-plated pincers. Incomplete metamorphosis. Picture shows: common earwig.

Order   PLECOPTERA   Stoneflies

4 membranous wings with many longitudinal veins, in repose lying flat over the body. Hind wings much broader than the fore. Long, bristle-shaped feelers. Mouth-parts for biting and chewing. Long thread-like tails (cerci). *Larvae:* predators in running water, with tufted gills mostly situated on underside of thorax. Incomplete metamorphosis. Lay eggs in water. Picture shows: stonefly.

Order   EPHEMEROPTERA   Mayflies

Very delicate. Long bodies with 4 transparent wings, fore ones larger, all very veined. Mouth-parts of adults vestigial. Do not eat. Short lived. Long cerci and usually also a middle tail filament. *Larvae:* aquatic, predators, with chewing mouth-parts; paired leaf-shaped tracheae-gills on abdomen. Incomplete metamorphosis. Lay eggs in water. Adults have winged sub-imago stage. Picture shows: common mayfly.

Order   ODONATA   Dragonflies

Large, slim, often very colourful; slight abdomen; very mobile head with 2 large hemispherical compound eyes and 3 simple eyes; short, bristle-shaped antennae; mouth-parts adapted for chewing; sharp toothed jaws (*odonata* means having teeth). 4 narrow, veined wings all similar; very expert flyers. Predator. Incomplete metamorphosis. Lay eggs in plant tissue. *Larvae:* aquatic, predators; equipped with rudimentary wings; extendible mask (adapted lower lip) for catching prey; 3 tail-like tracheae-gill-plates at the end of abdomen or internal anal gills.

Order   COLLEMBOLA   Springtails

Small; squat abdomen comprising 6 segments (often fused). Most have eyes; mouth-parts with or without chewing plates; short antennae. Last segment has leaping apparatus. Feed on algae, fungi, lichen, pollen, rotting vegetable and animal matter. On or in the ground, in holes, on the water, under leaves, stones, wood and moss, in human dwellings, on flowering plants. Picture shows: springtail.

Order   DIPLURA   Bristle-tails

Nocturnal. Eat vegetable and animal refuse, also flour, paste, sugar. Cause damage by chewing pictures and material. Live in human dwellings, in nests of ants, bees, wasps.

Order   THYSANURA   Bristle-tails

Nocturnal insects with large eyes. Long bodies, almost equally divided. Have a long cercus (articulated tail-appendage) between their pincers. Feed almost solely on algae, but organic refuse too. Prefer stony areas inland or on the coast. Picture shows: silver fish.

Family	Viewed from above	Viewed from side	Larva and Pupa	Peculiarities
Chafers (e.g. cockchafers) Powerful legs, antennae with fan-shaped leaves. Eat plants (causing damage) or dung (e.g. dung beetle).				♂ 7 ♀ 6 Leaf damage
Ground Beetles (e.g. violet ground beetle) Long legs, thread-like antennae; strong pincer-shaped jaws for biting; wing-cases striped and dotted, often with metallic sheen. Predators as are their larvae.				 * Except for *Anisoplia agricola*
Weevils (e.g. apple blossom weevil *Anthonomus pomorum*) Rather small. Head elongated in the shape of a trunk. Antennae mostly bent. Both beetle and larvae feed on plants. Can be very harmful.				
Long-horned Beetles (e.g. *Cerambyx cerdo*) Rather spectacular. Antennae often much longer than the body, like two enormous horns. Feed on plants. Often on flowers in sunshine, also on tree blossom. Larvae mostly under tree bark or in wood. Monotonous chirping of beetles caused by friction between edge of hind part of back and middle-back.	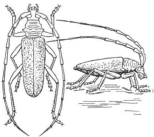			 Sound-producing organ

Family	Viewed from above	Viewed from side	Larva and Pupa	Peculiarities
Bark Beetles (e.g. typographer beetles) Small beetles with blunt heads and stud-antennae. Larvae eat characteristic passages under bark of trees.	5 mm long			
Leaf-Beetles (e.g. yellow-striped flea beetle or turnip fly) Small beetles. Short antennae. Oval arched bodies, often with metallic sheen. Small head, mostly directed downwards. Eat plants (harmful) leaving pattern of holes in leaves. Sociable.			Galleries of the larvae	Result of feeding
Carrion Beetles (e.g. the burying beetle) Club-shaped antennae, with blunt head. Prefer dead vertebrates in which to lay eggs as well as looking for beetles and larvae to eat.				

Fig. 54: The Important Beetle Families

COLOURFUL BEETLES   Plates 5 and 6

Order   COLEOPTERA   Beetles

Family   CARABIDAE   Ground Beetles

Calosoma sycophanta Plate 5, No. 1. Broad flat wing-cases in the shape of a long rectangle, metallic dark green with a red sheen; sides shiny golden-red, each with 3 longitudinal lines of dots. Well developed wings. *Larvae:* see p. 408. Pupates in small cavity in ground. Found in woods: in large numbers in "caterpillar years". Beetle and larvae climb trees destroying caterpillars, especially on the Continent those of processional moth, pine beauty, night moth.

Carabus auratus Plate 5, No. 2. Wing-cases golden-green with red side edges; each has 3 broad, blunt, unbroken ribs: in the male clearly, in the female deeply indented before the point. Legs and base of black antennae are red. Found in fields and dry places in woods. Roams in grass and on roads in the sun searching for prey.

Carabus auronitens Flatter than the previous species. Black underneath. Head and thorax purple, sometimes grass-green; wing-cases uniform gold-green with 3 dark ribs and black junction of the wing-cases. Top of head and thorax thickly covered with puckered dots.

Carabus intricatus Plate 5, No. 3. Slim, long oval, flat with long legs. Black underneath; blue or greeny-blue on top with lighter edges. Thorax almost longer than it is broad with deep central line, closely puckered and dimpled. Wing-cases each have 3 faint longitudinal lines. Found in woods under moss, bark, stones, decaying fallen trees.

VIOLET GROUND BEETLE *(Carabus violaceus)* 1.8 × 3.4 cm. Long elliptical shape. Black, with a dull sheen. Base and wing-cases have violet or golden edges to the sides. Wing-cases almost smooth, with very fine close granulation. Found in woods. Described by Fabre as a "frenzied murderer".

Carabus cancellatus Plate 5, No. 4. Arched body; wing-cases have strong chain-striped and raised secondary ribs. Found in woods, gardens, sunny fields, damp pastures; active after rain, in potato and turnip fields. Likes to winter in rotting tree stumps.

Carabus hortensis Plate 5, No. 5. Black or dark bronze; with a shimmer of bronze on thorax and wing-cases, which latter have 3 rows of pits that have a golden gleam, as have the edges of the sides; also delicate, regular, longitudinal stripes. Thorax rectangular, almost square. Found in woods.

Carabus granulatus Plate 5, No. 6. Flat body. Upper parts bronze; thorax fairly rectangular, oblique with narrow edges. Longish wing-cases each with 3 coarse chain stripes with 1 fine rib between them, and near on either side 1 more or less developed row of granulation. Found in fields, under stones.

Carabus arvensis Plate 5, No. 7. Can be coppery to greeny-bronze, violet or black on top. Wing-cases have fine chain stripes and between them 3 fine ribs, the middle one of which is often prominent. Found in woods in hilly country up to 3,000 m; found especially when snow melts, under stones. Winters in rotten wood.

Carabus silvestris Plate 5, No. 8. Coppery, occasionally greenish-bronze, on top. Wing-cases have 3 lines of large, shiny dimples. In mountain woods; under fallen trees and stones.

Carabus irregularis Plate 5, No. 9. Brown-copper on top; side edges and dimples lighter (golden-red or greeny). Wing-cases flat, confused pattern in front, longitudinal granulation behind; also 3 rows of large, deep, round dimples. In the mountains of central Europe, in fallen tree trunks, especially beech in which it bores galleries and winters.

Carabus nemoralis Plate 5, No. 10. Strongly built; black-green to bronze-brown on top. Rather arched wing-cases with dense longitudinally-puckered granulation and 3 rows of 8–12 dimples. In woods, under stones, moss, tree-bark. Not common.

Chlaenius vestitus Plate 5, No. 11. Top, metallic green; side edges of wing-cases yellow. Damp, marshy places and river banks.

Panagaeus crux-major Plate 5, No. 12. Covered with jutting hairs; broad, disc-shaped black thorax; each wing-case has 2 large yellowy-red patches and deeply pitted stripes. Likes marshy ground.

BOMBARDIER BEETLE *(Brachinus crepitans)* Plate 5, No. 13. Compact body, rather flattened. Broad, blunt wing-cases, uniform green or blue; antennae, legs, thorax rust-red. Gland near vent squirts out acid that volatilises on contact with air with an audible explosion, causes a burning sensation on human skin. Sociable, under stones in sunny places. Very common in some places.

*SMALL BOMBARDIER BEETLE *(Brachinus explodens)* 4–6.5 mm. Much smaller, but otherwise resembling previous beetle. Wing-cases are shorter and more curved and either unstriped or scarcely striped.

Sub-Family   CICINDELINAE   Tiger Beetles

Elaphrus riparius Plate 5, No. 14. Delicate, very quick. Strikingly large head with large, bulging eyes placed on the side. Matt bronze-green, occasionally coppery; indentations in head and thorax dull emerald. Wing-case of very coarse structure; sharply edged eye-patches. In stony, sandy banks of streams, etc.

GREEN TIGER BEETLE *(Cicindela campestris)* Plate 5, No. 15. Stocky body, slender legs. Grass-green on top; green thorax; abdomen metallic blue-green. Head, base, sides of thorax and legs have white hairs. Wing-cases have a few white spots. Colouring is variable. *Larvae:* see p. 408. Sandy ground; dry, light places in woods; heath.

Cicindela silvicola Plate 5, No. 16. Grey-green on top with gleam of bronze and white zigzags; underneath metallic or blue-green. Sandy, dry paths in woods. Hills and mountains.

Cicindela hybrida Plate 5, No. 17. Top mostly coppery-brown, underneath green; sides of thorax purple. White markings: shoulder-patch unbroken; transverse bars widening outwards. Patch at rear unbroken. Sandy paths in woods and in clearings, from spring to late summer.

Family   STAPHYLINIDAE   Rove Beetles

Staphylinus caesareus Plate 5, No. 18. Colourful; predominantly dark-brown to black; wing-cases reddish yellow-brown; antennae and legs yellow-red. Patches of thick, close-lying golden silky hairs on abdomen and as a border to base. Abdomen is often raised in a threatening posture, when emits unpleasant smell. Predator on insects, worms and snails. On paths, especially in woods.

Family   SILPHIDAE   Burying and Carrion Beetles

Necrophorus vespillo Plate 5, No. 19. 2 red-orange bars on black ground of wing-cases. Can make a chirping sound. *Larvae:* dirty white and blind. Found on dead animals. Is attracted by smell of carrion; undermines dead creatures which then sink into ground, when it buries them, and lays eggs on the carcase to provide food for the larvae.

Xylodrepa quadripunctata Plate 5, No. 20. Broad, oval body, very slightly arched. Rather small head. 4-jointed club-shaped antennae. Bare top with longitudinal ribbing, browny-yellow with black markings, i.e. 1 small, round spot, and sometimes another 2 towards the head. April to June on oak, beech and fruit trees. Hunts caterpillars as do its larvae, especially those of processional moth and loopers.

Oeceoptoma thoracicum Plate 5, No. 21. Rather flat, in outline a broad ellipse; dull black; head and thorax covered with velvety red hair; wing-cases turned up at the sides. In woods on carrion, excrement, fermenting efflux on oaks, rotting fungi.

Plate 5
Pictures of beetles mentioned on pp 265–274, life-size.

1. *Calosoma sycophanta*
2. *Carabus auratus*
3. *Carabus intricatus*
4. *Carabus cancellatus*
5. *Carabus hortensis*
6. *Carabus granulatus*
7. *Carabus arvensis*
8. *Carabus silvestris*
9. *Carabus irregularis*
10. *Carabus nemoralis*
11. *Chlaenius vestitus*
12. *Panagaeus crux-major*
13. *Brachinus crepitans*
14. *Elaphrus riparius*
15. *Cicindela campestris*
16. *Cicindela silvicola*
17. *Cicindela hybrida*
18. *Staphylinus caesareus*
19. *Necrophorus vespillo*
20. *Xylodrepa quadripunctata*
21. *Oeceoptoma thoracicum*
22. *Hylecoetus dermestoides*
23. *Trichodes apiarius*
24. *Thanasimus formicarius*
25. *Lygistopterus sanguineus*
26. *Rhagonycha fulva*
27. *Cantharis fusca*
28. *Malachius aeneus*
29. *Elater sanguineus*
30. *Corymbites aeneus*
31. *Chalcophora mariana*
32. *Dicerca berolinensis*
33. *Lampra (= Poecilonota) rutilans*
34. *Agrilus pannonicus*
35. *Agrilus viridis*
36. *Meligethes aeneus*
37. *Coccinella septempunctata*
38. *Bostrichus capucinus*
39. *Pyrochroa coccinea*
40. *Melöe proscarabaeus*
41. *Lytta vesicatoria*
42. *Systenocerus caraboides*
43. *Amphimallon solstitialis*
44. *Euchlora aenea*
45. *Polyphylla fullo*
46. *Phyllopertha horticola*
47. *Anisoplia segetum*
48. *Anisoplia agricola*
49. *Cetonia aurata*
50. *Gnorimus nobilis*
51. *Trichius fasciatus*
52. *Aphodius fimetarius*

Plate 5

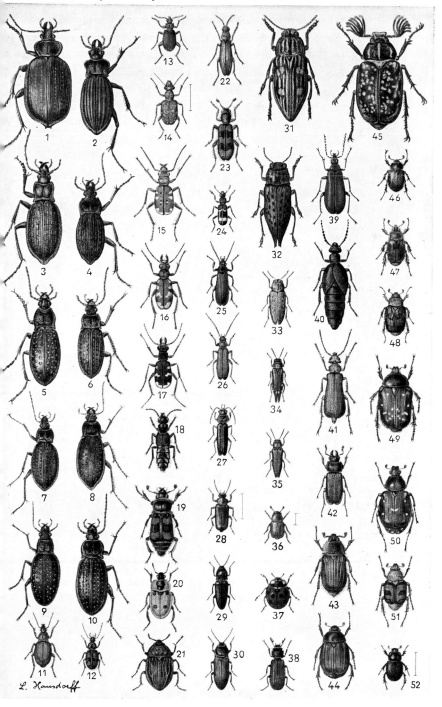

L. Hausdorff

Family   LYMEXYLIDAE

Hylecoetus dermestoides Plate 5, No. 22. Male 6–13 mm. Female 9–20 mm. Long, cylindrical body covered with fine hairs; yellowy-brown to dark-brown. Antennae serrated. Maxillary palpus in 2nd joint has large, bush appendage in male. Female yellow wing-cases, in male all black or with yellow points; antennae yellow. In woods and clearings. May to June in swarms in hot weather. *Larvae:* see p. 429. In deciduous woods.

Lymexylon navale 7–13 mm. Resembles the above, but body is long and narrow and covered with fine hairs, reddish-yellow; head very constricted, black. Wing-cases of male black with browny-yellow along the front junction; in female often only the ends are dark; legs and abdomen yellow. Lays eggs in cracks in felled oaks or standing ones with bark injuries. *Larvae:* see p. 430. Often found in wood-piles. Beetles found on old birch and chestnut trees, as well as oak. Flies May to June.

Family   CLERIDAE

Trichodes apiarius Plate 5, No. 23. Longish, with long, thick hair. Wing-cases red to yellow with 2 blue-black velvety bars and blue-black patch at end. Body otherwise blue-black. Wing-cases coarsely pitted. Larvae developed in the nests of wild bees and of the honey bee, eating bee grubs. Beetles are often on umbellifers, e.g. cow parsley and carrots.

Thanasimus formicarius Plate 5, No. 24. Body black, underneath, base and end of wing-cases red; head black; 1 white-haired bar in front and a 2nd behind the middle of the wing-case. *Larvae:* see p. 408. Beetle winters in pine groves. Ambushes large wood-gardener and bark beetles.

Family   CANTHARIDAE   Soldier Beetles, etc.

Lygistopterus sanguineus Plate 5, No. 25. Wing-cases and sides of thorax bright blood red. On *Compositae,* umbellifers, elder, lime trees; frequently found on edges of wood. Larvae in rotting tree-stumps, old oak trees and alders. Sociable.

Rhagonycha fulva Plate 5, No. 26. April to September. Body yellowy-red all over; only the points of the wing-cases are black. On flowers of umbellifers, especially in late summer.

Cantharis pallida Body 6–8 mm long; equal width throughout. Top yellowy-red; thorax and middle of abdomen black. Wing-cases granulated. May to July: on grasses.

Cantharis fusca Plate 5, No. 27. Head and antennae black; thorax yellowy-red with black patch reaching to fore-edge; wing-cases black with sparse grey hairs. Abdomen has broad red edging. Predator on smaller insects, also gnaws delicate young shoots. *Larvae:* see p. 409. Beetles often on umbellifers, corn, etc. Sometimes eat young oak shoots until the stems break over.

Family   MALACHIIDAE

Malachius aeneus Plate 5, No. 28. Body glossy bronze-green; front of head golden; fore-corners of thorax scarlet as are wing-cases except for a broad, green seam-patch. When agitated, protrudes on the sides of its thorax soft lobes of red skin with glands. Eats other insects, etc. e.g. larvae of the beetle *Meligethis aeneus*.

Family   ELATERIDAE   Click Beetles

Elater sanguineus Plate 5, No. 29. Deep black, shiny body; wing-cases scarlet sometimes almost turning bright or rust-red. Thorax pitted with longitudinal central furrow. Wing cases deep-ribbed. Found under bark of conifers, in old tree-stumps, on umbellifers. Common.

Corymbites aeneus Plate 5, No. 30. Very shiny; colouring varies: metallic green, coppery, reddish, bluish. Striped wing-cases. Larvae (wireworms) noxious. Found on deciduous or coniferous trees, on roads, in old timbers and under stones.

Family   BUPRESTIDAE

Chalcophora mariana Plate 5, No. 31. July. Underneath shiny copper colour. Upper parts bronze-brown; indented places coppery with brassy sheen; irregular longitudinal furrows. Found in pine woods. Larvae under bark of sickly or dying trees turning the wood into worm-dust. *Larvae:* see p. 431.

Dicerca berolinensis Plate 5, No. 32. June to August. Longish, oval body rather arched and pointed at rear. Tips of wing-cases elongated. Coppery or greeny-bronze: rows of darker specks on wing-cases. Found in beech woods; in hot midday sun on decaying copper-beech, hornbeam, and alder, in which its larvae develop.

Lampra (= Poecilonota) rutilans Plate 5, No. 33. May to June. Emerald green, outer edge coppery red. Wing-covers have black patches. Topside of abdomen steel-blue. Found on lime trees; in early morning creeps out of oval holes to hunt; at midday flies in tree-tops. Quick flight. Larvae in trunk and branches of old decaying, but still live lime trees, gnawing irregular galleries in the bark and sap wood.

Agrilus pannonicus (= biguttatus) Plate 5, No. 34. May to June. Elongated body, pointed at rear. Blue-green or gold-green. Each wing-case has a small white hairy patch on the seam well before its point. On oaks and beeches; also on young shoots. Larvae in thick bark of old oaks.

Agrilus viridis Plate 5, No. 35. Narrow, long body of a uniform metallic green or blue or coppery gold. Size and colouring vary. Found on oaks, beeches, alder, hawthorn, aspen, lime, birch, vines; also on willows, silver poplar. Chiefly on young trees, which it usually rings, thus plantations of young beech and oak can be endangered by its larvae. *Larvae:* see p. 430.

Family   NITIDULIDAE

Meligethes aeneus Plate 5, No. 36. Longish body of unvarying width. Wing-cases do not cover the whole body. Short antennae with 3-jointed club. Metallic green, blue or violet, rather shiny; has fine, close-lying hair. Female lays 1 or more eggs in flower bud; 6-legged larvae which eat blossom and young shoots; when mature drop to ground, pupate in a cavity in the ground. Beetle hibernates in ground, appears in spring; feeds on pollen and buds; flies round in sunshine. Often found in large numbers on flowering rape.

Family   COCCINELLIDAE   Ladybird Beetles

SEVEN-SPOT LADYBIRD *(Coccinella septempunctata)* Plate 5, No. 37. Body almost hemispherical, base black. Wing-cases a bright red or yellowy-red; 1 round black spot divided by the join and usually 3 others on each wing-case. Thorax black with 2 whitish-yellow frontal spots and whitish-yellow corners. Moves little. When touched ejects yellowish drops of blood from its knee-joints. Lays eggs in heap of from 10–12 in vicinity of an aphis colony. *Larvae:* see p. 407. Found on various plants. Very common. Both beetle and larvae avid eaters of aphis.

Sub-species: the wing-case markings vary considerably. Some of the 7 spots may be larger or smaller; some, even all, may be lacking *(lucida)* or there may be more of them (e. g. *maculosa* has 11) or some merge to from a transverse bar *(divaricata)* or a longitudinal stripe *(confusa)* or the wing-cases can be all black except for one patch of yellow at the join *(anthrax).* (There are 2–10, 14–18 and 22-spot ladybirds; 2-, 4- and 10-patch ladybirds, etc.)

Family   BOSTRICHIDAE   Boring Beetles

Bostrichus capucinus Plate 5, No. 38. May to July or August. Cylindrical black body. Abdomen and wing-cases red. Thorax steeply arched. Wing-cases coarsely pitted. *Larvae:* see p. 429. On timber stacks and where trees have been felled; sometimes in workshops and houses.

Family   PYROCHROIDAE   Cardinal Beetles

Pyrochroa coccinea Plate 5, No. 39. May to June. Long, flattened-looking, fairly soft-skinned black body. Base and wing-cases fiery red. Black head. Serrated black antennae. Wing-cases broaden towards the rear. Head tapers to a neck-line join. Penultimate joint of tarsus broad. *Larvae:* see p. 409. Beetle found on blossom on edge of woods. Reluctant to fly.

Family   MELOIDAE   Oil Beetles

Melöe proscarabaeus Plate 5, No. 40. April to May. Stocky, clumsy body, very abbreviated wing-cases covering only part of the abdomen; black with a bluish shimmer. Head and thorax coarse and closely pitted; wing-cases wrinkled like leather. *Larvae:* see p. 407. Beetle found in grass, on clover. Feeds on young soft blades of grass, *Ranunculus,* dandelion, violets, etc.

Melöe violaceus 1–3.2 cm long, blue, seldom almost black; wing-cases finely wrinkled along their length. More common than the previous species.

BLISTER BEETLE or SPANISH FLY *(Lytta vesicatoria)* Plate 5. No. 41. June to July. Long body. Thorax broader than it is long, narrowing considerably at the rear; groove down middle of head; elongated, narrow, soft, closely wrinkled wing-cases; the whole is metallic green. Ejects yellow fluid from joints that gives off acrid smell. Larvae eat honey in nests of bees built in ground. Found on shrubs and bushes, especially ash, often in great numbers. (Collected to obtain the blistering agent cantharadin, mainly contained in the elytra, which is used for pharmaceutical puposes.)

Family   LUCANIDAE   Stag Beetles

Systenocerus caraboides Plate 5, No. 42. Longish, shallowly-arched, glossy black body. Green or blue to black on top, occasionally with violet or bronze dots; no hair. Found in spring on the bursting buds of oak and aspen trees. Larvae in the dead wood of various deciduous trees (oak, beech, ash, etc.).

Family   SCARABAEIDAE   Chafers

Amphimallon solstitialis Plate 5, No. 43. June to July. Long, well-arched light-brown bodies. Wing-cases pale yellow with raised smooth longitudinal lines, indistinctly pitted, shiny, covered with long, jutting hairs. Flies towards sundown, swarming on fallow fields; nocturnal. Feeds on upper half of previous year's needles of pines and second bloom of deciduous trees. *Larvae:* see p. 410. Inflicts damage on pasture and in fields by eating roots.

Euchlora (= Anomala) aenea Plate 5, No. 44. June to July. Short, broad, well-arched body. Colouring varies: dark green underneath. Wing-cases bare, usually yellow with a shimmer of green; occasionally all green or dark blue. Wing-cases have lines of pitting. Lively flier in hot noon-day sun; found on bushes and pasture on sandy soil.

Polyphylla fullo Plate 5, No. 45. Flies June to July. Basic colour brown or black-brown. Wing-cases reddish-brown with white marking, looking as if sprinkled with flour; abundant white scaly hairs that are easily rubbed off. Fan-antennae of male have 7 leaves, very long and wavy; those of female are very small and 5-leaved. Can chirp loudly by rubbing sharp cross-ridges of penultimate abdominal segment against stout veins on the underside of the under wings. Found in pine woods, sandy areas, dunes. Feeds by night, especially on pine trees. *Larvae:* see p. 410.

GARDEN CHAFER *(Phyllopertha horticola)* Plate 5, No. 46. Flies in June. 8–12 mm long. Head and throax green or greeny-blue. Wing-cases dark brown; underneath green, blue or black. Male has long, female shorter, hairs on top. Feeds on leaves and flowers of roses and various bushes, also of oak, hazel, plum, etc. *Larvae:* see p. 410.

Anisoplia segetum Plate 5, No. 47. Body 1.0–1.2 cm long; black-green, rather glossy. Wing cases reddish-brown or -yellow, uniform in the male, but the female has fine, closely pitted patch on thorax; wing-cases edged with long, jutting bristle-hairs. Found especially on grasses and corn, of which it eats the anthers. Larvae at the roots of grasses. Prefers sandy soil.

Anisoplia agricola Plate 5, No. 48. June. Long body with jutting grey hairs. Head and thorax green; colouring of wing-cases varies, but is usually yellow with narrow black seam, broad black outer edge seam, a quadrilateral pattern on the shield and a central black transverse bar. Some may have a reddish tinge, or the black may be more widespread. Eats the anthers of grasses and corn. Larvae live on the roots of grasses.

ROSE CHAFER *(Cetonia aurata)* Plate 5, No. 49. Broad, shallowly-arched body; large shield in form of longish triangle ending in a rounded point; thorax somewhat rounded in front. Glossy light golden-green on top; coppery-red underneath; individual hairs. Wing-cases have small white transverse patches and some flat ribs. Found on flowers (elder, umbellifers) and on tree-juices. Destroys the stamens of roses. *Larvae:* see p. 410.

Gnorimus nobilis Plate 5, No. 50. May to August. Smooth on top, hairy underneath; square head shield; thorax much narrower than the wing-cases. Coppery-red underneath, golden-green, occasionally coppery, on top; wing-cases have narrow white patch especially in the middle. Found on blossom, especially of elder and spirea, often swarms in hot sunshine. Larvae in rotting stems of fruit trees.

Trichius fasciatus Plate 5, No. 51. June to August. Black body, head and thorax covered with shaggy yellow hair; the underneath and rear covered with white hair; wing-cases yellow with 3 black bars. Found in meadow flowers, especially thistle, bramble, eating the delicate parts. Larvae in rotting parts of deciduous trees.

Aphodius fimetarius Plate 5, No. 52. Long, arched body. Black head and abdomen. Thorax black except for fore edge; wing-cases vivid red, notched and striped. Lives in dung of cattle.

Family   Cerambycidae   Longhorn Beetles

Saperda carcharias Plate 6, No. 1. Browny-black body made to appear leathery-yellow by thick close-lying hairs. Wing-cases pitted. Lays eggs in cracks in bark at foot of a tree trunk. *Larvae:* see p. 428. Beetle found June to July on poplars and willows; feeds on juices flowing from tree wounds.

MUSK BEETLE *(Aromia moschata)* Plate 6, No. 2. Antennae of male longer or as long as its body. Thorax has a lateral spike on either side. Wing-cases each have 2 black longitudinal ribs and are closely wrinkled like leather and taper to the rear; usually metallic green, but can be blue, copper or even black. 2 musk-glands on underside of thorax give off a pleasant smell. Larvae bore into willows, especially pollard willow, and into the root-stock of osiers, see p. 429. Beetle seen in July on trunks and branches of willows, sometimes in numbers on old willows from which sap is oozing. Also goes to oozing sap of the aspen.

Rosalia alpina Plate 6, No. 3. Flies June to August. Dull black body with very fine pale blue hair that makes it look blue; one transverse velvety black patch on fore edge of thorax and 3 similar bars on wing-cases; the first and last bars having a wide break in the middle reducing them to a fleck on either wing-case. Larvae in old beech stumps, stacks of timber, also in pines. Found in highish mountains, on beeches.

Acanthocinus aedilis Plate 6, No. 4. Antennae of female 1^1/$_2$–2, of male 2–5 times as long as its body. Thorax hexagonal, on each side below the middle a protuberance. Light or grey-brown on top; wing-cases finely pitted and have 2 oblique darker bars. *Larvae:* see p. 427. Beetles found on pine timber.

Clytus rhamni Plate 6, No. 5. Dull black. Fore and hind rim of thorax and scutellum covered with thick golden hair. 1 narrow, yellow transverse stripe on each wing-cover just behind the base; these transverse stripes and the tips of the wing-cases hairy. Antennae of female more than half the length of the body, those of male more than that of the whole body. Beetles found May to July on felled oak-trees, on live oaks, beech, hedges and umbellifers. Larvae develop in shoots of various deciduous trees: oak, apple, etc. Sometimes damage oak by gnawing galleries deep into the timber.

Plagionotus arcuatus 9–20 mm. Black with orange markings. Resembles *Clytus rhamni*. Has 5 yellow cross bands on body, the 2nd winding and broken at the seam, often forming two spots. On felled oak trees and blossom. *Larvae:* see p. 428.

Saperda populnea Plate 6, No. 6. Body black and brown-black and covered with grey hair. Thorax has no protuberance, but is cylindrical with greyish-yellow longitudinal stripes on either side, often a third in the middle, narrower and not so distinct. Wing-cases coarsely pitted with an irregular line of small yellow or grey specks. Underneath greyish-yellow and more closely hairy than the top. Beetle found May to June on the twigs and leaves of aspen. Lays eggs. *Larvae:* see p. 429. They take 2 years to develop.

Phymatodes testaceus Plate 6, Nos. 7, 7a. Colouring varies, but the most common is orange with completely orange or browny-yellow wing-cases and legs; head yellowy-brown or black. Wing-cases not infrequently blue or violet and base red. Rest of body rusty-yellow. Thorax almost circular. Antennae of male much longer, of female shorter, than the body. Larvae in dead deciduous trees. Beetles fly at dusk May to June; found on blossom and dry oak wood.

Leptura rubra Plate 6, Nos. 8, 8a. Male has black thorax and yellowy-brown wing-cases; female has red thorax and wing-cases: often the female's thorax is black as well, only with narrow red edging. *Larvae:* see p. 427. Beetle July to August; in pine woods.

Strangalia maculata Plate 6, No. 9. Yellow wing-cases with 2 black bars, 1 in the front half, and 5 black spots. Head and thorax black with sparse yellowy-grey hair. Abdomen of female more or less yellow. Larvae live in birch. Beetle in July, on blossom in woods.

Callidium violaceum Plate 6, No. 10. May to June. Of rather stockier build than *Phymatodes testaceus*. Thorax rounded at the sides. Wrinkled and pitted and mostly dark blue on top, or violet, often with a green sheen. Brown underneath. Antennae slightly shorter than the body. *Larvae:* see p. 426.

Plate 6

(Size – lifesize, except where otherwise given.)

1. *Saperda carcharias*
2. *Aromia moschata*
3. *Rosalia alpina*
4. *Acanthocinus aedilis*
5. *Clytus rhamni*
6. *Saperda populnea*
7. 7a. *Phymatodes testaceus*
8. 8a. *Leptura rubra*
9. *Strangalia (= Leptura) maculata*
10. *Callidium violaceum*
11. *Rhagium bifasciatum*
12. *Rhagium inquisitor*
13. *Acmaeops collaris*
14. *Phytoecia coerulescens*
15. *Gaurotes virginea*
16. *Pachyta quadrimaculata*
17. *Toxotus cursor*
18. *Oberea oculata*
19. *Tetropium castaneum*
20. *Chrysomela (= Melasoma) populi*
21. *Chrysomela (= Melasoma) tremulae*
22. *Agelastica alni*
23. *Chrysomela (= Melasoma) aenea*
24. *Lochmaea capreae*
25. *Phyllodecta (= *Chrysomela) vitellinae*

26. *Leptinotarsa decemlineata*
27. *Crioceris asparagi*
28. *Crioceris duodecimpunctata*
29. *Lilioceris (= Crioceris) lilii*
30. *Lema melanopa*
31. *Phyllotreta undulata*
32. *Phyllotreta nigripes*
33. *Phyllotreta nemorum*
34. *Clytra quandripunctata*
35. *Cryptocephalus sericeus*
36. *Donacia aquatica*
37. *Cassida viridis*
38. *Cassida nebulosa*
39. *Apoderus coryli*
40. *Attelabus nitens*
41. *Byctiscus betulae*
42. *Byctiscus populi*
43. *Rhynchites cupreus*
44. *Phyllobius calcaratus*
45. *Phyllobius pomacius*
46. *Anthonomus pomorum*
47. *Anthonomus cinctus*
48. *Apion frumentarium*
49. *Baris cuprirostris*
50. *Curculio (= Balaninus) nucum*
51. *Cryptorhynchidius lapathi*
52. *Hylobius abietis*
53. *Pissodes piniphilus*
54. *Pissodes pini*

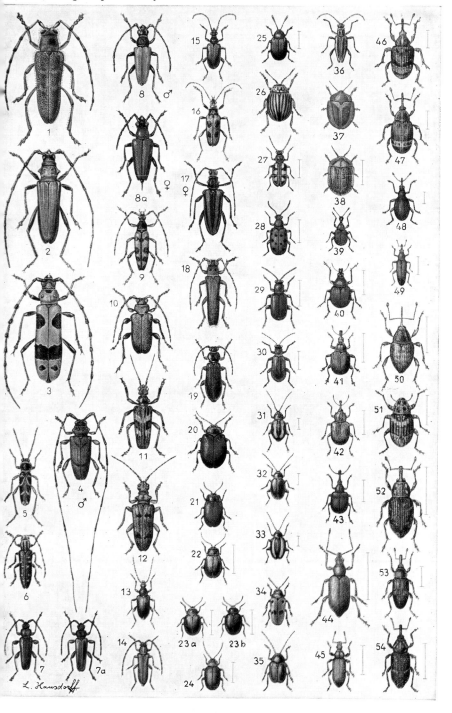

L. Hausdorff

Rhagium bifasciatum Plate 6, No. 11. Black body. Sides and points of wing-cases reddish-brown; 2 oblique yellow bars one in front of, the other behind the middle; 2–4 abbreviated longitudinal ribs; often only one yellow bar is distinct. Larvae under bark of old pines, spruce, firs, chestnuts. Beetles May to August.

Rhagium inquisitor Plate 6, No. 12. One pointed "thorn" on each side of base. Yellow wing-cases have patches of grey hair, and 3 longitudinal ribs and 2 dark more or less complete bars as well as a few scattered spots; sides black and without hair. *Larvae:* see p. 427. Beetles March to June on pine-blossom, or felled conifer timber.

Acmaeops collaris Plate 6, No. 13. Thorax narrower in front, slightly constricted front and back; wing-cases blue-black; thorax red, abdomen yellowy-red. Covered with fine upright dark hairs on top. On woodland blossom, especially in mountains.

*Phytoecia coerulescens Plate 6, No. 14. May to July. Black body covered with thick bluey-green or grey-green hair making it look green on top. In sunny patches of grass, on snake's head and other flowers.

*Gaurotes virginea Plate 6, No. 15. Short, broad, black body. Underneath red and so, often, is the thorax. Wing-cases blue or green with a metallic sheen; occasionally violet. On umbellifers and other flowers; quite common in mountains.

*Pachyta quadrimaculata Plate 6, No. 16. Black, not very shiny body. Head and thorax covered with grey hair. Wing-cases yellow or yellowy-brown, each with 2 large, sharp black spots. Common on flower clusters in mountains.

*Toxotus cursor Plate 6, No. 17. Male all black; female broader and also black, except for reddish-brown antennae, part of legs, side edge and 1 longitudinal stripe of each wing-case. Larvae in old trees of coniferous woods. In summer seen on blossom.

Oberea oculata Plate 6, No. 18. Black wing-cases with fine grey hairs; thorax yellowy-brown with (or without) 2 black dots. Found on young willow shoots. Develops in willow stems.

*Tetropium castaneum Plate 6, No. 19. Black body; antennae and legs partially reddish-yellow; reddish yellowy-brown wing-cases; often wing-cases or even the whole body are black as well. Wing-cases have 2 scarcely discernible raised longitudinal lines. Lays its eggs on the trunks of 60–100 year old trees, moving up the tree as it does so. *Larvae:* see p. 426.

Family   Chrysomelidae   Leaf Beetles

Chrysomela (= Melasoma) populi Plate 6, No. 20. June to August. Fat, egg-shaped body. Wing-cases vivid brick red to yellowy-brown; tips black. Underneath blue-black, sometimes black-green. Head and thorax dark green, sometimes with a shimmer of bronze-yellow, rarely black-blue or black. Found on poplars and willows. Both larvae and beetle eat the leaves. Initially sociable and eating leaves to the skeleton, later becoming lone and making only holes. *Larvae:* see p. 405.

Chrysomela (= Melasoma) tremulae Plate 6, No. 21. Resembles the foregoing, only smaller and its red wing-cases do not have black tips. *Larvae:* see p. 405.

Agelastica alni Plate 6, No. 22. Body black-blue to dark violet, slightly metallic. Thorax and wing-cases closely pitted. Colour of wing-cases varies between sky-blue, violet, coppery violet and black. Common on alder, the leaves of which they eat.

Chrysomela (= Melasoma) aenea Plate 6, No. 23. May or June to August or September. Long, egg-shaped; vivid metallic green on top with more or less bronze-yellow, or blue or violet; black-green underneath. Common on alder.

Lochmaea capreae Plate 6, No. 24. Black, bare body. Thorax and wing-covers browny-yellow. Wing-covers coarse and rather closely pitted. Found on willow, birch, alder. Beetles in spring on young shoots. Larvae eat leaves to skeletons.

Phyllodecta vitellinae Plate 6, No. 25. Oval body; vivid greenish brassy-yellow; shiny. Colouring varies: either pure brassy-yellow or dark bronze-green or blue, dark green, even dark steel-grey or black. On young willows and poplars. Beetles and larvae both destroy buds, young leaves, tips of shoots, young bark. *Larvae:* see p. 405.

COLORADO BEETLE *(Leptinotarsa decemlineata)* Plate 6, No. 26. Top yellow; wing-cases have 10 black longitudinal stripes; base has 10 or more irregular black spots; head has 1 triangular black spot. Female sticks yolk-yellow eggs in discs of 35–40 on undersides of leaves. Beetles hibernate in ground; 2 broods a year. Does great damage to potatoes. *Larvae:* see p. 406.

ASPARAGUS BEETLE *(Crioceris asparagi)* Plate 6, No. 27. Length 5–6.5 mm. Wing-cases greenish-blue each with 3 yellow spots and a yellow edge; base red. Hibernates in asparagus, also under leaves; on fences. When seized, makes a chirping sound. Fixes eggs vertically onto stalk and leaves of asparagus; eats plants and blossom from April on. *Larvae:* see p. 406. Pupate in ground. Mostly 2 broods.

Crioceris duodecimpunctata Plate 6, No. 28. 6 mm long; red wing-cases each with 6 black dots. Eggs laid horizontally (not vertically) on asparagus leaves and shoots; eats asparagus fruit. Chirps when touched. Larvae up to 8 mm; dirty orange-yellow. 2 broods. Otherwise as foregoing. *Larvae:* see p. 406.

Lilioceris lilii Plate 6, No. 29. 6–7 mm long. Shape and ways as preceding; almost uniformly red. Produces a chirping sound. Eats lily-of-the-valley, onions, leeks.

**Lilioceris merdigera* Body 6–7 mm long. All red on top. Beetles and larvae eat holes in leaves, flower and stalks of onion, leek, lily-of-the-valley; also asparagus. *Larvae:* see p. 406.

Lema lichenis 3–5 mm long. Shape as preceding; uniform metallic blue.

Lema melanopa Plate 6, No. 30. Shape as preceding; wing-cases greeny-blue to black-blue; thorax and legs reddish-yellow. Both species common in meadows and fields.

Halticines 2–4 mm long. Beetles of this group have strongly developed hind legs and leap like fleas. Oval shaped body. Uniformly dark or striped with yellow. Emerge in spring and in large numbers attack budding cabbage and other cruciferous plants, causing great damage by the holes they eat. Larvae up to 7 mm, whitish-yellow, live on rootlets; some mine in leaves, stems. Pupate in the earth.

Phyllotreta undulata Plate 6, No. 31. Body 3 mm long, blue or greeny. Each wing-case has a longitudinal yellow streak, bent in the middle and tapering at either end. Common and harmful to brassicas.

Phyllotreta atra 2 mm. Uniform black, metallic blue, green or bronze. Dots on wing-cases in distinct rows. Common and harmful to brassicas.

Phyllotreta nigripes Plate 6, No. 32. Length 2.6 mm. Greenish-blue to metallic green; dull silky sheen. Found especially in spring and autumn on cruciferous plants and mignonette.

Phyllotreta nemorum Plate 6, No. 33. 2.5–3 mm. Black with a shimmer of green; each wing-case has one straight, sulphur-yellow longitudinal streak. Tibia and tarsus almost always uniform reddish-yellow. Larvae olive-yellow; mines in leaves of radish, white turnip, mustard (not cabbage).

Haltica quercetorum Length 4–5 mm; egg-shaped, slightly arched. Pure metallic green, sometimes with a shimmer of blue, shiny. Sides of wing-cases longitudinally depressed. Found in woods, copses, on young oaks, the leaves of which it eats.

Phaedon cochleariae 3–4 mm long; oval; wing-cases lined with dots, black-blue or greenish. Beetle hibernates under heaps of twigs, stones or in the ground, emerging in May. Lays eggs in small heaps on leaves. Eats holes in leaves of horse-radish, mustard, cress, cabbage. *Larvae:* see p. 406.

Phaedon armoraciae 3–4 mm. Top dark blue, seldom green. Wing-cases more finely pitted. Otherwise as *P. cochleariae*. On cruciferous plants by water.

Clytra quadripunctata Plate 6, No. 34. 7–11 mm long; lanky. Underside, legs and head covered with thick grey-white hair. Body glossy black. Wing-case yellowy-red, each with 1 shoulder spot and 2 touching, almost merging black dots lower than the middle, either or both of which can sometimes be missing. Larva sits in a black, sack-like housing, closed at one end, made from its own excrement; eats ants'-eggs. Found on grass, bushes (oak and willow, etc.). Quite common. Larvae and pupae with red wood ants and meadow ants, see p. 382–3.

Cryptocephalus sericeus Plate 6, No. 35. Length 5–8 mm. Plump. Metallic green or blue or golden. Long, filament-shaped antennae. Larvae in cylindrical firm sack narrower at the mouth, which it carries about with it, crawling about backwards with it tilted up obliquely. Found June to July on the blossom of Compositae, especially dandelion.

Donacia aquatica Plate 6, No. 36. 7–10 mm long; body somewhat pressed in on top. Wing-cases golden-green with broad purple or brown-red longitudinal bands, which are seldom lacking. Underneath golden silky hairs. Thorax often shiny like brass, shot with violet or blue. May to August on bog-grass and aquatic plants.

Donacia crassipes 9–13 mm long. Metallic green or gold-green; base and wing-cases of male, coppery, of female with tinge of violet on black. Covered with silver hair underneath. Some rare specimens are uniform gold or deep violet on top. Lay eggs on undersides of water-lily leaves where a hole has been eaten. *Larvae:* white, plump, six-legged and have 2 brown "horns" behind the 8th segment of the abdomen with which it drills into plant tissue to obtain oxygen. Adults found on water-lily leaves

Cassida viridis Plate 6, No. 37. 7–9 mm long; oval shield-shaped; arched on top, flat underneath. Large pronotum that extends to cover the head. Male grass-green on top, black underneath. Wing-cases irregularly pitted. Base narrower than wing-cases and has rounded corners. Larvae broad and flat, armed with horns on the side; behind has a tail-fork that it carries curved up and forward holding a mask of dung over its back so that it appears like a bit of dirt and is inconspicuous. Beetle and larvae in damp places on labiate flowers (sage, hedge-nettle, water-mint). Eat holes in the leaves and their edges.

Cassida nebulosa Plate 6, No. 38. 5–7 mm long. Egg-shaped, somewhat arched; black underneath; rust-brown or green on top with black spots. Head, legs and side seam of abdomen browny yellow. Rear corners of thorax rounded. Wing-cases have longitudinal ribbing and rows of pitting; fine black seaming and distinct serration along the base.

Cassida nobilis 3.5–5.5 mm long; oval. Pale green to yellow or white on top; head, middle of thorax and abdomen black. Wing-cases each have 1 silver or gold longitudinal stripe near the seam, which disappears when the beetle dies; often they also have a few indistinct light-brown specks. Found on corn spurrey and daisies.

Cassida murraea 6–8.5 mm long. Reddish-brown or green on top; wing-cases mostly have black spots. Common on water-mint, June to July, or on scab-wort, mullein, thistles. Larvae carry mask of dung.

Cassida rubiginosa 6–8 mm long; broad oval; green to yellowy-green on top. Wing-cases black at root by base. Black underneath. May to August. On the flowers of Compositae.

Family   CURCULIONIDAE   Weevils

Apoderus coryli Plate 6, No. 39. 3.5–8 mm. Head has cheek-like bulges tapering to the rear and joining the thorax as a stalk. Wing-cases coarsely dotted. Black body; base, wing-cases, upper part of legs, red. Colouring can vary. Female cuts and rolls a hazel leaf into a cylindrical wrapper in which to lay her eggs (Fig. 55); this hangs down vertically and in it the larva lives and then pupates. Found on various deciduous trees, but especially hazel.

Attelabus nitens Plate 6, No. 40. 4–6 mm. Thickset, strongly arched. Thorax and wing-cases shiny red, the latter lined with rows of faint dots; the rest of the body glossy black. Rolls the oak leaf into a barrel (Fig. 55).

Female makes 2 vertical cuts one on each side of the leaf, meeting at the rib which is untouched. In each of these rolls it lays one egg. The larva leave the rolls after hibernating there and pupates in the ground. Common on young oak shoots, less frequently on willow, alder, hazel.

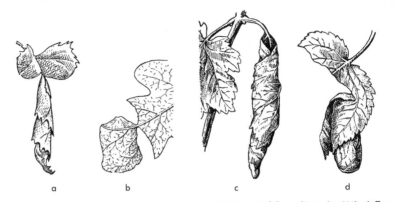

Fig. 55: **Leaf rolls of:** a) **Rhynchites betulae** (p. 295) b) **Attelabus nitens** (p. 281) c) **Byctiscus betulae** (p. 282) d) **Apoderus coryli** (p. 281)

Byctiscus betulae Plate 6, No. 41. 5.5–9.5 mm long; uniform golden-green or blue. Irregular lines of close dots on wing-cases. Causes the frass on vines, pear trees, eats buds, cuts off shoots; the female bores into leaf-stalk and twists leaf into a cigar-like roll in which it lays eggs. The larvae develop in these leaf-rolls when they have fallen off (Fig. 55) and pupate in the ground. Found on birch, aspen, lime, vines, etc.

Byctiscus populi Plate 6, No. 42. 4.5–6 mm long; greenish, perhaps with a tinge of blue, or, more seldom, copper, on top; snout and underside dark blue. Regular lines of deep, distinct pitting on wing-cases. Female pierces middle of leaf-stalk and rolls withering leaf into a cylinder in which it lays its eggs. Very common on aspen, especially on shoots.

Rhynchites cupreus Plate 6, No. 43. 4.5 mm long. Dark, coppery red, shiny. August to May. Hibernates in ground. Female gnaws the stalks of young fruit making a 1 mm hole in the flesh in which it lays one egg. Larvae May to July; up to 6 mm long; whitish with brown head; legless. Develop in fallen fruit, of which they eat the flesh, leaving the core, see p. 414. Pupate in earth.

Phyllobius calcaratus Plate 6, No. 44. 8–12 mm. Underside of body light coloured; legs reddish; wing-cases matt black; usually covered with green metallic glistening scales. Lives on trees and bushes, especially young alders. Eats leaves, buds, needles. Larvae eat roots.

Phyllobius pomacius (= urticae) Plate 6, No. 45. 7–9 mm long. Body metallic green; feelers and legs black or sometimes red. Wing-cases thickly covered with gold-green, small, oval scales. On nettles in hilly country.
Rhynchites bacchus See p. 414.

APPLE BLOSSOM WEEVIL *(Anthonomus pomorum)* Plate 6, No. 46. 3.5–4.5 mm. Wing-cases black-brown with an oblique faded bar of lighter colour in the final third of its length, forming an open angle. Legs red-brown. Hibernates under scales of bark, lichen and in litter on the ground. Climbs and flies in tree-tops. In spring lays eggs individually in buds of apple and pear blossom it has drilled. The larva is up to 7 mm long, footless, yellowy-white with reddish tinge and has a black head; feeds on stamen and stalk; the bud remains vaulted and closed, withers becoming brown and looks as if scorched. Later a yellowish pupa in the dead bud. *Larvae:* see p. 414.

Anthonomus cinctus Plate 6, No. 47. May to September. 4 mm long; brownish, like *A. pomorum*. Cross-bands of white hairs beyond the middle of wing-cases, not oblique and thus not forming an angle. Larvae 7 mm, whitish; no feet; brown heads; September to May; hibernates in buds the inside of which it has eaten; pupa in buds. Found on blossoming apple and pear trees. Young beetles do damage by eating shoots and leaves. Summer "hibernation" from June to August.

Apion frumentarium Plate 6, No. 48. 2.5–3.5 mm; uniform bright red. Found on grasses in summer, especially in damp pasture. Common.

*Baris cuprirostris Plate 6, No. 49. August to May. 3–4 mm long. Glossy greenish, sometimes bluish on top; snout coppery; wing-cases delicately striped. Lays its eggs in the rib and stalk tissue of the leaves of cabbage and rape. Larvae 4–5 mm, without feet, whitish; bore tunnels; May to August on cruciferous plants.

Curculio (= Balaninus) nucum Plate 6, No. 50. 6–9 mm long; egg-shaped; black with thick yellowy-grey hairs; thorax lighter as are the disc-shaped patches on the wing-cases. Lays eggs in developing hazelnuts. Larvae up to 10 mm long, white; eat the nut and leaves by boring a circular hole in the shell; hibernate and pupate in the ground. Not common. On hazels. *Curculio (= Balaninus) glandium* Behaves in the same way as *Curculio nucum* only is on oaks and larvae are in acorns.

Cryptorhynchidius lapathi Plate 6, No. 51. 7–9 mm. Can tuck its snout into a deep longitudinal groove running down the middle of the front part of its thorax; wing-cases short, tapered at the end into "trunk-shape"; black or black-brown; covered with black, brown or reddish-white scales; each wing-case also has 1 oblique whitish bar, while the last third of it also is white. Larvae eat straight ascending galleries, first just under the bark, later deeper in the wood and pupate in the upper end of the gallery which is curved in the shape of a hook. Found especially on young alder, also on willows, poplars, etc. Recognisable by the swelling of young stems caused by the wounds it inflicts.

Hylobius abietis Plate 6, No. 52. 9–13 mm; matt, dreary brown, sparsely covered with close yellowish hair. Wing-cases have stout shoulders on which is a regular pattern of pitting, ribbing and granulation: longitudinal rows of lighter coloured dots and a few transverse patches of rusty-yellow. Common in coniferous woods. Gnaws holes in the bark of young trees, or in places eats it away altogether. Lays eggs on dying or dead roots. *Larvae:* see p. 411. Beetles mostly roam on forest floor. Breed in places where trees have been felled.

Pissodes piniphilus Plate 6, No. 53. 4–5 mm. Rust brown; each wing-case has 1 large reddish-yellow scale-patch. Larvae on smooth, thin-barked trunks of young pines. Eat meandering galleries under the bark, in which they pupate. Beetle May to June on young pines.

Pissodes pini Plate 6, No. 54. 7–9 mm. Dark brown with a bar of lighter-coloured scales, consisting of 2 oblique spots, the near one of which can be a few specks, in front. Eggs and larvae mostly under the thick bark of old pine trees. Beetles are up in or near the crown of the tree. On pines and firs.

Pissodes harcyniae 5–6 mm. Very similar to the foregoing, but much smaller. Matt black; upper parts dotted with white upright scales; wing-cases have 2 light-coloured, more or less destinct bars: yellow dots in an oblique row and other spots in addition. Larvae eat galleries under bark destroying trees.

Pissodes castaneus (= notatus) 7–10 mm. Reddish-brown broken by markings consisting of lighter-coloured scales; thorax wrinkled and granulated and has 4 white spots. Wing-cases have 2 reddish-yellow bars, the front one of which is interrupted at the wing-seam, while the hind one carries over it, mostly yellow outside and white inside. *Larvae:* see p. 431. Beetles March to September. Like to rest in buds of young firs and eat young shoots.

Brachyderes incanus 7–11 mm. Very short, broad, thick snout, scarcely any narrower than the head; thorax a little wider than the head; oval wing-cases. Body pitch-black; antennae lighter or even rusty-brown; whole body covered with coppery and whitish scale-hair interspersed with fairly thick fine golden hairs. On young pines and firs. *Larvae:* see p. 411. Beetle hibernates under scraps of bark on the ground, feeds on needles in plantations of conifers.

BLACK, DARK-BROWN AND GREY BEETLES

Order COLEOPTERA Beetles

Family CARABIDAE Ground Beetles

Carabus coriaceus Body 3–4 cm; all black, matt. Slender head and thorax; strongly pitted wing-cases with leathery creases; no stripes. Mainly nocturnal, often emerges in dull weather in search of snails and worms. Solitary.

Zabrus tenebrioides Body 1.4–1.6 cm. Plump, strongly arched. Short antennae; black-brown or black, often with faint metallic sheen; lighter brown underneath. Antennae and legs brownish-red. Wing-cases with rows of pitting; glossy, though somewhat more matt in female. *Larvae:* see p. 405. Common in corn-fields, where beetle eats the soft grain in the ears at night.

Sub-Family CICINDELINAE Tiger Beetles

Cicindela sylvatica 1.5–1.7 cm long; bronze-black on top with silky sheen; metallic violet underneath, sometimes tending to green; tibia blue. Wing-cases have whitish-yellow markings, half-moon-shaped shoulder patches, wavy bars lower than the middle and a roundish spot before the tip; widely granulated. Larvae in tunnels in the earth. Found in sandy places in pine woods. Both beetle and larvae prey on insects.

Family STAPHYLINIDAE Rove Beetles

DEVIL'S COACH HORSE *(Staphylinus olens)* Longish body, 2.0–3.2 cm, of fairly uniform breadth. Head tapers behind like a neck. Wing-cases protrude, only just reach beyond hind section of thorax. Has underwings. Whole body a matt black, finely pitted, dark-haired. When threatened curls the abdomen up. Waits in a threatening posture and emits an acrid smell from glands that it pushes out. Preys on insects, worms, snails. Found on roads, under rotting vegetable matter, on carrion, in dung, etc. Especially common in woods.

Lomechusoides strumosa Body 5.0–6.5 cm; broad, plump, reddish-brown; wing-cases and legs a shade lighter; tuft of golden hair on abdomen. Broad thorax curving up at the sides. Rather like an ant in size and appearance. Lives in colonies of the blood-red slave-maker ant, which likes the taste of the juice secreted by the glands at its hair-tufts and for this feeds the beetle, the mouth-parts of which are atrophied. They communicate by trilling.

Family   Silphidae   Burying or Carrion Beetles

Necrophorus germanicus Black body 2.0–3.5 cm long. Colouring varies. Thorax rounded in front, tapering towards the rear; flattens out at side and rear edges. Found on dead bodies of larger animals and under horse-dung.

Silpha obscura Body 1.3–1.9 cm long, elliptical. Short head with no snout-like prolongation. Matt black. Bare on top. Wing-cases have 4 longitudinal ribs, sometimes one, faintly indicated. Larva the shape of a wood-louse, only pointed at rear; brownish-yellow. Found on bodies of dead animals. Beetles and larvae roam freely in fields eating carrion, live snails, worms and insects.

Phosphuga atrata 10–16 mm long, oval, flatly-arched body. Head elongated like a snout; thorax almost semi-circular. Wing-cases have 3 ribs, closely pitted on top, glossy, bare, black or reddish-brown. Larva cylindrical worm-shape with striking long antennae; feeds on live and dead snails, as does the beetle. Found under moss, in rotten wood, under mouldering bark on old tree trunks; in fields, on roads, under stones, clods.

Aclypea (= Blitophaga) opaca Flat, matt, black body 9–12 mm long. Gold-brown on top showing through thick close-lying hair. Thick head, broader than it is long. Wing-cases have longitudinal ribs, the outer of which are well raised and end in a big bulge. Larvae are 1.1–1.3 cm long, black with yellow edges to the sides; antennae and palps rust-red; legs brownish-yellow; back covered with sparse, close-lying hair. Pupate in ground. Beetles and larvae eat the leaves of plants of the turnip family. *Larvae:* see p. 407.

Family   ELATERIDAE   Click Beetles

Agriotes lineatus Narrow body 9–10 mm long. Each wing-case has 8 rows of black dots. Legs and the entire top covered with hair that makes them appear yellowy-grey. Wing-cases taper gradually from the middle. Arched thorax, the rear corners of which curve outwards. By moving its thorax the beetle is able to spring into the air from off its back making a "click" as it does so. *Larvae:* see p. 411. Gnaw tender grasses and young corn, mostly at the roots. Found in fields, meadows, on roads.

Agriotes obscurus Compact short body, 6–10.5 mm; black to dark brown. Base of antennae and legs reddish-brown. Thorax highly arched, broader than it is long, coarse and closely pitted, not very rounded; wing-cases broad as thorax. Fine stripes with coarse dots, flat in between. Larvae as those of *A. lineatus*. Common in fields and on roads. (A variant has wing-cases of a lighter reddish-brown, even rusty colour.)

Adelocera murina (= Lacon murinus) Broad oval body, 1.2–1.7 cm long; mouse-grey or grey-brown-black chequered with scaly red and white hairs. Red antennae with black root. Thorax strong and closely pitted; rear corners not very curved. Wing-cases as wide as the base, striped with coarse pitting, smooth in between. Wings yellowy-red. Larvae like those of *Agriotes l.* or *o.* Beetles fly in sunshine. On meadows, fields, in gardens. Larvae (wireworms) feed on potatoes, carrots, roots of lettuce, endive, roses, etc.

Family   LAMPYRIDAE   Glow-worms

GLOW-WORM *(Lampyris noctiluca)* June to July; long body 1.1–1.2 cm, of the same breadth throughout, with wing-cases that gape at the rear. Yellow-brown underneath; matt black-brown on top. Yellowish thorax. Brown middle. Female 1.6 to 1.8 cm; light brown-grey, rather velvety, maggot-shaped looking like a larva, small eyes, no wing-cases. The last 3 segments of abdomen have light-producing organs on the underside. *Larvae:* see p. 409. Found on the edge of woods, headlands and banks between fields; on hill-sides. Male flies in the evening, displaying a faint light, while the females lie glowing in the grass. Larvae

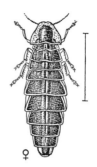

and pupae also give off light. Predators (on snails); have hollow jaws from which paralysing juice flows when they bite, and thus they decompose their prey.

Phausis splendidula Male 8–10 mm; thorax has 2 transparent oval spots on front edge. Wing-cases blackish, each having 3 raised longitudinal lines. Light luminous patch on the last 2

segments of the abdomen. Female is 9–10 mm long, oval, worm-shaped with 2 smaller scales instead of wing-cases. Light-producing organs similar to the male's, except that they also extend to the sides of the abdominal segments. Flies for only a few days at the end of July on the fringe of woods, on river-islands. Habits as *Lampyris n.*

Family   BUPRESTIDAE

Anthaxia quadripunctata Flattened, oval body 5–7 mm long. Head capsule short and rather broad, let into the thorax; its front and rear edges are almost straight. Wing-cases puckered and pitted; black to black-brown. Thorax has a shallow central groove and a transverse line of 4 "dimples", the outer of which extends to the side edge. Found in woods of conifers. *Larvae:* see p. 431.

Family   Tenebrionidae   Nocturnal Ground Beetles

Opatrum sabulosum Rather squat body, 7–10 mm long. Thorax as wide as the wing-cases, slanting, with rounded sides, rear corners projecting backwards. Black top, mostly dusted with grey. Thorax finely granulated. Wing-cases have dotted stripes of large shiny grains. Larvae cylindrical, but flattened on the underside. Beetle likes dry, sandy places.

Family   Lucanidae   Stag Beetles

STAG BEETLE *(Lucanus cervus)* Male 2.5–7.5 cm, female 2.2–4.5 cm. Male has broader head and upper jaw elongated into antler-shape. Female has a smaller head, with a normal, short upper jaw. Male's head is broader than the similarly rectangular thorax. Antennae brown-black; antlers and wing-cases dark chestnut. Feeds on sugary juices from wounds in the bark of oak trees, which it licks up with yellowy-brown hair-brushes on its lower lip and lower jaw. On thundery evenings in June or July makes swarm round oak trees in search of females over which they fight bloodless battles. They die after 4 weeks of life as beetles. Lay eggs on rotting wood of old trees. Larvae white, up to 11 cm long, and live for 5–6 years on mouldering wood, in which they pupate in firm, rounded cocoons, see p. 425.

Dorcus parallelopipedus 1.9–3.2 cm long. Flatly-arched body with parallel sides. Small eyes, partially divided. Antennae has a very narrow 4-limbed club. Upper jaw of male is only slightly elongated, that of female is ordinary (there are also males with ordinary jaws). Matt black wing-cases very thickly pitted and slightly creased. Thorax finely pitted. *Larvae:* see p. 430. Beetle flies May to June in twilight. Develops in rotting timbers of beech, oak, lime, willow, walnut and horse-chestnut.

Sinodendron cylindricum Lanky cylindrical body 1.2–1.6 cm long with a small head and a horn in front of it. Glossy black with dense coarse pitting. Thorax as wide as wing-cases, not shorter than it is broad, scooped out in front. In the larger male the frontal horn is as long as its head, and curved slightly backwards; at the thorax, on either side, is a rusty-yellow beard; the front half of the base is obliquely truncated, the shortened surface being rimmed with a 5-toothed edge, the middle tooth

being long and pointed. In the female the frontal horn is small, a mere pointed protuberance. Found in deciduous woods. Under bark. Larvae in rotting timbers of beech, oak, willow, chestnut.

Family   SCARABAEIDAE   Chafers

COMMON COCKCHAFER *(Melolontha melolontha)* May. Antennae are pointed "fans", those of the male with 7 points; of the female 6. The body is black with grey hair; the sides of the abdomen have triangular white patches; wing-cases brown; colour of thorax varies. The pygidium i.e. last segment of the abdomen (B) is powerful, lancet-shaped, gradually tapering. Flies especially on warm, windless evenings. Eats holes in the foliage of wood and fruit trees, especially oaks. Lays 60–70 white eggs the size of hemp seed in the ground, 10–30 at a time. Larvae (see p. 410) pupate in August of their 3rd year in small, smoothed-out holes in the ground; November new beetles that remain in ground until May. Generally takes 4, in south 3 years to develop, thus every 3rd or 4th year is a "Maybug year". On oaks, fruit and other deciduous trees.

Melolontha hippocastani Mostly smaller than the common cockchafer; pygidium (A) is smaller, trowel-shaped, broadening at the tip into a button-shape; side edges of the reddish-brown wing-cases, black; the male has a small tooth on the 3rd jaw of its antennae. In colder areas takes 5 years to develop.

DUNG BEETLE *(Geotrupes stercorosus [= sylvaticus])* Body egg-shaped, steeply arched, 1.0–1.6 cm long. Top not very glossy, with a blue to blue-black or green sheen. Underneath metallic blue or green, with black hair. Wing-cases have fine longitudinal stripes. Lives under dung, also on fungi; rotting plants, carrion and tree juices. Digs vertical holes up to 40 cm deep in the ground under the dung and makes a plug of dung to act as bed for one egg. *Larvae:* see p. 410.

DOR BEETLE *(Geotrupes stercorarius)* 1.6–2.4 cm long. Wing-cases have 7 deep longitudinal furrows. Top black with blue or green edges to the sides. Underneath metallic green or blue with black hair. Prefers stony ground or clay soil and open arable land. Found under dung of cattle and horses.

Geotrupes vernalis Body 1.4–2.0 cm long, so arched as to be almost hemispherical. Top smooth, glossy, black-blue or blue, sometimes a vivid metallic green (e.g. *G. autumnalis*). Busy by day carrying dung of sheep and deer into its brood-chamber. Found in woods, especially on sandy heaths.

Oryctes nasicornis June to July. 2.5–3.9 cm long; stocky, arched body a shiny chestnut-brown. Top smooth, underneath and legs covered with fox-red hair. Male has one strong, backward curving horn on its head; the female has a small, pointed protuberance on the forehead. Wing-cases have rows of fine pitting. Eggs the size of hemp seed. Very fat larvae which take several years to develop and live, like the beetles, in oak bark. Beetles, larvae and pupae found in greenhouses, gardens and tanneries; the larvae and pupae also in the dust of hollow oaks in woods.

Copris lunaris 1.7–2.3 cm long; shiny black, roundish, very arched body. Semi-circular head; male has one rather long, pointed, slightly curved horn on its brow, that of female being short. Wing-cases strongly striped, the stripes being slightly notched.

Typhaeus (= Ceratophyus) typhoeus 1.5–2.2 cm long, body looking rather flattened. Deep, glossy black. Underneath and legs covered with black hair. Male's thorax carries 3 forward-pointing horns, the middle of which is short and directed slightly upwards; in large specimens the two side horns stick out beyond the head; in smaller specimens the horns may not be so well developed; in the female the front corners of the thorax are drawn-out into points. Found in sandy woodland soil or open arable fields, on the dung of sheep, deer, hares, rabbits.

Sisyphus schaefferi Body 8–10 mm long, pointed at the rear; not very shiny; many have white-coated sides. Wing-cases with extensive stripes of pitting. Large base; shield not visible. Short wing-cases, with pointed tips that make the shape triangular. Fore-legs rather short, the tibia with 3 external "teeth"; the middle and hind legs are long with curved tibia. Feeds on dung

of cattle and sheep. Male and female shape dung into balls
which they roll away, moving backwards, then bury the ball,
lay an egg on top of it and cover this up with more dung. The
ball provides food for the larva. Found on sunny slopes and
pastures in central and southern Europe.

Osmoderma eremita 2.6–3.5 cm long; broad, shiny metallic
black-brown; wing-cases creased like leather and pressed-in
along the seam. The male has a "scooped-out" head with a
pointed protuberance on either side. The thorax has a central
groove, deeper in the male, not so deep in the female, with two
bulges before half way. Emits a strong smell like that of Russian
leather. Both beetle and larvae live in powdered wood of old
willows, limes, oaks and alders. May to August.

Aphodius fossor 0.8–1.2 cm long, cylindrical, steeply-arched,
glossy black body, often with red wing-cases, mostly with black
roots (e.g. *A. sylvaticus*). Under dung of cattle and horses.
Common.

Family   CERAMBYCIDAE   Longhorn Beetles

Cerambyx cerdo Flies June to July. Body 2.5–5.0 cm; large, slim,
tapering towards the rear. Very long antennae, those of the
male longer than its body; curved, jointed, carried like horns
(hence the name) on the head. Dark brown on top; wing-cases
tapering and becoming rust-red towards the tip. Thorax coarsely
puckered and has a strong "thorn" on either side. *Larvae:* see
p. 428, gnaw broad, winding galleries in wood and hollow out
smooth egg-shaped hollows for their eggs. Take 3–4 years before
they pupate. In old oaks, especially those the sun strikes, on the
fringe of a wood, in streets, etc. Beetle flies in the evening, and
can be found at twilight on the trunk and branches of oaks and
where sap is oozing out. Has a sound-producing organ, see p. 263.

Prionus coriarius Body 2.4–4 cm long; pitch-black or black-
brown, slightly glossy. Thorax covered with thick grey hair.
Antennae serrated, deeply in male, slightly in female. Articula-

tions of antennae fit into each other like a telescope. Thorax twice as broad as it is long; puckered and pitted with 3 teeth on either side. Wing-cases have 2–3 longitudinal lines slightly raised. Can produce a fairly loud chirping note. Lays eggs in mouldering wood in which larvae live (see p. 428). Found in mouldering stumps of conifers, oaks, cherry, beech, birch. The beetle does not emerge until the summer and spends most of the time sitting motionless on an old trunk or stump and in the twilight flies heavily about buzzing.

Ergates faber 2.7–5 cm long; male black-brown, female reddish-brown, smooth and shiny; thorax thickly covered with short hair. Wing-cases thickly puckered and pitted. *Larvae:* see p. 426. Solitary. Beetle August to September in places where trees have been felled and in timber yards. Flies at noon and during early afternoon; fertilised females will be found in rotten wood during same period.

Lamia textor Body 2.4–3 cm, plump. Bristle-shaped antennae that do not reach the end of the body in either sex. Wing-cases start by being broader than the thorax. Strong legs of medium length. Top matt, dirty brown with small blackish protuberances standing up from the yellowish hair that covers it. Thorax furnished with powerful "spike" on either side. Larvae live in roots of young willows, see p. 429. On willows and aspens.

Spondilis buprestoides Squat, cylindrical body 1.2–2.2 cm long with powerful jutting upper jaw which can give a painful nip. Antennae short and like a string of beads. Head and eyes about as wide as the thorax which is arched, rounded at the sides, not armoured, pitted. Wing-cases somewhat wider than the thorax, pitted; each with 2 inner and 1 slightly raised centre longitudinal lines. Black and only slightly glossy. Underneath covered with short, brown hair. Larvae have thoracic feet, live in old trunks of conifers, often in large numbers. (Woodpeckers eat them.) Beetle flies in the evening once darkness has fallen, in timber yards often in large numbers. *Larvae:* see p. 427.

Cerambyx scopolii Body 1.8–2.8 cm long. Longish head, narrower than the thorax. Antennae of male half as long again as its body, those of female the length of the body. Thorax as broad as it is long, strongly contracted in front, rounded at the sides and equipped with 1 pointed "thorn", has rough horizontal creases. Wing-cases at root almost twice the width of the thorax edge, long, rounded at the tip. Deep black on top with very fine grey hair. *Larvae:* see p. 428. Beetle May to July on blossoming hawthorn, guelder-rose, elder, spiraea.

Family   CURCULIONIDAE   Weevils

Otiorrhynchus niger Slim, egg-shaped body, 9–14 mm in length. Snout a little longer than it is wide in front (the base being narrower). Lacks under-wings and is thus unable to fly. Black body covered with sparse grey hair; wing-cases have lines of pitting; red legs. Beetle gnaws young shoots. Lays eggs in ground where spruce grows. *Larvae:* see p. 411. Pupates June to July in smoothed holes in ground. Beetle seen in May on young spruce trees. In mountain areas.

Philopedon (= Cneorrhinus) plagiatus 4.7 mm long; so closely covered with grey to brown scales that the black of the body is not visible. Sides and underparts covered with light grey scales and whitish bristles. Short snout. Short antennae. Wing-cases longitudinally striped, almost spherical. Common on sandy soil and on young pines. Beetle eats bark, buds and needles; also leaves of deciduous trees. Larvae underground at roots.

Strophosomus melanogrammus 4–6.5 cm. Whole body thickly covered with shiny copper-coloured scales, between which on head, thorax and wing-cases it has short bristles that stand up obliquely; a bare, black stripe down front third of wing-case seam. Wing-cases broad oval, steeply arched. May to October. On spruce, fir, oak nuseries, on hazel, birch, beech, rowan. Beetle gnaws at bark, buds, leaves, needles.

Liscus paraplecticus 1.2–2 cm long. Narrow, long, cylindrical body; long, narrow wing-cases ending in two points that fork away from each other; black with fine grey hairs; start life thickly powdered with yellow. Wing-cases have lines of fine pitting. Lays eggs in thick hollow stems of water-fennel, etc. Larvae mostly in stem-nodules; hiding places for the beetle: on riverside plants.

Cionus scrophulariae 4.5–5.5 mm without snout. Squat, round, black body. Thorax thickly covered with white or yellowish scale-hairs. Wing-cases dark slate-grey, the spaces in between the stripes chequered velvety black and white; a large velvet patch on front part of the seam and another at the rear. Larvae brownish-green; pupate on the plant on which they have fed, spinning and attaching to it a roundish, transparent cocoon (pictured in the margin). Very common on *Scrophularia*.

Anthonomus rubi Beetle 4 mm long, dark-brown; whitish shield; long snout. August to May; hibernates in ground. Lays series of single eggs in buds, then gnaws the stalk halfway through so that it bends over. Larvae 4 mm long, white, without feet, feed on the inside of the withering bud. On both raspberries and strawberries.

Rhynchites germanicus Beetle 4.5 mm, dark blue to dark green. September to May; hibernates in a hiding-place. Gnaws the leaf stalk so that it dries up above the bite. Larvae 5 mm long, whitish brown head, no feet; live in dried up leaf blade on the gnawed stalk. May to June. Pupate in the ground. On strawberries.

Rhynchites betulae 4.4 mm long; uniform glossy black. Wing-cases have lines of coarse pitting. Hind tibia of male enlarged. Found on birch, alder, hazel and hornbeam. Lays its eggs in a funnel-shaped roll made by making incisions in leaf blade and middle-rib (Fig. 55) of leaf which droops, slowly withering and providing shelter and food for the larva which falls to the ground with it when developed.

Otiorrhynchus ligustici 9–13 mm long; plump, black. Fairly thickly covered with yellowish-grey scales on top; wing-cases often mottled. Snout much longer than it is broad and noticeably longer than the head. Lays eggs in the middle of May in the ground 2–5 cm deep; pupates in July. Common in sandy places, especially in fields of lucerne, vineyards, etc. Often appears suddenly in large numbers. Beetle eats the bark of vines, peach and young fruit trees down to the wood, also buds, shoots blossom, sprouts, leaves of lucerne, beans, rape. Larvae eat the roots.

STRIPED PEA WEEVIL *(Sitona lineatus)* 3.6–5.4 mm long, longish oval brown-grey body. Striped wing-cases. Hibernate in the ground. Eats away edges of the leaves of peas, beans, lentils, vetch, clover, lucerne, destroying very young plant completely. Larvae 6.3 mm long, whitish; eat the roots and bacterial nodules of papilionaceous flowers. Pupate in ground beetles emerge in August. Beetle feeds on papilionaceous flowers especially common on clover.

WATER BEETLES AND BUGS

a) IN WATER

Order   COLEOPTERA   Beetles

Family   DYSTISCIDAE   Aquatic Carnivorous Beetles

GREAT DIVING BEETLE *(Dytiscus marginalis)* 3–3.5 cm long; dark olive-green with yellow edging; abdomen entirely or almost entirely yellow. Filament-shaped antennae. Broad, flat body without projections, looking as if out of a mould; broad head without any gaps between it and the stout plate of the thoracic section, on which thick wing-cases lie straight without grooves or notches. Fore and middle part of thorax firmly attached on underside by spines. Hind limbs adapted for swimming by being flattened and furnished with numerous bristles along one side like a large paddle. Expert swimmer underwater. Uses both legs at the same time. Fat excreted by numerous skin-glands which make top waterproof and smooth. Wing-cases of males always smooth, those of female have longitudinal furrows. Makes long flights overland by night or when home water dries out. To breathe it places itself with rear point of abdomen and hind legs on surface, admits air into space between wing-cases and lowered point of abdomen. Store of air in enclosed air space between wings and abdomen, where spiracles are sited. Feeds on smaller aquatic creatures, tadpoles and small fish, holding on to the prey with its fore-legs and breaking it up with the mouth-parts. Very greedy. In the male the first three basal segments of the fore and middle tarsi are disc-shaped and carry numbers of tiny bowl-shaped suckers. Thus without the use of muscles, but only by the elasticity of the chitin, it is able to adhere to smooth surfaces and it uses this power to hold on to its prey and also the female. Lays its eggs from spring to June. The female uses ovipositor to split the stem of an aquatic plant and push a white, long egg into the slit, making numbers of slits with one egg in each. In ponds and slow-moving streams with plenty of vegetation. *Larvae:* see p. 439.

Dytiscus latissimus 3.6–4.4 cm. Very broad, oval body; wing-cases have broad, broken edgings widening in the middle. Thorax edged with yellow. Wing-cases have a broad streak of yellow along outside (broader towards the rear) and a yellow transverse bar before the tip. Greenish-black on top; yellow underneath. Lives as *D. marginalis*. Rare in smaller ponds, etc. More often in larger stretches of water.

Acilius sulcatus 1.6–1.8 cm. Black-brown on top with a yellow transverse bar across the middle of the base; underneath black with a few spots of yellow. The male has disc-shaped enlargements to its fore legs; top and underside both closely and strongly pitted. The female has 3–4 smooth longitudinal ribs on each wing-case with thick hair between each rib. Larvae have strikingly small heads. Feeds mainly on small planktonic crustacea. In stagnant water.

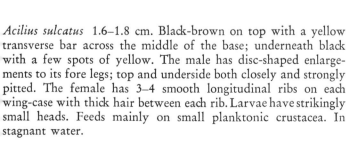

Deronectes halensis 4–4.5 mm long; black, yellow on top with black markings: 2 large triangles often of merged dots on the middle of the thorax. Wing-cases have dark seam and 6 black longitudinal lines that here and there spread into each other; the 2 outer lines being reduced to a few dark spots; female brownish-red underneath. Predator living in stagnant and flowing water.

Agabus bipustulatus 7–9 mm. Thorax has acute-angled rear corners and is as broad as the start of the wing-cases. Black with a faint leaden gloss in the male. Predator living in both stagnant and flowing water.

Family   HYDROPHILIDAE   Water-Scavengers

GREAT SILVER WATER BEETLE *(Hydrophilus piceus)* 3.7–4.7 cm long. Steeply arched and plumper than the true water beetles. Very large, oval body, pitch-black with a faint olive green sheen. Wing-cases have lines that come close together in pairs. Short antennae with final joint thickening into club shape with 3–5 hairy joints. Maxillary palpi longer than the antennae. Feeds on algae and soft aquatic plants. Rather a slow swimmer. Middle and hind legs having very few swimming bristles and in swimming, are used not together, but alternately. Renews its supply of air on the surface, holding its head and antennae out of the water. On each side of its head is a groove made of 2 partings in the hair which act as continuations of the gutter-like troughs in each of the hairy antennae, and down this air flows to the spiracles in the front of the thorax. This air passes through the tracheae and through the spiracles of the abdomen on the top and underside. The male has a broadened claw on the front pair of legs with which to hold on to the female while mating. The female emits white silky filament from the tip of the abdomen and uses this to make an open-mouthed sac in which she lays some 50 eggs; she then finishes this cocoon with a curving chimney and lets it float off on the water. It cannot capsize, the top being filled with air and thus lighter than the lower part. *Larvae:* see p. 439.

Hydrochara (= Hydrophilus) caraboides 1.4–1.8 cm. Oval, steeply arched body; black with slight green sheen. Reddish-yellow antennae with black club ends. Stripes on wing-cases only faintly indicated and there are few rows of pitting. Root of antennae reddish-yellow. Found in ponds and pools.

Family   HALIPLIDAE   Small Water Beetles

Haliplus ruficollis 2–2.5 mm; short, broad, boat-shaped body with very convex shoulders narrowing into almost a wedge-shape behind. The wing-cases widest at the shoulders. Yellow-brown or reddish-yellow; wing-cases have dark stripes and blackish spots. The hind (swimming) legs are moved alternately. Found in ponds etc. near the bank. Beetle and larvae predators in both stagnant and flowing water under washed-up matter, moss and algae.

Order   HEMIPTERA   Bugs

Family   NEPIDAE   Water Scorpions

WATER SCORPION *(Nepa cinerea [= rubra])* 1.7–2.2 cm. Long oval body, broad and flat, uniform grey-brown mostly wearing a crust of dirt. Very small head carried in a four-sided cut-out part of the front of the thorax; 2 protuberant round eyes at the side; very short, concealed antennae; short 3-jointed snout; shield an almost equilateral triangle; leather-like opaque fore-wings, only transluscent at the tip; membranous hind-wings, when closed, covering the back of the abdomen which is a vivid red-black colour. Fore-legs modified into 2 powerful clutching organs that are held out in front; the middle and hind legs slight and used for walking and swimming. The abdomen has long breathing tube consisting of 2 semi-circular spines which protrude slightly above the surface of the water. Is awkward both in swimming and walking and spends most of the time sitting motionless either on the bottom or on an aquatic plant, waiting for its prey. The feet close on the tibia like a knife, trapping any insect or small fish that swims past, which is then pierced by the beak and its body contents sucked out. In the spring

eggs are laid in a pad of algae, rich in oxygen, or the stem of a water plant from which only front end of the eggs, each equipped with 6–8 tracheae, sticks out. Larvae hatch out from May to July and take 5 months to become mature insects. Found in slow flowing, muddy water.

Ranatra linearis 3–4 cm long (without breathing-tubes); as slim as a straw with long thin legs. Grey-brown with red on the rear of the top of the abdomen; the sides are yellow. Flies only occasionally. Mostly sits motionless on the mud of the bottom or among plants in shallow water holding its fore-legs, modified into prehensile arms, in front of it. Its colour and immobility are its camouflage. It catches, kills, eats its prey and breathes in the same manner as *Nepa cinerea*. Lays its eggs in rows in stems of water plants. Each egg has two filament-like breathing tubes. Larvae hatch out May to July. Several moults. Found in stagnant, shallow water.

Family   NOTONECTIDAE   Water Boatmen

Notonecta glauca 1.3–1.6 cm long. Usually hangs upside down on the underside of the surface film of water; swims normally on its back. Longish body. Basic colour brown. Arched back, smooth and light in colour (camouflage). Head and fore part of the back are whitish; wings light brown. Abdomen is flat, hairy and dark in colour. Large head with big shining eyes; hind-legs, modified to act as paddles, are very long and strong, compressed and have hairs on either side, but no claws; with these it "rows" taking a wide sweep in each motion. Feeds voraciously on the body fluids of aquatic insects and their larvae, which it sucks out with its rostrum. Its sting can be very painful to humans. It comes to the surface every now and then and hangs with its rear end on the surface, unfolds two appendages, opening an air chamber that is ringed with long hairs and thus admits fresh air for breathing into 2 spiracles. Used air remains in the body, whereby the centre of gravity moves to its back and the lighter underside is turned up. Lays its eggs in slit cut in the stem of aquatic plants. Larvae have 5 moults. Common in stagnant water.

Family   NAUCORIDAE   Saucer Bugs

SAUCER BUG *(Ilyocoris [= Naucoris] cimicoides)* 12–16 mm
long; flat, oval body. Slightly arched back; shiny greenish-grey.
Hind legs have swimming-hairs. When catching its prey, can
close its fore-legs like a pocket knife against its thick tibia, the
undersides of which are covered with hair; then it pierces the
prey with its beak, injects poison, that can prove painful even
to humans. Obtains air from rear part of abdomen which is held
above the surface of the water; the close velvety hair covering its
body holds a layer of air that gives a silvery effect.

Family   CORIXIDAE   Lesser Water Boatmen

Corixa spp. 5–12 mm long; black-green on top; yellow underneath; base and wings yellow speckled with yellow. Fore-legs
short and with spines, widened to make oar blades. Hind legs
act as oars. Good at swimming and flying. Body is surrounded
by a thin coating of air and is lighter than water. Feeds on
unicellular algae and decomposed matter. Lives mostly on the
bottom. Body posture normal. Obtains air at the surface, which
its head and thorax break. Stores air under its wing-cases. In
summer flies by night from pond to pond.

b) ON THE SURFACE

Order   COLEOPTERA   Beetles

Family   GYRINIDAE   Whirligigs

Gyrinus natator 5–7 mm. Easily recognisable by its peculiar
mode of progression. Swims about in large numbers, swiftly
spiralling and circling, also diving swiftly to the bottom. Oval,
boat-shaped body, rather flattened; glossy black on top; truncated wing-cases leave the end of the body uncovered. Fore-legs
elongated; the middle and hind legs are broadened out into
flippers and have long swimming-hairs. The wing-cases have

11 rows of pitting, of which the inside ones frequently are only slightly marked or not at all. Predator on smaller aquatic creatures. 2 large compound eyes divided into an upper and lower half by a transverse ridge so that it can see above and below the surface at the same time. In fine weather circles on the surface of the water or suns itself on floating leaves; flies quite far at dusk; in bad weather stays by the bank or on the bottom. Attaches its eggs to roots and stalks underwater. Found on both stagnant and slowly flowing water. *Larvae:* see p. 440.

Order	HEMIPTERA Bugs
Family	GERRIDAE Pond Skaters

Gerris sp Up to 17 mm long and 9 mm across, they have silvery undersides but otherwise their narrow, long bodies are dark. They have 2 large protuberant eyes and freely outstretched antennae; they glide along the surface on 4 long, thin legs, very quickly and jerkily with occasional long jumps; often considerable numbers together. Almost the whole surface of the 4 long legs lies on the surface; the 2 short forelegs are held out in front and used to clasp its prey; a close matting of hair filled with air prevents the underside becoming wet. Mature specimens may have large, leathery wings or else quite short degenerate ones. Among them the larvae also move about, these being smaller and still having moults to go through. They feed on flies, beetles, caterpillars and smaller creatures that fall on to the water. On occasion they will suck out another aquatic insect as well if one ventures too near the surface. If food runs short, or the water dries up, they will go elsewhere, usually flying at night. Spend the winter concealed on the bank. Found in quiet inlets of stagnant ponds or brooks and rivers.

Family	VELIIDAE Water Crickets

Velia currens Orange underneath, otherwise black. Legs shorter and thicker than those of *Gerris* sp. Found particularly in small streams. Rather quick, jerky movements.

Family HYDROMETRIDAE Water Measurers

Hydrometra stagnorum Up to 12 mm long. Very narrow blackish body with fine, white, longitudinal stripes; underparts covered with thick, silky hair. Head almost as wide as abdomen, no neck-line constriction, but wider at front, like a wedge. There is almost twice as much of the head in front of the eyes as there is behind them. Legs almost all the same length. Crawls slowly across the water using all 6 legs. When disturbed takes quite short jumps. Sociable. Feeds chiefly on aquatic insects when they come to the surface to breathe. Common in all water which is stagnant or slow-flowing, by its banks; on water plants as well as on the water itself.

GROUND INSECTS OFTEN MISTAKEN FOR BEETLES

Order HEMIPTERA Bugs

Family PENTATOMIDAE Shield Bugs

GREEN SHIELD BUG *(Palomena prasina)* 1–1.5 cm long; legs and top green; membranous part of the wing-cases black-brown; underparts mostly red. Becomes chocolate-brown in autumn before hibernating. Lays greeny eggs on garden vegetation. 5 larval stages. Its evil smell often ruins fruit. Feeds especially on raspberries.

BISHOP'S MITRE *(Aelia acuminata)* 8–11 mm long and 5 mm across; head an elongated cone, narrowing in front and protruding like a snout; long, oval shape, a bright ochre-yellow with 3 dark, longitudinal stripes down the back. Hibernates on the edges of woods, etc. In April cuts stalks of corn and sucks the leaves and soft, milky grain in the ears. Found on grasses in clearings and on fringe of woods, more rarely on pasture land.

FOREST BUG *(Pentatoma rufipes)* 1.2–1.4 cm long. Yellowish or reddish-brown on top with black dots and bronze sheen; back of abdomen glossy black; antennae, legs, point of shield, reddish; base has a blunt prolongation on either side; in summer often sits on straws, crawls on tree trunks, often of birch; when disturbed whirrs away; sucks out small caterpillars and plants in orchards.

BRASSICA BUG *(Eurydema oleraceum)* 5–8 mm long; flattish body, green or blue with metallic sheen; the male has white patches; those of the female are blood-red; underparts similarly coloured, but in the male white with dark patches. Sits on cabbage or blossom; when sun shines is a lively flier, buzzing about sucking at cabbage, turnips, radish and other cruciferous plants, which, when present in large numbers, it can destroy. Those that have hibernated lay eggs May to June on undersides of leaves.

Sub-Family   SCUTELLERIDAE   Shield Bugs

Very large shields covering most or all of the abdomen.

SLOEBUG *(Dolycoris baccarum)* 9–14 mm long, hairy, olive-brown body with close pitting; whitish-yellow point to shield; underside has close black pitting; antennae have black and white rings; sides of abdomen similarly coloured. Hibernates in ground, under stones, etc. Flies about actively in spring eating noxious insects and sucking out soft fruits and young shoots. Sticks its eggs to leaves in small disc-shaped clusters, each egg separate. Takes until mid-summer to develop.

Eurygaster nigrocucullatus 1.1–1.3 cm long; arched back, flat underneath; yellowish, black-brown or black; shield, reaching to point of abdomen, often has 2 light coloured lateral patches at the root, leaving a narrow strip of the skin-covering free along the edges. Sits in bushes and on grasses.

Graphosoma italicum Blood-red, with longitudinal black stripes on top and black dots on underside. Often sits on umbellifers. Mostly in the south of Europe.

Family   LYGAEIDAE   Ground Bugs

Lygaeus equestris 1.4 cm long, elliptical body; back blood-red and black; wing-cases velvet black with white edgings and a large white patch in the middle. Sits in groups on old oak trees, on plants or on the ground.

Family   Pyrrhocoridae   Red Bugs

FIREBUG *(Pyrrhocoris apterus)* 9–11 mm long; black and blood-red; wing-cases without membrane; hind wings missing; often found in companies at the foot of old lime and elm trees, where it eats rotting matter and sucks juices from fallen fruit, dead insects and, occasionally, from tree roots.

Family   Reduviidae   Assassin Bugs

Rhinocoris iracundus 1.6–1.8 cm long; strikingly large snout; blood-red; abdomen has a sharp turned-up edge, rows of black spots; underneath 3 rows of black dots. Waits motionless on blossom for small flies and bees, which it seizes in its powerful arms. Can give a nasty sting.

Family   Coreidae   Squash Bugs

Enoplops (= Syromastes) marginatus 1.4 cm long; leathery appearance; rather rectangular head, with long protuberances on antennae that expand into a spike. Reddish-grey body with rows of fine black dots; red back to abdomen, shiny bronze wing-cases; half-cases protrude beyond the body at the rear, leaving the protruding sides of the abdomen uncovered. Rather active flier in hot weather, but spends much time sitting on bushes and umbellifers, living on what it can catch there; has a peculiar aromatic smell; hibernates under fallen leaves. On sorrel.

Family   Piesmidae   Beet Bugs

BEET LEAF BUG *(Piesma quadrata)* 3.5 mm long; with short, wide head; base a squat quadrilateral with curved sides and 3 ridges before the middle; to the side of each eye are 2 small notches. Adult is dark-grey with black patches. Female hibernates in bushes, grass, fallen leaves, etc. Flies from early April to early May on to beet or turnips, lays 150–160 eggs individually on the undersides of leaves; larvae hatch after 2–3 weeks; 4 moults when colour changes from yellow to yellow-green to green through which red stomach patch on abdomen shows; becomes mature by early June. Occasionally 2 broods. Places where it has sucked show white or brown patches, while the leaf itself puckers and withers. On sugar beet and turnips.

Family   MIRIDAE   Capsid Bugs

Halticus saltator 2.7 mm long; pear-shaped, glossy black body.
Head yellow to brown; yellow legs; long, thin antennae; very
protuberant eyes. No simple eyes. Hind femur very strong and
long, which helps it make great leaps like the flea beetle. Female
has short wings. Sits on the underside of the leaves of celeriac,
cucumber, melons, asters and stocks, causing them to shrivel, die
and fall off; prevents fruit forming.

Calocoris sexguttatus 6–8 mm long; black with bright yellow
patches; black femur, yellow tibia. June to September on celery;
lays eggs on leaves leaving a small, light-coloured patch that
later withers where they have sucked; leaf buds often crumpled.

Order   ORTHOPTHERA   Grasshoppers etc.   See p. 261

Family   BLATTIDAE   Cockroaches

GERMAN COCKROACH *(Phyllodromia [= Blattella] germanica)* 1.1–1.4 cm. Shy domestic vermin that shun the light
and hide in cracks and holes, emerging in swarms in the dark
to feed on remains of what people eat. Body yellow-brown;
antennae and legs lighter in colour; base has 2 dark brown
longitudinal stripes. Wings protrude beyond flat abdomen and
are apparently only capable of short gliding flight. Adhesive
pads on last toe-joint make it able to run along smooth overhanging surfaces. Abdomen of female is broad at rear, that of
male pointed and furnished with 2 short prongs. Will eat almost
anything. Female may produce a long, yellow-brown egg-case
(cocoon) containing some 30 eggs, at almost any time of the
year; she carries this around with her, attached to the rear end
of her body, for 4 weeks, when the larvae hatch; they take
4–6 months to develop going through several moults. Common
in all countries; in kitchens, cellars, breweries, etc.

COMMON COCKROACH *(Blatta orientalis)* Male 2–2.5 cm,
female 2.2–2.8 cm. Male chestnut, female almost black. The
male's wings cover two-thirds of the abdomen; in the female
the fore-wings are short, the hind ones rudimentary. The male
performs brief glide-flights at the most, but can run swiftly.
Stink glands in the abdomen cause a revolting smell. Avoids the

light, mostly remaining concealed and coming out by night to eat scraps of people's food, especially meat, but also milk, beer and water. Fouls food with its excrement. Female produces an egg-case with some 16 eggs which she carries for up to 5 days on the end of her abdomen. Hatched larvae go through 5 moults and, in Europe, take up to 3 or 4 years to achieve maturity.

AMERICAN COCKROACH *(Periplaneta americana)* 3.0–3.7 cm. Wings of both sexes perfectly developed and protruding beyond the abdomen. Flies by night. Body chestnut brown; base lighter in colour and has 2 dark patches in the middle and a dark rear edge. Female disguises her egg-case by sticking dung, sawdust, etc. on it. One female can produce 50 egg-cases each with 15–20 eggs. Larvae take 2–3 years to develop. Food and habits as others of the family. Despite its name the insect probably originated in Africa.

DUSKY COCKROACH *(Ectobius lapponicus)* 8–10 mm. Head and antennae black; front of thorax and abdomen also black but are edged with yellow, wide at the sides. Base carries a large dark patch in the middle, the outline of which is blurred. Brown-yellow fore-wing of male tapers to a point and juts beyond the abdomen; in female the fore-wings are rounded and reach only to 4th abdominal segment. Hind wings of male yellowish, of female rudimentary. Considerable variations in size and colour possible. Male flies actively from plant to plant in sunshine. Found at the outskirts of woods and in bushes. In Lappland also enters houses.

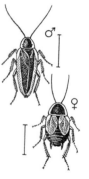

Aphlebia (= Hololampra) maculata 7 mm long; dark brown; white line round its crown; front and sides of thorax yellowish. Fore-wings of male longer than abdomen, brown with large dark brown patch at the tips; of the female half the length of the abdomen, yellow-brown, sometimes with a black patch at the end. On the fringe of deciduous woods, sometimes also in conifers.

Aphlebia punctata Body 7 mm; shiny black, with a yellow-brown edging round front of thorax. Fore-wings whitish-grey with fine black dots, those of the male being as long as abdomen, of the female only half its length. Found under dry leaves on edge of woods. May to June.

Family   GRYLLIDAE   Crickets   See p. 260

FIELD CRICKET *(Gryllus [= Liogryllus] campestris)* Body of male 1.9–2.6 cm, of female 2–2.7 cm long; fore-wings of male 1.3–1.7 cm, of female 1.4–1.7 cm. Ovipositor 1.1–1.4 cm. Thick, roundish head; broad back, and plump, almost round abdomen. Fore-wings lie horizontal and hind wings fold up like fan and protrude. Female has long, stick-shaped ovipositor. Shiny black body; dark brown fore-wings and sometimes a yellowish band across the base of them. Hind wings stunted, translucent. Underside of rear femur red. Soft eggs laid on bottom of living tube in little heaps of 30 or so. Larvae hatch out after 14 days, go through several moults, then hibernate. The chirping of the male is shrill and piercing, but attracts the female. Each cricket has its lair, a short tunnel slanting into the ground, which it defends bitterly against intruders. Defeated opponents are eaten. Otherwise feeds on delicate parts of plants, later in life on flies and other insects. Prefers sandy soil and sunny positions.

HOUSE CRICKET *(Acheta domesticus)* Body of male 1.5–1.9 cm, of female 1.6–2.1 cm; fore-wing 1.0–1.2 cm in male, 0.9–1.3 cm in female, whose ovipositor is 1.2–1.5 cm. Is thus smaller and daintier than the field cricket; yellowish-brown; hind wing protrudes beyond the body. Chirps in the evening and at night, a monotonous and melancholy sound. Does not dig itself a lair, but has hiding places in human dwellings; loves warmth. Moves usually at a run, seldom jumps. Mostly only emerges at night to search for vegetable refuse. Laying of eggs and the various stages of development can occur throughout the year. Found in kitchens, bakeries, breweries, etc.

WOOD CRICKET *(Nemobius [= Gryllus] sylvestris)* Body of male 0.9 cm, of female 1.0–1.1 cm; fore-wings 3–4 mm; ovipositor 8 mm (almost the length of the body). Fore-wings very stunted. Black head; dark brown body with lighter-coloured patches on abdomen. Hind tibia furnished with 6 long spikes. From June to July males chirp delicately from their hiding places in the afternoon and evenings. Swift runner; also able to jump. Found in open woods under leaves, moss and stones.

*Oecanthus pellucens Body of male 9–16 mm, of female 1.0–1.5 cm; fore-wings of male 1–1.6 cm of, female 1–1.2 cm. Ovipositor 7–8 mm. Delicate body covered with whitish hair. Bright yellow head. Very long antennae. Front of thorax bright yellow, a shallow cylinder in shape, very long. Fore-wings bright yellow and longer than the abdomen; hind wings translucent and longer than the fore-wings. Abdomen bright yellow. Ovipositor black serrated, straight. Male chirps in the evening and at night, a piercing sound that ceases at the least interruption. Feeds on leaves, insects (caterpillars, aphis). Lives free on plants, shrubs, trees, mostly sitting concealed under leaves. Found August to October especially in warmer parts of the Continent and particularly in vineyards.

MOLE CRICKET *(Gryllotalpa gryllotalpa)* Body 3.3–4.8 cm, fore-wings 1.5–2.1 cm. Grey brown, with shiny silky hairs. Strong, short antennae. Powerful head. Front of thorax large and stoutly armoured; oval, making the creature look a bit like a lobster. Fore-legs directed forward, large, spade-shaped, adapted for digging. Fore-wings short, parchmenty with dark-brown veining. Hind wings long, folded like a fan when at rest; fish bone-like appendages jutting beyond the abdomen between the two cerci. Hearing-organ concealed in deep longitudinal slits in fore-tibia. Lives mostly underground, where it digs galleries the thickness of a finger just under the surface, making small "molehills" in the process. Feeds on insects, seedlings, potatoes, turnips. Does considerable damage in gardens. Chirps lightly at night during June and July whilst on the ground; also leaves its dwelling and whirrs in heavy undulating flight close above the ground. Female has no ovipositor; lays 300–600 eggs in smoothed underground chambers the size of a hen's egg. Larvae hibernate.

Order   DERMAPTERA   Earwigs, etc.

Family   FORFICULIDAE   Earwigs

COMMON EARWIG *(Forficula auricularia)* Body 1.1–1.4 cm. Two halves of pincers touch, those of the male being curved,

those of the female straight, and close together with the tips crossing. Body dark brown, flat and very mobile; legs yellowish; wing-cases short, scale-shaped, strongly chitinised and no use for flying. Hind wings membranous as far as strongly chitinised fore edge, with radial veins, folded length-wise and across when at rest, when only a light coloured tip protrudes. Pincers are used for defence and for unfolding the wings. Flies only rarely and then at night. Feeds on plant and animal remains, damaged sweet fruits, dead insects, the more delicate parts of flowers and spores of fungi. In autumn female lays 50 to 60 eggs in small holes in the ground under stones, etc. and guards them and subsequently the larvae until the spring. Several moults before wings develop. Males die in autumn. Found under bark, stones, fallen leaves, on flowers and fruit.

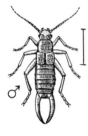

Chelidura acanthopygia Body of male 7–13 mm, of female 8–11 mm. No hind wings. In the male the two halves of the pincers do not touch. Reddish-brown, otherwise as others of the family. Lives in ground, under stones, in leaves, on bushes and trees.

Chelidura albipennis 7–10 mm long. Yellow-brown all over. Mostly have fore-wings, but no hind wings. Arms of pincers slightly curved. Hairy, pitted abdomen, mostly under bark, on flowers; summer and autumn.

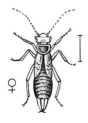

Labia minor 5–6 mm long, the smallest Continental earwig. Brick colour with black head. In male the base of the two pincer halves is separate. The female's pincers are slightly curved. Frequently seen flying by day round dung heaps and over fields where dung has been spread.

Labidura riparia 1.4–2 cm long. Yellowish with dark markings on front of thorax. Found under stones on the coast or on river banks.

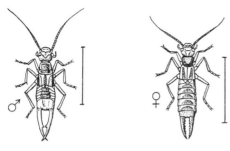

JUMPING GRASSHOPPERS

Order   ORTHOPTERA   Grasshoppers, Crickets, etc.

Family   ACRIDIDAE   Short-horned Grasshoppers   See p. 261

Oedipoda coerulescens Male 1.5–2.1 cm long. Fore-wings yellow-brown, dark at roots, two dark bars. Hind wings blue with dark, uneven band running from one edge to the other; tips lighter. Noiseless flight. Found in dry, heath-like country.

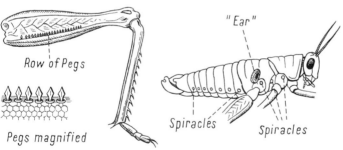

Fig. 55a: Short-horned grasshopper: sound-producing organ (left); sound-receiving organ "ear" (right)

Oedipoda germanica Male 1.8–2.3 cm, female 2.3–2.7 cm long. Wing span about 4.5 cm. Great resemblance to *O. coerulescens,* but rather larger and in flight displays its magnificent red hind wings. No sound as it takes wing. Found on dry, stony, sunny hill-sides in central and southern Europe.

Psophus stridulus Male 2.4 cm long. Black-brown body; red hind wings glow when in flight; only the tips of the wings are black. Makes a loud clapping sound as it takes wing, probably caused by some of the strong veins on the wings striking against each other. Sound is only heard as it takes off. Found on lush, rather damp pasture.

RUFOUS GRASSHOPPER *(Gomphocerippus [= Gomphocerus] rufus)* Male 1.5 cm, female 1.6–2.4 cm. Blackish thickening (club) at end of antennae, the tips of which are whitish in male, light coloured in female. Front of thorax red-brown with lighter sides. Black lengthwise stripe along edge of side. Abdomen red-brown on top, yellowish underneath. Fore-wings roughly as long as abdomen, red-brown. Hind wings brown. Found in light, grassy glades and forest meadows.

STRIPE-WINGED GRASSHOPPER *(Stenobothrus lineatus)* Male 1.9 cm, female 2.2–2.4 cm long. Head green; front of thorax green; edge of sides curves sharply inwards; 1 black stripe on the outside of the fore-half and another on the inside of the other half. Fore-wings longer than abdomen, green, seldom brownish, darker tips. Female has vivid sulphur-yellow lengthwise stripes near the fore edge. Hind wings uncoloured, slightly dark at the tip. Abdomen green with a red end in the male and a yellow one in the female. Blackish trochanter; hind tibia red or reddish-brown. Found on dry meadows. (Can be found on heather, but then is reddish-violet.)

Omocestus rufipes Male 1.4–1.6 cm. Female 1.9 cm. Fore-wings: male 1.2–1.6 cm; female 1.8 cm; brown with a white bar not far from the tip, and a few light patches; the back part of the female's wings being green. Hind wings slightly brownish. Hind femurs of male can be red, knee black, hind tibia always red; tibia of females brown; end of male's black abdomen red, yellow underneath; that of female brown on top, yellow-red or green-yellow underneath. In meadows.

Omocestus (= Stenobothrus) viridulus Male 1.4 cm, female 2.1–2.4 cm long. Head and front of thorax greenish. Fore-wings green, those of male brown with black veining in front, those of female greenish-grey. Hind wings faintly brown; legs green or grey-green. Hind femur brown-grey or green. Hind tibia green-yellow. Abdomen of male olive-green, of female green with dark patches.

(The female can be all green with red stripes close to the fore edge of the fore-wings and white side edgings to the front of the thorax.)

Stethophyma grossum (= Mecostethus grossus) Male 1.3–2 cm, female 2.6–3.1 cm long. Fore-wings of male 1.8 cm, of female 1.9–2.3 cm. Green-brown head; greenish front of thorax; brown-green fore-wings with darker tips and yellow or yellow-green streaks along fore edge. Hind wings transparent. Hind femurs red underneath; hind tibia greenish with black spikes. Black knees. Abdomen reddish-green on top with black patches: yellow underneath. Slight chirrup and also makes a striking click sound, when the hind femurs slide back along the end of the fore-wings. Very active. Marshy ground, ditches, water meadows.

Family   TETTIGONIIDAE   See p. 260

Bush-crickets or Long-horned Grasshoppers

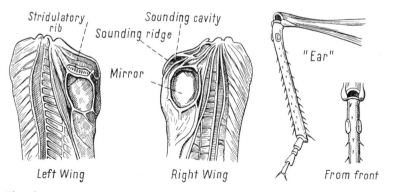

Fig. 55b: Great green grasshopper: sound-producing organ (left) **and sound-receiving organ "ear"** (right)

GREAT GREEN GRASSHOPPER *(Tettigonia [= Locusta] viridissima)* Body of male 2.7–3.4 cm; of female 3–3.6 cm long. Fore-wings of male 3.3–4.9 cm, of female 5–5.5 cm; ovipositor 2.6–3 cm. Green (protective) colouring on head, antennae, front of thorax; most have brown lengthwise stripes on top. Fore-wings green and longer than abdomen; base of the wings has brownish patch; hind wings transparent, colourless. Female has long ovipositor. Climbs sedately about plants; when threatened uses its strong legs to jump or flies with fluttering wings; otherwise wings act only as a parachute while gliding. Feeds on other insects on which it pounces; occasionally also on juicy parts of plants. Male's chirp a loud *zick-zick* in late summer and autumn from bushes and trees on edge of woods; this attracts the female. Eggs are laid individually in loose soil with ovipositor. Hibernates.

WART-BITER *(Decticus verrucivorus)* Male 2.5–3.6 cm; female 3.1–4.5 cm long. Fore-wings of male 2.4–3.3 cm, of female 2.2–3.1 cm; ovipositor 1.8–2.4 cm, half the length of the body. Crown of head and forehead yellow, sometimes with yellow spots; green antennae. Front of thorax green; side-flanges have a brown patch in the middle. Fore-wings are as long, or longer than the abdomen spotted with green or brown. Hind wings translucent. Abdomen yellow-brown or green on top, with spots of brown; lighter underneath. Male chirps as great green grasshopper, only shriller and only by day. Eggs in loose earth. Powerful hind femurs enable it to make long leaps. When cornered will bite, secretes brown juice from mouth, popularly supposed to cure warts. On grassland.

Meconema thalassinum (= varium) Body of male 1.1–1.4 cm; of female 1–1.4 cm long; fore-wing of male 1.2–1.3 cm, of female 1.2 cm; ovipositor 0.9 cm. Body light green with lengthwise yellow line on the base. Very long, fragile antennae. Fore-wings light green; hind wings membranous, translucent. Abdomen light green. Rudimentary sound-producing organ. Feeds on plants. Lays eggs in cracks in bark. Hibernates. In crests of trees and tall bushes, especially oaks.

Phasgonura (= Locusta) cantans Body of male 2.4–2.7 cm; of female 2.6–2.8 cm long; fore-wings of male 2.6–3 cm; ovipositor 2.3–3 cm. Brown or brown-green head. Front of thorax browny-green, darker on top. Fore-wings green, brownish at base, slightly longer than abdomen. Hind wings colourless, translucent. Legs and abdomen brownish-green or brownish. Male chirrups like great green grasshopper, but sound is higher and sharper. In fields and bushes in late summer and autumn.

Locusta caudata Body of male 2.1–2.6 cm; of female 3–3.5 cm; fore-wings of male 2.8–4 cm; of female 4.2–4.6 cm. Ovipositor 3.8–4.1 cm. Resembles great green grasshopper only its femurs are yellow and the rear ones have spikes with black rings; the ovipositor is somewhat longer than the fore-wings. Makes a peculiar buzzing sound. Found in cornfields, on trees and bushes in fields.

BUTTERFLIES AND MOTHS AND THEIR CATERPILLARS

COLOURFUL BUTTERFLIES OF THE OPEN COUNTRY

Plates 7, 10 and 11 (Life-size)

Order   LEPIDOPTERA   Butterflies and Moths

Family   PAPILIONIDAE   Swallowtails

SWALLOWTAIL *(Papilio machaon)* Plate 7, No. 1. Flies April or May to July or August. Sulphur yellow. Fore-wings have black patches and a broad black seam along the edge with a number of half-moon shaped yellow indentations. Hind-wings have small tails, blue bands along the edge and a large, rust-brown eye-spot on inner edge. Lays eggs on parsnip, carrot, burnet, dill, caraway, angelica. Caterpillar (Plates 10 and 11) June to August are fat, bare, green with black belts studded with red spots. Pupa attached to plant, dormant during winter. In Britain only in Wicken Fen, Cambridgeshire and Norfolk Broads.

*SCARCE SWALLOWTAIL *(Iphiclides [= Papilio] podalirius)* Plate 7, No. 2. Flies April to June; 2 generations. July to September. Straw-yellow wings; fore-wings have irregular black bands; hind wings long tails, black edgings with blue half-moons; on the inner edge small rust-yellow eye-spot. Lays eggs on sloe, plum, pears and apple trees. Caterpillar 4 cm, smooth, green with lighter back line, red-brown spots and yellow side stripes. Attached pupa dormant during winter.

*APOLLO *(Parnassius apollo)* Plate 7, No. 12. Flies June to August. White wings with large black spots. Hind wings carry 2 blood-red eyes edged with black. Egg dormant during winter. Caterpillar (Plate 10). May to June; black, velvet hair with steel-blue warts and rows of red dots; on its nape carries an orange-red fork of flesh that it can thrust out. In the heat of the day feeds on white stonecrop *(Sedum album)* otherwise is concealed under it. Found in Alps and other mountains from 250–2,000 m.

*ALPINE APOLLO *(Parnassius phoebus [= delius])* Flies June to July. Resembles the Apollo but has antennae ridged with black and white and the male has no black patch on the rear edge of the fore-wing; the female having a red patch there instead. Caterpillar July to August on saxifrage *(Saxifraga aizoides);* black with lemon-yellow spots. Confined to Alps from 1,250 to 2,500 m, and parts of Denmark.

Family	Cater-pillar	Pupa	Butterfly in flight	sitting

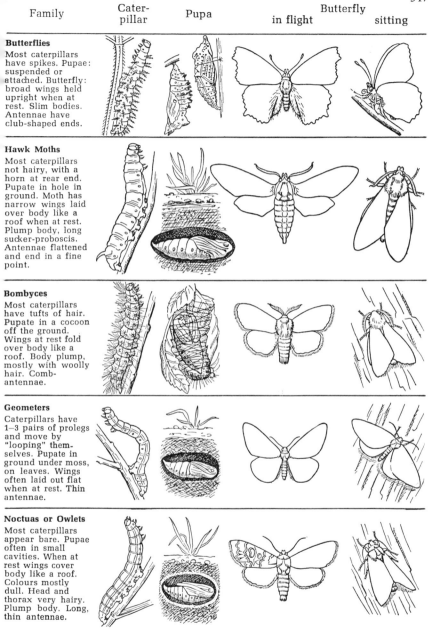

Butterflies

Most caterpillars have spikes. Pupae: suspended or attached. Butterfly: broad wings held upright when at rest. Slim bodies. Antennae have club-shaped ends.

Hawk Moths

Most caterpillars not hairy, with a horn at rear end. Pupate in hole in ground. Moth has narrow wings laid over body like a roof when at rest. Plump body, long sucker-proboscis. Antennae flattened and end in a fine point.

Bombyces

Most caterpillars have tufts of hair. Pupate in a cocoon off the ground. Wings at rest fold over body like a roof. Body plump, mostly with woolly hair. Comb-antennae.

Geometers

Caterpillars have 1–3 pairs of prolegs and move by "looping" them-selves. Pupate in ground under moss, on leaves. Wings often laid out flat when at rest. Thin antennae.

Noctuas or Owlets

Most caterpillars appear bare. Pupae often in small cavities. When at rest wings cover body like a roof. Colours mostly dull. Head and thorax very hairy. Plump body. Long, thin antennae.

Fig. 56: The Most Important Families of the Larger Butterflies and Moths.
(See text for individual families of butterflies)

Family   PIERIDAE   The Whites

ORANGE TIP *(Anthocaris cardamines)* Plate 7, No. 8. Flies April to May. In male the outer half of the fore-wing is orange with grey-black tip. Hind wings have yellowy-green spots underneath; female's lack the orange. Lays eggs on lady's smock and other cruciferous plants. Caterpillar June to July: 3.5 cm; blue-green, with fine black dots; 1 white side stripe. Grey-green underparts. Attached pupa dormant during winter.

BRIMSTONE *(Gonepteryx rhamni)* Plate 7, No. 9. Flies in early spring and from June on; butterfly spends winter dormant on ground under leaves. Wide wings; those of male lemon-yellow, of female greenish-white, each wing having an orange spot in the middle. Caterpillar up to 5 cm long; blue-green with white lengthwise stripes across the tarsi. May to June on buckthorn. Pupa attached to plant.

CLOUDED YELLOW *(Colias croceus [= edusa])* Plate 7, No. 10. Flies July to September. Wings orange have broad black edging, sulphur yellow below, orange towards the top. Caterpillar on sainfoin, lucerne and other clovers.

PALE CLOUDED YELLOW *(Colias hyale)* Plate 7, No. 19. Flies May and July to August; also September to October. Wings of male sulphur yellow, of female greenish-white; in middle of fore-wings a black spot, of hind wing an orange spot, the latter being double resembles an 8. Fore-wing black-brown at tip and along outer edge. Caterpillar June to July and autumn to April. 4 cm; green with black dots and yellow lengthwise stripes. On vetches, clover, lucerne. Occasional immigrant to Britain.

Family   NYMPHALIDAE

RED ADMIRAL *(Vanessa atalanta)* Plate 7, No. 3. Flies May to August. Dormant during winter as butterfly or pupa. Top-side of wing velvet black; fore-wings with brick-red oblique bars and white spots. Hind wings with red, black-spotted edges. Caterpillar (Plate 10): May to June and July to September; brown-yellow or black with yellow or whitish side stripes and yellow, branching spikes. Eggs laid individually on nettle-leaves folding the leaf over the egg and securing it thus with silk. Hanging pupa. Common. Often on fallen fruit, sucking the juice.

PEACOCK *(Nymphalis io)* Plate 7, No. 4. Flies early in the year and from June to late autumn; female spends winter dormant. Each wing has one jutting corner, in the fore corner a large blue eye; brown on top, brown-black underneath. In May lays green eggs on nettles and wild hops. Caterpillar (Plate 10) May to June and August to September; sociable; black with fine white dots; black branching spikes. Pupae hang by tails.

PAINTED LADY *(Vanessa cardui)* Plate 7, No. 5. Flies all summer; several generations; butterfly spends winter dormant. Wings brick-red on top, with black patches; white patches in point of fore-wing. Caterpillar 5 cm long; black-green; branching grey or brown spikes. In summer individually on thistles, nettles, etc. Pupa hangs by tail. Often migrate in mass.

SMALL TORTOISESHELL *(Aglais urticae)* Plate 7, No. 7. Flies June to autumn. 2–3 generations. Butterfly dormant during winter. Brick red on top; 3 dark patches on rear part of fore-wing; blue half-moons in a dark outer edging round all wings. Caterpillar (Plate 10) June to autumn in companies on nettles; black or grey with yellowish longitudinal stripes; short spike. Pupa hangs by tail.

LARGE TORTOISESHELL *(Nymphalis polychloros)* Plate 8, No. 14. Flies July to September. Butterfly hibernates. Upper side of wings yellow or red-brown with black patches; very similar to small tortoiseshell, but hind wings are larger and have round blue spots in dark margin (absent in fore-wings). Caterpillar (Plate 10, No. 10) black-blue with rust-brown lengthwise stripes and rust-yellow spikes. On cherry, quince, apple, pear, damson, willow, elm, poplar. Sociable. Pupa drops to ground.

SMALL PEARL-BORDERED FRITILLARY *(Clossiana [= Argynnis] selene)* Plate 7, No. 16. Flies until early July; sometimes 2 generations on Continent. End July to September. Brownish wings with dark spots. Hind wings underneath, basal and outer margins reddish-brown, often brushed with violet and silver speckles. Found especially on damp meadows.

QUEEN OF SPAIN FRITILLARY *(Argynnis [= Issoria] lathonia)* Plate 7, No. 18. Flies from end of April to October. 2 generations. Wings orange as *A. selene*. No line of half-moons on margin of fore-wings, but instead 2 rows of black dots before the marginal line. Undersides of hind wings have large silver spots in 2 rows with red-brown bars with silver dots on them in between. Caterpillar hibernates; is 4 cm long, grey-brown with white, broken back stripe; brick red spikes on red warts. Feeds on heartsease. Pupa hangs by tail-hook. Butterfly often sits on ground with outspread wings. Rare immigrant to Britain.

Family   SATYRIDAE   Browns

GRAYLING *(Hipparchia [= Satyrus] semele)* Plate 7, No. 13. Flies July to August. Brown on top with red-yellow bars which are rather indistinct in male; the "eye" is faint or missing in the male; ochre on the undersides of the fore-wing. Underside of hind wing brown with white marking; a deeply serrated white transverse line across the middle. Found in dry areas.

Plate 7

(Life-size)

1. SWALLOWTAIL *(Papilio machaon)* p. 316
2. SCARCE SWALLOWTAIL *(Iphiclides [= Papilio] podalirius)* p. 316
3. RED ADMIRAL *(Vanessa atalanta)* p. 318
4. PEACOCK *(Nymphalis io)* p. 319
5. PAINTED LADY *(Vanessa cardui)* p. 319
6, 6a. SILVER-STUDDED BLUE *(Plebejus argus)* p. 321
7. SMALL TORTOISESHELL *(Aglais urticae)* p. 319
8. ORANGE TIP *(Anthocharis cardamines)* p. 318
9. BRIMSTONE *(Gonepteryx rhamni)* p. 318
10. CLOUDED YELLOW *(Colias croceus)* p. 318
11. SMALL COPPER *(Lycaena phlaeas)* p. 321
12. APOLLO *(Parnassius apollo)* p. 316
13. GRAYLING *(Hipparchia semele)* p. 320
14. COMMON BLUE *(Polyommatus icarus)* p. 322
15. WALL BROWN *(Pararge megera)* p. 321
16. SMALL PEARL-BORDERED FRITILLARY *(Clossiana selene)* p. 319
17. LARGE HEATH *(Coenonympha tullia [= tiphon])* p. 321
18. QUEEN OF SPAIN FRITILLARY *(Argynnis lathonia)* p. 319
19. PALE CLOUDED YELLOW *(Colias hyale)* p. 318
20. SMALL HEATH *(Coenonympha pamphilus)* p. 321

Plate 7

L. Haundorff

WALL BROWN *(Pararge megera)* Plate 7, No. 15. Flies May to June and August to September. 2–3 generations. Browny-yellow on top with jagged brown bars. Large eye near the point of the fore-wing. 3 or more eyes with dots in the middle of them on the upper side of hind wings; underside has uniform brown marking. Caterpillar greenish with white back and side stripes; found in autumn on fescue-grass; hibernates. Pupa hangs by tail-hook. In vineyards, sunny places.

LARGE HEATH *(Coenonympha tullia [= tiphon])* Plate 7, No. 17. Flies June to July. Brown-yellow upper side with indistinct eyes, one of which is on fore-wing and several on hind wing. Eyes on underside are distinct, with white centres and light rims. Caterpillar August to May, hibernates; 2.5 cm long, green; found on cotton-grass and sedge. Wet meadows.

SMALL HEATH *(Coenonympha pamphilus)* Plate 7, No. 20. Flies March to October. 1, 2 or 3 broods. Wings ochre-yellow on top with dark margins and light fringes. Fore-wings have indistinct eye near the point. Grey underside; that of fore-wing has an eye with white centre and yellow rim; hind wing 3–6 lighter spots. Hopping flight, slow and low. Lays eggs on various grasses. In cornfields, pastures.

Family   LYCAENIDAE   Blues and Coppers

SILVER-STUDDED BLUE *(Plebejus argus)* Plate 7, No. 6. Flies mid-June to mid-August. Wings of male reddish-blue on top with narrow black margin and white fringe; those of female are dark brown on top; the hind wing has reddish-yellow round spots with black dots before the margin. Underside of hind wing on the margin side of the red spots has black dots with metallic green-blue centres. Eggs lie dormant during winter. Caterpillar colourful; April to July on bird's foot trefoil, gorse, clover, heather; has honey-gland which ants milk. Dry, sandy places, especially slopes up to 2,250 m in Alps.

SMALL COPPER *(Lycaena phlaeas)* Plate 7, No. 11. Flies April to May and July to October. Top-side of fore-wings shiny red-gold with broad, black-brown margin and angular black patches; hind-wing drawn out into a small tip; black-brown on top with an earthy-brown margin and grey-brown with black dots underneath. Caterpillar 2 cm dark green; back line and side stripes yellow or red. Found on sorrel, knotweed; hibernates. Dry grassland in open country.

COMMON BLUE *(Polyommatus icarus)* Plate 7, No. 14. Flies May to June and July to September; also October. 2–3 generations. Resembles *P. argus* which it equals in size. Upper side of male blue with reddish tinge, underside grey with black spots. Female brown on top, often with quite a lot of blue and reddish spots on both fore and hind wings. Caterpillar light green with a dark back stripe and yellow spots on its sides. On trefoil, etc. The commonest blue.

Colourful Butterflies of Woodlands and Parks

Plates 8, 10 and 11

(Life-size)

Family   NYMPHALIDAE

PURPLE EMPEROR *(Apatura iris)* Plate 8, No. 1. Flies July to August. Upper side of wings black-brown with broad, white band; male has blue iridescence, female does not. One eye on top of each hind wing and on undersides of both wings. Caterpillar (Plate 11, No. 16) hibernates in small cocoon. May to June on sallow; up to 5 cm, green with yellow side stripes in front, yellow oblique bars and 2 tall, blue-green fork-shaped horns; matt green pupa hangs by tail-hook. Chiefly oak woods with sallow. Butterfly often sits on puddles, on roads and also on carrion or dung.

*SMALL PURPLE EMPEROR *(Apatura ilia)* Flies July. Smaller than purple emperor, but very like it. Wings black-brown with magnificent bright blue iridescence on top and one eye on side of fore-wing. No zig-zag on white bar on hind-wing. Moist woods; mostly in mountains. Much more rare.

CAMBERWELL BEAUTY *(Nymphalis antiopa)* Plate 8, No. 2. Flies July to September. Hibernates and lives until end of April. Velvet brown top to wings with yellow margin and 2 yellow patches on fore-wing. Caterpillar June to July, 5 cm, black with yellow spots, black spike and rust-red spots on back; red abdominal legs; first in companies, then scattered. On willow, birch, polar, elm. Brown-grey pupa hangs by tail-hook. Rare immigrant to Britain, mainly in east.

*GREAT POPLAR *(Limenitis populi)* Plate 8, No. 4. June to July. Brown-black wings with white patches and a row of orange crescents inside the margin. Female has white bar, which in male is only indicated. Caterpillar (Plate 11, No. 17) May to June on aspen; grey-yellow with a double row of hairy warts on its back, on which the first behind the head stick out most. Hibernates in a leaf it has spun in together. Light deciduous woods.

WHITE ADMIRAL *(Limenitis camilla)* Plate 8, No. 5. Flies May to July. Brown-black tops to wings with a white bar down hind one; white spots on fore-wing almost form a bar; no orange marginal spots. Underneath reddish-yellow to red-brown with 2 rows of black dots on margin. Caterpillar 4.5 cm, green with delicate white dots. August to early June hibernating; on honeysuckles. Butterflies in forest rides; often settle on puddles.

DARK GREEN FRITILLARY *(Mesoacidalia charlotta)* Plate 8, No. 6. Flies June to August. Upper side reddish-yellow; black double line along margins, plus a row of black half-moons. Underside has iridescent spots; that of hind wing is greenish at root turning yellow towards the edge. Caterpillar 4.8 cm, from spring to May on violets; black-brown with fine white specks and white back stripes, red side spots, black branching spikes. Hibernates when still small. Light woods; outskirts of woods.

SILVER-WASHED FRITILLARY *(Argynnis paphia)* Plate 8, No. 7. Flies June to August. Ochre-yellow wings with 3 rows of black spots along the margin. The male's fore-wing has 4 broad, black veins. Underside of hind-wing matt green with 3 silver streaks and a distinct row of eyes; also a narrow, silver line along the margin broken with dark colour. Caterpillar August to May, 5 cm, fat, with brown and black stripes; bright yellow back stripe with black line down middle; long, yellow spikes, the fore pair elongated like antennae. On violets, raspberries. Hibernates while still small. Pupa hangs by tail- hook. Fringes of woods, glades.

LARGE PEARL-BORDERED FRITILLARY *(Clossiana euphrosyne)* Flies May to July. Very similar to foregoing, but underside of hind-wing has brick-red basal and outer bands and 1 spot of silver in yellow middle band. Caterpillar on violets, July–May, hibernating. In deciduous woods.

*MAP BUTTERFLY *(Araschnia levana)* Plate 8, No. 10. Flies April to May and July to September. In spring has red-yellow upper side with black markings, white spots on fore-wing and blue spots on margin of hind-wing; undersides rust-brown with white-yellow bars. In summer, upperside is black-brown with white or yellowish bars and narrow red-brown lines. Caterpillar 3.5 cm, black or blackish spikes, 2 on head; in companies on nettles.

HEATH FRITILLARY *(Melitaea athalia)* Plate 8, No. 11. Flies May to June and August. Markings vary considerably. Yellow-brown upper side with black bands; underside of hind wing has light band in middle and brown band nearer margin, both interrupted by black streaks. Caterpillar 3 cm, black-brown or black with lights dots and light brown spikes. On cow-wheat, plantain.

Plate 8 (Life-size)

1. PURPLE EMPEROR *(Apatura iris)* Male. p. 322

2. CAMBERWELL BEAUTY *(Nymphalis antiopa)* p. 322

3. LARGE BLUE *(Maculinea arion)* p. 327

4. GREAT POPLAR *(Limenitis populi)* Female. p. 323

5. WHITE ADMIRAL *(Limenitis camilla)* p. 323

6. DARK GREEN FRITILLARY *(Mesoacidalia charlotta [= Argynnis aglaia])* Female. p. 323

7. SILVER-WASHED FRITILLARY *(Argynnis paphia)* Male. p. 323

8. *Hipparchia fagi (= Satyrus hermione)* p. 325

9. SMALL WOOD NYMPH *(Hipparchia alcyone [= aelia])* p. 325

10. Spring 10a Summer MAP BUTTERFLY *(Araschnia levana)* p. 323

11. HEATH FRITILLARY *(Melitaea athalia)* Male. p. 324

12. *Euphydryas (= Melitaea) maturna* p. 325

13. COMMA *(Polygonia c-album)* p. 325

14. LARGE TORTOISESHELL *(Nymphalis polychloros)* p. 319

15. SPECKLED WOOD *(Pararge aegeria* var. *egerides)* p. 325

16. NORTHERN BROWN or SCOTCH ARGUS *(Erebia aethiops)* p. 326

17. *Erebia medusa* p. 326

18. 18a. MEADOW BROWN *(Maniola jurtina)* p. 326

19. SCARCE COPPER *(Heodes virgaureae)* p. 327

20. PEARL-GRASS BUTTERFLY *(Coenonympha arcania)* p. 326

L. Hausdorff

Euphydryas (= *Melitaea*) *maturna* Plate 8, No. 12. Flies May to July. Upper sides black-brown with a row of reddish-yellow spots; male also has yellowish-white spots; underside of hind wings orange with bright yellow middle band and moon-spots along margin. Caterpillar 4 cm, black with sulphur yellow back stripe; on plantain, scabious, violets and a few deciduous trees. Hibernates. Solitary. Forest meadows.

GLANVILLE FRITILLARY *(Melitaea cinxia)* Flies May to July. Upper sides yellowy-red, chequered with black like chess board; white diced wing-fringes. Underside of fore-wings have pale yellow tips with black dots; hind wings a row of yellow moon-spots along the margin. Caterpillar 4 cm, black with bluish-white dots; on plantain and hawk-weed. Hibernate in communal cocoon.

COMMA *(Polygonia c-album)* Plate 8, No. 13. Flies May to June and August to September. Hibernates as butterfly. Wings deeply notched; upper sides reddish-yellow with black-brown spots; undersides have a white C in the middle of the hind wing. Lays eggs individually on rasp-berry, gooseberry, wild hops, nettles, young elm. Caterpillar (Plate 10) black-blue with rust-brown lengthwise stripes and rust-yellow spikes. On cherry, quince, apple, pear, plum, willow, poplar, elm. Sociable. Pupa hangs on tail-hook.

Family   SATYRIDAE   Browns

Hipparchia fagi (= *Satyrus hermione*) Plate 8, No. 8. Flies July to August. Dark brown wings with yellow-white band and 2 eyes with white centres on fore-wing and one in rear corner of hind wing. Light band on fore-wing of male is tinged with smoke-brown. Caterpillar, May to June. 4 cm, reddish-grey with black back stripes. On honey-grass *(Holcus* sp.) hibernates. On dry, grassy clearings, sits on tree trunks. Becoming rare. Southern.

* SMALL WOOD NYMPH *(Hipparchia alcyone [= aelia])* Plate 8, No. 9. Flies June to September. Dark brown upper side with yellowy-white band dusted with brown. In this band respectively 1 and 2 eyes with white centres. Caterpillar yellowish with dark lengthwise stripe: found on grasses; hibernates. In dry pine woods during summer.

SPECKLED WOOD *(Pararge aegeria* var. *egerides)* Plate 8, No. 15. Flies April to June and July to September. Basic colour black-brown; fore-wings have pale yellow patches and one eye near the tip; hind wings have 3–4 white-centred eyes in a pale yellow band. Undersides brown and greenish marbling as well as light spots with brownish rims. Caterpillar June to July and September to October on couch-grass, 3 cm, dull green. Common in and around deciduous woods.

NORTHERN BROWN or SCOTCH ARGUS *(Erebia aethiops)* Plate 8, No. 16. Flies throughout the summer. Brown wings with red bands visible even on underside of fore-wings; towards top has 2 white-centred eyes close together and a third lower down. Hind wing has red band with 3–4 white-centred eyes. Caterpillar 3 cm, hides among grass, feeds only at night; reddish yellow-grey back line with white seam and dark brown side stripes; hibernates.

Erebia medusa Plate 8, No. 17. Flies end of May to early July. Both sides of wings brown-black with band of rust-red spots; in tip of fore-wing 2 large black eyes with white centres close together, sometimes merged; 3 other spots with small eyes or just dots. Hind wings of male have 2–3, of female 4–5 eyes on upper side, on underside no markings, but the eye-band. Caterpillar 4 cm light green; darker back stripe framed with white; pale side stripes. Until end of May on finger-grass, etc. Hibernates. Grassy paths and clearings in woods; ditches, etc.

Erebia (= Maniola) pronoe Flies July to September. Upper side of wings black-brown with lighter band ornamented with black dots and white-centred eyes. Underside: fore-wings rust-brown with lighter band; hind wings grey with violet sheen and dark-brown band. On grassy slopes in upper reaches of tree-zone.

Erebia gorge Flies early June to August. Each fore-wing has 2 oblique black-rimmed light eye-spots in the rust-red band. Grey-marbled hind wings have sharply outlined dark band. Stony ground above 1,500 m.

MEADOW BROWN *(Maniola jurtina)* Plate 8, No. 18, 18a. Flies June to August. Upper sides of male's wings uniform dark-brown, one eye with white centre and reddish rim near the tip. As well as this eye, the female has an orange band on fore-wing. Undersides are lighter with one band each. Caterpillar 3.5 cm, green; on grasses (especially poa); hibernates. Pupa hangs on tail-hook. Meadows, woods, railway embankments, country roads.

*PEARL-GRASS BUTTERFLY *(Coenonympha arcania)* Plate 8, No. 20. Flies June to August. Fore-wings reddish-yellow with black outer margins in which often one centred eye. Undersides have broad, white margin.

Hind wing dark-brown above; ochre-brown underside with white band and eye-spots. Caterpillar 3 cm, green; until May on pearl-grass. Especially on edges of woods with undergrowth; in hilly country.

Coenonympha iphis Flies June to July. Wings of male are uniform brown on upper side, hind wings of female darker with a few dark eye-spots. Hind wings of both sexes have a few irregular white spots on underside, occasionally merging into a band. Male has mostly one eye near the tip of fore-wing. Grassy rides, damp pastures. Solitary.

Minois (= Satyrus) dryas Flies July to August. Upper sides uniform brown; 2 eyes (female often has 3) on fore-wing with centres more blue than white. Grassy, damp woods; likes the shade.

THE RINGLET *(Aphantopus hyperantus)* Flies June to July. Wing-span about 4 cm. Uniform dark brown with light-coloured fringes; on upper side of each wing 2 indistinct small blackish spots often with white centres and yellowish rims. Undersides light brown; fore-wings usually have 3, hind wings 5, large eye-spots. Light woods, meadows.

Family   LYCAENIDAE   Blues

LARGE BLUE *(Maculinea arion)* Plate 8, No. 3. Flies June to July. Colouring varies considerably. Blue wings with chain of black spots on upper side and numerous eyes on underside; root of wings vividly dusted with blue. Lays eggs on flower of thyme. Caterpillar dirty red; on thyme. Red ants titillate the caterpillar and lick up its sugary secretion, carry it to their nest in the autumn, where it feeds throughout winter on their grubs, pupating in spring. Dry, sunny slopes with thyme. In Alps and southern Europe rather than the north. In Britain mainly in a few localities in S.W.

HOLLY BLUE *(Celastrina argiolus)* Flies mid-April to mid-June and July to August. Blue wings, those of male having a reddish sheen. Fore-wings of female have broad dark margins. Undersides bluish-white with black blue-edged spots. Caterpillar on buckthorn, etc. Grassy patches in and around woods; likes bramble blossom.

*SCARCE COPPER *(Heodes virgaureae)* Plate 8, No. 19. Flies end of June to August. One winter in egg stage. Wings of male are reddish-gold on top with black margins. Female's are more browny with rows of dark spots. Undersides of fore-wings yellow, dusted with red, a few black spots and lighter dots. Caterpillar 2.7 cm, dark green with lighter longitudinal lines. Pasture, light woods.

Insects

COLOURFUL EVENING AND NIGHT-FLYING MOTHS

Plates 9 & 11, (Life-size) and Fig. 56

Family   SPHINGIDAE   Hawk Moths

DEATH'S HEAD HAWK *(Acherontia atropos)* Plate 9, No. 1. Flies
only at night in summer. Wing span 11–12 cm. Fore-wing black-brown
with cloud-like streaks of yellow; hind wing ochre-yellow with 2 black
bands. Black thorax with yellow mark like a death's head. Abdomen
ringed with yellow and black, with blue stripe down the middle. By
expelling air produces a mouse-like squeak. Feeds only on sap from
wounded trees and honey of bees. Caterpillar (Plate 11, No. 1) up to
15 cm. Yellow thoracical section with greenish abdomen with oblique
blue streaks; S-shaped horn on rear end; feeds on potato plants and
thorn-apples. Deep brown pupa in smoothed cavity in ground.

EYED HAWK *(Smerinthus ocellata)* Plate 9, No. 2. Flies May to June
in the evening about flowers. Wing span *c.* 8 cm. Has large pink patch
at root of hind wing in which is a large black patch with dark blue circle
on it. Caterpillar (Plate 11, No. 11). June to September; 8–9 cm, blue-
green with fine white dots and white oblique streaks; blue horn. On
willows, poplars, fruit-trees. Reddish-brown, shiny pupa. Hibernates.

POPLAR HAWK *(Laothoe populi)* Plate 9, No. 4. Flies May to July.
Wing-span 7–8 cm. Colouring varies. Wings yellow- or red-grey, often
ash grey or brown. Several faded, dark wavy lines and bands on fore-
wings; characteristic large rust-red patch on root of hind wing. Outer
edges very notched. Caterpillar (Plate 11) June to October; 8–9 cm, yellow-brown with yellow spots and 7 yellow oblique streaks; often also
has 2 rows of reddish-yellow spots on the sides, or is annulated without
markings. Green, occasionally bluish, horn. On poplars, willows, birch.
Matt black-brown pupa; hibernates in cavity in ground.

LIME HAWK *(Mimas tiliae)* Plate 9, No. 5. Flies from April to July
at night; spends most of day sitting on stem of lime-tree. Wing-span
6.7 cm. Irregular zigzag outer rim on fore-wings. Colouring variable;
that of fore-wings mostly yellowish; matt green before margin, a dark
green bar in the middle, usually divided into 2 larger patches. Hind wings
brownish with darker band that has "run". Caterpillar (Plate 11, No. 8)
June to September 8.8 cm, green; yellow, oblique streaks edged with red
on top; bluish or green horn, granulated. On lime, elm, alder, birch, oak,
ash, pear and apple trees; hornbeam. Matt brown pupa, almost black in
front; long proboscis sheath, in loose soil or a few inches under grass or
in crevices in bark. Common.

LARGE ELEPHANT HAWK *(Deilephila elpenor)* Plate 9, No. 9. Flies May to June in evening and morning. Wing-span some 6 cm. Fore-wings olive green with two oblique bands and violet-red fore edge and seam; hind wing wine-red, black at the root. White fringes. Abdomen olive green, red at the sides. Caterpillar (Plate 11, No. 6) 8 cm, green and brown with darker streaks; 1 half-moon, brown and white rimmed eye-spot on each of 1st and 2nd abdominal segments. Short, black-brown horn. On willow-herb, bedstraw, sometimes vines. Yellowish-brown pupa with black dots; hibernates in rough cocoon on ground under moss etc.

SMALL ELEPHANT HAWK *(Deilephila porcellus)* Flies May to June and August to September. Wing-span not above 5 cm. Lighter coloured than foregoing, has pink patches on fore edge of fore-wing. Abdomen mostly red. Caterpillar 7 cm, grey-brown; only a small bump instead of a horn. In autumn on bedstraw, willow-herb, vines. Pupae hibernate.

HUMMING-BIRD HAWK *(Macroglossum stellatarum)* Plate 9, No. 13. Flies May and August to October by day. Hovers over flowers sucking nectar with long proboscis. Wing span 4–4.5 cm. Fore-wings dark grey with a couple of zigzag black bands. Hind wings reddish-yellow. Body grey on top, black behind, white side patches. Tail-like tuft of hair at end of abdomen. Moth hibernates. Caterpillar (Plate 11, No. 12) 5 cm, green with white side stripes and spots and one yellow foot stripe. Horn bluish with brownish-blackish tip. On bedstraw.

*BEE HAWK *(Hemaris fuciformis)* Plate 9, No. 14. Flies May to July. Wing-span about 4 cm. Glass-clear "panes" in middle of wing; reddish-brown, exceptionally broad margins and 1 short red-brown bar on fore-wing. Body olive green, abdomen has 1 brown and 1 yellow belt. Caterpillar (Plate 11, No. 13) 5 cm, light green with yellow lengthwise stripes or all pink; July to August on honeysuckle, snow-berry.

NARROW-BORDERED BEE HAWK *(Hemaris tityus)* Similar to *H. fuciformis,* but has narrow dark wing margins and no half-bar. Flies May to June. Caterpillar (Plate 11, No. 14) green, white back lines; on various kinds of scabious.

PRIVET HAWK *(Sphinx ligustri)* Plate 9, No. 15. Flies May to June; on garden flowers by night. Wing-span 9–10 cm. Fore-wings brown with 1 black and 2 white oblique lines along the outer margin. Pink hind wings with 3 black bands. Abdomen has black and red rings. Caterpillar (Plate 11, No. 2) 12 cm, light green with violet and oblique streaks; horn on abdomen black at tip, yellow below; on privet, lilac, viburnum, spiraea, ash. Pupa brown; proboscis close against thorax; hibernates in hole in ground.

CONVOLVULUS HAWK *(Herse convolvuli)* Flies May to June and August to September at dusk and by night. Resembles foregoing. Wing-span 10–11 cm. Wings mixed grey and brown; hind wings have 4 dark bands; abdomen has 2 red patches at top, right and left; then rings of pink framed with grey on top, black beneath. Caterpillar (Plate 11, No. 3) 15 cm, either brown with yellow oblique streaks running into darker-colour, dark back line and black horn; or green with oblique yellowish streaks running into black, and black spots on the side of a dark green back line; yellow horn with black tip. On bindweed. Brownish pupa with protruding, coiled proboscis sheath; hibernates.

SPURGE HAWK *(Celerio euphorbiae)* Plate 9, No. 8. Flies June to July and in late summer. Wing-span some 7 cm. Fore-wings grey-yellow brushed with red; root, middle, fore edge and margin from inner edge up to point dark olive green. Hind-wings red, black at root and along in-side of margin. Underside red with dark patch in middle of fore-wing. First abdominal rings white and black. Caterpillar (Plate 11, No. 4) June to October up to 9 cm, black-green, red back stripes, 1 yellow side stripe spotted with red as well as small and large yellow spots. On spurges.

BEDSTRAW HAWK *(Celerio galii)* Flies May to June. Resembles spurge hawk but has olive green fore-wing, grey-yellow underside and brownish antennae that are white only in front. Caterpillar (Plate 11, No. 5) at first green, then olive, has on either side of each segment 1 black-rimmed yellow eye spot, a red horn with a black tip. On spurge, willow-herb, sometimes in gardens on fuchsias.

Family   LASIOCAMPIDAE   Lackey and Eggar Moths

LAPPET *(Gastropacha quercifolia)* Plate 9, No. 12. Flies May to August in evening. Span about 8 cm, covered with thick woolly hair. Female much the larger. Wings rust-red with blue, very serrated edge. Closed in roof-form when at rest, with the hind wings curving down over the sides. Caterpillar (Plate 10, No. 23) earth-colour; flattened appearance reddish underside side flaps on abdominal segments and 1 peg on the last segment; two dark blue bars on neck. From August to October and after hibernation to July on sloe, fruit trees, poplar, hawthorn, rose. Pupa black-brown dusted with white in black-grey, opaque cocoon hung between twigs.

Family   SATURNIIDAE   Silk Moths

*TAU EMPEROR *(Aglia tau)* Plate 9. No. 10. Flies March to June. Male flies by day. Wing span 6–7 cm. Male reddish-brown; female ochre-yellow; black bands parallel to outer edge of all wings, each of which has eye-spot with deep blue centre and a white nail-shaped mark; black ring round it all. Caterpillar (Plate 11, No. 15) up to 6 cm, greenish, at first has red spikes on back, later without hair; numbers of yellow dots, whitish, narrow, lengthwise band and white oblique streaks; deep gaps between body segments which end in protuberances on its back. May to August especially on beech, also birch, alder, oak. Dark brown pupa hibernates in loose cocoon on ground below loose covering.

EMPEROR *(Saturnia pavonia)* Plate 9, No. 11. Flies April to May, the male in sunshine, female prefers it dull. Span of male 6–7 cm, of female 7–8 cm. All wings of female are light and dark grey, those of male more brown-grey and hind wings orange. In middle of each wing is a large eye with a black centre and light strokes surrounded by 1 yellow and 1 black ring. Fore-wings have reddish patch at tip and a light dark-rimmed zig-zag line parallel to margin; dark bar near the root. Caterpillar (Plate 10, No. 24) up to 6 cm, grass-green with 1 black oblique bar on each segment which carries at most 6 hairy yellow or red warts; instead of oblique bars often has just a black spot at base of the warts. May to August on sloe, rose, raspberry, bramble and various deciduous trees. Curved, black-brown pupa; hibernates in brown pear-shaped cocoon.

*GIANT PEACOCK *(Saturnia pyri)* Largest and loveliest European moth. Flies May. Span 12–14 cm. Wings browny-grey with light zigzag bars with dark frame; margin yellowish with distinct inner edge; corners of fore-wings lighter as far as band; each wing has large eye with black inside and silver stroke and ochre rim; whitish towards root and red semicircle: whole black circle round this.

Family   ARCTIIDAE   Tiger Moths

GARDEN TIGER *(Arctia caja)* Plate 9, No. 6. Flies July to August. Span about 7 cm. Fore-wings brown streaked with white; hind-wings cinnabar-red with big round black patches dusted with blue. Thorax and head dark brown, abdomen red with black bars. Caterpillar, the "woolly bear", (Plate 10, No. 25) black with white warts and long black hair on its back, red hairs on the sides and front segments. August to May, hibernating. On many plants. Pupa blackish, concealed on ground in cocoon that has caterpillar hair mixed with it.

JERSEY TIGER *(Euplagia quadripunctaria)* Flies July to September, also by day. Span 5–6 cm. Fore-wings black-green with yellow-white bars forming a V in the outer section; yellowy-white near margin. Hind wings cinnabar with large black patches. Abdomen reddish. At rest, hind wings are entirely covered by the fore.

CINNABAR *(Callimorpha jacobaeae)* Plate 9, No. 18. Flies May to June, even by day if disturbed. Span about 4 cm. Fore-wings dark grey with carmine along fore edge. 2 oval red patches at outer rim. Hind wings carmine, fore edge and margin black fading out towards the body. Caterpillar (Plate 10, No. 26) yellow with black belt on each segment. Black head (warning). June to August on cruciferous plants. Pupa reddish-brown in thin cocoon; hibernating. In open, dry country.

Plate 9

1. DEATH'S HEAD HAWK *(Acherontia atropos)* p. 328
2. EYED HAWK *(Smerinthus ocellata)* p. 328
3. GREEN SILVER LINES *(Bena prasinana)* p. 334
4. POPLAR HAWK *(Laothoe populi)* p. 328
5. LIME HAWK *(Mimas tiliae)* p. 328
6. GARDEN TIGER *(Arctia caja)* p. 331
7. SCARLET TIGER *(Panaxia dominula)* p. 333
8. SPURGE HAWK *(Celerio euphorbiae)* p. 330
9. LARGE ELEPHANT HAWK *(Deilephila elpenor)* p. 329
10. TAU EMPEROR *(Aglia tau)* p. 331
11. EMPEROR *(Saturnia pavonia)* p. 331
12. LAPPET *(Gastropacha quercifolia)* p. 330
13. HUMMING-BIRD HAWK *(Macroglossum stellatarum)* p. 329
14. BEE HAWK *(Hemaris fuciformis)* p. 329
15. PRIVET HAWK *(Sphinx ligustri)* p. 329
16. RED UNDERWING *(Catocala nupta)* p. 334
17. POPLAR HORNET CLEARWING *(Sesia apiformis)* p. 361
18. CINNABAR *(Callimorpha jacobaeae)* p. 332
19. FIVE-SPOT BURNET *(Zygaena trifolii)* p. 333
20. SIX-SPOT BURNET *(Zygaena filipendulae)* p. 333

Nos. 13, 14, 10 (male), 11 (male), 19, 20, and if disturbed 18, fly by day.

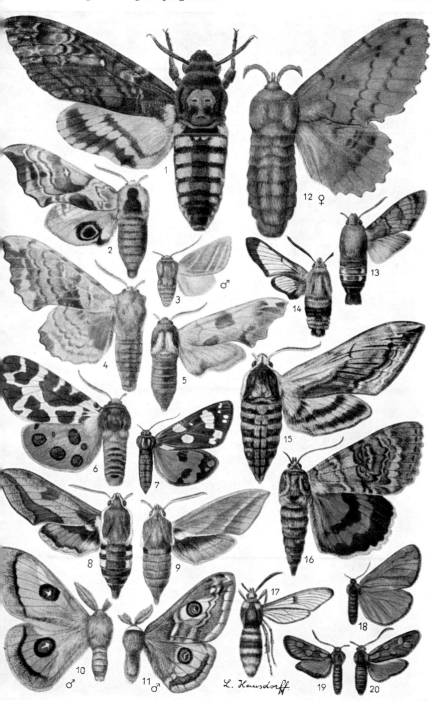

1

2

3 ♂

4

5

6

7

8

9

10 ♂

11 ♂

12 ♀

13

14

15

16

17

18

19

20

L. Hausdorff

SCARLET TIGER *(Panaxia dominula)* Plate 9, No. 7. Flies July to September. Span 5–6 cm. Fore-wings dark green often with blue sheen with patches of white and yellow. Hind-wings carmine; broken black bar on outer edge; black patch in middle of fore edge. Thorax dark green with 2 yellow vertical streaks.

Family   ZYGAENIDAE   Burnets and Foresters

Abdomen red with black streak down the middle. Caterpillar blue-black with yellow back stripe and 1 whity-yellow streak on each side; short, mixed yellow and black hairs. Eats and hibernates on nettles (stinging and dead), strawberries and raspberries, willow, poplar.

FIVE-SPOT BURNET *(Zygaena trifolii)* Plate 9, No. 19. Flies June to July. Body and wings blue-black. Forewings have 5 red patches, often merging. Hind wings carmine, broad black margin. On wet pasture land.

SIX-SPOT BURNET *(Zygaena filipendulae)* Plate 9, No. 20. Flies June to August. Span 3.5 cm. Long, narrow wings, in roof position when at rest; upper side of fore-wings black-green with 6 pink spots. Hind wings red with narrow black-blue margin. Plump black-green body. Club antennae. Caterpillar up to 3 cm; yellow with black spots; May to June on clover, plantain, hawkweed, etc. Meadows, woods, country roads. Often on thistle and scabious when in flower. Caterpillar Plate 10, No. 36.

TRANSPARENT BURNET *(Zygaena purpuralis)* Flies June to August. Span 3.5 cm. Fore-wings blue to green, slightly translucent; 3 red lengthwise stripes, the middle one being strikingly broad towards the outer edge. Hind wings red with black fringes. Caterpillar up to 2 cm, squat, yellowish; each segment has a black dot on either side. August to May on thyme, etc. Hibernates.

Zygaena scabiosae Flies end June to August. Span about 3.5 cm. Fore-wings blue-grey, slightly translucent, 3 lengthwise red stripes. Hind wings red with blackish margin. Common on flowers, especially scabious.

NARROW-BORDERED FIVE-SPOT BURNET *(Zygaena lonicerae)* Flies July to August. Span about 4 cm. Fore-wing black-blue with 5 red spots; front middle spot somewhat smaller than those below it. Hind wings almost all red, very narrow black seam.

Zygaena meliloti Flies June to July. Span 2.5–3 cm. Fore-wings dark grey, brushed with blue or green; red spots; front middle spot tiny, those below it mostly large and rectangular; underside grey-yellow. Hind wing red with dark seam.

Family   NOCTUIDAE   Noctuas (See p. 352 and Fig. 56)

RED UNDERWING *(Catocala nupta)* Plate 9, No. 16. Flies July to September. Span 7–8 cm. Fore-wing browny-grey with light and dark zigzag bands; hind wings carmine with bands following line of wing; the inner band not quite reaching inside edge of wing; light margins. Caterpillar up to 8 cm, grey or reddish-grey. May to June on willow, poplar.

DARK CRIMSON UNDERWING *(Catocala sponsa)* Flies July to early September. Span 6–7 cm. Wings like that of red underwing, but inner band on hind wing shaped as a W. Caterpillar up to 7 cm. Grey or reddish-brown; light protruberance on the 8th segment. On oak, Spanish chestnut.

LIGHT CRIMSON UNDERWING *(Catocala promissa)* Black middle band on red hind-wing slightly undulating, end curved inwards and not reaching the near margin.

CLIFDEN NONPAREIL *(Catocala fraxini)* Flies end July to September. Span about 10 cm. Largest European noctua moth. Fore-wing light-grey with double dark bands; hind-wings black with light blue band; white fringes. Caterpillar up to 9 cm, ash-grey. May to July on ash, poplar and other deciduous trees. Slim, active pupa dusted with blue; pupates on leaves spun together.

GREEN SILVER LINES *(Bena prasinana [= fagana])* Plate 9, No. 3. Flies April to June. Fore-wings green (paler in female) with 3 yellow (male) or white (female) bands. Margin and inner edge reddish in male and yellow in female. Hind wings of male yellowish, of female whitish, no marking. Abdomen green. Antennae red. Caterpillar yellow-green with 3 yellow back stripes and cream dots. Caudal disc has red streak. June to October, on oak, beech. Pupa hibernates. Deciduous woods.

BUTTERFLIES AND MOTHS WITH CONSPICUOUS WHITE MARKINGS

Family   PIERIDAE Whites

*BLACK APOLLO *(Parnassius mnemosyne)* Flies end May to June. Span 5–6 cm. Wings white with black patches; no red. Caterpillar April to May, 4–5 cm. Short-haired, black with orange spots. On larkspur. Mainly in mountains.

LARGE WHITE *(Pieris brassicae)* Flies April to June and July to October. Span 6 cm. White upper side of fore-wings have black corners; female also 2 round black spots and an oblong one on inner edge of fore-wing. Hind-wings of both sexes have 1 black spot. Underside of fore-wing 1 black spot, of hind-wing all yellow. Lays eggs on underside of cabbage leaves. Caterpillar (Plate 10, No. 4). May to June and August. Short, stiff hairs; when grown bluish-green, greenish-yellow on top with black dots; yellow sides and back stripe; underneath dull yellow. Head blue-grey. Sling-pupa, yellowish-green or yellow with black dots and patches; hibernates.

SMALL WHITE *(Pieris rapae)* Flies May to autumn. 2 broods. Span 4–5 cm. Fore-wings of female have 2, those of male 1, black spot. Shorter and not so heavy dusting of black on tip of fore-wing. Underside of hind wing and tip of fore-wing pale yellow and grey. Lays eggs individually on all kinds of cabbage, also likes fragrant mignonette. Caterpillar (Plate 10, No. 5). May to autumn; fine hairs, matt green; fine yellow stripe on back and both sides: brown-green head; yellow-green underneath. Sling-pupa, hibernating on foodplants.

GREEN-VEINED WHITE *(Pieris napi)* Flies May to late summer. 2 broods. Span 4 cm. Female has 2, male 1 (often missing) black spot. Underside yellowish with grey or black along the ribbing. Green eggs laid individually. Caterpillar 3 cm, matt green with black dots and white warts. Hibernates on rape, cabbage, turnip, mignonette.

BATH WHITE *(Pontia [= Pieris] daplidice)* Flies May and late June to August. Span about 4.5 cm white with patterns of black patches on point of fore-wing; female dark spots near edge of hind wing. Undersides have green and white patches. Caterpillars on mignonette and various cruciferous plants.

*ALPINE WHITE *(Synchloë [= Pieris] callidice)* Resembles Bath White *(Pontia daplidice)* but underside of hind wing is green only round the veins. In mountains.

WOOD WHITE *(Leptidae sinapis)* Flies May and August. Span 3.5 cm. Pure white wings; fore-wing of male has roundish black patch at tip; hind-wings have 2 faded grey bands on underside. In woods.

*BLACK-VEINED WHITE *(Aporia crataegi)* Flies late May to July. Span about 6 cm. Wings grey-white with black veins. Black-grey body. Female more slightly dusted; transparent centres to wings. Caterpillars (Plate 10, No. 3) June to May on hawthorn, apple, pear, cherry, medlar, plum, damson, apricot. Underneath of mature caterpillar is grey, on top black with 2 red-brown broken streaks. Sling-cocoon on leaves; hibernates. Meadows, heaths, tree tops. Now extinct in Britain.

ORANGE TIP *(Anthocaris cardamines)* Flies April to May. Female white on top with grey-black tips to fore-wings. Underside of hind wings spotted with yellow green. Male see p. 318.

Family   SATYRIDAE   Browns

MARBLED WHITE *(Melanargia galathea)* Flies June to August. Span 4.5–5 cm. Black patches, (sometimes brown) on white or cream ground. Caterpillar May to June, 3 cm, feeds by night on grasses; either vivid green or yellow-grey; hibernates. Meadows, glades.

*GREATER WOOD NYMPH *(Brintesia [= Satyrus] circe)* Flies June to August. Span about 8 cm. Wings velvety black with broad milk-white band, carrying one eye just before the tip. Bands are distinct on underside as well. Grassy woods. Central and southern Europe.

Family   NOTODONTIDAE   Prominents

PUSS MOTH *(Cerura [= Dicranura] vinula)* Flies May to mid-July. Span 7–8 cm. Fore-wings white with narrow zigzag line; black dots on seam. Hind wings of male almost pure white, of female grey. Abdomen has black rings. Male the smaller. Caterpillar (Plate 10, No. 11) green; large, red-brown head; pyramid-shaped bulge on 3rd thoracic segment; brown diamond-shaped back patch reaching to end of body. Carries its rear end high; 2 caudal discs transformed into long prongs. Spiracles white rimmed with black. Adopts threatening posture as defence against ichneumon-flies, drawing in head and thorax, while the red on fore-end grows more vivid and 2 pink threads appear from tail and wave threateningly over its head and body. In summer on willow, poplar. Pupa reddish-brown; hibernates in stout cocoon made of bits of bark and wood cemented together.

POPLAR KITTEN *(Harpyia bifida)* Flies May and July to August. Wings white-grey. Fore-wings have rows of black dots at roots, then broad, dark grey band; zigzag line near margin; large dark patch near tip. 1 row of dark dots along margins of fore and hind wings. Caterpillar similar to *C. vinula;* 4.5 cm; first black, then yellow-green; shiny, chestnut head, chestnut spot on nape; violet-brown back spots. 3rd segment carries pyramidal bulge. Last segment has 2 white half-moons. Ends in 2 forks, pale green and red prongs. June to September on poplars. Pupae hibernate.

Family   LYMANTRIIDAE   Tussock Moths

GYPSY MOTH *(Lymantria dispar)* Flies end July to September. Span 6.5–7 cm. Combed antennae. Wings almost white with brown zigzag bands. Thick, dirty-white abdomen with brown-grey hairs at the end. Lays flat heap of 300–800 eggs covered with down-like scales from the anal tuft of the female dormant on tree trunk, branch, wall, fence during winter. Caterpillar (Plate 10, No. 19) grey with tufts of long, stiff brown hairs; on 1st five segments 2 blue warts and on the others 2 red ones. Very greedy. Pupa in loose cocoon in crack in bark or between leaves. Caterpillar on fruit and wood of trees. Accidentally introduced into U.S.A. and has become a major pest of fruit trees but native stock in Britain is almost non-existent.

BLACK ARCHED TUSSOCK *(Lymantria monacha)* Flies July to August especially in the evening. Egg stage during winter. Span 3.2–4.2 cm (male), 3.8–6 cm (female). Fore wings white with brown-black zigzag bands. Hind wings brownish-grey. Sits on stem with wings roof-like over body. Abdomen partly pink. Caterpillar (Plate 10, No. 18) grey with black back markings and tufts of long hair. 2nd segment has white spot on top. Feeds April to July. Young caterpillars remain close together. Pupae shiny bronze with some thread-like hairs. Deciduous and conifer woods.

WHITE SATIN *(Leucoma salicis)* Flies June to July. Wings snow-white, silken gloss, no markings; black rings on tibia and tarsi; end of body not coloured. Eggs in glossy white froth on leaves of willow and poplar. Caterpillar blackish with a row of big yellow or white spots on its back; red warts toward the sides; May to June in groups on willow, poplar. Black pupa with white spots, long, yellow hair; in cocoon between leaves.

BROWN-TAIL *(Euproctis chrysorrhoea)* Flies June to August. Span 3 cm. Wings and thorax white. Abdomen brown, that of female has thick hair-tuft. Lays eggs on underside of leaves covered with "wool" from the anal tuft of the female. Caterpillar (Plate 10, No. 17), dark brown or black-grey; 2 reddish back stripes and reddish spots; white side streaks. Long yellow-brown hair in star-shaped tuft. The loose hairs can cause irritation on human skin. August to autumn and in spring to end of May on fruit trees, oak, sloe, rowan, hawthorn, beech, elm.

maple, poplar, willow, etc. Sociable. Share common "tent", the size of a fist, in which they also hibernate. Feeding-places marked by numerous threads covering everything. Pupae in transparent firm cocoons between remains of a leaf folded and fastened with silk.

GOLD TAIL *(Euproctis similis)* Flies June to August. Wings and body almost pure white, only the end of abdomen covered with bright yellow hair. Male often has black patch on fore-wings. Lacks 5th ribbing in hind wing. Lays heaps of eggs, covered with yellow "wool" from the anal tuft of the female, on underside of leaves. Caterpillar black with cinnabar back line and 1 broken white streak along each side. Long, sparse hair; warts have black and fine white hairs. Gregarious only at first; hibernate individually in small cocoons in cracks in bark, lichen on trunks or on the ground. Feeds August to June on fruit trees, oak, maple, lime, willow, sloe, hawthorn, etc. Pupa black-brown, in fine cocoon between leaves.

Family   ARCTIIDAE   Tiger Moths

WHITE ERMINE *(Spilosoma lubricipeda)* Flies May to July. Span 4 cm. White wings, the fore with many, the hind with fewer black spots. Head and thorax white; abdomen yellow with rows of black dots, white tips.

Family   COSSIDAE   Goat and Leopard Moths

WOOD LEOPARD *(Zeuzera pyrina)* Needs 2 years to develop, caterpillar hibernating twice. Flies June to August soon after evening dusk. Span 6 cm. Whitish wings with round blue spots. Abdomen black-blue with white rings. Female often sits low down on trunk of old trees. Eggs laid individually on buds, or in turned-over leaf. Caterpillar, see p. 436. In gardens and parks.

Family   HEPIALIDAE   Swift Moths

GHOST SWIFT *(Hepialus humuli)* Flies June to August. Span cm. Male's wing silver; female's fore-wings yellowish with or 2 blurred reddish oblique stripes; hind wings reddish-grey. Wings at rest roof-shaped. Caterpillar, see p. 412. In meadows, in grass skirting woods, up to a high altitude.

Caterpillars of Butterflies and Moths

Plate 10 (Life-size)

1. SWALLOWTAIL *(Papilio machaon)* p. 316
2. APOLLO *(Parnassius apollo)* p. 316
3. BLACK-VEINED WHITE *(Aporia crataegi)* p. 336
4. LARGE WHITE *(Pieris brassicae)* p. 335
5. SMALL WHITE *(Pieris rapae)* p. 335
6. RED ADMIRAL *(Vanessa atalanta)* p. 318
7. PEACOCK *(Nymphalis io)* p. 319
8. CAMBERWELL BEAUTY *(Nymphalis antiopa)* p. 322
9. SMALL TORTOISESHELL *(Aglais urticae)* p. 319
10. LARGE TORTOISESHELL *(Nymphalis polychloros)* p. 319
11. PUSS MOTH *(Cerura vinula)* p. 337
12. LOBSTER MOTH *(Stauropus fagi)* p. 346
13. PEBBLE PROMINENT *(Notodonta ziczac)* p. 345
14. BUFF-TIP *(Phalera bucephala)* p. 346
15. OAK PROCESSIONAL *(Thaumetopoea processionea)* p. 347
16. PALE TUSSOCK *(Dasychira pudibunda)* p. 349
17. BROWN-TAIL *(Euproctis chrysorrhoea)* p. 338
18. BLACK ARCHED TUSSOCK *(Lymantria monacha)* p. 338
19. GYPSY MOTH *(Lymantria dispar)* p. 338, 347
20. FOX MOTH *(Macrothylacia rubi)* p. 350
21. LACKEY *(Malacosoma neustria)* p. 349
22. PINE LAPPET *(Dendrolimus pini)* p. 350
23. LAPPET *(Gastropacha quercifolia)* p. 330
24. EMPEROR *(Saturnia pavonia)* p. 331
25. GARDEN TIGER *(Arctia caja)* p. 331
26. CINNABAR *(Callimorpha jacobaeae)* p. 332
27. TURNIP DART *(Agrotis segetum)* p. 353
28. CABBAGE DOT *(Mamestra brassicae)* p. 354
29. PINE BEAUTY *(Panolis flammea)* p. 353
30. SYCAMORE DAGGER *(Apatele aceris)* p. 354
31. MULLEIN SHARK *(Cucullia verbasci)* p. 356
32. BORDERED WHITE BEAUTY *(Bupalus piniaria)* p. 358
33. MAGPIE MOTH *(Abraxas grossulariata)* p. 341
34. WINTER MOTH *(Operophthera [= Cheimatobia] brumata)* p. 357
35. MOTTLED UMBER *(Erannis defoliaria)* p. 358
36. SIX-SPOT BURNET *(Zygaena filipendulae)* p. 333

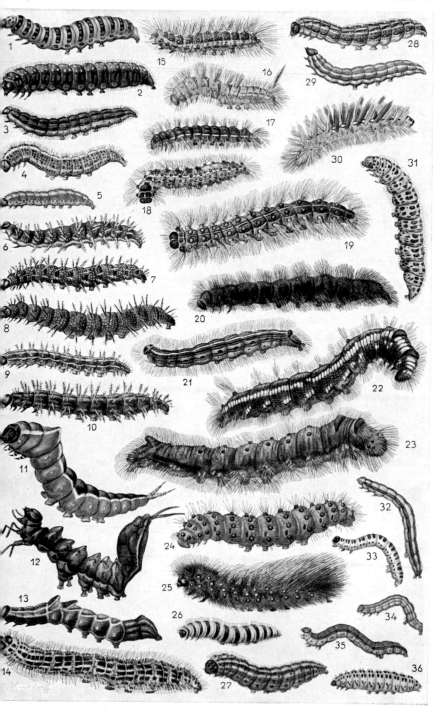

Family   Noctuidae   Noctuas

THE MILLER *(Apatele leporina)* Flies May to June. White
wings with black markings. Caterpillar green or yellow. Thick,
white, long hair on sides; sometimes has black tufts. Feeds
especially on willow, birch, alder. In deciduous tree areas.

Family   Geometridae   Geometers

PEPPERED MOTH *(Biston betularia)* Flies May to June.
5.5 cm. White wings with dark speckling imitating birch-bark;
occasional specimens more grey, even black. Caterpillar July
to October. Head deeply grooved, 2 pointed. Colouring varies:
on birch brown, on oak ashen-grey, on elm yellowy-brown, on
willow and poplar yellow-green. Disturbed, adopts rigid, jutting posture. Pupa hibernates in earth-cocoon.

MAGPIE MOTH *(Abraxas grossulariata)* Flies June to August.
Span 4.3 cm, white, black spots, yellow bands on fore-wings.
Body yellow and black. Yellow eggs on undersides of leaves.
Caterpillar (Plate 10, No. 33) May to June; looping progression; white with black spots, bottom and sides yellow. Feeds
in spring on buds and leaves to point of stripping. June, pupates
on leaves and twigs; September the caterpillar hatches, hibernates cocooned in a leaf or on the ground. In bushes on fringes
of woods or gardens; on gooseberry and raspberry.

Family   Syntomidae

Syntomis phegea Flies June to July, often sits on tree-trunks
and stones. Span 4–4.5 cm. Fore-wings much larger than hind.
Body and wings black-blue. On fore-wings mostly 6, on hind-
wings 2–3 white translucent spots. Abdomen has yellow belt on
1st and 5th segments.

Family Pyralidae   Pyralid and China Mark Moths

Scirpophaga praelata Small, white moth on water. Eggs
on stem of bullrushes. Young caterpillars spin threads and let
the wind carry them to other rushes, where they eat galleries
in the pith down to root-stock, hibernate there, in spring emerge
into water, bore their way back into rush, eat a gallery downwards, then upwards and pupate.

YELLOW SATIN GRASS-VENEER *(Crambus perlellus)* Flies in summer at dusk, often to lights. Span 2.5–2.8 cm snow-white shiny wings, perhaps dusted with green or blue. Hind-wings very broad in relation to fore-wings; used for short, gliding flights. Rests by day on grass-stalks; easily disturbed. Caterpillar feeds on grasses.

BROWN CHINA MARK MOTH *(Nymphula nymphaeata)* Span 2.1–2.6 cm. Flies June to August. Body of female whitish male brownish. Wings white with brown markings. True aquatic moth, flying close above surface. Lays eggs in rows on underside of a floating leaf. Caterpillars at first green, then brown; eat leaf-tissue; cut themselves 2 elliptical pieces out of a leaf, spin them with the edges together into a case; the following spring enlarge this air-filled case, which by the summer is 4 cm long and 2–3 cm across. From August on pupal cases can be found spun fast to plant stems just below the surface.

Family   TINEIDAE   Clothes Moths

BLACK-CLOAKED CLOTHES or TAPESTRY MOTH *(Trichophaga tapetzella)* Flies May to August. Span 1.2–2.4 cm. Milky or creamy-white with indistinct grey markings. Head and inner part of fore-wings black-brown. Hind wings grey. Yellow-white caterpillar with a black head. Eats fur, wool, furnishing material, carpets. Lives like clothes moth, but is not so common.

Family   YPONOMEUTIDAE   Ermine Moths

ADKIN'S APPLE ERMEL *(Yponomeuta malinella)* Flies July. Span about 2 cm. Fore-wings snow-white with 3 lengthwise rows of fine black dots. Hind wings grey. Caterpillar yellowish; head, head-capsule and warts black. Feeds in spring on buds and leaves, stripping them; later makes common large web on point of twigs; in June pupates inside web, each with a separate cocoon. Stone fruit, hawthorn, sloe, bird-cherry.

COMMON HAWTHORN ERMEL *(Yponomeuta padella)*
Flies June to July. Span 2.4 cm. Fore-wings white dusted with
grey; 3 lengthwise lines of black dots. Fore edge and underside
grey-brown. Hind-wings grey. Lays heap of eggs on twigs
covered by secretion. Caterpillar up to 2.2 cm, yellowish to
greenish. Head, nape-capsule and caudal disc dark. Dark spots
and hairy warts on each segment. September to June hibernates
under casing of egg-heap. Larvae in web damage plum trees by
their eating. Pupate in cocoon in web.

FULL-SPOTTED ERMEL *(Yponomeuta evonymella)* Very
similar to *Y. padella,* but fore-wings have 5 rows of black dots.
Hind wings grey. On apple trees.

Family   PTEROPHORIDAE   Plume Moths

LARGE WHITE PLUME *(Pterophorus pentadactylus)* Flies
May to August. Span 2.6 cm, snow-white. Fore-wing split into
2 "feathers", hind wing into 3; at rest folded together and held
out horizontally; long, narrow abdomen. Caterpillar pale green
with white hairs. September to May on convolvulus.

INCONSPICUOUS BUTTERFLIES AND MOTHS

MAINLY BROWN OR GREY

Family   LYCAENIDAE   Blues

PURPLE HAIRSTREAK *(Thecla [= Zephyrus] quercus)*
Flies mid-June to August. Span about 3.5 cm. Upper side black-
brown with blue sheen in male. Fore-wings of female have
2 whitish stripes running from root into middle. Undersides
light grey with white streaks, and hind wing has a red-rimmed
black patch before the "tail". Caterpillar April to June on oaks;
2.4 cm, flesh colour.

GREEN HAIRSTREAK *(Callophrys rubi)* Flies mid-April to
June and July to August. Blackish-brown on top, on fore-wing
of male a light oval patch before the middle of fore edge;
undersides green with or without white markings. Caterpillar

June and September 2 cm; green with yellow lengthwise line. On clover, bramble, heather, etc. Bushy areas, light pine woods, heath.

BROWN HAIRSTREAK *(Thecla [= Zephyrus] betulae)* Flies July to October. Egg remains unhatched during winter. Span 3.5–4 cm. Black-brown on top, male has faded yellow patch in middle of fore-wing; female has large, kidney-shaped reddish-yellow patch. Hind-wings have small reddish spot on the tip. Undersides yellow with lighter cross-lines. Bushes, edge of woods.

Family   HESPERIIDAE   Skippers

SILVER-SPOTTED SKIPPER *(Hesperia comma)* Flies June to August. Span about 3 cm. Male has dark, broad streak the shape of a comma across browny-yellow fore-wing, composed of scent-scale marks with a silver line inside; also a few lighter spots at tip of fore-wing and a broad, dark margin on both wings. The female has lighter, larger and more numerous spots. Hind-wings yellow-green on underside with distinct white dice-shaped spots. Caterpillar April to June 3 cm, black-grey. On grasses, spins cocoon of grass stalks. Open country, especially with dry, warm soil.

GRIZZLED SKIPPER *(Pygrus [= Hesperia] malvae)* Flies end April to June. Span 2.5 cm. Wings grey-brown on top with numerous white dice-shaped patches in rows before the margin. Fringe of black and white checks. Caterpillar 2.5 cm, dusty yellow-grey; pupates between leaves of bramble, strawberry, raspberry, cinquefoil, etc. Dry, sunny, open country; glades; prefers mountainous areas.

LARGE SKIPPER *(Ochlodes venata [= Augiades sylvanus])* Flies June to August. Span 3.5 cm. Browny-yellow wings, like silver-spotted skipper, only the male's scent-scale marks are narrower and not split, and the wing margins are not so dark: the female's more conspicuous dice spots are matt. On the underside, the hind wing and tip of the fore-wing are yellowish. Caterpillar 3 cm, dirty green; pupates in grass leaf rolled up spirally.

COMMON SMALL SKIPPER *(Thymelicus sylvestris [= Adopaea silvester])* Flies end June to August. Span about 3 cm. Wings ochre on top with narrow, dark margin, male having a long, narrow, slightly curving patch of scent-scales on forewings, with a gap in the middle. Hind wings greenish underneath with ochre inner margin. Caterpillar 3 cm; pale green with yellowy-white side stripes. On loosely spun grasses; hibernates.

Family   SPHINGIDAE   Hawk Moths

PINE HAWK *(Hyloicus [= Sphinx] pinastri)* Flies June to July at dusk and at night. Span 7–8 cm. Often hovers in front of honeysuckle flowers. Long, pointed browny-grey wings; folded in roof-shape at rest. In daytime motionless on trunk. Caterpillar (Plate 11, No. 10) July to September. 6 cm; light green with browny-red back stripes and black-brown horn with a cleft tip. Pupa 4 cm, brown with a short proboscis-sheath; 3 delicate points; hibernates under covering on ground. Pine woods.

Family   NOTODONTIDAE   Prominent Moths

PEBBLE PROMINENT *(Notodonta ziczac)* Flies May and July to August. Span about 4.5 cm. Fore-wings pale yellow-brown, white-grey at fore edge, dark half-moon from middle of fore-wing to outer edge. Hind wing yellow-grey, in female darker. Caterpillar (Plate 10, No. 13) 5 cm; violet-brown with large, brown, pointed bulge on 5th and 6th segment. Fore and rear ends of body red-brown. 11th segment raised in a pyramid. July and September on willow, poplar.

Pygaera anastomosis Flies April to August. Span about 4 cm, long tufts of hair on end of abdomen. Wings grey-brown. Fore-wings have red-brown tips, 3 light, narrow, dark-edged lines. Top of head and thorax deep black-brown, velvety. Caterpillar 5 cm, brown. Black back with white and red spots, 2 yellow side lines in which are red, hairy warts. 4th and 11th segment have humps. On willow and poplar.

COXCOMB PROMINENT *(Lophopteryx capucina [= camelina])* Flies April to June and July to August. Span 3.5 to 4.5 cm. Fore-wings rust-brown with darker transverse line ending in dark point; hind-wings yellowish-grey with dark patch on rear angle; long tuft of hair on thorax. Caterpillar 5 cm, green, light back and yellow side lines with red dots; sparse short hair; last segment has hairy red spike. On birch, lime. Dark brown pupa hibernates in ground at foot of trunk.

LARGE CHOCOLATE-TIP *(Clostera [= Pygaera] curtula)* Flies April, early June and July to August. Span about 4 cm, light-browny-grey. Crown of head and middle of thorax deep dark brown; red-brown patch on tip of fore-wing; hind-wings yellower. Summer brood often paler. At rest, hairy forelegs stretched out in front. Caterpillar 5 cm; blue-grey with tiny red-brown speckles. Willow and poplar.

PLUMED PROMINENT *(Ptilophora plumigera)* Flies May to July and late October into the winter; moth hibernates, egg dormant. Span 3.5–4 cm, thin scaled wings, translucent, bright brown-red. Hind wings lighter, dusted with red. Long hair on head, front part of body less, back part more hairy. Strikingly long teeth in comb of male's antennae. Caterpillar 3.5 cm, green with white lengthwise band. On maples, copper beech, sloe.

LOBSTER MOTH *(Stauropus fagi)* Flies April to May and July to August. Span 5–6 cm. Basic colour brownish-grey. Fore-wings long with zigzag yellowish bars; dark patches before outer edge. Hind wings short, well-rounded. Woolly thorax. Caterpillar (Plate 10, No. 12) 6 cm, bare; dirty light brown. Name of moth clue to unusual shape and posture of caterpillar: long thoracic legs, conical bulges on back; caudal disc modified into long prong; while it holds the front and rear segments upright, holding on with just its abdominal feet. On beech, oak, hazel, etc. Pupa black in web between two leaves, with which it falls to ground; hibernates.

BUFF-TIP *(Phalera bucephala)* Flies May to July. Span 5.5 to 6 cm. Fore-wings silver-grey with large yellow patch at the tip with splodge of rust in it. Hind wings are pale yellow with grey shadow-spot. Big head. Thorax brown-red with black rim. Abdomen yellowish-white with black side spots. Caterpillar (Plate 10, No. 14) 6 cm, black with yellow, broken longitudinal lines and yellow bars; soft, yellow-brown hair, (irritant). In autumn on elm, lime, oak, willow, birch, hazel, poplar, beech, hornbeam, maple, alder. Sociable.

Family   THAUMETOPOEIDAE   Processional Moths

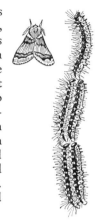

*OAK PROCESSIONAL *(Thaumetopoea processionea)* Flies August to September mostly in tree-tops. Span of male 2.9 cm, female 3.2 cm. Sits by day on oak bark with wings folded as a roof. Same colour as the bark: fore-wings brown-grey with black bars. Hind wings grey with indistinct dark bars. Female is the larger and lighter coloured. Eggs on oak trunk, dormant during winter. Caterpillar (Plate 10, No. 15). May to June, up to 4 cm, bluish dark grey, whitish at the sides; row of rust-brown hairy warts on back. Hairs are long and fragile and can cause irritation in people and animals. Common web in which they sleep at the foot of the tree or in bough-fork. In the end go in procession to the leaves to feed, each following a thread spun by the one in front. Also pupate in communal nest web. Pupae 1.5 cm, ochre to brown; each in own cocoon, grouped together.

*PINE PROCESSIONAL *(Thaumetopoea pinivora)* Flies May to July, spends winter as egg or pupa. Span 3–3.5 cm. Fore-wings grey, banded. Fringe of hind wing chequered with black. Caterpillar 3.5 cm, head black; Yellow-green underparts; on each side a green-grey band with fine dark dots, between which is a broad, dark, grey-green back stripe with a large black patch edged with red-yellow on each segment from 4 to 11; red-yellow warts with long hairs. Caterpillars in clusters on pine branches; no web nest, spin as they roam, always one behind the other. Pupae 1.5 cm, light brown to brown-yellow, 1.4 cm deep in sandy soil.

Family   LYMANTRIIDAE   Tussock Moths

GYPSY MOTH *(Lymantria dispar)* Flies end July to September. Span about 4.5 cm. Fore-wing grey with dark brown, very serrated bands. Hind wings brown-yellow with wide margins. Female see p. 338. Caterpillar Plate 10, No. 19.

COMMON VAPOURER *(Orgyia antiqua)* Flies June to September. Spends winter in egg form. Span 3–3.4 cm. Sexes dimorphic: male rust-brown with darker bars and 1 white patch near rear corner of fore-wing; female has only tiny stumps of wings, a plump woolly abdomen; very slow; lays 100–250 eggs on the cocoon she has left. Caterpillar 3 cm, ash-grey, white side lines, red warts on each segment, tuft of long black hair on first and last segments. The middle segments each have 1 bright yellow hair-tuft. June to July on deciduous trees, fruit trees, sloe, etc. Pupa in thick cocoon.

Caterpillars of Moths and Butterflies

Plate 11 (Life-size)

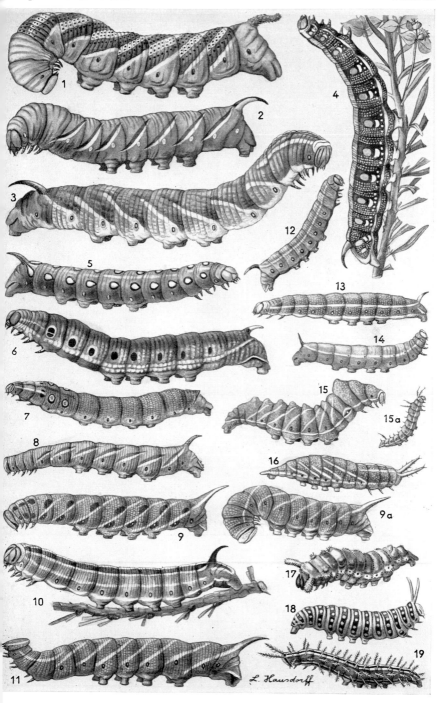

L. Hausdorff

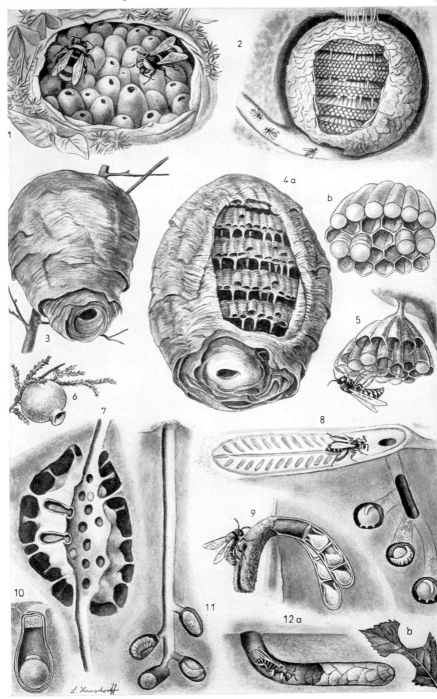

L. Hausdorff

PALE TUSSOCK *(Dasychira pudibunda)* Flies April to June. Span about 5 cm. Fore-wings white-grey with 3 dark-grey bands; hind-wings light grey; fringes spotted with black. When at rest stretches very hairy fore-legs out in front. Caterpillar (Plate 10, No. 16) end July to October, green-yellow with several thick yellow hair-tufts and one long fox-red hair-brush; velvety black gaps between body segments. Pupa in firm brown cocoon, usually in litter on ground. Woods, parks, gardens. Often on beech, elm, oak, hazel.

Family   LASIOCAMPIDAE   Lackeys and Eggars

LACKEY *(Malacosoma neustria)* Flies June to August. Span about 3.5 cm, female the larger. Colouring very variable, the whole moth uniform ochre to red-brown. Fore-wings have reddish-brown or yellowish bands; in female the strip between the two bands is darker. Egg does not hatch till spring. Laid in a collar round a twig. Caterpillar (Plate 10, No. 21) full-grown: blue head, white, brown, red and black lengthwise stripes on blue-grey ground. April to June sharing a common web-tent on fruit trees, blackthorn, hawthorn, in woods. Pupae blackbrown, soft, with brown hair; individually between folded leaves spun together or in crevices in bark.

♀

◄———

Plate 12

1. Nest of *Bombus terrestris* p. 366
2. Nest of *Vespa germanica* p. 372
3. Nest of *Vespa media* p. 373
4a. HORNET *(Vespa crabro)* p. 372
4b. Section of cells from HORNET'S nest
5. Nest of *Polistes gallicus* p. 373
6. Nest of HEATH POTTER WASP *(Eumenes coarctata)* p. 373
7. Nest of MINING BEE *(Halictus quadricinctus)* (front view), opened in clay p. 368
8. Nest of MINING BEE *(Dasypoda plumipes)* in sand p. 369
9. Nest of FLOWER BEE *(Anthophora parietina)* with tube structure p. 369
10. Nest of *Osmia papaveris* p. 369
11. Nest of MINING BEE *(Andrena ovina)* p. 370
12a. Nest of LEAF-CUTTER BEE *(Megachile centuncularis)*
12b. Rose leaf cut by LEAF-CUTTER BEE p. 370

PINE LAPPET *(Dendrolimus [= Gastropacha] pini)* Flies July to August. *Span:* male 6–6.5 cm, female 7.5 cm. Plump, grey-brown, sluggish, sits by day on pine trunk with wings in roof position. Female has rust-brown, male grey bands on fore-wings. Caterpillar (Plate 10, No. 22) ash-grey or brown with reddish hairs and 2 blue spots on front segment. Feeds from spring to August. Hibernates on ground. Mostly on old pines, seldom on spruce or larch.

FOX MOTH *(Macrothylacia rubi)* Flies May to June. Span about 5 cm. Male has brown, female reddish-grey fore-wings with 2 white bands. Caterpillar (Plate 10, No. 20) up to 8 cm. Velvet-brown with red-brown hairs and dark bars. In autumn on grasses, bramble, heather, oak, rose, apple, in mown hay-fields. When touched, rolls up tight; hibernates then pupates in grey cocoon in its winter quarters, late April to early May.

GRASS EGGAR *(Lasiocampa trifolii)* Flies July to September. Male brown-red, female red-grey; one white spot in middle of each fore-wing with a curving, broad whitish line between this and wing margin. Caterpillar up to 8 cm, has brown-yellow hair all over; black-blue between segments, white spots; broken yellow side stripes. Autumn to June on clover, etc. Pupates in brown cocoon.

OAK EGGAR *(Lasiocampa quercus)* Flies June to July, also by day. Span 6–7 cm. Wings of male chestnut with yellow band with sharp inner and blurred outer edge. Fore-wings have white spot in middle. Female is ochre and much larger. Lays eggs on oak, poplar, willow, hornbeam, hawthorn, heather. Caterpillar up to 8 cm with thick grey-yellow hair. Velvet black between segments; white side lines. August to May. Hibernates.

Family   ARCTIIDAE   Tiger Moths

WHITE ERMINE *(Spilosoma lubricipeda)* Flies June to July. Span 4 cm. Yellow body and wings. Dark spots, not always in line, on fore-wings. Abdominal rings have black spots in middle and at the sides. Female paler. Will often go into lighted room. Caterpillar has long thick browny-yellow hair and light back line; light coloured head. July to September on nettles, spurge, dandelion, etc. Often on roads. Pupae hibernate.

RUBY TIGER *(Phragmatobia fuliginosa)* Flies May to August. Hides by day. Cinnamon fore-wings, with one black spot. Hind wings pink with black along margin and several black patches near by. Abdomen pink with a black stripe down the back and a row of black dots on each side. Caterpillar either light grey, brown-grey or black; very hairy. Black-red head. June to July and September to April. Hibernates. On plantain, etc. in grassy areas.

Rhyparia purpurata Flies June to July. Span 4–5 cm. Body and fore-wings yellow with brown spots. Hind-wings bright red with black spots and yellow margin. Long, hairy blackish caterpillar with yellowish back and side stripes; back fox-red; yellow hairs on the sides. On many plants and shrubs. Hibernates. Only in dry, sandy places, fairly high up.

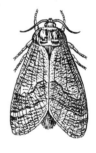

Family   COSSIDAE

GOAT MOTH *(Cossus cossus)* Takes 2–3 years to develop. Flies June to July. Span up to 9 cm. Strong, great body. Large abdomen. Male the smaller. Wings brown-grey with dark waves and black veining. Light rings round abdomen. Sluggish. Flies by night; when at rest closes wings round its body. Yellow eggs laid in heaps in crevices in bark. Caterpillar, see p. 436.

Family   LIMACODIDAE

FESTOON *(Apoda avellana)* Flies end May to July. Fore-wings ochre, those of male have a brown dusting and 2 darker straight oblique bars in shape of inverted V when wings closed. Female slightly larger, has no brown. Fore-wings have 3 lines. Hind wings blackish. Caterpillar yellowish-green, short, squat, like a woodlouse with 2 white lines and 3 rows of glossy warts on its back; 1 silver side streak. Has only suction pads instead of abdominal legs. Adult hibernates in firm, paper-like barrel with ready-prepared lid for pupating. In oak woods.

Family   PSYCHIDAE   Bagworms

OPAQUE SWEEP *(Canephora unicolor)* Flies June to July.
Male has abdominal tube, 1.2 cm, used for mating, during which
female remains in bag. Span about 3 cm. Wings only lightly
scaled, brown-black, yellow fringes. Female is wingless, white-
yellow, has 2 darker back stripes ind 3 brown back discs; only
abdomen protrudes from bag. Caterpillar grey-brown, with
3 back discs and 3 yellow lengthwise lines, spins out of bits of
grass, which jut out behind, a protective bag open at both ends
which it carries about with it. The male's bag bristles with bits
of dry leaves, that of female with dry grass stalk. Seals one end
of the bag to pupate, sloughs its skins, turns body head downwards to the still open end of bag. In dry open country, especially in dwarf tree zone.

SHINING SWEEP *(Fumaria [= Fumea] casta)* Flies end
June to July. Span about 1.5 cm. Shiny brown wings. Female
red-brown, yellowish wool on rear end. Caterpillar plump
grey bag covered with thin bits of plant; hangs obliquely from
stems, fences, etc. In May on low plants and shrubs. Mostly
in woods.

Psyche viciella Flies July. Span about 2 cm. Female rust-yellow. Caterpillar bag has transverse pieces of straw and stalks.
Lives on vetches.

Family   PTEROPHORIDAE   Plume Moths

CURTIS'S PLAIN PLUME *(Oidaematophorus tephradac
tylus)* Moth flies from June, hibernates. Span 2.4 cm. Wing
grey-yellow to reddish-brown, cleft as with white feathe:
moth, not so deeply; a few dark spots in middle and on rea:
edge of 2nd feather of fore-wing. Caterpillar on bindweeds

Family   NOCTUIDAE   Noctuid or Owlet Moths

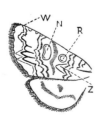

Appearance very similar. Mostly dark in colour with 3 charac
teristic "owl" markings on fore-wing: plug, kidney-ring-marks
also wavy lines towards outer edge. Robust, hairy thorax
Rather narrow wings, roof position when at rest. Caterpilla
usually bare and shuns the light, hiding by day, sometimes o:
colourful food plants. Mummy-shaped pupa, mostly in ground
seldom in spun cocoon.
(W = wavy line; N = kidney; R =ring; Z = plug)

PINE BEAUTY *(Panolis flammea [= piniperda])* Flies March to
May, also by day. Red-brown fore-wing with irregular light
bars and spots. Dark grey hind wings with white fringes. Rests
by day on trunk of pines, wings in roof position. Eggs laid in
rows on needles. Caterpillar (Plate 10, No. 29) May to July on
pines. Green with brownish head and white back stripe with
1 light streak on either side of this and 2 yellow side stripes.
Glossy brown pupa in ground-litter, in cavity of spun particles
of plants and dung. In pine woods.

LARGE YELLOW UNDERWING *(Noctua pronuba)* Flies
June to October, even November. Span about 6 cm. Hind wings
ochre with black margin; fore-wings have pale
brown-red to rust-coloured patches. Often
enters houses. Caterpillar up to 6 cm, earthen-
brown or green or yellowish; 3 light and
2 dark broken back lines. Feeds on cabbage,
carrot, beans, potatoes, hops, primula, vines.
Hibernates. Pupa glossy red-brown in cavity
on ground.

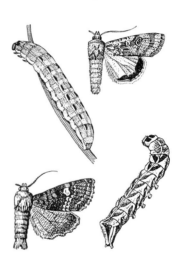

WHITE DOT MOTH *(Melanchra persi-*
cariae) Flies May to August. Span about
4.5 cm. Fore-wings violet-black; white kidney mark with brown centre; the wavy line
on margin the only one distinct. Hind wings
grey, darker at edge. Caterpillar 4–5 cm,
green, greenish-brown or reddish-brown;
triangular, dark open-angled mark on the
ring-mark. On fleabane, peas, beans, carrots,
rape, lettuce, strawberry, raspberry.

BROOM BROCADE *(Ceramica pisi)* Flies June to July.
Span 3.5 cm. Fore-wings red-brown and violet-grey mixed; the
bands double and slightly serrated. Zigzag wave-lines, yellowish-white. Hind wings yellowy-grey. Caterpillar up to
5 cm, red-brown or brown-green with 4 yellow lengthwise
stripes; July to September on peas, beans, etc. Red-brown pupa
in soft web; hibernates in ground.

TURNIP DART *(Agrotis segetum)* Flies June to July, only
at night. In southern Europe 2 generations: May to June and
August to September. Span 4 cm. Colouring varies. Fore-wings

yellowish-brown or grey-brown with darker patches: hind wings brilliant yellow-white. Female darker. Lays eggs individually on ground or on weeds. Caterpillar (Plate 10, No. 27) July to August and autumn to May; hibernates in ground; flat, grey or earth-brown, shiny; abdomen dirty-white with tiny black warts and white spiracles. Concealed by day rolled up in ground. Feeds only at night: leaves, stalks, roots, buds, preferring to gnaw through young plants on or just below surface. Pupa brown-red, in ground.

SYCAMORE DAGGER (*Apatele aceris*) Flies May to June. Span 1.9–2.1 cm. Fore-wings whitish-grey, dark-sprinkled. Large markings with double bars. Hind wings of male white, of female grey, darker at margin. Eggs on maple, horse chestnut, perhaps beech, lime, oak. Caterpillar (Plate 10, No. 30) 4–5 cm. July to September; thick hair, a black-framed silver spot on each segment and beside it 2 tall tufts of yellowish-red hair. Rolls up when disturbed. Will strip leaves of horse chestnut. Pupa hibernates.

SILVER-Y (*Plusia gamma*) 2–3 generations. Flies end April to October, by day and night. Span 3.5–4 cm. Fore-wings grey-brown with a silvery gamma mark in the middle; wavy margin. Hind wings yellow-grey with broad, black-grey band at margin. Dark grey thorax; light grey abdomen. Often on nettles, clover, flax, roots, corn, peas, beans, etc. Pupa matt black-brown, in a web off the ground. Migrant from the south.

CABBAGE DOT (*Mamestra brassicae*) Flies May to September. Mostly 2 generations. May to June and July to August. Span about 4.5 cm. Fore-wings yellowish and black on brilliant brown ground; kidney mark has white outline; wavy lines are yellowish-white near the margin. Hind wings yellowish-grey-brown. Flies by night. Eggs on cabbage and other cruciferous plants. Caterpillar (Plate 10, No. 28) up to 4 cm. Colouring can vary: light or dark green, brown or black; back has 3 light lines; where colouring darker back is blackish; 3 lighter back lines joined by cross-bars; side stripes yellow or whitish. Young ones gnaw holes in cabbage leaves, then bore galleries in the heart, which they foul with excrement. Pupa hibernates in ground.

BEAUTIFUL YELLOW UNDERWING *(Anarta myrtilli)*
Flies May to June and end July. Span 2–2.5 cm. Fore-wings
light and dark-brown with markings: white patch in middle.
Hind wings yellow; broad, dark brown seam. Caterpillar up
to 3 cm, green; 3 rows of yellow back spots and slanting white
side patches. June to July on heather and bilberry.

ORANGE BROCADE *(Trachea atriplicis)* Flies May to June
and July to September. Span 4.5 cm. Fore-wings brown mixed
with moss-green, serrated black cross-bars; short, thick, white
slanting line under the large marks. Caterpillar up to 6 cm.
At first green with 3 rows of white dots; 1 yellow side stripe,
last segment has 2 yellow spots. July to autumn on sorrel, knot-
grass, convolvulus. Red-brown pupa, hibernates in web on
ground.

GREEN-BRINDLED CRESCENT *(Allophyes [= Miselia]
oxyacanthae)* Flies September to October. Fore-wings light and
dark brown mixed; green ribbing and margins have strikingly
large markings. Hind wings brown-grey. Caterpillar up to 6 cm;
light or green-grey with dark streaks and spots; 2 pronged
protuberances on 11th segment. May to June on hawthorn,
blackthorn, apple and pear trees; concealed by day in cracks in
bark; fat, yellow-brown pupae in balls of earth.

HERALD MOTH *(Scoliopteryx libatrix)* Flies June to July.
Span about 4 cm. Fore-wings have very jagged outer edges;
violet-grey; root and middle tinged with red; white bands. Hind
wings dark grey to red-brown. Caterpillar up to 6 cm, green;
May to September on bindweed, poplar. Pupa dull black,
between leaves it has spun together. Moth hibernates in caves,
cellars, etc.

LARGE ANGLE SHADES *(Phlogophora [= Trigonophora]
meticulosa)* Flies April to June and August to November. Span
5 cm. Fore-wings jagged edges, brown with darker middle,
parallel yellow bands to outer edge. Hind wings light ochre,
darker margin. At rest wings lie close to body. Caterpillar up
to 5 cm, green or brown with white broken back line; dark
oblique streaks and yellow side streaks. April to June and
September to October; hibernates until May. Lives on dead
nettle, stinging nettle, sorrel, etc.

COPPER UNDERWING *(Amphipyra pyramidea)* Flies July to October. Eggs dormant during winter. Fore-wings grey-brown with light cross-bands; ring-mark has dark, oblong centre. Hind wings red-brown; grey-brown at fore edge. Fringes wavy, rimmed. Caterpillar up to 6 cm, green with white length-wise lines; pyramid-shaped bulge with red tip on 11th segment. May to June on hawthorn, most deciduous trees and bushes. Red-brown pupa in loose web.

COMMON SHARK *(Cucullia umbratica)* Flies June to July. Span 5 cm. Narrow, grey fore-wings with dark lengthwise streaks. Hind wings of male whitish with bluish margin, of female grey-brown. Mostly on posts, tree trunks. Caterpillar up to 5 cm, fat, dark brown, indistinct red-yellow streaks, close black dots; belly leaden-grey. July to September. On thistles *(Sonchus),* chicory.

MULLEIN SHARK *(Cucullia verbasci)* Flies April to end May. Fore-wings brown-yellow, darker by fore and inner edges; 2 light moon patches between middle and inner edge. Hind wings brownish but those of male are white at root and in the middle. Caterpillar up to 6 cm, white or cream with blue-grey cross-lines; on each segment 3 yellow spots with 2 black dots in front of middle spot; belly side has black patches. On mullein, figwort. Pupae hibernate.

RED SWORD-GRASS *(Xylena [= Calocampa] vetusta)* Flies August or September to June; hibernates. Fore-wings brownish-yellow in front, dark brown behind, whitish at root; most have only the kidney mark, the ring being missing. Hind wings dark-brown to brown-grey. In early spring on willow-catkins. Cater-pillar up to 8 cm, grass-green; 3 back lines and 1 side stripe all yellow; 3 white dots on each segment; rust-red, black-edged spiracles. June to August on knot-grass, sorrel, grasses, etc.

CLOUDY SWORD-GRASS *(Xylena [= Calocampa] exsoleta)* Flies September to June; hibernates. Similar to red sword-grass, being rather larger, grey, with kidney and ring marks both distinct.

BROAD-BORDERED YELLOW UNDERWING *(Lampra fimbriata)* Flies June to September. 2 generations. Span about 5.5 cm. Fore-wings: basic colour of female bright ochre and red, of male red-brown and olive green. Distinct cross-bands; middle patch has light edging. Hind wings: inner half and margin orange, outer half black. Caterpillar up to 6 cm, yellow-grey to brown-grey, light back line, light and dark streaks on sides. Hibernates until May. Prefers cowslips. Pupates in spring. Pupae red-brown: in cavity in ground.

DARK ARCHES *(Apamea [= Hadena] monoglypha)* Flies June to September. Fore-wings yellowish-brown, lighter and darker mixed, some quite dark or all brown-black; light cross-bands in wavy lines; large marks; hind-wings light grey. Caterpillar up to 6 cm, dirty white or black-grey; also pale-brown; light back stripes; dark warts with bristles. July to May, hibernates; on grass roots. Moths often come into houses.

FIGURE OF EIGHT *(Episema caeruleocephala)* Flies September to October. Span 4 cm. Fore-wings blue-grey; distinct bands; several large greeny-white patches. Hind wings light grey and 1 black patch on hind edge. Caterpillar up to 4 cm, green with inconspicuous light lengthwise lines; several black warts each with one short stiff hair. End April to June on fruit trees, hawthorn, hazel, lime, oak, feeds on buds. Red-brown pupa with blue rings, in cocoon fastened to bark.

Family   GEOMETRIDAE   Geometers

WINTER MOTH *(Operophthera brumata)* Flies October to December. Male has 2.5 cm span, thin delicate wings, the fore-wing pale grey-brown with cross wavy lines. Hind wings brownish-grey. Female incapable of flight; body 5–8 cm long, brown-grey stumps of wings with narrow bands. Eggs on buds during winter. Caterpillar (Plate 10, No. 34) April to July, up to 2.6 cm; looping motion; grey at first, becomes green with darker back line; 3 white lines on each side. Feeds on bursting buds of fruit and other deciduous trees, and strips leaves and unripe cherries; spins leaves and fruit together. Pupates in ground June to Autumn. Apple, pear, quince, medlar, cherry, damson, plum, apricot, peach, walnut, beech, maple, rowan, elm, willow, lime, hornbeam.

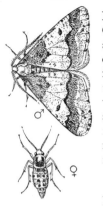

MOTTLED UMBER *(Erannis defoliaria)* Flies September to October. Span of male 4 cm. Yellowish wings. Fore-wings have a wealth of brown markings and 2 brown cross-bands. Body of female 1 cm, no wings, speckled black and white. Eggs on foliage hatching in spring. Caterpillar (Plate 10, No. 35) May to June, up to 3.5 cm; looping progression, lively, pale yellow with red-brown back, wine red spots and broad yellow side stripes; brown head; white spiracles with black rims. Feeds on foliage and fruit, particularly cherries, also apple, pear, quince, medlar, plum, damson, peach, apricot, walnut, oak, elm, alder, may and blackthorn.

BORDERED WHITE BEAUTY *(Bupalus piniaria)* Flies May to August with peak in June. Span 3–3.8 cm. Male ash-grey to black-brown; female ochre to rust-red; wings at rest carried upright like a butterfly. Caterpillar (Plate 10, No. 32) bare, yellow-green, with whitish or yellowish lengthwise stripes; looping progression. Feeds July to October. Pupates from October in ground-litter. On pine trees, seldom on spruce.

Butterflies with Predominantly

Green Markings

Family   Zygaenidae   Burnets and Foresters

FORESTER *(Procris [= Ino] statices)* Flies June to August. Span up to 2.9 cm, green metallic shimmer on black-grey fore-wings. When touched metallic "powder" comes away. Caterpillar colourful, varying. On sorrel; August to May. Hibernates. Common in flowery meadows.

Family   Noctuidae   Noctuas

*MALACHITE OWLET *(Calotaenia [= Jaspidea] celsia)* Flies July to September. Span 4.5–5 cm. Basic colour of fore-wings apple-green with a brown band through the middle with one jagged branch to either side; brown margin. No kidney or ring marks. Hind wings grey-brown. Thorax green with brown middle patch. Abdomen and antennae yellow. Caterpillar, yellowish and white-grey; June to August on grass-roots. Sandy, conifer woods.

MERVEILLE-DU JOUR *(Griposia [= Dichonia] aprilina)*
Flies August to October. Eggs dormant during winter. Span
about 4.5 cm. Apple-green fore-wings with simple black cross-
streaks; kidney, etc. markings large and distinct. Black patches
on fore-edge. Small white fringe. Hind-wings dark grey,
several marginal bands. Caterpillar up to 6 cm, brown-grey
April to June on oak, lime; by day in cracks in bark. Common in deciduous woods with oaks.

SCARCE SILVER LINES *(Pseudoips bicolorana)* Flies end
June to July. A little larger than green silver lines. Green fore-
wings with 2 yellowish-white straight, slanting lines. Hind
wings, body and fringes whitish. Caterpillar green; August to
May on oak. Hibernates. In oak woods.

GREEN SILVER LINES *(Bena prasinana)* See Plate 9, No. 3
and p. 334.

Family   GEOMETRIDAE   Geometers

LARGE EMERALD *(Geometra [= Hipparchus] papilionaria)*
Flies June to August. Span about 5 cm. Wings bright green with
several white patches before the margin; fore-wings have 2, hind
wings 1, white serrated cross-band. Caterpillar especially on
birch, hazel, alder; green with humps and 1 yellow line on each
side and 2 red bumps on segments 2, 5 and 8. Hibernates on
silk mat on twig. In deciduous woods; hides among foliage by
day.

Family   TORTRICIDAE   Leaf-rollers

GREEN OAK-ROLLER *(Tortrix viridana)* Flies June to July
in tops of oaks. Egg dormant during winter. Span 1.8.–2.3 cm.
Fore-wings light green; hind wings grey. Caterpillar up to
1.8 cm; blackish grey-green; head and warts black-brown. Web
on young leaves it has eaten; later cigar-shaped folded oak leaf.
Often strips a tree leaving it looking as if covered with white
veil. Pupates in chinks in bark. Common on oak trees.

Insects

Family   ADELIDAE

GREEN LONG-HORN *(Adela viridella)* Flies May to August. Span 1.6 cm. Very long antennae. Fore-wings dark green, brassy sheen; hind wings dark. Nuptial flight in dense swarm, in sunshine dancing up and down around bushes, after sunset rest in foliage with wings in roof position. Caterpillar yellow-white, head-and-nape disc black. Mine in leaves of beech and oak; later cut a long sack out of a leaf, let themselves fall to the ground in it and hibernate among fallen leaves. Common.

To identify leaf-rollers, clothes moths and pyralid moths see sections *Insect Larvae* and *Domestic Pests*.

INSECTS THAT GO THROUGH 4 MOULTS, AND MOST OF WHICH HAVE TRANSPARENT WINGS

BUTTERFLIES WITH GLASS-CLEAR WINGS

Family   SESIIDAE   Clearwings

Day-fliers resembling wasps, bees and colourful flies.

POPLAR HORNET CLEARWING *(Sesia apiformis)* Plate 9, No. 17. May to June, by day. Mostly sits on trunk of poplars, the appearance and buzz resemble a hornet. Long, glass-clear wings, only the outer edges and a small central band (on fore-wings) being scaled and dark. Long, fat body with fairly long hair. Yellow head; thorax has a yellow patch on either side; segments 2, 3 and 5, and the last two of abdomen, yellow; rest of body brownish. Caterpillar, p. 437.

Bembecia hylaeiformis Flies June to August. Span up to 2.7 cm. Brown-edged wings, fore-wing very narrow with black spots and only clear in the middle; hind wings entirely clear. Blue-black body. Abdomen 3–4 lemon-yellow belts; yellow rear-tuft. Wings close to body when at rest. Caterpillar, p. 437.

Fig. 57: Clearwings
a) **Maple clearwing;** b) **Currant clearwing;** c) **Raspberry clearwing**

RED-CURRANT CLEARWING *(Aegeria tipuliformis)* Flies May to July. Span 2 cm. Fore-wings narrow, glass-clear; only blue cross-bar and brown margins scaled; hind wings all clear, brown fringes. Abdomen blue-black with 3 (female) or 4 (male) yellow segments: rear left blue-black. Eggs laid individually on buds. Caterpillar, see p. 437.

SMALL RED-BELTED CLEARWING *(Aegeria myopaeformis)* Flies May and August. Span 1.7–2.2 cm. Glassy wings with brownish margins; fore-wings have dark cross-bands. Brown-black body. Abdomen has red band. Male white on underside of rear end. Eggs laid in chinks or wounds in bark. Caterpillar, see p. 437.

DRAGON-FLIES AND DAMSEL-FLIES

Plate 13

A. SMALL DRAGON-FLIES OR DAMSEL-FLIES

Small to medium size. Abdomen very long and thin. Fore and hind wings roughly the same size, held (joined together) vertically above the body, when at rest (except for *Lestes*). Relatively slow, fluttering flight. Broad, hammer-shaped head with eyes placed wide apart at sides.

DAMSEL-FLIES

Family   AGRIIDAE

DEMOISELLE AGRION *(Agrion virgo)* Flies May to September. Male has green-blue body with metallic sheen, dark blue wings; female metallic green body and drab grey-brown wings. Slow-flowing water, especially overhung and shadowy. Plate 13, No. 1.

BANDED AGRION *(Agrion splendens)* Flies May to September. Male has metallic blue body; wings have broad blue band in centre; female has metallic green body with a coppery sheen at the end; wings have no middle band, glass-like wide green veining. Flowing water with rather unshaded banks. Plate 13, No. 2.

Family   COENAGRIIDAE

COMMON COENAGRION *(Coenagrion puella)* Flies May to September. Very slender body, the male's sky-blue with black markings on top, the female's yellow-green on sides, black markings on back almost covering it completely. Wings pedunculate, i.e. there is a small "stalk" before the wing part broadens out. Stagnant and slow-flowing water, water-meadows. Plate 13, No. 3.

Family   PLATYCNEMIDIDAE

WHITE-LEGGED DAMSEL-FLY *(Platycnemis pennipes)* Flies May to September. Head of male bluish, female's yellowish, black on top with light cross-bands. Thorax of male blue, female yellowish with 2 light stripes. Basic colour of abdomen varies: blue or yellowish-white, blue, green or yellowish-brown. The markings vary too: black lengthwise lines more or less expanded. Lakes and slow-flowing water. Plate 13, No. 10.

Family   LESTIDAE

*Lestes viridis Flies mid-July to October. Top of body metallic green, underneath yellow; older ones have coppery sheen on thorax and first and last abdominal segments. Wings uniformly clear; at rest they are not folded back but held still, slightly spread; have distinct stalks. Often settle on bushes on bank. Narrow, long-legged larva with lithe body. Lays eggs under bark of twigs that overhang water, especially willow, alder, causing gall-like growth, out of which young larvae work their way to fall into the water. Stagnant and just-flowing water. Plate 13, No. 4. The green lestes (*Lestes sponsa*) and the scarce green lestes (*L. dryas*) are two emerald green species that occur in Britain.

B. LARGE DRAGON-FLIES

Strong abdomens; fore and hind wings not the same size, the latter most definitely broader than the fore-wings. At rest wings are held spread horizontally. Head hemi-spherical with 2 large eyes which almost meet (space between being smaller than their diameter).

HAWKER DRAGON-FLIES

Family   AESCHNIDAE

*Aeschna viridis Flies July to September. Wings dusted with brown. Black, horizontal lines on bluey-green brow. Red-brown legs. Male's eyes blue on top, yellow beneath and behind. Abdomen constricted at 3rd segment; 1st segment green with a brown spot, 2nd green and a little blue, the rest brown-black with green and blue spots and markings. Female: eyes olive-green on top, yellow underneath and behind; abdomen red-brown, only green markings. Sits on ground. Plate 13, No. 5.

SOUTHERN AESCHNA (*Aeschna cyanea*) Flies July to November. Male's face and sides of thorax green; female's face yellow, top of thorax dark brown with 2 large oval yellow-green spots, 2 black spots linked by lines on yellow-green sides. Abdomen constricted at 3rd segment, especially in male. Basic colour dark red-brown; in male green on top, blue spots on sides; in younger females blue and yellow-green spots; in old females green spots on top and at sides. Glass-clear wings. Especially pools in clay. Plate 13, No. 6.

EMPEROR DRAGON-FLY (*Anax imperator*) Flies June to September. One of the largest. Its large eyes move in line. Eyes contiguous in one line. Face, eyes, brow, green, latter has light blue line across top. Thorax green, with 2 small blue spots across at the root of the fore-wings. Black legs. Abdomen constricted at 3rd segment, male's being blue with brown or red back stripes and fine cross-bars; female's blue-green with wider, red-brown markings. Flies for hours without resting. Female bores holes in stalks of plants below surface with ovipositor, thrusting abdomen under water, she lays 1 egg in each hole. Plate 13, No. 9.

Family LIBELLULIDAE Darter Dragon-Flies

FOUR-SPOTTED LIBELLULA *(Libellula quadrimaculata)* Flies May to August. Wings yellow at root; hind wings have a large black triangle under this yellow patch. Green-white brow; yellowy-brown thorax with yellow sides. Abdomen brownish in front, behind black with yellow side patches. Stagnant water, especially in peat bogs. Flies over water, but also away from it.

BROAD-BODIED LIBELLULA *(Libellula depressa)* Flies May to July. Very broad, flattened abdomen. All 4 wings have large, dark brown root-patches. Yellow-brown brow; body dark brown-olive. Yellow-brown thorax, darkish brown at sides, white hair on top. Black legs with brown femurs. Abdomen of adult male blue-striped with yellow spots, the female's spots being broader and yellow-brown, acquiring blue stripes much later on. Usually only in ponds, etc. in clay soil. Plate 13, No. 8

Family CORDULIIDAE Hawker Dragon-flies

BRILLIANT EMERALD *(Somatochlora [= Cordulia] metallica)* Flies May to August. Body has strong metallic sheen. Male's abdomen constricted at 3rd segment; 2nd and 3rd segment with yellow patches, wing roots mostly yellow, whole wing yellow to yellow-brown. Female's wings deeper yellow. The three fore abdominal rings and thorax with strong green glow and red sheen. Stagnant and slow-flowing water. Prefers forest and mountain. Plate 13, No. 12.

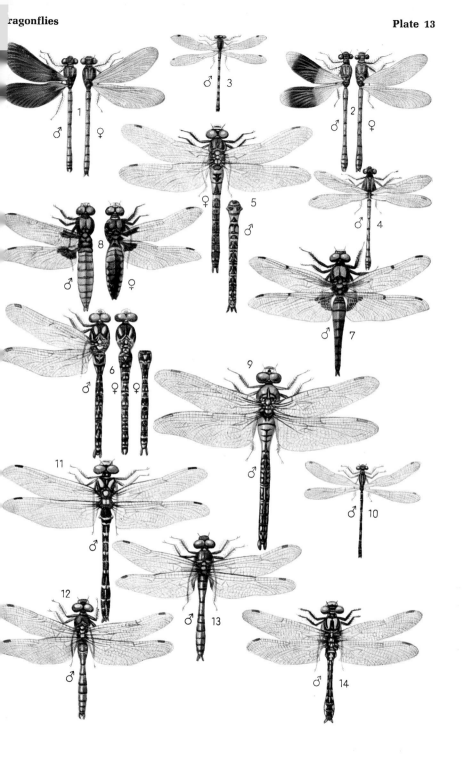

DOWNY EMERALD *(Cordulia linaenea)* Flies May to July. Body gold-green. Front of head, thorax, abdomen have no yellow markings. Abdomen relatively short, that of male slightly constricted, of female quite cylindrical. Particularly in low country. Hunts on any water, especially in evening sunshine on edges of woods, etc.; also at dusk and when sky is overcast. Plate 13, No. 13.

Family   GOMPHIDAE   Hawker Dragon-flies

CLUB-TAILED DRAGON-FLY *(Gomphus vulgatissimus)* Flies May to June. Blue-green eyes with wide gap between. Wings uniform light colour; thorax green-yellow with black stripes; abdomen, especially of male, constricted from 3rd to 6th segments with yellow to green-yellow spots. Black legs. Male likes sitting on ground with abdomen cocked up; the female tends to stay hidden. Streams, etc., especially where they flow through a wood. Metamorphosis almost exclusively in running water. Plate 13, No. 14.

Family   CORDULEGASTERIDAE   Hawker Dragon-flies

Cordulegaster bidentatus Flies June to July. Eyes contiguous. Yellow head with black cross-lines on front of head. Abdomen black with yellow rings, no side edges. Triangular space behind eyes black; middle abdominal segments have 1 yellow cross-band. Black thorax with 2 oval yellow spots on top and 3 yellow streaks on sides. Wings light with a hint of brown. Black legs. 7th and 10th segment of male all black, the female's 9th segment has yellow spot. Streams, river banks in mountains. Also hunts in woods, glades, etc. Plate 13, No. 13.

Cordulegaster boltonii Triangle on back of head yellow and middle segments of abdomen each with 2 yellow bars. Otherwise as *C. bidentatus.*

BEES AND WASPS

Plate 14 (Life-size)

Order   HYMENOPTERA

Super-Family   APOIDEA   Bees

Have feathered-hair – most have a sting. Larvae feed on pollen and honey. Divided into 2 groups according to their way of life.

A. SOCIAL BEES

HONEY BEE *(Apis mellifica)* Plate 14, No. 1. *Queen:* 1.5–1.6 cm. Abdomen strikingly long, protruding beyond tips of wings. Narrow head; compound eyes not contiguous at top. Short proboscis. Powerful sting. No pollen-basket. *Workers:* female 1.2 cm, abdomen only slightly protruding. Broad head, compound eyes not contiguous at top. Proboscis 6 mm long; powerful sting. Pollen-basket and pollen-collecting hairs on 1st femur; tibia and femur form pincers for holding wax while building honeycomb. *Drones:* (males) 1.5–1.6 cm. Plump bodies with fat heads, large compound eyes contiguous on forehead; short proboscis, no sting or pollen-collecting apparatus. Larvae are colourless grubs with neither eyes nor legs; turn their heads towards opening of cell in order to be fed. Queen grubs develop in 16, worker grubs in 21 and drone grubs in 25 days; the cells are then closed by worker-bees and the grubs pupate. Summer community contains 40–80,000 workers, queen, several hundred drones. Queen grubs are kept in especially large cells and given special food in excessive quantities; life 4–5 years. Mate once during nuptial flight. Only occupation to deposit one egg in each cell during spring, laying up to 3,000 each day. Workers live 4–6 weeks. Drones can live several months. After the first queen cell is closed, the preliminary or first swarm takes place, when the queen leaves the hive with roughly half its population; later there is the nuptial flight, when the drones and young queen make their flight and return to hive after mating. Males are then driven out or killed. No hibernation, but live on stored up honey and pollen.

BUMBLE or HUMBLE BEES Fat bodies; buzz in flight caused by vibration of vocal chords in spiracles on abdomen. Nest in cavities: finger-shaped wax-cells. Fertilised queen lives through winter to found new community in spring. Feed their grubs: *Nest:* see plate 12.

BUFF-TAILED BUMBLE BEE *(Bombus terrestris)* Plate 14, No. 2. Queen 2.4–2.8 cm; male 1.2–2 cm; worker 0.9–1.8 cm. Queen April to May on willow; males in August on thistles. Large thick body with thick hair. Basic colour velvet black, with broad rich yellow band on thorax and 2nd abdominal segment; snow-white rear end. Male's hairs are often quite yellowy-grey. Nest mostly underground, often 1 m or so, in old mouse or mole hole, where moss, leaves, etc. provide nest material. The lump of cells can be up to 50 cm and house apart from the males, the old queen-mother and up to 150 workers and 120 females. Not so common in the North. *Nest:* see plate 12, no. 1.

LARGE RED-TAILED BUMBLE BEE *(Bombus lapidarius)* Plate 14, No. 3. Female 2.4–2.7 cm; worker 1.2–1.8 cm; male 1.5–1.8 cm. Female April to May on dead nettles, common bugle, ground ivy; male in August on harebells, thistles and other Compositae. Big and plump. Smooth, velvety yet rather long hair. Basic colour velvety black; the last 3 abdominal segments brick-red. Female and workers give impression of 6th segment being bare and round, conspicuous against the red hairs. Subterranean nest, preferably under heap of stones, or in crack in wall.

SMALL GARDEN BUMBLE BEE *(Bombus hortorum)* Plate 14, No. 4. Female 2–3 cm; male 1.8–2.2 cm; worker 1.5–2.2 cm. Female April to May on dead nettle, sage, aconite; male in August on *Stachys,* clover, *Aconitus napellus.* Proboscis 2.1 cm. Basic colour black: 3 broad, yellow cross-bands; also on front and back of thorax, on shield and 1st abdominal segment. White hair on end of abdomen. Underground nest with up to 400 inhabitants.

EARLY BUMBLE BEE *(Bombus pratorum)* Plate 14, No. 5. Female 1.6–2 cm; male 1.4–1.6 cm; worker 0.9–1.5 cm. The first bumble to appear. March to April on willow catkins, gooseberry blossom. Male in July on raspberry, bramble and rose-bay. Shaggy hair. Basic colour black; red end to abdomen, on thorax and 2nd abdominal segment more or less yellow hair, often band-shaped; in male yellow hair more or less replaces the black. Nest mostly above ground, in abandoned squirrels' nests or in bushes, moss, etc. housing up to 50 females, 163 males and 125 workers.

Bombus pomorum Plate 14, No. 6. Female 2–2.4 cm; male 1.8–2 cm; worker 1.5–1.8 cm. Female in May on kidney vetch, primrose; worker on clover and thistles, especially in August. Long head, bristly hairs. Basic colour black. Rear end covered with fox-red hair; male has grey-white hair, and abdominal segments 2–6 covered with reddish hair as well as white. Nest underground.

Bombus confusus Plate 14, No. 7. Female 1.6–2.4 cm; male 1.5–2 cm; worker 1.2–1.6 cm. Female in May on clover, common bugle, dead nettle. Male in August in large numbers on thistles. Deep black. Very similar to *B. lapidarius,* the red at the end of its abdomen is less vivid and its hair quite short and velvety. Nest above ground in bushes or some hollow.

Bombus rajellus Plate 14, No. 8. Female 1.8–2 cm; male 1.5–1.8 cm; worker 1.4–1.5 cm. Pollen-collecting hairs on hind leg fox-red. Black coat of males mingled with light or brownish hairs.

MOSS CARDER BEE *(Bombus muscorum)* Female 2–2.2 cm; male 1.2–1.6 cm. Worker variable. Female in May on common bugle and dead nettle. Male in August to September on clover. Very short-haired, yellow to red, lighter at sides. Nest above ground, often between grass stalks in rough gardens; covering of moss and fine thread roots.

COMMON CARDER BEE *(Bombus agrorum)* Plate 14, No. 9. Female 1.8–2.2 cm; male 1.5–1.8 cm; worker 1.2–1.5 cm. Female in May on common bugle, ground ivy, dead nettle; male August to September on thistles. Head much longer than broad. Very like *B. muscorum*. Colouring variable. Basic: yellow, head and thorax more red to brown-yellow; abdomen more grey-yellow and coarsely haired, sometimes with faint ring markings; underside yellowish white. Male mostly lighter coloured. Nest mostly above ground (abandoned bird's nest, house-wall, barn, etc.). Very common.

KNAPWEED CARDER BEE *(Bombus sylvarum)* Plate 14, No. 10. Female 1.2–2.2 cm; male 1.5–1.8 cm; worker 1–1.6 cm. In May female on white dead nettle; in August male on thistle, scabious. Basic bright grey-yellow; front of head covered with light hairs; the black-brown cross-bar on thorax blurred, those on abdomen narrow; rear end covered with pale red hair with white-fringed edges; last abdominal segment almost smooth. Hair of male slightly paler. Nest mostly above ground, often in bird's nest.

B. SOLITARY BEES

MINING BEE *(Halictus)* Various *Halictus* bees nest underground in slightly clayey soil: you can see small holes and beside each a small heap of excavated earth and bees with "trousered" legs going in and out. Fertilised females hibernate under moss at the foot of a tree or in vertical side of a gravel-pit, etc. Mostly in large companies.

Halictus quadricinctus Plate 14, No. 11. 1.4 cm. Dark body: male's is elongated and narrow; female has small, bare, smooth lengthwise groove in the middle of the 5th abdominal segment; 4 white cross-bars on abdomen, the first 2 of which are broken. Female excavates in earth a honeycomb-like nest of 24 cells in horizontal lines, removes the surrounding earth so that the comb is left free, as if suspended from roof of vault supported only by small buttresses. 2 approach-pipes. Building begins May or June, on steep, clay faces. On hawkweed, scabious; in August on cornflower. *Nest:* see Plate 12, No. 7.

HAIRY-LEGGED MINING BEE *(Dasypoda plumipes [= hirtipes])* Plate 14, No. 12. 1–1.5 cm. The *Dasypoda* have the largest leg collecting-apparatus of all bees; long hair. Female has long, bushy, fox-red hair round hind tibia and tarsi; abdomen somewhat depressed, black hair with white bands. Male somewhat smaller, longer antennae, hind legs not so hairy. Likes to nest in companies: each excavates a nest-shaft up to 60 cm into sandy soil, at the end of which are several brood-chambers; shape of nest like bunch of grapes; in each cell or chamber is store of pollen damped with nectar and formed into a ball, then one egg is laid on it and the entrance closed with loose sand. Plate 12, No. 8. Pollen ball is supported on 3 feet, air preventing it going mouldy. Nest in large colonies in roadside banks, between paving stones. In high summer mostly on scabious, knapweed, hawkweed, etc.

LONG-HORNED EUCERA *(Eucera longicornis)* Plate 14, No. 3. 1.2–1.5 cm. Browny-yellow hair. Male has very long, thick antennae. Female plumper and hind-legs have bright side-patches. In May visits wild rosemary, anchusa and vetches. Nests usually alone on slope with sparse grass. Brood arrangements as with *Dasypoda plumipes*.

Anthophora parietina Plate 14, No. 14. 1.3–1.5 cm. Squat body and dense hair makes it resemble a bumble. Thorax and front part of abdomen conspicuous with yellow-brown hair. No light bands on abdomen. In central and northern Europe female's hair can be all black. Nests in large colonies in steep clay faces, sometimes on grassy slopes; nest-pipes identifiable by protruding, drooping clay plugs; horizontal main passage branches after 2–3 cm into numerous galleries each with 2–3 cells. Lid of one cell is floor of the next. Female fills each cell with pollen, lays one egg on it; downward-curving flight-pipes protect the entrance. Visits blossom of sage, ground ivy and anchusa. More in warmer climates. *Nest: see* Plate 12, No. 9.

Osmia papaveris Plate 14, No. 15. About 1 cm. Most of this genus nest in walls and partitions. Yellowish bodies with yellow-brown hair on thorax. Short, oval abdomen. One-celled nest in sandy soil, bottle-shaped underneath and lined with rounds of poppy leaf to prevent the walls caving in. Food-ball of pollen and nectar of cornflower with one egg laid on it. Entrance to brood-chamber covered with grains of sand. Cells can be lined with cornflower leaf instead of poppy. Collects pollen of harebell and cornflower June to July. *Nest: see* Plate 12, No. 10.

TWO-COLOURED OSMIA *(Osmia bicolor)* Plate 14, No. 16. 9–10 mm. Head and thorax covered with black hair; thick red hair on abdomen. April to May builds nest in empty snail shell: 3–4 cells inside the coil, each with a food-pellet of nectar and pollen and one egg on it; a cover of masticated vegetable matter closes the shell. In June builds an ingenious structure of pine-needles, grass-stalks, bits of moss, fixed with sticky saliva, to camouflage it. Sometimes uses hollow reeds to live in. March to June visits heartsease and common bugle.

MINING BEE *(Andrenidae)* Many species of this family with pollen-collecting apparatus on their legs. The outsides of the hind legs of the female have thick pollen-collecting hair. Early in year they visit the first willow-catkins, gooseberry, rape blossom. Nest in sandy soil which they mix with clay; slanting burrows lead 10–30 cm down, often branching and ending in round chamber for "nest" cells. Female lays 1 egg on food-pellet of pollen, then closes cell with lid of cemented sand. Prefers sunny slopes for nest. Common everywhere. *Nest:* Plate 12, No. 11.

Andrena ovina 1.3–1.4 cm. White hair on thorax; abdomen shiny black. Nest mostly in large colonies on south-east banks of roads, etc. Flies April to May, especially in flower meadows.

EARLY MINING BEE *(Andrena albicans)* 9–10 mm. White hair on female's head. Red-mottled thorax, bare, black abdomen with red-yellow hair on end. Brown-yellow hair on head of male, longer antennae. Visits flowers of willow, gooseberry; later dandelion, hawthorn, snowball.

TAWNY MINING BEE *(Andrena fulva)* Plate 14, No. 17. 1.2–1.3 cm. Long, fur-like hair, orange on top, black underneath and on legs. April to May on gooseberry.

Megachile circumcincta Plate 14, No. 18. 1.1–1.3 cm. Long yellow-brown hair; no bands. Nest in ground lined with discs of birch or berry-bearing alder leaf. Usually seen in the air with the disc of leaf held between the fore-legs. May to June on bird's foot trefoil.

COMMON LEAF-CUTTER *(Megachile centuncularis)* Plate 14, No. 19 1.1–1.2 cm. Plump, black body with sparse yellow-brown hair and white abdominal bands. Female has rust-brown collecting hair on underside of abdomen. Cuts discs and ovals out of rose leaves and carries them between its legs to nest, making with them a brood-chamber shaped like a finger-stall in some hollow plant stem, old post, crevice in wall, then fill it with pollen and lays one egg. Usually there are several brood-chambers side by side. June to August on thistle, cornflower, knapweed and bird's foot trefoil. *Nest:* see Plate 12, No. 12.

MASON BEE (Chalicodoma muraria) Plate 14, No. 20. 1.6–2 cm. Looks like a bumble. Female has all black hairs; legs have rust red collecting-hairs. Wings blackish with violet sheen. Male is smaller, slimmer, hair mostly orange, only blackish on abdomen; wings water-clear with brown tinge. Builds masonry nest on sunny rock faces, mixing sand and saliva into a cement-like mass sticking it to rock to make small cells, which it fills with food-store of pollen and nectar, lays one egg on this and then walls up the cell. 5–7 adjacent cells are then cemented over and strongly resemble mud spatter. Larvae pupate in autumn; pupae spend winter in mortar-nest. Flies May to June on sainfoin, sage, trefoil, common bugle.

Stelis nasuta 5–9 mm. Black body with 4 white spots on 2nd–4th abdominal rings. Red legs. Elongated head capsule. Creeps into nest of mason bees and beside their eggs lay 2 rows of 4 tiny eggs each. Often there are 6 *Stelis* larvae (or pupae) in a cell; the cocoons fill the cell completely. These parasitic larvae develop more quickly and so can feed on their host's stores of food. June to July on hedge-nettle, devil's claw, common bugle.

CARPENTER BEE (Xylocopa violacea) Plate 14, No. 21. 2–2.3 cm. Easily mistaken for bumble. Large, plump, somewhat flattened body with short, close-lying or sparse hair and thick head; uniform glossy blue-black; wings dark with steel-blue or greenish sheen. Back of tibia and tarsi have thick bristle-like hair for collecting pollen. Gnaws pipe-like galleries up to 30 cm long, first horizontal, then vertical, into dry wood (rotting tree, post, etc.) to accommodate the nest cells which lie in rows of up to 12, one behind the other; below is a special right-angled exit; at the bottom of the nest-gallery it places pollen mixed with honey, lays an egg on top of this, then covers it with lid of masticated saw-dust, then more pollen and nectar, another egg, and so on. Both sexes hibernate. Visit willow-catkins, dead nettle, lilac, wistaria. Mostly in the South.

Super-Family   Vespoidea   Wasps

Mostly yellow and black. Slim smooth bodies with "wasp waists". Narrow wings that fold along their length.

A. SOCIAL WASPS

Fertilised female = the queen. She hibernates, founds a colony; lives one year. Nest is of chewed-up wood: comb consists of hexagonal cells (Plate 12) with mouths pointing down; brittle external cases. Larvae feed on chewed up insects.

HORNET *(Vespa crabro)* Plate 14, No. 22. Female 2.6–3.15 cm; worker 1.9–2.3 cm; male 2.1–2.3 cm. Thorax black with tinge of red-brown; 1st abdominal segment red-brown, the others yellow with 2 or 3 small brown dots. Nest (Plate 12, No. 4) under rafters, in nesting box, hollow trees; up to the size of a person's hand, it has several horizontal combs, one above the other in layers; the top being the oldest, the underneath one the newest. Brittle outside case. When food is plentiful the population can be as much as 3–4,000, of which many are males, recognisable by their long antennae and lack of sting.

GERMAN WASP *(Vespa germanica)* Plate 14, No. 23. Female 1.7–1.9 cm; worker and male 1.3–1.6 cm. Flies from May onwards. Black with yellow markings and black hair on head and thorax. Abdomen more yellow. Head capsule yellow with 1 or 3 black dots. Rim round eye quite yellow at the back. Thicker lengthwise stripe before the wing-root. Nest (Plate 12, No. 2) underground, especially on sides of country roads, sometimes really huge, up to 10,000 cells. Average population 3–4,000 individuals. Habits the same as hornet. Goes to sweet things. Very pugnacious. Sting very painful. Male on ivy, September to October.

COMMON WASP *(Vespa vulgaris)* Plate 14, No. 24. Female 1.5–2 cm; worker 1.1–1.4 cm; male 1.3–1.7 cm. Flies from May. Black with yellow markings and fairly thick yellowish hair. Yellow head-capsule usually has a black zigzag line lengthwise down the middle. Eye-rims partly black behind. Underground nest in hole, suspended swung from roots, especially on fringe of a wood, under tree roots or a stone. Usually not a large population. Male flies September to October on ivy and umbellifers.

TREE WASP *(Vespa silvestris)* Female 1.7–2 cm; worker 1.3–1.5 cm; male 1.4–1.6 cm. Flies May to June. Rich yellow colouring makes it conspicuous; yellow ring-bands are almost straight. Yellow head-capsule, often has tiny black specks. Distinct gaps between edge of eye and root of fore-jaw. Round nest the size of an apple; above ground; on twigs, beams, in garden shelters, etc. free standing. Likes mountain woods. Male in August on umbellifers.

Vespa media Plate 14, No. 25. Female 1.8–2 cm; worker 1.5–1.6 cm; male 1.5–1.7 cm. In June female is very rare. Males on umbellifers with the workers in August. Second largest wasp. Female closely resembles a hornet: head and thorax rust-brown; narrow, yellow cross-line on thorax and a yellow line lengthwise on either side before the wings. Eye-recess quite yellow; 3 distinct simple eyes on crown of head. Builds a rather large, oval balloon nest (Plate 12, No. 3) in treetop or under eaves; outer case consists of shell-like curved scales that overlap like roofing tiles.

Vespa saxonica Plate 14, No. 26. Female 1.5–1.7 cm; worker 1.1–1.3 cm; male 1.3–1.5 cm. Black with yellow markings, hair more grey. Jutting tooth-like head-capsule with black lengthwise stripes; distinct cheeks; 2nd abdominal segment reddish. In female the rim of eye is only slightly yellow. Balloon nest of small dimensions, delicate, under eaves, etc. Has 3 envelopes: the first bell-shaped, the other two funnel-shaped. Flies May to June, especially on medlar; in August on umbellifers.

RED WASP (*Vespa rufa*) Plate 14, No. 27. Female 1.5–2 cm; worker 1–1.2 cm; male 1.3–1.6 cm. Black with yellow and red markings; bristly black hair. Fore part of abdomen reddish. More placid than its relations. Makes flat nest underground with only 3 huge combs, apparently holding up to 3,000 cells. Large nests have up to 700 females and 700 males. Males on umbellifers in August.

Polistes gallicus Plate 14, No. 28. 1–1.6 cm. Elongated oval abdomen tapered equally at either end. Black with a wealth of yellow markings. Segments have yellow notched bands. Males are yellow underneath. Antennae cilia reddish-yellow. Nest (Plate 12, No. 5) made of grey "paper" without a case. Mostly only 1 comb fastened by stout stalk to a stone, rock, clay-face, bush, plant, etc. Horizontal cells, many containing store of honey; up to 300 cells. In April to May only females on cypress spurge; often on willows; workers in May to August, males only in August to September, often in large numbers round bushes in the sun. Central and southern Europe.

B. SOLITARY WASPS

HEATH POTTER WASP (*Eumenes coarctata*) Plate 14, No. 29. 1.1–1.4 cm. Pretty little creature. From May to September on snowberry, thyme, umbellifers. Black and yellow markings. Thorax almost spherical; 1st segment of abdomen stalk-shaped; 2nd bell-shaped with faint dots; rear edge of all segments golden. Builds one-celled, thin-walled nest the size of a hazel nut (Plate 12, No. 6) using clay, fixed individually or a few together on walls of brick or wood, on straws or stalks, under bark, on pine needles, etc. Takes 3–4 looper caterpillars into each and then lays an egg; each nest has a short, neck-like prolongation at the point which seals it. Larvae hibernate.

Eumenes pomiformis 1.2–1.5 cm. Resembles *E. coarctata;* its 2nd abdominal segment is deeply pitted.

MASON WASP *(Odynerus [= Symmorphus] murarius)* 1.1–1.5 cm. Long body with black and yellow markings. Abdomen has no stalk. Difficult to distinguish from other species. Nests in groups on steep banks or not too hard clay-faces. In front of each entrance hole is a small down-turned flight or protective burrow made of friable earth. Looks like a tiny top. Female carries in several hairless caterpillars it has paralysed with its sting as food for larvae, then lays 1 egg; a new burrow is built for each egg.

Family   SPHEGIDAE   Digger and Sand Wasps

BEE-KILLER WASP *(Philanthus triangulum)* Plate 14, No. 30. 1.2 to 1.6 cm. Rich yellow markings on abdomen and its broad head make it conspicuous; hind wall of thorax pitted. Black abdominal segments have yellow bands, much broader at the sides. Legs yellow with black base. Clear wings. Digs in sunny slope a 10 cm gallery widening out into a brood-chamber. Different wasps often make their nests close together. They attack honey bees out searching for nectar, paralyse them and fly back to their nests with them, where they pile them up, lay a few eggs on them and wall them up to feed the larvae when they hatch. In July or August in sandy areas. Flies to thyme, clover and umbellifers to catch honey bees.

RED-BANDED SAND WASP *(Sphex [= Ammophila] sabulosa)* Plate 14, No. 31. 1.8–2.2 cm. Male often smaller. Slim, restless little creature, easily recognisable by its thin 2-jointed abdominal stalk that gradually turns into a club-shaped, black and red abdomen. The sides of the female's thorax and the male's head-capsule have silver hair. Nests in sunny sites with loose soil, in which it digs a slanting hole some 2.5 cm long with a pot-shaped enlargement underneath; carries little stones to it in its jaws and closes the entrance with them when it leaves. It catches hairless noctuid caterpillars, paralyses them with its sting, drags them to its hole, lays one egg on them and closes the hole with sand, which it rams in with its head; at once it starts digging another hole, and so on. From June to October in sandy places, on the flowers of thyme and other labiates sucking nectar.

Sphex maxillosus 1.8–2.5 cm. Short-stalked abdomen, almost covered by its yellowish wings; body black; has silvery white hairs on front of head and sides of thorax; base of abdomen usually a distinct brown. Long legs have spikes on them used in digging. July to August sucks nectar on wild thyme, stonecrop, dill. Nests in sandy soil on edges of woods; slanting gallery some 5 cm long with oval brood-chamber; often 2–3 compartments at end of the gallery. Paralyses grasshoppers by stinging them and drags them inside to feed its larvae when they hatch out.

BLACK BORER *(Trypoxylon figulus)* 8–12 mm. Long black body with slightly white hair. Uses abandoned galleries in tree trunks and posts, or hollow bramble stalks as nest-tube (or gnaws one in soft vegetable matter); these are about 20 cm long and contain up to 9 cells separated by clay partitions and closed with especially stout clay lids once spiders have been piled up inside and the egg laid. May to July often on leaves, posts, beams, old tree trunks.

Bembix rostrata Plate 14, No. 32. 2–2.5 cm. Stout build. Black with yellow (or other) cross-bands. Nests communally in sand, preferring sunny glades in pine woods, on coast or inland dunes. Begins building nest in July. While digging uses its wing to send sand swirling so violently as to create visible cloud of dust. Nest has oval entrance, broader than tall. Flies July to August. Visiting thyme, dragging off large flies, supplying its larvae with fresh ones until they pupate.

SAND-TAILED DIGGER *(Cerceris arenaria)* Plate 14, No. 33. 1.4 to 1.7 cm. Deep, ring-shaped incisions between nodular protruding abdominal segments. 1st segment considerably narrowed. Sides of head yellow, also thorax. Legs brown with yellow. Digs brood-galleries in sand in colonies, especially at the side of country roads. Feeds the larvae with bees and beetles it has paralysed. July to August in sandy areas. On white clover.

Family   POMPHILIDAE (= PSAMMOCHARIDAE)

Spider-hunting Wasps

BLACK BANDED SPIDER WASP *(Pompilus viaticus)* Plate 14, No. 35. 1.2–1.4 cm. Legs strikingly long and thin; sparse, black hairs; first 3 abdominal segments red with black-brown terminal edge; fore-wings brownish; black legs. In early spring on willow flowers; moves quickly with hops and jumps and quivering wings along the ground or on roads, catching and paralysing large spiders and dragging them into its nest-gallery. Female will even give people a nasty sting if annoyed. April to October where ground is sandy.

Family   SCOLIIDAE   Digger Wasps

Tiphia femorata 9–12 mm; shiny black; femur and tibia of middle and hind legs brown-red; distinct groove down back on 1st and 2nd abdominal segments. Eager visitor to umbellifers, often found on blossom at night. Develops in grub of *Amphimallus solstitialis*.

Family   MUTILLIDAE   Velvet Ants

Mutilla europaea Plate 14, No. 34. 1–1.4 cm; female wingless, resembles ant. Thorax brick-red, coarsely pitted; black abdomen with several silvery cross-bands, the rear ones broken; runs busily about. Male has wings with blackish sheen; abdominal bands more red-yellow; often on blossom. Female chirrups to attract the male; finely grooved cross-lines on back between 1st and 2nd segments that are more in opposition. Female forces her way into bumble bee's nest and lays eggs in its cells; live as larvae in bumble bee's larvae.

SMALL VELVET ANT *(Mutilla rufipes)* 4–7 mm long; black head; brown-red thorax; 1st and 2nd abdominal segments have white cilia at end; 3rd segment has white band. Female wingless, can chirrup. Common in sandy areas.

Family   CHRYSIDIDAE   Ruby-tails

Chrysis ignita Plate 14, No. 36. 6–12 mm. Size and colouring varies. Head and thorax metallic green and blue; abdomen deep red. Parasite: lays eggs on creatures the grub wasps have brought in. From May to September sits on old posts, tree trunks, faces of clay and plaster; seldom on umbelliferous flowers.

Family   CEPHIDAE   Stem Saw-flies

WHEAT-STEM BORER *(Cephus pygmaeus)* Plate 14, No. 41. Flies May to mid-July. 6.8 mm. Span 1.4–1.8 cm. Shiny, black body. Abdomen has lemon-yellow cross-bands. Legs spotted with yellow. Clear wings with dark veining. In sunshine sucks nectar from flowers. Lays eggs singly in top nodule of 10–15 barley or wheat stalks. *Larvae:* see p. 423.

Family   UROCERIDAE (= SIRICIDAE)   Wood-wasps

Cannot sting.

Urocerus gigas Plate 14, No. 39. Male up to 3.2 cm; female up to 4.5 cm. Black head and thorax, yellow antennae, femora and tarsi; male has red-brown abdominal bands; 1st segment black, last dark brown; in female black-blue band on bright yellow abdomen; at end of which is powerful boring "ovipositor". Female sits on felled tree trunk or moribund stem, drills its ovipositor 1 cm into wood and deposits 1 egg; repeats this elsewhere. *Larvae:* see p. 436. In hot summer weather flies actively and noisily in woods, especially in clearings, often in numbers.

Urocerus (= Paururus) juvencus Plate 14, No. 40. Flies June to September. 1.5–3 cm; blue-black, metallic sheen; orange legs; male has orange belt in middle of abdomen; eggs are laid as *U. gigas,* mainly in pine-wood. *Larvae:* see p. 436. Goes mainly for pines, but also firs and spruce. In hot weather swarms round tall trees.

Xeris (= Sirex) spectrum 1.5–3 cm; uniform black-brown with yellowish spots on head and lighter streak each side of top of thorax. Long antennae, reaching to abdomen. Ovipositor almost the length of the entire body. Lives as the foregoing.

Family   ICHNEUMONIDAE   Ichneumons

Slim, mostly curved with "waistline" abdomens.

Therion (= Exochilum) circumflexum Plate 14, No. 37. About 2 cm. Slight build: abdomen waisted and pressed-in; mainly reddish yellow; wings dulled with brown; swarms round bushes and trees; long hind legs stick out behind, antennae up in the air and abdomen curving downwards; occasionally alights on a leaf to suck the sugary excrement of an aphid or a drop of dew. Lays eggs in caterpillars of *Dendrolimus pini* (one egg in each). Found in pine woods.

Ichneumon pisorius Plate 14, No. 38. 2.2–2.8 cm. Slim; black head and thorax with brilliant yellow shield and 1 yellow line at each wing root; abdomen, tibiae and tarsi orange; antennae have white ring; females lay eggs in caterpillars of the larger hawkmoths (one in each). From June in woods of conifers.

Rhyssa persuasoria Up to 3.2 cm. Blue-black body with white spots; legs light rust colour. Ovipositor almost half as long again as the body; female walks about trunk, long antennae quivering, until they tell where a larva of the giant woodwasp is, then she cocks up her abdomen, draws a hair-thin drill out of its sheath and with sheath held vertically drills up to 6 cm through the hard wood and into the larva, laying one egg in it and withdrawing her ovipositor-borer. The whole operation takes about fifteen minutes. Influenced by the parasitic ichneumon larva, the wood-wasp eats its way up to the bark thus enabling the ichneumon to emerge easily. In conifer woods.

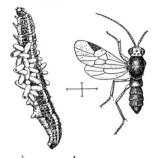

Family   BRACONIDAE

Apanteles glomeratus 2.5 mm. Black with yellowy-brown legs. Female stabs ovipositor into caterpillars of large white and lays in them. The hatched larva eats the inside of the caterpillar and breaks through its skin, spins for itself on the outside of the caterpillar's skin, a long, oval, yellow cocoon in which it pupates (wrongly called "caterpillar eggs"). After 10–14 days a round lid rises up on each cocoon and out comes a young ichneumon.

Pimpla instigator 1.1–1.9 cm; black; 4 fore legs have orange tibiae and tarsi; the two hind legs have yellow tibiae. Female with wings slightly raised runs about tree-trunk, hedges and clay faces, looking for caterpillars of butterflies which it stabs laying 1 egg inside it, then flies off in search of a fresh victim. Attacks harmful caterpillars of the tussock moths. In fields, woods, gardens.

Family   CHALCIDIDAE   Chalcids

Parasitic in eggs, larvae, pupae of other insects.

FAIRY FLY *(Anastatus bifasciatus)* About 5 mm. Egg-parasite; lays 1 egg in eggs of the gypsy moth *Lymantria dispar*, killing them.

Pteromalus puparum 3 mm; bronze-green; seeks out young, still soft-skinned pupae of garden white butterflies *(Pieridae)* and *Vanessidae,* thrusting a tiny egg between the segments of the pupa. Many larvae hatch out from this single egg (polyembryony) and eat out the butterfly pupae to the skin and make a hole through which they creep, so that at the end the pupa looks like a sieve.

Family   EVANIIDAE   Hunger-Wasps

Parasitic in egg-capsules of cockroaches.

Gasteruption abeillei (= affectator) 8–12 mm; black body with red spotted abdomen; very pressed-in sides; ovipositor about a quarter the length of the abdomen. Visits umbellifers for nectar. When sun is out, in light and graceful flight round tree stumps and bushes. Visits nests of bees *(Prosopus)* or potter wasps in which its larvae are parasites. In Alps up to the snow line.

Evania appendigaster 8–9 mm. Easily recognisable by peculiar shape of its black body, the abdomen being very pressed in at the sides and distinctly waisted: the waist being high up on the back of the rear thoracic segment, making it look as if the abdomen was missing. The female has a short ovipositor and lays its eggs in the egg-capsules of the oriental and American cockroach. Found in all areas inhabited by people.

Family   TENTHREDINIDAE   Sawflies

Plump bodies without waists.

BIRCH SAWFLY *(Cimbex femorata)* Antennae have club-like thickened ends. Big, plump bodies. Lethargic. Colouring varies, but mostly glossy black, often becoming yellow or brown-yellow halfway down the abdomen. Abdominal ring has, in the middle, a deep hollow filled with white skin. Wings

have conspicuous dark brown seam. Male has much thicker hind femora. Eggs thrust individually into leaves. *Larvae:* see p. 403. On trees and bushes in spring.

*Craesus (= Nematus) septentrionalis Flies from May on. Colouring: black and red; points of tibiae and 1st joint of tarsi on hind legs enlarged into shovel-shape. Eggs on undersides of leaves of birch, alder, hazel, etc. *Larvae:* see p. 403.

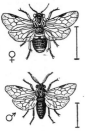

PINE SAWFLY *(Dirrion [= Lophyrus] pini)* Size of a house fly. Male 6–7 mm, slim black body with yellow legs; tip of abdomen red; broad comb-antennae. Female 9 mm, plump, dirty yellow with patches of black-brown; simple antennae; extendable sawing-ovipositor at end of abdomen with which it slits pine-needles lengthwise, laying (April to May) 10–20 eggs in the slit and then cementing it. *Larvae:* see p. 404.

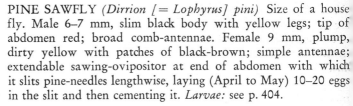

Arge (= Hylotoma) ochropus (= rosae) Flies end of May, early June. 7–10 mm. Body predominantly yellow. Head, middle of thorax and end of ovipositor black. Antennae of male have short, bristly hairs. Lays eggs in one long row in young rose shoots, which then curl up and shrivel. *Larvae:* see p. 403.

Plate 14

Nos 1–41 on pp. 366–377. Nos 42–56 on pp. 390–395

1. HONEY BEE *(Apis mellifica)* worker 2. *Bombus terrestris* 3. *Bombus lapidarius* 4. *Bombus hortorum* 5. *Bombus pratorum* 6. *Bombus pomorum* 7. *Bombus confusus* 8. *Bombus rajellus* 9. *Bombus agrorum* 10. *Bombus sylvarum* 11. *Halictus quadricinctus* 12. *Dasypoda plumipes* (= *hirtipes*) 13. *Eucera longicornis* 14. *Anthophora parietina* 15. *Osmia papaveris* 16. *Osmia bicolor* 17. *Andrena fulva* 18. *Megachile circumcincta* 19. COMMON LEAF-CUTTER *(Megachile centuncularis)* 20. MASON BEE *(Chalicodoma muraria)* 21. *Xylocopa violacea* 22. HORNET *(Vespa crabro)* 23. *Vespa germanica* 24. COMMON WASP *(Vespa vulgaris)* 25. *Vespa media* 26. *Vespa saxonica* 27. *Vespa rufa* 28. *Polistes gallicus* 29. *Eumenes coarctata* 30. *Philanthus triangulum* 31. *Sphex* (= *Ammophila*) *sabulosa* 32. *Bembix rostrata* 33. *Cerceris arenaria* 34. *Mutilla europaea* 35. *Pompilus viaticus* 36. *Chrysis ignita* 37. *Therion* (= *Exochilum*) *circumflexum* 38. *Ichneumon pisorius* 39. *Urocerus* (= *Sirex*) *gigas* 40. *Urocerus juvencus* 41. *Cephus pygmaeus* 42. GREEN BOTTLE (= *Lucilia caesar*) 43. *Calliphora erythrocephala* 44. *Larvaevora grossa* 45. *Larvaevora fera* 46. *Hypoderma bovis* 47. *Gastrophilus intestinalis* 48. *Chrysops caecutiens* 49. *Bombylius major* 50. *Anthrax* (= *Hemipenthes*) *morio* 51. *Scaeva* (= *Syrphus*) *pyrastri* 52. *Asilus crabroniformis* 53. *Helophilus trivittatus* 54. *Volucella bombylans* 55. *Tubifera* (= *Eristalis*) *tenax* 56. *Scopeuma stercorarium.*

L. Hemdorff

GOOSEBERRY SAWFLY *(Pteronidea [= Nematus] ribesii)*
7 mm. Reddish-yellow; brown head and thorax. Lays eggs on
ribbing on underside of leaves. *Larvae:* see p. 403.

*PEAR SAWFLY *(Eriocampoides limacina)* Flies May to
August. 5 mm. Glossy black; clear wings. Eggs under skin of
leaves. *Larvae:* see p. 403.

Eriocampoides annulipes Shiny black with white ring at base
of tibiae and tarsi. *Larvae:* see p. 403. Found on leaves of birch,
oak and willow.

Pamphilius stellatus Flies end of April to end of June. 1 cm;
black, reddish abdominal margins; head dotted and patched
with yellow. Lays up to 80 eggs individually on old reeds.

Pamphilius hypotrophicus (= Cephaleia abietis). 1.2–1.3 cm.
Flies May to June. Shiny black with bright yellow markings;
abdomen, legs, antennae all yellow. Female reluctant to fly,
climbs up tree trunks, lays 100–120 eggs in clumps of 4–12 on
needles of previous year's growth. *Larvae:* see p. 404.

Neurotoma saltuum (= flaviventris) 1–1.2 cm. Head and
thorax black with yellow patches; abdomen broad and flat,
orange in male, blackish with yellow side spots and yellow
cross-bars on underside in female. Clear wings with brownish
cross-bands on fore-wings. Lays eggs on leaves of hawthorn
and fruit trees. *Larvae:* see p. 404.

Cimbex variabilis Large black body with no hair; red-brown
or yellow abdomen. Antennae have button-shaped thickening
in front. Larvae yellowy-green; on birch, willow, alder. Yellowish
cocoon.

Family   CEPHIDAE   Stem Sawflies

Janus compressus Flies from middle of May. 6 mm. Span 1.3–
1.4 cm; black; reddish-yellow abdomen. Lays eggs individually
in slits made in bark on previous year's growth of pear, hawthorn and apple. *Larvae:* see p. 423.

ANTS WITH OR WITHOUT WINGS

Order   HYMENOPTERA

Family   FORMICIDAE   Ants

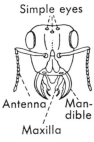

Simple eyes

Antenna   Mandible

Maxilla

Head broader than front of thorax. Waist where abdomen joins thorax. Antennae bent at an angle. Sting either absent or rudimentary. Always has poison gland in abdomen which secretes formic acid that is injected into wound made by jaws as means of defence. Upper mandibles strong and pincer-shaped. Long, rather thin legs. All ants are social. Males have wings, slim bodies, longish antennae and are short-lived. The queen is a perfectly developed, winged female that sheds its wings shortly after mating; at which stage she is recognisable by longer thorax; lives for years, lays eggs, founds independent colonies. Workers are imperfect females, wingless and incapable of reproduction; mentally highly developed, very active. Those of some species (e.g. *Formica fusca*) live to be six years old. Perfect metamorphosis. Minute eggs. Pupae in white cocoons spun by larvae wrongly called "ants' eggs".

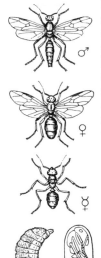

WOOD ANT (*Formica rufa*) Red back. Head and abdomen black. Queen and male 9–10 mm with yellow-tinged wings (differences see above), workers 5–7 mm, always wingless. Nest, mound up to 1.5 m tall; mainly built of conifer needles, up to 3 m in diameter and reaching deep into the earth; inside is a labyrinth of passages and chambers. *Food:* insects, worms, etc. do considerable good by destroying caterpillars; act as sort of forest rangers. Communicate by using antennae, which are also organs of touch and smell. Recognise smell of nest by palpitating with antennae. Entrance closed in the evening, opened in the morning, guarded during the day. Workers clean and lick the eggs and hatched grubs with their tongues, regurgitate fluid food in front of grubs, carry them to higher or lower levels according to the weather; help the young ant to emerge from its pupa-casing. On some sunny day in May or June all the ant communities of an area will conduct their nuptial flight. Swarms of males and females, like columns of smoke. The two columns mingle at some elevated point (crest of a hill, top of a tree, etc.). Mating takes place between ants of different nests in order to avoid inbreeding. Countless exhausted males sink dead to the ground, as do most of the winged females. The fertilised queen sheds her wings and founds a new community.

building a cell with earth and laying an egg in it. First workers
break through wall, run out and come back bringing fluid food in
their crop for the larvae. Queens live up to 20 years, laying
eggs in lowest chamber. All ants in a nest are the progeny of
one or very few queens. The population of a nest can be as
much as 50,000 or even 500,000. Some have branch nests near
by with ant-streets connected to the various heaps. Thus a
community can comprise millions. If an ant-street is blocked
the cut-off communities become independent. Found especially
in coniferous woods. Picture shows: *Clytra quadripunctata*
which pupates in nest of wood ant.

NARROW-HEADED ANT *(Formica exsecta)* 4–9 mm. Matt
black head and abdomen; front and middle of back blackish.
Nest on fringe of wood is not tall, but a flat curve.

Formica trunicola 6–11 mm. Head, back, waist and half abdomen are bright red. Irregular nest mostly on old tree stumps.

BLOOD-RED ANT *(Formica sanguinea)* 6–9 mm. Resembles
wood ant. Head brown-black; back and waist bright blood-red.
Head capsule has a semi-circular cut in the front of it. Small,
flat, irregular nest often built in the ground under stones, turf
or in a tree stump, seldom making a curved dome. Collects
building material only at edge of nest. Found especially on
sunny fringes of woods. Hordes attack the communities of other
smaller ants carrying off pupae and bringing those up as slaves
which take part in all the work and seem to feel quite at home.
Mixed communities with small black-brown fusca-slaves running
about among their big blood-red masters.

NEGRO ANT *(Formica fusca)* 5–7 mm; dark brown to
brown-black with brown-red legs and antennae. Abdomen covered with bloom-like hair. Nests mostly built underground or
under stones; populations not large. Are often plundered and
enslaved by *F. sanguinea.*

JET ANT *(Acanthomyops [= Lasius] fuliginosus)* 4–5 mm.
Deep, shiny black. Gives off a strong smell of acetic acid, when
held between the fingers. Rendered conspicuous by its well-
worn streets, often leading across paths, and always to a bush
or tree with aphis. Lives in large colonies mostly at the base of
an old tree or in a tree stump. Will go for rotting wood. Builds

brittle, black-brown nest with numerous passages and chambers, making a cement of wood-dust, fibre (or soil) and with a secretion from its mandible glands producing thin, cardboard-like walls. Builds by preference in hollow willows or poplars. Sometimes a nest that hangs free from the tree. Has both a summer nest and a winter one, deeper in the ground. Feeds mostly on honey-dew from aphides, but also on beetles, etc. of which it leaves only the outer shell.

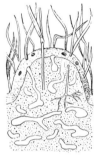

GARDEN ANT *(Lasius niger)* 3–4 mm. Head and abdomen black-brown to black; brownish thorax. Nest: where the ground is damp and well covered with grass it builds a dome that rises up to 30 cm above the vegetation to catch the sun; where it is warm and has little vegetation it nests in open soil; where the ground is stony it builds under a stone which protects the nest from the rain and acts as a heat-store, many brood-chambers being crowded immediately under the stone; in a shady wood will build in a tree stump, since the sun shines in where trees have been felled. Subterranean passages lead to places where there are aphides, on the secretion from which they chiefly feed. In gardens, fields, woods, meadows, old tree stumps.

YELLOW ANT *(Lasius flavus)* 2–4 mm; uniform pale yellow to brownish. Lives underground. Painful bite. Earth nest round a tuft of grass, only a small mound showing above ground, often with passages made of earth radiating from it. The structure proper is underground, and from it covered galleries lead to small heaps of earth concealed in the lower part of a tussock. These are aphis stables, where numbers of aphides are kept guarded by a few ants. The aphis sucks at the grass roots and secretes sugary juices for the ants. When female aphides return from nuptial flight the ants bite off their wings and drag them off to their stables where they look after them, collect their eggs and tend these till they hatch. In the turf on the edge of woods, at the feet of old trees, under stones.

Camponotus ligniperdus Black. One of the largest European ants, the female being 15–17 mm with brown-yellow wings (flight May to June), the male 9–11 mm with bright yellow wings. The workers have no wings and vary considerably in

size, from 8 to 14 mm. Live in stumps of pine trees and firs and also in healthy trunks, in which they gnaw away the soft wood leaving only the harder parts, thus constructing a wooden nest with numerous galleries and chambers, often extending 10 m up the tree. The ants enter and leave by small holes out of which fine dust usually trickles. As they destroy trees and breed aphides, they are regarded as pests.

SLIM INSECTS LIKE FLIES
SMALLER THAN DRAGON-FLIES BUT LARGER THAN FLIES

Order   NEUROPTERA   Lacewings

2 pairs of similar transparent membranous wings with a "lace-work" of veins. Mouth-parts adapted for biting or sucking. Complete metamorphosis. Legs mostly long and thin. First thoracic segment freely movable.

Family   CHRYSOPIDAE   Lacewings

Chrysopa carnea [= vulgaris]) About 8 mm. Wing span 2.7—3 cm. Dainty insect with 2 pairs of large, clear, green-veined wings and grey-green body. 2 large eyes with a golden gleam; 2 long thin antennae. Feeds on aphides. Lays stalked eggs in groups on leaves or twigs. Hibernates. On plants throughout the year.

Chrysopa perla Very similar to *C. carnea.* X-shaped spot between the antennae. Black abdomen; greenish at the sides. Common.

Family   MYRMELEONIDAE   Ant-lions

*Myrmeleon formicarius 63–65 mm. Rather like a dragon-fly with slender body and 4 large, transparent wings with lacework of veins, 2 club-shaped antennae. Mostly motionless by day with wings in roof-position, sitting on tree trunk. Slow, awkward flight in twilight. Feed on small insects. Found especially in conifer woods at low altitudes. Flies July to August. *Larvae:* see p. 409.

Order   MEGALOPTERA   Alderflies, Snakeflies

Family   SIALIDAE   Alderflies

Sialis lutaria 2.5–3 cm. Black body with brownish wings, held roof-like when at rest, jutting beyond the body. Especially during spring sits on plants in stagnant or slow-flowing water; flies only when sun shines, for short distances. Egg-mass over 1 cm across, brown, velvet appearance, on plants near water. *Larvae:* see p. 442.

Family   RAPHIDIIDAE   Snakeflies

Raphidia notata About 1 cm. Wing-span 2.5 cm. Shiny black body. Abdominal rings have yellow seams on underside; light brown legs. Small head narrowing behind to look like a neck; 2 compound eyes, 3 frontal eyes; long, bristle-shaped antennae. Mouth-parts adapted for chewing. First segment of thorax elongated like a neck and very mobile, usually held rather upright. 6 slender legs. 2 pairs of membranous wings of equal size, held in roof-position at rest. Female has long ovipositor and lays eggs under pieces of bark. *Larvae:* see p. 409. In summer on bushes, trees and bark; not very active.

Order   TRICHOPTERA   Caddisflies

Mostly uniform brown or grey, moth-like but with bodies densely covered with hairs instead of scales; thread-like antennae and long, narrow bodies; in summer usually sitting lazily on waterside plants; disturbed, they will run a short distance away or flutter in hasty rocking flight elsewhere. Many kinds soar by day in easy flight over the surface of the water; others swarm as dusk falls over water, having spent the day concealed. These are good fliers. Some kinds are as small as clothes moths, others as large as the cabbage white butterfly. They have long, wide wings, folded roof-wise when at rest. No sucking-proboscis; 2 large compound eyes mostly sited forward. Antennae stretched out in front when at rest. Slender legs with 5-jointed tarsi. Strongly degenerate mouth-parts; only food liquids such as nectar or water. Life-span about 8 days. Most species fly from about end of June to end of August. They are most familiar as larvae, see p. 443.

Family PHRYGANEIDAE

Phryganea grandis Flies April to June and August. Span 4–6 cm. Fore-wings lie close to body, haired, irregular patches of grey, brown or dark-brown; hind wings grey or light grey-brown with dark seams. Body brown-yellow to brown; grey hair on head and thorax; antennae brown-yellow or dark brown with light rings. Inactive by day, concealed in bushes or under tree-bark; in evening twilight fluttering about restlessly; will enter houses.

Family LIMNEPHILIDAE

Limnephilus rhombicus Flies May to August. Span 3–4.4 cm. Antennae about the length of the fore-wings, seldom shorter. Rather broad wings with little hair. Fore-wings shiny yellow or brown with large transparent patches. Hind wings transparent, iridescent. Head and thorax reddish or brown-yellow with sparse reddish or yellow hair. Bright red antennae. Abdomen grey-brown on top, reddish-brown underneath. By stagnant or sluggish water.

Order MECOPTERA Scorpion-flies

Head elongated downward into beak shape. Antennae long, bristle-shaped. 4 wings all same size, membranous, veined. Male holds end of body upturned over the back in a similar way to that in which a scorpion carries its tail.

Family PANORPIDAE Scorpion-flies

COMMON SCORPION-FLY *(Panorpa communis)* 2.7 cm. Slim, long-legged; head has beak-like elongation. 4 large wings with dark patches. Male has thickened rear-end, a short, thick pincer held aloft, resembling the sting of a scorpion. Female holds its thin awl-shaped rear end outstretched. Wings held horizontally when at rest, slowly dipping up and down. Flies only for short distances and is easy to catch. Feeds on dead, decaying insects, also live ones. Lays eggs in ground. Larvae are like caterpillars, rather sluggish, living in specially dug galleries. Moult and pupate. First scorpion-flies take wing in May. On bushes, where ground is not too dry.

Order   EPHEMEROPTERA   Mayflies

4-winged insects with 2 or 3 "tails".

Dance in swarms near water just before sunset on still warm evenings in May and June. Mate during nuptial flight. Lay eggs in water. Mature winged Mayflies live only 2 to 3 days or just a few hours without food. *Larvae:* see p. 439.

Family   EPHEMERIDAE

MAYFLY *(Ephemera vulgata)* Flies May to early June. Body 1.7 cm; fore-wings 1.7–2 cm; "tails" of male 3.2–3.6 cm, of female 2.4 cm. At tip of abdomen has 3 thin "tails" (cerci) of equal length. Slim, slight body with soft skin; brown-black head; short antennae, awl-shaped. Black thorax. Fore-legs of male very elongated; held in front like antennae when at rest. Transparent glossy wings; the fore-ones large, brownish or grey-green with dark patches and veining; hind wings small; fore-margin brown; the male has brown patch in the middle. At rest both wings are held upright. Abdomen mostly yellow to red-brown with lighter patches on back and sides; black or brown lengthwise line on each side of underneath. Vestigial mouth-parts. 2 compound eyes; those of male being particularly large. *Larvae:* see p. 439. Slow-flowing water where bottom is sandy or muddy.

Family   EPHORIDAE

*Ephoron virgo Flies July to early September. Body 1.6 cm. Fore-wings of male 1.2 cm, of female 1.5 cm; tails of male 2.5 cm, of female 1.3 cm. Recognisable by dull white wings and white tails. Male has 2 smooth, long side-tails with a tiny one in the middle; those of female are all almost the length of her body and hairy. Abdomen yellow-white. Sometimes when flying round a lamp near water they resemble snowflakes. Dead ones often cover surface of water or lie heaped on ground. Muddy bottom of larger rivers contain masses of their larvae.

Family   BAETIIDAE

POND OLIVE DUN (sub-imago) *(Cloeon dipterum)* Flies August to September. Body of male 0.5–1 cm, female 0.7–1.1 cm. Only 2 tails. No hind wings. Colouring and size vary considerably. Body yellow to black-brown. Wings of male colourless, female's have brown fore margin. Tails mostly white, alternatively broad and narrow, with dark rings or no rings. Ponds.

LITTLE CLARET SPINNER *(Baetis pumilus)* Flies June to August. Body 6 mm. Tails of male 1.2 mm, of female 8–9 mm; only two. Has hind wings. Wings clear, colourless, shiny. Legs white or grey-white. Tails of male white, of female brownish. Rivers and small streams.

Order   PLECOPTERA   Stoneflies

Family   PERLIDAE

STONEFLY *(Perla bipunctata)* Body of male 2.3–2.8 cm, of female 3.3–3.6 cm. Span 2–6.4 cm. Inconspicuous, inactive. 2 long tails, 2 pairs of membranous brown, translucent wings, held at rest flat over body. Long, bristle-shaped antennae. Usually on tree trunk or rock near road or swift stream; seldom flies and only for short periods. Life-span 4–6 weeks. Does not feed. Blackish eggs dropped into water in one mass. *Larvae:* see p. 442. Spring and summer, near swift-flowing water.

Perla abdominalis Body 2–2.5 cm. Span 3–5.8 cm. Head and thorax almost black; abdomen red-brown to brown. Mountain streams. Otherwise as *P. bipunctata*.

Family   CAPNIIDAE

Capnia nigra 1.6–1.8 cm. Dull colouring. Wings of male very diminished. Enjoys temperatures only just over 0° C. *Larvae:* see p. 442. Mountainous areas.

INSECTS WITH 2 MEMBRANOUS, MOSTLY TRANSPARENT WINGS

FLIES LIKE BEES, BUMBLE BEES AND WASPS

Plate 14

Order   DIPTERA   True Flies

Family   MUSCIDAE   House Flies

BLUE BOTTLE *(Calliphora erythrocephala)* Plate 14, No. 43. 9–13 mm; shiny steel-blue; red cheeks with black hair; deep hum in flight. Female comes indooors when it scents meat, lays long white eggs in it, or, out-doors, on carrion. Maggots often hatch while eggs are being laid.

BLUE BOTTLE *(Calliphora vomitoria)* Resembles *C. erythrocephala,* but has black cheeks with red hair, and is not so common.

Protocalliphora azurea Abdomen has a handsome violet or greeny sheen; metallic-sheened thorax has brownish lengthwise stripes. Lives as maggot in nests of swallows, starlings, etc. sucking at the underneath of the wings of the young birds and sometimes thereby killing them. Pupate in the nest. Rare.

GREEN BOTTLE *(Lucilia caesar)* Plate 14, No. 42. Size of a house fly; magnificent gold-green sheen. Lays eggs preferably on meat, in open wounds and running sores, into which swiftly growing larvae bore deep down. Often on human and animal vomit and excrement; also on carrion and umbellifers. Sucks nectar.

Lucilia bufonivora (= silvarum) Male blue-green, female has more of a coppery sheen; 2 strong bristles on 2nd abdominal segment. Flies attach common toad and lay their eggs in its nostrils. As they hatch, the larvae bore their way in, feeding, but sparing the brain, so that the toad remains alive; eventually bore their way out and pupate in the ground. In deci-duous woods.

Family   DOLICHOPODIDAE   Long-headed Flies

Dolichopus aeneus 6 mm. Slender legs, the hind ones being elongated. Golden-green bodies; black antennae; legs reddish-yellow; coxae and tars black; long black hairs on underside of femora; wings greyish.

Hunts other insects, mainly smaller Diptera: conspicuously active in sunshine. From May on through the summer in all damp places where trees and bushes grow.

Family   LARVAEVORIDAE (= TACHINIDAE)   Parasitic Flies

Numerous species differing in size and shape, many of them being like the house fly. Colouring mostly drab or dark with reddish spots. A minority are vivid metallic-blue or green. Characteristic of majority: shaggy appearance with a few protruding bristles on abdomen. Adults on flowers. Eggs are laid mostly on caterpillars; the larvae, when hatched, boring into the caterpillar, in which they live – parasites until full-grown, when they eat their way out through the skin, let themselves drop to the ground, pupate in litter on ground in brown barrel with distinct rings. Victims die. Tachinidae are astoundingly prolific. Useful in combatting pests.

Larvaevora (= Echinomyia) grossa Plate 14, No. 44. 1.6–1.8 cm. Glossy black body with thick bristle-like hair; head and wing roots orange. On flowers and leaves.

Larvaevora (= Echinomyia) fera Plate 14, No. 45. 7–12 mm. Fat, bristly; shaggy appearance; abdomen translucent rust-yellow with a black stripe down the middle. Antennae and legs rust-yellow. Quite common.

Family   OESTRIDAE   Parasitic Flies

GAD FLY *(Hypoderma bovis)* Plate 14, No. 46. About 1.5 cm. Flies June to July in particular. Looks like a bumble bee; mostly black, thick hair; black on 2nd and 3rd abdominal rings and yellow at tip of abdomen, otherwise white or grey-white; tibiae and tarsi yellow. Back has a few blunt lengthwise ridges. Grazing cattle try to escape it by running about wildly. Female lays sticky eggs on fore-legs and back, which the cattle lick off; hatching maggots get into gullet and stomach, pass through the animal's body to settle in the tissues of the skin on its back, causing suppurating sores (warbles), on the secretions of which they live; then, mature, work their way out, fall to the ground and become barrel-shaped pupae. Can develop in humans. Hides of affected animals are less valuable because of the holes. Fig. 58.

| Fig. 58: | Fig. 59: | Fig. 60: | Fig. 61: |
| Gadfly eggs on hair. Warble with maggot | Horse-bot fly eggs on hair. Larvae | Warble fly of deer | Bot-fly of deer |

HORSE-BOT FLY *(Gastrophilus intestinalis [= equi])* Plate 14, No. 47. Flies June to autumn. 1.3–1.7 cm. Brown-yellow, well covered with hair; large, opaque wings with brown cross-bands and patches. Abdomen and legs yellow-brown. Hovers buzzing loudly in front of horses, head towards them. Darts suddenly at them and sticks one egg on to a hair of front legs or shoulders; often laying as many as 700 over a period of hours. Eggs are licked off and so reach the mouth and stomach, where they anchor themselves to mucous membrane, often in large numbers close together. Live as parasites for 10 months, leaving the horse via its intestines and pupate in the ground. Larvae found in horse dung. Fig. 59.

Hypoderma diana Flies May to June. Rather large with front and rear of abdomen covered with white or yellow hair. Fastens eggs to hair of deer. The white maggots cause warbles and make coats look unkempt. Emerge March to April and fall to the ground, where they turn into barrel-shaped pupae in ground-litter. Fig. 60.

Hypoderma actaeon Resembles *H. diana.*

DEER-BOT FLY *(Cephenomya stimulator)* 1.3 cm. Femora yellowhaired. Hair on abdomen yellow shading into fox-red in middle and at sides. Flies often swarm round an eminence (tall tree, tower, etc.) in summer. Female squirts ready-hatched larvae into nostrils of deer, which then crawl up into throat and frontal cavity, where they grow and emerge from nostrils to pupate. Affected animals snuffle, cough, sneeze, become thin and can suffocate. Fig. 61.

Cephenomya auribarbis (= *rufibarbis*) Attacks red deer, sometimes causing death.

SHEEP-BOT FLY *(Oestrus ovis)* 1–1.2 cm; brown, almost naked; silky hairs on abdomen making it appear checkered; frons, dorsum and scutellum, covered with black warts. Flies August to September near where sheep graze; often in holes in walls, on tree trunks or walls. Female squirts eggs into nose of sheep. Maggots crawl into frontal cavity, where they anchor and feed on mucus which is secreted more copiously. When ready to pupate are sneezed out on to ground. Larvae are the cause of false staggers in sheep.

Family   TABANIDAE   Horse Flies or Clegs

THUNDER FLY *(Chrysops caecutiens)* Plate 14, No. 48. 7–9 mm. Iridescent eyes. Wings of male almost all brown, of female brown at root, front margin, tip and in the middle. Front half of abdomen bright yellow; male has orange side-spot on 2nd segment, female 2 oblique black lines; antennae, palps and legs black. Awl-shaped antennae. Visits blossom. On hot days will sting people and animals. Larvae aquatic. Common, especially in the vicinity of water.

Family   BOMBYLIIDAE   Bee Flies

Bombylius major Plate 14, No. 49. 1.2–1.6 cm. Stocky body with fur-like hair. Resembles bumble bee. Snout up to 1 cm, stuck out straight; active, jerky flight; sucks nectar as it hovers in front of flower. Black-brown body with thick yellow-brown hair; thorax and sides of belly white-haired; yellowish legs with brown tarsi. Roots and fore edge of wings brown. Larvae parasitic in other insect larvae, especially those of solitary bees. Common in summer, especially near water, on labiates, papilionaceous flowers, heartsease, etc.

*Anthrax (= *Hemiphentes*) *morio* Plate 14, No. 50. 10–14 mm. Deep black; front of thorax and base of abdomen covered with fox-red hair. Short proboscis; wings have dark root halves and clear tips. Balancers black with white tips. Lays eggs in larvae of Hymenoptera which are

ready to pupate (especially in nests of mason bees and parasitic flies). In light woods with dry soil. Hovering in air or sitting on sandy soil. Not common.

Family   ASILIDAE   Robber Flies

Asilus crabroniformis Plate 14, No. 52. 1.5–3 cm; grey-yellow with pure yellow streaks and spots on head and back, becoming yellow-brown down the femora; 3 first abdominal rings are velvet black, the last bright yellow; wings pale yellow, spotted with brown on hind margin. Sits on tree trunks, flowers or on the ground, waiting for its prey; flies up abruptly with loud buzz, keeping low over the ground, catches an insect and returns to its place. In autumn on heaths, sandy paths, fields. Eggs laid in dung.

Dioctria oelandica 1.5 cm. Narrow body, shiny black. Sides of thorax have bright yellow patches and there are similar streaks in the middle of abdomen. Long, black-brown wings. Orange legs. Sits on leaves and flowers waiting for small insects to fly past, stabs them with its sharp mouth-part and sucks them out. Larvae live in the ground, also predators.

Family   SYRPHIDAE   Hover Flies

Scaeva (= Syrphus) pyrastri Plate 14, No. 51. 1.2 cm; like wasp or bee: oval abdomen is shiny black-steel-blue with 6 bright yellow half-moon shaped patches arranged in pairs; clear wings. Flies in sunshine, hovers. Innocuous eater of pollen. Lays eggs singly on leaves inhabited by aphis. Greenish-grey grub with brown patches, lithe and stretchy; has two mouth-hooks. Moves with leech-like action, holding on with rear sucker, stretching front out gropingly, then fastening on and drawing rest of body up; seizes an aphis with mouth-hooks and sucks it out. Voracious. See p. 407.

Helophilus parallelus (= trivittatus) Plate 14, No. 53. Velvet-black with 2 light yellow lengthwise stripes. Yellow and black markings on abdomen.

Volucella bombylans Plate 14, No. 54. 1.4–1.6 cm. Resembles bumble bee *(Bombus lapidarius)*. Furry black body, fox-red at the back. Visits flowers, buzzing and moving like a bumble bee. Feeds on pollen and pollinates flowers. Lays eggs in nests of bumble bee, where larvae are parasites.

Tubifera (= Eristalis) tenax Plate 14, No. 55. 1–1.6 cm according to kind. Resembles bee. Fat body, very hairy wings, short legs and antennae; in summer and autumn often on umbellifers, especially near ponds, etc. Clear wings. Grub in muddy places, even in liquid manure. *Larvae:* see p. 441. Stagnant or sluggish water; especially sewage and slurry-pits.

Family SCATOPHAGIDAE

COMMON YELLOW DUNG FLY *(Scopeuma [= Scatophaga] stercorarium)* Plate 14, No. 56. Long oval abdomen somewhat flattened with thick yellowish coat of hair; red fore edge to wings which have a small black patch in the middle. Assemble on cow-pats. Partly a predator on other insects; as white maggot lives on excrement of humans and animals. Common.

GREY-BLACK AND SMALL FLIES

a) That do not sting

Family MUSCIDAE House Flies

COMMON HOUSE FLY *(Musca domestica)* 6–8 mm; ash-grey; abdomen indistinctly checkered black, 4 dark stripes on thorax; pale yellow belly, spherical head, 2 large compound eyes, 3 tiny simple eyes; proboscis with broad sucking surface with which it takes liquid or decomposed matter; does not sting, but pesters. Fore-wings clear; hind wings reduced to tiny balancers. 2 bolster-shaped sucker-pads between the claws of last joint of tarsi that remain moist. Female lays 120–150 white eggs, preferably on horse dung. White worm-like maggots, pointed at front end and mature in a few days. Pupae brown, hooped barrels. Several broods a year. Common.

LESSER HOUSE FLY *(Fannia canicularis)* Up to 6 mm. Grey-black thorax, male's has 3 darker, blurred stripes, abdomen dark tinged with grey, the female's being yellowish at base and has a more or less distinct black line down the back. Black legs. Does not pester. Often circles round lamp or other hanging object. Maggot has prickles; lives in rotting organic remains either in houses or in open.

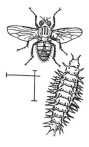

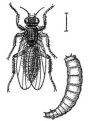

Family   PIOPHILIDAE   Cheese Skippers

Piophila casei 4–5 mm. Small, shiny black body. Lays eggs on rotting matter, also ham fat. Maggot 6 mm, white; pointed, very mobile, can leap up to 20 cm; finishes its growth in a week; small yellow barrel-pupa. Common.

Sub-Family   SARCOPHAGINAE   Flesh Flies

FLESH FLY *(Sarcophaga carnaria)* 1–1.6 cm. Brick-red eyes; large, fat sucker-pads on feet. Base whitish-grey with dark stripes; abdomen has dark and light checkering: opalescent. Viviparous, producing white maggots on fresh and rotting meat, or squirts larvae into live animals' open wounds (also of people); maggots whitish and conical. Pupae are black-brown barrels hidden away or buried close to surface of ground. In the open on carrion, dung, flowers; also in kitchens and larders.

Family   DROSOPHILIDAE   Fruit or Vinegar Flies

Drosophila funebris 3–4 mm. From late summer on, often in swarms, dancing about or settling on rotting fruit or fermenting juices. Characteristic hovering flight interrupted by sudden dropping on to some object. Brown-red head, reddish thorax, yellowish legs. Dark abdomen with yellow cross-bands, especially in female. Maggot lives on fermenting fluids and the yeast-fungi and mould developing in it. In storerooms and living-rooms: on jam, fruit-juice. Goes to excrement and can spread typhoid.

Family   CONOPIDAE   Thick-headed Flies

Myopa buccata Flies in early spring in flowering meadows. 1–1.2 cm; strikingly large head, puffed out, white jowls extending under the eyes. Female's body cylindrical, top turned downwards at the tip. Very long, thin, dog-leg proboscis. Sucks nectar in meadows; lays eggs on wasps and bumble bees; maggots rather large, white and soft, and eventually occupy the whole abdomen of their host where they pupate.

Family PHORIDAE Bee-flies

Borophaga (= Hypocera) incrassata Small, shiny black with matt grey abdomen; clear wings, pitch black legs. Bowed head. Upward curving thorax; down curving abdomen, thus appear hump-backed. Powerful legs. Elongated coxae; short stud-shaped antennae with large erect bristles on the back. Flies only short distances; runs swiftly to and fro about leaves, windows, etc. but always in a straight line. Larvae fee on putrid juices from rotting wasp and bees' nests.

Phora (= Trineura) aterrima Deep velvety-black. Front veins of clear wings show clearly. Found on rhododendron and laurel leaves. Quite common in cemeteries. Larvae often found in large numbers in coffins, when exhumations take place.

Family STRATIOMYIDAE Soldier Flies

SOLDIER FLY *(Stratiomys chamaeleon)* 1.4–1.6 cm; strikingly broad abdomen with 3 broken yellow markings. Head has thick, ledge-like jutting yellow cheeks and large eyes that, in male, are contiguous on crown of head. Fleshy proboscis with a dog-leg bend in it; drawn in when at rest. No sting; yellow scutellum with 2 spear-like spikes (hence soldier) directed obliquely backwards. Noiseless flight, but buzzes loudly if caught. Lays eggs on aquatic plants. Larvae grey earthen-brown, 12 segmented, pointed at both ends; spiracle at rear tip, hang with head under, breathing on surface of water (like larvae of gnat). Common, especially in neighbourhood of water.

Family TIPULIDAE Crane Flies

Tipula oleracea 2.2–2.6 cm. Big, long legs that easily break off ("Daddy-long-legs"). Tarsi longer than tibiae. Light streak behind fore margin of wings. Dancing, restless flight low over the ground. Female has pointed ovipositor, lays in loose earth. *Maggot:* see p. 412.

Tipula paludosa Yellowish wings with red-brown streak at rear of fore margin; otherwise as *T. oleracea.* Larvae gnaw through young grass plants. See p. 411.

b) Stinging

Family   MUSCIDAE

Sub-family   STOMOXYDINAE   Stable Flies

STABLE or BITING HOUSE FLY *(Stomoxys calcitrans)*
Roughly the size of a house fly, but its proboscis is directed
forwards, its body squatter, its wings held more open when at
rest. Both sexes suck blood of cattle and people, stabbing pain-
fully with proboscis. Development takes place particularly in
cow dung; larvae are milky-white, rounded behind, otherwise
cylindrical; often in large numbers. In summer especially in
cattle-sheds, etc.; also enters human dwellings.

Family   TABANIDAE   Clegs and Gadflies

Tabanus bovinus 2–2.4 cm; black-brown; abdominal segments
have reddish-yellow rear edges; top side of abdomen has white
triangles on it. Wings brownish-grey with yellow-brown veins.
Easy, buzzing flight; often hovers; likes sunshine. Female
attacks horses and cattle, especially on roads and pastures, inflicts painful sting and sucks blood. Male contents itself with
flower juices. Larvae have long, 11-segmented bodies; stump-
like fleshy warts help them to crawl; firm jaw-capsule with
2 hook-mandibles; predator; lives in loose, moist earth, eats
the whole inside of insect larvae. Does not propagate until the
spring.

Haematopota pluvialis 9–11 mm. Slim, dark brown with grey
spots on abdomen; wings black-grey with lighter marbling;
eyes have a purple gleam and occupy the entire head, so that
it is popularly thought to be eyeless and called "blind". Stings
cattle and humans and sucks blood, especially in hot, thundery
weather.

Chrysops caecutiens see p. 393 and Plate 14, No. 48.

Family   SIMULIIDAE   Black Flies

Simulium reptans About 2 mm. Male velvet-black; female
black-brown. Wings jut behind squat body. Torments people
and cattle, especially in spring evenings near water or in
woods; seeks out sensitive places (nostrils). Unlike other gnats
is at its most active in bright sunshine. Both sexes sting and
suck blood. *Larvae:* see p. 441.

Simulium hirtipes Small black, 2 mm. Antennae of male are long and covered with bushy hair. Closely related to midges, but sting and suck blood. Some species pester humans, their sting being very painful. Lay 3–4 cm long strings of eggs on surface of water or in small clumps on aquatic plants.

Family   CULICIDAE   Mosquitos, Gnats

Culex pipiens Male 5 mm; female 6 mm. One pair of narrow membranous wings. Slender body. Hind wings reduced to balancers. Long, thin legs. Long antennae, those of male having a long bristle-agitator. Long stinging proboscis. Dance in air near water on summer evenings, especially at some vantage point. Large swarms composed entirely of males, ascending and descending while softly buzzing. Swarm moves together as if at a word of command, sometimes also sideways. Females mostly sit still on undersides of leaves. Individual females that enter swarm are mated on surface of shallow, stagnant water and lay eggs in raft-like formation of 200–300 which then drift away. Common, especially in low country with marshy areas or much stagnant water. Usually only the females sting and suck blood, mainly of birds not mammals. The males live on plant juices. The female injects saliva into sting-wound preventing the blood coagulating and then sucks. *Larvae:* see p. 440.

Theobaldia annulata Dark brown and white rings on legs. Wings have 3–5 brown spots.

MALARIAL MOSQUITO *(Anopheles)* Deceptively like *Culex pipiens,* but holds its body tilted downwards in front, when at rest, while the latter holds its body parallel to what it is standing on. Not uncommon in marshy areas. In the South can transmit malaria.

Chaoborus crystallinus (= Corethra plumicornis) Flies May. 6 mm. In both sexes the stinging proboscis is short, only slightly longer than its head, weak and not suited for sucking blood. Identifiable by the way hair grows on it. Thorax dark grey on top with white side stripes. No spots on wings. *Larvae:* see p. 440.

SWARMING GNATS

Family   EMPIDIDAE

Small flies, the male of which flies in circling, dancing swarms low over water or in clearing and rides in woods as evening falls in spring and summer, while females sit on leaves nearby. Most species catch smaller insects on the wing and suck them out; others visit flowers or sting plants and suck juices. Larvae live in the ground, under bark or moss, feeding on tiny creatures.

Empis tesselata 4–5 mm; slender, long-legged, brownish-grey. 3 black stripes on upper side of thorax; shimmering lighter checks on abdomen; wings light brown and almost clear with brown line round rim and yellow roots. Male has cylindrical abdomen ending in a thickened clasping apparatus. Females live on plant juices and dance in sunshine. Males bring captured insects to eat in nuptial banquet. Often on umbellifers.

Family   CHIRONOMIDAE   Non-biting Midges

Closely related to the mosquitoes and in appearance very similar to them. Delicate, long-legged, only one pair of wings. Do not sting or suck blood. Form immense swarms flying up and down in pillar-like formation, often being mistaken for smoke. As well as the huge swarms of males, occasional smaller swarms of females. Each swarm produces a note, the pitch of which depends on the size and species of midge. The individual has the strange practice, when at rest, of raising its fore-legs and holding them out in front like antennae, and continually twitching them. When folded, wings are laid roof-like over the abdomen. Antennae of male have bushy hair; those of female are bristle-shaped. Vestigial stinging-proboscis. Larvae on stagnant or sluggish water in upper layer of mud. Eggs laid together in jelly-like lumps which the female drops into the water. Pupae very similar to those of mosquito. *Larvae:* see p. 441.

Chironomus plumosus Flies March and May to June. 10–12 mm. Middle of body light yellowish or greenish with 3 grey stripes. Milk-white wings with a black dot near the middle of the fore edge. Antennae of male brown with lighter edges to rings. Legs light rust colour. Large numbers in and on ponds, etc.

Family   Bibionidae

Bibio hortulanus Flies April to May. 8–10 mm; male has white hair on the side and the back of body. Thorax and abdomen of female yellow-red. Legs blackish. Hover in swarms. When in flight, hind legs hang down low. Eggs laid in humus or fresh stable manure. *Larvae:* see p. 412. Gardeners' and farmers' pest.

ST MARK'S FLY *(Bibio marci)* Flies end of March to April. 1.1–1.3 cm. Shiny black with black hairs. Larvae 2–2.6 cm; otherwise as *B. hortulanus.*

INSECT LARVAE

Leaf and Needle-eating Caterpillars and Pseudo-caterpillars

(Free-ranging)

The caterpillars of butterflies mostly have 3 pairs of thoracic legs and, in addition, 4 pairs of abdominal legs, or pro-legs, and 1 pair of claspers. Many of the owlet moths lack the first two pairs of pro-legs. All loopers have only 1 pair of pro-legs and 1 pair of claspers, hence their "looping" method of progression.

Most pseudo-caterpillars of sawflies have 3 pairs of thoracic legs and 8 pairs of pro-legs; thus normally 11 pairs of feet.

Characteristic Caterpillar-shapes of Various Butterfly Families

A. Caterpillars of the Day-fliers

Family Papilionidae (Swallow-tails): V-shaped fleshy organ they can protrude from a fold in the ring nearest the head.

Family Satyridae (Browns): spindle-shape; 2 spikes on end of tail instead of caudal disc. Lives among grasses.

Family Nymphalidae (Fritillaries): either slug-shaped with 2 horns on head (Plate 11, No. 10) or has spikes and fleshy "plugs" (Plate 11, No. 19); the others have rows of dorsal spikes branched and bristly.

Family Lycaenidae (Blues): shape of a wood louse or of a snail; short legs.

B. Caterpillars of Evening and Night-fliers

Family Sphingidae (Hawk-moths): horn on rear end of body (Plate 11).

Family Notodontidae (Prominents): smooth or scarcely haired; in many the final segment has been adapted; no caudal disc; 2 prongs at rear end or 2 humps. (Plate 10, Nos. 11 and 12). Mostly on poplar, willow and deciduous trees.

Family Lymantriidae (Tussock-moths): have 16 legs; mostly fat and sluggish; star-shaped having big warts or colourful, bushy tufts on back. (Plate 10, No. 19.)

Family Lasiocampidae (Lackeys and Eggars): large, soft; with thick, short hair and side-tufts; often have vividly-coloured cross-bands. Mostly on deciduous and conifer trees. Plate 10, No. 23.

Family Arctiidae (Tiger Moths): short, fat; warts with tufts; quick-walkers. Plate 10, No. 25.

Family Zygaenidae (Burnets and Foresters): short, squat, colourful, short haired. Especially on papilionaceous plants. Plate 10, No. 36.

Family Psychidae (Bagworm Moths): spin their own protective "sacks", open at both ends, covered on outside with particles of plant or grains of sand. Picture on p. 352.

Family Sesiidae (Clearwings): naked smooth body; gnaws galleries in plants. Picture on p. 361.

Family Cossidae (Goat Moths): bare body; eats galleries in plants. Picture on p. 351.

Family Hepialidae (Ghosts): as foregoing. Picture on p. 339.

Family Noctuidae (Owlets): mostly bare; 16-, 14-, or 12-legged; wave-shaped or looper-like gait. Those that stay concealed by day and feed at night are sombre-coloured; those that feed by day vividly coloured, but colouring is adapted to that of plant they feed on. Plate 10, No. 27–31.

Family Geometridae (Geometers): bare; only 1 pair of pro-legs and 1 pair of claspers, hence looping movement. At rest most are rigid, often stretch out at an angle. Plate 10, Nos. 32–35.

Caterpillars of the small butterflies (Families: Leaf-rollers, Clothes Moths, etc.) have 14 legs; most do not live free on food plants, but excavate or construct web-nests. Dangerous pests. Pp. 414–416, 419–421, 422–425.

IDENTIFICATION OF CATERPILLARS

Of butterfly: see Plates 10 and 11, also p. 316–360, 414–417, 420–422, 436–437, 472.

Of pseudo-caterpillars of sawflies (pp. 379–381).

*BROAD-FOOTED BEECH SAWFLY *(Craesus septentrionalis)* Larva greenish, yellow at either end; head black; 2 lengthwise rows of black spots on back. 1 lengthwise row of black ventral spots. One behind the other on edge of leaf, often with abdomen raised up and looking like a question mark. Eats leaf up to middle rib. Sawfly, see p. 379.

BIRCH SAWFLY *(Cimbex femorata)* 22 legs; green; yellowish stripe on head, and a dark one down the middle of back; sluggish; when threatened, rolls up into saucer-shape and squirts aggressor with greenish or light blood out of side spiracles. Feeds mainly at night on birch leaves, astride edge of leaf; spins oval, firm, dark brown cocoon which is cemented to twig and there passes the winter. Cocoon has circular lid, which the emerging sawfly bursts open. Sawfly, see p. 379.

ROSE SAWFLY *(Arge rosae)* 1.5—2 cm, bluish-green or yellowish with black head; eats leaves from edge in; voracious. 2nd brood end July, early August, the larvae of which hibernate in cocoons. Sawfly, see p. 380.

YELLOW GOOSEBERRY SAWFLY *(Pteronidea ribesii)* 1.6 cm. Black head; light green body with black hairy warts. Feeds on leaves starting well within the bush. Up to 5 broods a year. Pupae hibernate in ground. On gooseberry and red currant bushes throughout the summer. Sawfly, see p. 381.

PEAR SAWFLY *(Eriocampoides limacina)* 1 cm. June to July and August to September. Slug-like appearance; yellowish, covered with black slime; has 20 feet; feeds on top of leaves leaving only underskin of leaf between the veining. Hibernates in cocoon in ground. On stone-fruit (cherry), pear, hawthorn, rose, quince, birch, oak, beech. Sawfly, see p. 381.

RING-FOOT SAWFLY *(Eriocampoides annulipes)* Dirty light green: sometimes on limes in great numbers; also on birch, oak and willow. Sawfly, see p. 381.

PEAR SAWFLY *(Neurotoma saltuum [= flaviventris])* June to April. 2 cm; yellowish, shiny, light and dark lenghtwise stripes, black head; 6-legged; common web-nest soon fouled by excrement; eats leaves from edge inward. Early August descends on threads to ground and there hibernates in cocoons. On pear and plum trees, hawthorn, medlar. Sawfly, see p. 381.

PINE SAWFLY *(Diprion pini)* 22 legs, resembles butterfly's caterpillar with its green or brown-yellow basic colour and black markings; live in colonies, often resting in a pile; when disturbed assumes S-shaped defensive posture, swaying body violently up and back; eats pine-needles to middle-rib; several moults; spins long, brown cocoon, which it cements to needles at end of June. Sawfly hatches end July, bursting open round lid of cocoon; lays eggs and new brood of larvae start eating more leaves. Cocoons remain hidden in ground during the winter. Often mass appearance in the autumn. Sawfly, see p. 380.

*PINE WEB SAWFLY *(Pamphilius stellatus)* Olive-green to yellow, with red-brown stripes and dark spots on head; June to August first on new growth, then on older needles, eating up towards the tip; age-old trees often stripped; among twigs large numbers of web-sacks with quantities of red excrement in them. In August larvae fall to ground, where they dig themselves chambers in the earth where they hibernate for 2 or 3 winters, pupating usually in their third year. Mostly in old woods. Sawfly, see p. 381.

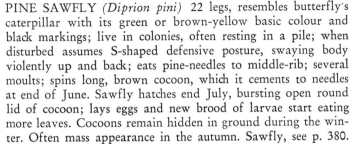

FRASS-SACK PINE SAWFLY Feeds mostly on young pine trees (3–4 years old); dirty-green; hangs individually in large web-sack, the bottom of which is at first covered with frass (excrement); eats its way up new growth; July to August takes to the ground.

*FIR WEB SAWFLY *(Pamphilius hypotrophicus)* Colouring varies: at first mostly grass-green with dark head, later becomes lighter and acquires a distinct X-shaped mark on brow. Feeds June to July towards point. Makes communal nest about the size of a hen's egg which contains a quantity of excrement. Larvae have individual web-cylinders inside the communal web-nest. In August larvae burrow up to 30 cm into ground. Generation takes 1–3 years; larvae spending 2 years in ground without pupating.

FREE-RANGING 6-LEGGED LARVAE ON PLANTS AND ON THE GROUND

Exception: Halfmoon Hoverfly legless (= maggot) p. 407.

a) 6-legged Leaf-eaters

Family   CARABIDAE   Tiger Ground Beetles

Larva of *Zabrus tenebrioides* 2–2.5 cm; elongated, flattened appearance; black-brown head; very light-shy; feeds on leaves of young corn, sucking out the juice. Beetle: see p. 285.

Family   CHRYSOMELIDAE   Leaf Beetles

Larvae live on leaves; most are vividly coloured and have warts, 3 pairs of powerful legs. Most have spear-shaped bodies strongly arched on top, small heads, antennae 3-jointed and small; eye-spots on either side; rather weak upper jaw. Strip leaves to a skeleton (the beetle makes holes). Many of the larvae mine.

*Larva of RED POPLAR LEAF BEETLE *(Chrysomela populi)* Up to 1.4 cm, tapered at either end; whitish with a black head, black lines and shiny black shields and warts in regular pattern. The warts on the abdominal segments have glandular tubes that can be protruded to excrete acrid smelling fluid. Pupa fastened to leaf by its rear end. Beetle: see p. 278.

*Larva of *Chrysomela tremulae* Dirty-white; head, neck-plate, legs, several rows of dots and the hairy warts are all glossy black. When disturbed secretes from wart of its back large drops of fluid with an unpleasant smell to repel enemies. Beetle: see p. 278.

Larva of *Phyllodecta vitellinae* Follows the sawfly pattern with 8 rows of black protruberances down the back. Basic colour a dull white; blackish down the middle of the upper side. See beetle on p. 278.

Larva of *Lochmaea capreae* Similar to *C. tremulae,* only smaller and has somewhat shorter legs; the warts are further apart as are the back plates which are also smaller.

Larva of COLORADO BEETLE *(Leptinotarsa decemlineata)* Up to 1 cm; fat, shiny reddish-yellow with black side spots. Head and legs black. Eats leaves of potato. Pupates in ground. Beetle: see p. 278.

Larva of ASPARAGUS BEETLE *(Crioceris asparagi)* Up to 8 mm; plump, grey-green, smeared with excrement. Black head. 1st generation May to June; 2nd generation August to September. Strips leaves of asparagus, weakening plants. Beetle: see p. 279.

*Larva of *Crioceris duodecimpunctata* Up to 8 mm, plump, yellowish to brownish, smeared with excrement. Yellow head. 1st generation May to June; 2nd generation July to August. Larvae of 2nd generation feed on asparagus berries. Pupate in ground. Beetle: see p. 279.

*Larva of *Lilioceris merdigera* 6–8 mm; dirty yellow, covered with slimy excrement. Beetle: see p. 279.

Larva of MUSTARD BEETLE *(Phaedon cochleariae)* Up to 6.6 mm; brownish-yellow, black head with 1 row of brown warts along each side of back. Eats holes in leaves of horseradish, mustard, cress, cabbage. Several broods. Pupates in ground. Beetle: see p. 280.

Psylliodes chrysocephala 4.5 mm; black to blue-green, shiny. Larva 6.7 mm, whitish; head and caudal disc dark brown; dark hairy warts on body rings. Eats leaf stalks and stems. Beetle eats holes in leaves of radish, cabbage, turnip, etc. Very harmful to rape.

Family   SILPHIDAE   Burying and Carrion Beetles

Aclypea (= Blitophaga) opaca   Beetle 9–12 mm; flat; dark brown with close golden-brown hair; outer rib of wing-case very raised with big lump at end. Larvae 1.5–1.8 cm. Shiny black with yellow side edges. Eats edges and holes in leaves of beetroot, mangold, etc. Beetle: see p. 286.

b) Destroy greenfly on leaves and delicate shoots

Larva of SEVEN-SPOT LADYBIRD *(Coccinella septempunctata)* 6 legs. Back covered with spikes and prongs. At first is all black, then becomes bluish slate-grey; line of delicate rib dots on back and the red sides to 1st, 4th and 7th segments. Very active. Lives free on plants, destroying numbers of greenfly; often in large numbers. To pupate fastens itself with tailhook. Beetle: see p. 271.

Larva of GREEN LACEWING *(Chrysopa perla)* Brownish, spotted, with big head; mouth-organs adapted as powerful pointed sucking-pincers with which it sucks out plant-lice, also millipedes, larvae of flea-beetles, shield-lice and small caterpillars. Pupates in cocoon the size of a pea fastened to a leaf or twig. Lacewings emerge and spend winter dormant. Often has a covering of skins of plant lice it has eaten.

Larva of HALF-MOON HOVER FLY *(Scaeva [= Syrphus] pyrastri)* Greenish-grey maggot with brown spots, agile and elastic, has two mouth-hooks as pointed fore-end; no feet. Moves like leech, holding on with hind fleshy warts groping forwards with front part, then taking hold with it and drawing up rest of body; impales greenfly on mouth-hooks and sucks them out. Voracious and useful. Common. Picture shows larva with captured greenfly. Hover flies: see p. 394.

c) In flowers lying in wait for bees

Larva of *Melöe proscarabaeus* Long, slim, 6-legged, each ending in 3 claws of which the middle one is longest; several bristles at end of abdomen. 1 eye and 1 multi-jointed antenna on each side of head. Lives on the white and yellow blossom of anemones, ranunculus, etc.; clutches hold of the hairy coat of a furry bee, allows itself to be carried to its nest. There leaps onto

bee's eggs and allows itself to be enclosed in a nest-cell, where it soon moults and is transformed into a soft-skinned larva like a cockchafer grub, which eats honey, then moves outside, turns itself into a pseudo-pupa that remains in its split larval skin, which becomes crumpled, and takes no more nourishment; after further moults becomes a true pupa. Beetle: see p. 272.

d) Hunting small creatures on tree-trunks on ground

Larva of GROUND BEETLE *(Calosoma sycophanta)* Lengthy body, rather broad in the middle, tapering at either end; deep black, 3 pairs of rather short legs. Rings of abdomen twice as broad as they are long, strongly up-turned at sides. Back-plates quite horny and black, with sharp margins. Appendages of last (9th) ring rather short, up-turned. Upper jaw pincers closed in front; small mouth-opening only for sucking. Antennae shorter than upper jaw (mandible), 6 simple eyes on either side of head. Agile runner and climber; hunts caterpillars and pupae. Often on trees in woods. Beetle: see p. 265.

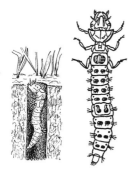

Larva of TIGER BEETLE *(Cicindela campestris)* Long body; head and thorax well-developed, dark metallic sheen. On each side of head 4 simple eyes; large pincer-shaped jaws. Back-plates on abdomen retrogressive. 5th abdominal ring has 2 powerful hooks mounted on protruberances and directed forward, used for maintaining position in its living hole, and almost vertical shaft dug up to 40 cm deep and the width of a quill. Larva lurks in mouth of this waiting for insects. Pupates in high summer or autumn at bottom of this shaft. Dry, sandy places. Larvae of other members of this family have same structure and habits. Beetle: see p. 267.

Larva of *Thanasimus formicarius* Long, rose-red body; short but powerful and sharp upper jaw. Short legs. Predator. Forces its way into galleries of the wood-boring beetles, *Blastophagus piniperda* and *Ips typographus*, consuming their larvae and pupae. Beetle: see p. 269.

Larva of CARDINAL BEETLE *(Pyrochroa coccinea)* Elongated, flat, brown body with 6 legs; large head with short antennae; last abdominal ring elongated into 2 large spikes used for holding on and pushing. Feeds on larvae of noxious wood-beetles. Found in large numbers under bark of dead trees, in old stumps. Beetle: see p. 272.

Larva of *Cantharis fusca* Longish, fat, cylindrical body with 6 short legs. Fine velvety hair. Dark colouring, often with red or white spots and legs. Powerful biting mouth-parts; 1 large simple eye on each side of head. Lives concealed in ground; during winter under leaves and stones. Digs deep gallery in earth, where it also hibernates, closing entrance with stones. Consumes plant lice, small caterpillars, etc. Emerges occasionally during winter, especially during a thaw, and crawls about the snow in large numbers. Beetle: see p. 270.

Larva of GLOW-WORM *(Lampyris noctiluca)* 2–2.3 cm when full-grown; same width throughout, longish; male black on top, lighter underneath; 1 orange spot in the hind corner of each abdominal ring. 3 pairs of fairly short legs. Jaws curved like sickle, pointed, with fine hollow canal, down which paralysing fluid flows into wound and decomposes prey (small snails). Beetle: see p. 287.

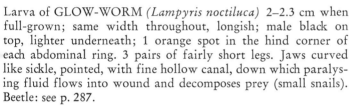

Larva of SNAKEFLY *(Raphidia ophiopsis)* 1.2–1.4 cm; long, thin and flat; 1st thoracic segment elongated; strong legs that enable it to run quickly backwards and forwards. Voracious predator, like the imago, feeding on insects, then larvae, pupae and eggs. Penetrates into feeding-galleries of *Ips typhographus;* hibernates in crevices. Pupae like larvae, very mobile, run almost as fast, backwards and forwards. Snakefly: see p. 386.

*Larva of ANT-LION *(Myrmeleon formicarius)* 1.2 cm, 5 mm broad; brownish, squat, very hairy head with powerful pincer jaws; first thoracic segment constricted like a neck. Predator. Makes traps on sunny places on edge of woods, where ants are, digging little craters in loose, sandy soil; many only a few mm across, others up to 8 cm wide and 5 cm deep. Ants slide on loose sand into these holes; the ant-lion emerges and with swift movements of head spatters sand over the escaping ant, making it slip back, kills it and sucks it with its hollow pincer jaws. See p. 385.

LARVAE LIVING UNDERGROUND

a) Root-eaters

Larva of COCKCHAFER *(Melolontha melolontha)* Up to 5 cm. Fat, soft-skinned, whitish, curled-up body; last abdominal segment swollen like a full sack. Red-brown, roundish, horny head; 4-jointed antennae. Strong mandible with oblique sheath. 3 pairs of well-developed legs, 2nd pair longer than first, third pair longer still. 9 pairs of spiracles: one on the side of the thorax, and one on each of the first 8 abdominal rings. Each segment has a row of long hairs across the back; rings 1–6 covered with thick, tiny prickles; the last ring with hair and bristles. Feeds on the delicate rootlets and root-bark of most cultivated plants. Pupates in August of its 3rd year in a small, smoothed-out hole in the ground. Takes usually 4, in the South 3, years to develop. Beetle: see p. 290.

Larva of ROSE CHAFER *(Cetonia aurata)* Up to 3.6 cm, often confused with the foregoing, but body is shorter, squatter and less curved, while last segment is much fatter and more swollen; legs are much shorter and weaker; head smaller; antennae smaller and thicker, without appendage on penultimate joint. Hair longer and thicker on the underneath; hair on back reddish. First thoracic ring has a distinct horn-plate on each side. Feeds on compost, occasionally roots. Beetle: see p. 273.

Larva of *Amphimallon solstitialis* Up to 3 cm. Resembles and often taken for young cockchafer larvae. Feeds on roots of grass and on freshly planted young pine trees. Beetle: see p. 273.

Larva of GARDEN CHAFER *(Phyllopertha horticola)* Up to 2 cm like cockchafer larva; feeds on roots of grasses, cabbage, conifers, roses. Beetle: see p. 273.

*Larva of *Polyphylla fullo* Up to 8 cm. Very like cockchafer larva. Feeds on roots of young pine trees, also of birch and dune-grasses. Beetle: see p. 273.

Larva of DUNG BEETLE *(Geotrupes stercorosus)* Often confused with cockchafer larva, but has very short antennae, and last pair of legs very reduced. Very sparse hair. Prickles on back of abdominal rings not strong. Feeds on "broad-pills" of dung. Does not eat roots, but improves the soil. Beetle: see p. 290.

Larva of WEEVILS Characteristics: no legs; slightly curled inwards, mostly colourless, soft, bare or with only few hairs; head strongly chitinised. Powerful mandible.

*Larva of *Otiorrhynchus niger* Up to 1.2 cm long and 4.5 mm thick; wedge-shaped pads across back which are used to move it along. Brown-yellow hairs. Takes 3 years to develop. Feeds on roots mostly of young firs and pines in nurseries, causing the needles to go yellow, then red. With roots eaten away, the young tree can be drawn easily out of the ground. Beetle: see p. 294.

Larva of *Hylobius abietis* Eat up roots of pine trees, etc.; first to the inner bark, then deeper. A root attacked by larvae is left looking like a grooved pillar, the grooves often full of dust. Not so harmful as the beetle: see p. 284.

*Larva of *Cneorrhinus plagiatus* Eats the roots in pine nurseries. Beetle: see p. 294.

*Larva of *Brachyderes incanus* May to June eats rootlets of young pines and firs, killing them. Beetle: see p. 284.

Larva of WIREWORMS *(Agriotes)* Some 2–3 cm; long, round, yellow-brown, tough-skinned due to smooth, hard chitin armour; 3 pairs of short legs. Heads have 2 simple eyes; 2 short 3-jointed antennae; mouth-parts for biting. Live concealed in ground, humus; others as miners in live plants. Eat the filament roots of grasses and corn, get into the main root of lettuce and other garden plants and into tubers. Hibernate 2–3 times. Pupate in ground. Beetle: see p. 287.

*Cutworm of *Agrotis segetum* Plate 10, No. 27 and p. 353.

*Cutworm of *Agrotis tritici* As the foregoing.

Larva of DADDY-LONG-LEGS *(Tipula paludosa)* Up to 4 cm; earth-colour, cylindrical, fat, has a head; rear end has fleshy pointed structures. Feeds by day on roots, tubers, by night on parts of plant that are above ground. Very harmful to young cabbages, peas, beans, lettuce, also grasses, etc. Adult: see p. 397.

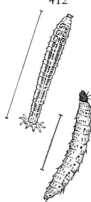

Grub of *Tipula oleracea* 3.5–4 cm; Cylindrical, ash-grey. Feeds as T. *paludosa*. Adult: see p. 397.

Grub of fly *Bibio hortulanus* Up to 1.5 cm. No legs. Head almost black with a grey-brown gloss. Leathery, wrinkled, granulated skin, with a fleshy spike on each ring. Hibernates, doing most of its harm in the spring, when it eats the soft rootlets of vegetables, flowers and lawn-grass. Common in hotbeds. Pupates in May in ground. Adult: see p. 401.

Grub of ST MARK'S FLY *(Bibio marci)* Appearance and damage similar to that of the foregoing. Adult: see p. 401.

b) Larvae that mine in roots, tubers, bulbs, rape

GHOST MOTH *(Hepialus humuli)* In ground, August to May, up to 5 cm; yellowish with a few black hairs; brown head. Gnaws galleries in roots of hops, sorrel, nettles, carrots, etc.; hibernates. Pupates in the ground in tubular cocoon. Pupa brown with striking short wing-cases. Abdominal rings rimmed with prickles. Very active. Adult: see p. 339.

Root-gall of *Ceuthorhynchus pleurostigma* Beetle 2.3–3.2 mm; black with fine, grey-white hair. In spring lays eggs in holes bored in roots of cabbage, radish and other cruciferous plants. Larvae 5 mm; yellow-white; eat tissue; morbid growth round larvae, size of a pea, gall. (Plate 15.) Pupates in ground. Beetle hatches and produces 2nd generation, which passes winter in gall. On cruciferous plants, especially *Brassicae;* common.

Larva of WIREWORMS *(Agriotes)* See p. 411.

Family   PSILIDAE   Carrot Rust Flies, etc.

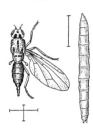

CARROT FLY *(Psila rosae)* Flies May to July and August to September. 4–5 mm; shiny black; brown head, yellowish legs. Eggs in roots of carrots or in ground near the plant. Several broods. Pupa hibernates in ground. Whitish larva, without head or feet, 6–8 mm long, makes brown galleries in carrots just below the surface of the ground.

Family   MUSCIDAE

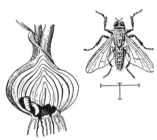

ONION FLY *(Delia cepetorum [= Phorbia antiqua])* Flies May and July; 6–7 mm long, blackish, thickly dusted with grey; black legs. Lays eggs singly on leaf. Larvae May to June, 6–8 mm, whitish, without head or legs. Causes leaf-bud to wither and white grubs can be seen eating at bottom of bulb.

CABBAGE ROOT FLY *(Erioischia [= Chortophila] brassicae)* Fly 6 mm; grey with red brow-spot. Male has 3 dark stripes on thorax, and on abdomen narrow dark cross-bands and 1 dark lengthwise stripe. Lays eggs at neck of root. Larvae up to 8 mm; shiny, white, May to June; July; September. First eat delicate rootlets, then penetrate inside root, causing the cabbage to become leaden in colour and remain small, while leaves wither; finally plant dies, the side roots having been eaten. On cruciferous plants, cultivated plants of cabbage family, rape, radish. Pupae remain in ground over winter or in cabbage stalk.

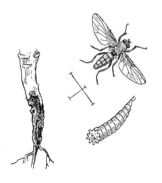

Erioischia (= Chortophila) floralis Larva and fly similar to foregoing, but larger. In July larvae gnaw galleries in bulb of radish.

Egle (= Anthomyia) radicum Whitish larva with black granulation. Lives like the two foregoing. Pupa and adult hibernate.

FEEDING AND MINING LARVAE IN BLOSSOM, FRUIT,
SEEDS, FUNGI

Family   CURCULIONIDAE   Weevils

Larva of APPLE BLOSSOM WEEVIL *(Anthonomus pomorum)*
Up to 7 mm; yellowish-white with reddish tinge; dark head;
legless. Eats into flower-buds, pistils, stamens; gnaws into base
of petals, so that bud does not open but turns brown, appearing
scorched. Fruit does not set. Adult: see p. 283.

Larva of *Rhyncites bacchus* Up to 9 mm; white to yellowish;
brown head. May to July. Gnaws galleries in flesh of young
apples, destroying most of core. Walls of galleries often felty
white. Fruit falls prematurely. Pupates in ground.

Rhynchites cupreus Larva up to 6.5 mm, whitish with brown
head and no legs. Adult lays eggs on young fruit and nicks the
stalk. Hatched larva bores near base of fallen fruit, eats the
flesh, but does not harm the kernel. Pupates in ground. Adult:
see p. 282.

Family   BYTURIDAE

RASPBERRY BEETLE *(Byturus fumatus)* Larva 6 mm; yellowish with dark brown stripes; short hair, 6 legs, with 2 little
hooks at rear. Eats into fruit of raspberry. Pupates in whitish
web in cracks in post, etc. or in ground. Beetle 4–5 mm, lives
on blossom, hollows out buds of raspberry and bramble.

Family   TORTICIDAE   Leaf-rollers

Ernarmonia (= Carpocapsa) pomonella Flies May to July;
span about 1.6 cm. Fore-wings grey-blue with lighter cross-lines
on base and in the middle. Hind wings simple grey-brown.
Rests by day, flies in twilight. Lives only a few days, laying

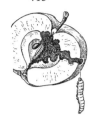

20–80 eggs singly on young fruit. Larva, up to 2 cm, at first whitish with black dots, then reddish; brown head. Bores from calyx to core, eats the pips and tunnels its way out. Excrement hangs from opening in the "worm-eaten" fruit. In July lets itself down fruit (still on tree) on silk and pupates throughout winter under bark or in the ground. In a hot summer there can be a 2nd generations also laying eggs in August. Larvae in stored fruit pupate in cracks. On apple, pear, quince, apricot, cherry, plum.

Ernarmonia (= Laspeyresia = Grapholitha) funebrana Flies June to July; span 1.5 cm. Fore-wings dark grey-brown; hind wings lighter. Lays eggs on ripening plums. Larva July to October up to 1 cm, reddish; dark brown head. Damage and excrement on stone, while outside of fruit discoloured. Larva spends winter in web under bark or on ground. Pupates in the spring. Especially on plums and damsons.

Clysiana (= Clysia) ambiguella Flies May and July; span 1.2–1.3 cm. Fore-wings yellowish with broad, brown cross-bands hind wings grey-brown. Eggs on flower buds of vine (May); larva up to 1.2 cm; grey-green to red-brown with rows of brown warts; head and neck-plate glossy brown-black. Sits by day in tubular web, by night feeds on buds, stamen and fruit-bud. Pupates in inflorescence. Adult of 2nd generation emerges in July, lays eggs on unripe fruit which, once gnawed, remains sour. Pupa brown, in whitish cocoon often in crack in vine bark or in split in post.

Polychrosis botrana Mostly 2 broods. Span 1.1–1.2 cm. Fore-wings yellow-brown with irregular grey and dark spots and bars. Hind wings grey. Caterpillar green-yellow; yellow head and neck-plate. Lives as foregoing.

Sparganothis pilleriana Flies July to August. Span 2–2.4 cm. Fore-wings yellow or greenish or bronze. 2 brown cross-bands and margin, but many specimens lack these markings. Eggs on topside of vine leaves; larva up to 2.5 cm; greenish or grey-white; head and neck-plate black or black-brown; moves swiftly in jerks. Damages green grapes and leaves, which are wound round with silk, curled up and brown. Spends winter in cocoon in some concealed place; pupates between shrivelled leaves. Causes damage in spring.

Ernarmonia (= Laspeyresia) dorsana Flies May to June. Span 1.8 cm. Fore-wings dark olive-brown, 1 white half-moon on rear margin. Lays eggs singly on young pea-pods. Larva up to 1.4 cm, orange; head brown to black. June to September in pod, eating peas. Hibernates in web on ground. Pupates in spring.

Ernarmonia (= Laspeyresia) nigricana Flies May to June. Span 1.2–1.6 cm, dark, also light olive-brown; margins dusted with ochre; mirror slightly lighter; leaden grey set with 4 black spots. Caterpillar whitish with dark dots; head light-brown. Does same damage as *L. dorsana.*

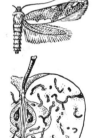

Family   YPONOMEUTIDAE   Ghosts

COMMON ROWAN-BERRY ARGENT *(Argyresthia con-jugella)* Flies May to July. Span 1.4 cm. Fore-wings yellow-grey with violet sheen; wide rear margin, white or yellow; oblique brown band. Lays eggs in young fruit. Caterpillar up to 7 mm, reddish. Brown head. June to September. Feeding leaves narrow, winding galleries in flesh of fruit, later fine holes in skin, where it has bored its way out. Pupa spends winter in web on ground or on bark. On apple, rowan, sometimes pear.

BRINDLED ARGENT *(Argyresthia cornella)* Caterpillar 6 mm, white to reddish; brown head. April to May. Eats inside flower-buds. Pupates in ground.

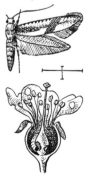

BLOTCHED ARGENT *(Argyresthia pruniella)* Flies June to September. Span 1.2 cm. Wings red-brown with long fringes. Fore-wings have dark oblique bands and white near margin. Abdomen and hind legs stretched obliquely upwards when at rest. Egg on bark, bud-scales during winter. Caterpillar up to 6 mm. Greenish to bluish. Head, neck and abdominal plates light brown. April to May on cherry, plum, apple, pear, haw-thorn. Eats stamens, seed-buds of several kinds of blossom. *Traces:* eaten-out calyx with excrement covered with web. Pupates in cocoon in ground.

Family   PLUTELLIDAE

GREY AND DIAMOND-BACKED SMUDGE *(Plutella maculipennis)* Flies May and July to August. Span 1.6 cm. Forewings grey to dark brown; light yellow, wavy stripe on rear margin. Lays eggs on leaves. Caterpillar up to 10 mm; at first yellowish, later green; head black; slightly hairy. Mines first in leaves of cabbage, lettuce, etc. then eats holes and even strips; also on cauliflower. June; July to August; August to September. Pupa hibernates in web-like cocoon on leaf.

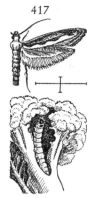

Family   TENTHREDINIDAE   Larger Sawflies

APPLE SAWFLY *(Hoplocampa testudinea)* Flies May; 6–7 mm; black-brown on top; yellow underneath; 4 clear wings with dark veining. Females cuts with "saw" into calyx of apple-blossom and introduces one egg. *Larva:* May-March, 1 cm, whitish brown head, 10 pairs of legs and smells of bed-bug (that of the apple leaf roller is reddish, has 16 feet and no smell). Destroys 4–5 fruits, causing them to fall off when the size of a walnut with a large hole full of excrement. Entrance holes remain open.

PEAR SAWFLY *(Hoplocampa brevis)* Attacks pears in the same way as *H. testudinea* attacks apples. 1 larva destroys 3–5 fruits, which turn brown and fall off.

*Hoplocampa minuta Flies May to June. 5 mm, shiny black with small yellowish hairs on head and thorax. Antennae and legs reddish brown-yellow; 4 clear wings. Egg in point of calyx of blossom. Larva May to July, 1 cm; yellowish; brown head; 10 pairs of legs, smells like a bed-bug; destroys several fruits one after another, spends winter in the ground. Pupates in March. Signs of presence: unripe plums acquire premature blue-tinge, have hole in skin and are hollow inside; always small beads of resin or lumps of excrement thrown out.

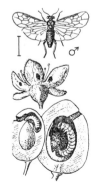

Hoplocampa flava Yellow-brown sawfly, otherwise similar to foregoing.

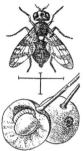

Family   TRYPETIDAE

Rhagoletis cerasi Flies May to July. 6 mm. Shiny black; yellow plate; yellow markings on front of thorax; yellow legs; clear wings with 3 brown cross-bands. Lays eggs singly where stalk enters cherry as it begins to turn colour; a yellowish-white, legless maggot hatches and bores into the fruit, eating its flesh, establishing itself between the stone and stalk; becomes up to 1 cm long; turns in the ground into a sulphur-yellow, barrel-shaped pupa that hibernates. Maggot lives in fruit of cherry and honeysuckle.

Ceratitis capitata 5 mm; head bright yellow to orange; thorax black with stripe of short grey hair; abdomen orange; eyes blue-green; brown-yellow cross-bars on wings and blackish streaks and dots. Eggs in flesh of fruit. Larva 8 mm, whitish, no head or legs. Pupates in ground. Recently introduced from citrus fruits. Attacks peaches.

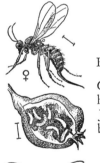

Family   CECIDOMYIIDAE   Gall Midges

Contarinia pyrivora Larva 4 mm, white to yellowish, no legs or head. Several in each young fruit which is made to bulge. From July larvae in ground; pupae hibernate. *Adult:* 3 mm, dark brown, clear wings; flies April to May. Lays eggs in flower bud.

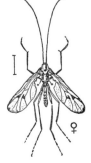

Family   MYCETOPHILIDAE   Fungus Gnats

Very long, bare, glossy, cylindrical larvae without pro-legs. Feed on decaying plant and animal matter and bore into fungi, sometimes destroying whole crops of mushrooms. Only a few mm in size, mostly dull-coloured with slender legs and 6–7 abdominal rings.

Sub-family   SCIARINAE

Sciara (= Lycoria) pectoralis Larva 7 mm, brownish with black head and no legs. Feeds on fungi (cultivated mushrooms); pupates in cocoon in ground or dung. *Adult:* 2–3 mm, black-grey.

Sciara frigida Larva 6–7 mm, shiny white, black head. Gnaws galleries in stalks and caps of fungi; also in seedlings of other plants and pot-plants. Adult 5 mm, black; lays its eggs in humus or dung.

LEAF-MINERS

Many insect larvae eat only certain layers of the leaf-tissue, mining into the fabric of the leaf, leaving the upper and lower skin intact. The resultant space, or leaf-mine, is both their dining and living-room. This is done only by the larvae of certain butterflies, beetles, flies, gnats and sawflies.

In autumn on young oaks milky-white spots can be seen, often in large numbers. Apart from the oak-leaf miner moth, the caterpillars of some 20 different kinds of butterfly and the larvae of 4 different kinds of beetle mine the leaves of the oak in a variety of ways. There is the site-mine, when a larva remains in one place eating round it; there is the gallery-mine when the larva eats its way forward following the same direction. There is a blister-mine, which is an inflated site-mine. There is also a spiral-mine. Many larvae line the inside of their mines with threads of silk. The caterpillars of the Lithocolletis family of butterflies attach threads at intervals and, as they dry, these shrink causing charactersitic pleats, known as fold-mines.

Family   CURCULIONIDAE   Weevils

Rhynchaenus (= Orchestes) fagi 2.8–3.2 mm without proboscis. Oval, pitch-black body with fine, glistening hair. Antennae and tarsi yellowish. Wing-cases long, oval shape with regular lines of pitting. Adult beetle hibernates in early May; gnaws small holes in leaves of copper beech. Female lays her eggs singly under the upper skin of leaf, close to the middle rib. Larva eats winding galleries between upper and lower skins, which broaden out towards the edge of the leaf and end up near the tip, where the larva enlarges its mine into a translucent web and pupates. The adult emerges from mid-June. Damaged leaves turn brown in summer, looking as though affected by frost. Fig. 62a.

Rhynchaenus (= Orchestes) quercus Adult beetle reddish-brown; lives as fore-going. In October female lays eggs in middle rib. Larva eats first along the main vein, then as *R. fagi.*

*Rhynchaenus (= Orchestes) populi On poplar and willow. Forms blister-mines, often several on one leaf.

Family   GRACILLARIIDAE

Gracillaria syringella Moth flies May and July. 2–3 broods. Span 1–1.4 cm. Fore-wings yellowish-brown, with cross-bands of white patches and dark brown dots. Caterpillars on lilac, ash, privet; first transparent, flattened-looking, without legs or hair; then covered with white or greenish bristles and with a dark grey line down its back; head brown-ish. Has legs, pro-legs and claspers. Eats out blister-mines which some-times cover most of the surface of the leaf, causing striking brown colour in leaf. Several together, starting at tip of leaf on underside, will roll a leaf up into a funnel-shape. Rolling is achieved by using silk threads which dry in 1–2 hours. The rolled-in upper side of leaf is eaten. They then go on to make a fresh roll. Pupae hibernate in a rolled leaf, or on bark or the ground.

Family   LYONETIIDAE

Lyonetia clerkella Winding gallery-mine that gradually widens; under top-skin, starting from middle rib reaching almost to the edge then curling back. Caterpillar glossy green with brown head; leaves its mine and pupates on underside of leaf or on bark. Moth is milk-white or grey or yellow-grey, shiny; outer area has brown markings. Fig. 62b.

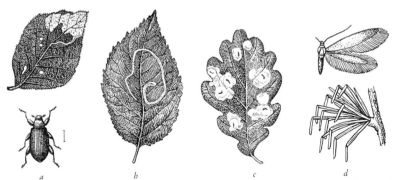

Fig. 62: Leaf-miners: a) **Rhynchaenus (= Orchestes) fagi**; b) **Gallery-mine of Lyonetia clerkella**; c) **Blister-mine of Tischeria complanella**; d) **Coleophora laricella**

Family COLEOPHORIDAE

BAGWORM *(Coleophora laricella)* Flies by day, May to June. Span 1 cm; grey; fore wings brownish with long yellow-grey fringes. Caterpillar on larch; reddish-brown; mines in needles of larch; in September bites off the hollow, whitish part of needle with open end, which becomes a sack for the caterpillar in which it goes about with its head and thoracic segments protruding. Winters on bud or bark. Starts feeding again in spring. Lets itself hang on thread and is carried away on the wind. Pupates in May inside the sack which it first hangs up. Fig. 62 d.

Family LYONETIIDAE

Tischeria complanella Flies May to June. Span 9 mm. Fore-wings brownish-yellow. Hind wings grey with long fringes. Pale yellow, flattened-looking caterpillar; legs degenerated to mere protuberances; gnaws into inside of leaves making large blister-mines with transparent rim, but middle covered with web and thus opaque. Caterpillar winters in mine, then pupates in cocoon. Quite common on oak, Spanish chestnut. Fig. 62c.

Family STIGMELLIDAE

Stigmella (= Nepticula) centifoliella Flies in spring and summer. Span up to 6 mm. Fore-wings dark with light cross-bands with silvery sheen. Head covered with jutting hair; short antennae. Inconspicuous, amber-yellow caterpillar; gnaws brown winding galleries in leaves of garden roses, leaving a black line of excrement down the middle. The caterpillar is at end of mine.

Stigmella (= Nepticula) prunetorum On leaves of prunus and crataegus. Gallery first straight, but soon becoming a close spiral looking like a round patch (spiral mine). Caterpillar is green, the moth brown-black with greenish-gold at the base of the wings, which have silvery cross-bands. Span 4.5 mm.

Family MUSCIDAE True Flies

Pegomya hyoscyami Maggot up to 9 mm. White-greeny-yellow; gnaws first a whitish, winding gallery; later a broad brown blister-mine in the leaves of mangold, beetroot, spinach, which wither and break off. Pupates in ground, where it hibernates. Fly 6 mm, light grey to olive-green according to colour of host-plant; has 3–5 dark stripes on thorax. Lays eggs on underside of leaves. 3–4 broods, first in April.

Mining Larvae in Young Shoots

Family   Curculionidae   Weevils

Ceuthorhynchus rapae Damages cabbage and rape, eating galleries inside the stems which curl. Larvae 5 cm, whitish, legless. Beetle 3.5 cm, first brownish, later slate-grey. Fine stripes on wing-cases with fine, whitish hair in between them. Hair short, scale-shaped. Lays eggs in stems. August to May, wintering as larva, then free in the ground. Not uncommon on cruciferous plants.

Ceuthorhynchus quadridens Eats galleries in stems and leaf stalks of young cabbage plants, killing them. Larvae 4 mm, whitish, no legs, dark head. Pupates in earth. Beetle 3 mm, grey-brown.

Family   Pyralidae   Pyralid Moths

EUROPEAN CORN BORER *(Pyrausta nubilalis)* Eats galleries in stems of maize, millet, hemp, hops; especially in the panicle-stems of maize which bend over, and also in spadix. Caterpillar dirty grey-brown with dark back line; number of darker dots on each segment, blackish head and brown neck-plate. Eats into stem, eats a gallery 8–10 cm long upwards; winters in stem just above the ground; pupates in spring. Moth flies in July. Span about 3 cm. Fore-wings of male brown with 2 yellow cross-bands and 1 yellow central patch; hind wings grey with light middle band. Female's fore-wings with 2 zigzag cross-lines and middle patch; hind wings yellow with grey roots, grey middle line and grey marginal band. Casual immigrant to Britain becoming established in S. England.

Family   Cosmopterygidae

Blastodacna putripenella In spring eats pith of end-shoots and blossom of apple trees. Caterpillar up to 5 mm, yellowish with red confined to rings; head and prothoracic plate brownish; yellow lengthwise side stripes. August to May, wintering in bud. Moth flies July to August; span about 1 cm. Brownish wings with yellowish patch and white dots. Lays egg on bud or leaf stalk.

Family   TORTRICIDAE   Leaf-rollers

Evetria buoliana Flies June to August. Span 2 cm. Fore-wings uniform brown. Lays eggs singly on buds or needle-sheaths. Caterpillar up to 2 cm long; light brown with black head and dark prothoracic plate. Eats into side-buds of first year's growth, hibernates and in spring eats the young shoots, so that they either wither or droop; in the latter case they can recover. June to July pupate mostly in lower part of a May shoot.

Family   TENTHREDINIDAE   Larger Sawflies

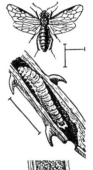

Ardis brunniventris (= *bipunctata*) Pseudo-caterpillar up to 1.5 cm, whitish; bores into rose-shoot and eats up it to a height of 12 cm, eating the pith so that tip of shoot droops and withers. Pseudo-caterpillar winters in cocoon in ground. Sawfly 5–6 mm, black. April to July eggs individually on top of rose-shoots.

*Monophadnus elongatulus Pseudo-caterpillar up to 1.5 cm, whitish; bores into rose-shoot and eats out the middle for about 12 cm. Presence betrayed by excrement that trickles out. Shoot does not wither. Sawfly 6–8 mm, black.

Family   CEPHIDAE   Stem Sawflies

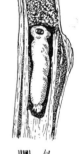

*Janus compressus Larvae hatch early June; 7 mm legless, ivory-yellow, stuffed appearance, tight rings; head darker with a horn-knob behind; bores spirally into the pith of the shoot upwards for 7–10 cm, filling the gallery behind it with excrement; in autumn gnaws an exit-hole, then spins itself a web at the bottom of the gallery where it winters, pupating in April. The shoot gradually dies. See p. 381.

WHEAT-STEM BORER *(Cephus pygmaeus)* Larva 1 cm, distinctly jointed, glossy yellow-white, bores into stalk and downwards until just above or just under surface of ground; in autumn spins itself a web at the bottom of its shaft, sealing itself in with a plug of gnawed material above which it has gnawed a ring; pupates the following spring. Damaged stalks remain short, turn colour prematurely and their ears remain unfilled and upright or they can break off at point of entry. Normally harvesting leaves the larvae unhurt. Harmful to corn. See p. 376.

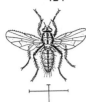

Family   MUSCIDAE   True Flies

Phorbia platura Maggot 6–7 mm, whitish; headless and legless.
Eats galleries in leaf bud and root neck of bean shoots, which
wither. Pupa winters in ground. Fly 4–6 mm, grey brown. Eggs
laid on sprouting beans.

Family   TRYPETIDAE   Large Fruit Flies

Platyparea poeciloptera Flies April to June; 6 mm; brown zigzag
stripes on wings; brownish body with light grey abdominal bands
and reddish-yellow legs. Eggs laid behind the scales of young
asparagus heads; maggots shiny yellowish-white; no head or
feet; 1 cm. Eats gallery downwards as far as woody root, which
then rots. Young asparagus wilts and curls.

Family   CHLOROPIDAE   Fruit Flies

GOUT FLY *(Chlorops pumilionis [= taeniopus])* Flies 3–4 mm.
Body shiny yellow; antennae, frontal triangle, 3 longitudinal bars
on thorax and 4 cross-bands on the abdomen all black. Clear
wings. 2 broods a year; lays eggs in May on upper leaves of
wheat and barley. Maggot yellowish-white 5–7 mm; yellow-
brown pupa. Stem swells, but does not grow; the ear remains
in the sheath, empty. Pupates end of June to July in gallery
it has eaten; 2nd brood flies from August on, laying eggs on
winter-grown wheat or wild grasses. Larvae hibernate. In spring
an onion-like swelling appears at base of affected shoots, which
gradually die. (Early sowing is a method of prevention.)

FRIT FLY *Oscinella [= Oscinis] frit)* Fly 2–3 mm, shiny black
with metallic sheen; thick down makes antennae look white.
Maggot 2–4 mm; whitish with lateral rings. Cylindrical light
brown pupae; 3 broods a year. Fly emerges mid-May, feeds on
nectar and pollen, lays eggs singly on underside of leaves of
young corn. Larvae eat the heart of the seedling. Pupates. Eggs
of the 2nd brood are laid particularly on leaves of oats. The
larvae eat the milky young grain, leaving the leaves which grow
pale and die. Eggs of the 3rd brood are laid on winter-sown
crops. Larvae hibernate in ground. Damage usually not apparent
until harvest-time.

Family   CECIDOMYIIDAE   Gall Midges

HESSIAN FLY *(Mayetiola [= Cecidomyia] destructor)* Fly
3.5 mm; span 6.5 mm. Flies in second generation: end April to
early May and August to September. Dainty fly, velvet black
or black-brown; female has black hair and red abdomen; male
orange hair; dirty red abdomen; both sexes have red bands on
abdomen; antennae brownish with orange-yellow spots; hairy,
brownish legs; dull grey, fringed wings. Eggs laid on young
wheat, rye and barley. Maggot forces in between straw and
leaf-sheath, sucks the straw becoming plump and oval, finally
pupates in the last moulted skin, in which it resembles linseed
in size and appearance. Affected straws wither and yellow above
the 1st or 2nd nodule, bend over or break off. Eggs of 2nd brood
laid on winter-sown plants near the root, causing gall-like
swellings on stems and the young plant withers. Introduced from
southern Asia along with wheat and said to have been taken to
America in straw by Hessian cavalry in 1776-7.

INSECT LARVAE IN BARK, SOUND AND ROTTEN WOOD

a) Larvae of Beetles

Fig. 63: Larva and pupa of the stag beetle

Family   CERAMBYCIDAE   Longhorn Beetles

Larva of the STAG BEETLE 2–3 cm, whitish and soft except
for its chitinised head; sparse hair on body, tapers towards the
rear, flattened top and underside. Head sunk into much wider
1st thoracic segment. Mouth-parts sited towards the abdomen,
strong, dark-coloured. Body segments sharply defined. Pads (for
moving) on the back divided into little warts (distinguishing it
from larva of *Callidium violaceum*) 3 pairs of pro-legs visible
only under microscope. Eats galleries especially in sap-wood,

(also along the edges of squared timber), occasionally in heart-wood; oval, often cave-like widening, usually filled with up to 1 mm of excrement. Spends 3–4 years as larva, but can be as much as 10 or 12 years. Pupa's cradle near the intact upper surface, 1.6–2.2 cm, separated from feeding-gallery by coarse gnawings. Exit-hole an elongated oval of 6–10 mm, outside rim mostly smooth, inner rim frayed. Flies from mid-June to end of August. Attacks only stacked or worked timber of coni-fers; especially in roofs, staircases, floors.

Larva of *Callidium violaceum* Similar to the foregoing only its progression-pads are flatter and smooth. It attacks timber with bark on it, especially when fresh, eating shallow galleries that often expand and cross, in bark and sapwood, only a few mm deep in the latter; the galleries filling with wood-dust and excrement: to pupate bores a hook-shaped shaft 1–2 cm into timber. In stacked timber the pattern of damage resembles that of the stag beetle. Exit-hole oval with both edges smooth. *Adult:* see p. 276.

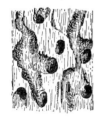

*Larva of *Tetropium castaneum* Attacks only growing spruce or those recently felled that still have their bark, preferably in lower part where bark is thick. Gallery runs between bark and wood, first in inner bark, when oval and very narrow, later also in sap-wood and then wider but more shallow; finally in parts very wide, winding irregularly and often very broad on the curves, packed with coarse gnawings, those of the inner bark brown, of the sap-wood white. Disturbs the flow of sap and harms the tree. Finally makes a flat oval place in which to pupate, 1–3 cm into the wood then turning sharply downwards for another 2–5 cm. Oval exit-hole up to 6 mm across. On pines and firs. *Adult:* see p. 277.

*Larva of *Ergates faber* Up to 8 cm, yellowish, as thick as one's finger. Each progression-pad has 2 transverse pads on top and below. Small feet, just discernible. Breeds only in dead woods of conifers, especially pine. In stumps. Also damages telegraph poles, etc. in the ground. *Adult:* see p. 293.

Larva of *Leptura rubra* Up to 3 cm, whitish; pointed mandible; distinct line down middle of back, small legs; no spike at rear end. Only in conifers, especially in stumps of felled trees or dead branches. Often in telegraph poles, etc. or beams of wood, bridges, if these touch the ground. Damage mostly at ground level. Needs a lot of moisture. Section of gallery oval. Exit-hole more or less circular; 5–7 mm across. *Adult:* see p. 275.

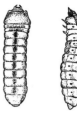

*Larva of *Leptura maculata* Lives in birch.

*Larva of *Spondilis buprestoides* 2.5–3 cm; flattened appearance. Head and part of thoracic segment covered with reddish-brown chitin. First thoracic segment twice as wide as it is long, has 2 lines running back. 2 small spikes before end of abdomen. Mostly in trunks of old conifers, especially pines; also damages building-timber at ground level, posts, etc. *Adult:* see p. 293.

Larva of *Acanthocinus aedilis* 1.6–1.8 cm, long-headed, yellowish-white, fine hair, no legs, fine warts on pads. Discernible simple eyes. Pupa has long antennae wound round the body several times. Attacks freshly felled trees, stumps with bark, deteriorating timber, especially pine. Gnaws shallow, winding galleries in inner bark, damaging sap-wood little or not at all. Pupates in narrow, oblique oval chamber that only just enters sap-wood. Pupa cradle ringed with long gnawings; entrance plugged with wood-dust. Oval exit-hole in bark. Adult flies early in the spring. See p. 275.

Larva of *Rhagium inquisitor* Whitish, almost transparent; wide, flat head tapering into wedge point; legs only slightly developed. In conifers, especially pine; stumps with bark, trees with thick bark or dead. Wide, winding galleries packed with wood-dust and excrement only in inner bark; sap-wood not harmed. When tree is barked, pads of brown dust remain on surface of timber. Large pupa cradle like a bird's nest, oval, lined with gnawings. *Adult:* see p. 277.

Larva of *Cerambyx cerdo* Up to 8 cm, thickness of one's finger; somewhat flattened, yellowish-white, dark brown band on front of head and brown band across thoracic segments. Small pro-legs. Wide, finely humped progression-pads furrowed in either direction and distinct groove down middle. Attacks oaks; mostly trees with injuries; galleries at first between bark and wood broad, shallow, sharp-edged, winding, then deep in sap and heart-wood, packed with wood-dust. Oval section, 1.5–4 cm across; fungus growth makes walls black. Takes 3–4 years to develop. Makes hook-shaped pupa cradle 2–5 cm across, with oval, smooth-walled chamber. *Adult:* see p. 292.

Larva of *Cerambyx scopolii* Gallery first in inner bark, then oval hook-gallery into wood ending in pupa cradle, which is plugged with gnawings and 2 mm thick lid of chalk. Attacks weakly trees or those with bark wounds. Especially beech. *Adult:* see p. 294.

Larva of *Prionus coriarius* Lives in old rotting trunks of deciduous trees and conifers. Black-walled galleries similar to those of *Cerambyx cerdo.* No actual damage. *Adult:* see p. 292.

Larva of *Plagionotus arcuatus* Shallow gallery in bark sapwood layer, then oval one in heart-wood, running 2–6 cm straight into timber, making up to 14 cm in all. Oval exit-hole. Often causes considerable damage to stacked oak, beech or hornbeam. Develops in 1 year. See p. 275.

Larva of *Saperda carcharias* Up to 3 cm, no legs, shiny. First thoracic segment widened with well-chitinised granular brown plate on top, and 1 small brown plate on either side underneath. Progression-pads have distinct lengthwise groove. Attacks poplar, aspen, willow. First remains under bark, visible as a swelling, later oval gallery of about 2 cm across running mostly in direction of wood fibre. Coarse gnawings are mostly brushed outside through special hole leaving pile at foot of tree. Galleries free of dust here and there. Pupa cradle cut off by plug at either end. Affected tree dies. *Adult:* see p. 274.

Larva of *Saperda populnea* Larva eats ascending gallery in heart of branches and young trunks of poplar causing nodule-like swellings or galleries, usually the death of the tree. *Adult:* p. 275.

Lamia textor Up to 4 cm long and 1 cm thick. Differs from *Saperda carcharias* in that head-plate is quite narrow; the chitin plate on first thoracic segment is not granulated and the pads are not ribbed. Attacks old willows, sometimes aspen. *Adult:* see p. 293.

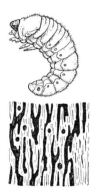

Larva of MUSK BEETLE *(Aromia moschata)* Up to 3 cm Attacks willows: trunks of young trees and branches of others. See p. 274.

Family   BOSTRICHIDAE

Larva of *Bostrichus capucinus* Attacks the root-stock of oaks, even oak parquet floors and barrels. Also other deciduous trees. *Adult:* see p. 272.

Family   LYCTIDAE

Lyctus fuscus (= linearis) 5–7 mm; white, with brown head; very like grub of *Ptilinus pectinicornis,* but a magnifying glass will show that a) spiracle on 8th segment is brown and much larger; b) legs are small and only 3-jointed, instead of 5-jointed. Attacks mainly oaks, but also walnut, ash, elm, Spanish chestnut poplar and willow, especially on timber in houses. Galleries always twisting and packed with fine wood-dust; eats everything but the outer layer. Beetle emerges through round hole 1 mm across; mainly May to June. Takes 1 year to develop.

Family   LYMEXYLIDAE

Larva of *Hylecoetus dermestoides* 1.2–2 cm; yellowish cylindrical. Front thoracic segment raised like a cowl, long forked tail appendage with pointed prongs. Attacks both sound and ailing trees and freshly felled ones. Cross-section of galleries round, about 2 mm across, mostly winding; near branch, going about 20 cm into wood. Larva feeds on ambrosia fungus placed on egg by female; larvae breed these fungi; therefore keep their galleries free of wood-dust and excrement; pushing out this dust between sap-wood and bark causes characteristic bulges. Wood-dust can also be seen on bark and on the ground. Adult emerges through hole 3–4 mm across. Later, dead fungi stain walls of galleries dark brown. Flies end April to June. Often ruins oak, beech, pine, spruce by boring holes into both sap- and heart-wood. *Adult:* see p. 269.

Larva of *Lymexylon navale* Up to 1.5 cm, very slender. Front thoracic segment raised like a cowl; blunt, cylindrical rear-appendage directed upwards. Only found in oak. Hair-fine entrance holes; as larva grows galleries become 1.5–2 mm wide. No fungi and no discolouration of walls. First horizontal main gallery, much of it straight, then branches of up to 6 cm up and down following run of wood-fibres. Adult emerges through hole 1.5–2.2 mm across. See p. 269.

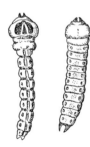

Larva of LESSER STAG BEETLE *(Dorcus parallelopipedus)* 2.5–4 cm; dirty white with reddish-grey showing at rear; curled like a cockchafer grub; semi-cylindrical, same thickness all over. Head as wide as body, arched, smooth, glossy yellow. 3 pairs of thoracic legs. Lives in rotten wood attacked by fungi; preferably of beech or oak. *Adult:* see p. 289.

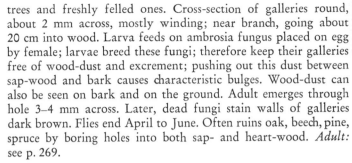

Family   BUPRESTIDAE

Two types of larva:

a) with greatly expanded, flattened thoracic segment;

b) thoracic segment only slightly widened, the other segments almost round; 2 chitinised spiracles at rear.

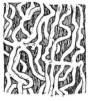

Larva of *Agrilus viridis* Up to 2 cm; white, soft-skinned; gnaws galleries between bark and wood. Several larvae will leave a confused pattern (see margin) of winding, intersecting galleries that can ruin the sap-conveying layer, though only the surface wood is furrowed. The branch will often die, sometimes twist. Individual galleries about 50 cm long. Pupa cradle 0.5–1 cm into wood with entrance opening gnawed by larvae, exit by young beetle. See p. 271.

*Larva of *Anthaxia quadripunctata* Under the bark of dead conifers, also attacks fencing and deal planks. *Adult:* see p. 288.

Larva of *Chalcophora mariana* Lives under bark, especially of felled pines, often turning it all into wood-dust. Larva in margin is of type a).

Family   CURCULIONIDAE   Weevils

Larva of *Pissodes notatus* Gnaws galleries down the trunks of young pines just under bark, causing tree to shrivel. Digs egg-shaped cavities in wood, which it lines with gnawings; these are pupa cradles. Beetle emerges by round hole. See p. 284.

b) Bark-beetles and their larvae

Family   SCOLYTIDAE   Bark-Beetles

A. Breed in Bark

Ips typographus 4.2–5.5 mm; squat, shiny black with brownish hair; wing-cases often brown with rows of coarse pitting; chasm (= deep gap at end of wing-cases) matt, with 4 teeth on either side, of which the 3rd is the stoutest. Wing-cases somewhat larger than base. Prefers mountainous country, where lives in the bark of large spruce trees (if short of food will also go to smooth bark of young trees; seldom to larch or pine). Galleries provide a more or less regular pattern, all in inner and outer bark, seldom touching the sap-wood. In spring young male bores a hole in bark, gnaws small "nuptial chamber" to which one or more females come. Female gnaws 1 vertical corridor between bark and wood with egg-niches off it, in each of which it lays one egg. Each larva, as it hatches, eats away from corridor a passage that becomes progressively wider and ends in pupa cradle; the resulting regular pattern with its rows like lines on a page has earned the insect its German name of typographer. Young beetles on emerging bore through the bark. You can also find a branching vertical corridor with numbers of horizontal passages off it. When the male is bigamous there are two corridors extending 5–25 cm both upwards and downwards (with several ventilation holes) from the nuptial chamber; when the male is polygamous there can be 3 or more such corridors; the horizontal passages are only 5–10 cm long.

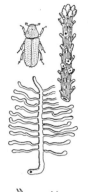

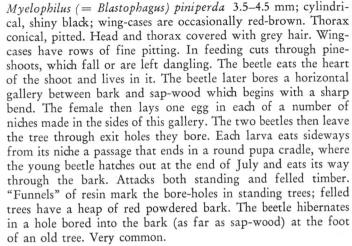

Myelophilus (= Blastophagus) piniperda 3.5–4.5 mm; cylindrical, shiny black; wing-cases are occasionally red-brown. Thorax conical, pitted. Head and thorax covered with grey hair. Wing-cases have rows of fine pitting. In feeding cuts through pine-shoots, which fall or are left dangling. The beetle eats the heart of the shoot and lives in it. The beetle later bores a horizontal gallery between bark and sap-wood which begins with a sharp bend. The female then lays one egg in each of a number of niches made in the sides of this gallery. The two beetles then leave the tree through exit holes they bore. Each larva eats sideways from its niche a passage that ends in a round pupa cradle, where the young beetle hatches out at the end of July and eats its way through the bark. Attacks both standing and felled timber. "Funnels" of resin mark the bore-holes in standing trees; felled trees have a heap of red powdered bark. The beetle hibernates in a hole bored into the bark (as far as sap-wood) at the foot of an old tree. Very common.

Hylesinus (= Blastophagus) minor 2.6–4 mm black; wing-cases mostly red-brown, seldom black. The space between the 2nd and 3rd row of pitting at the end of the wing-cases (where it slopes down) is not hollowed in a groove (as is that of *M. piniperda*) and has a row of granulation. Lives as *M. piniperda,* but is not so common and found more in dry bark of pines. It makes two-forked corridors.

Pityogenes chalcographus 1.8–2.2 mm. Black thorax. Wing-cases chestnut, the rest of the body more or less yellowish-brown. Pitting on the wing-cases stops just beyond the middle. Each side of the "chasm" has only 3 teeth. Under spruce bark, preferably thin bark; thus is found mostly in young timber or the crests of older trees. Its corridors make a star pattern with curving brood-passages (only slightly in sap-wood) and numerous larval corridors. No visible nuptial chambers, these being mostly concealed inside the bark.

Pityophthorus micrographus 1.3 to 1.9 mm, narrow, cylindrical, deep brown, rather shiny, sparse grey hair. Wing-cases strongly pitted; has a wide, smooth fork on the "chasm" beside the seam, occupying the last third of the wing-cases. Attacks the thin-barked parts of spruce trees, upper sections of the trunk and branches. Star-shaped pattern of galleries with distinct nuptial chambers gnawed out of sap-wood with 2–5 brood-galleries leading off from it. These are 2–4 cm long and also gnawed out of sap-wood. Late swarmer.

Pityogenes (= *Ips*) *bidentatus* 2–2.8 mm. Side edges of wing-case "chasm" furnished with long, thin hooked-teeth and on top, near the seam, one protruberance. Galleries gnawed entirely out of sap-wood in star pattern of 3–7 arms. Nuptial chamber visible. Brood-galleries slanting or following the grain of sap-wood. Egg-niches and larval corridors made rather far apart. On pines and larch. Common.

Polygraphus polygraphus 2–3 mm. Eyes arranged in 2 parts. Cylindrical body tapering in front, rounded behind, pitch black; dark brown wing-cases and yellow legs. On spruce, seldom on pine. Gnaws in bark of young trees indistinct star pattern of irregular galleries. Polygamous. Often only 2 arms lead from each nuptial chamber. The brood-corridors are visible only when bark is stripped, as the larval-corridors are mostly in different layers, so that occasional pieces tear off. The pupa cradles are sometimes in bark, sometimes in sap-wood (when bark is thin). Does most damage to spruces of 15–40 years.

Pityoctines (= *Ips*) *curvidens* 2.5–3 mm; narrow, cylindrical, pitch black, slightly shiny, has very long brown hair. Wing-cases very deeply pitted. Area between its 4 large "chasm" teeth rectangular and distinctly broader than long. Found in trunks of silver fir, sometimes in spruce, larch, pine. Brood under thicker bark, mostly in pairs; from one entrance shaft running under the bore-hole (no similarity to nuptial chamber) 2 twin-armed slant-ing corridors branch off; occasionally there is one or more (all linked together). Side-corridors, according to the number of females. Not common.

LARGE ELM-BARK BEETLE *(Scolytus scolytus)* 4.0–5.5 mm, cylindrical, usually tapering in front; shiny black; wing-cases mostly brown with stripes of fine pitting; reddish antennae. Thorax finely pitted. Thick yellow hair in middle of brow; long, yellow hair on thorax; tail-end of male has a transverse tuft of bristles with long points at either end. Especially on elm, under the bark; exceptionally on poplar, willow, ash, hornbeam. At end of May beetle eats at joint between new shoot and old. Pattern: thick vertical shaft 3–5 cm and numerous, first horizontal, then winding larval-passages at relatively large intervals.

Dendroctonus micans 8–9 mm, cylindrical, strongly arched, black-brown with a faint gloss, covered with long, grey-yellow hair. Head and base pitted; wing-cases have rows of pitting. On spruce, especially trees 20–40 years old; prefers damaged parts lower down the tree. Eggs are laid in heaps; larvae gnaw together, between bark and bark-fibre, a spacious area as family corridor that ends in branching, finger-like galleries; later young beetles hatch out there among wood-dust. Sometimes 6–8 together. The damage causes a considerable efflux of resin, visible on outside, which can kill the tree. Late flier.

Hylesinus fraxini 2.5–3.2 mm, short, squat, egg-shaped, matt, black. Upperside has unequal patches of rust-red and dark scales. Wing-cases have lines of fine pitting. Common on ash. Beetle eats green bark of tree tops causing cankerous swellings of up to 2 cm. For brood-galleries prefers the smooth bark of weaker trunks in which it gnaws, often deep into the sap-wood, two-armed, long cradle-corridors, off which are short, very regular perpendicular larval galleries, where bark is thick in the inner-bark, where it is thin in actual wood. Swarms early in April.

Eccoptogaster (= Scolytus) rugulosus 2-3 mm, oval, tapered almost equally at either end; pitch-black; antennae, tibia and tips of wing-cases red-brown; often the entire wing-case is red-brown. Thorax longer than it is broad, tapering in front, deeply pitted. Wing-cases narrowing considerably towards the rear, pitted. Larva up to 3 mm; brood-corridor some 3 cm, vertical. Larval-galleries close together, often intersecting; up to 20 of them on each side of the brood-corridor. Found under bark of fruit trees.

Scolytus mali 3.5–4.5 mm; cylindrical, glossy black; wing-cases dark brown or black, often lighter; antennae and legs red-brown. Wing-cases pitted; thorax very finely pitted. Found under the bark of fruit trees, causing the branches or stems it attacks to wither. Characteristic pattern of galleries: a long broad corridor leading vertically upwards from bore-hole under the bark, often starting with a small, ragged enlargement. Larval-galleries and round pupa cradles, as well as brood-corridor partly gnawed out of sap-wood.

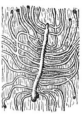

B. Breed in Wood

Anisandrus (=Xyleborus) dispar Big difference between sexes: female 3–3.4 mm, squat, cylindrical, highly arched, deep black or black-brown, sparse hair; thorax as long as it is broad; antennae and legs reddish yellow-brown; male: 2mm, short and egg-shaped (back to front) and only slightly arched; seldom completely coloured, mostly brown or yellow; has longer hair. Wings stunted; thorax longer than broad, almost round. Wing-cases of both sexes coarsely pitted; front half of base coarsely granulated, rest almost smooth. On almost all deciduous trees, including alder, vines, exceptional on conifers. Eating causes strong efflux of juices that will kill tree, or young ones may break off at the eaten place. Fertilised female bores into branch on thick trunk making an entrance shaft straight into wood; at the bottom of this gnaws to the right and left brood-galleries that roughly follow the annual circles and from which other, secondary brood-galleries branch off at right angles, roughly in the direction of the grain; the female lays an egg in both brood-galleries. The larvae do not eat wood and bore no shafts, but live communally in the galleries living on the ambrosia fungi that proliferates on them.

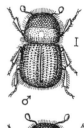

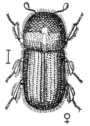

Trypodendron (= Xyloterus) lineatum 2.8–3.3 mm, cylindrical, round head; black; thorax and wing-cases yellowish-brown, latter finely pitted. Only in cut conifer wood, especially of silver fir; seldom on standing timber, then only if diseased; make black brood-galleries in white sap-wood in ladder pattern. From end of entrance shaft 2 roughly horizontal brood-galleries following the annual rings of the wood; these have egg-niches at regular intervals both above and below. The larvae gnaw short corridors which then look like the rungs of a ladder; the beetle bores its way out through the bark. Larvae feed on fungi cultivated by the beetle (hence the black discolouration of the galleries). (Ambrosia = little piles of nutritious cells.) Escaping beetles are covered with spores. (This fungus causes the blue mould on conifers.)

C. Larvae of Wood-Wasps

Up to 3 cm whitish, soft-skinned, cylindrical; 3 pairs of stunted thoracic legs; distinctive is the "shorn-off" head and the spike on the abdomen (for pushing itself along), both dark-coloured. Round galleries of progressively greater diameter, often curved first parallel to the axis of the stem, then turning and penetrating deeper, up to 20 cm in; packed with gnawings. To pupate they return to near the surface of the wood and make oval pupa cradle lined with glossy skin. Exit hole round, with smooth edges, 4–7 mm across. Attack pines, spruce, fir. Lays eggs in freshly felled trunks, diseased standing timber or trees with bare places (due to lightning, sun or man). Dry or constructional timber is not attacked. Larvae take 3–4 years to develop.

Wood-wasps often do not hatch out until timber has already been incorporated in a building and in this way cause damage. See p. 376 and 377.

D. Caterpillars (Larvae of Butterflies and Moths)

Caterpillar of GOAT MOTH *(Cossus cossus)* p. 351. Up to 10 cm; when young is dark flesh-pink, full-grown red-brown on top with black head and a few hairs; has strong smell of goat or wood-vinegar. Eats ascending galleries in stems and branches of willow, fruit and walnut trees, oak, beech, elm, lime, sycamore, birch, poplar and ash. Dust trickles out from opening at bottom. In May of its 2nd or 3rd year pupates near its exit in a cocoon of gnawed-up wood; pupa is red-brown; abdomen has prickles.

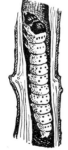

Caterpillar of LEOPARD MOTH *(Zeuzera pyrina)* Up to 4.5 cm, fat, glossy yellow with black warts with bristles; head, neck-plate and legs black; gnaws ascending galleries up to 20 cm in trunk of oak, ash, birch, elm, sycamore, beech, lime, poplar, horse-chestnut, fruit trees. Excrement cylindrical, reddish or brown-yellow, disposed of through bottom mouth of shaft. Makes firm case of gnawed wood in the exit hole for brown-yellow pupa. Moth: see p. 339.

Caterpillar of HORNET MOTH *(Sesia apiformis)* Naked, white, with brown head; bores into young poplars, eats first under bark, then hollows in sap-wood an ascending shaft up to 20 cm long, then a side-gallery back to the surface, where in the following spring it pupates in a firm cocoon of spun gnawed-wood. Presence betrayed by crumbling excrement on outside. Particularly found on black poplar, sometimes in considerable numbers. Moth: see p. 361 and Plate 9, No. 17.

Caterpillar of SMALL RED-BELTED CLEARWING *(Aegeria myopaeformis)* 1.8 cm; yellow with red sheen; head and back-plate dark brown-red. Eats galleries out of sap or heart-wood of branches or trunks of apple trees; often large numbers on one trunk. Cause cankerous places. Pupate in cocoons which protrude from feeding-hole shortly before moth is due to emerge. Mostly on apple, but sometimes on plum, pear, apricot and hawthorn. Moth: see p. 361.

Caterpillar of RED-CURRANT CLEARWING *(Aegeria tipuli-formis)* 2.2 cm, whitish with bluish neck-plate and dark stripe down back; hairs here and there. Makes galleries downwards from bud in branches of red-currant, raspberry and gooseberry, eating out the core. July to May wintering and pupating in feeding-gallery. Moth: see p. 361.

*Caterpillar of RASPBERRY CLEARWING *(Bembecia hylaei-formis)* Up to 3 cm; whitish yellow-grey with yellowish head. Bores first into roots of raspberry or bramble, then into core of previous year's growth, where it pupates. Presence betrayed by cankerous swollen stem and bush withering. Moth: see p. 361.

INSECT LARVAE IN WATER

LARVAE WITH RUDIMENTARY WINGS (= nymph)

Larvae of DRAGONFLIES On the bottom in shallow water dull-coloured insects several centimetres in length, either waiting for their prey half hidden in the mud or crawling about slowly on long, weak legs. Catching sight of small insect it darts out its "mask" which has lateral hooks, catches it and conveys it to its mouth. The mask is its adapted lower lip. Swift, jerky forward movement achieved by abrupt expulsion of water from anal opening. (Jet propulsion.) The rectum has air-filled tracheae in its skin folds and regularly takes in fresh water which washes round these tracheae-gills promoting the exchange of gases. The rectum is thus also an organ of breathing and propulsion. The wing-stumps increase in size with each moult. After several years, during which it develops, the mature larva or nymph leaves the water, climbs up the stem of some plant, pumps into itself enough air for its expanding thorax to burst the skin on its back.

a) Without lateral tracheal-gills on their abdominal rings

Larva of LARGE DRAGONFLY (*Aeschna* sp.) No external rear gills, but breathes solely with internal rectal gills. Both parts of its grasping pincers curved like a helmet; the teeth fit into each other and when at rest they cover not only the lower part of the mouth, but also the sides and top; hence the term "mask".

Larva of SMALL DRAGONFLY *(Agrion)* 3 leaf-shaped tail gills. Flat "mask" that covers only the lower part of the mouth.

b) With lateral tracheal-gills on their abdominal rings

Larva of a MAYFLY Caterpillar-like body with head, thorax, 9 abdominal rings, 2 long antennae, 2 compound eyes that are particularly large in the male, dagger-like upper jaw; 3 pairs of legs with 1 rear claw; tail-bristles at rear of abdomen and tracheal-gills on each side. Common on lakes and ponds; important food for fish. They themselves feed on organic particles, tiny creatures and algae on stones and aquatic plants. Moults. Mature larvae or nymphs recognisable by wing-sheaths that cover the first few abdominal rings. The nymph's skin splits along the back and an insect capable of aerial activity emerges.

Larva of *Ephemera vulgata* 1.5 to 2.3 cm. Yellowish. Has 3 feathered tail-bristles half the length of its body. Each upper mandible has a long appendage with outward curved point that juts beyond the rim of the brow. On the abdomen are 7 pairs of 2-armed, fringed tracheal gills which lie across the back. Mandibles and fore-legs act as drills when boring galleries in mud of slow flowing water or inshore area of lakes. *Adult:* see p. 388.

LARVAE WITHOUT RUDIMENTARY WINGS

Larva of GREAT DIVING BEETLE *(Dytiscus marginalis)* Spindle-shaped body 5–6 cm long; 3 pairs of articulated thoracic legs, no claspers; feet have 2 claws; 2 pairs of antennae, 1 pair of pointed hollow mandibles adapted for sucking. Swims with its hairy legs and bristle-fringed rudder tail (last few abdominal rings) which it flicks from side to side. Voracious predator. When it bites, it secretes a yellow-brown fluid down its hollow mandible which paralyses and kills its victim, dissolving it into a pulp which the larva sucks in through its mandibles. Mostly remains still on bottom, lurking. Feeds on insect larvae, isopods, tadpoles, young fish. Breathes air through last pair of spiracles on abdomen which it raises above surface and opens. Pupates in small cavity under turf of wet bank. *Adult:* see p. 296.

Larva of GREAT SILVER WATER BEETLE *(Hydrophilus piceus)* 7 cm. Body similar to the foregoing but plumper and its feet have one claw, tail has two small filaments; mandibles adapted as feeding-pincers. No swimming bristles on legs or tail. Lurks to catch and eat tiny creatures. Sluggish swimmer, crawls slowly;

attacks snails, breaking their shells and eating the inside bit by bit. Breathes air through holes at end of abdomen. *Adult:* see p. 298.

Larva of WHIRLIGIG *(Gyrinus natator)* 1.5 cm; long, slim, yellowish-white body without rudimentary wings; has 3 pairs of thoracic legs and all the abdominal segments have long, narrow, feathery tracheal gills. Feet have 2 claws. Mandible adapted as sucking pincers. Voracious predator. Especially June to July. Agile swimmer or crawls on bottom, but mostly concealed in mud or under stone. *Adult:* see p. 301.

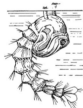

Larva of MOSQUITO *(Culex pipiens)* 8–9 mm, slender, spindle-shaped with distinct "separate" head; broad, unringed thorax; no legs or pseudopads; 7 abdominal segments with tufts of bristles. Breathes air through 1 air tube at end of abdomen which has 2 openings into tracheal system, round holes rimmed with chitin which expand when out of water and below the surface contract into a cone shape closing both breathing openings. Feeds on all sorts of organic matter. Somersaulting, wriggling swimming action. After the moult pupates: pupa has huge cephalo-thorax with 2 horny appendages, breathing horns which protrude above surface while it floats quietly just below. Does not feed. If threatened, dives then drives itself jerkily up again with flicks of its abdomen, the end of which has a fan-shaped paddle. Eggs take 6 days, larvae 15–21, pupa 10 days to develop. Some 6 broods in a summer. *Adult:* see p. 399.

Larva of MALARIAL MOSQUITO *(Anopheles maculipennis)* Lies horizontally below surface, as its 2 breathing apertures are in a shallow depression on the back of its 8th abdominal ring.

←

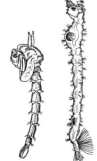

Larva of *Chaoborus crystallinus* (= *Corethra plumicornis*) 1.2–1.5 cm. Transparent body floats vertically. 2 pairs of air containers enable it to float at different depths. Jerky progression. Predator. Antennae adapted for grasping. Feeds mainly on tiny crustaceans. Pupa hangs vertically in water without tucking its abdomen under cephalo-thorax. *Adult:* see p. 399.

Larva of *Simulium reptans* Up to 1.5 cm; slender, maggot-like brownish body with club-shaped expanded hind end; attaches itself by abdominal sucker to plant or stone, holding its soft body erect; needs plenty of oxygen so is found only in fairly fast-flowing water. 2 small fans of comb-shaped bristles make a sort of basket in front of its mouth with which it sieves its food (small algae and organic waste matter) out of the flowing water. Able to detach itself and move like a leech. Shortly before pupating spins a cone-shaped, flat, yellow or brownish cocoon which it fastens underside down to a stone, with the opening in the direction from which the water flows. 2 bunches of white filaments protruding from this opening, aid breathing in the water and also when drying out in the air. Both larvae and pupae usually congregate. *Adult:* see p. 398.

RAT-TAILED MAGGOT Larva of fly *(Tubifera [= Eristalis]* sp) Up to 2 cm, ugly. Dirty-grey with 7 pairs of short leg-stumps furnished with hooks and a tail-like appendage, its breathing tube, that leads vertically up to the surface of the water. This consists of three sections, that, like a telescope, can be pushed in and drawn out, depending on the depth of the water, having a maximum length of over 10 cm. Winters in mud. Pupates on land in barrel-shaped pupa. *Adult:* see p. 395.

BLOODWORMS, larvae of *Chironomus* Length according to species from 2 mm to 2 cm. Long, worm-shaped body with 12 segments, can be red, yellow, white, green or grey-brown, the red being found especially in the upper layers of mud in large numbers. Those of other colour among underwater plants. Heads are distinct as such. On each of first and last segments is a pair of stumps with claws, so-called pseudo-legs, which it uses to grasp with while slowly crawling; it swims by curling up then expanding the ends of its body. These are numerous enough to be one of the staple diets of fish. *Adult:* see p. 400.

Larva of BITING MIDGE *(Ceratopogon niveipennis)* Up to 1.5 cm. Swims twisting and turning in tangles of algae.

Larva of SOLDIER FLY (*Stratiomys* sp) 3–5 cm; maggot-like body tapered at either end; head and thorax in one; no pseudopads; 12 segments; brownish-earthen-grey, very compressed at sides. Elongated tail-point with opening for breathing with a ring of long, feathered bristles, which spread in star pattern on surface of water, when the larva hangs there in vertical position. When disturbed, 4 star-tail closes into a ball that encloses a bubble of air, which is a reserve for breathing, when the larva submerges in a wriggling dive. The jaws are always moving, swirling particles of food (algae) into the mouth opening. Pupa floats horizontally on surface.

Larva of ALDERFLIES *(Sialis)* Large brown head with powerful pincer-like jaws. Body tapers towards the rear, ending in a long, thin, finely-haired articulated tail filament. First 7 abdominal segments have movable, long-bristled gill-filaments or tracheal gills. Feed on small aquatic creatures. Pupate in moist earth of shore in following spring. No cocoon. Curled-up pupa has 2 pairs of wing-sheaths. Not closely related to the true flies. *Adult:* see p. 386.

Larva of STONEFLIES (*Perla* sp) 1.6–2.1 cm. Resembles the larva of the mayfly but has only 2 tail-bristles and tarsi are 3-jointed with 2 claws (whereas those of mayfly have 1 joint and 1 claw). 2 large compound eyes, 2 long, thin antennae and numerous tactile hairs. Breathe through skin, the tracheal system being still closed. Only the larger species have filament-shaped tracheal gills in clumps on the sides of the thorax or between the tail filaments. As they need plenty of oxygen, they prefer flowing water, especially clear streams. Mostly hide under stones or crawl slowly among aquatic plants. Feed on tiny creatures, especially the larvae of the mayflies and plant matter. The larger species take 2–3 years, the smaller 1 year to develop. Older larvae are identifiable by their large, dark wing-sheaths. Climb out on to bank for final metamorphosis. The skin splits on back and the adult emerges ready to fly and mate. It lives for 4–6 weeks taking no food, but consuming its own fat. *Adult:* see p. 389.

Larva of STONEFLY (*Capnia nigra*) 7 mm; slim body yellow at first, with darker V-shaped mark on middle and hind section of thorax; shortly before emerging the V-formed figure becomes dark brown, wing-sheaths black and abdomen has black dots. *Adult:* see p. 389.

Larva of STONEFLY *(Chloroperla grammatica)* 1.2 cm; yellow head, darker in front with broad, black transverse stripe. Forepart of thorax broader than it is long, yellow with black rims; rest of thorax, abdomen, legs and tail filaments, yellow. Abdomen has black rings.

Larva of CADDISFLIES (Trichoptera) Caterpillar shape. 3 pairs of thoracic legs and pseudo-pads on abdomen. Two forms: one builds itself a quiver-shaped case in which it lives; the other lives free in water and, at most, spins itself a simple case. Regarding the case-makers the axes of head and body are at a right angle, whereas with the others they are a straight line. *Adult:* see p. 256.

The case-makers have their soft bodies in the case and their down-curved head and legs only emerge when they wish to eat or move. They will not leave their cases of their own accord and it is difficult to force them out.

The foundation of the case is a silk web, the secretion of a silk-gland that solidifies in water to make a tough thread which it weaves with its feet into a tube that it covers with foreign bodies (using its fore-legs). The larvae do not even emerge to moult. As they grow they build a wider section on to the end of the case and bite off the other end which has now become too narrow. Each species prefers its own building material and builds its own style. The choice of material will also depend on place, season and age of the larva. Thus the building material reveals at most the family, not the species, which however is at once revealed by the style of structure. For example many species lay the pieces of straw across, others parallel to the longitudinal axis of the case. One species lays pieces of plant of equal length in a spiral pattern, another lays one beside the other lengthwise. The larvae of the caddisflies feed on algae as well as fresh and rotting particles of plants. To pupate the larva attaches its case in some hidden place or to the stem of a plant, reduces the width of the two openings and finally closes them with a sieve-like lid of spun silk, thus allowing water for breathing to reach it. The pupa inside the case sways its body from side to side, thus renewing the water. When ready, the pupa emerges, swims to the surface and crawls out of the water in order to moult. The perfect, winged insect emerges and flies away.

The larvae that live free in the water feed on small aquatic creatures or plant matter. Many construct funnel-shaped nets between stones or plants, with the opening facing upstream, and catch algae and tiny creatures in them.

444 *Tiny Arthropods on Plants*

TINY ARTHROPODS ON PLANTS

Those that leap:

Flea-beetles and spring-tails

a) Flea-beetles: see p. 279 and Plate 6, No. 31.

b) Spring-tails in greenhouses, hot-beds, flowerpots.

Order   COLLEMBOLA   Spring-tails

Family   Isotomidae

Folsomia fimetaria 1 mm; lean, white; 1st thoracic segment almost entirely hidden by 2nd. Leaps. Several generations. In flowerpots, etc. Also on roots of onion, in which it eats holes.

Family   Achorutidae

Achorutes (= Hypogastrura) armatus 1.5–2 mm; greenish-grey, black-blue or wine-red, with short hairs, single spike at end of abdomen. Leaps. Claws are toothed. Several generations. In flowerpots, mushroom beds: feeds on cap, stalk.

Family   Smynthuridae

*Bourletiella pruinosa 1–1.5 mm; round body with indistinct articulation. Able to leap. Black, brown or greenish, with lots of small white spots. Eats shoots of cucumber, etc. On grass *Smynthurus viridis* is common; while on trunks of felled or standing trees, it is the brown species *Allacma fusca (= Smynthurus fuscus).*

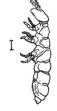

Family   Onychiuridae

Protaphorura (= Onychiurus) armata 1–2.5 mm; slim, white; its 3 thoracic segments quite distinct; cannot leap. Several generations Lays eggs in the ground. On shoots of cucumber, etc. in which it eats holes.

LEAPING OR FLYING SUCKERS OF SAP

Grasshoppers and flea-beetles

Order   HEMIPTERA   Bugs

Family   TYPHLOCYBIDAE   Leaf-hoppers

Typhlocyba rosae Shape of sharp wedge. Full grown 3.5 mm; yellow-white-greenish; translucent fore-wings tinged with brown; hind wings milky white, close-lying, when at rest in roof position over abdomen. Big eyes. Elongated hind legs, capable of leaping: when leaping spreads its wings and flies. Eggs laid on bark. Wingless larvae hatch in spring; later become yellowish with wing-sheaths; adult emerges end May to early June. In all stages on underside of rose leaves, where sucks along the ribbing, hopping away when disturbed. Also on apple trees. Leaves that have been sucked have white dots on upper side.

Family   TETTIGONIELLIDAE

Tettigonia viridis 6–9 mm. Thorax and wings blue-green or grass-green framed in yellow; back of head yellow; has 2 large black spots and 2 simple eyes.

Family   JASSIDAE   Leaf-hoppers

Cicadula sexnotata 3–3.5 mm; yellowish with black markings; at rest wings folded in roof position over abdomen. Eggs laid under top skin of plants. Larva black-brown. Does damage at all stages by sucking. On pasture, oats and barley, also on sugar-beet, turnips and potatoes. Often in hundreds of thousands.

Family   CERCOPIDAE   Frog-hoppers (Cuckoo-Spit Insects)

Philaenus leucophtalmus (= *spumarius*) 5–6 mm; yellow-brown; 2 white cross-bands on fore-wings. 2 large compound eyes and at back of brow 3 simple eyes. Legs for leaping. 4 glassy, transparent wings of equal size, held roof-shaped when at rest. Yellow antennae, but 3rd joint is black. Hops and flies. Eggs dormant during winter. Larva greenish, sedentary; bores with beak into stem, sucks out sap and surrounds itself with tough, mucous-like cuckoo-spit that provides good protection against rain, drought and ants. While mucus is liquid, air is expelled from last tracheae making foam which it pushes onto its back with its hind legs. Sucks at grasses and other meadow plants.

Aphrophora spumaria (= alni) Larvae in big lumps of foam on the stems of brambles and creeping buttercups. Adults also on willow and poplar, recognisable by 2 large patches separated by slanting dark brown bands.

Aphrophora salicis Larvae live in companies in large lumps of foam on willow bushes. Eggs laid under bark of willow shoots, making them fragile.

Cercopis (= Triecphora) vulnerata About 1 cm; vivid red and black; brow strongly inflated. When alarmed hops and flies. Often in numbers on plants.

Family   MEMBRACIDAE   Tree-hoppers

Centrotus cornutus 7–10 mm; grey-brown, with a pointed process on each side of fore-part and 1 curved down the middle of the back reaching almost to the end of its body. On bushes.

Family   CHERMIDAE   Jumping Plant lice

APPLE SUCKER *(Chermes mali)* April–June. *Larva:* flattened, yellowish to greenish, 6-legged, wingless. Moults and develops 4 transparent wings that lie in roof position over abdomen, when at rest. *Adult:* June to September. 3 mm; yellowish to red-brown; able to leap. Eggs laid on bark of young twigs; dormant during winter. Larvae and adults destroy flower buds, young shoots and leaves by sucking, leaving white spots and crumpled, shrivelled leaves; secretion of honey-dew; breeding ground for harmful smut.

PEAR SUCKER *(Chermes pyrisuga)* 2.5–4 mm; hibernates as beetle in crack in bark. Eggs laid on shoots, buds and undersides of leaves. From June mature insect, at first bright green, then red-brown; 4 translucent wings; leaps. Damages buds, blossom, fruit. Opens way for smut.

Trioza viridula June to July. *Larva:* 3 mm; flat, oval, greenish; body fringed with ring of shiny wax-hairs; fastens on to suck, and stays put. When mature 3 mm, yellow-green with yellowish wings and brown-red eyes; wings clear; swims and jumps, but does not fly much. Hibernates on conifer and deciduous trees, then in May to June moves to carrots and sucks at underside of leaves which curl up harming the crop.

NON-JUMPING, FREE-MOVING, WINGED OR WINGLESS

Plant lice, bark lice, frayed-wings, mites

Class	*INSECTA*	Insects
Order	HEMIPTERA	Bugs
Family	ALEYRODIDAE	White-flies

GREENHOUSE WHITE-FLY *(Trialeurodes [= Aleyrodes] vaporariorum)* 1 mm; 4 wings lying in roof position over abdomen and powdered with white wax as is the whole body. Larva like shield-louse, first moving, then sedentary, with stiff, translucent skin on back; oval, flattened body; back has fragile wax threads that at first are erect. Shed larval-skin is white. Mostly occurs in large numbers sucking underside of leaves, especially in greenhouses or hot-beds, seldom outdoors. Places where it sucks show as small, light-coloured spots that later wither. Discharges a shiny sugary waste, honey-dew. Lets in smut spores. Attacks tomatoes, cucumber, melons, potatoes; also beans, dahlias, vines, etc.

Family	APHIDIDAE	Greenfly

GREENFLY *(Macrosiphum rosae)* Wingless female up to 3.3 mm; green or brownish; plump, pear-shaped body with soft skin; male has 4 membranous wings folded in roof position when at rest, covering abdomen; head and thorax black; abdomen has rows of black spots; 2 relatively long antennae. With a magnifying glass it is possible to distinguish one dark compound eye behind each antennae and 3 simple eyes on the crown. Its weapons of defence are 2 tubes on its back, which secrete drops of fluid that swiftly become sticky and clog the mouth-parts of hostile insects. Sucking-beak with 2 pairs of stabbing bristles. Slender legs, slow movements; mostly sedentary; young and old remain

together in colony. *Development:* egg dormant during winter, aphid hatches and in about 10 days after 4 moults has become a wingless viviparous female; its young produce their young in another ten days and brood follows brood; in high summer winged roving-females appear which fly to plants of a different species. Towards autumn, come wingless females and winged males; the fertilised females then lay eggs in chinks in bark (where they remain during winter) in vicinity of buds; Food: the plant-juices they suck have a lot of sugar and little albumen, thus surplus sugar is secreted as a liquid discharge, honey-dew, which delights ants, flies, wasps. Honey-dew is also culture-medium for smut spores, a thick, black covering on leaves; prevents the leaf becoming vigorous. Sucking of juices prohibits growth of shoots. Changes hosts from rose, pear, etc. On shoots, buds, pedicles and underside of leaves of roses. Up to 10 generations a year.

Myzus persicae Wingless female 1.8 mm; greenish to glossy brown on top, greenish underneath. Winged male 2 mm, head and thorax black, abdomen yellow-brown on top with a large black patch and dark, sometimes merged, spots. Sucks at underside of peach leaves, the edges of which then curl under. Shoots contort. Host can be peach, or cabbage-type plants, tulip, hyacinth, etc. In June on potatoes; carrier of potato virus disease.

Appelia schwartzi 2.4 mm; yellowish-green with brownish cross-bands and large, dark back patch. Causes peach leaves to curl and fall.

Doralis fabae Wingless female 2.2 mm; black or green-black, oval. Antennae and legs partially white. Antennae shorter than body. Abdomen often has white bands on top; secretes wax. Winged female 2.6 mm, egg-shaped; head and thorax black to brown; abdomen green to brown-black with black cross-bands. From May to September several parthogenetic generations. Change of host-plant between rape, fodder-bean, Syringa, poppy, rhubarb, spinach. Bean shoots die, become stunted; leaves and flower of mangold and beetroot curl up. Transmits mosaic disease.

Myzus cerasi Wingless: 2.6 mm; shiny black. Winged: 2 mm. Sucks at leaves of morello cherry causing blisters.

Myzus pruniavium Very similar to *M. cerasi;* sucks at leaves of sweet cherry; which roll up tight. Stunts growth.

Hyalopterus pruni Wingless: 2.8 mm, greenish dusting with wax gives floured appearance. Winged: 2 mm; head and thorax black-brown, abdomen green, light lengthwise stripes; lightly powdered with wax. On plums, apricots, peaches, sloes. Shoots and fruit deformed.

Brachycoudes cardui Wingless: 2.2 mm; greenish; large, dark patch on back of abdomen. Winged: 2 mm; head and thorax black, otherwise as the unwinged. On shoots and leaves of plum. Leaves roll up.

Sub-family   ERIOSOMATINAE   Woolly Aphis

WOOLLY APHIS or AMERICAN BLIGHT *(Eriosoma lanigerum)* Wingless female up to 2.3 mm; pear-shaped, brownish body; secretes blood-red fluid; striking bluish-white waxen threads on back and abdomen which provide protective envelope for whole colony. Winged roving male about 2 mm, has 4 wings, longish legs and antennae; previously nymph with 4 rudimentary wings; no wax secretion; not common. No change of host-plant. Hibernates in root or at neck of root. Especially on apple trees; sucks the juices of twigs causing lumps and blistering the bark. Twigs die.

Family   PHYLLOXERIDAE   Dwarf Aphis

Viteus (= Phylloxera) vitifolii Larva hatches from eggs laid on vine (above ground) the previous autumn, sucks at leaf, causing gall (Plate 15) in which, without being fertilised, lays up to 500 eggs (parthenogenesis); from these hatch a) short-beaked larvae which suck at the leaves, causing galls in which they lay eggs repeating the process; b) larvae with long probosces which roam to the vine-roots and suck there, causing root galls and multiplying also by parthenogenesis and killing the vine. In summer and autumn such larvae become winged females which leave the ground and lay a few eggs on the parts of the vine above ground from which females and males hatch. These have no beak. Mate, whereafter female lays one egg that lies dormant through the winter to hatch in the spring and start the process again. Some beaked larvae hibernate.

The cycle of development frequently differs, e.g. in Germany those causing leaf-gall are seldom well-developed and often do not occur at all.

The short-beak larvae are 1.5 mm; wingless, yellow-green to orange. Those with long proboscis 1.35 mm; yellow to brownish with dark spots on upper sides; all are females. Winged female is 1 mm; yellow-green to yellow-brown. Those that mate are 0.3–0.5 mm; yellow, wingless. Leaf-gall is a green to reddish bulge on underside of leaf with hairy opening on top side. The root-gall is long swelling on the thread roots. Plate 15.

Order	PSOCOPTERA Book lice, Bark lice
Family	Psocidae Bark lice

Amphigerontia bifasciata Small and delicate with 2 pairs of glass-clear wings with indistinct markings, the hind wings being smaller and narrower than the fore. Mostly sits on tree bark with wings in steep roof position. Tarsi 2-jointed. From spring to autumn on branches, trunks that have lichen growing on them. Eggs dormant through winter.

Family   Stenopsocidae

Graphopsocus cruciatus Span about 1 cm; translucent wings with darker patches. Larva and adult feed on fibres and spore of fungi, lichen and all sorts of organic stuff. Eggs protected by small web, dormant during winter. Larvae, too, stay under a fine web. June to October on bark of deciduous trees, especially oak.

Order   THYSANOPTERA Thrips

Family   Thripidae Thrips

Mostly only 1 mm, slight, yellowish or brownish to black, with beak-shaped mouth-parts for stabbing and sucking. Legs have 2 foot-claws and sucker-bladder they can inflate. Many species have 4 narrow wings fringed with hairs; some run. 2 large compound eyes. Incomplete metamorphosis. Particularly active in thundery weather, sometimes in large numbers. Irritate the skin. Eggs laid in tissue of food-plant; sucking causes white "thrips spots". Adults hibernate in vegetable litter.

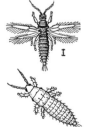

Heliothrips haemorrhoidalis Young ones at first white, then yellowish and reddish, finally brown-black with the end of the abdomen red. Very harmful in greenhouses. All year round. On almost all plants, which wilt and wither.

Kakothrips robustus Young are grey-yellow, later yellow-red with black end to abdomen; adults black all over. Suck at blossom, shoots, pods, leaves, causing tips to wilt and white spots to appear on leaves and fruit, blossom withers and pods shrivel.

Thrips flavus 1.2 mm; yellow with dark bristles. Sucks at leaves and blossom of different plants: apple, plum, fodder-beans, cucumber, carnations, etc. which wilt and shrivel.

Thrips fuscipennis (= tabaci) 1 mm; yellowish to brownish. Damages tobacco, onions, tomatoes, potatoes, cabbage and ornamental flowers.

Taeniothrips inconsequens Damages buds and blossom, leaves and young fruit of pear, apple and plum making them wither.

Thrips physapus Black-brown. Destroys base of roses and rose-buds, which wither.

Class	*ARACHNIDA* Spiders
Order	ACARI Mites
Family	Tetranychidae

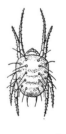

RED SPIDER MITE *(Paratetranychus pilosus)* Female 4 mm; red, white bristles and protruberance on back. Male 3 mm; yellow to yellow-green. Sucks at underside of leaves. Eggs red and grooved; dormant during winter. Leaves small light, later brown specks; fine threads on underside of leaves which become "foxy" and fall off. On apple, pear, plum, cherry, vine, rose, red-currant, etc.

Bryobia praetiosa Up to 0.8 mm; dark red, roundish; wrinkled across abdomen; side edges "padded-out"; 1 very long pair of legs. Red eggs dormant during winter behind scales of buds and bark of gooseberry, often in great numbers. Larvae suck at young leaves causing white specks and leaves remain small and fall prematurely; fruit is stunted; sometimes whole bush will die.

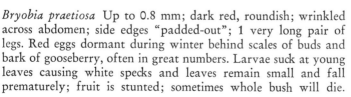

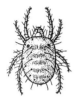

Tetranychus urticae 0.5 mm; reddish to yellowish. Eggs in fine web on underside of leaves; when in numbers webs often extend from leaf to leaf. Proliferate in heat. Suck juices, leaving leaves speckled and with fine threads on underside; leaves wither, plants can become stunted. Especially harmful in greenhouses, but also in the open on beans and tomatoes, etc.

Tetranychus telarius Scarcely 0.5 mm; oval, greenish-yellow or reddish larva with 6 legs. Often in large numbers on lime-trees, leaving delicate white veils on undersides of leaves looking like a floury mass. Hibernates in the ground.

Tetranychus altheae Causes copper blight on hops, whose leaves become copper-red, wither and fall.

GALL MITES are the smallest arthropods, mostly parasitic on one kind of plant on which they cause galls, leaf-curling, etc. Plate 15.

COCCID BUGS (that attach themselves)

Class	INSECTA	Insects
Order	HEMIPTERA	True Bugs

Parasites with considerable differences in adaptation and modification. The young are mobile, like tiny mites, and have legs, 2 simple eyes, antennae and sucking-beaks. Female larvae usually moult 3–4 times, remain like larvae all their lives; some of the females keep their legs and crawl about the food-plant, but the majority plunge stabbing bristles into plant tissue and remain in that one position all their lives becoming incapable of movement: lose their wings, their legs become stunted and their bodies swell and acquire a protective shield. Males go through at least 2 larval stages and 1–2 pupa stages, and when mature are very delicate and small, but they retain their antennae, eyes and legs; one species is winged (1 pair of fore-wings) but has rudimentary mouth-parts.

Family   COCCIDAE   Scale-insects

BROWN SCALE *(Eulecanium corni)* Female 4–6 mm long, 2–4 mm broad; yellow to dark brown, shape of half an egg, smooth, with a hard shell; on twigs often in large numbers. When a shell is shed a white speck of excreted wax remains. Female lays up to 3,000 eggs under its shell and dies; young larvae roam and hibernate, though still without scales. Unfertilised females also lay eggs. On damson, plum, peach, vine, red-currant, walnut, oak, ash, elm, alder.

Eulecanium bituberculatum 4–6 mm long, 3–5 mm wide; grey to brown, glossy; 2 dark brown protruberances on the back.

MUSSEL SCALE *(Lepidosaphes ulmi)* Small, club-shaped lumps covering trunk, twigs and leaves like scurf. Scale 2–4 mm long and 1 mm wide; the shape of a comma or mussel; dark brown to dark grey with an orange spot (boss) at small end; whitish to yellowish; parthenogenesis. Under each scale at pointed end is 1 female, the rest of the space occupied by eggs which are dormant during the winter. On a variety of trees and bushes, with a preference for fruit.

Pulvinaria vitis Female 4–8 mm long, 3.5 mm across; brown; shape of half an egg with 1 long stripe and dark cross bands. Strong woolly secretion of white wax; white egg-sac protrudes from under abdomen 4 mm x 6 mm, and 5 mm deep. Male is very small, brick-red and has 2 long tail bristles. Especially on vines, birch; but also on other plants.

Aspidiotus (= Quadraspidiotus) perniciosus May to August. Scale 2 mm in diameter, round, delicate, with faint concentric rings; grey to blackish, with light-grey to yellowish boss in the middle. August yellow. Female viviparous, some 400 progeny: 4–5 weeks to develop; at least 4 generations with about 3,000 million progeny in a year. Larva from August to May. Hibernating. Effect seen best on apples and pears: dark red spots in the middle of which the tiny grey scale of the bug can be discerned. This can be removed. (In Germany its presence has to be notified.)

Aspidiotus (= Quadraspidiotus) ostreaformis Scale of female 1–2 mm; robust, grey-green to black-green; boss in middle dark yellow to orange. Bug greenish-yellow. Scale can be removed. Eggs underneath it. On fruit and other deciduous trees. A microscope is needed to distinguish these from the foregoing. In the margin are pictured: end of abdomen of the female of (top) *Q. perniciosus* and (bottom) *Q. ostreaformis,* greatly enlarged.

GALL-MAKERS

As a chemical reaction to the stings, egg-laying and larva-hatching of various wasps, flies and bugs, plants form gall-tissue that provides food and shelter for the hatched larvae.

Oaks in particular have a wealth of galls. In central Europe some 200 different kinds of them have been found.

OAK-GALLS

Rhodites (= Diplolepis) quercus-folii Small black wasp lays eggs, May to June, in leaf tissue. The plant then forms a layer of food rich in albumen and fats round the larvae; this made of cells with thick external walls able to resist pressure and enemies, covered with strong bark tissue. The leaf gall, called a "cherry gall", is about 2 cm and acquires red checks in autumn; falls to the ground either on its own or with its leaf. In November or December the female hatches, bores into a winter-bud, lays eggs in it, from which in spring males and females will hatch. Plate 15, No. 1. Cherry gall.

Biorrhiza pallida 5 mm long wasp with yellowish front part and brown-red roots to its abdomen, which otherwise is black-brown; wings translucent, light with brownish veining. Wingless female with black bands lays eggs December to January in an oak bud, which turns into a juicy, spongy, yellowish oak-apple with a red tinge, that later becomes brown and is about 4 cm across; this has numerous oblong chambers each with one gall wasp larva in it. Matures in June. Does not fall off, but hardens once the insects have hatched. Plate 15, No. 3. Oak apple.

Neuroterus quercus-baccarum Causes leaf-gall, the common spangle gall, in numbers on underside of oak leaves; up to 6 mm across; flat, lens-shaped; contains one larval-chamber. In late autumn galls detach themselves and fall to ground; pupation in the gall; female emerges in March, lays egg in oak-buds which develop into round, greeny, translucent currant-galls, up to 8 mm across; on young shoots, leaves, flowers and stamen filaments. Male and females hatch, June. Female lays eggs on young oak leaves giving rise to lens-shaped galls. Plate 15, Nos. 4 and 5. Common spangle galls and currant-galls.

Neuroterus numismalis Gall a round disc with swollen edges in numbers on underside of oak leaves; thickly haired that makes it glitter like a gold coin. Sexual generation produces in spring, insignificant galls. Plate 15, No. 6. Silk-button gall.

Neuroterus albipes On top and underside of oak leaves. Resembles lens-shaped gall, but reddish and has lobed or up-turned edge. Shaped like a slouch hat, or sometimes a cocked hat. Sexual generation produces oval 2 mm spring-galls on the edges of young leaves (leaf-edge hairy gall). Plate 15, No. 7. Smooth spangle gall.

Andricus fecundator Bud-scales greatly enlarged; resembles fruit of hop or larch; up to 1.5 cm case enclosing brown, hard, egg-shaped gall, pointed at top and up to 9 mm long. Scales have brownish hairs. Mature September to October. Gall falls off. Plate 15, No. 2. Artichoke gall.

Adleria kollari 5 mm long, brownish gall-wasp which lays eggs singly in spring in buds of young oak trees *(Quercus robur)*. These cause hard round marble galls about 18 mm long. Females only emerge from these,

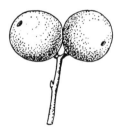

usually in August or September of same year. These lay eggs in buds of turkey oak *(Q. cerris)* which cause soft oblong galls 3 mm long in April. In May or June males and female gall-wasps emerge and after mating females lay eggs in Q. *robur* to start the cycle again.

GALLS ON VARIOUS PLANTS

On COPPER BEECH *(Fagus sylvatica)* Up to 1 cm; smooth, shape of a pointed egg, woody, often reddish; falls off when mature. Inside is white larva of a gall-gnat *Mikiola fagi*. Plate 15, No. 8. Pointed gall.

On ELM Sucking of wingless queens of aphis *(Tetraneura ulmifoliae)* produces club-shaped galls on leaves the size of a bean (up to 1.2 cm across); at first light green, then reddish-brown; mostly on upper side, often in large numbers. Leaf-tissue bulges like a sack, first with an opening on underside, then closed; houses juice-sucking plant aphis. Matures June to July, opening at side in form of a slit. Later gall dries. Plate 15, No. 10.

On ELM *(Ulmus)* Blister-shaped, irregular, up to 8 cm. Lumpy, hairy surface, pale green or reddish. Rest of the leaf pushed downwards or mis-shapen. With maturity irregular openings are made, finally becomes brown, dry: does not fall off in autumn; conspicuous on bare branches. Caused by aphis *Eriosoma lanuginosum*. Plate 15, No. 9.

On WILLOW, caused by sawfly *(Pontania vesicator)* Oblong or bean-shaped gall with thin walls, up to 2 cm long and 1.5 cm wide; like a blister on both sides of the leaf, often covering half the area; greenish, often with a tinge of red. Plate 15, No. 11. Bean gall.

On LIME Up to 1.5 cm horn-shaped galls scattered about upper surface of leaf; first red, becoming yellowish-white or light brown. Hairy open-ing on underside; has long hairs inside. Caused by mite *Eriophyes tiliae*. Plate 15, No. 12. Nail gall.

On POPLAR *(Populus nigra pyramidalis)* More or less oblong galls at upper or bottom end of leaf-stalk, up to 1.5 cm, reddish and woody; opening at the tip. Caused by aphis *Pemphigus bursarius*. Plate 15, No. 13. Purse gall.

On POPLAR Oblong galls at top or bottom of leaf-stalk, up to 1.5 cm, curled, reddish and woody. Opening at the tip. Caused by aphis *Pemphi-gus spirothecae*. Spiral gall.

On HAZEL Individual buds swell into balls up to 1.5 cm across. Scales thickened and enlarged with lumpy growths on inside. Caused by micro-scopic gall-mite *(Eriophyes avellanae)* that spends winter in the bud. Affected buds do not unfold. Large numbers can destroy the bush. Plate 15, No. 14.

On RASPBERRY Gall wasp *(Diastrophus rubi)* 2.8 mm, black; shiny abdomen, red-brown legs, 4 clear wings with chestnut veining; flies May to June. Eggs laid under bark. Larva 3–4 mm, whitish. June to March, hibernating in separate chambers in spindle-shaped gall. Plate 15, No. 15. Stem gall.

On WOOD-POA *(Poa nemoralis)* Stalk swollen above one joint and numerous threads at first whitish, then light brown, up to 1 cm, following line of the stalk, but with a middle-parting. These threads are aerial roots. Caused by gall-gnat *Pomyia poae*. Larva live between leaf-sheath and stalk.

On FRUIT TREES Caused by gall-gnat *Contarinia privora*. See p. 418.

On DOG-ROSE *(Rosa canina)* Caused by gall-wasp *Rhodites rosae,* 3 mm, black; front half of abdomen red; legs orange; pierces bud and lays eggs inside, giving rise to a round gall, some 5 cm across, with thread-like branching growths looking like moss; most have several chambers inside with 1 larva in each, very hard, tinged with red. Mature in summer. Plate 15, No. 17. Bedeguar gall.

On SPRUCE Caused by aphis *Adelges abietis*; 1.5 mm, greenish or brownish, covered with woolly wax secretions. Female lays tiny eggs on base of young twig-buds and sucks at their young needles, which are irritated and swell up into shield-shape so that one touches another to form small enclosed spaces in which the young plant-lice suck juices; later, the swollen needles shrink thus allowing the winged plant lice to escape. The dried-up woody galls remain on the twigs for years. Plate 15, No. 18. Pineapple gall.

On PINE Resin-gall shoot moth, *Petrova (= Evetria) resinella*, flies May to June; span 1.6–2 cm. Fore-wings black with shiny lead-grey cross-bands; hind wings brownish. Yellow-brown caterpillar has large head; gnaws young shoots. Exuding resin forms gall in which the caterpillar passes 2 winters and then pupates. Pupa pushes one end through resin warmed by sun, so that the moth can emerge. Plate 15, No. 19. Resin gall.

On RASPBERRY Gall-gnat, *Lasioptera rubi,* 2 mm, black, clear wings; yellow-brown legs. Bands of white hair across abdomen. Yellow hair on base. May to August. Lays eggs in bark. Gall 3 cm × 2 cm asymmetrical; several larvae in large cavity. Plate 15, No. 16. Stem gall.

On WILLOW Caused by gall-mite of *Eriophyes* species.

ARTHROPODS AS VERMIN ON ANIMALS AND PEOPLE

Class   *INSECTA*   Insects

LEAPING INSECTS: Fleas

Order   SIPHONAPTERA   Fleas

Wingless bodies flattened at the sides, well adapted to sliding along. No compound eyes and, at most, 3 simple eyes. Short antennae that can be laid in grooves. Hard chitin-case with number of bristles that point backwards and serve as supports. Hind legs developed into powerful jumping-legs. Mouth-parts adapted for piercing and sucking. Feeds on the blood of host. Complete metamorphosis. Lays eggs in gaps and beween boards and dirty corners. Worm-shaped, whitish maggots, feed on organic refuse, spin roundish cocoons with particles of dirt woven in, which house the free pupa.

HUMAN FLEA *(Pulex irritans)* Mainly on people, also on dogs, cats, pigs. Breeds in crevices in floors or straw mattresses. Takes 4–6 weeks to develop.

DOG FLEA *(Ctenocephalides canis)* Mainly on dogs, but also on people, and cats. Breeds where dogs sleep.

CAT FLEA *(Ctenocephalides felis)* Mainly on cats, but also on humans, and dogs. Breeds where cats sleep.

EUROPEAN RAT FLEA *(Nosopsyllus fasciatus)* Mainly on rats. Can spread plague, sucks in bacilli of plague-ridden rat with its blood and these pass through its intestine unharmed.

Species are distinguished by the bristles on the underside of the head and on the hind end of the front of thorax; heads are of different length and breadth.

Fig. 64: **Heads of** a) **European rat flea;** b) **Cat flea;** c) **Dog flea;** d) **Human flea**

Order   DIPTERA   True Flies

Family   HIPPOBOSCIDAE   Forest Flies and Sheep Keds

DEER FLY *(Lipoptena cervi)* 5.2–8 mm. After shedding its wings fly looks very like a louse. Legs widely straddled, powerful, with pressed-in femora and powerful clutching claws on feet. Tough, leathery skin. Parasite, sucking blood of red and roe-deer, but also flies on to people. Later in life wings break off at the root. Not uncommon in forests in late summer and autumn.

FOREST FLY *(Hippobosca equina)* Long wings retained all its life jut well beyond the abdomen. Body shiny rust-yellow; thorax chestnut on top; base pale yellow. Parasite on horses, donkeys, cattle, hares, especially on belly and other parts with little hair.

SHEEP KED *(Melophagus ovinus)* 4 mm; wings reduced to a pair of tiny studs. Lives on sheep.

Stenepteryx hirundinis 5 mm; narrow, sickle-shaped wings, but scarcely able to fly. Sucks blood of swallows and swifts on which it lives.

Bugs, Lice, Mites, Ticks

Order   HEMIPTERA   Bugs

Family   CIMICIDAE   Bed Bugs

BED BUG *(Cimex lectularius)* 5–6 mm; wingless; dark to yellowish brown; fine hairs. Proboscis can be tucked away in a groove. 2 tiny scales on either side of the base are the remains of fore-wings. Flat, pressed-down-looking body. Shuns the light, is attracted out from cracks in walls at night by the smell of humans asleep and lets itself drops onto them, sucks their blood and retreats into its hide-out. Can fast for weeks on end. Lays 6–50 white, oblong eggs behind wallpaper, etc. Moults 4 times before adult.

Order   ANOPLURA   Lice

Family   Pediculidae   Human Lice

HEAD LOUSE *(Pediculus humanus capitis)* Male about 2.5 mm; female 3 mm; wingless body a pointed oval. Colour adapted to that of host. 9 abdominal segments indistinctly separated. 3 pairs of legs with a strong claw for clinging and climbing in hair. Continuation of tibia can be laid firmly against the single joint of the tarsus that ends in a sharp claw. 5-segmented antennae. 2 large black eyes. Mouth-parts for piercing and sucking. Sucks blood, causing troublesome itch. 50—60 eggs or nits cemented individually to hairs. Egg has tiny lid to provide an exit. At the age of 2–3 weeks, after 3 moults, it is capable of reproduction. Almost only in dirty, neglected human hair. Infection due to contagion.

BODY LICE *(Pediculus humanus corporus)* Male 3 mm; female 4.2 mm; body very similar to that of *P. capitis,* only larger and has less hair. Lays eggs especially on inside of clothes; one female laying up to 300. Develops in 2–3 weeks. Blood-sucking pest and carrier of disease.

CRAB LOUSE *(Phthirus pubis)* 1–1.5 mm; broad, grey body with powerful legs and claws; long hairs on lateral prolongations of abdomen. Female cements 20–30 eggs on to pubic hairs of humans. Larvae hatch after about 8 days. Development takes 3 weeks. Sucks blood.

Family   Haematopinidae   Animal Lice

PIG LOUSE *(Haematopinus suis)* Male 4 mm; female 5 mm. Long head elongated into a beak. Small eyes are scarcely visible. Parasite on domestic and wild pig, living particularly on inside of the thigh.

DOG LOUSE *(Haematopinus setosus [= piliferus])* 2 mm; yellowish-grey. Has fine hairs on underneath of abdomen.

Order   DIPTERA   Two-winged Flies

Family   BRAULIDAE   Bee Lice

BEE LOUSE *(Braula coeca)* 1–1.5 mm; wings are lacking. Flattened, broad, red-brown louse-like body; short, 3-segmented antennae, sunk in deep cavities. 1 pair of small, simple eyes at the side behind antennae. Powerful legs with claws like teeth of comb on feet, which cling on to host. Parasite, mostly singly, on honey bees.

Order   ANOPLURA

Sub-order   MALLOPHAGA   Biting Lice

Differ from "true lice" in that head is enlarged and broader and mouth-parts adapted for biting and chewing; do not suck blood; feed on hair, feather, flakes of skin. Short antennae. Most have eyes. Can be present in large numbers without causing any great harm. Colouring mostly adapted to that of host: on coot black, on swan white, on golden oriole sulphur-yellow.

Family   TRICHODECTIDAE

Trichodectes canis (= latus) 1.5 mm; yellowish, broad, flat body with short head slightly indented in front. Short legs each with a strong claw. Lives on neglected dogs.

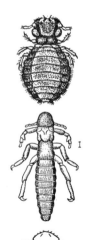

Bovicola bovis (= Trichodectes scalaris) Male 1.2 mm, female 1.5 mm; whitish body with dark cross-bands on abdominal rings. Otherwise as *T. latus.* Lives on cattle.

Family   PHILOPTERIDAE

Gonicotes hologaster Male .7 mm, female 1 mm. Each leg has 2 retractable claws. Head rounded in front and red-brown at edges. Sides of abdomen strikingly wavy. Parasite on domestic poultry and pigeons.

Lipeurus caponis (= variabilis) Male 2.2 mm, female 2.4 mm. Long, whitish body with black edges. Legs relatively long. 5-segmented antennae with prolongation on 3rd segment. Parasite often on domestic poultry; also on pheasants and guinea fowl.

Lipeurus baculus About 2 mm. Very narrow, long body, similar to *L. caponis*. Often on domestic pigeons.

Trinoton querquedulae (= luridum) 4–5 mm. Lateral spots on abdominal rings. Parasite on ducks and other swimming birds.

Class   *ARACHNIDA*   Spiders

Order   ACARI   Mites

Insignificant, most are almost microscopic creatures. Parts of bodies fused together (no articulation). Shaped like an egg, a sack or a worm. Mouth-parts adapted in many for biting. In others for piercing and sucking. 4 pairs of legs. Breathe mostly only through the skin, though one or two have tracheae. Lay eggs that hatch out 6-legged larvae which are not immediately capable of reproduction and generally go through 3 different stages as nymphs.

Family   THROMBIDIIDAE   Harvest Bugs

Thrombidium holosericeum Up to 3 mm; covered with plush-like scarlet hair. Soft, high-arched body. 2 eyes. Predator. Lives in ground, hunts plant lice. Larvae attack ants and all insect groups including spiders, attaching themselves by the mouth-parts to their host. Picture shows the underside.

HARVEST-MITE *(Thrombicula autumnalis)* 6-legged larvae often occur in large numbers in wet places; look like tiny red dots in high summer and autumn on grass, corn, attack small mammals and humans, sucking their blood and causing red pimples and an intolerable itch.

HYDRACARINA   Water Mites

Mouth-parts in form of conical beak for piercing and sucking. All are predators and most have vivid, lovely colouring. Feed on

Daphnia, Cyclops and larvae of small insects. Their tracheae lead into 2 air-chambers that lie on the mouth-part. Thin membranes that seal the outer end of the tracheae obtain oxygen out of the water. They presumably also breathe through their skins. Do not go up to the surface to get air. The stiff swimming-hairs on their legs are characteristic. 4 eyes on each side, in front of which at least one pair usually fused into a double eye. Development differs considerably. The larvae of many species are parasites on aquatic insects. Water beetles and water bugs frequently have round, red little patches on their undersides, which are the larvae of water mites that have bored their mouth-parts into them in order to suck. Other species leave the water early, climb up on the bank and attach themselves to dragon-flies and other aerial insects that live by or on the water. These transport their parasites from one stretch of water to another.

MUSSEL MITE *(Unionicola bonzi)* Lives in the gills of the freshwater mussel.

ROUND WATER MITE *(Hydrarachna globosa)* Female up to 5 mm; almost spherical, plump, blood-red body. Numerous swimming-bristles on the 3 hind legs. Bustles about in the water, but movements not especially quick. In weedy ponds and pools.

Hydrarachna geographica Up to 8 mm; almost spherical scarlet body with black spots on back and underside. Hind pair of legs have bristles to help it swim. Lays numerous pink eggs in a shallow layer on undersides of leaves of aquatic plants or on stones. When the 6-legged larvae hatch, they bore into the skin of a water-beetle or water-bug using their strong, piercing, sucking mouth-parts and on it they live and grow as parasites.

Family   IXODIDAE   Ticks

SHEEP TICK *(Ixodes ricinus)* 1–2 mm. When replete the female is about the size of a pea, flattened, and black-brown with leathery, elastic skin. 4 pairs of legs, long sucking proboscis that has barbed hooks in front and, if tick is torn off violently, will remain in the wound. Lives on only one host (large mammals, humans); female sucks for a week becoming the size of a pea and red to bluish-brown, glistening with fat; then drops to the ground, lays almost 3,000 eggs and dies. The larvae climb to the tops of bushes, and wait for a bird, can fast for 19 months, finally sucks itself full of blood, falls to ground and moults; then attacks fox, dog, deer, sheep, hedgehog, squirrel or human, bores its proboscis into the skin, becomes up to 1.1 cm, then falls replete to ground, moults, etc. Sucks only once in each stage of its development. Can transmit diseases of human and domestic animals, even cause paralysis.

Boophilus annulatus Blood-sucker and carrier of Texas fever, especially in America.

Family   ARGASIDAE

PIGEON TICK *(Argas reflexus)* 4–6 mm. Pale yellow with dark-red stripes and light underside. By day in crevices; attacks the pigeons at night, sucking for half an hour. Larvae remain on birds for days. Also on hens, geese, humans. Painful bite and irritation. Picture shows underside.

Family   DERMANYSSIDAE   Bird Mites

Dermanyssus gallinae .7–1 mm. Flat, oval, brown-red with whitish markings on fore-edge of body. Female has long needle-shaped mouth organs. By day in chinks and crevices, emerges at night to suck blood of domestic poultry, pet birds. Also on horses, cattle, people.

GALLS   Plate 15 (Pages 454–457)

1. Cherry gall 2. Artichoke gall 3. Oak apple 4. Spangle galls on oak leaf 5. Currant-galls on oak flower 6. Silk-button galls on oak leaf 7. Smooth spangle galls on oak leaf 8. Pointed galls on copper beech 9. Hairy galls on elm 10.a) Club-shaped galls on elm b) Elm gall aphis 11. Bean galls on willow 12. Nail galls on lime 13. Purse gall on poplar 14. Bud gall on hazel 15. Stem gall on raspberry 16. Stem gall on raspberry 17. Bedeguar gall on rose 18.a) Pineapple gall on larch b) Gall in section c) Nymph d) Winged pine aphis 19.a) Resin gall on pine b) Resin gall shoot moth 20.a) Leaf gall of *Phylloxera vastatrix* b) Root gall of *Phylloxera vastatrix*

L. Hausdorff

L. Hausdorff

Family   GAMASIDAE

Gamasus crassipes 1 mm. Golden brown. Predator. Lives on forest floor. Attacks dung-beetles, burying-beetles, etc. often in large numbers, attaching themselves, not sucking blood, but letting themselves be carried about.

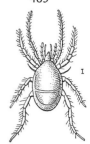

Parasitus fucorum About 1 mm. Often by the hundred in nests of bumble bees, eating their excrement. Brownish larvae often in numbers on bumble bees, long-horn beetles, etc. which they use as transport. Not parasite.

Family   ANALGESIDAE   Feather Mites

Analgopsis passerinus .5 mm, reddish-grey. Often in large numbers on song-birds, especially on neck and under the wings.

Megninia cubitalis Red or yellow-brown. Sucks blood of hens, sitting at base of feathers. Large numbers can cause death to chickens. Also comes into houses and on people.

Falculifer rostratus Attacks domestic pigeons, penetrating into their insides.

Cytolichus nudus .5 mm, just visible as tiny grey dot. Plump body like a tortoise; has 3 pairs of small spikes on its back; 4 pairs of legs with suction-pads. Often by the thousand in respiratory tract of poultry and pheasants; can cause suffocation.

Family   ACARIDIAE   Mange Mites

Knemidocoptes mutans Male .25 mm, female .45 mm; dirty yellow, 2 long hairs on rear end. Gnaws galleries in the skin especially of legs, causing whitish-grey thick bark-like crust. Irritation causes bird to peck at it; can lead to exhaustion. Picture shows underside.

Plate 16
Webs of

1. GARDEN SPIDER *(Araneus diadematus)*. Orb-web p. 480   2. *Araneus redii* p. 482   3. *Cyclosa conica* p. 483   4. *Argiope bruennichi* p. 483   5. *Meta segmentata* p. 483   6. *Steatoda bipunctata* p. 484   7. *Tetragnatha extensa* p. 484   8. HOUSE SPIDER *(Tegenaria domestica)* p. 485   9. *Hyptiotes paradoxus* p. 491   10. LINYPHIA SPIDER p. 484   11. LINYPHIA SPIDER in young spruce. Hammock-web p. 484   12. Hammock-web of a LINYPHIA SPIDER in the grass of an unfrequented forest path p. 484   13. LABYRINTH SPIDER *(Agelena labyrinthica)* p. 485. Sheet-web.

Acarus siro (On humans.) Reddish-grey. Female up to .45 mm with 4 pairs of short legs, the 2 fore pairs having stalked suction-cups, long bristles on body; male up to .3 mm with suction-cups on all legs, only 3 pairs ending in long bristles. Larvae have 6 legs. Tunnels into the skin especially between the fingers, round elbow or knee, filling the space with excrement and eggs. Develops from egg to egg-layer in 6 weeks. Female lays about 30 eggs. Cause of scabies. Picture shows underside.

Family   PSOROPTIDAE   Mange Mites

Acarus canis Cause of mange on dogs. Mange on puppies usually caused by *Demodex canis*.

Notoedres cati Causes mange on cats and rabbits.

Family   DEMODICIDAE   Hair-follicle Mite

Demodex folliculorum Female up to .4 mm, worm-shaped; long ringed abdomen; no eyes or tracheae. 4 pairs of legs with claws. Lives in hair follicles and in grease glands of skin causing inflammation, then small white swelling. Feeds on sebum. On humans causing whitish pimples. Also on dogs, cats and other mammals. Picture shows underside.

Class   *CRUSTACEA*

Order   BRANCHIURA   Fish lice

Family   ARGULIDAE   Carp-lice

FISH LOUSE *(Argulus foliaceus)* Up to 8.5 mm. Quite flat with shield-shaped shell; body comprises disc-shaped forepart and stunted, 2-lobed abdomen with a broad tail. Discernible on underside: maxilla becomes 2 strikingly large suction-caps; mouth with suction-tube and poison sting (adapted mandible); then, towards rear, 1 pair of claspers, then 4 pairs of long, cleft swimming-feet. On upperside: 1 pair of compound eyes sited in side of head. Parasite on the skin of fishes, sucking their blood fluids. Swims free in order to mate and lay eggs. On carp, perch, pike, stickleback, tench, etc.; occasionally also on larvae of toad and frog. Picture shows underside.

ARTHROPODS THAT ARE DOMESTIC PESTS

White maggots are "worms" on meat, cheese, fruit, vegetables, mushrooms

See pp. 390, 395, 396, 413–419 and 424.

Class   *INSECTA*   Insects

Order   COLEOPTERA   Beetles

Family   CUCUJIDAE

SAW-TOOTHED GRAIN BEETLE *(Oryzaephilus [= Silvanus] surinamensis)* 3 mm long, narrow, flat, dark brown body with fine yellow-grey hair; thorax has 3 fine lengthwise ridges and 6 teeth on either side. Wing-cases covered with rows of hair. Larvae 6-legged, yellowish-white. In houses; beetles and larvae feed on remains, larvae, pupae and excrement of noxious insects. Occasionally also lives in stored grain (maize, rice, semolina, etc.).

Family   LYCTIDAE   Powder Post Beetles

Lyctus fuscus (= linearis) 2.3–5 mm long, yellow-brown or dark brown; female lays eggs in tissue of wood. *Larvae:* see p. 429.

Lyctus brunneus 3–5 mm, brown-yellow with very fine hairs; otherwise as foregoing.

Family   DERMESTIDAE

BACON or LARDER BEETLE *(Dermestes lardarius)* 7–9 mm; rather long, oval, black body; wing-cases have wide yellow-grey crossbands with serrated rear edges and a few black spots: "knotted" antennae. A few yellow specks on thorax. Larvae cylindrical with red-yellow hair. Lays eggs singly on food-stuffs. In storerooms and larders. Beetles and larvae feed on cured meats, sausages, etc.

Attagenus pellio 4–5.5 mm black-brown with 1 silver spot in the middle of each wing-case and 2 very small spots with white hair behind each shoulder-hump. *Larvae:* 9 mm, 6-legged, brown, little body hair, tapered towards the rear; conspicuous tail of hair; jerky movements. Eggs laid either on or near (in chinks or cracks) what larvae will eat. Outdoors, beetles in blossom of hawthorn, spiraea, umbellifers, etc. Often powdered with pollen; larvae on furs, woollens (also in unmanufactured stage).

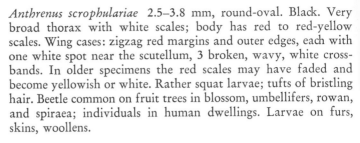

Anthrenus scrophulariae 2.5–3.8 mm, round-oval. Black. Very broad thorax with white scales; body has red to red-yellow scales. Wing cases: zigzag red margins and outer edges, each with one white spot near the scutellum, 3 broken, wavy, white cross-bands. In older specimens the red scales may have faded and become yellowish or white. Rather squat larvae; tufts of bristling hair. Beetle common on fruit trees in blossom, umbellifers, rowan, and spiraea; individuals in human dwellings. Larvae on furs, skins, woollens.

MUSEUM BEETLE *(Anthrenus museorum)* 2–3.2 mm long, oval; dark brown hair on top, grey hair underneath. 1 small patch on thorax before the scutellum and 3 blurred cross-bands on wing-cases all covered with ochre scales. Larvae up to 5 mm. Squat, reddish-brown; 3 pairs of tufts of hooked bristles at rear end which it spreads fan-like when agitated. Beetle in summer on umbellifers, swarming towards evening; enters houses to lay eggs, hence often found on windows. Larvae in hard timber; in houses destroy furs, skins of animals and birds.

Anthrenus verbasci 1.8–3.2 mm. Brown-black in middle of thorax and between the markings on the wing-cases; otherwise covered with ochre and white scales. Wing-cases have 3 white, zigzag cross-bands often broken, framed by ochre scales. Larvae have brown hair; live almost as *Attagenus pellio*. Outdoors on flowers. Found in many parts of the world.

Family   PTINIDAE   Spider Beetles

WHITE-MARKED SPIDER BEETLE *(Ptinus fur)* 2–4.3 mm. Male lanky, female oval. Almost round thorax waisted behind. Wing-cases of female shorter and more rounded, shoulders rounded; rust or black-brown. Underside and legs have fairly thick yellow-brown hair; base of both sexes has 2 strips of yellow hair reaching half way down it. Wing-cases hairy, well pitted. Beetle inert by day, lively at night. March to October. *Larvae:* curved, whitish, 6-legged; brown head, no eyes; short antennae. Common in houses, wool stores, barns, on dry plant remains, fresh bones, etc. Larvae in seeds, flour, woollens and furs.

GOLDEN SPIDER BEETLE *(Niptus hololeucus)* 4–4.5 mm. Club-shaped thickening of end of femora; wing-cases spherical with very fine stripes, brown; entire body covered with close felt of golden hair; wing-cases also have long rows of erect hairs. Beetle hibernates. Female lays 15–40 eggs in autumn. Larvae, 5–7 mm, pale yellowish-white, like cockchafer grubs, thick hairs. Pupates in cocoon. Found in the house, shops selling leather goods, barns, warehouses, woodyards; mostly sociable. Beetle can be found throughout the year, at times in large numbers. Feeds on feather, bristles, woollen goods, leather, paper, bread, paste (in books and framed pictures), tea, cigars, drugs, raw products. Can be a great roamer.

Family   CERAMBYCIDAE   Longhorn Beetles

HOUSE LONGHORN BEETLE *(Hylotrupes bajalus)* .8 to 2 cm, flattened, black body with fine white-grey hair. Wing-cases sometimes pale brownish yellow, closely grooved with pitting in grooves, two distinct white cross-bands. Female has long extendible ovipositor. Hind parts narrower than thorax which is oblique, rounded and the width of the wing-cases. Larvae gnaw galleries in deal, especially in houses. Young beetles eat their way out through oval holes.

Family   TENEBRIONIDAE   Nocturnal Ground Beetles

Tenebrio molitor 1.4–1.7 cm, long with parallel sides hairless, glistening, upper side pitch black, underneath dark red-brown; wing-cases grooved lengthwise. Larvae 2–2.25 cm, oblong, smooth, rather hard, yellowish gloss; short legs and rather quick wriggling gait. Found on flour, animal refuse, in houses and outdoors; in the rotten wood of old trees. Larvae (mealworms) in flour. Bred commercially as food for insectivorous cage-birds.

Blaps mortisaga 2–3 cm; large, oblong, pitch black; wing-cases taper to narrow points. When threatened secretes evil-smelling secretion from anal stink glands. Male also possesses scent-apparatus on its underside between 1st and 2nd abdominal segments, which is fringed with brown-yellow glandular hair. Larvae resemble mealworm, but are somewhat larger, lighter in colour and end in a simple point at end. Found in cellars of old houses, damp rooms, badly-ventilated larders. Beetle emerges only at night. Larvae mobile; feed on flour and bran.

Family   BRUCHIDAE   Pea and Bean Weevils

PEA WEEVIL *(Bruchus [= Laria] pisorum* Beetle 4–5 mm, short, powerful. Final or tail segment has 2 black, hairless spots at the tips. Broad, oval black body with thick rust-grey hair and patches of white-grey hair; wing-cases strongly pitted and have white markings; thorax-carries white spot. Feeds on petals and gnaws narrow slits in the soft tissue of pods and stems. Passes winter inside seed of pea in a hole with a round lid which the hatched beetle removes in the spring. Eggs laid singly on young pea pods where these curve over the seed. Larvae 6 mm, yellowish-white, curled, gnaws a cavity in young pea in which it pupates. Pea is then unable to germinate.

Bruchus rufimanus (= Laria rufimana) 3.5–5 mm; slimmer and darker than *B. pisorum;* has patches of yellow and white hair. Larvae, several together, in beans and peas. Otherwise as foregoing.

Bruchus atomarius (= Laria atomaria) Beetle 2–3.5 mm. Number of white hairy spots. Larvae in beans, peas, lentils. Hibernates in the seed.

Bruchus (= Laria) lentis Beetle 3–3.5 mm. Wing-cases uniform black with very thick grey hair that hides the basic colour, and in among it numerous oblong, white-grey latticed spots that often almost amount to 2 cross-bands. In lentils, each larvae destroying several. Will also move on to other plants.

Acanthoscelides obsoletus 2–5 mm long; wing-cases yellow-green with light-grey lengthwise patches. Underside and rear end orange. Lays eggs loose among stored seed. Larva eats the inside of the bean and gnaws a round "window" for the beetle that will hatch later. Introduced from abroad with imported haricot beans. In Europe does not attack actual bean until after harvest.

Family   ANOBIIDAE   Furniture Beetles

Attack sawn timber. Fly spring to summer. *Larva:* see picture in margin.

COMMON FURNITURE BEETLE *(Anobium punctatum)* 3–4 mm. Upperside black-brown with a shimmer of grey from thick, fine, silky hair covering. Thorax narrower than wing-cases, which have lines of pitting and curve down steeply at the rear, the ends being blunt and rounded. Larvae white, like tiny cockchafer bugs; thick in front, tapering behind; abdomen curled inwards. Head narrower than thorax, covered with sparse hair. Lays eggs in cracks, chinks and old galleries. Beetle eats its own round hole to emerge (1–2 mm across); these being the only external indication of its presence. In old standing conifers, in beams and furniture in houses. Common.

Anobium pertinax 4.5–6 mm; brown or black-brown; very short, fine grey hair; matt. Lozenge-shaped depression at end of base, in the rear corner of which is a patch of golden hair. Wing-cases striped with pitting. Stubbornly feigns death. Larvae similar to *A. punctatum*. Round exit hole for beetle up to 3 mm across. Flies April to May. In timber of conifers, beams, old fences, etc.; prefers pinewood. Not common.

DEATH WATCH BEETLE *(Xestobium rufovillosum)* 5–9 mm; upper side chestnut dappled with grey-yellow; fine, close granulation. Outdoors lives singly in old decaying oaks, hornbeam, birch, alder, poplar, willow, also Spanish chestnut; but mostly in houses (beams and posts). Taps at mating time (April or May). Not found everywhere.

Ptilinus pectinicornis 3–6 mm; narrow body, brown to black, with fine grey rather silky hair. Antennae of male have very long combs; antennae of female strongly serrated. Wing-cases finely wrinkled. In old deciduous trees, especially beech and oak; also on willow; poplar, elm and conifers; can damage furniture. Bores holes till wood looks like sieve. Often in association with death watch beetle.

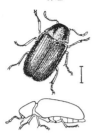

Stegobium paniceum (= Sitodrepa panicea) 2.2–4 mm; short, cylindrical, brown. Wing-cases fine rows of pitting; fine short hair and longer cover-hair. Larva builds itself a bag of particles of food and saliva in which it pupates; it is only when young it can crawl about properly. Beetle lives and develops in houses in food or drugs; when in numbers can do great harm. Will gnaw through tinfoil to lay eggs in chocolate, etc. Damages bindings of books, etc. Larvae eat dry pastry, cake, flour, cocoa, dry paste on back of wallpaper, etc. Also leather and raw meat, etc.

Family   CURCULIONIDAE   Weevils

GRAIN WEEVIL *(Sitophilus granarius [= Calandra granaria])* Beetle 3.5–4.8 mm, black to dark-brown. Upper side glossy. Wing-cases have lines of pitting. Underwings stunted and mere useless stumps. Eats grain either nibbling or hollowing it out. Female bores into grain making one hole in which she lays one egg. Larva is short, squat, maggot-like, white with a brown head; legless. Whole development takes place inside a grain of corn, in the empty shell of which it pupates. In granaries, especially on rye and wheat, but also on barley, oats, rice, millet and maize.

RICE WEEVIL *(Sitophilus [= Calandra] oryzae)* Beetle 2.3–3.5 mm, similar to foregoing, but each wing-case has 2 reddish spots, and there are lots of small round "dimples" in the base. Feeds on, and breeds in, rice; also wheat, barley, rye and other grains.

Order   LEPIDOPTERA   Butterflies, Moths

Family   TINEIDAE   Moths

COMMON CLOTHES MOTH *(Tineola bisselliella)* Moth May to September; flies at dusk. 2–4 broods annually. Fore-wings uniform ochre, without spots, but often darker at fore edge; hind wings more grey-yellow; head rust-red. Males fly, as do females once they have laid their eggs. Females mostly concealed, quick runners. Lay over 200 eggs, in clothes or furs; ivory-coloured caterpillar with yellow head, feeds on wool, fur, felt, horse-hair upholstery, feathers; spins long open-ended tube. Pupates in specially prepared web with local material woven in.

Tinaea granella Flies at night in spring and early summer; span 1.2 cm. Fore-wings yellowish-grey, dusted with brown and black spots. Hind wings grey, with long fringes. Fore-wings fringed only on outer edge. Head and thorax light yellow. Eggs laid between grains of corn. Caterpillar yellowish with red-brown head. Grains spun into a lump. Feeds on corn, especially rye. Pupates in spring in hollow grain and in crevices; often causes considerable damage in granaries.

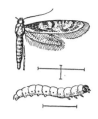

CASE-BEARING CLOTHES MOTH *(Tinaea pellionella)* Flies June to July. Span 1.2 cm. Fore-wings glistening clay-yellow, with 2 fine dark dots above the middle and 1 longer one below. Hind wings yellowish light grey. Yellow head. Caterpillar white with shiny brown head; spins a sheath in which it goes about feeding; no web on material it attacks; to pupate attaches its sheath to some support. On furs, feathers, carpets, but not often in private dwellings.

Family   PYRALIDAE

HONEYCOMB MOTH *(Galleria mellonella)* Flies May to September. Span 3 cm. Fore-wings violet-grey or red-brown with darker patches on hind margin. Hind wings brown-grey, those of male darker than female's. Characteristic is the salient between outside and lower edge of fore-wings. Lays eggs in cracks and crevices in bee-stock. Caterpillar dirty grey; feeds on wax, finally destroys the grubs. Firm white cocoons often close together.

COMMON HONEY MOTH *(Achroia grisella)* Moth flies July to August. Span 2.1 cm. Brown-grey, glistening fore-wings and light grey hind-wings. Light grey caterpillar with reddish head. Damages bees' honeycombs, dried fruit and sugar.

Ephestia sericarium (= kuhniella) 1 mm. Span 2.5 cm. Fore-wings blue-grey or brownish with zigzag cross-bars in darker frames and a row of small dark spots before outer margin. Hind wings grey with darker outer margin. Flies all the year round in mills, warehouses. Lays eggs in flour and flour products, also on flour dust on walls. Caterpillar white with darker head, fouls flour etc. with its silk and frass.

Order	PSOCOPTERA Book lice
Family	Trogiidae (= Atropidae) Book lice

BOOK LOUSE *(Trogium pulsatorium)* 2 mm; white or faintly yellow; often darts away when old books are opened. With a magnifying glass its powerful legs, long antennae, 2 hemispherical compound eyes on side of head, short wing-stumps and small rust-red spots on middle rings of large abdomen can be seen. Feeds on organic matter in books, herbaria, pillows, carpets. Harmless. Larvae moult several times.

Liposcelis (= Troctes) divinatorius About 1 mm; whitish; wingless; long antennae, thickened hind legs. When escaping runs about swiftly or takes little leaps. Found in same places as the foregoing.

Order	THYSANURA Bristle Tails
Family	Lepismatidae Silver Fish

Lepisma saccharina Up to 1 cm, flattened, tapering to a point with 3 tail bristles; covered with white, silvery scales. Compound eyes. Swift. Nocturnal. Feeds on vegetable and animal particles, also on flour, sugar, paste; often gnaws books, materials. Lays eggs with ovipositor in cracks in planks or crevices. In houses.

Class	*ARACHNIDA* Spiders, Mites
Order	ACARI Mites
Family	Tyroglyphidae Cheese and Flour Mites

CHEESE MITE *(Tyrolichus casei)* Scarcely visible to the naked eye, except as white speck. Microscope shows oblong, stout body with long bristles. Legs end in small suction pads. Found in old, hard cheese.

Tyroglyphus farinae Whitish, but scarcely visible to naked eye. Often in large numbers in flour stored in damp place. From it comes a nauseating sweet, honey-like smell. Flour is ruined.

Glycyphagus Prefers dry fruit, where it is difficult to eradicate. Prolific. Can cover furniture, etc. with a thick layer of live grey "dust". The domestic form is

FURNITURE MITE *(Glycyphagus domesticus)* .3–.5 mm, whitish with relatively long legs.

TINY LEAPING INSECTS FOUND ON POOLS, GLACIERS, FOREST-FLOOR, ROCKS

Class	*INSECTA*	Insects
Order	MECOPTERA	Scorpion Flies
Family	BOREIDAE	

SNOW FLEA *(Boreus hyemalis)* 3–4.5 mm. Resembles grasshopper larva. Slender body with long hind-legs, long antennae and rudimentary wings that, in male, are narrow upcurved appendages and, in female, small, close-lying scales. Female has upturned ovipositor the length of its down-pointing proboscis. Very large eyes especially in male. Brownish-green body with dark metallic sheen. Crawls about slowly; if disturbed feigns death or takes little leaps. Cannot fly. Sometimes in pine woods. From October to March on snow, especially on sunny days during a thaw. Also on moss; vanishes with the return of warmer weather. Feeds on dead or injured insects. Lays eggs in moss. In summer as a caterpillar-like larva in litter covering ground; pupates in a cavity in ground with a web.

Order	COLLEMBOLA	Spring-tails
Family	HYDROPODURIDAE	

Hydropodura aquatica 1 mm; fat, squat body with rolls and folds; consists of head, 3 thoracic and 6 abdominal segments; short antennae. Body pitch-black, legs and antennae reddish. Abdomen fitted with retractable "vaulting-pole" with which it leaps. Breathes through skin. Feeds on rotting matter. In pools, sides of ditches, ponds, lakes, often in such numbers that the surface of the water appears covered with mass of black dots. When disturbed, leaps most actively, without sinking in; when masses moult their cast skins look white.

Isotoma saltans (= *Desoria glacialis*) Up to 2.5 mm, black body, long hairs; long antennae. Long fork-like appendage on abdomen, its "spring-tail" for leaping. Appears like fine soot

on glaciers, often in such numbers as to give cracks or fissures a dark colour. When disturbed, leaps away in bounds up to 10 cm high. Feeds on remains of insects that storms have carried and killed up there, also other tiny creatures and wind-borne pollen from conifers. Only leaves glacier to lay eggs in area of moraine. Often mass migration.

Family   SMYNTHURIDAE

Smynthurides penicillifer Almost spherical body, indistinctly articulated. Hardly any interval between breast and abdomen. Male .3 mm, female slightly larger. Hops about surface of water. Male has hooks on antennae with which it catches the antennae of female. On pools and ponds.

Order   THYSANURA Bristle tails

Family   MACHILIDAE Bristle tails

Praemachilis hibernica (= *Machilis polypoda*) 8–10 mm, elongated abdomen with 3 "tails", the middle one of which is very long and flexible, used to propel the body forwards. Long antennae; 1 pair of large compound eyes and simple eyes. Body covered with scales; grey-white band down metallic brown back. Active climber on rough, sunny rocks and stones; feeds on lichens; if threatened takes great leaps away. At night in cracks and crevices.

Halomachilis maritimus Crawls about seaside rocks in the surf-zone. Quite common in North Sea and Baltic.

MILLIPEDES AND TERRESTRIAL ISOPODS

Class   *CHILOPODA*   Centipedes

Broad, segmented body, hind segments having 1 pair of legs each. Predators, killing their victims with poison.

Lithobius forficatus 2–3 cm; shiny chestnut, large multi-jointed antennae; 15 body segments each with 1 pair of legs: 1st pair pincers, from the claws of which poison flows when they close. Moves with serpentine motion. Predator. Feeds on insect larvae, spiders, isopods, earth-worms. Common in gardens, woods, under rotting bark, on old stumps, under planks, moss, fallen leaves. Bite not dangerous to people.

Geophilus 2–4 cm. 40–70 pairs of legs. Shiny, ochre to rust-yellow; very long antennae. When threatened rolls up, belly out, and glands in its belly secrete a fluid that scares insects away. Lives underground on fleshy roots and nodules. Eggs laid in heaps in the earth; female coils round them and guards them. Under stones, in flower beds, etc.

*A large, light yellow variety, *Geophilus flavidus*, about 3.5–6.5 cm, having 61–75 pairs of legs, occasionally occurs in central and eastern Europe.

Class   *DIPLOPODA*   Millepedes

Bodies usually round; most segments have 2 pairs of legs. Slow creatures, they feed chiefly on particles of rotting vegetation; when threatened mostly roll up and feign death.

Family   BLANIULIDAE

SPOTTED SNAKE MILLIPEDE *(Blaniulus [= Julus] guttulatus)* 1–1.8 cm; thread-like, white to yellow-grey with some 40 bright carmine spots on either side. Common in hot-houses; in south-west of Continent also outdoors, especially in gardens. Feeds mainly on rotting vegetable matter; gnaws strawberries, turnip, asparagus, greens, cauliflower, seedlings. Stinking glandular secretions spoil fruit. Has a preference for human excrement. Often in large numbers.

Family   IULIDAE

Iulus terrestris 1.5–5 cm; black or black-brown; when threatened emits yellow, stinking fluid or rolls itself up in a spiral. Found under leaves, stones, etc. *Tachypodoiulus niger* is a common black millipede found in Britain.

Schizophyllum sabulosum (= Julus sabulosus) Male 2–4, female 3.6–4.6 cm; shiny, dark brown or black; 2 yellow stripes down back; on each body segment except the first 4 and the last, has 2 short, weak legs, up to 100 in all. Not very supple, ponderous, slow. Coils up and feigns death when threatened; if attacked secretes evil-smelling fluid from numerous glands. Feeds on rotting vegetable matter. Found among fallen leaves, on tree stumps, under felled trunks and on fungi, mainly on sandy soils.

Family   POLYDESMIDAE

Polydesmus complanatus 1.6–2.8 cm; dull yellow to brown; body made up of 19–20 rings. No eyes, but antennae, in particular, are sensitive to light. Back-plates on ring strikingly extended over sides. Shuns the light. Feeds on decaying plants. Several sub-species. In damp woods, bogs, etc. especially where there are protruding stones; likes chalk. Hides under rotting leaves, planks, stones, in the mould of old trees.

Family   GLOMERIDAE   Pill-millipedes

COMMON PILL-MILLIPEDE *(Glomeris marginata)* 7–20 mm; full grown, is uniform shiny black. Female has 17, male 19 pairs of legs. When disturbed curls up into half the size of a pea, when its 2 antennae and many thin legs are no longer visible. Like a woodlouse in shape. Do not confuse with *Armadillidium*, the pill woodlouse (see p. 479). Feeds on rotting leaves. Especially in beech woods in damp places.

Glomeris pustulata 4.5–14 mm; deep black, shining, with whitish edges to rings which have 2 lines of yellow to red dots down them. Under stones, straw, leaves, moss in open country; also in rotten tree stumps.

Class   *CRUSTACEA*   Crustaceans

Order   ISOPODA   Isopods

Sub-Order   ONISCOIDEA   Terrestrial Isopods

Short abdomens with 6 rings tapering towards the rear, the first 5 of which have, on their underside, gills covered with narrow plates. The rear pair of legs juts out on either side of the abdomen like 2 prongs. Shuns the light; harmless; it lives in wet places and feeds on decaying matter. Female carries eggs in delicate-skinned appendages under her thorax. Young are very similar to the adults, and are carried on the mother's thorax for a long time.

Oniscus asellus Up to 1.8 cm. Rather shiny light grey-brown on top, with 2 rows of light spots down the back, and light side edges. One of the commonest isopods. Deciduous woods, thickets, on walls, under stones, in greenhouses and cellars.

Porcellio scaber Up to 1.6 cm; grey or black-grey with large, yellow spots, but very variable. Close transverse lines of granulation on upper side. External antennae 8-segmented. Found both outdoors and indoors. In this and the two following species the outer parts of the 2 front pairs of abdominal legs have air-tubes for breathing, like tracheae, with openings at the side.

Porcellio laevis Up to 1.8 cm; smooth on top; dark grey to grey-brown with light lines on each side of the middle of the back; the rear abdominal ring rounded. Mostly in cellars, greenhouses; very fond of warmth.

Armadillidium vulgare 1–1.5 cm. High-arched body; can roll up completely (do not confuse with the pill-millipede *Glomeris* see p. 478). Mostly dark slate-grey, uniform or with light speckles, but colouring very variable. Often in large colonies in sunny, dry places.

SPIDERS AND FALSE SCORPIONS

Class   *ARACHNIDA*   Spiders, etc.

Order   ARANEAE   Web Spiders

Head and thorax fused together (cephalo-thorax) under plate; 6 or 8 eyes. First pair of mouth-parts (chelicerae) has curved, retractable claws each with a poison gland with an opening just before the point of the chelicerae; this is the spider's main weapon. The second pair of mouth-parts, the labial palpus, has chewing appendage and palps or pedipalps. To enable them to run along threads of gossamer the two main claws on all 8 feet are furnished with fine comb-teeth. A third, smaller claw, the anal claw, is used for weaving, the spiders using them to direct the thread in the right direction. Abdomens are soft-skinned, inarticulate and joined to the front part of the body by a stalk; on the undersides of them are 1 or 2 pairs of lung-spiracles of even or uneven numbers of tracheae. Have silk-producing warts (spinnerets) at the end of their abdomens.

Family   Argiopidae   Orb-web Spiders

Characteristic is the cartwheel web with sticky threads often linked with the spider's lair by signal or touch-threads. Spiders often spend their entire lives in one spot, the species increasing by the young spiders letting the wind blow them away on their threads. Males roam. Webs of the different species differ in diameter, number of spokes and density of the concentric circles, etc.

GARDEN SPIDER *(Araneus diadematus)* Female 2 cm, male 1.1 cm. Abdomen has white, often blurred patches arranged in the shape of a cross on a light and dark brown base with grey shade. Eyes positioned as illustrated in margin. Female has large, round abdomen; cephalo-thorax: female 6.6 mm; male 2.5–4.5 mm. The male is much slimmer, so that cephalo-thorax and abdomen are about the same size, and its legs are several times the length of its body. 3 pairs of spinnerets on abdomen have numbers of tiny tubes for producing silk. Web, suspended vertically, has trapezoid frame of some 18 cm across, usually with 20 spokes and 24 spiral threads; spokes end in close hub-web in the centre; the gummed ring-threads are in a spiral, from it the bridge-thread leads to the lair, from which a signal thread leads to the inner zone of the trap-circles. The spider lurks either at the hub, sitting head downwards, or in the lair. Sense of touch in its many hairs leads the spider to its struggling victim, aided by its sight. It kills its prey by biting it with its chelicerae (poison-fangs) in its maxillary palpus, frees it from the web, so as to be able to turn it about and truss it unhindered, then sucks it out. Female lays a large number of eggs in the autumn and dies; spherical, compact cocoon of golden matted silk. The spiderlings hatch out in the spring. No metamorphosis, but they moult several times. *Life span:* 2 summers. In May, all at the same time, the spiderlings leave the egg-cocoon and for the next week remain together in a huddle without feeding; they then scatter, spin tiny webs about 2.5 cm across, and by autumn have grown to about 4 mm. They hibernate in rolled-up leaves, under bark, etc. and emerge in April to start making progressively larger webs, though always of same pattern. In September to October each female prepares several egg-cocoons, dying beside the last when it is complete with eggs inside. The construction of an orb-web takes about 40 minutes. Plate 16, No. 1.

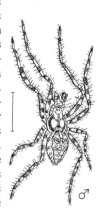

Araneus marmoreus Abdomen up to 1.1 cm. Male up to 5 mm. Colour very variable. Abdomen yellowish-white, yellow or faint red, with white patches arranged in a triangle or cross on the front part. Orb-web usually slightly excentric, suspended between tall grasses, perennials, or on outside of bushes and trees. Hub some 50–80 cm above the ground; lair in plants roughly, casually spun together. Common, but mainly in damp places. Rare in Britain but variety *A. m. pyramidatus* frequent.

Araneus sclopetarius Abdomen of female up to 9 mm, of male up to 5 mm. Basic colour grey to grey-brown. Lighter stripes of hair distinguish head from thorax and continue round edge of abdomen. Circular web. Catching area up to 70 cm across; up to 20 spokes. Distance between spirals 1 cm. Often in companies. Sometimes webs so close together as to touch or share the same frame-threads. Nocturnal. Only spiderlings attend the web by day as well. On bridges and other structures; rocks and in the neighbourhood of water.

Araneus ceropegius Abdomen of female up to 1 cm, of male up to 5.5 mm; oblong pointed at either end with yellowish oak leaf marking in the middle of back; dark band in middle of underside and yellow lengthwise stripes. Abdomen protrudes over the spinnerets. Side view depicted in margin. Orb-web suspended between low bushes, grasses or a hedge; has a preference for straws of corn beside field tracks. Hub some 50 cm above the

ground. Spider waits beside the web on flat plate-web or on the hub itself. A shadow on it is enough to make it seek the safety of the ground. Preys on insects. In open, sunny places. Very rare in Britain.

Araneus cucurbitinus Abdomen of female up to 5 mm, of male 3 mm; 4–5 pairs of black dots on upper side. Basic colour of the mature female greenish to yellowish; immature spiderlings before hibernation are reddish to red-orange, after hibernation, olive-brown. Orb-web mostly on solitary bushes, up to 2 metres up; oblique to horizontal, often on a large leaf; 20–30 spokes and 10–15 spirals; often departs from cart-wheel shape. No lair. Common.

Araneus redii 7 mm. Abdomen covered with thick down. Basic colour brown. Front part of back of abdomen has a patch in middle framed in yellow. Abdomen of female up to 5 mm, of male up to 3 mm. Web hung vertically between plants. Hub 40–70 cm off the ground. Builds in vicinity of web a small basket into which it retreats in cloudy weather, a guy-rope at its foot, but in fine weather sits on hub. Common especially in low country, in sunny uncultivated places. The spider does not leave the plants on which it was born for the first year. After a night of mist and frost the area will be a mass of webs with drops of moisture and ice-crystals like strings of beads. Picture is view of abdomen from above, showing how it is broader than long. Plate 16, No. 2.

Araneus cornutus (= *Aranea foliata*) Abdomen up to 9 mm, (male's 4 mm); basic colouring of females light, often white, but variable. Web hung between tall grasses, reeds, low bushes, on positions ranging from horizontal to vertical; up to 60 cm across; spaces between spirals, most 15–20 spokes. Webs often close together. Close to each web is a funnel, open at the bottom end, which is the lair: straws, stalks, etc. spun closely together forming a dwelling-chamber between them. Nocturnal; spends day in lair. In open, low country, especially beside water. Very common. After mating female attacks, and eats, male.

Araneus adiantus Abdomen 4–5 mm (of male 2.5 mm), viewed from above a long oval (drawing in margin). Web on low bushes, especially heather; catching area some 20–24 cm across; up to 40 spirals and 30–42 spokes. Beside web has funnel-shaped lair with its opening at the bottom, where are signal threads. By day, spider is mostly on the hub. Common on moors and heaths.

Cyclosa conica Abdomen up to 5 mm (male's 2.5 mm). At end of abdomen blunt, upturned protruberance, narrowing like a cone. Orb-web 1.5–2 mm off the ground, some 40 spokes and 20–30 spirals; about 28 cm across. Often has vertical screens woven on, above and below the middle, with the spider sitting in the space between them. Remains of prey arranged one above the other in line with the net and the spider (camouflage). Chiefly on conifers. Plate 16, No. 3.

Cyclosa oculata Similar to *C. conica*.

Argiope bruennichi Abdomen up to over 1 cm (of male 3 cm) with conspicuous wasp-like bands of yellow and black, and similarly ringed legs, though the male's colouring is usually not so vivid. Web between plants, almost vertical. Hub some 30 cm off the ground. Characteristic are the 1 or 2 radial vertical partitions woven on and the fine threads spun across the hub making it visible for quite a distance as a white blob. Mostly 32 spokes: catching area some 30 cm in diameter. Spider waits on the hub, head down and legs straddled. Catches mostly grasshoppers. Male is eaten by female after mating. Egg-cocoon with 300–400 eggs, hung between grasses. Spiderlings hibernate in cocoon. In sunny places: waste-land, heath, pastureland. Quite common. Plate 16, No. 4. (Local in Britain in southern counties only. An introduced species.)

Meta (= Reticulata) segmentata Typical garden spider shape; clay- to green-yellow with dark spots and dark streaks on front of abdomen. Web always has open hub (a large hole in its centre) made by biting away the threads there; usually in an oblique position. Makes no special lair. Female is almost always in the middle of the web; male on outside, on a twig, with one leg on a signal thread. A couple remain together on one web throughout the autumn; the male hurrying up as soon as female has mastered the prey. Spider usually spends the night concealed under a leaf, but connected to the hub by a thread. In autumn on low plants. Very common. Plate 16, No. 5.

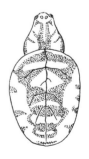

Family   THERIDIIDAE   Comb-footed spiders

Spherical abdomen. Web consists of two horizontal bracing-threads with a number of vertical, gummed trap-wires in which victim becomes entangled. Males do the entire construction.

Steatoda bipunctata 4–7 mm. Abdomen a short oval, flattened on top. Fore-part dark brown-red; abdomen dark chestnut on top with lighter middle streak and light margin at top and half way down the sides. Makes a very loose structure (e.g. on the angle of a window-frame) from which a few threads lead down which have drops of adhesive on their lower ends. If an insect bumps into one, it sticks to it, the thread snaps, contracts and so pulls the insect off the ground; the insect struggles and gets entangled in the other threads; the spider hurries up and paints it with adhesive from its glands using a special brush on its hind feet. By this method it can capture even blue-bottles and ants. Male has stridulating organ and serenades the female, rubbing the sharp fore-edge of its abdomen against 2 grooved plates in the hinder part of its back. The most common house spider, but also outdoors on tree trunks, rock-faces. Plate 16, No. 6.

Theridion lunatum About 5 mm. Round abdomen is whitish-yellow, often with reddish band down it and 2 rows of black dots at the back. Eyes pictured in margin. Attaches round, bluish egg-cocoon to a leaf and guards it until the spiderlings hatch; these remain with the mother for considerable time afterwards.

Family   TETRAGNATHIDAE

Closely related to the orb-web spinners.

Tetragnatha extensa 15–20 mm. Lanky, rod-shaped body with very long legs; while lying in wait 2 pairs of legs are stretched out straight in front and 2 pairs straight out behind. Legs and cephalo-thorax reddish-yellow, abdomen mostly yellowish-white with a pattern of red-brown leaves with dark edges on its back. Maxillary palpi as long as the cephalo-thorax. 8 eyes in parallel rows. Vertical orb-net with wide mesh, fairly low off the ground in wet places or at water's edge between rushes, grasses, reeds. Plate 6, No. 7.

Family   LINYPHIIDAE   Hammock-Web Spinners

Small web-spinners at most 6 mm long. Many species. Web mostly a lightly concave like hammocks or umbrellas stretched between twigs; above the curve a criss-cross of almost invisible "trip" threads to catch their prey; on the underside of the web individual bracing threads. The spider sits, back downwards, on the underside of the web and if an insect flies into the "trip" threads and falls onto the web, catches it. In bushes, or on pine and larch; often in great numbers. Plate 16, Nos. 10, 11 and 12.

Family   AGELENIDAE   Sheet-Web Spinners

Mostly have long spinnerets and long legs.

Tegenaria domestica About 1 cm. Ochre with darker markings: 3rd pair of legs shorter than the rest, which are roughly of the same length. Spinnerets jut out from oval abdomen like a little tail. Web made in corners, cellars and houses. Rather large, horizontal triangular sheet-web in the angle of a wall, has a depression in the middle; ends at the apex in a dwelling-funnel open at either end. Flies etc. do not get stuck to the web, but are hampered by the numerous layers of thread arranged one above the other. The spider waits in its funnel for a capture, attacks like lightning, kills its prey, and takes it to its funnel and there sucks it out. In margin: male above, female underneath. Plate 16, No. 8.

Agelena labyrinthica 8–14 mm; grey-yellow cephalo-thorax with 2 black-brown stripes down it. Abdomen grey and yellow mixed with a stripe of reddish hair down the middle ending in a patch of orange over the spinnerets; yellow coxae and femora, orange tibiae and tarsi. Horizontal sheet-web, like a hammock, carefully anchored to grasses with a funnel-shaped, open-end tube either at one side or in the middle, which is the spider's lair. Where hunting is good the web may be only the size of one's hand, but in areas where game is scarce it can be 40–60 cm across. Makes a spherical egg-cocoon which it hangs up in bushes; the actual cocoon is suspended hanging free from numerous guy-ropes inside a roomy hemispherical cover-web, which serves to shelter the spiderlings during the winter. In sunny places. Either on the ground or in low bushes. Common. Plate 16, No. 13.

Family   ARGYRONETIDAE   Water-Spiders

Males about 15 mm, females about 8 mm; drab grey-brown. Lives the whole time underwater; makes a web diving-bell between aquatic plants. A layer of air adheres to hair on body making it look silvery. Renews this air supply every now and again by thrusting its abdomen and 4 pairs of legs up out of the water

and with the air obtained fills its dwelling-diving bell which can hold 10–12 "loads". Feeds, moults, mates and brings up its young in these special diving-bells.

Argyroneta aquatica   Male 1.5 cm, female 8 mm; head-part strikingly high and quite distinct from thorax part (of cephalo-thorax). Multiple-toothed claws on the feet of fore-legs. A dull grey-brown in colour. 8 eyes, six of them arranged in a slight curve in front, with the other two behind the middle of it. Legs mostly have prickles. Abdomen covered with very fine white hair. Feeds on insect larvae, mites, water isopods, etc., which it catches as it crawls about the aquatic plants. In swimming keeps its back held down. Underwater, the abdomen with its covering of air looks like an oblong silvery bladder. The underneath of the spider's hairy thorax is also coated with air. Constructs between plants a stout, airtight diving-bell of web, rises to the surface and in diving again takes with it a bubble of air adhering to its rear which it releases under its diving-bell; it repeats this until it has made a largish store of air. Instead of this diving-bell it may make use of an empty snail-shell between roots or something similar as a nest, collecting air in it, and, for the winter, closes the opening with a lid of web or spins plant-stems across it. Either eats its prey in the air, hauling it up the stem of a plant to above the surface, or consumes it in its diving-bell. The female sticks the flattened egg-cocoons against the ceiling of the diving-bell which serves as her first dwelling. Found in stagnant or slow-flowing water, mainly dykes, ponds with plenty of aquatic vegetation, especially duck-weed. Seems to prefer moors.

Family   Pisauridae   Hunting Spiders

Closely related to the wolf spiders, but different in the position-ing of their eyes and method of procreation. Large, round egg-cocoon not spun on to spinnerets, but carried about with female held between maxillary palpi and only hung up under a shelter of grasses spun together, where it is guarded by female, shortly before the spiderlings are due to hatch.

PIRATE SPIDER *(Dolomedes fimbriatus)*   Male 1 cm, female up to 2 cm. One of the largest European spiders. Long legs covered with thick hair. On top is a uniform rich red-brown with or without a few white spots (but never has a lighter zigzag band down the middle). Cephalo-thorax and abdomen fringed with a broad margin of white or yellow. Runs swiftly about the surface of water without sinking in, for its feet, which are covered with hair, do not break the surface film, just dent it slightly. Dives under, if threatened. Preys on insects that fall on to the water, also water insects; but feeds on the bank. Lives on the banks of reedy waters and in boggy places where trees grow.

Pisaura mirabilis (= listeri) 1.1–1.3 cm. Abdomen light brown on top with broad, light jagged stripe in dark frame down the middle. From May on, on plants and low bushes in open country. In sunshine numbers can often be found on leaves. Male feeds the female with parcelled-up flies, mating with her while she eats. Common in low country, rare in the mountains.

Family   LYCOSIDAE   Wolf Spiders

Powerful build with sombre colouring; cephalo-thorax tapers towards the front, arched. Eyes in 3 rows (see illustration below) those in front being the smallest. Hindermost legs are the longest. Make no webs. Swift runners and agile hunters, stalking their prey, pouncing on them and overpowering them, "like a wolf". Females attach their egg-cocoons to their spinnerets and then take them about with them. Spiderlings live for a while on the backs of the females. Sociable, that is to say, are found in one place often in large numbers.

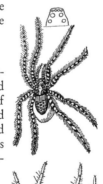

Lycosa amentata (= saccata) 5–7 mm, brown-grey to black-grey with a yellow patch on cephalo-thorax; sombre-coloured hair; legs brownish-yellow with black rings. Runs in a series of swift jerks, often taking little leaps. Hibernates in a web-lined cavity in the ground. Female makes flat-shaped egg-cocoon (end of May) which she attaches to her under-abdomen and carries about; has the spiderlings on her back. Young spiders take occasional aerial trips.

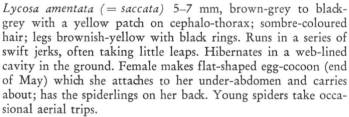

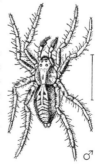

TARANTULA (Tarentula inquilina) Male 1.2 cm, female 1.8 cm (without legs) one of the largest European spiders. Legs have both hair and prickles. Prepares pits the shape of a finger-stall in the ground or in moss, which it lines with web; then lies in wait for passing insects which it overcomes and sucks out. Hunts by night. Bite is harmless. Found on commons, heaths and under stones in chalky soil.

Family   Dysderidae   Six-eyed Spiders

Have large filter-tracheae with 2 pairs of spiracles, one behind the other, close behind the fan-tracheae. Mostly under stones, bark or moss.

Segestria senoculata Up to 1.6 cm. Long, oval cephalo-thorax a glossy deep brown, almost twice as long as it is wide, cylindrical, both ends blunt. Abdomen brownish-yellow, cylindrical, hairy, with dark brown markings, spots one behind the other, on the back. Medium lengthed living tube-web, open at both sides with trip-threads radiating in various directions. By day, lies in wait in entrance to tube-web, feels when an approaching insect stumbles over a trip-thread. Egg-cocoon is almost round. Spiderlings hatch in the middle of summer. In holes in walls, crevices in rocks, in houses. Quite common.

Family   Clubionidae

Mostly hunt at night and make no webs, but stalk their prey. Spend the day in thin dwelling-sacks which they weave under bark, between leaves, etc. Always have 2 exits, which are sealed off before moulting, hibernating or egg-laying.

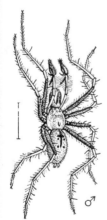

Cheiracanthium virescens (= nutrix) Female about 1 cm, mostly yellowish-brown. Maxillary palpi have teeth on their sides. Has 2 claws on feet. Spins low, pointed plants (grasses etc.) into a dwelling-bell the size of a pigeon's egg with the opening at the bottom, and here the female guards her lens-shaped heap of eggs. Common. Bite causes nausea and even loss of consciousness, in humans. Not common in Britain and no records of biting humans.

Agroeca brunnea 5–7 mm, with 2 broad, brown stripes down the sides of the cephalo-thorax and brown spots on abdomen. Nocturnal in habits; makes no web, but roams about predator-like, concealing itself by day under moss or bark. Striking egg-cocoon: a delicate, snow-white lantern on a short stalk suspended from heather or the stem or branch of some other plant 20–60 cm off the ground. The spider often covers it with a protective coating of earth, which is both camouflage and armour against parasitic wasps; this cocoon consists of an egg-chamber at the top with a moulting room underneath which is used by the spiderlings when they have hatched. Particularly on the ground of heaths, between grass, on moss and bushes.

Family   SPARASSIDAE

Swift hunters. No web. Only one European species.

Micrommata viridissima (= roseum) 1.1–1.3 cm. Vivid bright green on top, red stripe down the middle in males only. Lies in wait for insects on leaves. Very pugnacious.

Family   THOMISIDAE   Crab Spiders

Seldom more than 1 cm in length. Flattened-looking bodies with 4 very long fore-legs, longer and stronger than the 4 hind-legs. Holds its legs out sideways like a crab and runs very swiftly either sideways or backwards. Makes no web or web-chamber for living, moulting, hibernating, but many do spin leaves together to make an egg-nest; roam about free, adapting their colouring to their surroundings. Can wait almost motionless for days on end on a sprig, grass, flower, for its prey. Some species can change colour and are easily overlooked. Infinitely slow stalk of prey ending in a sudden clasp of legs (catching insects and other spiders often its superior in size and agility, such as bees, bumble bees, etc.). Kills its prey with poison from fangs and sucks it out. Spiderlings able to produce thread, which they do on fine autumn days and on this the spiderling travels through the air. (Gossamer.)

Xysticus cristatus (= viaticus) Male 4.5 mm, with light prong-marking on top of cephalo-thorax. Abdomen is seamed with white and has light, jagged markings; 4 fore-legs are yellow from the knee down. Female is 7 mm, yellowish-brown with same markings as male; mostly lives among leaves which she spins loosely together and places her egg-cocoon between them; these she guards and defends with determination.

Diaea dorsata Grass-green with a large brown patch on top of abdomen. Lies in wait for prey on leaves.

Misumena vatia (= calycina) Colouring adapted to surroundings, ranging from bright yellow, and cream to pure white. Depressions in abdomen make it look like a face. Lurks on yellow and white flowers. There is a variety with 2 long crimson stripes on the back of the abdomen.

**Diaea tricuspidata* Only lighter and darker specimens, or those with darker or blurred markings on back, can change colour.

Family   SALTICIDAE   Jumping Spiders

Squat bodies with powerful legs; often very colourful. Have the best-developed eyes of any spider; these are in 3 rows, the middle two in the front row being unusually large. Active by day, they spring on their prey, which they sense when 20 cm away and then stalk. They make no nets for hunting, but a lair-sack from which the spider keeps watch, and also moulting and hibernating chambers. Many pass the night under stones or bark. Male performs a courtship dance in front of female, who guards her egg-cocoon and spiderlings.

Salticus scenicus (= Epiblemum scenicum) 5–6 mm, oval, dark cephalo-thorax with white markings; long, oval abdomen, velvet-brown or black with wavy white cross bands. Eyes as in diagram in margin. On sunny walls of brick or wood keeping a look-out for flies etc. which it stalks, then leaps upon, thrusting in its poison-fangs, then sucking them out.

Family   ERESIDAE

CARMINE JUMPING SPIDER *(Eresus niger)* 9–10 mm. Male basic colour black; abdomen a flaming carmine on top with 4 black spots; fore-legs have white rings, the hind-legs are scarlet to the middle. Female less colourful. Prefers sunny, rocky places; rock gardens. Very rare in Britain.

Salticus zebranus (= olearii) About 5 mm; grey, with faded black markings. Often on the trunks of pine trees. Very rare in Britain.

Family   ULOBORIDAE

The only family that does not have poison glands. Spins webs
similar to orb-webs, but instead of trapper-threads they have
twining-threads; hub is always horizontal.

Hyptiotes paradoxus 4–5 mm. Lumpy on top. Colouring varies.
Horizontal web at the height of a person, but almost solely on
spruce; triangular so that it looks like a segment from an orb-net.
4 spokes lead off from 1 signal-thread. With its fore-legs the
spider holds the web to the signal-thread, while it has its hind
legs hooked on to a coiled-up safety-line running from its spinnerets to the branch. The moment a fly touches the web, the spider
releases the coil of thread which uncoils and lengthens causing
the web to sag entangling the fly, whose capture is completed by
further coiling and uncoiling of the safety-thread. Plate 16, No. 9.

Order   OPILIONES Harvestmen

Short round bodies of cephalo-thorax and abdomen. 8 legs;
scissor-shaped chelicerae; maxillary palpi long and bow-shaped.
Most have 1 pair of simple eyes on slight elevations on cephalo-
thorax.

Family   PHALANGIIDAE Harvestmen

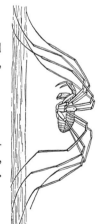

Legs easily discarded (autotomy) and most strikingly long. Feed
on plant matter, dead and live creatures. Lay eggs in ground,
crevices in rock, tree-stumps, etc.

Opilio parietinus 8–10 mm. Light brownish body with black-
brown markings on the back and whitish underside. On walls,
under stones, in gardens.   →

Phalangium opilio (= cornutum) Body 9 mm; brownish-yellow, with several blackish markings on cephalo-thorax. Dark stripe, diamond-shaped in female, serrated in male, down the middle of abdomen. Whitish on underside.

Nemastoma chrysomelas Body 2–2.5 mm with metallic golden spots on the sides. Under moss and stones.

Order   PSEUDOSCORPIONES False-Scorpions

Insignificant small, flattened inhabitants of cracks and crevices. Cephalo-thorax and abdomen of 10–11 segments more or less fused; does not have a tail-segment with a poison fang as scorpions do. In front has 1 pair of powerful maxillary palpi that serve as pincers. Breathe through tracheae. Well-developed sense of touch. Tactile hairs (setae) scattered all over the body.

Chelifer cancroides 3–4.5 mm; reddish-brown; 2 eyes; cephalo-thorax divided into 3 by 2 cross-grooves. Very agile, moves forwards, sideways or backwards. Feeds on mites and book lice. In woods, under bark in birds' nests, in houses among dusty books, in herbaria, insect collections, linen cupboards.

Neobisium muscorum 2.5–3.5 mm; yellow-brown body with dirty-yellow legs. 4 eyes in front of head. No grooves on cephalo-thorax. In woods and open country; both in lowland and mountain, especially on moors and boggy places, under leaves and stones.

CRUSTACEA (See p. 251)

I. MALACOSTRACA Higher Crustaceans

Number of abdominal segments a constant 20. Abdomen never ends in forked tail, but last segment is usually a complete disc or plate. Bodies usually stoutly chitinised.

Order   DECAPODA   "Ten-footed"

Family   Astacidae   River Crayfish

CRAYFISH *(Astacus astacus)* 8–25 cm, female 1–2 cm smaller than male. Dark olive-green to black, like the ground its on, when boiled is red; long body, cylindrical, with a conical point in front, covered with armour; cephalo-thorax finely granulated; pointed frontal spike between 2 mobile eyes on stalks; a flat transverse groove (nape furrow) marks the rear limit of the head; thoracic section has 2 grooves down it (between which the armour is attached to the back) and externally forms a hollow space on either side which are gill cavities. The muscular abdomen, popularly called the "tail", consists of 6 arched movable segments and at the end has 5 broad plates, the so-called tail-fan, which is the organ for swimming backwards. Next to the 2 pairs of antennae in front, come 6 pairs of mouth-parts: first a pair of maxillae (upper jaws) with stout, toothed mandibles and one short 3-segmented feeler; then 2 pairs of short, thin plates, the lower jaw, which present the food to the upper jaws; then 3 pairs of jaw-feet, the 3rd pair of which takes the particles of food to the mouth organs. Next come 5 pairs of thoracic segments which are walking legs; the large claws of the 1st pair of thoracic legs seize the crayfish's prey; the smaller claws of the 2nd and 3rd pair cut it up. On the abdomen are 5 pairs of abdominal legs (swimmerets) used in swimming and also by the female to hold on to her eggs. Balance: at the base of each of the 1st pair of antennae is a hollow, the so-called "hearing-sack" inside which are "sense-bristles" (setae), on which are "hearing-stones" (balancers), that the crayfish loses in moulting and replaces with heavy objects, e.g. grains of sand. A true creature of the twilight and night. Feeds on aquatic insects, worms, snails, mussels, amphibians, tiny fish, carrion, aquatic plants. In autumn female carries irregular balls of eggs between its swimmerets and in the following May or June young crayfish roughly 9 mm long hatch from them; they cling to the female for a while, using their claws.

They moult a number of times. While soft-skinned and defenceless, they remain concealed for about 8 days until the new armour plates harden. Lens-shaped chalk formations on wall of stomach, so-called "eyes" dissolved and secreted by the blood to form armour. Close-season Nov. 1 to May 31. In water with overhanging banks, tangles of roots, stones with hollows under them, etc. where crayfish can hide. The species native to Britain is *Astacus pallipes* but *A. astacus* has been introduced and has colonised some rivers in the south of England. *A. pallipes* is slightly smaller, varying from 4–10 cm in length.

*_Cambarus affinis_ Has a striking red patch on its abdomen, but otherwise is very like the ordinary river crayfish. Introduced from America in 1890, being immune to crayfish disease.

*_Astacus torrentium_ 7–8 cm with particularly narrow, almost cylindrical cephalo-thorax; feels rough to the touch. Whitish legs; eggs greenish-grey. Lives in clear mountain gravel streams in southern Europe.

Family   GRAPSIDAE

CHINESE MITTEN CRAB *(Eriocheir sinensis)* 4–6 sided back-plate, 6–7 cm long; 9 cm broad; the large claws covered with a thick felt-like layer of long hair, which in the adult male covers the entire "hard". Olive green, with dark mottling. Has all the other characteristics of the crab or short-tailed decapod *(Brachyura)*: rudimentary abdomen wrapped under the disc-shaped cephalo-thorax. Spawn in brackish water of estuaries. Young travel up-river, climbing weirs, locks etc. and make short overland journeys to lakes, ponds. Nocturnal. Feeds mainly on mussels, snails, dead fish. Native of China brought to Germany by ships about 1910 and now established in the river systems of Rhine, Elbe, Weser, Oder etc. as far as Lake Constance; also in France. Makes deep galleries in river banks, undermining them. Not fit to eat. Single specimen taken in Thames in 1935.

Order   AMPHIPODA

Family   GAMMARIDAE

FRESHWATER SHRIMP *(Gammarus pulex)* Female 1.5 cm, male up to 2 cm; whitish, greenish or yellowish. Long body curled in a bow and pressed in at the sides. 2 pairs of long antennae and 2 bone-like feelers on the under lip. 7 free thoracic segments each with a pair of legs, the fore 2 pairs being graspers, the next 2 walking-legs, the last 3 jumping-legs, with very thick femora and long tibiae, pointing well to the rear. At the base of their hind-legs are the gills. There are 6 abdominal segments, first 3 of which carry a pair of pronged swimming-feet which, moving continually, keep the gills supplied with fresh water; the hind 3 segments have jumping-legs directed backwards. Jerky swimming action of alternate curling and straightening of abdomen; on the bottom often slithers along sideways, or shoots upwards with a powerful jerk of its abdomen. Feeds on detritus, preferably plant-matter. On land the gills dry. Passes the winter buried in mud or moist sand. Eggs are laid in a tube of bristles, open at both ends, on the underside of female. Very common in running water (streams, rivers, dykes with plenty of aquatic plants to provide its nourishment; also on sea-coast); mostly on the bottom in shallow water, especially under large stones or bits of wood, often in large numbers. Has an importance as food for fish.

Order   ISOPODA

Family   ASELLIDAE   Water Isopods

WATER LOUSE *(Asellus aquaticus)* Female 8 mm, male 12 mm; brownish-grey to dark violet with lighter patches. Long body of roughly uniform width, shallow; 1 pair of long and 1 pair of short antennae. Eyes distinctly pigmented. Abdominal rings fused into one large plate with two forked abdominal legs. Crawls about the bottom, climbs slowly up water plants or swims about agilely. Cares for its young. Throughout the year females can be found with brood-sacks made out of the 4 fore pairs of thoracic legs enclosing first the eggs, then the incompletely developed young, which the female carries about for 3–6 weeks. Feeds on particles of dead plants. If water dries out in summer, buries itself in mud beforehand, a sort of summer hibernation until the next rain. Able to grow new legs or antennae segments if damaged. In stagnant or slow-flowing water with rotting vegetable matter, especially in pools in beech woods. Picture shows first upper side, then underside.

II. ENTOMOSTRACA   Lower Crustaceans

Bodies only slightly chitinised, often in a hinged shell of 2 plates; other than in the parasitic forms, abdomen ends in a forked "tail". Number of body segments varies, often only detectable by their appendages.

Order   COPEPODA   (Having oar-like feet)

Family   CYCLOPOIDA   Cyclops

Cyclops agilis Up to 1.45 mm; colourless to yellow, with eye in front of head; long, clear articulated body, the last segment bearing a tail-fork serrated on outer margins with long feathered bristles that it uses as balancers; 2 pairs of mouth-parts; 3 pairs of oar-like legs on thorax; no feet on abdomen. Feeds mostly on algae. Breathes through surface of body. Carries its eggs in two sacs attached to abdomen. From these hatch nauplius larvae, which grow more limbs with each moult. Prolific. Common everywhere in fresh water.

Cyclops fuscus 2–2.5 mm. Close-lying egg-sacs. One of the loveliest and most colourful of its kind. Otherwise as the foregoing. In most lakes and ponds.

Order   BRANCHIOPODA   Fairy Shrimps

Thoracic legs all leaf-shaped, lobed and have flat gill-sacs. Number of body segments varies.

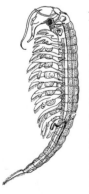

Family   BRANCHIPODIDAE

Branchipus stagnalis (= *schaefferi*) Up to 2.5 cm; pale yellow with vivid coloured markings. Long body; no shell; 2 large eyes on stalks on each side of head and small frontal eye. 11 pairs of thoracic legs with leaf-shaped lobes and flat gill-sacs; long abdomen has no legs, tapers into 2 strong bristles. 1st pair of antennae small, thread-like; 2nd pair longish and in male have become powerful pincers which are used to hold the female. Swims quickly on its back; legs move to and fro rhythmically swirling food to it. In pools etc. in sunny places; often in large numbers in spring. Eggs, if dried, will survive for months or years.

Family   CHIROCEPHALIDAE

Chirocephalus grubei 2–3 cm. Male has broad, toothed frontal appendage between its antennae (the same as the long filaments of *B. stagnalis,* which it otherwise resembles). Common. *Chirocephalus diaphanus* is a similar species found in Britain in temporary pools.

Family   BRANCHINECTIDAE

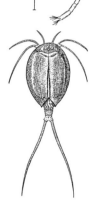

*BRINE SHRIMP *(Artemia salina)* Up to 1.5 cm. No frontal appendage. 8-segmented abdomen; short leaf-shaped tail bristles. Usually only in brackish inland waters.

Family   TRIOPSIDAE

Triops (= Apus) cancriformis Up to 10 cm including its 2 tail bristles. Body covered on top with broad, shield-shaped scales up to 3 cm long, and on these in front are sited its 3 eyes. Has 60 pairs of swimming-feet. The final abdominal segment has no plate, its end is indented. First pair of legs end in 3 long lashes. Swims on its back. Colouring: yellowish to brownish. Males few and far between. Reproduction mostly through unfertilised eggs. Small freshwater pools. Eggs survive long periods of dryness and frost; hence the sudden occasional appearance of large numbers.

Lepidurus apus (= productus) Similar to foregoing, but has 41 pairs of swimming-legs. Abdominal segments ends in a tongue-shaped, carinated plate between the two tail filaments, which the foregoing lacks. Appears in spring in pools of flood water.

Family   DAPHNIIDAE   Water-Fleas

Daphnia pulex Female 1.5 mm, male 0.8 to 1 mm. Yellowish to yellowish-red body, pressed in at sides, has a saddle of 2 hinged transparent scales which also cover the head, which has a distinct join and is elongated into a beak, like a helmet. At the rear it tapers into a spine. Abdomen tucked under the belly.

Fore antennae curled; hind antennae form divided paddles that have large swimming bristles at the end. Jerky, leaping swimming action. One large black compound eye on head. Eggs carried by wind, able to survive through a winter or long periods. Main constituent of the plankton that fish eat. Common in pools which, when present in large numbers, they can colour pink. Picture shows female with 3 eggs in brood-chamber.

Daphnia magna Female up to 7.5 mm, male is smaller. Back ridge of abdomen shows a deep indentation. Otherwise is as foregoing.

Phylum   *MOLLUSCA*

Soft, plump, inarticulated bodies with 2 symmetrical sides or spiral arrangement. Head more or less distinct or else lacking (mussels). No articulated limbs, but, instead, muscular underside acts as organ of locomotion (foot). Skin has a wealth of glands which form a fold or mantle and secretions form the calcareous shell, which, however, is often rudimentary or lacking. Between the mantle and the intestinal sac is the mantle-cavity which contains the organs for breathing and the openings of the intestines and sexual organs. Sexual reproduction. Many are hermaphrodites. Most live in water.

SPECIAL CHARACTERISTICS OF UNIVALVES

Shell in one piece, secreted by the glands in the mantle, or body skin, consists of epidermis, prismatic and mother-of-pearl layers. The simplest structure is that of the cap-snail. In other snails the growing body is

Fig. 65: Snail shell (lengthwise section)

always surrounded by a protective tube that is either on one plane or cone – or spindle-shaped with expanding coils arranged in a spiral. In

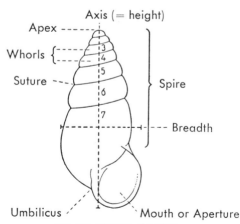

Fig. 66: Diagram of a Shell

most the shell coils to the right, i.e. when looking at the point, the shell coils in such a way that the mouth points to the right, the coils turning clockwise.

The turn is round the central axis or spindle, which can be bored down its length, in which case one speaks of an umbilical shell, but if the spindle is closed underneath, it is called non-umbilicate. The umbo depression in the middle of the underside of the shell is formed by the convolutions departing more and more from the imaginary centre line. When the umbo is very narrow it is called pierced. The thickening of the edge of the mantle that sometimes peeps out from the rim of the shell is well supplied with shell-forming glands. Transverse stripes (year rings) are caused by interruptions in growth. Foot has a broad, flat sole. Secretes mucus to keep this smooth. Head has feelers, eyes and mouth.

Respiration is purely water-breathing in the case of the gill-snails which can remain under water permanently; but all land-snails and shell-less water-slugs have lungs. The lung is a cavity on fore-part of the shell, between mantle and body, that is filled with air; a network of blood vessel tissue in the wall of the cavity effects the exchange of gases. The breathing-hole leading to the lung cavity is a round opening that lies at the edge of the mantle in the case of the shell-less molluscs, in those whose shells turn to the right, on the right hand side, and, in the case of those that coil to the left, on the left hand side.

All lung-breathing slugs, both of land and water, without shells, as well as the gill-breathing species, *Valvata*, are hermaphrodites. Each individual

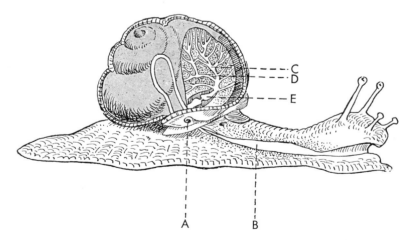

Fig. 67: Part of the body of an edible snail: A = vent; B = intestine; C = breathing hole; D = blood-vessels; E = heart

can act as male and female. The gill-snails and their relatives on land that have shells are sexually distinct, being either male or female. The eggs of the water-snails are thin-shelled and covered with a slimy adhesive coating so that they stick to things easily. Snail spawn differs according to the species. Under the influence of warmth it hatches in a matter of a week or two.

CHARACTERISTICS OF THE MUSSEL

The two movable halves or valves of the shell are attached to the back of the mollusc by a hinge-ligament, a piece of cartilage that when wet is very elastic. In many species the inner edge of the upper rims of the two shells has interlocking teeth preventing sideways displacement. Together with the ligament and the ridges they form the lock. 2 shallow depressions on the inside of either end of each valve denote the places where bunches of strong muscles will grow.

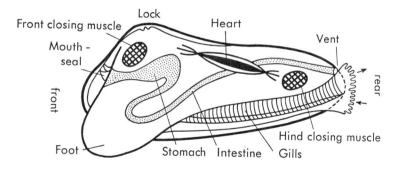

Fig. 68: Structure of a Mussel

These muscles that span the inside of the mussel at either end form the closing-mechanism. To move, the mussel protrudes an axe-shaped foot out of the bottom of its open shell, bores this into the mud, digs the point of it in, then contracts its foot, so that the whole body, shell and all, is drawn forward, leaving a furrow. The valves (shells) have 3 layers: on the outside a non-calcarous, horny skin, the periostracum; underneath the prismatic-layer of carbonate of lime, the ostracum, and then the iridescent layer of mother-of-pearl. There are growth or year rings.

The oldest part rises from each valve like a hump near the edge. It is called the umbo crown and is often badly corroded, especially in soft water. Normally the mussel lies motionless on the bottom, its foot and blunt fore-end of the shell deeply buried in the mud, leaving only the more pointed hind end with its 2 slit-openings protruding. Water is swirled in through the lower and larger opening and expelled through the upper and smaller opening or siphon. Large, leaf-shaped gills hang down from the trunk on either side of the foot. These, like the surface of the mantle, are covered with mucus and innumerable hairs (cilia) which beat rhythmically inducing a flow of water from which they gather particles of food and pass them to the mouth opening. The delicate gill-tissue extracts oxygen from the water, which thus both feeds the mussel and enables it to breathe. Tiny creatures and decaying plant matter are swirled through the triangular flaps around the mouth, which lies between the two parts of the seal just in front of the foot. Undigested food is expelled, along with used breathing-water, through the exhalent siphon. The in-flowing and out-flowing water also carries the sperm cells from the male into the female. The fertilised eggs develop into larvae in the gill-plates which are perforated like trellis-work. After some months, the female opens her valves and shuts them again so abruptly that the growing larvae (glochidia) are expelled. Should the long sticky byssus thread of one of these innumerable larvae now floating about on their own, brush against a fish, it will stick to it. The mussel will then anchor itself to the fish's skin by the sharp hooks it has at the tip of each valve and for the next 2–3 months will live on the fish's body juices, developing meanwhile into a proper mussel, when it will free itself and sink to the bottom.

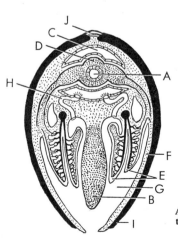

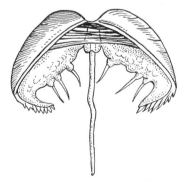

Fig. 70: Glochidium larva of a mussel showing byssus thread (natural size about .25 mm)

Fig. 69: Section of a river mussel:
A = intestine; B = foot; C = pericardium; D = ventricle; E = gills; F = mantle; G = mantle-cavity; H = kidney; I = shell; J = hinge-ligament

Being stationary on the bottom, a mussel is exposed to two particular dangers: being crushed (by a falling stone or gravel) and being washed away; it thus needs a stout shell that closes firmly to make the exposed area as small as possible. The same thing is true of the snail, whose shell is a long tube made into a spiral thus reducing considerably the area exposed to attack, as well as its resistance to the flow of water, as is also the case with the mussel, so that there is less risk of being swept away.

In this connection it is interesting that

1. The shells of mussels and other molluscs in calm water (sheltered bays, etc.) are thinner than those in more agitated water.

2. Mussels in ponds are larger, the calmer the water is.

3. Water-snails in still water stretch out further than those in water that is not so still.

Where breathing is concerned there are various degrees of adaptation discernible. Mussels and other molluscs with gills can remain permanently under water. Small orb-shells and pea-shells (see p. 516) with their long, tubular feed-pipes can bury themselves deep in mud or sand without interrupting their water-breathing. In inland waters that easily dry out, means have had to be found to make survival possible, so, instead of gills, the breathing cavity is equipped with a tissue of blood vessels that allows direct breathing of air. Pond snails *(Lymnaea)* will go up or down for breathing; but in late autumn and winter, you will not see them coming up for air, for they are also able to obtain oxygen direct from the water, as various parts of the body are adapted for breathing through the skin. Down the outer and inner edges of its broad triangular antennae run blood vessels with a network of veins between them. Similarly the loose mantle skin, which envelops the whole shell is adapted for breathing. The operculate snails are better adapted to life in the water and possess gills.

Class   *GASTROPODA*

LAND SNAILS

Order   PULMONATA   Lunged Snails

Family   HELICIDAE

ROMAN or EDIBLE SNAIL *(Helix pomatia)* Shell up to 5 cm high and 4 cm across; almost round with the umbilicus covered by the turned-back inner rim. *Colour:* a light or dark brown-yellow with 5 darker, blurred bands; surface surrounded by growth rings. 5 whorls rapidly increasing, the last being large and bulgy. Rounded almost circular mouth with slightly out-turned edges. Body worm-shaped, about 10 cm long. Slimy, yellow-grey skin. Arched back; underside a flat muscular foot rounded in front and slightly pointed at the rear. On the head, 2 retractable horns; 2 longish eye-supports, thick like a club at the end, each with a black dot (an eye) at the tip; 2 shorter, eye-less feelers. On the underside of the head is a mouth-opening with a thin, elastic upper lip. Inside the mouth is a radula, a rasp-like tongue with innumerable horny teeth, that breaks down particles of plants. Mating takes place in May or June, preceded by snails thrusting a chalky harpoon-like "love dart" deep into the side of each other's foot after which there is a mutual exchange of spermatophores. In winter the sole of the foot secretes a hard slime membrane that seals the shell. (This is dissolved again in the spring.) Lays several batches of almost pea-sized eggs with white skin-shells in some damp hole it digs in the ground. Hatch out after some weeks. Common, in gardens, bushy places, etc., especially where soil is chalky.

GROVE SNAIL *(Cepaea [Helix] nemoralis)* Shell 17 mm × 23 mm, globular, lemon-yellow to orange or red to brown-red with or without black-brown bands. 5 rather flat whorls; umbilicus is closed in adults; black-brown mouth margins, dilated, turned back. Feeds on fresh greenery. Mostly in hedges, tree-nurseries, less often in woods.

GARDEN SNAIL *(Cepaea [= Helix] hortensis)* In shape, colour and banding similar to *C. nemoralis,* but is somewhat smaller and the mouth of the shell is narrower with white margins. Lives more in woods than the foregoing.

COPSE SNAIL *(Arianta [= Helix] arbustorum)* Shell 12–22 mm high, 18–25 mm across; globular; shiny chestnut flecked with straw-yellow and dark brown bands. 3–6 whorls. Mouth margin has shiny white lip, curved back at the umbilicus, which it covers completely. On tree trunks, in hedges, deciduous woods.

Fruticicola sericea Shell 5.5 mm × 7.5 mm; globular, thickly covered with long, soft hair; thin, yellowish to reddish-brown shell, 6 somewhat arched whorls, the last rounded and widening at the mouth; deep groove; narrow, partially concealed umbilicus. Half-moon shaped opening with a sharp edge. In woods, meadows in hilly or mountainous country.

Helicella itala (= ericetorum) Shell 6–8 mm × 12–18 mm; flattened into disc-shape; uniform yellowish-white or may have light brown bands. 6 rather arched whorls with a deep groove. Mouth almost round, sharp edge. Wide umbilicus showing in whole convolution. On dry, warm slopes with short grass, mostly on chalk.

Helicella (= Xerophila) obvia Shell 7–9 mm × 15–20 mm; flattened like a disc; rather thick shell almost chalk-white with 4–6 dark brown to black bands, often broken up into streaks and spots. Narrow umbilicus, only widening towards the mouth. On dry, grassy slopes, embankments, in glades, often together in colonies. Largely in central and southern Europe.

Zenobiella incarnata (= monacha) 1.3–1.6 cm × 0.9–1 cm. Flattened; globular; matt, very thick, finely granulated shell, grey-yellow to reddish-brown; deep, but narrow boss, uncovered or half-covered; 6 whorls, not very arched, the last having blunt edges rising away from the mouth, which is set obliquely, has a sharp edge, dilated and turned back, with a stout, flesh-pink lip inside that shows reddish-yellow on outside. In woods and bushes, but more in mountainous than in low country.

Fruticicola (= *Eulota*) *fruticum* Shell 14–15 mm × 18–20 mm; spherical, almost transparent, uniform ash-grey to grey-white, or yellowish, or reddish to red-brown. 5–6 well arched whorls, the last big and bulging. Mouth margin sharp, scarcely dilated at all, turned slightly outward. Umbilicus open to the tip. Among bushes, in woods, in grass. In dry weather often on the underside of leaves.

Family   VITRINIDAE   Glass-shells

Vitrina pellucida Shell 3–4 mm × 4.5 mm; flattened spherical, greenish, glassily-transparent; no umbilicus; 3 whorls only slightly raised, quickly increasing, a little arched, the last rounded, moderately dilated. Mouth as wide as the rest of the shell. In damp, cool places. In summer, concealed deep in moist earth, coming to the surface, when the weather is cooler.

Family   ZONITIDAE   Glass Snails

Retinella (= *Hyalinia*) *nitidula* Shell 4.5 mm × 8–9 mm, flattened, brown horn-colour, shiny. 4^1/$_2$–5 faintly arched, slowly increasing whorls, the last expanding only slightly at the mouth. Milk-white round the wide, deep umbilicus; all the convolutions visible. Found in the foliage of oak and beech.

Family   DAUDEBARDIIDAE

Daudebardia rufa Shell 5 × 3 × 2.5 mm, delicate, glassily translucent, shiny, yellow-greenish to red-brown, flatly arched; 2^1/$_2$–3 whorls, the last increasing rapidly; mouth wider than it is tall; edge of spindle partly covering the umbilicus. Small shell cannot accommodate the whole of the large body. Lives in damp earth; carnivorous (snails, earthworms, woodlice) even cannibal.

Family   SUCCINEIDAE   Amber Snails

AMBER SNAIL *(Succinea putris)* Shell 2.2 cm × 1.2 cm, in shape a swollen oval, thin walls, lighter or darker amber-yellow or a pale greenish-yellow, glassy. 4 quickly expanding whorls, rather arched, the last very bulging. Brown oval mouth, somewhat oblique, at least half the height of the whole shell. Body contains a lot of water and cannot be wholly accommodated, so that snail is not entirely covered. Those that live by water are of darker colour. Often by water or in moist pasture, especially on reeds and other bog-plants, sometimes even submerged. Intermediate host of *Distomum macrostomum,* a parasite flatworm (fluke), the gill-tubes of which grow into the snail's horns causing irregular swellings and colouring them brightly (green and white rings) so that song birds are attracted to eat them.

Family   ENDODONTIDAE   Discus Snails

Discus (= Goniodiscus) rotundatus Shell 2.5 mm × 6–7 mm, flattened, disc or lens-shaped, umbilicus large; strongly fluted; yellow-grey with red-brown flecks in a ray pattern. $4^{1}/_{4}$–$6^{1}/_{4}$ whorls with a blunt keel that disappears near the mouth. Feeds chiefly on mould. In wet, shady places: under stones, leaves, wood, in shady woods, under bark, on rushes.

Family   CLAUSILIIDAE   Door Snails

TWO-LIPPED DOOR SNAIL *(Laciniaria [= Clausilia] biplicata)* Shell 16–20 mm × 4 mm; spindle-shaped, turning anticlockwise; 12–14 gradually expanding convolutions, the last being one-third of the toal length. Narrow mouth that can be closed with a tongue-shaped door, the clausilium, which rests on and is guided by lamellae in the mouth. On mossy rocks, walls, tree stumps, and on the ground; among bushes, in woods; among leaves, humus, stones. Especially where there is chalk.

Family   ENIDAE   Bulins

Latin *bulinus,* a little blister

Ena obscura (= Buliminus obscurus) Shell 9 mm × 4 mm; tower-shaped, finely striped, dark brown, coiling clockwise, 7 whorls; mouth margins slightly bent out with a weak, white lip. Shell often thickly covered with earth. In woods and bushes on the ground and on tree trunks. Hides in ground during drought, emerging when it rains.

Buliminus detritus (= Zebrina detrita) Shell 2 cm × 1 cm; elongated oval; thick, shiny, uniform white or has brown streaks; 7–8 slightly arched convolutions, the last some two-fifths of the total length. Almost vertical mouth with sharp margin and weak lip. In uncultivated chalky soil; on grass of sunny slopes.

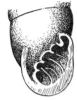

Family   PUPILLIDAE   Chrysalis Snails

Abida (= Buliminus) frumentum Shell 6.5 mm × 3 mm; elongated oval and pointed top shape; brown-yellow; 9 whorls, the last whitish. 8 folds in mouth; 2 on walls of mouth, 2 on column of spindle, and 4 on roof of mouth. Margin of mouth has thick, whitish translucent swelling. Likes heat and chalk. On dry slopes with short grass in limestone hills; on ground, under roots of grass. Intermediate host of lancet leech.

MOSS SNAIL *(Pupilla muscorum)* Shell 3.5 mm × 2 mm; short, cylindrical, like a bee skep, brown to horn-colour, 6–7 gradually increasing whorls, the last of which has whitish, tooth-like protuberances on the wall of the mouth. In the turf on sunny, not too dry places where there is some chalk. Also gardens, hedges. Common.

Family   FERUSSACIIDAE   Spire Snails

BLIND SNAIL *(Caecilioides acicula)* Shell 5 mm × 1–1.4 mm; slim, spindle-shaped; transparent whitish with strong gloss; when snail dies, becomes milk-white and opaque. 6–7 convolutions. Narrow mouth with sharp margin. Snail has no eyes. Found on particularly chalky, rather wet places in moss, under stones, in the ground beside roots or bones. Empty shells found in rock-dust, where rivers have overflowed, mole-heaps, tangles of roots.

Family   COCHLICOPIDAE   Agate Snails

SLIPPERY SNAIL *(Cochlicopa [= Cionella] lubrica)* Shell 6 mm × 3 mm; long oval, smooth, glossy, translucent, yellowy horn-colour; 6 faintly arched whorls, the last as long as the other 5 together. Egg-shaped mouth with a reddish, somewhat thicker margin. Damp places: meadows, woods, especially under leaves.

TERRESTRIAL SLUGS

Order   PULMONATA   "Lunged slugs"

Family   ARIONIDAE   Round back slugs

LARGE BLACK SLUG *(Arion ater)* Up to 15 cm. When fully grown is brick-red *(A. a. rufus)* brown or black with red foot-seam; juveniles are yellowish or whitish-green, sometimes with black head and horns. Back wrinkled and carries a mantle-shield, in which, towards the foot, is the slug's breathing hole and close under it the sexual opening. When touched contracts, withdrawing its front towards its rear (the opposite way to *Limax*) making itself almost hemispherical. Feeds on fungi, withered plant matter, fresh green-food. Lays calcareous shelled eggs on theg round under moss, stones, etc. Life span about one year. Woods, among bushes, on meadows. Common.

BOURGUIGNAT'S SLUG *(Arion fasciatus [= circumscriptus])* 4—5 cm; grey or olive to brownish; juvenile is light or reddish-grey. Dark side bands with sharp lower edges. Broad fringe of lighter colour between dark band on side and light edge of sole. The sole is white. Most have a white keel-line down the middle of the back. Colourless slime. Vegetarian. Otherwise as the foregoing. Woods, gardens.

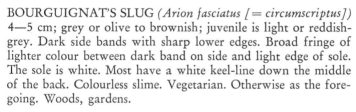

GARDEN SLUG *(Arion hortensis)* Up to 5 cm. Basic colour is dirty black. Middle of back is darker with a blurred lighter line round it. Light grey sole. Orange-coloured slime. Small grains of lime under the shell-plate. In chalky country. Gardens, quarries, vineyards; less often in fields; not in woods. Solely vegetarian. Spends the day in worm tunnels or under thick vegetation.

DUSKY SLUG *(Arion subfuscus)* 5–6 cm contracting to 1 cm. Fine lengthwise wrinkles, yellow to reddish-brown with dark lengthwise bands; finely granulated mantle-shield with dark lyre-shaped mark. Yellowish-white sole. Orange slime. Small grains of lime under the plate. On beech leaves of the same colour as it or on the needle-strewn floor of fir-woods; also on fungi, on which it feeds.

HEDGEHOG SLUG *(Arion intermedius [= minimus])* 1.5 cm, flat, rounded rear end; yellow-grey, back and mantle-shield mostly darker; side bands faded; whitish-yellow sole; golden-yellow slime. Has small round pin-heads on skin. Mainly in conifer woods. Feeds on fungi.

Family   LIMACIDAE   Keelback Slugs

GREAT GREY SLUG *(Limax maximus)* 12–15 cm; long, slim tapering body ending in a sharp point; either grey or has 2 broken blackish bands down the sides, or grey-black; sole uniform white. Sharp keel along hinder part. Mantle-shield short and broad, rounded in front, pointed behind. Found particularly in woods under bark on trees, under stones, leaves, etc.; feeds on fungi.

SLENDER SLUG *(Limax tenellus)* 3.5–6 cm. Slight, translucent body, yellowish body, sometimes with faint lengthwise bands; yellow slime. Slight "keel" on end of tail. Mantle-shield rounded both in front and behind. Bright yellow sole. Shield mostly darker, sometimes orange. Found on fungi, on which it feeds.

FIELD SLUG *(Agriolimax [= Deroceras] agrestes)* 3–6 cm. Spindle-shaped, tapering to a point behind with sharp keel along end of back. Whitish to brown with irregular dark spots and streaks. Sole yellowish-white. White slime. Short mantle-shield rounded at the back with broad wavy line. In fields and gardens, especially on heavy land; never on sandy soil deficient in lime. Causes damage by eating plants. Emerges from the ground and other places of concealment at night. Lays 200–250 eggs in the summer.

TREE SLUG *(Lehmannia marginata [= Limax arborum])* Up to 7 cm; spindle-shaped. Mantle-shield rounded in front, pointed behind, concentrically corrugated. Grey with 2 dark stripes down it and between them a light keel stripe with sharp edges; hind part of body translucent. Sole uniform white-grey. Colourless slime. On bark of trees and rocks, for which particularly suited because takes up water in body. In dry weather in knot holes; in winter in ground. Feeds on lichens.

SHELL-BEARERS IN FRESH WATER

Order   PULMONATA

Family   LYMNAEIDAE   Pond Snails

GREAT POND SNAIL *(Lymnaea stagnalis)* Shell 5—6 cm; horn-coloured, glistening, fine stripes, coils to right. Slender whorls, drawn into a point, almost as long as the mouth. Different habitats. 6–8 whorls, first expanding slowly and scarcely arched at all, then expanding rapidly. Spindle hollow right up to the tip. Broad head, flattened on a slant. Breathing and sexual vent on the right. One pair of triangular, lobed horns that are not retractable. Eyes at the base of the horns. Capable of steady slide on a ribbon of slime secreted by the glands in its foot. Often moves along such a band on the surface of the water, with its foot uppermost and shell pointing down. Grazes on algae on aquatic plants, stones, etc. Obtains air at the surface. When threatened expels air and sinks rapidly. Rises by reducing the pressure of its mantle. Hermaphrodite. Mostly unisexual reproduction. Spawn a transparent ribbon of jelly stuck to stones, water-plants, etc. Tiny, fully developed snails hatch out. Mostly in stagnant water with muddy bottom and water plants.

DWARF POND SNAIL *(Lymnaea [= Galba] truncatula)* Shell up to 10 mm; horn-yellow, coils to the right; finely striped. 5–6 steeply arched and stepped whorls, together somewhat higher than the mouth, which is egg-shaped with a sharp margin. Spire slightly spiral. Umbilicus slit narrow. In small bodies of water, pools, ditches, on stones, plants, etc. at the water's edge; sometimes emerges from water and can be found in meadows. Lies buried in mud during drought. Intermediate host of *Fasciola hepatica,* the liver-fluke that attacks sheep.

MARSH SNAIL *(Lymnaea [= Stagnicola] palustris)* Shell 2–2.7 cm × 1.1–1.7 cm; elongated oval drawn out into a point; surface often wrinkled, mostly blue-grey to black; grooves yellow-white. 6 whorls only slightly arched, expanding quickly and regularly. Often has a brown seam before rim of mouth, which latter is half the height of the whole. In stagnant or slowly flowing water with little vegetation, or in marshes, seldom in lakes.

Lymnaea (= Radix) auricularia Shell 2.5–3 cm × 2–3 cm; coils to right; pointed short whorl jutting beyond the mouth. Last whorl large and extended like an ear-shaped blister. Shell of juvenile pointed oval, the last whorl not expanded into ear-shape. Shape varies where there is movement in the water. Spawn is a string of eggs the shape of a caterpillar. In stagnant water with plenty of vegetation (still water form).

GLUTINOUS SNAIL *(Myxas [= Amphipeplea] glutinosa)* Shell 10–15 mm × 8–11 mm; delicate, thin, translucent, smooth, glistening, almost as clear as glass or yellowish, finely striped. 3–4 whorls, the first only slightly raised, the last constituting almost the whole shell. Wide, oval mouth. Snail itself is fat, very slimy, olive with black flecks. Mantle yellow-brown with black marking enveloping almost the entire shell. Stagnant water with lots of vegetation; boggy pools, backwaters; either on plants or on the bottom.

Family   PLANORBIDAE   Ram's Horn Snails

GREAT RAM'S HORN SNAIL *(Planorbis corneus)* Shell 12–14 mm × 25–32 mm. Thick walls, glistening, olive to red-brown; coils to left, disc-shaped, completely round with 5½ whorls that expand rapidly, higher than they are wide, arched on top with a deep groove between. The convolutions all on one level, deeply grooved on surface. Mouth kidney-shaped. Snail itself is ashen-grey or velvety black. Sole is lighter. Long, bristle-shaped horns. Food and habits like *Lymnaea stagnalis.* Stagnant or slowly flowing water with plenty of vegetation.

RAM'S HORN SNAIL *(Planorbis [= Tropidiscus] planorbis)* Shell up to 4 mm × 17–20 mm; stout walls, yellowish to horn-brown, glistening; 6 whorls broader than deep, coiling to the left in one plane in shape of disc; whorls expand slowly. Steeply arched on top, flat underneath; keel near the underside; mouth oblique oval. Stagnant water with muddy bottom; both in lowlands and hills. Prolific.

KEELED RAM'S HORN SNAIL *(Planorbis [= Tropidiscus] carinatus)* Shell 2–3 mm × 14–17 mm; thin walls with almost regular stripes; reddish horn-colour; 4–5 whorls very compressed, coiled to left in one plane, expanding quickly and with a sharp keel on the middle of the whorl. In clear, chalky water, stagnant or with slight motion. Not so common as foregoing.

Family   PHYSIDAE   Bladder Snails

BLADDER SNAIL *(Physa fontinalis)* Shell 10 mm × 6–8 mm; oval, thin and fragile, yellowish horn colour, translucent, smooth, glistening. Coils to left, 3–4 whorls, the first 3 very small, the last greatly inflated and constituting almost the entire shell. Snail itself very active; long horns with eye at the base but on the inside; mantle flecked with black enveloping, with finger-shaped appendages, the greater part of the shell. Long, thin foot. Very large breathing-hole. Circular spawn, contains 10–30 eggs. Clear water with plenty of vegetation, especially among the plants in streams.

MOSS BLADDER SNAIL *(Aplecta [= Physa] hypnorum)* Shell 12–15 mm × 5 mm; long oval, brownish; smooth, glossy; thin translucent walls; 6 whorls coiling to the left, only slightly arched, the last whorl being elongated and not inflated. Mouth half the height of the whole. Snail itself is black-blue with long awl-shaped horns, mantle grey with black flecks. Rises to the surface every now and again to breathe. Ditches, pools, especially on moors, alder-swamps, in low country and hills. Mostly in large numbers, especially in spring.

Family   ANCYLIDAE   Freshwater Limpets

RIVER LIMPET *(Ancylastrum fluviatile [= Ancylus fluviatilis])* Shell up to 4 × 5.7 × 4–5 mm; shaped like a cap or a bowl, no convolutions; has a blunt point on top curving slightly back-wards. Curls towards the right. Fine radial stripes cross the con-centric growth stripes. Most have thin, translucent walls, whitish or yellowish or red-brown. Snail is not curled up, but spherical and wholly contained in the shell. Mantle is almost shield-shaped and does not extend beyound the shell. Short horns. Broad disc-foot by which attaches itself to stones; never rises to surface. Breathes through its skin, the lung-cavity being rudimentary. Spawn in shape of an hour-glass, transparent, a disc some 2–4 mm across fixed to some object. Flowing water, seldom in shore-zone of lakes.

LAKE LIMPET *(Ancylus [=Acroloxus] lacustris)* Shell 2 mm × 7 mm × 3 mm; shield-shaped; very thin, horn-yellow to brownish; covers its much smaller mollusc like a roof; whorl slightly tilted to the left (in *A. fluviatile* to the right). On plants or pieces of wood in stagnant water.

Order PECTINIBRANCHIATA (= MONOTOCARDIA)

Family   VIVIPARIDAE   River Snails

RIVER SNAIL *(Vivipara [= Paludina] vivipara)* Shell 3–
4 cm × 2.4–3 cm. Fat creature with a long beak-like snout and
broad foot. Shell fat cone, green-brown with 3 dark bands
(seldom uniform colouring), 6–6^1/$_2$ steeply-arched whorls set off
by very deep grooves. Delicate, sharply protruding point. Open
operculum. Round oval mouth; horny lid (operculum), reddish-
yellow with concentric growth-rings, when snail stretches out,
lies behind the shell. Both horns of female thin; right horn of
smaller male is thicker and shorter than the left. Comb-shaped
gills line the whole length of the breathing-cavity. Feeds on
animal matter. Mostly on bottom, will swim to surface when
the sun shines. Sexes distinct, viviparous. All summer ovary is
filled with embryos at various stages of development as only
1 is born at a time, being already 1 cm and having a shell with
4 whorls. Stagnant, muddy, boggy water with vegetation, especially in low country.

LISTER'S RIVER SNAIL *(Viviparus fasciatus)* Shell 2.5–
3.5 cm × 2.1–2.6 cm; very like the foregoing. Slim shell. Covered
boss. 5–6 flat whorls, not stepped. Shallow grooves. Blunt point.
In slow flowing water.

Family   VALVATIDAE   Valve Snails

VALVE SNAIL *(Valvata piscinalis)* Shell 6 mm × 5 mm, round,
top shape, greenish or yellowish, shiny. Whorls almost as high
as the mouth. Fairly stout walls with fine ribbing stripes. 4–5
roundish whorls with fine growth stripes. Operculum and mouth
almost circular; yellowish, translucent, not retractable. Long,
comb-shaped gills protrude from gill-cavity. Muddy bottom of
stagnant and slowly flowing water. Common.

LAND WINKLE

Family   POMATIASIDAE   Land Winkles

The following species, although related to the winkles, has mig-
rated to land.

ROUND-MOUTHED SNAIL *(Pomatias [= Ericia] elegans)*
Shell 10–15 mm × 8–12 mm. Egg-shaped to top-shaped, blunt,
stout walls; surface latticed with cross and spiral lines, yellowish-
violet-grey or dark flesh-colour, mostly with bands broken in
spots. 5 almost cylindrical whorls. Mouth nearly circular. Lung-
breathing land snail. Feeds on dead leaves. On chalky soil, in
vineyards, ruins; hidden under leaves and bushes. Sociable.

Class *LAMELLIBRANCHIATA* Bivalve Molluscs

Family   UNIONIDAE   River Mussels

PAINTER'S MUSSEL *(Unio pictorum)* 7–10 cm × 3–4 cm ×
2.5–2.8 cm. Thick walled, tongue-shaped, rounded in front,
narrow and with a rounded point at rear. Upper rim almost
straight, with obtuse angle to rear edge, lower rim straight and
parallel to upper rim, gradually rising behind. Shell of juvenile
reddish yellow, becoming olive-yellow and yellow-green behind.
Locks with tall teeth and long sharp ridge. Inflated umbones with
2 protuberances. Especially on sandy bottoms of moving water
of rivers and lakes. Various local races and sub-species. The shells
were fomerly used by artists to hold their paints. Picture shows:
U. p. platyrhynchus, the form found in muddy lakes.

Unio grassus (= batavus) 5–6 cm. Valves swollen and with
thick walls, dark or greenish, sometimes have rays; oval outline,
always the same width at either end; lower rim almost straight,
slightly concave in the middle; rear part 2–2½ times as long
as the front part, rounded with a slight point. Strong, brown-
yellow ligament. Umbones mostly corroded. Mother-of-pearl
layer varies: bluish or yellowish-white, even pinkish. Picture
shows greatly corroded shell of the form found in the muddy
streams and lakes of northern Germany.

SWOLLEN RIVER MUSSEL *(Unio tumidus)* 6.5–9 cm × 3.4 cm
× 2.5–3.5 cm. Thick walls, pointed egg-shape; widely rounded
in front, narrowing quickly and evenly behind, lower rim convex.
Shell olive-green or greenish-brown, with radiating rays.

Anodonta complanata 8 cm × 4.5 cm × 2 cm. Shell sometimes vividly coloured, shiny; very flat, thin elliptical oval, round-pointed in front; more pointed at the rear. Upper rim almost straight, ascending, rear rim gradually falling away. Umbones only slightly protuberant. Slow-flowing water with muddy bottom. Picture shows form found in Upper Danube. Locally distributed in Britain.

SWAN MUSSEL *(Anodonta cygnea)* 7–20 cm. Broad, egg-shaped, stout shell, bulbous. Greatest height under the whorl; broadly rounded in front, rear section 2¹/₂ times longer. Lower rim curved throughout its length. No teeth on locking edge. Umbones only slightly protuberant. In larger ponds and slow-flowing river with muddy bottoms.

Family   MARGARITIFERIDAE   Pearl Mussels

PEARL MUSSEL *(Margaritifera margaritifera)* 12 cm × 5 cm × 3 cm. Egg- to kidney-shaped shell, rather compressed, very thick, dark brown to black, only slightly glossy. Upper rim slightly curved throughout its length; lower rim shallowly grooved. Locks only with main teeth, has no long ridge or side teeth. Umbones scarcely protruding, broad, very close to the fore-edge, mostly badly corroded. Mother-of-pearl bluish-white, also pink, sometimes flecked with oil-green. In clear mountain streams; can contain pearls. Picture shows: *M. m. freytagi,* as a juvenile.

Family   SPHAERIIDAE   Orb Mussels and Pea Mussels

RIVER PEA MUSSEL *(Pisidium amnicum)* 11 mm × 8.5 mm × 5 mm. Elongated oval shell, considerably longer than tall, shiny, with close concentric ribbing; broad whorl, only slightly protruding, placed close to rear rim. Main teeth duplicated in either valve. Juveniles yellow, becoming almost brown; growth rings are darker. Very slender body. Long, lancet-shaped foot. 2 gills on either side, the hinder one stunted. Lives in rough water of rivers and lakes.

POROUS-SHELLED PEA MUSSEL *(Pisidium obtusale)* 3.5 mm × 2.5 mm × 2.3 mm. Rounded egg-shaped, very bulbous shell with fine stripes thin, yellowish horn-colour; outline has no corners. Round, wide, protuberant whorl. Mostly in small, stagnant pools, also in moors; seldom in lakes.

Sphaerium (= Musculium) lacustre Shell up to 8 mm × 5.5 mm × 3.5 mm; white or yellowish, rather rhomboid with rounded corners, only slightly inflated; upper rim almost straight, lower rim has shallow curve. Umbones almost exactly in the middle, elongated like a tube, short, tilted slightly forward, with a distinctly horizontal cowl (the shell of the initial stage). Lives in the mud of stagnant, foul water. Seldom in flowing water.

HONEY ORB MUSSEL *(Sphaerium corneum)* Shell 15 mm long, 11 mm high, 8–9 mm thick. Thin, fragile walls, shiny; horn-grey, growth rings are sometimes yellowish. Round-egg-shaped outline, with or without slight hint of a corner; whorl in middle, mostly broad, not very protuberant, no cowl. Muddy ponds, ditches, alder-swamps.

Family   DREISSENIDAE   Zebra Mussels

ZEBRA MUSSEL *(Dreissensia polymorpha)* 3–4 cm × 1.5–1.8 cm × 2–2.5 cm. Triangular shell looks a small overturned skiff; thin with growth rings rough to the touch, green-yellow with wavy brown bands. Upper side steeply arched, under side almost flat, gaping in the middle. Pointed whorl right up at fore end and tilted slightly downwards. Straight rim to lock, no teeth or ridge. The edges of the mantle are fused except for 3 small slits, through which the foot can protrude and a bundle of byssus threads, that come from glands in the foot, by which the mussel attaches itself to larger mussels, stones, ships, etc. In lakes in low country and in rivers as far up as they are navigable.

NON-PARASITIC WORMS

Phylum   *ANNELIDA*   Ringed Worms

Bodies composed of a series of rings or segments separated by grooves. Intestine runs from front to rear, ending blind in a number of species. Mouth-opening overshadowed by head-lobe. No articulated limbs. Nervous system consists of ropeladder-like ventral nerve-cord and brain (a pair of ganglia above the gullet). Sense-cells distributed all over the skin. Have a system of blood vessels and body-cavity. Breathe through the skin or by means of gills.

Class   *OLIGOCHAETA*   Earthworms and Freshwater Worms

Small number of bristles (setae) placed individually or in bundles in wall of body. Live in freshwater or damp earth. Hermaphrodites. Development without metamorphosis.

Family   Lumbricidae   Earthworms

Long, cylindrical bodies; numerous short rings; 1 cone-shaped head-lobe forming an upper-lip; on each ring 4 groups each of 2 hooked bristles not visible to naked eye. Well-developed senses of touch and taste, sensitive to light. Breathe by the skin. Red blood in young worms. The main blood vessel above the intestinal tract is visible to the naked eye. Back and abdominal muscles connected by cross-tubes. In breeding season there is whitish or yellowish glandular swelling of the "saddle" with the sexual organs, which takes up several rings. Being hermaphrodites each fertilises the other, for which the rings secrete adhesive to provide a grip. Later, each of the two worms forms yet another slime-ring in which it lays its eggs and which it then sloughs. As it shrivels, the ring hardens, forming a protective case (cocoon) round the eggs, and this is placed close under the surface in some damp place for the brood to develop.

Worms dig deep tunnels thrusting the moist earth aside and eating the dry; excreted earth deposited in tunnel or piled as worm-cast at mouth of hole. By day mostly in dwelling-tunnel; at night above ground. Some species pull leaves into their holes to rot. Feed on decomposing plant tissue and the microscopic creatures absorbed with the earth. After lengthy rain come above ground as otherwise in danger of suffocating. In winter rest coiled up at lower end of tunnel. Beneficial to agriculture as they loosen, aerate and mix up the soil and make humus.

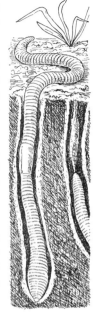

Lumbricus terrestris (= herculeus) 9–30 cm × 6–9 mm. Saddle on rings 32–37. Dark brown-violet on top with darker streaks down the hinder part; lighter colour underneath. Prefers clay.

Lumbricus rubellus 6–15 cm × 4–6 mm; saddle on rings 27–32. Red-brown on top, yellowish-white underneath. In soil rich in humus and medium moisture content; also in old tree stumps. Common.

BRANDLING *(Eisenia foetida)* 6–13 cm × 3–4 mm. Saddle on rings 26–32. Each ring has one broad, red, purple or brown, cross-band. Light grooves between rings. Among decaying vegetable matter and in manure. Never comes out of concealment. Common.

Eisenia (= Allolobophora) rosea 2.5 cm × 3–4 mm; yellowy flesh-colour to blood-red, translucent because without pigment.

Family   Tubificidae   River Worms

RIVER WORM *(Tubifex tubifex)* Up to 8.5 cm. Reddish, translucent; keeps its front end buried in vertical mud-tube, while the rest sticks up and is in continual motion, providing a supply of fresh water for breathing. Often present in thousands so close together as to make the surface of the mud look like a red lawn. A sudden blow on the water will make them all vanish into the roomy shafts they have dug. Thin, thread-like bodies distinctly ringed, with bristles on the rings. Feeds indiscriminately on mud, which is conveyed through its intestine into the water. Beneficial as mixer of sediment. Swift reproduction by simple splitting. In muddy ditches, especially where there is effluent from factories, breweries, mills, etc. Sold for feeding aquarium fish.

Family   NAIDIDAE

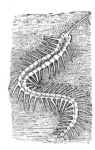

Stylaria lacustris Up to 1.8 cm; locomotion like a snake's; good swimmer; has long, antennae-like extension of the head-lobe that flickers about in groping and feeling. Down each side is a row of tufts of long hair-bristles. Mouth-opening is under the front end. 2 eyes. Brownish in colour; transparent. Reproduction both sexual and by asexual splitting, when a chain of them is formed. A new head grows on each section that splits off. On aquatic plants, especially duck-weed, in mud and on posts in the water. Ponds, lakes. Common.

Nais elinguis Up to 1.2 cm. No thread-like extension of head. Light brown. 2 eyes. Chain reproduction. Very active. Among aquatic plants or swimming free; also in mud on bottom. Even more common than the foregoing.

Class   *HIRUDINEA*   Leeches

Elongated, flattened bodies, almost smooth, no bristles; fine rings and with a sucker at either end. The front sucker, through which runs the mouth-opening, is used both for holding on to prey and sucking in food; the hind sucker is for clinging on. Hermaphrodite. After mutual fertilisation each leech, by turning and twisting its body in the moist earth near the water's edge, makes a hole in which to lay its eggs. The surface of its body secretes a foamy, spongy mass that hardens and surrounds the leech like a broad ring. In this it lays up to 15 eggs; then it wriggles out of its ring, which is elastic and contracts into a cocoon some 2–3 cm long. Many leeches attach their egg-capsules to water-plants. The young leeches hatch out after a few weeks and go on growing for 5 years, their life-span being up to 20 years. They pass the winter in a torpid state, buried in the mud. Well-developed body muscles make great mobility possible. Agile swimmer, wriggling action; on ground moves like looper attaching fore and hind suckers alternately. Breathes through the skin, which is frequently cast. Quickly dries and dies out of water. All leeches live on animal substances, either sucking blood or truly carnivorous, devouring whole, or pieces of other small creatures. Many kinds suck the blood of larger animals. Once replete a leech can wait over a year for its next meal.

Sub-order   GNATHOBDELLAE   Leeches with Jaws

Family   HIRUDIDAE

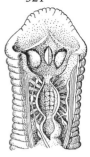

MEDICINAL LEECH *(Hirudo medicinalis)* Up to 15 cm long. Upper side arched; mostly dark green with 6 rust-brown lengthwise stripes broken by black spots; underside flattened, yellow-green with black spots. On the front ring are 5 pairs of black dots, so-called eyes, supposedly some organ of smell. In the root of the fore sucker is a mouth with 3 slits and 3 so-called jaws, each of which is semi-circular mass of firm muscle, the outer edge of which has sharp teeth; these move like a cross-saw causing the characteristic 3-rayed wound. Tending to shun light, they usually rest under stones, between plants, etc. As juveniles feed on invertebrates, then on amphibians (frogs, toads), fish; as adults suck the blood of mammals and humans. Glands in mouth secrete an anti-coagulant. Stores a considerable quantity of blood in 11 pairs of sacs opening out of intestine. Great elasticity of walls of stomach and body allow the leech's body to stretch to 3 or 4 times its original size. Lays its eggs in the earth on the bank or lake shore in late summer. In the old days much used by doctors for blood-letting and specially bred for their use. In calm, shallow water with plenty of plants, especially in moors. Now rare in Britain.

HORSE LEECH *(Haemopis sanguisuga)* 6–10 cm long. Back is a dirty brown with darker patches (no lengthwise stripes); the sides are framed with a yellow line. Underside yellow-grey with black spots. "Eyes" in same position as *H. medicinalis*. Shuns the light; but often swims about actively or crawls about the bottom or on stones using its suckers (looper action). Feeds on worms, snails, and other small, soft-skinned aquatic creatures, which it devours completely. Does not live up to its family name, for only occasionally will it fasten on to a small frog. Is only dangerous to larger animals (horses), if it should get into their throats while drinking and fastens on there. Common in stagnant and flowing water, preferring swamp with plenty of plants, or ponds with clay bottoms.

Sub-order   PHARYNGOBDELLAE

Family   ERPOBDELLIDAE

Erpobdella octoculata (= Herpobdella atomaria) Up to 5 cm, somewhat flattened looking. Brown-green with indistinct lighter rings. 4 pairs of "eyes". Toothless gullet. Feeds on animal and vegetable matter. In young ones that are reddish translucent, the working of the blood-stream can be observed. Swims or crawls with looper action; rolls up to rest. Common in ponds and running water where there are water lilies.

Sub-order   RHYNCHOBDELLAE

Family   PISCICOLIDAE

Piscicola geometra Up to 10 cm. Cylindrical, rod-shaped. Mouth-disc distinct from body; circular. Sucker twice as broad as the middle part of the body. Mostly 2 "eyes" placed behind the middle of the mouth-disc. Variegated greenish-brown and green-grey. Agile swimmer. At rest lies obliquely in the water. Sucks on to fish, especially carp and tench; but quite often swims about by itself. Common. Can cause damage in fish-hatcheries, as its sucking can kill young fish. The provision of large stones on which the fish rub them off, helps to get rid of them.

Phylum   *PLATHELMINTHES*   Flatworms

Bodies more or less flattened. Shapes vary considerably.

Class   *TURBELLARIA*

Family   DENDROCOELIDAE   Planarian Worms

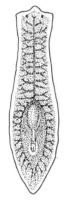

Dendrocoelum lacteum 1.2–3 cm. Long, flat body, cut off short in front, where it has 2 side-lobes, feeler-shaped, which it can move; rear end of body pointed. Slimy. Milky-white with the intestine and the food in it showing through darkly. This branches towards the rear. Two dark-coloured eyes in front. Without changing shape it crawls along slowly, flat against a stone or it can hang, upside down under the surface film of the water and crawl about there. It moves with the help of the cilia with which its whole body is covered. Feeds on flesh and carrion; is easily tempted by a bait of fish. A nasty predator, it will attack anything smaller than itself: insects, snails, spawn; also eats the rotting remains of dead animals, thrusting forward its proboscis-like pharynx and with powerful suction, tearing pieces off its prey and swallowing them. Can fast for very long periods. Hermaphrodite. Sexual reproduction by means of eggs, which are laid in hard-shelled, stalked egg-capsules or cocoons in sheltered places. Asexual reproduction by splitting and regeneration. Stagnant and flowing water. Under stones between the leaves of reeds; on the underside of water lily leaves.

WORMS AS INTERNAL PARASITES OF HUMANS,
ANIMALS AND PLANTS

Class   *NEMATODA*   Threadworms

Thread-shaped, cylindrical, pointed at either end. Male always
smaller than female. Firm, thick skin, smooth or ringed. Mouth
exactly at front end; vent on underneath near the rear end. Alimentary canal: fore-, middle- and terminal intestine. Gullet
mostly muscular, for sucking. Sexes separate. Breathe through
skin. Locomotion by turning and twisting. Reproduction by
means of eggs: in parasitic forms eggs are in very large numbers
and have great powers of resistance. No actual larval stage, but
they do moult. Mostly very small – up to 1 mm long – but some
large.

Family   ASCARIDAE

MAW-WORM *(Ascaris lumbricoides)* Male 15–17 cm; female
20–25 cm. Rear end curled inward. Host: human or pigs. Usually
present singly or in small numbers. Eggs retain power to germinate even after years. Outdoors. Transmitted in dirt, especially
in spreading liquid manure. Lives in small intestine, but occasionally occurs in stomach.

Parascaris equorum (= Ascaris megalocephala) Male 15–26 cm,
female 18–37 cm. In small intestine of horses, mules, donkeys.

PIN WORM *(Oxyuris vermicularis)* Male 2.5–5 mm; female
1–1.2 cm and .4–.6 mm across. Circular, thread-like, whitish.
1 female produces up to 12,000 eggs. These can enter humans
by way of the mouth. Lives in small or large intestine. Females
leave the intestine when ready to lay causing irritation. Infected
children can have eggs in traces of excrement under their finger-
nails and may re-infect themselves. Can be spread with excrement that has dried, powdered and been blown by wind on to
fruit, vegetables, etc.

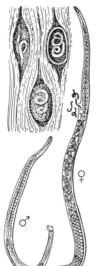

Family   TRICHOTRACHELIDAE

Trichinella spiralis Male 1.5, female 3–4 mm. Viviparous. 2 stages of development: larval stage in muscle, adult in intestine. Larvae coiled spirally inside a small calcareous cyst in the muscle (e.g. of pigs) survives for years without nourishment. When a cyst is dissolved by gastric juices the trichina is freed and becomes parasitic in the intestine (e.g. of a person). The female here produces thousands of live offspring, only .1 mm long; these get into lymph and the blood-stream, where they absorb juices causing fever and exhaustion of the host, etc. (trichinosis). Or intestinal trichinae penetrate into the finest blood vessels and muscles, where surrounding muscle-tissue secretes calcium carbonate to protect itself, which encapsulates the larva, a thing that does not harm the host. In the small intestine of pigs, rats, humans, etc. As trichinae can only be in certain definite parts of a pig's carcase, in most countries all pork has to be tested by law.

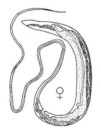

Trichuris trichiura 4.5 cm. Front of body thin, hair-like, bores into mucous membrane of large intestine; hind part of body thick, bluntly rounded. Eggs keep up to 1 or 2 years in water or the earth. Parasitic in the small intestine of humans. Develops without intermediate host. Can cause mass illness.

Family   ANCYLOSTOMIDAE   Hookworms

HOOKWORM *(Ancylostoma duodenale)* Male 9–12 mm; female 15–20 mm; pale flesh-colour, when dead grey or white. Mouth-capsule strikingly large and fitted with powerful hooked teeth. Lives in small intestine of humans, causing bleeding. Common in workers building tunnels and in coal mines, as they mostly work in a temperature of 25–30 °C, that most favourable to their development. Transmitted either via the mouth, by eating or drinking what is infected, or by larvae penetrating the skin via the pores. One of the most dangerous intestinal parasites in humans.

Family   ANGUILULIDAE   Eelworms

Of small size and mostly transparent.

VINEGAR EEL *(Anguillula aceti)* Male 1 mm, female 2 mm. In fermenting vinegar and sour paste; especially in wine-vinegar where it feeds on yeast-germs.

Tylenchus (= Anguina) tritici Male .9–2.5 mm, female 3–5 mm, coiled up in a spiral and motionless. Cause of "ear-cockles" in wheat; crinkling, bump excrescences and curling-up of leaves; ears covered with green to black galls in which are the adult worms, eggs are laid and larvae hatch. Galls fall off and rot. Spread with the grain, straw, by animals. Grains are smaller, rounded, black, with a thick, hard husk and powdery inside.

Tylenchus (= Ditylenchus) dipsaci Male .9–1.6 mm; female .9–1.8 mm. Slim, with distinct head part. Cause of stem disease in rye, oats, buckwheat, onions and narcissus: this is when stem grows at expense of shoots. Leaves twist like corkscrews. Larvae penetrate into plants through slit-openings or wounds.

Heterodera schachtii Size varies considerably according to the host plant. Male 1.2–1.6 mm, cylindrical; female .4–1.4 mm, shape of a lemon with a neck, protruding sexual opening. Causes "wilting" in roots, especially sugar-beet ("beet-sickness"): drooping leaves, premature yellowing of outer leaves, roots form on sides and, June to October, milk-white brood capsules, full of eggs, appear on roots and later fall off. Female penetrates on to rootlets. Can spread to a whole field. Can also effect other cruciferous and papillionaceous plants. Spread by implements, draught animals and dirty seed. Picture shows: root with brood-capsules and worms.

Phylum   *PLATHELMINTHES*   Flatworms

Classes   1. *TURBELLARIA* p. 522   2. *TREMATODA*

3. *CESTODA*

Parasites with attaching organs.

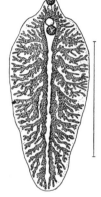

Class   *TREMATODA*   Flukes

LIVER FLUKE *(Fasciola hepatica)* 1.8–4 cm × .4–1.3 cm. Leaf-shaped, broad in front, tapering to the rear. Mouth-sucker on conical fore-end; 3–4 mm, behind it is a larger sucker. Cycle of development: mature worm in bile duct of sheep, cattle, horse, donkey, pig, etc.; eggs expelled with excrement; easily desiccated, develop only in water becoming microscopic, swimming, ciliated larvae (miricidia) that get inside dwarf pond snails *(Lymnaea truncatula),* where they turn into sporocysts inside which sexless creatures with just intestines and mouth are produced (rediae). These grow quickly and produce again without fertilisation new creatures, cercariae, which have sucker, mouth and intestine. These leave their intermediate host and attach themselve in a capsule to stalks of grass beside water, and can then be eaten by sheep or cattle. Very harmful.

Dicrocoelium (= Distomum) lanceatum   8–10 mm. Slim, lancet-shaped. Abdominal and mouth-suckers of equal size. Cycle of development as foregoing. Not so common, nor so harmful.

Class   *CESTODA*   Tapeworms

Range in length from a few mm up to 10 m, in breadth up to 2 cm. Internal parasites without intestines; almost always able to reproduce when in intestines of vertebrates. Very long bodies. Small heads mostly no more than the size of a pin-head with organs for clinging to host; then comes the neck, a short inarticulated growth-zone, then a chain of from 3 to over 4,000 distinctly separate, very flattened segments. No breathing organ, blood vessels or intestine. Takes in nourishment through the skin. Each segment has a hermaphroditic sexual apparatus, which is mature somewhere in the middle of the worm; last segment is full of eggs in an ovary with multiple branches; these detach themselves and are evacuated with the excrement. Segments near the growth-zone are always broader than they are long, but towards the rear are mostly longer than broad. Almost all tapeworms are hermaphrodites. Mostly individual segments fertilise themselves; but various segments of the same or different worms can fertilise each other. Eggs develop in ovary to larvae with 6 hooks; these are expelled along with the excrement of the host and arrive in the intermediate host by way of the mouth (feeding); the gastric juices of the intermediate host dissolve the surrounding shell and the larva bores with its hooks into the wall of the intestine, gets into the blood-stream, settles in some organ and there develops into a bladderworm, on the inner wall of the head of which the future tapeworm comes into being, reaching the intestine of its host by being eaten in the flesh of the intermediate host; there it thrusts its head out, fastens on to the wall of the intestine, casts its bladder and the head then acquires a neck and growth zone. In many cases there is also asexual reproduction of the bladderworm by inner and external gemmation.

Family   TAENIIDAE

SOLITARY TAPEWORM *(Taenia solium)* Sexually mature in humans, 2–3 mm. Head has protruding stub, a double crown of hooks and 4 suckers. Ovary with 7–10 branches, some forked. Bladderworm, *Cysticercus cellulosae,* up to 2 cm × 1 cm; size of a pea or bean. In pigs as intermediate host; in muscle; transference to human through eating pork or vegetables fouled with human excrement. Picture on p. 526 and 527. The commonest tapeworm found in man on the Continent.

TAPEWORM *(Taenia saginata)* Sexually mature in humans. Up to 10 m. No crown of hooks on head, which has 4 suckers. Ovary has 25–30 or more appendices. Bladderworm, *C. bovis,* up to 1 cm × .5 cm; in cattle as its intermediate host, in muscle. Transference to humans by eating raw beef. The most common tapeworm in humans in Britain. Picture in margin shows head and segment.

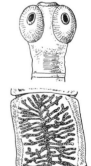

Echinococcus granulosus (=Taenia echinococcus) Sexually mature in dog. 3–5 mm × .33 mm; 3–4 segments. Head has protruding studs, double crown of hooks and 4 suckers. Bladderworms round variety, in size from that of an egg to that of a child's head, form sub-bladders with heads inside or out. Come into being in small brood-capsules. Transference to humans and various domestic animals, especially sheep, by dog's excrement getting into food. Uncommon, but very dangerous. Bladderworms in liver and lungs of sheep, cattle, pigs and humans can lead to death.

STURDIE or STAGGERS WORM *(Taenia coenuris)* Host is dog. Up to 60 cm. Pear-shaped head with double ring of hooks; ovary has 18–26 appendices. Bladderworm size of a pea to that of a hen's egg; in brain of sheep and cattle. Can develop several hundred worm heads by gemmation; the pressure on the brain causes staggers in sheep, the outcome of which is fatal. Bladder of the worm dissolves in stomach of dog. Eggs expelled with dog's excrement and taken in on grass the sheep eats; dog acquires it by eating head or brain of sheep.

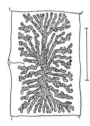

Taenia marginata Mature in dog. 1.5–3 m. Rectangular head with a double crown of hooks. Ovary has side-branches with 4–5 forks. Bladderworm can also be in humans and is the size of a hazel nut or even of a person's fist; in fleece of sheep on chest or belly, in entrails, liver, of sheep, cattle, pigs, deer, but seldom in humans for whom it is not dangerous.

Taenia crassicolis Mature in cats. 15–60 cm. Multiple segments. Strong head with 3 crowns of hooks; short, thick neck. Segments are square with jutting corners (mature segment, not shown in picture). Bladderworm in mice and rats.

Family   DIBOTHRIOCEPHALIDAE

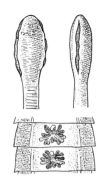

Dibothriocephalus latus Mature in humans and dogs. 5–9 m. 3,000–4,000 short, wide segments. Distinct head has 2 oblong sucker-like slits, no crown of hooks. Ovary has numerous coils that make it look like a rosette (visible to the naked eye). Larvae live free in water; have crowns of sickle-shaped hooks and are not bladderworms. Intermediate host can be a fish (pike, elvers) or small crustacean *(Copepod)*. Quite common in certain areas.

Family   DIPYLIDIIDAE

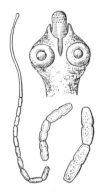

Dipylidium caninum Final host can be a person, dog or cat. 10–35 cm; multiple segments, each the shape of a cucumber seed and pale pink. Head has club-shaped knob and 4 irregular crowns of hooks; 2 suckers. Eggs or segment reach skin round rectum with excrement, are eaten by flea-larvae, in which they develop into juvenile form, the dog bites at its skin, by which means they enter the mouth. Transference to humans by association with dogs or cats.

APPENDIX

BIRD SONGS

It is difficult for the beginner to single out the song of any one bird from the general chorus and fix it in his memory; thus it is best to begin a study of bird songs as early as possible in the spring, before they are all singing. Before the trees burst into leaf it is often possible to get a close look at the bird on its bare branch.

You should always make a note of the date and time, so as to be able to eliminate those species which have not yet started to sing or which have already stopped.

Because the blackbird sings sitting free in the immediate vicinity of people and produces such a wealth of melodies it is, perhaps, easiest to identify and is the obvious one to start with. Song thrush and nightingale are grouped with it. The striking, and thus easily identifiable, part of the song thrush's song is its loudness and the repetition of its motif. When a string of notes of the same pitch rings out loudly or comes soft and flute-like from low bushes, it is immediately recognisable as the song of the nightingale.

Before even going out, you should memorise the groups into which the various songs and calls are arranged. The page headings give the main characteristic, so that when one is heard you know at once where to look for further identification.

The main purpose of writing the song as music is to provide a visual image of the bird's voice and so make it easier to identify and remember. To play this on an instrument can give the rhythm and the melody, but cannot properly convey the timbre. In a number of cases old popular jingles or phrases provide a good idea of the rhythm, at least, of a song without any musical notation. Often it is enough to write the notes and give no indication of the pitch, as often it is impossible to determine this exactly. In these cases the notes are given without the usual ledger lines. Timbre, modulation, structure and length of the phrase are far better means of recognition than pitch, which it is often exceedingly difficult to determine.

When, in a descending or ascending sequence, the individual notes come closer to each other than can be indicated in our system of notation, dots are put instead of notes. Sometimes, too, it is preferable to use a simple diagram instead of notes.

The very quick repetition of the same note is described as trill, twitter, bleat, churr, rattle, bell-note, jingle, whirr, or cooing, depending on the timbre. The expression "warble" is used only when the sound resembles that of a tremolo whistle. In music, of course, a trill is the quick alternation of two different notes.

Obviously you cannot expect musical annotation to give you the exact sound of every bird song. There are good and bad songsters among every kind of song-bird, beginners and masters; in fact the song of one bird can change in timbre, loudness, etc. with its mood and age, and this must be borne in mind.

BIRD VOICES IN ORCHARD, GARDEN, PARK AND WOOD

BLACKBIRD, THRUSH, NIGHTINGALE – the 3 best
Plate 2 and pp. 125 and 128

BLACKBIRD Individuals can start singing in the first mild day of February, but in general they sing without interruption from March up to and into July, and even then still fairly regularly. When singing, likes to perch on some high point: ridge of a roof, tree-top, etc. *Song:* loud, melodious, flute-like; each phrase different from the preceding and has a cadenza of weaker, sharp, or compressed notes; often a favourite phrase, that is frequently produced.

Blackbird song has been studied for many years by Heinz Tiessen, who used to play interesting motifs on the piano and write them down. His studies have shown that the blackbird's range is considerably more than an octave and varies with individual birds like the rest of their musical performance. The longest interval he recorded is the descending eleventh as in the following:

Others too have drawn attention to the considerable similarity between the musical powers of the blackbird and ours. Tiessen's recordings have shown "that the musical language of the blackbird ranges in its harmonic association from the style of the simplest signal or nursery song to the material of the 20th century; and the notes and observations made show that this range is not the result of any influence exerted by man but must have come about independently. How little the blackbird depends on man's example is indicated by the fact that the song of those in lonely woods is no less varied than is that of those that live where they can hear our music. Their talent as mimics is no more than an additional ability."

The recorded examples show there is no limit to the number of rhythms the blackbird uses. It is shown to be musically more imaginative than any other song-bird.

The good ideas of the most talented blackbirds are close to man's own music. It is characteristic of blackbird song that individual stanzas often rise towards the end.

The blackbird's song, taken as a whole, is an unconstrained stringing together of individual motifs that are not arranged in any formal pattern; though, of course, many blackbirds have a favourite motif.

Blackbirds will practise until their motifs are polished as they wish them. This has been described by Tiessen, who relates how the blackbird rehearsed tirelessly, making slight experimental alterations, trying out two motifs; one with a small interval:

the other with one of a fifth:

Some six hours later this partial motif had been made into a whole and the fifth become, triumphantly, an octave:

Use of the Blackbird Motif in Music

According to Tiessen the most famous of all the blackbird's motifs is the final motif from Beethoven's violin concerto. Tiessen himself heard a blackbird sing it, the only difference being that D had become E.

Beethoven   Blackbird

"It is reasonable to suppose," he writes, "that Beethoven, who had a passionate love of nature, also heard it in this or similar form sung by a blackbird. In their admiration of nature, Beethoven and other masters like Liszt, Wagner, Bruckner, Carl Loewe, have been glad to record and use her gifts."

Tiessen also records having had "the following blackbird motif with an interval of a ninth that is to be found note for note in the 2nd Act of Mozart's *Marriage of Figaro*," sent him by Martin Grabert:

Blackbird 1)

Mozart: Marriage of Figaro

Another instance is to be found in *Siegfried*, Act 2, "Forest Murmurs".

There is another faithfully reproduced blackbird's song at the start of Richard Strauss' *Rosenkavalier*, played by the 1st clarinet at bar no. 13 with all sorts of birds' voices.

1)

Tiessen says that "this intricate twittering" most nearly approaches the following blackbird's song that he himself had recorded:

1)

Blackbird motifs have also been used by Armin Knab in his pieces for piano and recorder.

In inventiveness and range the blackbird is far ahead of all our song-birds.

SONG THRUSH Sings from early March until well into the summer (about mid-July), especially in morning and evening twilight. Ardent, loud and flute-like, as with the blackbird, but consists of short motifs, each of which is repeated several times. Where volume of sound, clarity and the cleanness of its intervals are concerned, it is among the best. Its motifs are simple and easily remembered. For example, one often hears the two syllable *Philipp Philipp* (stress on 1st, or 2nd syllable); often the sound is *tratü tratü* (stress on the 2nd syllable). Professor Hoffmann wrote down the following:

The song thrush also shows that it has a gift for variation. One example of this has been recorded by Professor Hoffmann:

There are not many examples of the song of the song thrush being used in music. Professor Hoffmann suggests that the Swan Knight motif in Wagner's *Lohengrin* is one such. This is the well-known motif, that Lohengrin sings as he takes leave of his swan and which recurs frequently:

Nun sei bedankt

Hoffmann writes, "This motif was obtained from none other than *Turdus musicus l.* which seems to have a great liking for this phrase and often sings it almost exactly, only an octave higher. The rhythm and metrics, it is true, are usually different, for the thrush mostly sings:

"What in particular strengthens our contention is that Wagner repeats the motif more times than in itself is called for – in one or two places thrice in succession, for example, where the choir bursts out in its admiring cry:

Wie ist er schön und hehr zu schauen, dem solch ein Wun-

which is exactly the number of times that the thrush usually repeats its motifs."

MISTLE THRUSH Sings from late February or early March for not quite a full three months, and not often in June. Only in spring, flute-like notes, especially like the song of a blackbird in its sonority and melodic structure. Apart from time, can be identified by its hurried delivery: short, simple motifs from which most depart only very slightly.

NIGHTINGALE Sings from the 2nd half of April to about end of June, seldom for more than 2 months; especially at daybreak and in the evening twilight, though many sing all night, especially on first arrival. Sings in parkland or woods, from low bushes, several phrases, that is a series of notes separated by short pauses produced whistled or warbled, lingeringly or quickly. For example, a longer or shorter series of hard *terrterrterrterr* is followed by a series of sonorous *diudiudiu,* now higher, now lower, now loud, now soft.

As it is clearly not a melody, so much as a series of notes of the same pitch, the nightingale's song is best reproduced by syllables. As the syllables change, the pitch naturally changes too. The sequence is often concluded by a higher note.

Of the many phrases, the following syllables are quoted:

The crescendo phrase and the loveliest of them all consists of smooth, flute-like notes that begin quite softly, stay at the same pitch in solemn tempo and express a soulful increase in feeling and mood in the swelling of each subsequent note.

tioo-tioo-tioo-tioo-tioo-tioo

Dull pealing set of sharp distinct notes remaining on the same pitch, often of a melting character:

cheek chook

The *vati-vati* motif:

vati - vati - vati

The trill motif ending in a high note:

r - - - cheek

There is a great wealth of different rhythm and timbres: smooth flute-like notes alternating with loud pealing and "lip-smacking" ones, plaintive alternating with gay, melting with trilling.

The call-note is a prolonged *huit,* more sonorous than that of the redstart or willow warbler, or a sharp *wheet, wheet-tack.*

Warning-note or alarm-call a deep, hard *karrrrr.*

The *vati-vati* motif provides a good combination of notes and syllables:

cheek cheek cheek cheek   vati   vati   vati   r - - - - - cheek

cheek-judik i i djordji-kud-cheek-kuwud-cheek- wud-cheek

Composers who have heard and used the nightingale's song in their music are: Johanna Matthieux, in whose *Bird Cantata* the crescendo phrase with added *rrrrr*-phrase and characteristic high concluding note can be heard:

Beethoven, at the end of the 2nd movement of whose *Pastorale* Symphony comes the flute-like song of the nightingale:

While Wagner also uses its call, in somewhat freer form, played by the clarinet in the "Forest Murmurs" in *Siegfried:*

Wagner was a great lover of nature and the nightingale also appears in the "Forest Birds", again in *Siegfried,* and among the bird motifs is the *Meistersinger.*

The nightingale has often been called the queen of song-birds. Certainly there is no end to the variety of its stanzas, the differences in timbre and pitch, to say nothing of crescendo and diminuendo, the coaxing, the sobbing, the tempo now stormy now restrained, that seem to express yearning, pain and lament, as well as gay jubilation. Undoubtedly it is the best artist among the song-birds. And yet its song lacks the definite melodic intervals that that of the song-thrush has and especially the ingenious melodies of the blackbird.

*THRUSH NIGHTINGALE Song has the same timbre as nightingale's but has a different melodic structure. Song-motifs all like the thrush's and also repeated once or more often as the thrush does.

BIRD SONGS RECOGNISABLE BY MERE REPETITION
OF THE MOTIF

SONG THRUSH see p. 533.

NIGHTINGALE see p. 535.

GREAT TIT p. 141. Sings frequently in spring, on sunny days in February to June; less in summer, seldom in autumn. Song is loud, in quick tempo, a clear *teacher-teacher* repeated twice or thrice, or more often. Frequent variations, even inversion. Professor Hoffmann has noted these examples:

Anton Bruckner said that in the 1st movement of his 4th Symphony he copies the voice of the great tit:

The theme is taken up by all the instruments and you can easily hear the little tit motif everywhere, freely though Bruckner has treated it.
Richard Wagner has used it very delicately in *Die Meistersinger,* that is, the minor third of its spring call which, as so often in nature, ascends.

CHIFFCHAFF Plate 3 and p. 129. Sings from end of March to September, individuals perhaps also in October; continually up to midsummer or beyond; in autumn not so complete or so continuous. From early morning till towards evening, not so continuously in afternoon. Song uniform, regularly separated between 2 notes, in this sort of way:

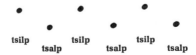

Sounds almost like the scolding of starlings, being not so hard, but more pleasant and soft.

COAL TIT Can best be observed either before or after nesting in thickets in the edge of the wood or in tree-nurseries. Spring call is an unbroken, buoyant

tee-chu, tee-chu, tee-chu

with variations, but always more hurried than the great tit and in a thinner voice.

It also has various song forms with piping or twittering notes; rather long.

A short, more delicate "conversational" note *sit sit,* rather like a gold-crest, but becomes louder being produced again and again until it is a buzing *sirrrr.*

STARLING Sings from March to June. (Arrives on Continent in February and begins to leave in August.) Some sing for a few weeks from September on, as in the spring. Song, when continuous, repeats each phrase two or three times, sometimes clicking, chattering or gurgling; the whole is multitude of whistles, pipes, clicks and shrills. Also imitates the voices of other birds, e.g. golden oriole and tree creeper. Call *stoair* or *stoek.* Plate 2 and p. 123.

*ICTERINE WARBLER Plate 3 and p. 130. Sings from May to high summer; still fairly regularly in the first half of July, but gradually less and less until it stops altogether. Sings all morning from dawn and also in the afternoon; in leafy gardens and parks and bushy fringes of woods; song is very hurried, high and diversified, with shrill notes alternating with soft motifs, and produced without pauses and with frequent im-mediate repetitions. Its more artistic and elaborate motifs are repeated 2 or 3 times, the short, shrill ones 6 or 7 times, or even more. Often imitates whole stanzas of other birds, (swallow, swift, lark, blackbird chatter, nuthatch) and also imitates grasshoppers and cats. The main characteristic of its song is its allegro motif with incisive shrill high pitch, like:

dee dee   zee   dee dee   zee

or

dee dee   zee   dee dee   zee

It has a pleasantly resonant, animated arpeggio motif, like a harp:

STRIKINGLY LOUD, SHORT WHISTLE WITH
TIED NOTES

Plate 2 and p. 124

*GOLDEN ORIOLE Sings from early May onwards, especially the first part of June; later less frequently, stopping in the first half of August. Sings from top of trees, a striking, short, sonorous whistle with characteristic ending *leeoo-keoo;* tied notes; everything in a hurried tempo.

The simple form of its call is:

A few variants that are often heard are quoted by Tiessen:

The golden oriole's call usually begins with a step upwards, then descends. This is usually repeated along with other notes, so that the motif has 2 melodic climaxes, with main stress on the second. The last note is usually the deepest.

There is a great similarity between the motif recorded by Professor Hoffmann and Wagner's second "Forest Birds" motif in *Siegfried:*

Golden Oriole   Wagner

Again, in "Forest Murmurs" Wagner gives the flute an extended golden oriole's call:

LOUD, HURRIED TWITTERING, REMAINING AT THE SAME PITCH,
THAT COMES FROM BUSHES

BLACKCAP Plate 3 and p. 128. Sings from second half of April, at first rather unskilfully, but practises diligently from early morning until late in the evening, being loudest at about midsummer. In the first half of July still sings regularly, but stops in early August. In parklands, gardens and woods, from low bushes. One of the loveliest bird songs. The first part is low, quick twitter that can easily be missed; then, without a pause, comes the second part, the so-called "turn", of 10 or more loud, flute-like notes, striking in their swift tempo and beauty of timbre, sung all in one breath.

GARDEN WARBLER Plate 3 and p. 129. Sings from early May until after midsummer; in the first half of July still sings fairly regularly. From early morning until sundown, from low bushes, a rather loud, melodious song of rougher timbre produced at great speed in one breath, of small compass and equal volume; it lacks the long, flute-like notes of the blackcap.

*BARRED WARBLER Plate 3 and p. 129. Sings from May to midsummer, almost all day, but mostly in the early hours; often sings in flight. Song resembles that of garden warbler and whitethroat. See p. 129.

SONG EASILY RECOGNISABLE BY CHARCTERISTIC NOTES

a) Characteristic beginnings

ROBIN Plate 2 and p. 127. Sings from 2nd half of March until well on in the summer; never so constantly or loudly as in the spring, but rather a mere twitter without an actual melody. Song has one bar pitched strikingly high, recognisable by beginning with 2–3 very high, shrill notes squeezed out almost in an undertone; then without a pause in very quick tempo follows a ripple of descending notes or a descending trill, often ascending again, to end in a low, flute-like note. Hoffmann gives two forms of the robin's main motif, from which you can easily see the basic form:

REDSTART Plate 2 and p. 126. Sings from first week of April to end of July. In orchards, parks and light woods; a full-toned short little song, easy to recognise from the start: a stressed high note that it tends to hold followed by 2–3 short equally stressed notes somewhat lower than the first:

Often, the beginning note has a quite short grace note. The song is mostly quite short and often contains imitations of other birds: the *svee-svee* of the tree pipit, the endings of willow warbler and chaffinch, etc.
The melody goes more or less

WREN P. 144. Sings the whole year round, though rarely between August and November; sings in January and February. Most diligently when the sun shines; sings most and loudest from end of March to early May; still does so regularly in July and early August. From mid-October into December only individuals sing. In undergrowth, clearings in woods and by streams; a fresh, ringing, short little song, recognisable by:

1. A clear, ringing string of notes, like a canary, but shorter, mostly a series of 3–6 penetrating staccato notes with equal pitch.

2. The accentuation introduced between these series, that is to say somewhat lengthened notes.

3. The emphatic and lower trill of the last or penultimate series.

The song begins quite softly, usually with 1–3 notes held slightly, followed by 3–6 ringing staccato notes, like:

PIED FLYCATCHER P. 141. Sings from end of April to early June in gardens and light woods. A rather melodious song, consisting of unvarying, ascending and descending notes, rather draggingly produced, the characteristic start is:

wheet-i-wheet-wheet-i-

First, usually are a few high notes; or 3 notes held and then the characteristic opening, thus:

zee zee zee   wheet-i-wheet-i   zee zee zee   wheet-i-wheet-i-wheet

b) Characteristic sounds introduced into the melody

GOLDFINCH Plate 1 and p. 119. Sings from March to July and mid-August. At almost all hours of the day; occasionally in autumn too, even on fine winter days, when they sun themselves in whole companies. Orchards, avenues, near villages (never in woods), short little song, rather like that of the linnet, easily recognisable by the call *didlit* inscribed in it:

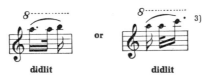

didlit   didlit

In *Die Meistersingern* Wagner includes the goldfinch's call along with those of the nightingale, lark and pelican. David sings:

Die Stieg - - litz-weis'

The chief things in the goldfinch's song, as the example shows, are the triplet at the beginning of the motif and the weaker beat that follows it and that is why Hoffmann holds that the accompanying part Wagner gave his goldfinch motif was not entirely accidental.

c) Characteristic song-endings

CHAFFINCH Plate 1 and p. 119. Sings from early March to end of June or early July, but most are silent by the middle of July. The loud, warbling finch song begins high and soft, sinks in quick staccato notes and is followed by an almost toneless roll, next a few tied notes that again rise, then the powerful final figure. This is the main identification mark, the three syllable motive with the emphasis on the last syllable but two.

cheweeo

Can be better recorded in syllables or verse than written as music, e.g. *cheep-cheep-cheep-till-till-till-cherry-erry-erry-zee-zee-cheweeo*

Often you get a 4-syllable ending like *Friedericia* or a 2-syllable one like *Rite-tsup*.

Rite-tsup

Frequent variations, examples of which Tiessen has noted.

WILLOW WARBLER Plate 3 and p. 130. Sings from the 2nd week of April into July, or even the beginning of August (occasionally into September) very diligently, from early morn till evening, but most continuously during the morning just before sunrise. Sings in deciduous woods, parks and copses; song has a descending melody line and sounds a bit like a soft chaffinch song, something like this:

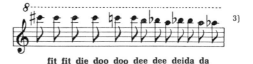

fit fit die doo doo dee dee deida da

There is no roll, as with the chaffinch, and towards the end it gets softer and softer, not ringing out like the chaffinch's. The first couple of notes are often enciphered *feet feet* . . . (hence the German name for the bird *Fitis*). Introduction and end can vary considerably.

YELLOWHAMMER Plate 1 and p. 122. Sings from sunny days in February and March; somewhat amateurish at first, but has perfected its song by the end of March, and goes on singing. Sings at all hours of the day, on the fringe of a wood, in a hedge in a field, by the roadside, from the top of a tree, a telephone wire, etc. 1–10 rather rough short notes of the same pitch and timbre, with 1 (or 2) held, deeper, broader and louder concluding notes, thus:

little   bit   of   bread and   no   cheese

The last note but one, little and soft, is often missing altogether. The last note loud and flat.

Richard Wagner included the song of the yellowhammer in his "Forest Murmurs" in Act 2 of *Siegfried;* indeed, it begins it.

SISKIN Plate 1 and p. 121. Sings at almost any time of the year except the latter half of the summer and the first part of autumn, when it moults. A twittering song characterised by a long squeezed out note that is almost a screech at the end. Only in conifer woods.

*SHORT-TOED TREE-CREEPER P. 145. Sings from the first mild days in March until June or July. Song is a clear, high whistling of 6–7 notes, the 2nd and last being the highest; between them tied notes, all of good timbre, thus:

titi   tirroiti

TREE-CREEPER P. 145. Sings from the fine days of February well into the summer, particularly in March and April; a very delicate short little song, even finer than that of the blue tit. Stretched, introductory notes, almost out of tune, like *sree sree,* then comes the descending series of purling notes, very reminiscent of the blue tit ending in an ascending-*huit* (wheet) that can be heard farthest off.

si   si   si   sis sis iss   iss   issi ssissi huit

EASILY RECOGNISABLE BECAUSE SUNG ON THE WING

Lark, see p. 560. Whitethroat, see p. 559.

TREE PIPIT P. 137. Sings from Mid-April to July; until the middle of June sings almost all day until evening twilight in light woods, on the fringe of woods, in grassy or heathery clearings in conifer woods. Sings from a bare branch, or rises up in the air and sings as it floats down again with legs drooping. Its normal song consists of:

Part 1. A warbling string of about 7 notes, rather like a canary's song.

Part 2. A clamour of out-of-tune down-drawn notes, the pitch remaining the same; or, again, a string of higher notes, the grace-note phrase, that strikes upwards, the *svee-svee* phrase.

Svee Svee Svee

Or this can be a series of rising whistle-notes or a warbling like the 1st part, only somewhat deeper.

Part 3. A roll. This can be missed out or come 4th instead of 3rd.

Part 4. A long run of soft, descending, beautiful notes, the *seea* motif:

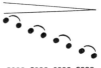

seea seea seea seea

This *seea* motif is the surest means of identification. Professor Hoffmann insists that the third bird in Richard Wagner's "Forest Murmurs" *(Siegfried)* is the tree pipit.

WOOD WARBLER Plate 3 and p. 130. Sings from 2nd half of April until nearly midsummer. In deciduous woods. Sings:

a) In gliding descent of display flight, consisting of up to 10 very high, staccato, quick notes ending in a buzzing trill that is loud to begin with, but grows fainter and fainter and finally dies away, thus:

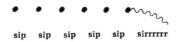

sip   sip   sip   sip   sip   sirrrrrr

Often the trill is kept at the pitch of the staccato notes right to the end.

b) While perched, 2 lovely, plaintive gentle whistle notes that curve down, also a whole run at the same pitch, thus:

piu piu piu

Mating call: separate whistles of *piu*.

UNIFORM CHATTER, TRILLING, WARBLING, TINKLING

Uniform notes of the nightingale in first section; plaintive piping of the great tit, p. 551; *gigs-gigs* sound of the blackbird, p. 531. Warbling of the tree pipit and trill of the wood warbler, p. 546.

LESSER WHITETHROAT Plate 3 and p. 129. Sings from end of April to beginning of September, most industriously from early morning until evening. Song is a rather rough chatter on the one note, produced at speed, thus:

didl didl didl didl didl didl didl didl . . . . .

This chatter is preceded by a brief, soft twittering that one usually fails to hear.

MARSH TIT Pp. 551 and 142. Sings particularly in the spring. *Mating call:* a series of notes in quick succession, mostly *sjezjezje* 6–8 times . . . chattered like the lesser whitethroat, but softer and often becoming a soft *djüb djüb* or a distinct *djep djep*.

BLUE TIT p. 142. Sings mostly in the spring months, even on fine days in January. Song consists of 2 or 3 very high, drawn-out notes that end in clear trill mostly on the same pitch, though often the trill will be slightly lower than the initial note, thus:

zi zi gurrrr

CRESTED TIT P. 142. Mostly in the spring, but also on mild days in January. Particularly in pines. Song is an often repeated *zizi gurr*; like the blue tit, but deeper and fuller. The purring *gurr* is deeper than the *zizi* that precedes it.

LONG-TAILED TIT P. 142. Sings particularly in the spring and autumn in woods and gardens with lots of bushes. Has a sort of "conversational" *sisisisi*, very high, soft metallic whistle that gets fainter and drops a little. Warning note is a deep *zerrr*, rather like the whirring *zerrr* of the wren. Its actual song is insignificant.

GOLDCREST P. 143. Sings from early spring well into summer, and also in the autumn and on fine winter days. In conifer woods sings a short, delicate little song so high and soft that most people fail to hear it. The melody runs in a straight line, scarcely rising or falling, with one or two expressive accentuations. A whole lot of it clear, tied notes, getting quicker and stronger towards the end, thus *sisisi-sisisi-sisisi-sirr*. Call note a delicate *sisisi*.

*FIRECREST P. 144. Sings from April into the summer, in parklands and conifer and mixed woods, a short, delicate, silvery song of 8–10 quick, staccato notes on the same pitch, getting quicker and louder towards the end, but without accentuation and distinctly ascending; mostly with a distinct descending concluding note.

GREENFINCH Plate 1 and p. 121. Starts on fine sunny days in February and sings until well on in the summer, but mostly in April and May; still fairly regularly in July. In gardens and light deciduous woods, but never deep in a wood. Song is a rather loud, rapid trill on one note, thus:

As well as the trill one often hears a pleasant

or, more seldom, this can be an ascending whistle like *tswee*.

*SERIN Plate 1 and p. 121. Sings from mid-April until well into August from early morning on; those that do not migrate can also be heard in the winter. In gardens, avenues and in the country. A high, uniform trilling song, all in one breath, without pause. The timbre is that of the yellowhammer and the melody alternates between 2 closely related, high, scratchy notes, thus:

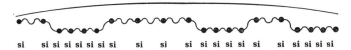

The singer perches on a bare branch, the top of a tree, a roof-ridge or the top of a wall.

Often there is also a rippling phrase, thinner than the blue tit's, but still sonorous; this is sometimes inserted into the song.

LINNET Plate 1 and p. 120. Usually starts singing on fine days in late February or March and continues into July or early August from early morning until nearly evening, but most in the morning. In orchards, parks and bushy places; often sings from the top of a low tree, a short varied song characterised by:

1. At the start a soft call consisting of a longer or shorter series of *geg*'s, some high, some lower:

● ● ●

gegegeg

which is frequently repeated in the melody.

2. Slower, delicate whistle notes interspersed among those *geg*'s and made into a harmonious phrase. Great variety in the songs, with a preference for simple, clean intervals. The following are two variants recorded by Voigt:

gegege   **gegege**   **gegege**   3)

The triplet gives the *gegegeg*. Shorter songs usually end with an ascending note that is almost a "crow". When changing position between tree and tree, the song is often confined to *gegs*.

BLACK REDSTART Plate 2 and p. 126. Sings from early March until early August, the occasionally on into October. Sings from early morning until after twilight from posts, rooftops and trees. Song is monotonous and in 3 parts: first a quick succession of 4–5 sonorous notes on the same pitch, a low, forced throaty note, followed by 2 or 3 short whistles on the same note as the first part.

Call note: *fuid-tack-tack.*

DULL, HOLLOW COOING

STOCK DOVE P. 163. From early March until the end of June, only occasionally in August. In woods with hollow trees. Dull coo that seems to be hauled up from depths, getting quicker and quicker and swelling

hoohoohoohooh
hoo
hoo
hoo

into almost a hoot, like *hooh*   with 7–10 or more syllables in a phrase. Another individual will make an ascending phrase more of a coo, every call having 2 syllables, thus: *oore oore oroo ooroo ooroo ooroo;* one will make the break down, another up.

After this comes a uniform coo, a sort of *hoovay* repeated 6–9 times in a row; each phrase with a cooing short and ascending; often each call has 3 syllables, like *hooh hoo oot* with the emphasis mainly on the 3rd syllable.

WOOD PIGEON P. 163. From early March to the end of September wherever there are trees. Its deep coo usually consists of 3 similar phrases of 4–6 syllables, like:

groo groohgroo groogroo groogroo groo groohgroo groogroogroo groohgroo groogroo goog

The 2nd syllable is always higher and more stressed. When the phrase is repeated the accented syllable and the three following are somewhat higher than at the beginning of the stanza. The whole ends with a raised *gug*. There are often variants especially in late summer and into September.

TURTLE DOVE P. 163. From early May to early August in dry conifer woods, small woods in farmland, the cooing of the cock bird being on the pitch of the cuckoo: 3–5 regular whirring *toorr* from 1 phrase, the 3rd *turr* being somewhat higher; or there may be 3 or 4 *turr* at the same pitch, or that following the 3rd *turr* is a little higher than the preceding ones. Usually coos in early morning or evening.

turr turr turr   or   turr turr turr turr   or   turr turr turr

INDIVIDUAL CALLS OR PHRASES, MEDIUM-LOUD TO SOFT

a) Short, more or less clear calls individually or in a string

GREAT TIT P. 141. Call note: a short, clear *pink*, seldom just once, usually repeated several times. Also a bleating "cry for help" of 4 or more clear notes, crowded together, on the same pitch, like *dzedzedzedze;* often repeated quite soon, another often slightly changed.

BLUE TIT P. 142. A string of short notes on same pitch, like *tetetet*, which can be preceded by 1–3 high, prolonged notes, like *tititetetetet;* the short notes following slightly held or rippling and slightly descending. Again: a *zerrrrretet* rather like the great tit's "cry for help", but ascending.

MARSH TIT P. 142 and 547. Another "cry for help" *zjededede* like the great tit.

*ICTERINE WARBLER Pp. 539, 554. From a tall bush or tree of medium height. Alarm-note: a hard smacking *tze* or *tzek;* when agitated *errrr*.

CHAFFINCH Plate 1 and p. 119. Call-note: a clear *pink*, by itself or 2–4 in a row. Flight-call: *djoo* or *joop*.

PIED FLYCATCHER P. 141. Call-note: a short, soft *beet beet*.

RED-BACKED SHRIKE P. 139. Short, rather rough *ge* or *geck* coming from a hedge or low tree.

BLACKBIRD Plate 2 and p. 125. Alarm-note: a subdued *duckduckduck* or *derkderkderk*.

SONG THRUSH Plate 2 and p. 125. Call-note: *zip*, rather rarely *zeezeezeezee*.

YELLOWHAMMER Plate 1 and p. 122. Call-note: *zeech* from low trees or fruit trees. In flight, *zeechzeech*.

WREN P. 144. From ground or bushes, a short hard *zeeck* or *tjeeck*, by itself or up to 8 in a string.

ROBIN Plate 2 and p. 127. Call-note: a sharp *tsick* or *tsee* or just a metallic *ts*, coming from close to the ground, sometimes one on its own, or a string of them.

HAWFINCH Plate 1 and p. 119. Call-note: from a tall tree, a short hard *zeeicks* or *tzeeit*.

TREE PIPIT P. 137. Short call, half "under its breath" of *dzee, dzee*.

GREENFINCH Plate 1 and p. 121. Call-note: a clear *gjeeck*, mostly strung together: *gjeeckgjeeckgjeeck* with a rippling metallic sound.

All warblers, when anxious have a hard *tzek* call, like hedge shears snapping shut.

WHITETHROAT Plate 3 and p. 129. A hard smacking *tze,* like shears snapping together, comes from bushes.

Alarm-note: *ved ved ved* or a subdued *voeed voeed voeed* or

    deed   deed
voi   voi

*SHORT-TOED TREE-CREEPER P. 145. A clear, high whistle repeated 2–4 times: *tee tee tee.*

b) Long notes, either held or ascending or descending slightly, single or repeated

BLACKBIRD Plate 2 and p. 125. Long *tseeay.* HAWFINCH's is similar.

WOOD WARBLER Plate 3 and p. 130. From brushwood, mating-call: single *dju.* Alarm-note the same *dju* but loud, declining and plaintive, often repeated for minutes on end.

NUTHATCH Plate 4 and p. 144. Call-note: a loud, short *two-it* or *seet,* singly or in quick succession.

CHIFFCHAFF and WILLOW WARBLER Plate 3 and p. 129–130. From young decidous trees or young plantations of spruce a long whistle *who-eet* or *djoo-eet.*

REDSTART Plate 2 and p. 126. Call-note: *foocet* produced with rather a flourish and often brought up with a *teck teck teck.*

NIGHTINGALE Call-note: protracted *heweet,* with more resonance to it than in the call-notes of the two preceding birds.

YELLOWHAMMER Plate 1 and p. 122. Individual high rather out-of-tune *sseay,* like a robin's but not so high and sometimes descending.

ROBIN Plate 2 and p. 127. High, protracted *tseeay.*

SISKIN Plate 1 and p. 121. Call-note: *day ah,* often as two syllables. Also an ascending *bee-a yb,* rather like a canary.

BULLFINCH Plate 1 and p. 120. Call-note: soft, whistling, descending *dee-oo,* not unlike the peeping of a lost chicken.

STARLING Plate 2 and p. 123. A shrill *spree-n* several times in a string, then as many again ascending, then descending order broken off in the middle.

CHAFFINCH Plate 1 and p. 119. Rain-call: a protracted *treeaif* or *vreed* on the same note.

GREENFINCH Plate 1 and p. 121. A broad, squeezed-out *shvoinsh,* distinctly descending at the end and more drawn-out than the chaffinch's.

WHITETHROAT Plate 3 and p. 129. Out of low bushes a striking *tshe, tshre* or *tshrah.*

c) Whirring or rattling sounds

WREN P. 144. Call-note: penetrating, long whirr: *tserrrrrrr* on a short hard note, like winding up a clock.

ROBIN Plate 2 and p. 127. Alarm-note: mostly from the ground a clear chattering, like two pebbles being struck together.

LONG-TAILED TIT P. 142. Alarm-call: from branches of tree a not very hard whirring *tserrrrrrr* rather like a wren's, but a little lower and can descend.

CRESTED TIT P. 142. Alarm-note: a soft whirring *tserrrrr.*

NIGHTINGALE Plate 2 and p. 128. In dense bushes a low woody churring *karrrr* often preceded by upward drawn *hooeet,* but only by bad songsters.

d) Call-phrases of 2–4 different notes

REDSTART Plate 2 and p. 126. Call-note a drawn-out whistle, mostly with 3 following short, clear sounds on same note, thus: *fuit teck teck teck.*

NIGHTINGALE Plate 2 and p. 128. High, drawn-out whistle followed by a deep churr, like *whoit karrr,* often only *karrr.*

GREAT TIT P. 141. Especially in early spring, a clear *see* followed by a drawn-out whistle *who-it* like:

see-tooyt   see-tooyt

sometimes followed by a *see* or *tooyt* or both.

BLUE TIT P. 142. Especially in spring, call-note: thin, sharp or, more often, 3–6 thin extended notes, the last 2 or 3 sometimes lower.

MARSH TIT P. 142. From deciduous trees, a striking, sharp *tseeday* with rising *ee,* thus:

tsee-day

and variations.

GOLDFINCH Plate 1 and p. 119. In parklands and orchards; call-note: *deetleet deetleet* on almost the same note.

*ICTERINE WARBLER Plate 3 and p. 130. Alarm-note: hard, smacking *tsee,* that may be followed by its characteristic *dedehooy* and *dedeho-ee.*

LOUD, RESOUNDING SINGLE AND MULTIPLE CALLS

BUZZARD P. 152. A cat *like mew* high in the air. *Heeay.*

JAY P. 134. A soft *heeay* in thickets or woods. Very like that of a buzzard. Usual note a loud, harsh *skaak, skaak* like the tearing of cloth.

GOSHAWK in flight. P. 153. Call rather like a buzzard's.

SPARROW HAWK In July (while attending to brood) above the tree-tops or from nest in the crest of a tall tree *geegeegeegeeg,* often more than 20 times, all on the same note, or rising and falling.

KESTREL P. 155. Above or in the crest of trees in a wood, a clear repeated *kleekleekleeklee, geekgeekgeek,* or a rather deeper *gegegege* timbre, pitch and loudness rather like the goshawk's. Most frequent in April and May, when looking after chicks.

CUCKOO Plate 4 and p. 149. Calls from end of April to early July, from then only morning and evening, falling silent about middle of the month, though a few may continue up to August. Calls at all hours of the day and often in the night also. Male calls from perch: *cuck-coo*. When pursuing hen-bird or rivals often gives a deep, hoarse *hachachach* which you have to be quite close to hear.

The "giggle" of the hen-bird in flight consists of 6–10 notes all on the same pitch, slightly higher in the middle: *kvickkvickkvick*, or even *coocookoocook*, ringing call that can be heard for quite a distance.

HOOPOE Plate 4 and p. 149. Calls from its arrival in mid-April (on the Continent arrives a fortnight before the cuckoo), all day from early morning; becomes quieter and stops about the end of July. In woods in wooded country, especially on pasture land with old trees. Male's call a hollow-sounding *hoop poop* repeated up to 4 times in quick succession. Timbre almost that of the cuckoo, slightly muffled.

WRYNECK Plate 4 and p. 149. Calls from mid-April to end of June. Very eager at first, it is less constant later on and mostly in the morning; a series of 8–12 resonant, drawn-out notes, each falling slightly, like *quee quee* . . . . repeated up to 20 times moderately quickly. Pitch rising at first.

NUTCHATCH Plate 4 und p. 144. Sings from first mild day in February until mid-May; rarely heard in June. Parks, gardens, deciduous woods. Mating-call: ringing, clear whistle of 4–8 notes linked in a sequence; 2 tied, splendidly drawn-out notes, like the peeping of chicks, or else each with two descending notes:

tweet-tweet   tweet-tweet   or   weet - weet   weet - weet

Call-note: a clear *seet* or *tweet*.

*MIDDLE SPOTTED WOODPECKER Plate 4 and p. 148. Calls from February to May or June. Especially in low-lying woods with aged oaks. A series of drawn-out, grating out-of-tune notes, the first softer and deeper, then louder and higher, the final two being duller again, individual notes at the end dropping. Mostly when changing tree a series call *gehgehgeh* at moderate speed.

Calls loudly in the spring (mating season). Drums like a great spotted woodpecker or not so loudly.

LESSER SPOTTED WOODPECKER Plate 4 and p. 148. Calls from March into June, in thin woods, parklands, orchards. A series of quick, sharp *geekgeekgeekgeek* in quick succession, soon becoming more of a squeak or whistle-scream.

Drums like the great spotted, but less forcibly. Calls a lot, above all in the spring (mating call).

GREAT SPOTTED WOODPECKER Plate 4 and p. 147. Calls from March into June. When climbing, both male and female give short, sharp *kjick*, repeated once after a long pause (the middle spotted woodpecker practically never gives a single call); during the mating season this can also be repeated several times in succession, but the pauses are longer than with middle spotted.

In flight a shrill *geegeegeegeegeeg,* but not so sharp.

In flight, too, a deeper, rougher, jarring *grehgrehgrehgreh,* very quick.

The woodpeckers stop calling in June. During the mating season a drumming *arrrr* that can be heard at a distance.

GREEN WOODPECKER Plate 4 and p. 148. Calls often from February and into high summer; individuals also in September. Especially in the morning from March into May, a mating call like a ringing laugh, the first syllable somewhat drawn-out, the subsequent ones getting quicker and quicker, falling either at the beginning or at the end; even the individual notes tending down, thus:

quea   quea   quea   quea   quea   queaqueu-queu-queu

The hen-bird's call is shorter, slightly deeper and not so clear. In summer, also single calls, like a golden oriole's *gleeau* or *gjep* or *quee-eh.*

*GREY-HEADED WOODPECKER Plate 4 and p. 148. Calls from March into June, especially in the forenoon; a very loud call like the laugh of the green woodpecker, but not so sharp, but soft and slower, sounding rather plaintive, especially at the end with its slow notes. Call-notes descending, or the first one or two on the same note then descending, like:

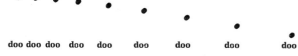

doo doo doo doo   doo   doo   doo   doo   doo

Drums frequently, but not so violently as the great spotted.

*BLACK WOODPECKER Plate 4 and p. 149. Starts in March earlier or later depending on the weather, and on into the autumn.

Perched on the trunk, it calls only a few times a loud, ringing descending

Kleea

When flying gives a ringing call, on the same note, often drawn out.

During the mating-season (March and April) often gives a succession of 10–20 rather melodious *quickwick wick* ... in which the *quicks* are distinctly drawn up from below.

Drums very strongly, but not so furiously as the great spotted; starts in March, sometimes even in January if the sun is shining; especially frequently in July and August; very seldom heard in winter.

ROUGH CROAKING SINGLE OR MULTIPLE CALLS

ROOK P. 133. In flight a deep rough *craa craa* or *garb garb* deeper than the carrion crow's.

CARRION CROW P. 134. In flight: rough *craa craa,* but higher than the rook's and mostly tending to fall away.

HOODED CROW Like carrion crow.

MAGPIE Loud, clear call, a succession like *shakakak* or *rrekekek*.

JAY Very loud jarring *skaak, skaak* (also imitates other bird's voices).

SHRILL SINGLE CALLS AND MUFFLED MULTIPLE CALLS HEARD IN THE EVENING OR AT NIGHT

LITTLE OWL P. 160. At night from the crest of a tree in garden or field a high, piercing *coowiff coowiff* ... the accented 2nd syllable being higher than the 1st; or else a loud shrill *kooit koiit ot,* also, a shrill whistling *geevcukgeevcuckcucuc,* the first syllable being stressed and higher.

TAWNY OWL P. 161. From the end of March onwards, a high barking *koowit,* ascending two notes. In spring there is the mating call, a high-

huu   hu   huuuu   huu

pitched howl that begins with 2 loud, barking notes, then a quiet note, then swells again and rises, before finally dropping.

According to Professor Hoffmann, in the "Wolf's Den" scene in the *Freischütz,* Karl Maria von Weber uses the call of the tawny owl in the chorus of spirits *(oohoo oohoo)* in the phrase:

LONG-EARED OWL P. 161. Especially at night, half a shriek, half a whistling howl, rising to begin with, then falling like *hooooo-oooooo.* Courtship flight in spring, a deep, dark *hooooooooo.*

WOODCOCK P. 180. Courtship flight in spring, at dusk and at night over heath and woods, a deep, muffled *koo-orr – koo-orr* and a high, whistling *pseeb* or *heebst.*

NIGHTJAR Plate 4 and p. 151. From mid-May into the first half of July on quiet nights. "Song" or courtship-note a "purring", while perched: a repeated, chattering churr of 2 alternating notes, like *airrrr airrrr,* with the 1st syllable always longer and higher than the 2nd.

In flight: a call-note *dak dak habit habit* or a high *quick quick* with a loud clapping of wings over its back; also in display flight.

BIRD VOICES IN THE HEDGES, ROUND WOODS OR IN OPEN FIELDS

YELLOWHAMMER See p. 545.

WHITETHROAT Plate 3 and p. 129. Sings from early May until well into the summer, almost all day; from hedges pretty well everywhere, but especially in the vicinity of water; a quick chattering twitter conspicuous by some rough notes, often with some better-sounding high notes at the beginning. A typical warbler's song with nothing but staccato notes in a shallow wavy line, but slower in tempo than with the other warblers; a less strong beginning is followed by a loud final phrase:

didudidoidida

The song is sometimes arranged in one very soft section that is seldom heard and one loud one. During the first part it creeps about restlessly in the thickest of the foliage, but for the 2nd part perches on the swaying end of a twig, on a telephone wire, or sings it in display-flight above the hedge.

In the thick foliage it is often *voidvoidvoid* or *ved ved,* or also
    eed   eed, eedeedeed
void   void   void void
or something similar.

Call-note a harsh *tse,* like shears snapping together.

DUNNOCK Plate 3 and p. 132. Sings on sunny days from the end of March on, at almost all times of the day, especially in early morning. In woods, hedges, gardens, parklands, often from the tip of a tree branch, not very loud, a somewhat "barrel-organ" song of some 10 notes produced in one breath, all high notes at the same pitch, with 2 or 3 notes standing out in the middle and falling away at the end. Timbre reminiscent of the wren's, but softer and without trills. Undulating melody like the goldcrest's, but rougher and not so high.

RED-BACKED SHRIKE P. 139. From early May onwards especially from hedges in farmlands; a short, rough call *gek gek gek,* then swiftly repeated when agitated. Sings mostly unconcealed, on the point of a twig, on a low tree or telephone-wire. Very soft, pressed-out twitter; also imitates other voices.

SONGS AND CALLS IN OPEN COUNTRY, FIELDS, MEADOWS, WASTELAND, COUNTRY ROADS, AVENUES
SONG FLIGHT

TREE PIPIT P. 551. ROCK PIPIT P. 137. WOOD WARBLER P. 546 and 552.

WHITETHROAT P. 552 and 559.

SKYLARK P. 135. Sings from February to after midsummer. Young cock birds sing in autumn before migrating, if the weather is fine but not so loudly or continuously as the adults. Song-flight in the open fields with trills without pauses; flies up the first few yards silently, then starts singing in almost vertical flight. Very industrious songster from sunrise to a quarter of an hour after sunset. Sings only 1st morning song and last evening song sitting.

*CRESTED LARK P. 136. Sings from fine February days until well into summer. In late summer and autumn the imperfect attempts of the young cock birds rehearsing. Begins before daybreak, sometimes even at night, mostly in flight, but sometimes also from the ground. Song a soft trill with pauses; also sings perched on an elevated point; in flight sings only from a certain height. Flight is more sluggish, more hovering and fluttering than the lark's.

WOOD LARK P. 136. Sings from mid-March into July. The old birds sing best in the morning and evening, but also at other times of the day, even at night, particularly about midnight. The young cock birds of the year sing from August into October, especially in the forenoon in fine weather, where there are low trees and bushes. Song-flight: phrases with pauses between; also sings at night. Begins singing first some 20–30 m up; soulful trills and melodies.

*TAWNY PIPIT P. 137. Sings roughly from May to the end of June, almost all day. In August and September young and old often sing together on plough land. Rises singing until over tree height, then flies in a downward curve singing

gridelin   gridelin

or a 2 syllable *zeerrlee*.

Call-note: *deedleehoo* and a sparrow-like call *deelem*.

MEADOW PIPIT P. 137. From mid-April until nearly July, sings diligently from morning until nearly evening. *Song:* cock bird flies steeply upwards and as it descends sings an unusually long phrase, which it ends as it lands on some elevated perch. Main phrase is either a 1 syllable *dip dip dip* or *dzee dzee dzee* or *djeh djeh djeh;* whichever it is repeated 25–30 times at the same pitch, in the tempo of the chiffchaff.

WHEATEAR Plate 2 and p. 127. Sings from March until summer, also at night. Sings from a stone, etc. but also in flight, rising obliquely 3–7 m, then plunging down to another perch. Song is a short twitter.

Call-note: a hard *geev,* often followed by a smacking *terk terk.*

SONG FROM EXPOSED PERCHES

SERIN P. 548. RED-BACKED SHRIKE P. 559.

CORN BUNTING Plate 1 and p. 122. Sings from March until well into the summer; sometimes also in September just after its moult. Sings from telephone wire or the top of a tree at short intervals a song like the clatter of a knitting-machine, consisting of several quick, staccato notes, followed by a whirring sound that gets louder, then softer again and descends thus:

zick zick zick zick   schnirrrrps

*ORTOLAN BUNTING P. 122. Sings from end of April to end of June, often at night. Industrious songster. Along country roads and in fields where soil is sandy. Song has a soft, almost melancholy sound; varies considerably; mostly 3–4 somewhat drawn-out notes on same pitch and 1–3 somewhat lower, thus:

jif jif jif jor jor

or else the 2nd part consists of 3 linked notes and often a lower concluding note as well.

WHINCHAT Plate 2 and p. 127. Sings soon after arrival or towards mid-May, starting about an hour before daybreak and continuing most of the day and into the night; will even sing in the middle of the night. Only in grassy farmlands, from a tall bush, tree or telephone wire, a short interrupted song, mostly of 3–7 notes, including 1 or 2 grating sounds (like the redstart's) and 1–4 better whistle-sounds. Mostly not linked in any definite way.

Call-note: a muffled snorting *teck teck*.

STONECHAT P. 127. YELLOW WAGTAIL P. 138.

CALLS FROM CONCEALMENT

PARTRIDGE P. 166. In fields on warm evenings of spring and autumn, a loud *geerrheck* or *geerheck*.

QUAIL P. 166. In fields during summer, a 3-syllabic *boockerrook*.

Beethoven has used the quail's call, as well as those of the cuckoo and nightingale in his *Pastoral* Symphony, and it can also be heard in Haydn's *Seasons*. Also Franz Schubert uses it in a song with that title.

PHEASANT P. 167. A rather unmelodious crowing in field or coppice in spring and summer is the courtship-cry of the cock. In autumn and winter there is just the unlovely *oeroerk* or *goek goek*.

SONGS FROM INLAND WATERS

BLUETHROAT Plate 2 and p. 128. **DIPPERS** Plate 2 and p. 124. **WREN** P. 542. **ROCK PIPIT** P. 137. **WHITE and GREY WAGTAIL** P. 137 and 138.

REED BUNTING Plate 1 and p. 123. Sings from April until well into the summer, from early morning and at almost all times of the day, often also at night. In reed beds. A short, stuttering little song ending in a magnificent upward swing or a slight trill, often like this:

tweet tweet tweet tit itick   3)

Call-note: an updrawn whistle like:

tseep

*GREAT REED WARBLER Plate 3 and p. 131. Sings from early May to mid-July, from morning till evening, mostly early, when day starts to break; shortly after arrival sometimes all night. In large reed beds.

Very loud, long song; changing from a deep squawk to high whistling, almost squeaking, with rhythmical delivery, like:

karr   karr   karr   kiet kiet kiet karr karr karr

REED WARBLER Plate 3 and p. 131. Sings from early May to late summer; at its best in July; very industrious. Starts at break of day and sings all day until late evening, almost without interruption, but rarely into the night. In reeds. Song similar to that of great reed warbler, consisting of 1 and 2 syllable sounds, somewhat hoarser, but rhythmical, like:

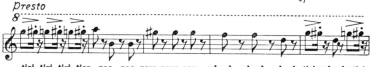

tiri tiri tiri tier   zac   zac zerr zerr zerr   scherk scherk scherk tiri scherk tiri

SEDGE WARBLER Plate 3 and p. 131. Sings from arrival until early August at all times of the day, also in light nights, mostly at daybreak and dawn. On inland waters, also in cornfields. Song like reed warbler, both having drawn-out, jarring notes, but the tempo of the sedge warbler's song is not so mechanically regular, being fresher and more lively and tends more to repeat the phrase it likes best. A good identification is its *voidvoidvoid* phrase, that recurs now and again.

MARSH WARBLER Plate 3 and p. 132. Sings from end of April or early May into July; sings mostly all day and also at night. In bushes in damp places and in cornfields. Song like the icterine warbler with repetition of individual notes, but not so strong and without the sharpness of the latter's song. Characteristic are its trilling, twirling notes, which the other does not have. Song often begins with a short series of *teep* sounds or *veet veet,* then comes a resonant jingling string of notes with a rising tendency,

3)

or downwards drawn whistle-notes like *tsah tsah tsah* at the end of the tree pipit's song. Smacking sounds are interspersed. Also imitates other birds.

GRASSHOPPER WARBLER Plate 3 and p. 131. Sings from May onwards on wet pasture land with bushes, in thin woods. A monotonous mechanical *seerrr* ... rather like the noise of certain grasshoppers, or the unwinding of a fisherman's reel, the phrase of the song lasting anything from a few seconds up to 2 minutes.

INDEX TO COMMON NAMES

INDEX TO SCIENTIFIC NAMES

Arrangement of

Class: **Mammals**

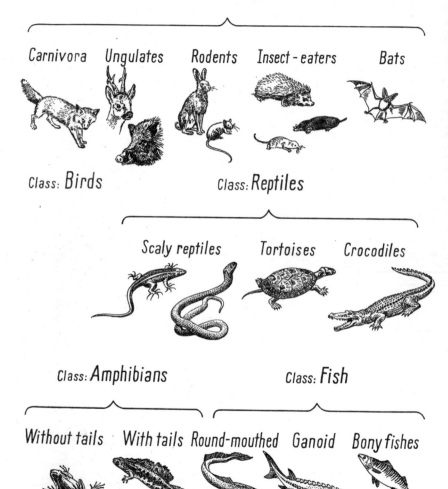

Carnivora   Ungulates   Rodents   Insect-eaters   Bats

Class: **Birds**   Class: **Reptiles**

Scaly reptiles   Tortoises   Crocodiles

Class: **Amphibians**   Class: **Fish**

Without tails   With tails   Round-mouthed   Ganoid   Bony fishes